HISTORY OF THE MINISTRY OF MUNITIONS

VOLUME V / I

WAGES AND WELFARE

Part I Control of Men's Wages
Part II Control of Women's Wages
Part III Welfare: the Control of Working Conditions
Part IV The Provision of Canteens
Part V Provision for the Housing of Munition Workers

The Naval & Military Press Ltd

in association with

The Imperial War Museum
Department of Printed Books

Published jointly by
The Naval & Military Press Ltd
Unit 10 Ridgewood Industrial Park,
Uckfield, East Sussex,
TN22 5QE England
Tel: +44 (0) 1825 749494
Fax: +44 (0) 1825 765701
www.naval-military-press.com
www.military-genealogy.com
www.militarymaproom.com

and

The Imperial War Museum, London
Department of Printed Books
www.iwm.org.uk

In reprinting in facsimile from the original, any imperfections are inevitably reproduced and the quality may fall short of modern type and cartographic standards.

CONFIDENTIAL
For Official Information only   *Crown Copyright Reserved*

HISTORY OF THE MINISTRY OF MUNITIONS

VOLUME V

WAGES AND WELFARE

PART I

THE CONTROL OF MEN'S WAGES

1922

Volume V

WAGES AND WELFARE

PART I
THE CONTROL OF MEN'S WAGES

CONTENTS.

CHAPTER I.

The Adjustment of Wages before the passing of the Munitions of War Act, 1915.

	PAGE
1. The Settlement of Wages before the War	1
(a) Wages and Industrial Unrest	1
(b) Organisation of Employers and Employed	2
(c) Methods of Remuneration	5
(d) Collective Bargaining and Government Control	7
2. The Movement of Wages, August, 1914—July, 1915	9
(a) Rise in the Cost of Living	9
(b) Demand for Labour	12
(c) The First Advances	13
3. Government Intervention in Wages Questions, August, 1914—July, 1915	17
(a) Wages and Labour Supply	17
(b) The Treasury Conferences of March, 1915	19
(c) Appointment of the Committee on Production	23
4. Conclusion	26

CHAPTER II.

The Ministry's Powers of Wage Regulation.

1. Powers under the Munitions of War Act, 1915	29
(a) Part I	29
(b) Sanction of Changes in Wages in Controlled Establishments	31
(c) Schedule II	32
(d) Works Regulations	33
(e) Leaving Certificates and Power of Embargo	33
(f) The Fair Wages Clause	35
(g) Summary	37

CHAPTER II.—*cont.*

		PAGE
2.	Munitions of War (Amendment) Act, 1916	37
	(a) The Central Munitions Labour Supply Committee	37
	(b) Demand for Control by Order	39
	(c) Provisions for Control by Order	40
	(d) Amendment of the principal Act	42
	(e) Extension of the Area of Regulation	42
3.	The Dilution Bill of 1917	43
	(a) Object of the Bill	43
	(b) Provisions in first Draft	44
	(c) The Bill in Parliament	45
4.	The Commission on Industrial Unrest	47
5.	Negotiations with Trade Unions and Employers, 1917	48
	(a) Extension of Awards	48
	(b) Acceleration of Arbitration Proceedings	49
	(c) Protection of Piece-Rates	50
	(d) The Repeal of the Leaving Certificate Provisions	51
	(e) Rejection of Bill by Amalgamated Society of Engineers	55
6.	The Munitions of War Act, 1917	56
	(a) Re-introduction of the Bill as a Wages Measure	56
	(b) Repeal of Leaving Certificate Provisions	56
	(c) The Skilled Time-Workers Clause	57
	(d) Section 4	59
	(e) Rejected and Deferred Provisions	59
7.	Inadequacy of the Ministry's Statutory Powers of Wages Control	60

CHAPTER III.

The Settlement of Munition Workers' Wages outside the Department.

1.	Local and Sectional Awards by the Committee on Production	65
2.	Cycles of Advances	67
3.	The "Embargo" on Advances	70
	(a) Policy of Checking Wage Increases	70
	(b) Increasing Discontent of Workers	73
4.	The Second Cycle of Advances	76
5.	The Movement towards National Advances	77
6.	National Awards	80
7.	Low-rated Districts	85
8.	Conclusion	86

CHAPTER IV.

The ordinary Wages Administration of the Department.

		PAGE
1.	Introductory	89
	(a) Effects of Dilution Policy on Wages	89
	(b) Types of Wages Questions before the Department	90
2.	Administration of the Fair Wages Clause	91
	(a) Scope of Department's Responsibility	91
	(b) Procedure	92
	(c) Problems Raised	93
	(d) Effects of the Application of the Fair Wages Clause	96
3.	Changes of Wages in Controlled Establishments	99
	(a) Procedure	99
	(b) Refusals of Advances	99
	(c) Registering Wage Movements	101
	(d) Protection of Piece-Rates under Section 4 (2)	104
	(e) The Effect on Wage Advances of the Policy of "Sanction"	109
4.	Administration of Circular L.3 and the Dilution Policy for Men	110
5.	Compulsory Extension of Awards	115
	(a) Demand for Extension of Awards	115
	(b) Extension by Administrative Pressure	116
	(c) Extension under the Act of 1917	118

CHAPTER V.

Payment by Results.

1.	The Spread of Payment by Results, 1914-15	121
	(a) Attitude of Labour towards Piece-Rates	121
	(b) Attitude of Employers	123
	(c) Policy of the Government	123
2.	Official Propaganda before 1917	126
3.	Propaganda by Employers	126
4.	Payment by Results in National Factories	129
5.	Propaganda in the Shipbuilding Industry, 1917	132
6.	Negotiations with the Engineering Unions and the Munitions of War Act, 1917	137
7.	Payment by Results in the Aircraft Industry	141
8.	Departmental Policy, 1917-18	150

CHAPTER V.—*cont.*

		PAGE
9.	Departmental Policy, 1918	151
10.	Some Questions of Principle	153
	(*a*) Methods of Payment by Results	153
	(*b*) Premium Bonus System	154
	(*c*) Output Bonuses	156
	(*d*) Opposition of Trade Unions	158
	(*e*) Difficulties of Settling Piece-Rates	162
	(*f*) Policy of the Department	164

CHAPTER VI.

Time Wages and the Problem of the Skilled Time-Worker.

1.	The Origin of the Problem	167
2.	Statutory Power to deal with the Problem	169
3.	The Skilled Day-Workers' Committee	172
	(*a*) The Committee's Problem	172
	(*b*) Proposals Submitted	172
	(*c*) The Department's View	175
4.	Adoption of the $12\frac{1}{2}\%$ Bonus	177
	(*a*) Consideration by the Minister and the Department	177
	(*b*) Departmental Differences and the Cabinet Decision	179
5.	Reception of the Bonus	180
	(*a*) Demands from excluded Time-Workers	180
	(*b*) Extension to Semi-skilled and Unskilled Workers and to Shipyards	182
6.	The Cabinet Committee on the Bonus	184
7.	The Spread of the Bonus	186
	(*a*) Extension to Time-Workers in other Industries	186
	(*b*) Extension to Piece-Workers	187
8.	Conversion to a General Advance	191
	(*a*) Procedure in making Awards	191
	(*b*) Conclusion	192

CHAPTER VII.

The Problem of Co-ordination.

1.	Introductory	194
2.	Wages and Contracts	195
	(*a*) Limitation of Wages	195
	(*b*) Compensation for Wage Advances	199
	(*c*) Limitation of Prices and Sliding Scales	203

CHAPTER VII.—*cont.*

	PAGE
3. The Problem of Wages in the Building Industry	205
4. Extension of the Coal Controller's Awards	212
5. The Co-ordination of Departmental Action by the Cabinet	219

CHAPTER VIII.

Conclusion.

APPENDICES.

I. Rates and Earnings in November, 1915 239

II. Circular L.3 243

III. Difficulty of Enforcing Awards on Methods of Payment 245

IV. Proposals for the Regulation of Payment by Results agreed on by the Engineering Employers' Federation and the Amalgamated Society of Engineers, and suggested as a Second Schedule to the 1917 Amendment Act, 15 June, 1917 247

V. Documents illustrating the Skilled Time-Workers' Bonus' 248
    1. Interim Report of Chairman of Skilled Day-Workers' Committee 248
        (*a*) Memorandum and Proposals by Employers' Representatives 249
        (*b*) Memorandum and Proposals by Trade Union Representatives 252
        (*c*) Memorandum by Official Representatives .. 253
    2. Final Report of Committee on Rates of Skilled Day-Workers 254
    3. Memorandum by the Labour Committee of the Ministry of Munitions 255
    4. Extract from a Memorandum by Sir Lynden Macassey, Director of Shipyard Labour 256
    5. The Skilled Time-Workers (Engineers and Moulders) Wages Order, 1917. 259

VI. Cost Variation Clauses in Contracts (Wages) 260

VII. Table of Statutory Wages Orders relating to Men .. 262

CHAPTER I.

THE ADJUSTMENT OF WAGES BEFORE THE PASSING OF THE MUNITIONS OF WAR ACT, 1915.

I. The Settlement of Wages before the War.

(*a*) WAGES AND INDUSTRIAL UNREST.

The adjustment of wages to changing industrial conditions is always a delicate and complicated task. The war, by accelerating industrial change in every direction, put a new aspect on the problem and compelled the adoption of new methods of dealing with it. On the Ministry of Munitions, as the authority charged with the organisation of the country's industrial resources for the purposes of the war, fell the chief burden of devising and applying these new methods. Much had, however, happened before the Ministry was established; the Ministry's policy is therefore intelligible only in the light of the changes that took place and the measures that were adopted between the outbreak of war and the passing of the Munitions of War Act. These in their turn require some understanding of the wages situation on the eve of the war.

The years immediately preceding the outbreak of war were years of exceptional industrial unrest, in which wage-rates and wage-relations were subject to frequent change. For a generation wage-rates had lagged behind the increase in the cost of living. The year 1900 being taken as 100, wholesale prices rose from $88 \cdot 2$ in 1896 to $116 \cdot 5$ in 1913 and retail prices in London from $91 \cdot 7$ to $114 \cdot 8$; the average rise in the wage-rates recorded by the Labour Department of the Board of Trade in the same period was from $90 \cdot 2$ to $106 \cdot 5$, the rise in the recorded rates of skilled engineers being even less, viz., $96 \cdot 7$ to 105. The rise in prices does not represent exactly the rise in the cost of living, since rents in most parts of the country rose only slightly; but the combined rise was sufficient to be felt as a hardship. Wage-rates again are not an exact measure of the wage-earners' income, since an average of wage-rates makes no allowance for the movement of population from lower-paid to higher-paid occupations, for promotion of individuals to higher grades, for overtime, and for increased facilities of earning on piece-work due to general improvements in methods of production. But rates and their relation to the cost of living are the issues on which differences about wages usually turn. The workman does not regard it as a reason for accepting a lower nominal or real rate that he can increase his income by working longer hours or undertaking more responsible work; the increased yield of piece-rates, so far as it is not due to increased dexterity, he regards as his due share of the general increase in the productivity of industry; while a reduction in the rate of any trade, due to an influx of labour from lower-paid occupations, naturally strikes the workpeople in that trade as a loss, although there may be a net gain to the wage-earning class as a whole.

Since 1910 the adjustment of wages had been accompanied by a succession of trade disputes. Wage-rates had risen, on the average keeping pace with prices, but the advances had been unevenly distributed in preceding years, and had not been sufficient to make up the ground lost. In the five years before 1910 the average number of disputes beginning each year was 456, and the average number of workpeople directly involved 211,000 ; in the years 1910–13 the average number of disputes was 947 and the average number of workpeople involved 915,000. The records of voluntary conciliation and arbitration boards reveal a similar increase in activity, the number of cases considered rising from an average of 1,734 in the earlier period to an average of 3,418 in the later. The figures for 1913 were 1,497 disputes, involving 689,000 workpeople, and 4,070 cases considered by conciliation boards. The work of the Chief Industrial Commissioner's Department under the Conciliation Act of 1896 showed a similar increase. It is worth noting, since one of the results of the war was to institute compulsory arbitration, that the proportion of disputes settled by arbitration in 1913 was smaller than in any of the previous nine years, and the chief national agreements providing for the settlement of disputes in munitions industries, those namely negotiated by the Engineering Employers' Federation, the Shipbuilding Employers' Federation and the Midland Employers' Federation, made no provision for arbitration.

(b) ORGANISATION OF EMPLOYERS AND EMPLOYED.

The relations between employer and employed were largely governed by collective agreements between employers' associations and trade unions. There was in the years preceding the war a marked growth in the membership of trade unions, which is illustrated in the following table :—

	1910.	1911.	1912.	1913.	Estimated Industrial Population 1914.
Iron & Steel Manufacture	53,000	60,000	69,000	80,000	210,000
Ironfounding	37,000	39,000	45,000	49,000	63,000
Engineering	177,000	199,000	236,000	272,000	684,000
Shipbuilding	75,000	82,000	92,000	97,000	181,000
Miscellaneous Metals	28,000	35,000	37,000	40,000	—
Total Metal, etc., Trades	370,000	415,000	479,000	538,000	1,803,000
Cabinetmaking, etc.	14,000	17,000	18,000	25,000	144,000
Coachbuilding	12,000	13,000	16,000	20,000	36,000
Other Woodworking Trades	13,000	15,000	17,000	19,000	—
Total Woodworking, etc.	39,000	45,000	51,000	64,000	338,000
General Labour	119,000	227,000	252,000	391,000	—
Female T.U. Membership : Non-Textile Trades	38,000	60,000	79,000	100,000	—
Mining and Quarrying	731,000	752,000	757,000	916,000	1,174,000
Transport Trades	245,000	514,000	515,000	700,000	—
Building Trades	157,000	173,000	204,000	249,000	806,000
All Unions	2,446,000	3,019,000	3,288,000	3,987,000	—

It will be noticed that the most remarkable increases in the period are in the organisation of general labourers, transport workers and women; the skilled men's unions, however, including as they did the irreplaceable workers in each industry, were the chief factor in collective bargaining. It will be noticed also that the number of trade unionists is in few industrial groups approximate to the number of persons engaged. The explanation is partly that general labourers and in many cases semi-skilled workers are organised outside the unions specialised to the industry, and that the industrial population in any group includes clerical, transport and other workers likely to be outside these specialised unions. But the chief explanation is that trade unionism, except in a few very highly organised trades such as coal, was "patchy," the organisation being strong in most districts and firms, but very weak in some, or inclusive in the skilled grades and weak or negligible in the semi-skilled and unskilled grades. The existence of national unions had not brought about national rates of wages, standard rates being nearly always district rates and of varying authority at that; the standard time rate for example for a turner recognised by the Amalgamated Society of Engineers in October, 1913, varied from 24s. a week in Redruth to 46s. in Grays, with 31 intermediate rates, and many workers were regularly paid above the standard rate.

Outside the metal, engineering and shipbuilding group of industries, the workpeople affected by munitions contracts were not well organised. The general labour unions, especially the Workers' Union, were establishing sections for semi-skilled and unskilled labour in different industries and thereby supplementing the organisation of the more specialised unions; but they had not in 1914 succeeded in organising a majority of the workers in these grades. Among women especially organisation was weak. The chief women's union, the National Federation of Women Workers had at the end of 1913, 12,152 members, the Workers' Union had 5,200 women members, the National Union of General Workers, 4,380, and the Dockers, 4,806. If these figures are compared with the membership of the same unions after four years of State regulation of wages, it will be seen that State regulation is not necessarily hostile to trade union organisation and may very well be the reverse.

In the organisation of employers the local association was the important unit. In engineering most of the local associations (52 in number in 1912) were combined in the Engineering Employers' Federation, which thus represented (1912) 830 firms employing between 500,000 and 600,000 workpeople, or about 75 to 80 per cent. of the trade. In shipbuilding the National Employers' Federation not only gave the support of a national organisation to the local associations, but negotiated national wage-settlements. A large part of the miscellaneous metal industry of the Birmingham, North Worcestershire and South Staffordshire area, hitherto ill-organised, had been organised in the Midland Employers' Federation, formed in 1913, which had a collective agreement with the three chief general labour unions in the area, establishing minimum time-rates and providing a procedure for the settlement of disputes.

Negotiations about wages were the subject of collective agreements over the greater part of the metal, engineering and shipbuilding industries. In the engineering trades they had been governed until March, 1914, by an agreement made in 1898 and revised in 1907. This provided for the settlement of disputes without stoppage of work, in the first instance by deputation to the employer; or an official of the union could approach the local secretary of the employers' association; or either party could bring the question before a local conference between the local association of employers and the local representatives of the unions; failing settlement locally, the question would be referred to a central conference consisting of members of the executive board of the employers' federation and members of the central authority of the union or unions concerned. The agreement also dealt with the general principles governing piece-work, overtime, rating of skilled workmen, apprentices, and the manning of machine tools. The detailed working conditions were the subject of local agreement between local employers' associations and the unions. Wage-rates were not usually specified in agreements, but the national agreement laid it down that general alterations in the rates of wages in any district should be negotiated between the employers' local association and the local representatives of the trade union or unions concerned. In this the employers' policy corresponded with that of the chief union concerned. The Amalgamated Society of Engineers, while providing for a central control over finance, left wage-negotiations to the district organisations; indeed a revision of rules carried through in 1912 had very much cut down the powers of the Central Council to control the districts and correspondingly enhanced the activity and independence of the district authorities.

The parties to the agreement of October, 1907, with the Engineering Employers' Federation were in 1914 the Steam Engine Makers' Society, the United Machine Workers' Association, the Toolmakers, the Scientific Instrument Makers, and the two national unions of Smiths and Strikers. In addition the Electrical Trades' Union, the two Brassworkers' Societies, while not parties to the general agreement, were parties to the provisions for avoiding disputes. The Amalgamated Society of Engineers had withdrawn from the agreement and from a supplementary agreement, authorising and prescribing conditions for the premium bonus system, in March, 1914, mainly owing to its objection to the clause in the general agreement dealing with the manning of machines, but partly also owing to complaints of the delay in the settlement of grievances. The Central Council was, however, in September, 1914, authorised to enter into negotiations for a new general agreement, and agreed on a provisional procedure for avoiding disputes.

Similar provisions for preventing stoppages governed the shipbuilding industry; but in this agreement general fluctuations in wages due to the general conditions of the industry were the subject of national, not local, negotiation, and applied to all firms in the Federation and all trades, party to the agreement, at once. Such general changes could not be made until at least two conferences had been held to discuss them, or within six months of the last general change, and they were limited at any one time to 5 per cent. on piece-rates and 1s. a week or ¼d. an hour on time rates. One important trade union in the industry, the United Society of Boilermakers and Iron and Steel Shipbuilders, withdrew from the agreement in 1912; it remained, however, a party to a number of local agreements of narrower scope.

The agreement between the Midland Employers' Federation and the General Labour unions concluded in July, 1913, for twelve months, laid down standard rates of 23s. a week for adult unskilled male labour and 6s. for girls of 14 rising to 12s. at 21; piece-rates it left to be settled by mutual arrangement between the employer and workman, but guaranteed the workman's day-rate irrespective of his piece-work earnings. It also provided for the settlement of disputes on lines similar to those adopted in the engineering trades.

In the whole of this industrial group the actual conditions of work and rates of pay were governed more by local agreements than by any national or even provincial settlement. The agreements were in most cases only in part reduced to writing, many of the factors being customary observances. Just as standard time-rates varied from district to district even for the skilled grades, so the standard week, allowances for overtime and night work, the arrangement of shifts, procedure for fixing piece-rates and other bases for payments by results, group payments and sub-contracting arrangements, varied. The Engineering Employers' Federation was urging its constituent associations to substitute written agreements for unwritten custom, but the latter still regulated relations between employers and workpeople over the larger part of the field of their relations.

In the iron and steel trades the wages of the majority of the workpeople employed were regulated by sliding scales, under which the rate per ton paid to the workpeople was made to rise or fall in accordance with prescribed advances or reductions in the selling price of the product. This automatic provision for the general movement of wages had the effect of confining within very restricted limits the number of disputes between employers and employed. To deal with such as arose and to consider modifications and adjustments in the sliding scale, however, a number of conciliation boards existed. They were usually constituted of representatives of individual works, not of employers' associations and trade unions; trade unionism in the industry was, however, so strong that the difference was not very material. There were no national agreements in these trades, the unit of organisation being usually the district.

(c) METHODS OF REMUNERATION.

The customs and agreements regulating wages illustrate well the complexity of the problems involved in any attempt on the part of the State to control wages. Methods of remuneration vary with the varying circumstances of different trades. In engineering, time-rates were the rule; these rates varied from district to district and from craft to craft, so that in the aggregate they numbered some hundreds. Piecework was however allowed under the national agreement,[1] prices to be arranged in the shop, overtime and nightshift allowances to be paid, and the time rate to be guaranteed. Of the 267,000 workpeople covered by the returns under engineering and boilermaking in the Wages Census of 1906, 22·9 per cent. were piece-workers and 4·6 per cent. paid on some bonus system. Time wages with a bonus on output were common in blastfurnace work. Certain shipbuilding processes, especially riveting, plating and caulking, were usually done on piece-work, about one in three of the whole number of workpeople covered by the returns in shipbuilding being piece-workers. In iron and steel manufacture the more responsible work was usually paid piece-rates, although only 28·3 per cent. of the workpeople employed were piece-workers; many of the piece-workers were sub-contractors, receiving a tonnage rate, and paying time-wages to some or all of their helpers. In the allied industries, such as railway carriage and wagon building (67·6 per cent.), light iron castings (45·3 per cent.), cycles (52·8 per cent.), nails, screws, nuts, etc. (48·2 per cent.), the proportion of piece-workers was much higher.

The proportion of workpeople on bonus systems in engineering in 1906 was small. Between 1906 and 1914 a great deal of experiment in bonus systems took place. The limited amount of simple repetition in commercial engineering gave few opportunities for straight piece-rates. Any system of payment by results therefore that was to be of general application must provide for a large number of individual arrangements and allow a margin of error that is unnecessary where production is uniform and standardised. The system that seemed to employers to satisfy these conditions best was the premium bonus system—the system under which each job is timed, and the workman paid a bonus on his ordinary time-rate if he completes the job in less than the base-time.

Bonuses and piece-rates might be paid to the individual on his output or they might be collective, *i.e.*, paid to a group in specified proportions on the group's output. Certain unions were opposed to any system of payment by results, the chief unions in the woodworking crafts being particularly dogmatic in their assertions of the ill effects of such systems. On the other hand, piece-work was the rule in the minor metal trades.

Changes in the general level of wages were usually the result of special negotiation, which was usually conducted in the district, but might be, as in the case of shipyard labour, conducted nationally. In the iron and steel trades, which the demand for munitions was to affect, such general changes were made, as has been indicated above, automatically in accordance with a sliding scale.

In the coal-mining industry changes in the selling price were a principal, though not the sole, factor in determining changes in wages;

---

[1] From which the Amalgamated Society of Engineers withdrew in 1914.

sliding scales were in operation in most fields, subject to a minimum below which, and a maximum above which, wages did not fluctuate.

The other provisions found in collective agreements had usually some bearing on the problem of wages even if they were not concerned directly with the fixing or varying of rates. The regulation of hours by the establishment of a standard week (or day) limited the amount of work that should be given for a given wage, and, in conjunction with provisions for special overtime rates, might give rise to earnings in excess of the nominal rate. The regulation of entry to the trade and the allocation of work or manning of machinery were parts of a policy which aimed at preventing any sudden influx into the trade and so at giving security to wages in it. Trade union policy may be said to aim at such a control of the conditions of employment as would serve to prevent any sudden or extensive change in wages to the disadvantage of the union members. Any alteration in the conditions of employment, such as those involved in a policy of dilution, might therefore involve a challenge to trade union policy (unless made with the consent of the union), and the attitude of the union would depend largely on the extent to which it considered that its standard rates were imperilled. Even if the representative leaders of a union were convinced of the necessity of a change, the working members would react instinctively against any proposal that threatened the security of their income.

(d) COLLECTIVE BARGAINING AND GOVERNMENT CONTROL.

The control of wages by voluntary collective bargaining, while it secured the continuous adaptation of wages to changing industrial conditions, was ill-adapted to dealing with changes so rapid and extensive as the war was to bring with it. The number of unions involved was great; an employer in the case of a large engineering works might have regularly to deal with more than twenty; and the extent of joint action between the different unions was limited. The number of consultations to be made and bargains to be struck was increased by the practice of negotiating changes in the district rather than nationally—a practice which also led to variations in the amount and time of advances in different parts of the country. The ordinary process of dealing with a disputed question, by reference from the works to the local conference and from local conference to central conference, although amply justified in ordinary times as a method of securing agreement and avoiding stoppages, was slow in itself, and the channels were liable to be clogged when there was any unusual number of difficult questions to be dealt with. Another obstacle to prompt adaptation to change was the condition of trade unionism itself, which exhibited many of the symptoms of a transition stage. The relations between unions in the same industry were being changed by federation and amalgamation; the distribution of duties between central and local authorities was a matter of controversy; the objects of trade unionism (if the articulate minority may be trusted) were broadening and becoming more revolutionary. The official spokesmen of the unions were reluctant to commit their constituents, and often debarred by their constitutions from so doing, on most important issues. An organisation that is undergoing extensive internal changes cannot act promptly in its external relations; yet any general change could be introduced only by the consent of the unions. A final obstacle to easy handling of national wage-questions was the large number of unorganised workers, whose wages normally followed those of their organised fellow-workers, but could not be made the subject of any general change with ease or certainty.

Thus, while the governing conditions of the wages problem before the war were relatively simple—the existence of standard rates in most trades, established and changed by collective bargaining; a regular procedure, in a more limited but still considerable range of trades, for effecting changes either in rates or in conditions affecting wages; and the strike or lock-out as the ultimate resort in a deadlock—it was not a simple thing to base a policy on these conditions, once State interference with wages became necessary. The conception of the standard rate was simple, but the thing itself was very complicated, since rates varied with occupation and with district and differed very much in the extent to which they received recognition. Similarly collective bargaining was effected through an enormously complicated machinery of very varying efficiency. And the resort to a stoppage in cases of deadlock, though the only way that had been discovered of finding a solution that might be expected to stand, had its dangers and disadvantages multiplied manifold by a state of war.

Government interference with wages before the war had been very limited in extent. In certain trades, characterised by low wages, a large preponderance of women workers, and a lack of trade union organisation, Trade Boards had been established under the Trade Boards (Minimum Wage) Act of 1909. In coal-mining similar machinery had been set up under the Coal Mines (Minimum Wage) Act of 1912. The effect of these was to establish legal minimum rates; but these rates were actually fixed by a process very similar to that of voluntary collective bargaining. Outside these exceptional trades the chief contact between the Government and the settlement of wages was through the Chief Industrial Commissioner's Department of the Board of Trade. Under the Conciliation Act of 1896, the Board of Trade had powers to inquire into industrial disputes and to endeavour to bring the parties to a dispute together; to appoint, on the application of either party to a dispute, a conciliator, who should endeavour to effect a settlement by agreement; and to appoint, on the application of both parties to a dispute, an arbitrator who should settle by an award. The exercise of these powers ensured an intimate contact between the Chief Industrial Commissioner's Department and the industries of the country, although the great majority of wage-questions were settled without his intervention. His work assisted and supplemented the machinery of voluntary conciliation without seeking to supersede it, and in general the State may be said to have left wages to be settled by the interplay of economic forces which it did not seek to control.

II. Movement of Wages, August, 1914—July, 1915.

(a) RISE IN THE COST OF LIVING.

On the outbreak of war there seemed no reason for interfering with, or even supplementing, this elaborate organisation for dealing with wages. The leaders of the workpeople's unions spontaneously recommended an industrial truce,[1] and the number of workpeople involved in disputes commencing in the last five months of 1914 was only 23,000. The general economic changes that the war led to made it impossible, however, to stereotype wages, and in the early months of 1915 the industrial truce showed signs of breaking down. The defects of the ordinary provision for dealing with wages began to show themselves, and the Government took its first steps in the direction of regulating wages. By the time the Ministry of Munitions came into existence, these steps were still very limited and tentative ; they were confined to supplementing rather than superseding the ordinary provision.

In the period between the outbreak of war and the establishment of the Ministry, changes in wages took place, but not of a magnitude to correspond with the changes that were taking place in the position of the wage-earner ; they took place without any co-ordinating control by Government policy, and they were hampered by the existence of the industrial truce ; they were uneven and partial, not uniform and general. They had the effect, therefore, of seriously altering the relations between the wages of different classes of workers without establishing any new basis, with the result that wages were in an unstable condition when the Ministry came into existence.

In the following table the general movement of wages is illustrated. The figures represent the effect of a change in the rate for a full week's work ; they do not therefore show the effect of short-time or overtime.[2] For the purposes of comparison some figures illustrating the change in the cost of living and the number of disputes are also given.

Months.	Percentage Rise in Retail Cost of Food over level of July 1914.	Net Increase (+) or Decrease (−) in Wages reported to Board of Trade.	Number of work-people receiving an Increase.	Amount of Increase.	Number suffering a Decrease.	Amount of Decrease.	Number of New Disputes.	Number of work-people directly involved.
		£		£		£		
1914								
August	—	− 178	18,706	1,010	36,200	1,188	15	1,975
September	10	+ 173	2,142	173	—	—	23	2,972
October	12	+ 2,117	58,081	2,297	9,182	180	27	5,046
November	13	− 1,883	31,452	3,502	147,405	5,385	25	4,665
December	16	+ 3,692	49,658	3,692	—	—	17	1,190
1915								
January	18	+ 1,916	44,770	4,240	77,535	2,324	30	3,436
February	22	+ 17,889	149,988	18,181	3,650	292	47	26,129
March	24	+ 72,713	446,267	72,713	—	—	74	12,982
April	24	+ 12,894	192,655	12,894	—	—	44	5,137
May	26	+ 188,485	969,680	188,485	—	—	63	39,913
June	32	+ 20,003	179,876	20,003	—	—	72	17,954
July { 1st / 31st }	32¼ / 34	—	80,700	2,900	754	—	40	202,095

[1] Vol. I, Part II, Chap. II, p. 31.   [2] Cf. Appendix I.

The reductions in wages in August and November, 1914, and January, 1915, were due to a fall in selling prices in industries and districts in which wages varied automatically with selling prices. The rise in February, 1915, is exclusive of a war bonus of 3s. and 2s. a week to railway workers. The great rise in May is accounted for by the advance, varying in the different fields, but normally about 15 per cent., in the coal-mining industry. The advance in June was subsequently supplemented by a 5 per cent. advance in cotton-spinning, arranged in July to date back to June. The large number of workpeople involved in disputes in July were almost all of them accounted for by the South Wales coal strike. The general result of the table is that wages were "frozen" from August, 1914, to January, 1915; from February onwards unprecedented advances in money wages were secured by those classes of workmen whose labour was in demand for the purposes of the war; but even these were not sufficient to compensate for the increased cost of living. These two factors it was, the rise in the cost of living and the growing demand for labour for war purposes, that made wage-changes inevitable.

The rise in the cost of living was the ground on which, almost exclusively, trade union spokesmen in conferences and arbitration hearings based demands for increases in wages. The profits that employers were alleged to be making were adduced as an additional reason, but the demand was pressed even when no attempt was made to rebut the evidence brought by employers that profits were small. It would be difficult, the spokesmen argued, to induce the rank and file of the unions to continue to observe the industrial truce, unless the rise in the cost of living was stopped or wages adjusted to meet it. Members of the Labour Party in Parliament protested against the rise and argued that, if the prices of commodities were allowed to rise in accordance with the law of supply and demand, wage-earners should be free to take advantage of the same law and raise the price of labour.[1] The Prime Minister's statement on 11 February, 1915, in the House of Commons on the rise in the cost of living, in which he gave the impression that it was unavoidable and that little could be done to check it, was strongly criticised by Mr. Clynes, Mr. Anderson and others, and provoked much resentment among organised workers in the country. Of the two alternatives, keeping prices down and forcing wages up, the trade union leaders expressed themselves as preferring the former; they were compelled, however, to aim at the latter.

The situation was the more difficult, because wage-earners were feeling the pressure of the rise in the cost of living before the war. They had been prevented in many cases by long term agreements from securing a corresponding advance in wages, in spite of the fact that industry generally was prosperous. In the cotton spinning industry, for example, wages were governed by a five years' agreement made in 1910. In the engineering trades, wages were largely governed by local agreements with a term of three years, and when, as in the Clyde and London districts, an agreement was due to terminate towards the end of 1914,

---

[1] *e.g.* 15 March, 1915. *Parliamentary Debates*, 1915 (H. of C.), LXX, 1823

the men were looking forward to its termination to give them an opportunity of securing compensation for the rise in the cost of living that had taken place since the agreements were made.

The negotiation of new long-term agreements was not easy in the abnormal conditions of war. The rise in the cost of living proceeded all the time negotiations were going on, markets had changed and were changing, the labour situation was changing every week. In spite of this the normal procedure was followed in a number of cases and new long-term agreements concluded. Thus in November new agreements were made in the engineering trades in London on the basis of a 3s. advance in time-rates, in Birmingham and Leicester of a 2s. advance, the new rates to stand for two years in each case. On the Clyde, although the form and amount of the unions' claims were determined before war broke out, and were based on the pre-war rise in cost of living and the pre-war prosperity of the industry, quite apart from war changes, no agreement could be reached, and after a serious strike the question was referred for settlement to the Committee on Production, who, on 23 March, awarded an advance of 1d. an hour (half the union's claim) as a war-wage.

The employers' case against making advances rested on the fact that their contracts were usually based on a labour cost based in its turn on a long-term agreement. Contracts made before the war or during the depression of August, 1914, were still running.[1] It proved impossible, however, even where agreements had still some time to run, to refuse advances. The example was set by munitions centres. In the Sheffield engineering trades an advance of 1s. a week was granted early in October, in spite of a three years' agreement raising wages 2s. a week concluded only the previous March. A further 4s. was conceded in March, 1915, when other districts were getting their first advance. On the Tyne a similar advance was granted in March, although wages were governed by an agreement with fifteen months still to run. The first award of the Committee on Production, a national award in the shipbuilding industry of 4s. a week, 1d. an hour or 10 per cent. on piece-rates, on 1 March, set a standard generally adopted in the ensuing months. These advances were supplementary, designed to meet the increased cost of living due to the war, and were extended generally to the engineering trades in the course of the spring and summer of 1915. A similar movement was going on outside the munitions industries, the railway workers receiving a bonus of 3s. or 2s. in February and the miners an average advance of about 15 per cent. in May.

Apart from advances in the standard district rates and bonuses extending to all workpeople, individual advances and bonuses were common wherever the demand for munitions made itself felt. Bonuses on output, bonuses on time-keeping, "hallelujah" rates, "time and a bit," remunerative systems of payment by results, and abundant

---

[1] Committee on Production Hearing: Manchester Engineering Employers: 19 April, 1915.

overtime were offered to induce an extra application from the worker or to attract workers from other firms and districts. Even where there was no intention of raising wages, abnormal earnings were in many cases made possible by the fixing of piece-rates at a high level, on work of which they had no experience, by firms undertaking the manufacture of munitions for the first time. Employers who needed labour, however, needed it very badly, and were willing to offer concealed advances, where for any reason a general advance in the district rate was objectionable. The growing shortage of labour was making itself felt and enabling the unions to press their demands.

(b) The Demand for Labour.

Some measure of this shortage and of the general demand for labour is afforded by the Board of Trade returns on the state of employment.

The first effect of the war was to depress employment outside a limited range of munition industries. Certain industries, notably cotton, were already affected by a general decline in employment due to causes quite unconnected with the war; and the extent of the decline was masked by the endeavour of many employers to avoid discharging any portion of their staffs by putting all upon short time. There was, however, in August an increase in the number of members unemployed in the case of all the trade unions making returns to the Board of Trade except shipbuilding. The average increase was 4·3 per cent., from 2·8 per cent. to 7·1 per cent., an average made up of figures that varied from an increase of 13·8 in the case of cotton to a decrease of 0·3 in the case of shipbuilding. Even in the case of industries like engineering and coal mining the first effect was a contraction of employment, since the volume of private work adversely affected by the war was so much greater than the volume of public work to which the war gave rise.

The first effect of the war, therefore, on wages was adverse. Although reductions were unusual, the movement upwards that characterised the first part of the year was checked, and the workpeople were unable to secure any compensation for the increased cost of living. The Government's policy of concentrating munitions contracts on a small number of established armament firms accentuated the evil, since it prevented the war demand from affecting any but a limited number of areas. The result was that engineering firms in Manchester and shipbuilding firms in Glasgow took on private contracts, with a view to keeping their works going, at prices that would not allow of an advance in wages. The influence of the set-back to trade at the outbreak of war continued to be felt as long as these private contracts ran, and constituted an obstacle to wages advances as late as the following spring, when food-prices had advanced over 25 per cent.

Where munitions contracts were placed, on the other hand, advances were made in order to stimulate workpeople to greater exertions and to attract labour from other districts. Such advances as those in the engineering trades in Sheffield in October and in London in November destroyed the normal relation between rates in these districts and rates in other engineering centres. Government contracts, while improving the demand for labour in the country as a whole, exercised an uneven influence; some industries they hardly helped at all, and they affected only certain districts in the industries on which their influence was greatest.

The effect of enlistment was felt more generally. It was not, however, until December that it overtook the contraction in men's employment, and, of course, it did not, except indirectly, affect women's employment at all.

The industries affected by Government contracts began to draw on other industries for labour to replace the labour of enlisted men in October; by December they had drawn in more labour than they had lost by enlistment. But there was a large group of industries, of which building and cotton were the most important, in which the contraction of employment in December was still much greater than the reduction by enlistment in the supply of labour. Moreover, every industry showed a considerable amount of short time, while overtime to a greater or less extent was being worked elsewhere in the same industry.

There was a general improvement by February; but depression persisted in certain industries, and short time was being worked even in the industries most affected by Government contracts. By April the first effect of the war may be said to have ceased. The number of women in employment reached pre-war level; the contraction of employment among men had already by December been overtaken by the proportion of men enlisting. A great deal of overtime was being worked, while few were on short time.

(c) THE FIRST ADVANCES.

The form and basis of the advances that the workpeople secured varied very much. In the first period, while the attempt was still being made to maintain pre-war rates unchanged, such changes as took place were in the form of ordinary advances, taking the place of lapsed agreements, establishing new rates, or following the movement of selling-prices in accordance with a sliding scale. In 1915, when it was becoming obvious that some alteration in wages was unavoidable, the practice of giving a bonus, explicitly supplementary and designed to meet the increased cost of living, became general. Existing standard rates and agreements were, nominally at any rate, left intact.

When the Committee on Production, early in 1915, intervened in wage-settlements, it questioned representatives of the two sides on the bearing of war conditions on permanent agreements.[1] There was general agreement that the two should be considered separately, and the Committee, in making its awards, adopted the form of a bonus

---

[1] *e.g.*, Hearing of Manchester Engineering Trades, 19 April, 1915.

or war wage to be "recognised as due to and dependent on the existence of the abnormal conditions now prevailing in consequence of the war."

Inevitably other questions than the cost of living, questions, for example, affecting allowances for "dirty" work, overtime and methods of remuneration, came up for consideration, and the Committee was prepared to consider them, if necessary, provided that no stoppage of work took place; but the necessity was regarded as regrettable. "We do feel as a Court very strongly," said Sir Francis Hopwood from the chair on one occasion, "that questions of that sort, which rather govern the constitution and the working of trade over long periods of time, in fact the life history of trade, should, if possible, be deferred until after this grave national crisis has passed away." Mr. Arthur Henderson, the spokesman of the workpeople at the hearing, concurred.[1]

Even when old agreements terminated and new agreements fell to be negotiated, there was a strong body of opinion that only temporary adjustments should be made, any change in the basic conditions of employment being deferred until after the war. This opinion was held by the Prime Minister, and was the basis of the Chief Industrial Commissioner's recommendations after his enquiry into the South Wales Coal dispute in June, 1915.

"The claim that a new wage agreement should now be settled on normal peace lines, with an attempt to dismiss from the mind the conditions of war, is, in my opinion, impracticable. Certain essential features of such an agreement would be inoperative during the war, and the possible conditions after the war, to which it is thought the new wage agreement should apply, may be quite as abnormal as the present conditions. I suggest, therefore, that the conditions both during and for some time following the war are likely to be so different from ordinary peace conditions, to which it is admitted the wage agreement is intended to apply, that any such agreement would be in practice valueless."[2]

That this view was not confined to official circles is shown by the speeches of Labour Members in Parliament. Mr. Anderson, for example, while pressing the Government to take action to stop the rise in the cost of living, deprecated any attempt to exploit the present difficulties. "Workpeople," he said, "are in a better position than ever they were to take advantage of the law of supply and demand for themselves if that is going to apply to the question of the price of food. I hope that neither workpeople nor employers are going to do anything of the kind."[3]

There was hesitation and difference of opinion as to the proper basis of such bonuses. Should the bonus be proportionate to existing rates, in which case the higher-paid worker would get the larger bonus? or proportionate to need, in which case the lower-paid worker would get

---

[1] Committee on Production Hearing: Bristol Channel Engineering and Shipbuilding Trades, 23 March, 1915.
[2] M.W. 20552.
[3] *Parliamentary Debates*, 1915 (H. of C.), LXX, 1823.

the larger bonus? or should it be uniform for all workers? If it was to be uniform, should it take the form of a definite weekly sum payable to time-workers and piece workers alike ? or should it take the form of a definite sum to time-workers and a percentage on earnings in the case of piece-workers ? Finally, should it count as part of the ordinary wages for the purpose of calculating supplementary payments, such as overtime ? Every variety was tried, and consistency had not been attained when the war ended. Thus, the settlement on the railways in February, 1915, differentiated between workers earning less and workers earning more than 30s. a week, and gave the higher bonus to the lower-paid class ; the awards to the miners in May were percentage advances and therefore proportionate to earnings. In March, in the engineering trades, there were advances made in Sheffield, in Barrow, on the North East Coast ; in the case of the first the skilled grades received 4s. and labourers 3s. ; at Barrow the skilled men received 3s. and the labourers 4s. ; on the North East Coast both received 4s. Some local authorities discriminated between married men and single men, and in at least one important branch of private employment the same was done.[1] On the whole the workpeople's representatives objected to such discrimination, on the ground that the different workers were " expending the same labour energy " ; they objected also to overtime earnings being brought into account and used as an argument against advances proportionate to the increase in the cost of living. Employers' spokesmen varied, in some cases objecting to flat rate advances,[2] in another arguing that an advance to meet the cost of living should take no account of the differences between the rates of different grades.[3] For the elimination of such local variations a national authority was needed. This was provided ultimately by the Committee on Production ; but the variations persisted long after the Committee was established.

This attempt to treat the war period as a thing apart was obviously influenced by the general belief that the duration of the war would be short. Most of the early war bonuses were fixed for the duration of the war. Had it been possible systematically to keep war conditions and the normal basis of wages apart, much subsequent trouble might have been saved ; but in practice many agreements were made, taking the place of lapsed agreements or establishing an entirely new basis in a trade, which took the form and were intended to have the effect of agreements made under normal conditions. A notable example was the South Wales Coalfield settlement of July, 1915, which, in spite of the Government's opposition, in effect conceded the workpeople's claim to a new agreement.[4]

Throughout the first year of the war the spirit of the industrial truce predominated. The Government hoped to stereotype the rates

---

[1] Committee on Production Hearing : S. Wales Copper Works v. Dock Wharf, etc., Union, 21 May, 1915.

[2] Committee on Production Hearing : Clyde Smiths and Strikers, 27 April, 1915.

[3] Committee on Production Hearing : Manchester Engineering Trades, 19 April, 1915.

[4] Vol. IV, Chap. I, Sect. 3.

obtaining when war broke out, and the trade union leaders were just as anxious to confine changes to the barest adjustment to meet the rise in the cost of living. Conditions, however, were such as to disturb the pre-existing rates of wages and the relations between rates of different classes. Owing to the action of individuals, rates and earnings tended to rise in certain industries and certain districts, and might have been forced higher, had Labour exploited its opportunities to the full; in other industries and districts, earnings fell and rates might have been depressed, had employers exercised pressure in that direction. On the whole both parties showed great restraint; the number of general changes (apart from changes under sliding scales) in the first six months was small, and any attempt on the part of Labour to exploit the country's needs was discountenanced by its leaders. The big changes that began in February, 1915, were far from compensating all workers for the rise in the cost of living. The engineering and shipbuilding trades showed a general advance of 3s. or 4s., coal-mining an average of about 15 per cent., iron and steel rather more; the equally well organised cotton industry secured no advance till June, when the spinning section secured a bonus of 5 per cent. The well-organised but less highly paid railwaymen received 3s. or 2s., transport workers at the ports usually more. In general, advances were secured where the demand for labour was greatest and was backed by organisation; in other words, wages were settled in much the same way as in peace time, by the relation of supply and demand. The same conclusion is suggested by a comparison of advances in different districts of the same trades; munitions centres showed advances long before other centres, and retained their advantage when general advances were made.

From the point of view of the subsequent problems of the Ministry of Munitions the irregularity of the advances is the most important feature of the year. Instead of a general movement of employment with a corresponding movement of wages in all industries, there were sporadic movements. Unco-ordinated individual, local and sectional advances took the place of general advances. Departures from standard rates were common, bonuses and other extra payments being made to individuals and groups to stimulate their exertions or merely to retain their labour. Even where no advances were made in the rate of remuneration, opportunities of making exceptional earnings were common on overtime or some system of payment by results.[1]

The ordinary difficulties of settling wages questions were, therefore, accentuated by the time the Ministry of Munitions was established

---

[1] In a hearing of the Clyde Engineering and Shipbuilding Trades before the Committee on Production, on 22 March, 1915, the employers' representative stated that a comparison of average earnings between four weeks in June and four weeks in December, 1914, showed, on Government work of all classes (returns from 26 firms), an advance of 23·5 per cent., on marine engineering for warships, an advance of 26 per cent., Government and merchant work (returns from 77 firms), an advance of 20·5 per cent. Yet overtime in the whole district averaged only 7 hours per man, and there had been no advance in rates (Cf. Appendix I).

and entrusted with its limited powers of controlling wages. For the comparisons between district and district and trade and trade, and between changes in the cost of living and changes in wages, which form the staple of the pleadings on conciliation boards and before arbitration courts, could lead to no stable settlement when relations were changing as much and as frequently as in the first year of the war. The industrial truce assumed the maintenance of pre-war rates as the basis of industrial peace; the alteration in these rates, in accordance solely with changes in the supply of and demand for labour, undermined that basis.

III. Government Intervention in Wages Questions, August, 1914—July, 1915.

(a) WAGES AND LABOUR SUPPLY.

In the first year of the war the Government was reluctant to face the issues that would be involved in any policy of controlling or adjusting wages. Burdened with other responsibilities and relying on the industrial truce, it aimed, so far as possible, at maintaining pre-war wages intact. Even after considerable changes had taken place, on the eve of the establishing of the Ministry of Munitions, the view was still authoritatively held that the war bonuses conceded between February and June constituted a settlement by which the Government should stand.[1] But the problem of munitions supplies, which was leading to an ever-increasing extension of Government control of industry, was inseparably linked with the problem of wages. In the first place, the output could not be increased without either increasing or economising the supply of skilled labour, and the attempt to secure such increase and economy turned largely on questions of remuneration; in the second place, output was endangered by stoppages due to disputes over wages.

The bearing of remuneration on supply was brought out first in the relatively unimportant case of allowances to transferred workers. The protracted negotiations to which it led are recorded elsewhere;[2] they are important in the history of wages, not only because they constituted the first interference by the Government with the course of wages and showed that such interference was practicable, but because they are typical of the way in which Government action directed

---

[1] "The Committee on Production have already given nearly forty decisions on wages questions covering directly about 750,000 workpeople, and agreements and decisions on similar lines have been adopted in many other cases, the total involving in the aggregate very large additions to the wages bill. Such a process cannot be again followed without serious difficulty . . . The local leader on the Clyde has made no secret of his determination to exploit to the utmost the needs of the nation for the benefit of the members of his Union. . . . The continued increase in the prices of food and other articles seems likely to be again used as a cover for the exercise of the power which, owing to the shortage of labour, is now in the hands of many Unions." Memo. by Sir George Askwith, 1 June, 1915. (HIST. REC./R/180/33).

[2] Vol. I, Part II, Chap. II; Part III, Chap. III.

to a specific and limited object was used as a precedent in support of a general claim. The Shipbuilding and Engineering Unions cited the payment of subsistence allowances to mobilisation labour when they demanded similar allowances in all cases in which labour was transferred from one district to Government work in another. The shipbuilding conferences on the Clyde and Tyne in November and at Carlisle in December, and the engineering conferences at Sheffield in December, all broke down on this point, although there were other but less important points of disagreement. In principle the demand was conceded by the War Munitions Volunteer scheme adopted by the Government on the recommendation of the National Advisory Committee in June, 1915.[1] By this scheme it was hoped to place a supply of mobile skilled labour at the disposal of the Minister of Munitions for employment wherever the exigencies of Government work required ; travelling expenses and subsistence allowance were a condition both of mobility and of voluntary enlistment.

The opposition of employers was due not only to the expense involved ; this might have been transferred to the Government ; but rather to the reaction of allowances upon their other employees. Complaints were made that the Admiralty terms for emergency workers had an unsettling effect on the other workers, who received no allowance, and provoked demands for equivalent wage advances. The Shipbuilding Employers' Federation argued that the additional payments demanded by the unions would merely result in men changing their jobs in order to qualify for them, and thus increase costs without increasing output. The unions' case was that travelling and subsistence allowance were the established custom of the trade when men were employed away from home, and the necessary labour would be forthcoming if this custom were extended to the new cases. The institution of a special corps, subject to special obligations which marked them off from other workers, met the difficulty, since it made it possible to extend special privileges to members of the corps without provoking comparisons which would cause a general demand for these privileges. Even so, there was hesitation on the part of large employers about taking members of the corps.[2]

Similar problems arose over the employment of Belgian immigrant labour and imported Dominion labour. Complaints were made by the unions that Belgians were being employed at rates or on conditions inferior to those of British labour on the same or similar work. To prevent any such evil the recruitment of Belgian labour for munitions work was confined to the Labour Exchanges, and the granting of rates and conditions not inferior to those of British labour required of contractors. The introduction of Dominion labour was at first opposed by the chief armament firms on the ground that it might cause trouble with the other workers ; when, subsequently, a number of Canadian engineers were introduced, the terms of employment, though including fares and a guarantee of six months' employment, included no subsistence allowance.[3]

---

[1] Vol. IV, Part I, Chap. I. [2] *Ibid.* [3] Vol. I, Part II, Chap. I.

(b) The Treasury Conferences of March, 1915.

The question of allowances was important only on the assumption, made by the trade union leaders, that there was in the country an adequate supply of skilled labour that merely needed transferring to Government work. Employers from the outset took the view that the supply would be inadequate to the need, and the Government, as represented by the Board of Trade, came to hold the same view. The problem therefore presented itself as one of economising and making the most effective use of the limited supply of skilled labour available. The problem was a problem of wages, directly, because it raised the question of the rates of less skilled workers introduced to skilled men's work and of skilled workers transferred to more responsible jobs, and also indirectly, because the rules and practices governing the allocation of work and the methods of remuneration were the principal safeguards on which the skilled worker relied for the maintenance of his standard rates. Stoppages, again, which it was essential to prevent, were due more frequently to wages disputes than to any other cause, and the frequent change of job by workmen attracted by the chance of higher wages was another failure of economy, which could be dealt with only by restricting the freedom of movement of the wage-earner or controlling wages.

The question of the rate arose as soon as the proposal to introduce labour of less skill to skilled men's work was put forward. The sanctity of the standard rate is the basis of trade union policy. At the shipbuilding conference on the Clyde on 9 November, 1914, the rates to be paid to the unskilled men whom it was proposed to introduce was one cause of difference. The problem was more important in engineering, and here the employers' federation met the unions' claim in principle. At the third conference of the Federation with the unions, convened in Sheffield on 13 January, 1915, as a result of an appeal to the two sides from the War Office to come to agreement, the employers in their proposals undertook, " That workpeople shall receive the rates of wages and work under the conditions recognised in the shop in question for the trade at which they are for the time engaged." This conference failed to reach agreement; but agreement was reached, so far as the production of shells and fuses was concerned, at a subsequent conference on 5 March, held after the two sides had met the Committee on Production separately. The rate was safeguarded more specifically by making the district practice the standard : " Where semi-skilled or female labour is employed in place of skilled labour the rates paid shall be the usual rates of the district obtaining for the operations performed." Later in the same month, at the Treasury Conference of unions concerned with the production of munitions, the question was considered again and a settlement embodied in the following formula :—

> " Where the custom of a shop is changed during the war by the introduction of semi-skilled men to perform work hitherto

performed by a class of workmen of higher skill, the rates paid shall be the usual rates of the district for that class of work.

The relaxation of existing demarcation restrictions or admission of semi-skilled or female labour shall not affect adversely the rates customarily paid for the job. In cases where men who ordinarily do the work are adversely affected thereby, the necessary readjustments shall be made so that they can maintain their previous earnings."

The last sentence was inserted to safeguard the interests of skilled men who might be transferred to more responsible work which carried with it diminished opportunities of earning. The guarantee of rates contained in the first clause was intended to cover time rates, that in the second piece-rates; the words "time and piece" were, however, inserted before the word "rates" when the agreement was incorporated as Schedule (2) in the Munitions of War Act the following July.

Thus the principle that the rates of the skilled men, whose province was to be invaded by less skilled labour, should be guaranteed was formally accepted by the Government and by them imposed on employers. But the subsequent history of the control of women's wages was to show that the conferences had been very far from anticipating and providing for all the possible questions that might arise in the application of the principle. The final formula was indeed as precise as is necessary in a voluntary collective agreement that can be referred back for interpretation or amendment to the parties that adopted it; it lacked the precision and elaboration needed in a rule that is to be enforced by legal process in the courts.

A guarantee of the district rates was only one method by which the skilled workers' representatives sought to secure their constituents' position. Much more serious than any temporary departure from these rates was the menace to them in the future involved in the breaking down of the various safeguards on which the skilled man's superior rates depended. More stress was laid at the Treasury Conferences on this aspect of the question than on any other.[1] The Chairman of the Amalgamated Society of Engineers put their difficulty very clearly:—

"The most grave aspect of the case is this. What is going to happen after the termination of the war, in regard to a lot of people who will be brought into the engineering industry, who have not the necessary credentials and qualifications for the work? That is what we are concerned about. Because the introduction of unskilled and semi-skilled labour into this industry is a standing menace to the skilled. We have no desire to prevent any one rising in the social scale, but we do not think we are called upon to allow him to rise in the social scale to the detriment of the skilled workers."

---

[1] Verbatim Report of the Conference. (Copy in HIST. REC./R/180/17.)

At the second Treasury Conference between the Government and the Amalgamated Society of Engineers, Mr. Brownlie again devoted the first and longer portion of his speech to explaining the importance to the skilled men of the safeguards and privileges it was proposed to suspend. Mr. Button, another member of the Executive Council, put their position very plainly:—

" . . . we represent certain interests—if you like, vested interests and a monopoly in skill which it is our duty to safeguard. . . . The job for which we are paid is to protect the interests of the operative engineer."

Mr. Ryder, an Organising District Delegate, explained that it was the attitude of the working members that they had to consider:—

" It is not altogether so much that we require to be convinced as our members generally . . . if we can go to our members with the present needs accurately defined, and with the safeguards accurately defined, then we can do some good and can convince our members and carry them with us. . . ."

Another delegate reached the heart of the trouble in a question he put to Mr. Lloyd George:—

" . . . could you see your way clear to give guarantees and assurances that, at the end of the war, semi-skilled men will be removed?"

The Chancellor of the Exchequer: "That is an essential part of the bargain."

The Delegate: "But could you devise ways and means of eliminating the skilled knowledge which the semi-skilled men will have acquired?"

The Chancellor of the Exchequer: "Well!"

To meet these very natural fears the Committee on Production in their interim report had recommended that employers should give a guarantee to restore pre-war conditions when the emergency was past. The same undertaking was embodied in the Shells and Fuses Agreement concluded between the Engineering Employers' Federation and the engineering skilled unions on 5 March, and an amplified version of the Committee on Production's formula was embodied in the Treasury Agreement of 19 March. Even then the Amalgamated Society of Engineers were not prepared to recommend the agreement for adoption by the unions; they required also definite assurances that the sacrifice of their safeguards should be for the benefit of the State alone and that the responsibility for restoring the safeguards would be accepted by the Government. These assurances the Government gave them, supplementing the Treasury Agreement of 19 March by a memorandum of 25 March, putting it on record that profits on war work were to be limited, relaxation of trade practices to be restricted to war work, war work to be certified as such by the

Government, the undertaking to restore conditions to be extended by analogy to new inventions, and the influence of the Government to be used to restore pre-war conditions.

The suspension of demarcation rules was refused by the shipbuilding unions in the shipbuilding conferences, but accepted as part of the Treasury Agreement to which they were signatories. It was accepted by the engineering unions by the Shells and Fuses Agreement, subject to the condition that the making of tools and gauges and the setting up of machines should be restricted to fully skilled men of some branch of the industry. The question of methods of remuneration arose in the shipbuilding conferences, the employers urging that the additional incentive of an extension of piece-work would increase output and so compensate in part for the shortage of labour. Similarly in engineering, employers in many cases introduced or extended piece-work and bonus systems, to which much of the new war production lent itself. The Amalgamated Society of Engineers had, however, just before the war withdrawn from the agreement with the Employers' Federation recognising these methods of remuneration, and there was a general prejudice against payment by results in trades with time-work traditions, due to the fear that in the process of fixing piece-rates for varying kinds of work and bargaining with individual workmen, the employers would find opportunities of depressing standards of wages. In the Treasury Agreement no explicit reference to methods of remuneration was made ; but the extension of systems of payment by results could be construed (and subsequently was construed) as falling under the head of relaxation of trade practices, essential to acceleration of output.

The Cabinet's other great object in convening the Treasury Conference, the suspension of the right to strike, had as important a bearing on wages. The trade unions recognised in principle that strikes to secure increased wages were inadmissible, but the rise in the cost of living and the difficulty in securing any corresponding adjustment of wages made it difficult for them to restrain their followers. Their difficulty was referred to by Mr. Ryder in the second Treasury Conference, and on more than one occasion by Labour Members, who were also trade union officials, in the House of Commons. It should be noted that it was an embargo on stoppages, not an embargo on advances, that Mr. Lloyd George asked for ;[1] but the comparison of wages advances and actual strikes made above suggests that the one was connected with the other.

It was the more difficult for trade union leaders to restrain their members from pressing their claims by the strike, since piecemeal advances were showing the possibility of higher wages on every side.

---

[1] Cf. Conference, 19 March, 1915.
" Mr. Arthur Henderson : You do not want to prevent our men making an effort to get something, but you do not want them to stop work."
" The Chancellor of the Exchequer : That is it; we do not want them to stop work." HIST. REC./R/180/17.)

These piecemeal and individual advances were the inevitable outcome of attempting to prevent a general rise in the wages of a class of labour that was in keen demand when the cost of living was steadily rising. It led to an unnecessary movement on the part of workpeople and a restlessness on the part of those who did not actually move which constituted a serious obstacle to smooth working and increased output. The ill-effects of this " enticement " of labour by the offer of high wages were brought to the notice of the Board of Trade, when it undertook its canvass of employers with a view to securing the release of skilled labour for munitions in January, 1915, and they were represented very strongly to the Armaments·Output Committee by deputations from Birmingham and Manchester in April. The evil was realised by the Committee, the Chairman stating that since the previous August, of every 100 men who had gone to Elswick 35 had left, and that at three works of Messrs. Vickers the number of men leaving in April and May amounted to nearly half the number taken on.[1] A " labour turnover " of this extent was a novelty in the United Kingdom ; that it was due to the breaking of the normal uniformity of rates for identical grades is suggested by a comparison with the United States, where standard district rates in engineering are almost unknown and an even greater " labour turnover " is normal.[2]

The development of the Government's policy in relation to the supply of skilled labour is described elsewhere.[3]

(c) Appointment of the Committee on Production.

Wages questions, like the other problems involved, were left in the first instance to the ordinary machinery of collective bargaining. As it became obvious that the necessary changes in trade practices would be delayed and the preservation of industrial peace would be endangered by the slow procedure of voluntary conferences, the Board of Trade in December intervened in a conciliatory capacity.

No great success attended this effort, and in January and February the Government began tentatively to consider steps, on the one hand, to conciliate labour, by allotting to the workpeople a share of the profits of manufacture for war purposes, on the other hand, to coerce labour by making striking and inciting to strikes punishable offences. The first part of this policy was announced by Lord Kitchener in the House of Lords on 15 March. Objections however were raised in private conferences by the employers concerned ; it was difficult to fit in Woolwich and other Government establishments with such a scheme, and it was discovered that labour itself did not like the policy. The other part was deferred on the advice of the Chief Industrial Commissioner until a final attempt should have been made to secure a suspension of the right to strike by agreement.

---

[1] Armaments Output Committee Printed Minutes, pp. 5, 10.
[2] Cf. Boyd Fisher, *Industrial Loyalty*, 1918.
[3] Vol. I, Part II.

While these measures were still under consideration on 4 February, the Committee on Production, consisting of the Chief Industrial Commissioner with a representative each of the Admiralty and the War Office, was appointed " to inquire and report forthwith, after consultation with the representatives of employers and workmen, as to the best steps to be taken to ensure that the productive power of the employees in engineering and shipbuilding establishments working for Government purposes shall be made fully available so as to meet the needs of the nation in the present emergency," and this Committee's reports shaped the policy finally adopted.

The first report, issued on 16 February, after conference with the shipbuilding unions and employers, dealt with the loss of time in shipyards due to broken squads of riveters, and recommended that the Government should call on employers and unions to agree on some method of making up broken squads, or, if they were unable to agree, to refer any outstanding differences to the Committee " for immediate and final settlement." The second report, issued on 20 February, after conference with the engineering unions and employers, dealt with the production of shells and fuses, with avoidance of stoppage of work and with guarantees that changes should be for the duration of the war only. Under the first head it pointed out the evil of any restrictive rules or customs, and recommended, first, that the Government should require its contractors to give an undertaking not to cut piece-rates unless methods of production were materially changed, and, secondly, that an increased use should be made of female labour. Without further intervention on the part of the Government the employers' federation and the unions were able to give effect to these recommendations in the Shells and Fuses Agreement of 5 March. Under the second heading, they recommended that the Government should ask the adhesion of its contractors and the trade unions to an undertaking to refrain from stoppages in Government work and to refer any differences that could not be settled to an impartial tribunal to be nominated by the Government. The Government at once acted on this recommendation, and nominated the Committee on Production itself to act as the impartial tribunal; thus the Committee was placed in a position that was subsequently to make it the chief influence in controlling wages in the country as a whole. Under the third head the report suggested a form of guarantee, to be signed by all Government contractors, safeguarding the unions against any permanent sacrifice of the control they were able to exercise over wages by their rules and practices, and again recommended that any difference in the adjustment of changes under this guarantee should be referred for settlement to the impartial tribunal. The third report, issued on 4 March, recommended the suspension of all demarcation restrictions, subject to certain safeguards, the chief of which were the maintenance of the rate for the job, the keeping of a record of all changes, and the guarantee of restoration after the war; and the utilisation of semi-skilled and unskilled labour on work normally done by skilled men, subject to the guarantee of restoration recommended in the second report. In cases of disagreement the matter was to be referred for settlement in the case of the suspension of demarcation restrictions to the Board of Trade, in the case of the utilisation of semi-skilled and unskilled labour to the impartial tribunal recommended in the second report. The fourth report, which was not published, pointed out the necessity, if labour was to be induced to sacrifice the practices by which it exercised its control over wages, of limiting the profits of the employers for whom they worked; it thus foreshadowed the "bargain" concluded in the Treasury Agreements of 19 and 25 March, 1915, and embodied in the Munitions of War Act the following July. On 1 March the Committee issued its first award as an arbitration court; the award was a national award, in settlement of a difference between the Boilermakers' and Shipwrights' Societies on the one hand and the Shipbuilding Employers' Federation on the other, and granted 4s. a week (or 1d. an hour) to time-workers and 10 per cent. to piece-workers, " to be regarded as war wages and recognised as due to and dependent on the abnormal conditions now prevailing in consequence of the war." The unions had claimed 6s.

The policy of the Committee was to rely on the moral authority of an appeal from the Government in time of war. This authority had enabled them to settle the Clyde strike at the end of February, and was still preferred to statutory powers. The reports did little to elaborate the terms on which the suspension of the various safeguards to wages should be effected and adjustments of wages made to meet the changing economic conditions. This they left to be settled by collective bargaining in the ordinary way, with reference to the Chief Industrial Commissioner or to the Committee itself in the last resort in place of the strike or lock-out. The problem was regarded as a temporary problem, to be dealt with by temporary arrangements, the permanent requirements of both sides being safeguarded by the guarantee that no temporary arrangement should prejudice a return to the *status quo*. No attempt was made to state principles in accordance with which trade practices should be modified and wages adjusted, doubtless because the duration of the war was not expected to be so long that permanent changes would be necessary; empirical adjustments by the parties concerned, or if they failed to agree, by an arbitrator, would, it was thought, meet all needs. At the same time a term would be put to the tedious and annoying negotiations that had been the rule before the Government intervened, and the strikes and lock-outs that in normal times put a term to such negotiations would be prevented. The recommendations amounted to a procedure rather than a policy.

The Treasury Conference was convened on 17 March to secure the explicit consent of the unions to this procedure. The Chancellor of the Exchequer appealed to the unions to forgo their right to strike and to suspend all practices restrictive of output, and promised to limit the profit of the employers. The conference did something, as is indicated above, to elaborate principles which should govern wages adjustments as a result of dilution; in the main, however, the agreement reached relied on reference to arbitration to settle any question that might arise and on the guarantee of restoration of pre-war conditions to safeguard the permanent position of the skilled worker. The miners' and cotton unions refused to agree to suspend their ordinary procedure in favour of the proposed procedure for avoiding stoppages·; but their abstention was due, not to any intention of exploiting the strike weapon, but solely to faith in the efficacy of the existing conciliation machinery, and an undertaking was given in each case to settle disputes without stoppages.

IV. Conclusion.

Thus in the first year of the war wages questions continually demanded the attention of the Government and led to action by the Government. But the problem that led to this action was conceived as the problem of labour supply and was never approached as a wages question. No attempt was made to devise a consistent policy of wages control. The Government stated its needs, and left it to the employers and trade unions to devise in negotiation with each other solutions of the wages questions involved in satisfying those needs. When it was forced to intervene, its interference was confined to substituting reference to arbitration for the strike, and to carrying through with the unions the negotiations over restrictive practices which employers had initiated and failed to carry through. When the Ministry of Munitions was established, it was still generally assumed that wages and wage questions could be left to the ordinary machinery of collective bargaining, working on the basis of pre-war rates. The Board of Trade, like the Ministry of Munitions subsequently, was reluctant to add the control of wages to its other duties until forced to do so. It might almost be said that the Government and the unions were at cross purposes, the former seeking to confine attention to output, the latter to the protection of wages.

The policy of piecemeal adjustments made the task of labour regulation, which the Ministry of Munitions was about to take up, much more difficult than it would have been, had the changes in wages in the first year of the war been controlled in accordance with some definite principles. As has been shown, the system of rates, which it was sought to adjust by arbitration, was seriously dislocated long before the machinery of arbitration was complete. The normal relations between the wages of different classes and grades of workers in the same industry, between different industries and between different districts had been altered and the new relations had neither authority nor stability.[1]

The practice of employers—and of the employing Departments of the Government itself—of inducing skilled workmen to leave their places by offering higher rates or opportunities of earning higher wages, which did perhaps more than anything else to break the standard

---

[1] For illustrations of the divergence of earnings in the first fifteen months of the war, see Appendix I.

rates, could be dealt with only by preserving uniformity of rates or by prohibiting the free movement of labour. The Board of Trade was reluctant to adopt the second course, and made no attempt to preserve the former condition. An attempt to prevent unnecessary movement was made by Regulation 8B of the Defence of the Realm Act on 29 April;[1] but it failed, the regulation remaining unused until it was revived in connection with an attempt to secure a more economical distribution of skilled men in 1918; a direct limitation of the worker's freedom to sell his labour in the best market was embodied in Section 7 of the Munitions of War Act.

The ordinary machinery of collective bargaining, on which it was intended to rely, was thrown out of gear and with important sections of the workers discredited. It had been found too slow in its operation to meet the needs of a period of rapid economic change, and it had been proved to depend for its effectiveness on the right to strike or lock-out, which was now suspended. It was ill-adapted to rapid change, because the system of reference from one conference to another, which increased the chances of peaceful settlement in normal times, took so long that the necessary adjustments could not be completed before further changes, requiring further adjustments, had occurred; it depended on the strike or lock-out, because negotiations might be prolonged and concessions refused indefinitely, if the fear of a stoppage in the last resort was not there to precipitate a settlement.

The failure of this machinery to preserve industrial peace was not yet apparent when the Ministry was formed; but it was obviously subjected to a serious strain by the continuous rise in the cost of living and the evidence of high profits. The Munitions of War Act carried out the Government's pledge, given at the Treasury Conferences, to limit profits; but the limitation of the profits of firms making munitions did nothing to check the rise in prices and corresponding inflation of profits in the trades supplying the needs of the ordinary wage-earner. The alleged "profiteering," from which the wage-earner suffered, and the "profiteering," which the suspension of his trade practices and union regulations would facilitate, were indeed independent issues confused in popular discussions. The Treasury Agreement and Munitions of War Act dealt with the latter, but did nothing to check the former. The Government's control of profits therefore failed to dispel industrial unrest, and was of use only as giving the Government a moral right to insist on the suspension of restrictive practices.

The Treasury Agreement had not the effect that was hoped. It was necessary to embody it in the Munitions of War Act, which gave statutory force to its terms. While the leaders of the trade unions, with whom alone the Government could get into direct contact, needed no convincing of the evil of strikes and were persuaded of the necessity of suspending restrictive practices, the rank and file, on whom the carrying out of the bargain really depended, were not convinced. As always, they reacted instinctively against the threat to their standard

---

[1] Vol. I, Part III, Chap. V.

rates; and the threat was serious, when they were asked at one and the same time to agree to a suspension of the principal safeguards and the disuse of the strike weapon. Even if there had not been this instinctive opposition, the continuous rise in the cost of living would have made general agreement difficult to secure. State control of wages was foreshadowed in the attempt to place restrictions on the movement of labour after higher wages, in the suspension of the right to strike, and in the beginning of the practice of national war advances awarded by a national arbitration authority. The implications of State control of wages were also foreshadowed in the suggestion put forward by the trade union spokesmen at several hearings of the Committee on Production that the Government should use its " control " over shipbuilding or engineering works to compensate employers for the cost of wages advances which their contracts would not otherwise enable them to bear.

CHAPTER II.

THE MINISTRY'S POWERS OF WAGE REGULATION.

I. Powers under the Munitions of War Act, 1915.

At the outset, the Ministry of Munitions was entrusted with very limited powers of wages control. The negotiations that preceded its establishment and led to the grant of its large powers of controlling the movement and regulating the labour of workpeople were, as has been shown, concerned very materially with wages, and the Treasury Agreement, on which the first Munitions of War Act was based, was in effect a bargain in which the protection of wages was a principal factor. But the Act placed on the Ministry no obligation and gave it no power to afford this protection.

The parts of the Act affecting wages are Part I with Schedule I, limiting the right to strike or lock-out in munitions industries and laying down procedure for the settlement of differences; Section 4 (2), requiring the consent of the Minister of Munitions to changes in wages and salaries in controlled establishments; Schedule II giving statutory force to the provisions of the Treasury Agreement about changes in practice and rates of wages; and also indirectly, Section 4 (5), which made works regulations for the ordering of work under certain conditions binding, and Sections 7 and 10, which limited the free movement of work-people in pursuit of higher wages.

(a) PART I.

Part I enacted that a difference which was not settled by the parties themselves might be referred by either party to the Board of Trade. The Board should take such steps as seemed expedient to promote a settlement; if suitable means existed under any agreement, the Board might refer the difference for settlement in accordance with these, or they might refer it to arbitration according to the provisions of the first schedule. This schedule provided three alternatives; the Committee on Production, a single arbitrator agreed on by the parties or appointed by the Board of Trade, and a special court consisting of an equal number of representatives of employers and work-people with a chairman appointed by the Board. The award on any such settlement would be binding on both parties; it might be retrospective; a contravention of it would be an offence under the Act. Strikes and lock-outs were made illegal, unless the difference should have been reported and twenty-one days have elapsed without the Board of Trade referring it for settlement. The differences to which this part of the Act applied were defined as—

"differences as to rates of wages, hours of work or otherwise as to terms or conditions of or affecting employment on the manufacture or repair of arms, ammunition, ships, vehicles, aircraft, or any other articles required for use in war, or of the metals, machines or tools required for that manufacture or repair,"

but the provisions might be extended by Proclamation to differences in other industries "on the ground that in the opinion of His Majesty the existence or continuance of the difference is directly or indirectly prejudicial to the manufacture, transport or supply of Munitions of War." This general power of extending the Act was, however, limited by the provision that no proclamation should be made in the case of any industry in which the Minister was satisfied that effective means already existed to secure a settlement without stoppage, a provision inserted in accordance with an undertaking to the miners' and cotton operatives' unions to exclude them from the scope of compulsory arbitration.

Part I thus embodied the policy of relying on the ordinary arrangements for collective bargaining to settle all wages questions, with the substitution of arbitration for the strike or lock-out. Even arbitration was deferred until every other resource was exhausted ; the Board of Trade was not bound to refer to arbitration, a provision intended to safeguard the Government against collusive action between employers and employed ; and the extension of the Act by Proclamation outside the defined field of munition industries was limited to industries in which adequate voluntary agreements for securing a settlement did not exist. Thus, formally, at any rate, the responsibility for adjusting wages to changing conditions was left with the unions and employers' associations, and the desire of the miners' and cotton operatives' unions to be excluded from the scope of compulsory arbitration was respected.

The powers of the Ministry of Munitions were limited to "reporting" differences. Since the control of munitions production rested with the Department, and the responsibility for carrying out the Government's pledges to the unions was naturally placed by the unions on its shoulders, this restriction was unfortunate ; the Ministry's officers inevitably came into contact with the differences first and were appealed to in connection with differences. The principle of the Act was, however, to disturb the ordinary provision for dealing with disputes as little as possible, and it was consistent with this principle to leave the administrative responsibility for arranging reference to arbitration to the Department which was already charged with conciliation and arbitration under the Act of 1896.

The independence of the arbitrating authorities followed from the same principle. There was no question as yet of fixing wages by administrative order ; the arbitrators, if they were to serve their purpose and make stoppages unnecessary, must be independent of departmental control.

(b) The Sanction of Changes in Wages in Controlled Establishments.

Section 4 (2) read as follows :—

"Any proposal for any change in the rate of wages, salary or other emoluments of any class of persons employed in the establishment or of any persons engaged in the management or the direction of the establishment (other than a change for giving effect to any Government conditions as to fair wages or to any agreement between the owner of the establishment and the workmen which was made before the twenty-third day of June, nineteen hundred and fifteen), shall be submitted to the Minister of Munitions who may withhold his consent within fourteen days of the date of submission :

"Provided that if the Minister of Munitions so directs, or if the Minister's consent is withheld, and the persons proposing the change so require, the matter shall be referred for settlement in accordance with the provisions of the First Schedule to this Act, and the consent of the arbitration tribunal, if given, shall in that case have the same effect as the consent of the Minister of Munitions.

"If the owner of the establishment or any contractor or sub-contractor employing labour therein makes any such change, or attempts to make any such change without submitting the proposal for the change to the Minister of Munitions or when the consent of the Minister has been withheld, he shall be guilty of an offence under this Act."

It was the only section of the Act giving to the Ministry definite administrative powers of controlling wages and was drafted in terms that might seem to give the Ministry complete control of wages. The Ministry's powers were actually very limited. In the first place they were confined to controlled establishments, a limited class covering at first no trade or industry as a whole. Hence the Ministry's powers did not extend to the control of changes in standard rates and in practice could not be exercised without running the danger of creating disparities between the wages of workpeople in controlled establishments and others of the same class in other establishments. The exemption from any need of sanction of "a change for giving effect to any Government condition as to fair wages" limited the Ministry's action in the same way. The Fair Wages Clause in Government contracts required controlled establishments to "pay rates of wages and observe hours of labour not less favourable than those commonly recognised by employers and trade societies . . . in the trade in the district where the work is carried on." A change in the district rate by agreement between employers or unions or by an arbitration award would effect a change in wages in a controlled establishment without any sanction from the Ministry. In the second place, there was an appeal possible from the Ministry's decision to arbitration in accordance with the provisions of the First Schedule of the Act;

the Ministry's decisions were always therefore liable to be upset by an authority independent of it. In the third place, although it was early realised that the control would be ineffective if it did not include the sanctioning of all changes in piece-rates,[1] it proved impracticable to require employers to submit all such changes.

The object of the Section was indeed much more limited. Mr. Lloyd George pointed out in addressing the first Treasury Conference that with the limitation of profits there would be a danger of collusion between employers and workpeople; this Section, it was explained in the debates on the Munitions of War Bill in the House of Commons, was intended to enable the Minister to prevent such collusion and to protect the tax-payer. While this was the object with which the clause was inserted in the Act, it was of course capable of other uses, and on 15 September, 1915, an announcement was made through the press that the Minister would use the powers conferred by it in order to prevent the reduction of piece-rates as a consequence of the increase of output due to suspension of restrictive practices.[2]

(c) Schedule II.

Schedule II embodied the terms on which at the two Treasury Conferences the trade union representatives had agreed to recommend to their members the suspension of all restrictive practices.[3] The only change from the formula embodied in the Treasury Agreement was the insertion in the fourth paragraph, which guaranteed rates in cases in which semi-skilled men were introduced to perform work hitherto done by skilled men, of the words " time and piece " before " rates." By Section 4 (4) of the Act itself the owner of a controlled establishment was deemed to have entered into an undertaking to carry out the provisions of this Schedule, rendering himself liable to a penalty (under Section 14 (1)) of £50 for any breach of the undertaking. The enforcement of the provisions in the Schedule was, however, left to private initiative; the question whether any particular rule or practice was restrictive was to be settled (under Section 4 (3)) by the Board of Trade or referred by them for arbitration like any other difference, while it was left to aggrieved workpeople and their representatives to detect and establish before a munitions tribunal any breach of the undertaking by an employer. It was expected that the principles set out in the Schedule would be applied by agreement between employers and trade unions locally; but the opposition to dilution among branch executives and the rank and file of the workers that had signed the Treasury Agreement was too strong to permit such agreement, until pressure was brought to bear by local Dilution Commissions. Without going to the extent of a prosecution, the Ministry could receive complaints and forward them to firms in the same way as breaches of the Fair Wages Clause were dealt with. Such complaints came in large numbers through the National Advisory Committee appointed after the Treasury Conference.

---

[1] C.R./2339, 2 September, 1915.   [2] See below, p. 125.   [3] See above, p. 19.

CH. II]   MINISTRY'S POWERS OF REGULATION   33

(d) WORKS REGULATIONS.

Section 4 (5) is a clause making binding any regulations with respect to the general ordering of work applied to a controlled establishment by the Minister of Munitions. It had a bearing upon the regulation of wages inasmuch as "due observance of the rules of the establishment" was one of the objects, and rules might be made governing the method of remuneration, penalising bad time-keeping and requiring work-people to work overtime. Such provisions were included in the code of rules drawn up for its members by the Engineering Employers' Federation,[1] which required work-people to work "on piece-work or the premium bonus system, as and when required by the Company, time rates in the case of piece-work being guaranteed." The prejudice against payment by results was not overcome by this simple device; it was decided that where men had been employed time-rate and the employer without their consent proposed to pay piece-rate, an order to work piece-rate was not a "lawful order" and disobedience was not punishable,[2] and the extension of payment by results was still the subject of controversy when the Ministry's operations ceased. In any case the final authority in deciding what rules should be enforced was left by the Minister's regulations not with the employer or even the Ministry, but with a local munitions tribunal; the Minister's regulations of 14 July, 1915, instructing owners of controlled establishments to post rules and work-people to comply with them, provided "that no person shall be liable to a penalty under the Act for failing or refusing to comply with any rule, if the Munitions Tribunal is satisfied that the rule is an unreasonable one, or that the person had just cause for his failure or refusal to comply with it." Experience soon proved that only the Ministry's model rules could be enforced, and these contained no provision of the sort indicated.[3]

(e) LEAVING CERTIFICATES AND POWER OF EMBARGO.

Section 7, like Section 4 (5) affected wages only incidentally, but its influence was much greater. It was as follows :—

(1) A person shall not give employment to a workman who has within the last previous six weeks or such other period as may be provided by order of the Minister of Munitions as respects any class of establishment, been employed on or in connexion with munitions work in any establishment of a class to which the provisions of this Section are applied by order of the Minister of Munitions, unless he holds a certificate from the employer by whom he was last so employed that he left work with the consent of his employer or a certificate from the munitions tribunal that the consent has been unreasonably withheld.

---

[1] Vol. IV, Part II, Appendix I.
[2] National Projectile Factory v. Fagan. M.A.R., p. 75.
[3] Cf. Vol. IV, Part II, Chap. I, Section 9.

(2) If any workman or his trade union representative complains to a munitions tribunal in accordance with rules made with respect to those tribunals that the consent of an employer had been unreasonably withheld that tribunal may, after examining into the case, if they think fit, grant a certificate which shall, for the purposes of this Section, have the same effect as a certificate from the employer.

(3) If any person gives employment in contravention of the provisions of this Section, he shall be guilty of an offence under this Act.

The order, applying it, defined the establishments to which it should apply as :—

"Any establishment being a Factory or Workshop, the business carried on in which consists wholly or mainly in engineering, shipbuilding, or the production of arms, ammunition or explosives, or the substances required for the production thereof."

This definition differed from that of "Munitions Work" adopted in the First Part of the Act, being taken from Regulation 8B, made on 29 April, under the Defence of the Realm Act, with the same object as Section 7 of the Munitions of War Act. Hence its scope was different both from the provisions of Part I, and of the regulations governing controlled establishments, yet the categories of workers affected were largely the same and the decision in any doubtful case could be made only by reference to a munitions tribunal.

The object of Section 7 was disciplinary.[1]

It was pointed out by Mr. Pringle that its effect would be to limit wages. "The workman in this country," he said, "is to be the only man who cannot sell the only commodity he has, namely, his labour, in the open market."[2] But it was the obstacle to output offered by the frequent movement of workers, not its indirect effect in forcing up wages, that employers impressed upon the Government and the latter sought to remove. Like the prohibition of strikes, it was part of a policy of removing obstacles to output ; taken with that prohibition, it also deprived workpeople of the normal means of protecting wages and securing advances. The trade unions urged and the Government subsequently admitted that these restrictions placed a corresponding obligation on the Department to safeguard wages, at any rate the wages of women munition workers. The disciplinary effect of

---

[1] Mr. Lloyd George :—" The third thing is the prevention of the practice which has done more to destroy discipline in the yards than almost anything— that is the practice of employers in pilfering each others' men. It is absolutely impossible to obtain any discipline or control over men if a man who may be either slack or disobedient to a reasonable order is able to walk out at the moment, go to the works which are only five or ten minutes off, and be welcomed with open arms without any question being asked." *Parliamentary Debates*, 1915 (H. of C.), LXXII, 1199.

[2] *Parliamentary Debates*, 1915 (H. of C.), LXXII, 1230.

the restriction, however, was the cause of its unpopularity at first. It was only as the cost of living rose and a marked divergence appeared between earnings on time-work and earnings on the system of payment by results that the inability to move was felt as a serious hardship. By the summer of 1917 employers were complaining of "poaching" of labour in spite of the leaving certificate,[1] and feared that if the leaving certificate were abolished it would be impossible to prevent a big movement of skilled time-workers to less skilled piece-work; and the Department found itself compelled to ask for power to regulate time-workers' wages before it could relinquish the leaving certificate provision.

Section 10 attacked the same problem, the obstacle to output offered by the frequent movement of labour, from the other side, by enabling the Minister to impose restrictions on the employers' freedom to engage labour. It amended, by adding the words, printed in italics, paragraph (d) of Section 1 (1) of the Defence of the Realm (Amendment) No. 2 Act (March, 1915), and ran as follows :—

"(d) to regulate or restrict the carrying on of any work in any factory, workshop, *or other premises, or the engagement or employment of any workman or all or any class of workmen therein,* or to remove the plant therefrom with a view to *maintaining* or increasing the production of munitions in other factories, workshops, *or premises, or to regulate and control the supply of metals and materials that may be required for any article for use in war.*"

This section represented an earlier policy than Section 7,[2] an attempt to stop the poaching of labour by dealing with the poacher. It had not proved practicable to pursue it, and no use was made of the power until Section 7 was repealed. Even then it was applied to an object different from that of its original intention, being used to enable the Department to "ration" skilled labour. But the Minister had relied on it, when deciding to relinquish Section 7, to enable him to prevent poaching of labour;[3] its unpopularity with labour proved as great as that of Section 7, and for the same reasons. By limiting the workman's freedom of movement, it limited his power to secure better terms of employment; as a trade unionist put it, it substituted a "starting certificate" for a leaving certificate.

(f) The Fair Wages Clause.

In addition to its limited statutory powers the Ministry exercised some control of wages through its administration of the Fair Wages Clause. The powers of wages control taken by the Minister of Munitions were indeed so limited in the first instance, because it was thought

---

[1] Employers' Advisory Committee Minutes. (L.R. 5581).
[2] Vol. I, Part II, Chap. III.
[3] Employers' Advisory Committee. Report of Meeting, 17 July, 1917. (L.R. 5581).

that all necessary adjustments could be left to ordinary collective bargaining, and the Government need in the main intervene only to enforce the carrying out of the terms so reached. The Fair Wages Clause, inserted under a resolution of the House of Commons in all public contracts, ran as follows :—

" The contractor shall in the execution of this contract observe and fulfil the obligations upon contractors specified in the Resolution passed by the House of Commons on the 10th March, 1909, namely, the contractor shall . . . . pay rates of wages and observe hours of labour not less favourable than those commonly recognised by employers and trade societies (or in the absence of such recognised wages and hours, those which in practice prevail among good employers) in the trade in the district where the work is carried out. Where there are no such wages and hours recognised or prevailing in the district, those recognised or prevailing in the nearest district in which the general industrial circumstances are similar shall be adopted. Further, the conditions of employment generally accepted in the district in the trade concerned shall be taken into account in considering how far the terms of the Fair Wages Clause are being observed. The contractor shall be prohibited from transferring or assigning directly or indirectly to any person or persons whatever any portion of his contract without the written permission of the Department. Sub-letting other than that which may be customary in the trade concerned shall be prohibited. The contractor shall be responsible for the observance of the Fair Wages Clause by the sub-contractor."

In normal times, it relieved Government Departments of the difficult task of deciding what were fair terms of employment and settled the relations of the Government to terms of employment by a method which the trade unions had themselves devised. In the abnormal conditions of the war it was no longer an adequate method, for two reasons. In the first place, the sanction by which a Department compelled a contractor to observe the conditions of the clause was inapplicable ; that was to exclude him from further contracts, an impracticable procedure when the Government could not get on any terms the full amount of supplies that it wanted. In the second place; the clause assumed stable and easily ascertainable terms of employment, and sufficient organisation on the part of the workpeople concerned to secure attention to any failure to observe the clause. These conditions did not apply to much of the work given out by the Ministry of Munitions : the work itself was novel, or was undertaken by firms and districts to which it was new, or by methods which were new, and the workers were in a large proportion women, who were not organised in any numbers and were in many cases new to industrial employment of any kind. While, therefore, the Fair Wages Clause played an important part in determining the relations of the Department with wages, specially the wages of the skilled grades, it did not prevent a demand for more direct and extensive control of wages.

(g) SUMMARY.

A survey of the wages provision of the first Munitions of War Act therefore shows clearly that the control of wages was no part of the policy which led to the establishment of the Ministry. Wages, in war as in peace, were to be adjusted by the employers and workpeople directly concerned. Arbitration was substituted for the strike as the ultimate resort in cases of difference, and certain conditions, settled once for all at the Treasury Conferences, were to be observed in return for the trade unions' undertaking to suspend all practices restrictive of output. Neither in the Act itself nor in the memoranda on which it was based are there any signs of the revolution in the attitude of the State towards the problem of fixing wages which the war was to bring about. Consistent with this is the slight administrative provision made for handling wages questions. In a review of the work of the Secretariat in regard to labour dated 14 September, 1915,[1] beyond a bare mention that control of controlled establishments includes control of wages and a reference to the administration of the Fair Wages Clauses, wages questions are not mentioned. In a report of the Labour Department, three months later (2 December)[2] the inevitable growth of work in connexion with wages is indicated. A large number of wages questions had been dealt with mainly under three heads, the Fair Wages Clause, Section 4 (2) of the Act, and by way of interpreting the recommendations of the Minister as to the remuneration of workers replacing skilled men under dilution. But in November, 1915, it was still thought that wages questions would not occupy the full time of more than a single official. Wages questions were incidental; the control of wages was neither sought nor desired; the policy of the Government was to interfere as little as possible with pre-existing methods of settling wages. Even when the Ministry found itself entangled in wages questions, the policy was to rely so far as possible on suggestions and recommendations rather than orders, and to proceed by the method of diplomacy rather than administration.

II. The Munitions of War (Amendment) Act, 1916.

(a) THE CENTRAL MUNITIONS LABOUR SUPPLY COMMITTEE.

The necessity of taking powers to control wages by Order arose from the policy of dilution. The Treasury Agreement nominally ensured the co-operation of organised labour in any measures that might prove necessary to increase the output of munitions, but in practice, as is shown elsewhere, the Agreement failed.[3] Nor was it sufficient to embody the Agreement in the first Munitions Act, thus making all restrictive practices illegal. Opposition to the substitution of women's and unskilled male labour for skilled men continued; the shortage of skilled

---

[1] D.M.R.S./153; HIST. REC./R/300/24.
[2] D.M.R.S. 259.
[3] Vol. I, Part II, Chap. IV.

men became more urgent as the programme of national factories developed and the demands of the combatant forces grew ; and the appeal made by the National Advisory Committee, appointed under the Treasury Agreement to advise and assist the Government in carrying out its terms, for volunteers under the war munition volunteers' scheme had definitely failed to meet the needs of the situation by September, 1915. The Department, therefore, was forced to give more detailed consideration to the possibility of economising skilled labour by means of dilution.

In the middle of September, after consulting the National Advisory Committee and the adjudicators who had advised on transfer under the war munitions volunteers' scheme, the Minister appointed the Central Munitions Labour Supply Committee to advise and assist the Department on the dilution and transfer of skilled labour. The chief work of this Committee was to lay down the principles on which women munition workers should be paid ; a full account of its work is therefore given in connexion with the history of the control of women's wages.[1] Its function was to promote dilution ; its interference with wages was unexpected. The composition of the Committee, however, with its large representation of trade unions, explains the direction of its activities. As in the negotiations that culminated in the Treasury Conferences, an appeal by the Government for increased output was translated into a treaty for the protection of wages. The Committee realised that the root of the opposition to dilution lay in the threat to wages inherent in dilution. One of its first acts was to appoint a sub-committee to draw up terms on which substituted labour should be employed, and the recommendations drafted by this sub-committee formed the basis of the Ministry's control of wages.

The Committee met for the first time on 22 September. The Sub-committee on wages two days later drafted a statement concerning the remuneration of women over 18 on men's work ; this they elaborated in a series of regulations, which, slightly modified, were subsequently issued by the Ministry as Circular L.2.[2] On 1 October, the Sub-committee also drew up regulations to govern the employment and remuneration of unskilled and semi-skilled men on skilled jobs ; these similarly became Circular L.3. The two series of draft regulations were forwarded to the Minister on 4 October. Later the Committee drew up regulations for the employment and remuneration of women on munitions on which they did not take the place of men. In forwarding these to the Minister as Chairman of the Committee, Mr. Henderson admitted that the employment of these workers was less directly connected with the problem of dilution ; but urged that experience showed some such statement to be necessary if the employment of women on a large scale was to be effected.[3]

On receipt of the two first proposals of the Committee, Dr. Addison pointed out for the Minister that he had no power to promulgate

---

[1] Vol. V, Part II. See also Vol. IV, Part I, Chap. IV.
[2] Vol. V, Part II, Chap. II.
[3] Vol. V, Part II, Chap. V.

binding regulations on these matters except in national factories. He proposed to circulate the recommendations for comment to the organisations of the parties concerned, and provisionally accepted them for the establishments directly under the Ministry. The Committee, however, pressed for the immediate issue of the regulations, on the ground that the progress of dilution was held up by the question of wages, and on 18 October the Ministry agreed to issue them as recommendations, with certain minor amendments, to which the Committee agreed, the chief of which were the substitution of the Minister for the Committee as the authority to interpret the recommendations and the making of the rates definite instead of minima.

(b) THE DEMAND FOR CONTROL BY ORDER.

The issue of recommendations by the Minister was an important change of policy. The mere fact that the Central Munitions Labour Supply Committee found it necessary as their first task to draw up wages regulations pointed to the inadequacy of the Treasury Agreement as a settlement of the wages problem involved in dilution; the issue of them by the Minister led inevitably to statutory control of wages.

In the first place, the issue of authoritative recommendations was a breach of the principle that all questions arising out of the Treasury Agreement should be settled by an independent arbitrating authority; the Chief Industrial Commissioner complained that the Circular L.2 was constantly quoted in arbitration proceedings. The position, then, that wages questions could be left to collective bargaining, as in normal times, was undermined. In the second place, the chief trade unions concerned with dilution demanded that the circulars should be made binding as a condition of their support to the policy of dilution, and it was difficult for the Ministry, after committing itself to the rates and conditions contained in the circulars by recommending them, to refuse to make them binding. This demand was made by the Executive Council of the Amalgamated Society of Engineers, whom the Committee met to discuss the circular on 27 October. They were persuaded for the moment to accept as a compromise the suggestion that their cooperation in dilution should be asked only where employers undertook to observe the recommendations contained in the circulars, and the principal other unions accepted the same compromise two days later; but the demand for compulsion was renewed when an amending Bill was brought forward.

As is explained elsewhere, an amending Act for other purposes was decided on at the end of September.[1] The draft was submitted to the National Advisory Committee for comment on 11 November. The National Advisory Committee considered the draft in detail and then urged the inclusion of a number of new clauses, including the provision for remedying the grievances of the worker under the existing operation of the leaving certificate rule and provision for taking power to establish

[1] Vol. IV, Part II, Chap. III.

standard rates for women in controlled establishments. Further, the Committee, at a joint meeting with the Council of the Federation of Engineering and Shipbuilding Trades and members of the Amalgamated Society of Engineers and the Boilermakers, decided to convene a conference on the Amendment Bill. At this conference, held in the Central Hall, Westminster, on 30 November, and attended by representatives of 55 unions, amendments under the same heads were urged, the proposal under the head of wages being that the Minister should take powers to enforce minimum rates and conditions for all women engaged on munitions work to which the leaving certificate Section of the Act applied.

(c) Provisions for Control by Order.

The Amending Bill, when presented in Parliament on 9 December, conceded this wider demand. In a draft clause submitted to the National Advisory Committee on 17 November, the power to regulate wages by Order was limited to the case of "female labour introduced to perform work which before the war was ordinarily performed by male labour"; the clause in the Bill extended the power to all female munition workers subject to the leaving certificate regulations. Thus it empowered the Minister to enforce regulations such as those drafted by the Central Munitions Labour Supply Committee, governing the remuneration of women who were not replacing men, and Dr. Addison, in moving the second reading of the Bill, used the argument that the restriction on their freedom imposed by Section 7 of the principal Act entitled them to this protection.

To meet the difficulty that the fixing of wages by Order was inconsistent with the settlement of wages questions by arbitration under Part I of the principal Act, the Government added a clause in Committee, empowering the Minister to constitute a special arbitration tribunal to arbitrate on differences reported under Part I of the principal Act, which related to the employment of women whose wages and conditions were subject to the Minister's directions, and to advise him as to what directions he should give.[1]

The principle of wages control by Order received a further extension before the Amending Bill became law. At a conference held on 30 December the Amalgamated Society of Engineers resolved to withhold its support to the dilution scheme, unless all the amendments it had urged at the conference on 30 November were embodied in the Bill, and instructed a deputation to lay this decision before the Prime Minister and Minister of Munitions. The deputation was received the next day.[2] After a long discussion, the representatives of the Government agreed to take powers to make Circular L.3 as well as L.2 binding, on condition that the concession put a term to the Amalgamated Society of Engineers' demands and really secured its co-operation in giving effect to the policy of dilution. The deputation passed a resolution to this effect, which the

---

[1] M.W. 58604/95. [2] Vol. IV, Part I, Chap. IV.

Chairman and Secretary of the society signed. The Bill was recommitted on 4 January, 1916, and a clause introduced giving the Minister the power to carry out his part of the undertaking. The clause relating to the special arbitration tribunal was also amended to enable the Minister to appoint a second tribunal to perform the same office in relation to male substitution as the tribunal already proposed would perform in relation to female substitution. The provisions, therefore, in the Bill as it was finally passed empowering the Minister to regulate wages by Order, were as follows :—

6.—(1) Where female workers are employed on or in connection with munitions work in any establishment of a class to which the provisions of section seven of the principal Act as amended by this Act are for the time being applied by an order, made thereunder, the Minister of Munitions shall have power by order to give directions as to the rate of wages or (subject so far as the matter is one which is dealt with by the Factory and Workshops Acts, 1901 to 1911, to the concurrence of the Secretary of State) as to hours of labour or conditions of employment of the female workers so employed.

(2) Any directions given by the Minister of Munitions under this section shall be binding on the owner of the establishment and any contractor or sub-contractor employing labour therein and the female workers to whom the directions relate, and any contravention thereof or non-compliance therewith shall be punishable in like manner as if the order in which the direction is contained was an award made in settlement of a difference under Part I of the principal Act.

(3) No direction given under this section shall be deemed to relieve the occupier of any factory or workshop from the obligation to comply with the provisions of the Factory and Workshops Acts, 1901 to 1911, or of any orders or regulations made thereunder, or to affect the liability of any person to be proceeded against for an offence under the Employment of Children Act, 1903, so, however, that no person be twice punished for the same offence.

7. The Minister of Munitions shall have power by order to give directions as to the rate of wages, hours of labour, or conditions of employment of semi-skilled and unskilled men employed in any controlled establishment on munitions work, being work of a class which, prior to the war, was customarily undertaken by skilled labour, or as to the time rates for the manufacture of complete shell and fuses and cartridge cases in any controlled establishment in which such manufacture was not customary prior to the war ; and any direction so given shall be binding on the owner of the establishment, and any contractor or sub-contractor employing labour therein, and the workers to whom the directions relate, and any contravention thereof or non-compliance therewith shall be punishable, in like manner as if the order in which the direction is contained was an award made in settlement of a difference under Part I of the principal Act.

8.—(1) The Minister of Munitions may constitute special arbitration tribunals to deal with differences reported under Part I of the principal Act which relate to matters on which the Minister of Munitions had given or is empowered to give directions under the last two preceding sections, and the Board of Trade may refer any such difference for settlement to such tribunal in lieu of referring it for settlement in accordance with the First Schedule to the principal Act.

(2) The Minister of Munitions may also refer to a special arbitration tribunal so constituted, for advice, any question as to what directions are to be given by him under the said sections.

(3) The tribunal to which matters and questions relating to female workers are to be referred under this section shall include one or more women.

(d) Amendment of the Principal Act.

Other provisions in the Amendment Act met grievances connected with wages, which had been urged on the Commissioners appointed to enquire into the grievances of munition workers on the Clyde and at the conferences convened by the National Advisory Committee. Section (2) amended Section (1) of the principal Act, requiring the Board of Trade to refer differences to arbitration within twenty-one days of their being reported. There had been bitter complaints of delays in securing settlements of differences. Section (5) amended Section (7) of the principal Act, among other provisions requiring a munitions tribunal, in determining whether the grant of a leaving certificate had been unreasonably withheld, to

> "take into consideration the question whether the workman has left or desires to leave his work for the purpose of undertaking any class of work in which his skill or other personal qualifications could be employed with greater advantage to the national interests, and whether the employer has failed to observe the conditions laid down in the Fair Wages Clauses required by resolution of the House of Commons to be inserted in Government contracts, and whether the workman has left or desires to leave his work because he has recently completed a term of apprenticeship or period of learning his trade or occupation and desires to obtain the full standard rate of wages applicable to fully qualified workmen in his trade or occupation."

(e) Extension of the Area of Regulation.

More important than these alterations in detail, which affected the position of the munitions worker rather than the powers of the Ministry, were the alteration in the definition of munitions and the extension of the Minister's power to declare establishments controlled. The former made possible a great increase in the number of establishments to which the leaving certificate sections of the Acts could be applied and in which, therefore, the Minister's powers of giving directions as to wages could be used ; and the latter, since the leaving certificate sections were applied to all controlled establishments, had the same effect. The Ministry became directly responsible for the wages of an increasing number of munitions workers, and these the workers whose remuneration raised the most difficult questions.[1] The special arbitration tribunals appointed under Section 8 of the Amendment Act, by taking over the task of advising the Minister on wages undertaken hitherto by the Central Munitions Labour Supply Committee, relieved the Minister of some of the responsibility for the directions given, and by dealing with differences under Part I of the principal Act kept alive the principle of settlement by arbitration ; but this division of responsibility did not diminish the importance of the change of policy affected. The Ministry had accepted the obligation to protect wages which the trade unions associated with its powers of controlling labour, and had forthwith to build up an administrative machine that could discharge that responsibility.

III. The Dilution Bill of 1917.

(a) OBJECT OF THE BILL.

Towards the end of 1916 it was decided that another Amendment Act would be necessary. The increasing demand of the army for munitions, the increasing need of the army itself for skilled artificers, the danger that the economic stability of the country would be undermined if more men were withdrawn from private industry, led to a renewed attempt to make a better use of the limited number of skilled men available. This economy, it was thought, could be effected best by extending dilution to private work.[2] An amending Bill was needed because the powers of the Ministry to declare establishments controlled, and so to secure the prohibition of restrictive practices, were confined to munitions work as defined in the 1916 Act. A further difficulty was that the Government had pledged itself not to extend dilution from Government to private work at the second Treasury Conference in March, 1915, and the Minister thought that the extension could not take place, although circumstances had changed since the pledge was given, without the consent of the unions to whom it was given.[3] At a conference in November, 1916, most of the unions agreed on conditions, but the most important union of them all, the Amalgamated Society of Engineers, which had originally exacted the pledge, refused compliance and would take no part in the negotiations over conditions that followed the Conference. No other method of attaining the Ministry's object, however, was suggested, and an Amending Bill was presented on 27 March, 1917.

---

[1] Chap. III, and Vol. V, Part II.
[2] Circular M.M. 142.
[3] *Parliamentary Debates*, 1917 (H. of C.), XCIII, 1903.

(b) Provisions in First Draft.

As originally presented the Bill had only three clauses. The first, which embodied the object of the measure, empowered the Minister of Munitions, where he was satisfied that it was of national importance that all or any of the provisions of the Munitions of War Acts should be extended to work of any particular class, or work in any particular establishment or class of establishment, to issue a certificate to that effect and to direct by Order that the provisions should extend accordingly; thereupon those provisions were to have effect as though reference to munitions work included reference to the work specified in the Order.

A proviso made it impossible to extend the provisions which imposed restrictions on the liberty of the workmen (*e.g.*, suspension of restrictive practices) without making the employer subject to the corresponding provisions affecting employers (*e.g.*, obligation to restore suspended practices after the war). The object of this proviso was to preserve the balance of the compromise between the interests of employers and the interests of workpeople embodied in the Treasury Agreement.

If this clause were passed, it would become possible for the Minister to control private and commercial firms and to assign to them war munitions volunteers.

The second clause was intended to improve the position of the war munitions volunteer. In the original Munitions Act priority of employment after the war was ensured to employees who had enlisted from a firm or were in the employment of the firm when it became a controlled establishment (Schedule II, Par. 3). This preference was now extended to workmen who had been assigned to some other establishment under Section 6 of the Act.

The third clause of the Bill was the only one bearing directly on wages control and also the only one of the three that became law. One of the most frequent complaints of trade union officials affected by the Munitions Act had been that arbitration awards took a long time to secure, and, when secured, a long time to enforce. Awards given under Part I of the Munitions Act were binding, but only on the actual parties to the difference. Even if the parties were representative associations of employers and workpeople, the award was not binding on the trade as a whole, since it did not bind firms outside the membership of the Federation; and the unions could make it effective throughout the trade only by the slow piecemeal procedure of complaints against individual firms that they were not observing the Fair Wages Clause in their contract with the Ministry. Some speedier procedure was desirable; the reform was the more important, because the employers' federation and the principal unions in the engineering and foundry industry in February, 1917, concluded an agreement to suspend their customary procedure for settling wages questions and to submit instead a joint application to the Committee on Production at four-monthly intervals. To this agreement, which placed on the Committee on Production the definite responsibility for controlling wages in the industry, and which was soon copied by the shipbuilding, chemical and other industries, a memorandum was attached recommending the Government to make arrangements " whereby all employers in any trade or trades affected should be subject to the awards which may be made by the Committee on Production in virtue of the agreement ";[1] the most important union concerned, the Amalgamated Society of Engineers made its participation conditional on such arrangements being made. Clause 3 accordingly provided that the Minister of Munitions might by Order direct that an award should be binding on other employers and persons engaged in a trade and specified in the Order, and that in such case the award should be binding on them in like manner and with the like consequences as if it had been made under Part I of the Munitions of War Act, in respect of a dispute affecting these employers and persons.

(c) The Bill in Parliament.

In moving the second reading of the Bill on 27 April, Mr. Kellaway announced that two or three new clauses would be put down by the Government " very largely as a result of questions addressed to me in the last two or three weeks, and of representations made to the Ministry from the country."[2] The clauses he specified were, first, a clause for expediting hearings of arbitration cases; second, a clause to deal with refusal to give a leaving certificate to a workman on the expiry of six weeks from his leaving his place, and, third, a clause tightening up the provision for preventing the cutting of piece-rates. Suspicion of such rate-cutting was, Mr. Kellaway said, " the real and substantial ground " of the recent trouble at Barrow. The Bill with these provisions added may be taken as the first draft of a bargain which the Ministry sought to drive with the unions in the course of the ensuing summer, by which it was hoped to secure the assent of the unions to the extension of dilution to private work by conceding their demands for the remedy of grievances under other heads. It also marked the beginning of a change which was to transform the Bill from a measure for extending dilution, of which opportunity was taken to effect a minor reform in wages administration, into a measure for removing the munitions workers' grievances under the head of wages, with all the dilution provisions left out.

Mr. Pringle moved the postponement of the Bill, until the existing restrictions on the freedom of employment of munitions workers had been removed. He insisted that Section 7 of the original Act was the chief grievance of the worker; but referred also to the doubts that were entertained that suspended practices and customs would after the war be restored, and pointed out that, since the excess profits tax was imposed, munitions manufacturers were under no special disability in the matter of profits, so that the compromise between the interests of employers and workpeople embodied in the original Act was

---

[1] See below, pp. 48 and 78–79.
[2] *Parliamentary Debates*, 1917 (H. of C.), XCII, 2743.

disturbed. Mr. W. C. Anderson seconded the rejection, asserting that the Ministry was under a moral obligation to see that the employer did not take unfair advantage of the leaving certificate provision to prevent the worker from getting the fair wage he could get elsewhere.[1] The Bill, however, was read a second time.

At the committee stage on 7 May, Mr. Kellaway said that it was intended to modify Section 7.[2] An amendment to exclude Section 7 from the provisions that the Minister might extend by Order was negatived; so was a proposal to make extension of the provisions of the Munitions Act to new work conditional on the trade unions representing the workers concerned giving their consent. The clause amending paragraph (3) of the second Schedule, extending the right of priority of employment after the war to workpeople assigned to some other establishment by the Minister, was passed. Amendments were inserted extending the scope of awards which might be made binding by Order, from wages alone to wages and " hours of work or otherwise as to terms or conditions of or affecting employment," and allowing the Minister to make any modifications that might be necessary to make the award applicable to the special circumstances of the firm to which it was extended.

Section 7 was amended first by making it incumbent on employers to issue leaving certificates at the end of the period of employment, and, secondly, by substituting " shall " for " may " in subsection (2) of Section 7, which permitted munitions tribunals, but did not require them, to issue certificates where they held that employers had withheld them unreasonably. A new clause was inserted, enabling the Minister of Labour to make rules for preventing delays in the settlement of differences under Part I of the original Act; and another gave the promised protection to piece-rates in the following form :—

" The following paragraph shall be inserted in the Second Schedule of the Munitions of War Act, 1915, after paragraph (5) :

(5) *a*. Piece prices, time allowances, or bonuses on output, once fixed in the establishment, may not be altered except by express agreement unless a substantial change in the method of operation or in the machinery or tools is introduced, and where such a change is introduced the altered piece prices, time allowances, or bonuses on output, shall not be such as to be less favourable to the workmen from time to time employed in the establishment."

With these additions and amendments the Bill was reported; but on an appeal from Mr. Pringle, who pointed out that several of the principal opponents of the Bill had been absent, further steps were postponed for the moment. The strike of engineers in all the important munition centres had shown clearly how unpopular any extension of dilution would be, and gave to the opponents of the Bill a backing in the country which they lacked in the House.

---

[1] *Parliamentary Debates*, 1917 (H. of C.), XCII, 2763 *et seq.*
[2] *Ibid.* XCIII, 830 *et seq.*

IV. The Commission on Industrial Unrest.

On 25 May, in the House of Commons, the Prime Minister was asked by Mr. Snowden to postpone further consideration of the Bill until the Commission which he had promised to enquire into industrial unrest should have reported. He refused on grounds of urgency, especially in merchant shipbuilding. It was not, however, until 14 August that the Bill appeared in the House again. The interval was occupied by negotiations with trade unions and employers, which transformed the Bill; while the course of events in the country discouraged any attempt to extend dilution.

The introduction of the Bill had almost coincided with the withdrawal of the trade card scheme of exemption from military service. The two incidents together, acting on the mass of pre-existing misunderstandings and grievances, precipitated a great strike, extending to all the important engineering centres, in April and May. The outbreak was unofficial, as it was illegal, but the repudiation of it by official trade union leaders did not end it. When it was ended, the official leaders mediating between the Government and the actual strike leaders, the Prime Minister promised an immediate enquiry into the alleged grievances. This promise was fulfilled by the appointment, on 12 June, of the Commission on Industrial Unrest, which sat in eight divisions in different parts of the country and reported on 17 July. In the " brief summary " of the Commissioners' findings submitted to the Prime Minister by Mr. G. N. Barnes, the first four of the fourteen points mentioned had a bearing direct or indirect on wages. They were—

" (1) High food prices in relation to wages, and unequal distribution of food.

" (2) Restriction of personal freedom and, in particular, the effects of the Munitions of War Acts. Workmen have been tied up to particular factories and have been unable to obtain wages in relation to their skill. In many cases the skilled man's wage is less than the wage of the unskilled. Too much centralisation in London is reported.

" (3) Lack of confidence in the Government. This is due to the surrender of Trade Union customs and the feeling that promises as regards their restoration will not be kept. It has been emphasised by the omission to record changes of working conditions under Schedule II, Article 7, of the Munitions of War Act.

" (4) Delay in settlement of disputes. In some instances ten weeks have elapsed without a settlement, and after a strike has taken place the matter has been put right within a few days."

Among the recommendations were two that had a bearing on the Bill; first, that the greatest possible publicity should be given to the abolition of leaving certificates, which the Government had promised while the Commission was sitting, and second, that a system should be inaugurated whereby skilled supervisors and others on day rates should receive a bonus. Some of the commissioners recommended also that agreements made between employers' federations and trade unions should be made binding on the trade, and that local arbitration tribunals should be set up.

V. Negotiations with Trade Unions and Employers, 1917.

The negotiations between the Ministry and the trade unions and employers' representatives had brought out the same needs in the industrial situation, and the Ministry had already, as in the case of leaving certificates, anticipated some of the Commission's conclusions. At a conference of trade union representatives on 10 May a committee was appointed to negotiate with the Ministry, with Mr. John Hill as chairman. Negotiations were carried on with the Amalgamated Society of Engineers separately but concurrently. In the course of the discussions the fears and grievances of workers and administrative difficulties of employers were fully explored, and a measure devised which it was thought would reconcile Labour to the extension of dilution to private work.

The chief points on which the discussions with the trade union representatives turned were the leaving certificate clause, the safeguarding of piece-rates, the form that the provision for extending awards should take, the delays in obtaining awards, provision for consulting the workpeople's representatives in effecting dilution or introducing any other changes, and the guarantee of restoration after the war of suspended customs and practices. The last two have no bearing on wages administration, and in any case did not reach the stage of actual legislation ; the others, which all bear directly on wages, resulted in the chief provisions of the Bill that actually became law.

(a) EXTENSION OF AWARDS.

The principle of extending awards was not in question ;[1] there were, however, one or two points about the form the provision should take. In the Bill as introduced the Minister was empowered to make an Order extending an award if he was satisfied that it " affects the majority of the employers " in a munitions trade. The trade union committee urged that the important point was whether a majority of workpeople was affected ; the condition was accordingly altered to read " the Minister of Munitions is satisfied that the award *is binding upon employers employing the majority of the persons* engaged on or in connection with munitions work in any trade or branch of a trade either generally or in a particular district."[2] Again, the Minister was empowered to make an Order making the award binding " either without modifications or subject in any particular cases to such modifications contained in the direction as the Minister may consider necessary

---

[1] See above, pp. 44–45.   [2] L.R. 139/9.

to adapt the award to the circumstances of such cases, and in particular in order that no such employer shall be *compelled to pay greater or enabled to pay less wages* than an employer who was originally bound by the award." The original intention was to allow an employer who had been paying above the district rate to pay less than the whole award. The Employers' Advisory Committee objected to the words in italics, on the ground that the object of the provision was the enforcement of advances, not the establishment of a minimum.[1] The words italicised therefore were omitted. With these alterations the section was passed as Section 5 of the Act.

(b) Acceleration of Arbitration Proceedings.

Complaints of delay in the settlement of differences under Part I of the principal Act were common. When that Act was presented to a conference of trade unionists, just before its introduction into the House of Commons, Mr. Duncan had urged the need of very greatly increasing the staff available for the work of conciliation and arbitration, on the ground that delays prejudiced arbitration and were a principal cause of discontent.[2] Two years later, as we have seen, the Commission on Industrial Unrest reported to the same effect. The complaints were not, however, confined to the representatives of Labour; the Government Departments concerned found that they were at times unable to secure the settlement of a dispute of which they were aware, because neither of the parties to it would report it.

Two provisions in the Amendment Bill were directed to remedying this delay. Clause (6) Subsection (1) was as follows:—

" The Minister of Labour may make regulations with respect to the reporting of differences under Section 1 of the Munitions of War Act, 1915, and with a view to preventing undue delay in negotiations for settling such differences may by those regulations prescribe the time within which any such difference is to be reported to him."

Clause 7 should be taken with this:—

" At the end of the First Schedule to the Munitions of War Act, 1915, the following paragraph shall be inserted:—

" (4) The tribunal shall make its award without delay, and where practicable within fourteen days from the date of reference."

The unions in pressing these complaints of delay had urged that there should be a fixed time-limit for the settlement of differences. It was, however, considered impossible to impose on an arbitration tribunal the duty of issuing its award within a specified time, since what was a reasonable time in a simple case might be quite inadequate for a complicated and important case.[3]

---

[1] L.R. 139/21. [2] Hist. Rec./R./300/5.
[3] Notes on the Munitions of War Bill, 1917. Hist. Rec./R./221·1/41.

Subsection (2) of Clause (6) gave Government Departments the power to report differences for settlement. It amended subsection (1) of Section 1 of the principal Act by inserting the words "by or on behalf of any Government Department" after the words "by or on behalf of either party to the difference." The power was needed particularly to enable supply departments, that heard of a difference first because it interfered with supplies, to report the matter at once to the Ministry of Labour.

(c) PROTECTION OF PIECE-RATES.

The negotiations over the section by which piece-rates were safeguarded are described elsewhere.[1] In the earlier drafts of the Bill, the provision was that rates should not be changed without consultation with the representatives of the workpeople concerned. The union leaders asked for "consent" to be substituted for "consultation."[2] The employers objected to the provision in either form,[3] and a compromise was adopted, by which rates and prices once fixed were not to be altered "except in accordance with any procedure which has been adopted by agreement between the owner of the establishment and the workmen or their representatives ... or by direction of the Minister of Munitions, which direction shall not be given except in accordance with an agreement between the owner of the establishment and the trade unions representing the workmen affected by the alteration, or failing agreement after consultation with the parties concerned."

As amended the clause provided an agreed, elastic and adequate procedure to prevent unauthorised alterations in piece-rates, instead of imposing a general prohibition. It gave a new sanction to any existing procedure that was satisfactory to both parties, and it enabled the Minister to enforce any future agreement that might be made. In other words, it extended to changes in wages due to the special conditions of payment by results the procedure applied to changes in district rates by Section 5 of the Act. Since changes in piece-prices under the clause could be made only by consent, it was not necessary to treat such changes as a change in working conditions under paragraph (7) of Schedule II of the original Act; they were therefore exempted from the scope of the paragraph by subsection (2) of the clause. The Admiralty had at one time suggested that piece-rates could be most easily protected by bringing them under this paragraph.[4]

Two exceptions were made to the clause. First, the provision did not apply to shipbuilding or ship-repairing yards, but as respects such yards the Minister of Munitions or the Admiralty might make rules regulating the alteration of the rates or prices under systems of payment by results therein. The Shipbuilding Trades Joint Committee had been asked to suggest a procedure similar to the procedure agreed on

---

[1] See below, pp. 137–141.
[2] L.R. 139/9.
[3] L.R. 5581.
[4] L.R. 139/31.

between the engineering unions and employers' federation, when it was proposed to attach that agreement to the Act as a schedule. They replied that the existing procedure was adequate, and that paragraph (5) of the second schedule of the original Act gave all protection needed.[1] The Admiralty also asked for the exemption of shipyards on similar grounds;[2] and the shipbuilding employers objected to certain provisions, particularly the prohibition of carrying forward debit balances, in the engineering trades' agreement.[3] Since the clause contemplated enforcing not a uniform procedure, but only agreements made by each trade itself, it is not obvious what object was served by the exemption of shipbuilding.

The other exception was as follows :—

"Provided that this provision shall not apply where the alteration is made in accordance with the directions as to the rates of female workers given by the Minister of Munitions, under section six of the Munitions of War (Amendment) Act, 1916 . . ."

This exception was necessary, because the majority of female munition workers, unlike the men, were not organised in unions, and there were no agreements between employers and the unions representing the female workers like those regulating payment by results in the men's trades. The effect of the clause, therefore, if the exception were not made, would be practically to make any change in piece-rates illegal.[4] These workers moreover were already protected by the power of the Minister, under Section 6 of the Amendment Act of 1916, to give binding directions as to their wages.

The exclusion of female workers made necessary a slight alteration in the form of the Bill. The provision protecting piece-rates was at first in the form of an amendment to Schedule II of the Act of 1915. The class of female workers to be excepted from it however was defined by reference to Section 6 of the Amendment Act of 1916. It was impossible to refer in a schedule to an Act of 1915 to a provision in an Act of 1916; therefore the piece-rates provision was given the form of a clause in the Bill instead of an amendment to the Schedule.[5]

(d) THE REPEAL OF THE LEAVING CERTIFICATE PROVISIONS.

The discussions with the trade unions, like the evidence given before the Commission on Industrial Unrest, made it clear that the leaving certificate provision of Section 7 of the principal Act was the chief grievance of munition workers. On 7 May in the House of Commons, Mr. Kellaway was still unwilling to admit the need of repeal; by 4 June the Ministry had become convinced that repeal was necessary, and Dr. Addison proposed repeal at a conference of trade unionists. The discussion on the provision may be divided into three periods. In the first the Ministry was trying to find means of saving the

---

[1] L.R. 139/40.   [2] L.R. 139/32.   [3] L.R. 139/90.
[4] L.R. 139/185.   [5] L.R. 139/185.

provision by amending it; in the second, while agreeing to repeal it, it hoped to effect repeal in the measure for extending dilution and was trying to devise safeguards against the dangers attendant on repeal; in the third, it decided to repeal the provision, although it had given up for the time being the hope of securing dilution on private work by consent, and only arranged to postpone the actual repeal until the attendant safeguards could be put into force at the same time.

The Bill as it emerged from Committee in the House of Commons amended Section 7 of the principal Act to the extent of making the issue of a certificate compulsory after six weeks had elapsed from leaving work or a tribunal had found the withholding of a certificate by the employer unreasonable. In the negotiations that followed it was proposed, first, that the conditions under which the issue of a certificate was compulsory should be widened and the following draft clause was considered to come at the end of Section 5 (5) of the 1916 Act.[1]

> "In determining whether the grant of a certificate has been unreasonably refused a tribunal shall take into consideration whether the workman has suffered a reduction in his rate of wages or has had his earnings materially reduced by reason of his transfer to less remunerative work or by reason of a change in the method of his remuneration, and in the event of the tribunal being satisfied of the existence of any of the above conditions the tribunal shall, unless there is good reason to the contrary, forthwith issue a certificate or order the issue of a certificate by the employer."

This provision would have safeguarded the worker's wages against reduction but not enabled him to move about after higher wages. This did not, however, satisfy the opponents of the section. Another proposal, to allow the workman to change his place of employment by giving three weeks' notice, was unsatisfactory to the employers. While protesting against the proposed repeal of the section, the Employers' Advisory Committee preferred repeal to the amendment.[2] The chairman, Mr. Allan Smith, pointed out, however, that the Ministry would have to take far greater control in the matter of parcelling out labour, and that it might be necessary to prohibit employers taking on men at more than the district rate.

Dr. Addison suggested the repeal of Section 7 at a conference with the Amalgamated Society of Engineers on 4 June. The decision was not made without full consideration of the risks involved. Not only were there protests from employers and supply departments,[3] but the officers of the Labour Regulation Department regarded the step with misgiving. The objections to the repeal were set forth in a memorandum at the time. It was pointed out that the provision was originally introduced with the limited object of stopping "poaching" by employers and unnecessary migration of labour; the inevitable pressure on the workmen had been materially eased by the changes introduced by the Amendment Act of 1916; and the results of repeal now, however

---

[1] L.R. 139/14.   [2] L.R. 139/21.   [3] L.R. 139/145.

advantageous the political reactions on Labour, would be very serious economically. The memorandum continued :—

"(a) In the first place, it must be remembered that there are considerable variations between the various engineering trades in point of wages. Efforts have been made as far as possible to level rates in the same occupation, but the divergences between one occupation and another are considerable. A skilled man could easily adapt himself to a slightly different machine, and if he had complete freedom to leave and found that a new shop and a new machine would give him higher wages he would be very likely to leave.

(b) It will be remembered that considerable dissatisfaction has been produced in the engineering shops because the unskilled and semi-skilled men on machines have been earning higher rates than the skilled men who had continued to work on purely skilled jobs on time rates. It has been a very difficult matter to induce the skilled men to leave the machine to go on to purely skilled work because removal from the machines reduces their earnings. There is no doubt that the skilled men, if Section 7 were removed, would return to semi-skilled work where their earnings would be much higher.

(c) It should be noted further that in the case of certain occupations there are inferior classes of lower rated work which must necessarily be performed by the same mechanic in the course of the whole job. . . . The firm's right to remove men to the lower paid work has been upheld by the tribunal and by the High Court. In peace time economic pressure gives the employer the necessary hold, but in war time it is essential that he should be given some additional strength."

The Ministry could not rely on the possibility of military service deterring men from changing their occupations, since the Ministry could in no case allow them to leave industry, and the normal fear of unemployment was inoperative owing to the great shortage of labour.[1]

To these objections Sir Stephenson Kent added the fear that munition volunteers, soldiers released from the colours, and army reserve munition workers would want the same freedom.

Mr. Kellaway, while admitting the force of these objections, stated that they were far outweighed by the advantages which would be derived from the disappearance of a restriction which had irritated labour more than anything else. The decision to take the risk was based on considerations of public policy.[2]

Two conditions, Dr. Addison pointed out, must be attached to the abolition of the leaving certificate. Employers must be prevented from taking men from munitions to private work ; and the poaching

---

[1] L.R. 139/3.   [2] L.R. 139/30. Cf. L.R. 139/87.

of labour must be prevented. The use of the workers' unemployment insurance book was suggested as a means of tracing and checking such transfers, a proposal to which the Amalgamated Society of Engineers' spokesmen raised no objection; they approved also the proposal that firms which held out inducements to the employees of another firm to leave should be stopped from engaging more men.[1] The same proposal of an embargo was discussed at considerable length with the Employers' Advisory Committee. The representatives of the Department preferred the use of the embargo to any overt provision for checking attempts to increase wages;[2] but the employers pressed for a specific prohibition of any enticement by offering higher wages. The matter was discussed with the trade union committee and the expedient devised, which is embodied in proviso (b) in the following draft clause :—[3]

(1) It shall not be lawful for a person to give employment to a workman who has, since the passing of this Act, been employed on or in connection with munitions work of the class specified in paragraph (a) of subsection (1) of section nine of the Munitions of War (Amendment) Act, 1916, or of any other class which may be specified in an order of the Minister of Munitions or on work to which the Munitions Acts, 1915 and 1916, have been applied by an order under this Act

(a) where the work on which he is to be employed is not work on or in connection with munitions work without the consent of the Minister of Munitions which consent may be given either as respects an individual case or generally as respects work of any particular class or description;

(b) where the work on which he is employed is work on or in connection with munitions work if the rate of wages (including any bonus or other consideration) offered or from time to time paid to him is higher than that for the time being applicable to other workmen employed in similar capacities by the person giving the employment; and if any person contravenes this provision he shall be guilty of an offence, triable by a munitions tribunal of the second class, under the Munitions of War Act, 1915, unless he proves that he did not know that, and had taken all reasonable steps to ascertain whether, the workman had been so employed :

Provided that in the case of a workman to be employed on or in connection with munitions work, it shall not be an offence to offer or pay him wages (including any bonus or other consideration) at a rate higher than that applicable to other workmen employed in similar capacities by the person giving the employment if the rate is not higher than that which the workman

---

[1] L.R. 139/22.
[2] L.R. 139/21; L.R. 5581, Minutes of meeting, 17 July, 1917.
[3] L.R. 139/38.

received in his previous employment, and that nothing in this section shall prevent him being employed in a higher capacity than that in which he was employed in his previous employment.

(e) Rejection of Bill by Amalgamated Society of Engineers.

With these conditions attached the repeal of the leaving certificate section was embodied in the Bill, and the Bill accepted by the Executive Council of the Amalgamated Society of Engineers subject to a ballot of their members. The members were asked to vote on it in a circular issued on 21 June, in which the Executive Council recommended it. The circular summarises the advantages of the Bill from the point of view of its critics.[1] Power was taken to extend dilution to private work, but the extension was safeguarded by the giving of 21 days' notice in each case and by the retention of the right to strike on private work. In return, the guarantee of restoration of suspended practices was made explicit and strengthened by higher penalties, and the guarantees of priority of employment were extended and also strengthened. The security for restoration was also strengthened by the restoration of the right to strike at the termination of the war instead of twelve months later. Leaving certificates were abolished subject to the conditions given above. The compulsory extension of arbitration awards was secured, and provision made for speeding up arbitration. A promise had been secured that the Minister would not press the general adoption of payment by results, and the Bill secured workmen already under that system from any cutting of prices. There was a clause prohibiting victimisation on the ground of trade union activity—an important provision at a time when official strikes were illegal and trade union aggression depended largely on unofficial leaders—and local joint committees were promised, if a workable system could be devised.

The result of the ballot was the rejection of the Bill by a large majority. Meanwhile the report of the Commission on Industrial Unrest had made clear the seriousness of the Labour fears of dilution and the need of certain of the other provisions of the Bill. The new Minister urged the need of the Bill on a conference of trade unionists in the Central Hall, Westminster, on 1 August, and appealed again for their advice and for assistance in getting over difficulties. Some support for going on with the Bill was forthcoming from members of the Committee which negotiated the amendments; but the chairman of the Amalgamated Society of Engineers insisted that it would be unwise and would defeat its object to pass the Bill against the opposition of his members.[2] The Employers' Consultative Committee, with whom Mr. Churchill discussed the Bill on 14 August, expressed doubts whether the dilution provision was worth the trouble it would excite; dilution on private work could be put into effect only by agreement, and

---

[1] L.R. 139/105; Circular M.M. 142 of 1917.
[2] L.R. 139/186.

agreement could be obtained without legislative powers.[1] It was decided, therefore, to postpone for the time being the extension of dilution and the more controversial among the other provisions of the Bill, but to proceed with the Bill as an agreed measure for removing certain pressing grievances which the discussions over it and the enquiries of the Commission on Industrial Unrest had revealed.[2]

This meant a short Bill embodying the repeal of Section 7 with consequential amendments, the clauses affecting wages, and the clause directed against victimisation.

VI. The Munitions of War Act, 1917.

(a) REINTRODUCTION OF THE BILL AS A WAGES MEASURE.

The Bill was reintroduced on 14 August and considered in Committee the next day. There were only a few days before the adjournment for the recess. Certain members misunderstood Mr. Churchill, until he explained the object of his amendments.[3] The Bill was no longer a dilution Bill. On the other hand, after the pledge had been given to abolish the leaving certificate provision, he did not like to be left for the six weeks of the recess without the means of giving effect to it. He asked for certain safeguards. Other amendments embodied agreed provisions extending awards and safeguarding against victimisation. In Committee he explained that the Bill was merely an "instalment, a necessary instalment." It was welcomed by the chief opponents of the Bill in its original form, Mr. Pringle, Mr. Anderson, and Mr. Tyson Wilson, and passed through all stages without further alteration. The Royal Assent was given on 21 August.

(b) REPEAL OF LEAVING CERTIFICATE PROVISIONS.

Certain changes made subsequently to the rejection of the Bill by the ballot of the Amalgamated Society of Engineers require explanation. Section 7 of the principal Act was not repealed outright; Section (2) said "The Minister of Munitions, on being satisfied that the provisions of section seven of the Munitions of War Act, 1915, as amended by any subsequent enactment, can consistently with the national interests be repealed, may by order repeal these provisions."

The provision for delay was due to the necessity now recognised of making some provision for the skilled time-workers, who might be tempted on getting their freedom to move to less skilled, or at any rate less useful, but better paid work.

The conditions that were to come into force on repeal of Section 7 were also different from the July draft. The provision that prohibited the employment on private work, without the consent of the Minister,

---

[1] Verbatim Report in HIST. REC./R/340/6.
[2] L.R. 139.
[3] *Parliamentary Debates*, 1917 (H. of C.), XCVII, 1121-22.

of a workman who had since the passing of the Act been employed on munitions work stood ; but the other condition, prohibiting employment at wages higher both than those which were being paid by the employer to other men on similar work and than those which the man had been receiving in his previous employment disappeared. The views of the officers of the Department prevailed, and reliance was placed on the device of an embargo imposed under Defence of the Realm Regulation 8A (b).[1] The Minister stated in Committee in the House of Commons that he was relying on this regulation. " I shall hold myself free," he said, " to utilise that to prevent poaching."[2] It was also intended to amend Regulation 8B, under the Defence of the Realm Act, which prohibited enticement but had been found difficult to administer, by making it possible for an aggrieved employer to prosecute merely with the consent of the Minister, and by placing the onus of proof that he did not entice on any employer who had entered into negotiations with a workman.[3]

The other safeguards against undue movement after repeal of Section 7 were provided in Sections 3 and 1 of the new Act. Section 3 provided that if Section 7 of the principal Act were repealed, a contract of employment in connection with munitions work should not be determinable by either party except by a week's notice or on payment of a sum equal to an average week's wages. Exception was made in cases in which a longer notice than one week was already required, in ship-repairing and in other discontinuous work which the Minister exempted by Order, and in cases of misconduct. The Minister stated that he relied on this as the substantial provision to prevent sudden dislocation.[4]

(c) The Skilled Time-Workers' Clause.

Section (1) enabled the Minister to fix special rates for skilled time-workers. It was as follows :—

> " If at any time during the continuance of the present war the Minister of Munitions considers it necessary, in order to maintain the output of munitions, that directions should be given with respect to the remuneration to be paid for work (being munitions work or work therewith or work in any controlled establishment), which at the time when the directions are given is paid at time rates, he may, subject always and without prejudice to any agreement made between employers and workmen with the consent of the Minister with respect to the remuneration of such work, by order give such directions with respect to the remuneration of such work as he may consider necessary for the purpose of the maintenance or increase of output."

---

[1] Employers' Advisory Committee Minutes, 17 July (L.R. 5581).
[2] *Parliamentary Debates*, 1917 (H. of C.), XCVII, 1306.
[3] Hist. Rec./R./221·1/41.
[4] *Parliamentary Debates*, 1917 (H. of C.), XCVII, 1122.

The origin of this section is to be found in a proposal put by Mr. Wolfe to Mr. Kellaway on 2 July, as a substitute for the provision then in the Bill prohibiting enticement by the offer of higher wages, under which a workman might move from place to place carrying a higher rate with him.[1]

" It is designed," he stated, " to meet special cases such as the tool-maker on day work leaving that work for semi-skilled repetition piece-work. The provision would enable the Minister to make Orders regulating the wages of skilled men so as to equalise them provided that they remain in the trade. This seems the least clumsy and most effective way of achieving a very necessary purpose." The difficulty had been brought prominently before the Ministry by a dispute at Messrs. Crossley Motors, Manchester, where the time-workers threatened to strike unless they received a bonus on the total output of the shops. The Commission on Industrial Unrest emphasised the same point a few days later. The draft clause was opposed by the Employers' Advisory Committee on 17 July, on the ground that a definite prohibition of enticement by the offer of higher wages was essential ; they were also still raising objections to the abolition of leaving certificates, of which this proposal was a corollary.

The proposal was put before the trade union conference on 1 August, at which the Minister emphasised the anomaly of the skilled time-worker's wages. The officers in charge of dilution reported that the fear of loss of wages by skilled men was an important factor in the opposition to dilution.[2] When it became necessary to revise the Bill by dropping dilution, Mr. Wolfe put forward the proposal again ; the question of the skilled time-worker's wages must be settled in connection with the Bill ; it was the most pressing matter before the Department. The employers would accept the proposal only on conditions ; first, that it was confined to piece-work establishments ; second, that it was not used where piece-work had been offered and refused ; third, that increases under the clause were confined to the war period ; and, fourth, that employers were reimbursed by the Government. The first two of these conditions could not be accepted, the first because a man might want to move from a day-work establishment to a piece-work establishment when it was necessary to keep him at the former ; the second because it would be in effect to make piece-work compulsory, which the Ministry had refused to do. The third condition was accepted and embodied in the Act, the fourth could be arranged.[3] The clause was put before a conference of engineering and shipbuilding unions on 13 August, at which Mr. Churchill said that consideration of the question must precede abolition of the leaving certificate. It was argued that all day-workers were affected but the question was not further discussed, the conference being taken up with the question of dilution.[4] The Employers' Advisory Committee considered the clause on 10 August. They objected to it and proposed an alternative embodying the conditions indicated by Mr. Wolfe.[5] The clause

---

[1] L.R. 139/138. [2] L.R. 139/185. [3] L.R. 139/193.
[4] L.R. 139/165. [5] Hist Rec./R./340/6.

appears in the Act, however, substantially in the form in which Mr. Wolfe drafted it, with the provision that any difference arising respecting matters on which the Minister had given directions under the section should be referred to a special tribunal constituted under Section 8 of the Amendment Act of 1916.

(d) SECTION 4.

Section (4) of the Act followed necessarily from the abolition of the leaving certificate, but it had substantial and independent importance. Under Section (6) of the Amendment Act of 1916, the Minister had power to regulate by Order the wages of female workers " employed on or in connection with munitions work in any establishment of a class to which the provisions of Section 7 of the principal Act . . . are for the time being applied. . . ." With the repeal of Section 7 of the principal Act the differentia of this class of workers went too. In its place the Minister's powers under Section 6 of the Act of 1916 were made to apply to female workers " employed on or in connection with munitions work in establishments of all classes." This represented a considerable concession to the women's unions, who had always pressed for a widening of the area of control, and a considerable increase in the powers and responsibilities of the Ministry. The War Office had objected, on the ground that the extension might lead to interference with the wages of workpeople engaged on work for the War Contracts Department.[1] The Ministry's powers, however, were limited to munitions work within the meaning of the Munitions Acts.

(e) REJECTED AND DEFERRED PROVISIONS.

No further addition was made to the statutory powers of the Ministry to control wages, although the Amendment Act of 1917 was admittedly only provisional and partial. Certain additional proposals that were considered may be noted. Mr. (later Sir) Lynden Macassey had urged, in April, that provision should be made for statutory introduction of payment by results.[2] He pointed out also that the general provision against restrictive practices, Section 4 (3) of the original Act, was largely inoperative, because an arbitrator might rule that a practice was restrictive without being able to say what should take its place, and because the Ministry could not refer a case to arbitration where employer and workmen refrained. He suggested amendments, first, empowering the Board of Trade or an arbitration tribunal to decide the " manner, extent and conditions in, to or upon which any rule or system proposed to be substituted for the suspended rule, practice or custom shall be put into operation " ; and, second, empowering the Ministry to refer to arbitration the question whether any rule or practice was restrictive. The difficulties in which the Ministry of Munitions found itself in securing assent to its Bill were too great to permit of these extensions, and they were not taken up.

---

[1] L.R. 139/14.   [2] L.R. 139/39.

Certain other provisions were deferred for inclusion in the Bill it was intended to bring in, extending dilution and giving the unions the security for restoration of suspended practices which they asked. The unions had asked for a provision making the Munitions Acts binding on Crown establishments, so that the Admiralty and War Office could be compelled to go to arbitration under Part I. The War Office objected on the ground that an award or Order affecting a limited class of munition workers would affect all other branches of Government employment; their employees should therefore come under the special Conciliation and Arbitration Board for Government Employees.[1] The Admiralty objected on the similar ground that employment in the Royal Dockyards was a self-contained system with standards and provisions for change of its own. The Ministry of Munitions supported the unions' claims, on the ground of mutuality, the Government establishments enjoying the benefits of the Munitions of War Acts. The Cabinet decided in November that the Acts should be made binding on Government establishments, since the present position of the Arsenals and Dockyards stood in the way of the co-ordination of the Government Departments dealing with Labour, and gave instructions that a clause to this effect should be inserted in the next Amendment Bill.[2]

VII. Inadequacy of the Ministry's Statutory Powers of Wages Control.

Negotiations over the Amendment Bill, which were concerned chiefly with the securities for restoration of trade union practices, had not issued in a Bill when the Armistice came. Meanwhile the inadequacy of the powers of wages control given by the Munitions Acts had been revealed by a movement of workpeople after higher wages and a divergence of actual wages from nominal district rates which became marked in 1918. The Ministry had full control of wages only in national factories. In controlled establishments its sanction was required for any change; but this power was, as has been shown, much more limited than appears at first sight, since sanction was not needed for changes due to collective agreements or general awards or for changes affecting individuals only; it was subject also to appeal to arbitration under Part I of the original Act, and in any case the controlled establishments over whom it was exercised numbered only 6,000 firms out of over 30,000 engaged on munitions. While the Ministry's powers of checking an advance were limited it had greater powers of compelling an advance. Under the first Amendment Act it could fix by Order wages of substitutes, male or female, on skilled men's work; under the second it could give directions with respect to the payment of time work. These powers enabled it to control the wages of women munitions workers fairly effectively. In relation to men's wages, however, its powers corresponded with the theory that wages should be settled by collective bargaining, arbitration

---

[1] L.R. 139/77. [2] L.R. 139/126.

being substituted for the strike or lock-out in the last resort. The Chairman of the Committee on Production had even protested against the Order giving the 12½ per cent. bonus to skilled time-workers as a dangerous interference with the Committee's control of the problem.[1] So long as the leaving certificate provisions were in operation, bargaining was not free; the individual workman was hampered in exploiting the shortage of labour; and, although complaints of poaching continued, the movement of labour was not great. When the leaving certificate was abolished and it had proved impossible to confine the special 12½ per cent. bonus to the limited class of skilled time-workers for whom it was designed, a situation developed in which powers of control more comprehensive than the piece-meal provisions of the Munitions Acts were needed. These were to hand in the Defence of the Realm Regulation 8 A., originally devised with a view to preventing the movement of labour and little used, and the Ministry was considering a proposal to use these powers to establish effective control over wages in munitions industries as a whole when the Armistice came. The memorandum containing this proposal was submitted by Mr. Campbell, the head of the Wages Section, to Sir Stephenson Kent, on 3 October, 1918. By him it was submitted to the Minister the next day with a strong minute calling attention to the administrative difficulties and the disastrous results that followed on the insufficient powers of the Ministry to deal with sectional advances and the unrest which the wages situation was causing. By the Minister it was referred to the Munitions Council on 13 October. A summary of this memorandum will indicate the wages problem with which the Ministry was faced in the last year of the war and the needs of the situation as perceived by its officers.[2]

The memorandum begins by pointing out that the policy of restricting changes in wages to general advances to meet increases in the cost of living and, apart from these, maintaining recognised pre-war standard rates and conditions had broken down. Bargaining had been freed by the abolition of the leaving certificate; competition for labour was constantly forcing wages up; standard rates had disappeared. The pre-war basis, it was argued, was no longer adequate;

> "The distinctions between industries, due to their respective economic conditions when conducted as private undertakings in peace time, have to a great extent lost their validity now that the war has brought about a fundamental re-orientation of the whole position. The truth is that to-day there are no longer a number of separate industries serving separate and distinct demands, but one single munitions industry, serving one demand only, that of the Government. This revolution involves a revolution in all the factors hitherto determining the various industrial wage systems. Unfortunately for administration these systems had never a very scientific basis. Based on conditions which the war has suspended they are in danger of falling rapidly

---

[1] L.R. 5997/11   [2] L.R. 26039/2.

into chaos. The changes now necessary cannot be given any real permanence for the war period if they merely take the form of patching here and there the breaches made in the existing framework. The war situation is so abnormal as to require to be handled without too close a regard to post-war conditions which must be so fundamentally different. Essential post-war problems such as the restoration of Trade Union customs must be made to depend as little as possible on the administration of wages during the War."

It will be noted that on this view the second Schedule of the original Act and the wages Orders issued under the first Amendment Act, which together formed the foundation of the statutory regulation of wages and were based mainly on " a regard to post-war conditions," would be discarded.

It is then pointed out that the powers conferred by the Munitions of War Acts are wholly insufficient for dealing with the situation. The regulation of wages through contract prices and conditions, *i.e.*, the method of the Fair Wages Clause—is also inadequate ; wages standards are in a state of flux and the method is too clumsy, dilatory and indirect to be effective in a quickly changing problem ; while important, it can be used only as auxiliary to other methods. A general centralised control by the State is needed. The State is the real employer, private employers and work-people only trustees for it. Just as the prices of material for munitions have been fixed, so it is inevitable if stability is to be maintained that the war price of labour should be fixed. Without stability there will be incessant labour unrest.

Coming to policy, it is pointed out that the time-rates actually paid exceed the recognised rate in a great many cases—the men's claim that in the London district the skilled engineer is receiving $5\frac{1}{4}$d. an hour above the recognised rates (exclusive of Committee on Production war bonuses) is probably justified ; that recognised rates vary from district to district, a variation with no justification under war conditions ; and that rates vary for the same work in different industries and cannot be adjusted without reactions throughout industry. The suggestion is then made :—

" If the freedom of men to change their employment is not to be limited, it will be necessary to establish the greatest practicable uniformity of wages between establishment and establishment, district and district, industry and industry for men of the same occupation. Districts must be as few and large as possible ; it may even be advisable for war purposes to regard Great Britain as a single district. Within the new districts the same rate must be paid to all men of the same trade, with such differentiations only between different industries as are directly proportionate to the difference in the working conditions of each."

Once new and uniform time-rates are established it would be necessary to adjust earnings under systems of payments by results. The variety of systems in operation is too great to standardise them, but limits might be imposed beyond which rates should not move, a lower limit of 25 per cent. and an upper limit of 75 per cent. over time-rates being suggested. This would involve going back on the famous piece-rate pledge ; but that pledge, it is pointed out, has been " one of the chief factors tending to the existing anomalies in wages," and its object, the maintenance of workpeople's confidence in payment by results, should be attained in some other way.

The skilled time-worker's grievance should be met by a high time-rate, granted within very carefully defined limits, the receipt of which should exclude from any participation in payment by results.

The machinery for revision of present wages proposed is described as follows :—

"The delimitation of districts and the settlement of time-rates and working conditions . . . . could be carried out under the authority of the Committee on Production. Time rates and conditions would be determined having regard to—
- (a) The actual rates paid at present to all men of the same occupation in any industry ;
- (b) the traditional relationship between one grade and another and one industry and another ;
- (c) the relative value of the various working conditions applicable to men of the same occupation working in different jobs ;
- (d) pre-war rates and working conditions ;
- (e) the cost of living."

The standardisation of wages under systems of payment by results should be done by local joint committees with a Government representative on them. Their experience, when co-ordinated, might in time provide the materials for standard systems of payment by results.

To administer the new principles and prevent any departure from them, ample and effective powers would be needed. It is suggested that these might be found in Defence of the Realm Regulation 8A., the " embargo " regulation. Though intended primarily to regulate the engagement of work-people, it had been used in the case of the London sheet-metal trade to enforce certain wage-standards, by prohibiting the employment of workers (without the permission of the Minister) at other than the standard rate. As used in this case, the Order allowed an exception in the case of any worker receiving more than the standard at the time of the issue of the Order, and allowed such a worker to take his higher rate with him to a new place ; but it could be used simply to enforce the standards and conditions decided in accordance with the principles outlined above.

The regulation contemplated would involve withdrawing the guarantee that the dilutee on skilled work should have the same wage as the skilled man. He might receive the skilled man's pre-war rate ; but the irritation arising from anomalous relations would persist if the skilled man saw the unskilled dilutee receiving the same wage as himself. The safeguard which the skilled man required of restoration of pre-war conditions should be given in some other way.

Finally, such a re-organisation should be accompanied by an equivalent regulation of contractors' profits. Sir Stephenson Kent added that a definite statement of the Government's labour policy and an attempt to restore the authority of the trade union leaders should be made at the same time. " In my view," he said, " labour unrest in this country at the present time is more acute and more dangerous than at any period of the war."

Thus the responsible officers of the Ministry, by the end of the war, had been forced to the conclusion that they could exercise effectively the control over wages forced upon them only if they were empowered to control wages completely. The practical proposals put forward were only tentative and had not gone beyond the stage of preliminary discussion when the Ministry came to an end ; they had not yet secured the serious consideration of the Minister, and it may be doubted whether in any event they would have been adopted ; but they make clear the position to which the administration had been reduced. The attempt to preserve the *status quo* had broken down ; and the principal factors in bringing about that break-down were the very measures—the piece-rates pledge, the guarantee of skilled rates to substitutes, and the preservation of the ordinary methods of private bargaining—which had been designed to preserve the *status quo*. In an earlier part of this history,[1] it is pointed out that the tendency for labour to drift in the direction of higher wages, which the leaving certificate was designed to check, might have been dealt with by equalising the rates of wages, but that method was not contemplated, and that the attempt to introduce uniformity into the endless variety of wages paid would have been to attack the question on its most intricate side. By the end of the war the Ministry had been compelled to contemplate that method as the only effective method.

---

[1] Vol. I, Part IV, pp. 38–39.

CHAPTER III.

SETTLEMENT OF MUNITION WORKERS' WAGES OUTSIDE THE DEPARTMENT.

I. Local and Sectional Awards by the Committee on Production.

It has been pointed out in the last chapter that the Ministry of Munitions had no general power to control munition workers' wages during the first eighteen months after its establishment. Such control as it exercised consisted essentially in the support of standard district rates in munition establishments, and the adjustment as far as possible of proposed changes of wages in accordance with these recognised rates. But these established rates, on whose existence the possibility of centralised control of wages as administered by the Ministry necessarily depended, changed constantly though irregularly after the first six months of the war, either as a result of voluntary agreements between associations of workpeople and employers, or as a result of awards by the Committee on Production ; while an isolated award by the Committee, or by a single arbitrator appointed by the Chief Industrial Commissioner, on a wage dispute in some important individual firm, although it did not establish a new district rate, yet often served as a precedent for a stream of applications to the Ministry for sanction to similar advances by firms in the same district and area.

The Committee on Production was therefore the principal authority controlling wages. Appointed in February, 1915, by the First Lord of the Treasury, to enquire into and report on questions connected with production in engineering and shipbuilding work, on 21 February, 1915, its terms of reference were extended by empowering it to deal with any differences referred to it by persons engaged on Government work. Between this date and the beginning of the following July, it issued awards on thirty-nine cases. On the passing of the Munitions of War Act it became a statutory arbitration tribunal under the Act, to hear and determine disputes between employers and employed arising out of munitions work. The original members of the Committee were Sir George Askwith, Sir Francis Hopwood, Sir George Gibb. In August, 1915, Sir David Harrel took the place of Sir Francis Hopwood, and subsequently Lord Balfour of Burleigh was appointed an additional member. On 1 May, 1917, the Committee was reconstituted and enlarged, representative employers and workmen being added, so that by sub-division into several panels it could deal with the increased work brought to it. Its members were then as follows :—
Sir David Harrel and Sir G. Gibb (Chairmen), Mr. F. S. Button, Col. Denny, Messrs. J. D. Elliott and G. J. Rowe. A third panel was added in July, consisting of Messrs. W. W. Mackenzie, J. W. White, and

W. Mosses. In 1918, Judge Walworth H. Roberts, and Mr. E. C. K. Gonner were added as Chairmen. Mr. H. J. Wilson acted as its Secretary from February, 1915.

The records of the awards issued by the Committee, which ranged over the whole wide and indeterminate field of munitions labour, therefore supply the key to the periodic wage movements in the munition trades as a whole. Obviously, its work as measured by the 641 awards issued up to 1 January, 1917, and the 3,754 issued by the end of 1918, in no way superseded voluntary local settlements and adjustments of wages. These, however, tended increasingly to fall into line with the binding awards issued by the Committee.

The claims for advances in wages which were reported as " differences " to the Committee on Production fall roughly into three classes, (1) those based on the increased cost of living due to the war; (2) those which turned partly on the rise of prices, but which also contained demands for the adjustment of local inequalities of wages in cases where the remuneration in one firm or area was said to be markedly below that of the district or industry as a whole, or for similar adjustments between one class of worker and another—the ironfounder and fitter, the steel drawer and furnaceman—within the same industry ; (3) those which involved special customs, again peculiar to the firm, district, or industry, with regard to the payments for overtime, Sunday, or holiday work, the remuneration of apprentices, etc., or which turned on the intricacies of the local application of piece-work or of premium bonus systems of payment.

The two latter classes, interesting though they may be in the industrial history of the country, and important though the awards of the Committee on Production were in laying down lines of policy and in helping to reduce to order some portion of the local eccentricities in remuneration which modern industry has inherited, are yet chiefly of local and sectional interest. The great majority of the applications considered by the Committee on Production fell ultimately into the first class, and depended on the rising prices directly due to the war, and it was therefore possible to treat them on consistent lines.

The awards of the Committee dealt principally with the shipbuilding, foundry and engineering trades, to which the great majority of male munition workers belonged. The iron and steel, woodworking and chemical workers, and the members of all the 40 and more trades engaged on munition work, also came within its sphere, and received awards, while other men and women engaged on Government work of many kinds—dock labourers, cotton and flax and jute workers, sail makers, building men, gasworkers, army boot and shoe makers, ropemakers, tramwaymen, also appealed to it, voluntarily or compulsorily, for the settlement of their disputes. But the movement of wages in the highly organised shipbuilding and engineering trades served constantly (as appeared in the agitation over the $12\frac{1}{2}$ per cent. bonus in the winter of 1917) as a precedent for wage demands in all other' munitions trades. Therefore, a summary of the main advances in wages, based on increased cost of living, in the engineering and shipbuilding trades, indicated the main lines of advances throughout the munitions trades.[1]

II. Cycles of Advances.

These advances fell into seven main periods, and, with local modifications, involved the following changes in rates of wages in trades represented by the 30 or more trade unions signatory to the standing agreement with the Engineering Employers' Federation, and the trades signatory to or moving parallel with the standing agreement with the Shipbuilding Employers' Federation.

	Approximate dates covered.	Kind of Advance.
1st Cycle	February, 1915 to September, 1915	4s. on time rates, 10 per cent. on piece-rates.
2nd Cycle	May, 1916 to November, 1916	3s. on time rates only.
3rd Cycle	April, 1917 (National Agreement)	5s. to time and piece-workers.
4th Cycle	August, 1917 (National Agreement)	3s. to time and piece-workers.
5th Cycle	December, 1917 (National Agreement)	5s. to time and piece-workers.
6th Cycle	June, 1918 (National Agreement)	3s. 6d. to time and piece-workers.
7th Cycle	November, 1918 (National Agreement)	5s. to time and piece-workers.

By the end of the year 1918, therefore, timeworkers in these trades had received a total war advance of at least 28s. 6d., due to the "abnormal circumstances of the war." Piece-workers had received an increase only of 10 per cent. on their pre-war rates, but had also received a weekly bonus of 21s. 6d. under the national awards of 1917–1918. It was expressly stated that this sum and the similar advance of 1916, while they were to be taken into account in calculating overtime payments, etc. (*i.e.*, they were not to be treated merely as war bonuses), were not to affect piece-rates. New piece-work prices fixed after 1915 were accordingly understood to be based on the pre-war time rates plus the war advance of 4s. given in 1915.

In addition to these advances the great majority of time-workers throughout the munition trades (and subsequently many other trades) received in the autumn and winter of 1917, a special advance of $12\frac{1}{2}$ per cent. on earnings, "not to affect or become part of their time

---

[1] Two large classes of workers must be excepted. (1) Women munition workers were granted advances on a lower scale by a separate tribunal; and (2) wages in the iron and steel trades advanced under sliding scale schemes, normally in accordance with the selling price of their product.

rates," while a very large number of piece-workers received, early in 1918, a similar advance of 7½ per cent. These advances were not primarily aimed at meeting the increased cost of living, nor were they, in their early stages, administered by the Chief Industrial Commissioner's Department. Their contentious history will, therefore, be considered separately.

As a result partly of these special advances and partly of the comparative stability of prices since the December national advance, the Committee on Production rejected, in February, 1918, the application for further increases from the engineering and shipbuilding trades, which would, if granted, have added yet another cycle of advances on standard rates.

The process by which some of these advances were secured is worth recording in some detail. It illustrates the gradual breakdown of the system of sectional changes in wages, a breakdown which led up to the important movement for national advances developed in the engineering and other trades in 1917, and, secondly, the delays involved in the established systems of settling disputes between federated firms and trade unions. These delays (strictly the result of constitutional procedure described above) were probably responsible for a large portion of the complaints of tardiness in settling disputes during the war, when industrial conditions and prices were rapidly changing.

The advances in wages obtained in the first year of the war have been summarised above.[1] Of these the most important was the advance of 4s. a week or 1d. an hour, and 10 per cent. on piece-rates, awarded to Clyde shipbuilding workers on 1 March, 1915. This was the first award made by the Committee on Production. It was followed by an award of the same amount to the engineering workers in the same district, in settlement of the dispute that led to the February strike on the Clyde, and instituted the first of a series of comprehensive awards by which the Committee came to regulate wages gradually.

Following these awards came a series of further advances, spreading slowly over the whole country. The waves broke very irregularly over different areas. Well-organised districts such as Sheffield, London, Newcastle and Edinburgh got their 4s. and 10 per cent. advance for skilled workers in the course of the next two months. To others, where the engineering trade unions were less strong, similar advances came in sections and at intervals. Thus at Preston the engineering trades received an advance of 3s. and 7½ per cent. in April, and 1s. and 2½ per cent in June, 1915; at Lincoln there were advances in these trades of 2s. in April, 2s. in November, 1915; at Weymouth, 2s. in February, 2s. in December, 1915; at Huddersfield, 2s. in May, 1915, and a second 2s. only in January, 1916.

Unskilled labour in the same industry also obtained advances, generally without having recourse to arbitration at this time, but on less good terms than were awarded to the skilled men. Thus employers, having agreed or being compelled to give advances of 3s. or 4s. to

---

[1] Chap. I.

their skilled workmen, not infrequently made, spontaneously, similar but rather lower advances, 2s. or 3s. a week, on the low wages of their labourers; these advances were often given only by way of bonus, not of an addition to their standard wages.

The amount of friction caused by these spasmodic advances, and the negotiations leading up to them, is of very great importance in judging the relationship of labour and capital in the first year and a half of the war. By the end of 1915, however, almost all of the districts covered by the organisation of the Amalgamated Society of Engineers had obtained—in most cases by agreement not by arbitration award—their 4s. and 10 per cent. advance for skilled workers. This represented for those employed on time work an increase of about 10 per cent. on pre-war rates, as against a corresponding rise of food prices claimed on the authority of the Board of Trade to be 42 per cent. in January, 1916. The shipbuilding trades had received the same increased rates.

The advances which had so far taken place had been arranged either by negotiation or award between local associations of the engineering employers and trade unions, or by similar agreements or awards for individual firms. The Committee on Production dealt, at this period, with a considerable number of purely "domestic" applications for increases in wages based on the general pressure of increased cost of living.

Claims for a second series of advances were beginning to be made in the autumn of 1915 by the engineering and shipbuilding trade unions, whose representatives urged that the increase of wages obtained was, on the statistics quoted above, quite incommensurate with the increased cost of living. To this, however, both employers and the Government offered resistance. The Secretary of the Shipbuilding Employers' Federation, in reporting to the Chief Industrial Commissioner's Department their refusal to consider even an informal conference with the trade unions concerned on the question of a further increase, urged that the policy of further wage advances—claimed not on general grounds but on those of increased cost of living—was one for the Government's immediate consideration.[1] "Every effort was being made to carry through all government work with reasonable economy in the best interest of the whole country."

The attitude of the Government was made clear within two days of the despatch of this letter.

On 1 December, at a conference of a thousand representative trade unionists at the Central Hall, Westminster, an appeal was made on behalf of the Government that more demands for further wage advances should, in the national interest, not be pressed. The Prime Minister explained the urgent need for economy. War votes since August, 1914, had reached £1,662,000,000. Four and a half million workpeople had already received advances of wages averaging 3s. 6d.

---

[1] M.W. 67820.

a week, while the increase in earnings would be considerably greater. Mr. McKenna, the Chancellor of the Exchequer, urged the necessity of thrift with much vigour.

"Those who demand higher wages," he said, "must show themselves worthy of higher wages. They must show they can save in the interests of the State and their neighbours, their families and themselves. And when they have shown they can save, then with clean hands they can come into court and say 'our labour is worthy of higher pay. We have earned it from the State and we are helping the State not only with our hands but with our money.' Until you can do so, you are not justified in asking for higher wages for a special trade to the injury of all other classes of the community."

The audience did not accept with unqualified approval this initiation of the War Economy Campaign, for some months later looked on with distrust by numbers of working men.[1] After some debate, however, they resolved to commend to the trade unions which they represented the earnest and favourable consideration of the statements laid before them.

III. The "Embargo" on Advances.

(a) POLICY OF CHECKING WAGE INCREASES.

In furtherance of this policy of checking wage advances in the interests of national economy the following minute of November, 1915, was communicated by the Government to the Committee on Production.

"His Majesty's Government have given earnest attention to the financial position of the country, to the great and increasing demands which will still be made upon its resources to meet the needs of the war and to the imperative need for economy in all forms of expenditure and consumption, both public and private. They have also had regard to the general advances of wages that have already been given since the beginning of the war and to the measures already taken to tax or limit the profits of undertakings. H. M. Government have come to the conclusion that in view of the present emergency any further advance of wages (other than advances following automatically from existing agreements) should be strictly confined to the adjustment of local conditions, where such adjustments are proved to be necessary."

The Committee on Production accordingly, when giving its decision on various applications for advances at the end of 1915 and the beginning of the next year, found the men's claims not established.

---

[1] "Economy has been the bane of our existence. We have had to exist under its influence from our infancy upwards," said the spokesman of the Engineering and Shipbuilding Trades Federation on the deputation of 22 June, 1916, referred to below.

Manchester led the way in an application to the Engineering Employers' Association from the joint committee of twelve engineering and kindred trades unions for an advance of 6s. per week on time-rates and the equivalent on piece-rates, on 28 October, 1915. The established procedure took its course and the demand was discussed at a local conference on 17 November, and at a central conference on 10 December; no settlement having been arrived at, it was referred to the Committee on Production, which heard the claim on 4 January, 1916, and on 7 January, having "regard to all the circumstances and to the communication of His Majesty's Government," decided that the claim was "not established."

A similar application was heard by the Committee on Production on 20 January, on a claim for 2d. an hour on time-rates and an equivalent advance on piece-rates from the Federation of Engineering and Shipbuilding Trades (Clyde District Committee), representing seventeen trade unions and including for the first time representatives of the unskilled workers (the Clyde engineers had since the previous spring endeavoured to obtain a further advance on that awarded to them by the Committee on Production in March, 1915). At this hearing,—which represented the first claim for an advance by industry rather than by craft—the employers' associations—the North-West Engineering Trades Employers' Association, the Clyde Shipbuilders' Association, the Scottish Sheet Metal Workers Employers' Association, the Scottish Coppersmiths' Employers, the Scottish Steel Makers Wages, the National Light Castings Ironfounders' Federation and the Scottish Employers' Federation of Iron and Steel Founders—desired to record their protest at the procedure adopted by the unions in formulating a collective claim, notwithstanding the existence of agreements providing, in the case of some of the unions, recognised machinery for the discussion of wages and other questions.

In this case the Committee referred to its award of 23 March, 1915, and found that the claim for a further advance had not been established except in the case of those semi-skilled and unskilled workmen who had only received an advance of 3s. or $\frac{3}{4}$d. per hour in the previous year. Their advance was increased by another 1s. or $\frac{1}{4}$d. per hour, with a similar advance in piece-rates to 10 per cent.

Other claims, though on a less comprehensive scale, were refused at this period—from the Clyde Coppersmiths, the Engineers and Allied Trades of Sheffield (in March), the Scottish Ironmoulders, the Engineering and Shipbuilding Trades of Liverpool, Birkenhead and Mersey Districts (whose rate had been brought up to 46s. for repairs and 43s. for new work by July, 1915) in April; the Southampton Engineers in May, etc. A long drawn-out dispute on a claim for a similar advance was heard on 16 December, 22 February and 5 April, between the Shipbuilding Employers' Federation and the Shipbuilding Trades Agreement Standing Committee representing the Shipwrights' Association and nine other unions having members in the shipyards. They claimed an advance of 15 per cent., but were refused (13 April). On the same day a claim from the boilermakers for a second advance, this time of 2s. on time and 5 per cent. on piece-rates, was refused.

Similar refusals were given to the employees of a number of individual firms throughout the country—Messrs. Fairfields, machine-men (13 April); Messrs. Harland & Wolff, platers' helpers (25 May); plumbers at Messrs. Cammell Laird, Birkenhead (9 June, 1916), etc.

Altogether some 70 applications were refused by the Committee on Production, while some 110 were granted or partially granted out of all the cases (not all involving munition work) brought before the Committee on Production between 1 December, 1915, the date of the meeting above described, and 22 June, 1916, when a formal deputation on the question of prices was received by the Board of Trade.

Exceptions to this policy of refusal were made in the cases of certain districts and occupations which in 1916 had for various reasons only received 3s. or $7\frac{1}{2}$ per cent. advance in 1915. Thus Bradford, Leeds, Halifax and Barrow received an extra 1s. or $2\frac{1}{2}$ per cent. for members of the local Engineering Trades Joint Committee on 27 May. Only a few groups of skilled engineers belonging to the organised trades still remained to claim such an advance in 1916—an advance bringing their time wages normally to about 42s.

In most districts, however, the labourers and semi-skilled workers had only had at most 3s. advance (or $\frac{3}{4}$d. an hour) in 1915. There had been few arbitration awards for them. Employers had generally granted their advances in the wake of the skilled men though on a lower scale (as on the Clyde). In 1916, however, partly as a result of the growing activity of the unskilled and semi-skilled workers' unions, a very considerable number of claims were received and awards made by the Committee on Production for labourers (of all types, not only those concerned with the engineering trades).

The low earnings obtained by the engineering and foundry labourer if he were paid on time-rates, and had no opportunity of putting in extra hours of work, made such an advance in rates most important to himself and his dependents. Thus on 7 January, 1916 (when it refused the claim for a 6s. advance from the skilled workers of the same district), the Committee on Production awarded an advance of 1s. a week with the conversion of their 3s. a week war bonus into war wages, for Manchester unskilled and semi-skilled men in the engineering trade. These men were receiving a minimum rate of 21s. a week with 3s. war bonus dependent on time-keeping, and the National Union of Gas Workers and General Labourers, the Workers' Union and the British Labour Amalgamation were claiming from 9 October 6s. advance on these time rates, and $17\frac{1}{2}$ per cent. on piece-rates. The claim had been discussed at a local conference on 11 November, and at a central conference on 10 December without result. On 10 January, the wages of the Sheffield labourers employed by the Sheffield Engineering Trades Employers' Association and Messrs. Hadfield, were raised by 1s. above their previous minimum time-rate of 23s. 6d. a week plus 3s. war bonus, and this was extended on 15 March to all classes of semi-skilled and unskilled workmen on time rates who had received less than 4s. a week advance. Similar advances were made in a number of districts.

The principle which led to the Government's discouragement of wages advances,—a principle whose application the Committee on Production was left to enforce—was that the munition workers like other members of the community should take their share in the national burden caused by the rise in prices,[1] and in many cases, it was admitted, the munition worker was in fact obtaining a much larger " real " as well as " nominal " income, than he had before the war. The Prime Minister, however, had explained in answers to questions in Parliament on 20 January and 7 March, and to a deputation from the Parliamentary Committee of the Trade Union Congress that the Committee on Production was not fettered by the Government's communication with regard to all classes of labour. The Government had no wish to limit finally the wages of any class of low-paid wage earners or of those who had not received adequate advances to recompense them for the rise in the cost of living.

(b) INCREASING DISCONTENT OF WORKERS.

In spite however, of this discrimination in favour of some classes of industrial workers, much discontent was growing up among munition workers in the spring and early summer of 1916, owing to the constant rebuffing of their claims. Overtime with its opportunities of extra earnings was being curtailed, prices were still rising, there was constant suspicion of " profiteering," and the whole process of fruitless negotiation by successive conferences and by arbitration was a weariness to the flesh even of the most buoyant trade union organiser. Such discontent readily assimilated with that produced by other causes, such as the operation of the Military Service Acts and the spread of dilution then beginning to be felt. Discrimination, however reasonable in itself, was certain to produce discontent among the workers whose claims were ignored. Moreover, the Government's policy was never made clear to Labour. The Cabinet's minute to the Committee on Production was not made public until the Committee had acted on it for two months; the grounds for restricting advances and the exceptions that would be made were not explained early enough and fully enough; and the Committee on Production was required to give effect to a policy that was never clearly defined.

The embargo was indeed a fundamental breach of the principle on which the regulation of wages had been based. In effect it reduced the Committee on Production to the position of an instrument of the Executive Government, and substituted control by administrative instructions for unfettered arbitration. The unions perceived this quite clearly.

Thus on 5 April, when the application of the Shipyard Trades Standing Agreement Committee to the Shipbuilding Employers'

---

[1] On these grounds, the income tax had been, by the Finance Act of 1915, extended to the weekly wage earner.

Federation was being heard, Mr. Wilkie explained that the embargo was shaking the workers' acceptance of the whole system of compulsory arbitration.

"It was a big fight to get the workmen to agree to arbitration, and in some cases it was a bigger fight to get the employers to agree to it. Some of us have been fighting for reason to settle these matters instead of force all our lives, sometimes with success, sometimes not. Our men are skilled artisans who understand the thing just as well as we do here, and they are very strong up against this action of the Government, which is reducing arbitration before you to a farce. That is a point I want to press. . . . The Committee on Production should not be bound by the views of the Government. The men hold very strongly that the Government in itself has no more right to override the Act of Parliament than any other body or any other citizen."

On 25 May, 1916, accordingly, an appeal was sent to the Prime Minister on behalf of the Engineering Trade Unions.

"I am directed by the Engineering Trade Unions to bring to your notice a discussion which took place at a Central Conference at York between the Engineering Employers' Federation and the engineering trade unions with reference to wage advances and the ever-increasing cost in the commodities of life.

"We gave consideration to the almost universal demand on the part of our members for wage advances owing to the enormous increases in the cost of living since the outbreak of the European War. We further gave consideration to constant refusal both by the Committee on Production and the Engineering Employers' Federation, to grant wage advances, and the consequent irritation and unrest which exists in the workshops and homes of our country.

"In asking your Government to give consideration to this important problem, we desire to bring to your notice the fact that 4s. for a weekly advance appears to be the basis upon which it is difficult to secure any advance in wages to our members. This sum represents roughly 10 per cent. on the total weekly wages of our members. It is unnecessary in this connection to remind you of the fact that the increase in the cost of living represents about 50 per cent.

"Our members are arguing that £1 is worth no more than roughly 11s. for the purposes of purchasing food and the other primal necessaries of life. . . I am therefore requested to send in for the consideration of your Government, that steps be at once taken to limit the prices of food stuffs, or alternatively to agree to such advances in wages as shall be regarded as a fair compensation. Our only desire is to co-operate in every possible way with the Government in harmonious working for the final victory of our country. Will you please regard this as an urgent matter?"

The whole position with regard to the adjustment of wages to prices was discussed at a deputation from the Federation of Engineering and Shipbuilding Trades and the Trade Union Parliamentary

Congress to Mr. Harcourt at the Board of Trade, on 22 June, 1916, when Dr. Addison was present.

Mr. J. Hill stated the case for the Federation of Engineering and Shipbuilding Trades in arguments repeated scores of times by others before the Committee on Production and on labour platforms.

"We ask the Government to immediately reduce food and fuel prices to their pre-war level, or alternatively to remove the embargo placed by them on the Committee on Production against the general advance of wages to meet increases in the cost of living. We have decided to give preference rather to the reduction of the cost of living than to the increase in wages because this does not work out fairly. Some strongly organised trades can get advances, and I believe we have cases of certain trades in this federation who have had advances for sections of their members almost equivalent to the increase, but that is the very rare exception. All of us in this federation have had some advances of wages, and generally our advance has amounted to something like 4s. per week on time-rates and 10 per cent. on piece-rates."

Prices, he urged, had risen by at least 60 per cent. Unfair profiteering was taking place in some quarters. "We are not profiting by the position we are in; we are losing." The Committee on Production had become a by-word. Instead of being a fair arbitration court it had acted for the Government in keeping down wages.

The next labour spokesman repeated these points with emphasis. Exploitation was rampant throughout the country, and the only sufferers were the working classes. The men had carried out the obligations entered into in March, 1915. If the Government did not propose to do so equally in its dealings with capital it should free them from their undertaking. The Committee on Production had been most disappointing as a court of arbitration.

Mr. Harcourt in reply held out little hopes of a different policy either with regard to wages or control of prices. He pointed out that the so-called embargo was not intended to apply to the lowest paid workers. The Committee on Production had already levelled up earnings in many ill-paid trades. The 4s. and 10 per cent. advances already awarded in no way represented the increase of earnings by most munition workers. Thus in the case of a firm in the North of England, where a claim for an advance had been sent in on behalf of 5,000 employees, the average increase in rates of payment between 1914 and 1916 had been 3s. only, whereas the increase of earnings had been 19s. 6d. per week. The average increase of earnings among the workmen appearing before the Committee on Production had been about 40 per cent. This fully counterbalanced the rise in the cost of living which, excluding taxation, amounted to 40 per cent. Increased opportunities of family earnings further added to the weekly incomes of many munition workers.

"The fact is," he stated, "we must all sacrifice something and adjust our scale of living, except the very poorest, and these, it is admitted, cannot do so." A committee had been appointed to enquire into food prices, but so far " all experts were against fixing maximum prices, the failure of which in Germany was well known. . . . . It is better to have plenty dear than a scarcity still dearer by competition by consumers for the purchase of insufficient supplies. . . . . I promise you," he concluded, " to continue to watch the relation of wages to the cost of living, but I can say no more than that, and I make no definite promise of any immediate change."

IV. The Second Cycle of Advances.

After this conference, although no definite change of policy was announced, a second cycle of advances in wages began, initiated as before by awards of the Committee on Production to the engineering trades in highly organised districts and followed by agreements in individual firms between non-federated employers and their men. The normal award at this period consisted in an advance of 3s. to timeworkers only, " not to apply to or affect piece prices," and was intended in part to rectify the disproportion, already complained of, between the earnings of the timeworkers and the pieceworkers who were frequently less skilled but better paid.[1] Thus the principle of adjusting the share in the common burden of high prices to those best able to bear it was maintained. These advances spread in the course of the autumn to the less organised districts and the less skilled workers. The Cardiff and Bristol engineers had their 3s. advance in July, the boilermakers and shipbuilders and the engineers of Glasgow, Birmingham, Newcastle and Sheffield in August, those of Weymouth in September, Lincoln (2s. only) in October, Preston, Blackburn, Halifax in November, Grantham and Ipswich in December.

The men at this time normally claimed advances of from 6s. to 10s., and much discontent was shown, especially at Barrow and Sheffield, on the Clyde and Tyne, at the small increase given.[2] In the hearings before the Committee on Production, their pent-up irritation over their previous rebuffs found vent. Prices, they said, had gone up at least 50 per cent. (70 per cent. in Sheffield, according to the representatives of the smaller engineering trade unions in that district) ; time wages even after the last rise had only increased by 7s., 15 to 20 per cent. at most, on their pre-war rates.

In industries connected with the engineering trades, such as some of those engaged on steel production, wages had advanced from 60 to 80 per cent. while the skilled workmen who dealt with the same material in its later stages had a much smaller increase. It was, they urged— and this was repeated a hundred times in successive hearings—grossly unfair to consider earnings rather than rates of wages in fixing advances required by increased cost of living. Clearly a man should not be penalised for wearing himself out in overtime work, by having the income thus secured quoted as a reason for not increasing his standing wages.

---

[1] cf. Committee on Production awards, 56, 57, 59, 63, 65, 71, of 1916.
[2] cf. *A. S. E. Journal.*

"The previous replies we have got," urged the representatives of the shipbuilding trades during an arbitration in August, 1916, between themselves and the Shipbuilding Employers' Federation, "have struck deep into the roots of the shipyard workers against what is called compulsory arbitration. They think they have not got fair play in this matter. Some of us have been blamed because we have helped to get these things into force for the sake of our country."

The employers, on the other hand, while professing their complete readiness to pay any advance prescribed by the Committee on Production for timeworkers, and especially for low-paid timeworkers, normally represented that they themselves were constantly urged to economy by the Government and especially by the Departments from which they received their contracts; that in a very large number of cases workers could greatly improve their income by better time-keeping; and that the admittedly large earnings of some timeworkers and of most pieceworkers must logically be taken into account in arranging compensation for the phenomenon of increased cost of living.

Between these two groups of arguments, constantly repeated, the Committee on Production had to decide; and the 3s. advance to time-workers represented in its findings the point of equilibrium.

V. The Movement towards National Advances.

During the autumn of 1916 the failure of the established system of providing for changes of wages in the engineering trades became evident. The trade unions, by their local representatives, continually asked for advances in wages. These applications were referred to local conferences, at which almost invariably no agreement was reached, and thence to the monthly Central Conference at York, at which again the parties normally failed to agree; the question was then reported to the Board of Trade as a difference under Part I of the Munitions of War Act, and was referred by the Board of Trade to the Committee on Production.

The same barren routine was followed in the shipbuilding trades, while in both groups of trades during the preliminary negotiations, at conferences, and at the hearings before the Committee on Production, the same facts and arguments were perforce reiterated by employers and workmen, the same calculations about the rise in the cost of living were made, based on quotations from the Labour Gazette and supplemented freely by the speakers' domestic experiences; the same attempts were made to distinguish between wages and earnings as a basis for war advances; the same criticisms of the workers' time-keeping were offered by employers and rebutted by workmen; the same readiness was expressed by the workers to shoulder a share of the national burden of high prices, so long as that share was fair and profiteering in all its forms was restrained, and by the employers to raise wages so long as the necessity for this could be definitely proved by the incidence of high prices on the workers.

This process clearly involved much waste of time and temper among all the parties involved; and since the output of munitions and not the adjustment of wages was at the time the more obvious national necessity, it became increasingly desirable to curtail the existing procedure.

After the monthly Central Conference of 11 October, 1916, between the Engineering Employers' Federation and the Engineering Trade Unions at York, when all the twelve district applications for wage advances received were refused by the employers, action was taken by both trade unions and employers to remove the deadlock.

The Amalgamated Society of Engineers' monthly journals of February and March, 1917, thus described the society's part in the succeeding negotiations.

> "A special conference of organised district delegates of the Amalgamated Society of Engineers was held, owing to a letter from the Executive Committee to the Engineering Employers' Federation giving notice of the society's intention to raise the question of suspending the holding of central conferences on wages applications during the period of the war. The result of recent central conferences with reference to wages applications in which the employers had made offers totally inadequate to the merits of the case which could not be accepted by the Executive Committee . . . justified the Council in suggesting a suspension of these conferences during the present national emergency."

The employers replied that they would refer this question to their Emergency Committee and meanwhile all wage references discussed at local conferences were referred, so far as the Amalgamated Society of Engineers was concerned, to the Committee on Production direct.

At the beginning of the next year (1917) the Chief Industrial Commissioner communicated with the Amalgamated Society of Engineers and fifteen other trade unions connected with the engineering and foundry trades, suggesting for their consideration (as for that of the Engineering Employers' Federation) "Whether a more simple procedure could not be adopted with regard to the various pending claims for advances of wages, due chiefly to the increasing cost of living, taking care to preserve for the period after the war, and to avoid infringing upon, the various arrangements of Conciliation Boards, Conferences, etc."

Conferences of representatives of these trade unions met under the chairmanship of Sir G. Askwith and considered this proposal on 30 January and 5 February, 1917, and the following memorandum of agreement was drawn up between them and the Engineering Employers' Federation, providing for the consideration by the Committee on Production, at four-monthly periods during the war, of the need for general alterations in wages—awards on such general alterations to be of national application to all federated firms in the trade concerned.

Memorandum of Agreement between the Engineering Employers' Federation and the Unions connected with the Engineering and Foundry Trades, arrived at in February, 1917.

It is agreed that, having regard to the special circumstances of the war, the following shall be the principles upon which wages changes shall be arranged for the period of the war :—

1. That existing agreements or practice under which applications for general alterations in wages are dealt with shall to that extent be suspended until the termination of the war or for such further period as may be agreed upon by the parties thereto. This shall not refer to agreements or practice whereby the wages of any trades in any district or department rise or fall with the fluctuations in another district or industry not covered by this agreement.

Nor shall it prevent the Unions bringing forward for special consideration at the hearings referred to in paragraph 2 (*a*) the case of any district in which they claim that the rates of wages are unduly low or that the total amount of war advance is not adequate.

On the other hand, the Federation shall be entitled to bring forward for similar consideration any special cases they desire.

2. During such period of suspension the following procedure shall be observed, provided the consent of the Committee on Production is obtained :—

(*a*) The Committee on Production shall in the months of February, June, and October, after hearing parties, consider what general alteration in wages, if any, is warranted by the abnormal conditions then existing and due to the war.

(*b*) The award of the Committee on Production shall be an award under the Munitions of War Acts and shall be of national application to all federated firms in the branch of trade concerned.

(*c*) The first award shall take effect in all districts on the first full pay day in April and the altered rate shall continue until amended by a further award in accordance with the provisions hereof. Subsequent awards shall specify the date upon which the alteration awarded shall take effect.

The following Memorandum was also agreed between the parties :—

"The Engineering Employers' Federation and the Unions whose signatures are appended hereto recommend to His Majesty's Government that arrangements should be made whereby all employers in trade or trades affected should be subject to the awards which may be made by the Committee on Production in virtue of the agreement hereto attached."

As is explained above, the principle of the rider was accepted by the Government and embodied in the 1917 Amendment Act.[1]

---

[1] See above, pp. 44 and 48.

VI. National Awards.

At the first general application to the Committee on Production under the terms of this agreement, the Chairman of the Executive Committee of the Amalgamated Society of Engineers claimed on behalf of his society and thirteen kindred organisations, an advance of 10s. on time rates and 25 per cent. on piece prices, since food prices had advanced 89 per cent. since July, 1914. It is worth noting that the trade unions represented included in this case, though they were not all heard together, the four chief general labourers' unions, whose members were therefore no longer reduced to following in the wake of the awards to skilled workers. "The award," stated Mr. Brownlie, "will in all probability affect one million persons." In applying for these considerable advances, he was, he stated, only acting "in accordance with the opinions expressed by the members of his society, several hundred branches having during the past six months forwarded resolutions to that effect." The rise in cost of living had been between 89 and 93 per cent. Even if the advance were conceded the workers would still be "sharing with the country the losses of the war."

The Committee on Production awarded from 1 April "as a war advance, intended to assist in meeting the increased cost of living, to be recognised as due to, and dependent on the existence of the abnormal conditions now prevailing in consequence of the war," 5s. to men, 2s. 6d. to boys under 18, to be paid weekly both to time workers, piece and premium bonus workers, such advance to be taken into account in fixing payments for overtime, etc., but not to be taken into account as part of the time rates for fixing new piecework prices or premium bonus rates. When in federated districts less than 7s. advance had been given since the outbreak of war, this was to be made up to a total of 12s.

Members of the following societies received 5s. or 2s. 6d. a week under this award of the Committee on Production (*i.e.*, the award covered the members of these societies working in the shops and foundries of the Engineering Employers' Federation) : the Amalgamated Society of Engineers ; the Steam Engine Makers' Society; the United Machine Workers' Association ; the United Kingdom Society of Amalgamated Smiths and Strikers ; the United Journeymen Brass-founders', Turners', Fitters', etc., Association ; the National Brass-workers and Metal Mechanics ; the Electrical Trades' Union ; the Associated Blacksmiths' and Ironworkers' Society ; the Society of Amalgamated Toolmakers ; the United Patternmakers' Association ; the Scientific Instrument Makers' Society ; the Friendly Society of Ironfounders ; the Amalgamated Society of Coremakers ; the Iron, Steel and Metal Dressers' Trade Society; the Amalgamated Machine, Engine and Iron Grinders' and Glaziers' Society ; the National Amalgamated Union of Enginemen, Firemen, Mechanics, Motormen and Electrical Workers ; the Dock, Wharf, Riverside and General Workers' Union ; the National Amalgamated Union of Labour ; the National Union of General Workers ; and the Workers' Union. It was extended, after separate hearings in the course of the next two months, to include members of the Sheet Iron Workers' and Light Platers' Society, the Northern United Enginemen's Association ; the British Steel Smelters' Association ; the Amalgamated Moulders' Union ; the Amalgamated Society of Carpenters and Joiners, and a number of other unions. By October, 1917, 48 unions had given their adhesion to the national agreement with the Engineering Employers' Federation.

A third cycle of advances was thus inaugurated.[1] The "national" award for the engineering and foundry trades attracted much attention among the munition firms which were technically outside its scope, and this was intensified by the extension of its application throughout the engineering trades by the action of the Department[2]—even before the acquisition of the compulsory powers for this purpose under the Munitions of War Act of August, 1917. It was adopted—sometimes voluntarily, sometimes after arbitration—by a number of non-engineering firms, both in the metal trades (such as the Scotch light castings and the stove grate and light metal trades, which obtained awards in April) and in the chemical trades, which had hitherto showed little unity of action.

The Boilermakers and Shipwrights made an independent agreement in March with the Engineering Employers' Federation, on identical terms with that of the engineers, while the same advance was awarded on 1 March to these societies and to the other signatories to the shipbuilding trades' standing agreement, with regard to their members employed by the Shipbuilding Employers' Federation.

Subsequent combined applications for increased wages in the engineering and shipbuilding industries were duly heard by the Committee on Production at four-monthly periods. On 19 June, 1917, a three hours' session of the usual Committee was held, when some 120 trade union representatives, with 12 members of the Engineering Employers' Federation, appeared to argue the merits of a fresh advance of wages in accordance with the recent increase in prices.

No less than 50 trade unions were represented or were invited to attend, and the occasion was noteworthy for the fact that it was the first, when the whole industry in all its grades was represented at the same time. The Amalgamated Society of Engineers sent 20 members to represent it, but the smaller skilled unions also sent their delegates, while the 4 unions definitely representing the semi-skilled workmen and the labourer had over 30 representatives, and expressed their views with much distinctness. The arguments brought forward reproduced many that had been produced before, but some of them are worth summarising by way of recapitulation of the pros and cons of the adjustment of wages to prices on which so much of the relation of the Government to Labour depended during the war.

---

[1] Cf. Awards, 76, 80, 81, 93, 94 of 1917.
[2] See below, pp. 116–117.

After the Chairman of the Committee on Production (Sir David Harrel) had explained that those present had been summoned by a letter from the Committee, intimating its readiness to hear combined claims of the unions signatory to the national agreement if they so desired, Mr. Brownlie claimed, on behalf of the Amalgamated Society of Engineers, 100 per cent. advance to journeymen and apprentices on the rates obtained in July, 1914. The cost of food had, according to the Board of Trade returns, risen by 102 per cent. since that date. The workmen's family which spent 25s. a week (out of a weekly wage of, say, 40s.) on absolute necessities before the war must, or should now pay 50s. This increased cost was clearly due to the war. Wages ought to be a first charge on industry, and the increase which was demanded was clearly justified.

Mr. J. Hill (Boilermakers' Society) then claimed on behalf of the majority of the skilled trades represented, 10s. advance for men, and 5s. for boys, and the equivalent for piece-workers. Up to the present, the time-workers had only received 12s. weekly advance, which represented 30 per cent. increase on a pre-war wage of 40s. The present claim, if granted, would only mean a 55 per cent. advance in all.

> "It has been said to us," he urged, "again and again, that we should not claim to be in a position exactly equivalent to what we were in pre-war times, that we should take some share of the burden of the war, and we say so too. We say we should take a share, and we have been taking a very large share up to the present time."

The workmen were not alone responsible for the "vicious circle" of rising wages and prices.

> "We adhere to the position which we took up at the beginning, namely, we protest against the unjustifiable advances in the cost of living, not brought about by claims for advances of wages but brought about by those who have control of the production and distribution of the necessaries of life, and by our own Government who have neglected their duty in not taking charge of these affairs. . . . We have applied to Parliament, and Parliament says it cannot 'redress the balance in the way we wish.' Parliament says it can only be done by an adjustment of wages. You are the authority to adjust wages, and your duty, according to the Government, is so to adjust wages and rates that we will not suffer as a result of the rigging of the market by those who control the market to-day. . . . We think what we have asked for is fair. . . . It does not cover the difference in the cost of living, but if we get this advance for all the trades represented here to-day, we will manage to get along and maintain efficiency."

After Mr. Dawtry, on behalf of the Steam Engine Makers' Society, had explained afresh the grievance of the skilled time-worker as compared with the semi-skilled piece-worker, the delegates from the labourers' unions urged the necessity of an increase of weekly wages for the lowest paid workers, who were feeling the effect both of the increased cost of living and the diminished opportunities of overtime and Sunday work. Mr. Bevin, of the General Workers' Federation, stated that 75 per cent. of his members were paid 35s. or under for a normal week's work, and this and not the irregular earnings (if any) from overtime work, should be the basis for an advance. It was essential that the whole 10s. claimed should be awarded, instead of the fraction of the claim usually given in arbitration awards. He had gone from town to town urging the men to accept the last award honourably, but with all sense of responsibility, he would no longer attempt to restrain their discontent unless justice were done to them. Mr. Will Thorne equally urged that the workers must be given the whole sum claimed, although he admitted that they would not even then be satisfied. The present demand was based largely on the increased cost of living, but it was by no means only on these grounds that the claim was based. " Surely we as wage earners as well as producers have a right to participate in the increase in the wealth of the country that is taking place and has been taking place now for a great length of time." Mr. J. W. Frost (Ironfounders), when urging the claim of his very arduous trade to a 15s. and 7s. 6d. advance, also went beyond the cost of living argument, and discussed the effect of the Munitions Acts on the free play of supply and demand. " It is quite clear that if labour had exercised the same freedom in selling its labour power—if the law of supply and demand had been allowed to operate during the period of the war in the same way as it has operated in the selling of the necessaries of life which the worker has to purchase—then we have no hesitation in saying that wages would undoubtedly have been very much higher than at present." If limitations were placed on the worker's liberty of bargaining, corresponding measures were necessary for his protection.

The employers' representatives replied briefly to the men's arguments, declining to enter into the question of the theoretic basis on which wages should depend. They felt, said successive members of the federation, the greatest possible sympathy with members of the trade unions with regard to the cost of food. They had already met the men's representatives on this point, and had sent a resolution to the Government asking that prices should be regulated. They had no sympathy with profiteers, either in the engineering or food trades.

The real increase, however, in the cost of living, was not more than 65 per cent. according to the Board of Trade estimate, allowing for the use of certain substitutes for people's normal dietary. This advance in prices had already been practically met by the increase of wages given to labourers, and nearly if not quite by that to skilled workmen. The men's often repeated contention that earnings by overtime work or extra exertions on piecework should not be considered in assessing advances of wages was valid in peace time, but it did not apply under present conditions, since the high cost of food and the increased opportunities of earning were both phenomena directly due to the war. The suggestion that engineering firms were earning high profits and could well afford to share these with the workmen in higher wages was based almost entirely on misunderstanding. A further advance in wages might mean the closing down of certain works. If, however, the Committee on Production held that further advances in wages were due to their employees, they would, of course, readily submit to its award. They protested, however, against any increase in piece-rates (such as had been commonly given two years before), and urged that any advance should be given by way of a bonus in addition to earnings. Incidentally, they pointed out that since the cost of living had only risen some 10 per cent. since the previous general award, the men (assuming that strict attention was to be paid to Board of Trade statistics and that the previous awards of the Committee on Production were adequate) were only entitled to an advance of rather more that 1s. a week, instead of the 10s. and 15s. claimed.

The Committee on Production, after hearing these conflicting opinions, made an award of 3s. for men, 1s. 6d. for boys under 18, to be paid to piece and time workers equally, like the previous national award, from the beginning of August, 1917.

Since 45 unions were represented at this hearing, and the award (issued on 14 July) was made applicable to all their members when in the employment of the 1,400 firms included in the Engineering Employers' Federation, fewer supplementary awards were necessary after its issue than after that of the previous general award. The Committee issued on the same day identical findings with regard to the organised workmen employed by the Shipbuilding Employers' Federation (in this case again labourers' unions were included with the skilled men's unions which normally negotiated with the Federation) for the Scottish Ironfounders, for the National Light Castings Ironfounders' Federation, for engineers and bricklayers in steel works in Scotland, etc., and a few days later an award, similar in effect though slightly different in terms, was awarded to members of the Workers' Union and three other general labourers' unions, employed by members of the Wages Committee of Chemical Manufacturers. This was the first hearing in this hitherto ill-organised industry on the basis of a " national agreement."

The 3s. and 1s. 6d. advance of August spread through the munition trades of the country in the summer and early autumn of 1917, accompanied by a parallel advance of 2s. 6d. and 1s. 3d. to women and girl munition workers, enforced by statutory order on the recommendation of the special arbitration tribunal for women's wages, and by orders for the " extension of awards " issued under the Munitions of War Act of August, 1917.

Agreements on the same lines as the agreement in the engineering and foundry industry were made in the course of 1917 and 1918 by the following organisations :—[1]

The Mersey Ship Repairers' Association and the Employers' Association of the Port of Liverpool on the one hand, and the Federation of Engineering and Shipbuilding Trades (Mersey District Committee) and the Liverpool District Joint Committee of Engineering Societies

---

[1] *Twelfth Report of Proceedings under the Conciliation Act, 1896:* p. 38.

on the other; the National Association of Master Heating and Domestic Engineers and the National Union of Operative Heating and Domestic Engineers; the Chemical Employers' Federation and the National Federation of General Workers, etc., and Joint Committee of Salt and Chemical Workers; the Soap and Candle Trades Employers' Federation and the National Federation of General Workers and Joint Committee of Salt and Chemical Workers; the Wages Committee of Explosives Manufacturers and the National Federation of General Workers; the Drug and Fine Chemical Manufacturers' Association and the National Warehouse and General Workers' Union and others; Scottish Building Trades (Employers) Wages Board and Building Trades of Scotland Standing Committee; Employers and Operatives' Associations and Federations connected with the Building Trades of England and Wales.

In the case of a number of other trades, for example: shipbuilding, Scottish iron and steel trades, dockers (Great Britain), carters (Great Britain), clay industry (Great Britain), railway shopmen, London County Council, the principle of a four-monthly revision of wages by the Committee on Production, without the other clauses of the agreement, was adopted. The trades covered by these agreements and arrangements were of such importance that they exercised a predominant influence on wage movements throughout the rest of the war.

VII. Low-rated Districts.

In October, the Committee on Production was already hearing fresh applications for periodic advances and it granted in November a series of increases of 5s. and 2s. 6d., under the same conditions as those granted in April and August, to take effect from the first full pay day in December, 1917. The engineering unions at their hearing on 23 October repeated their claims made in the previous July, with the additional demand of a 50s. minimum wage for labourers.

It also spent two days in hearing in detail applications brought forward under a provision of the engineers' national agreement of the previous February for " special consideration " in the case of some 48 districts in which it was claimed that the engineering wage was unduly low or the total amount of war advance was inadequate. Among the 48 districts included was a group of 13 towns in Lancashire and Cheshire, a group of 15 towns in Yorkshire, a group of 6 towns in East Anglia, together with some areas isolated industrially, such as Stroud, Chepstow, and Bath. In each of the first groups of cases it was claimed that wages should be raised uniformly to at least those of the highest rated towns in the district.

The Committee, after detailed consideration, resisted this attempt to standardise wages throughout districts, and only sanctioned advances of 1s. to 3s. a week to special grades of workpeople at Aberdeen, Carlisle, Keighley, Otley, St. Helens, giving as the reason for their refusal that " It is not sufficient to show that the rate in some other district or districts was higher previous to the war or is higher at the present time, without regard to the conditions affecting the districts compared which gave rise to the differential rates." The terms of the national agreement only provided for special local adjustment of rates when these were " unduly low having regard to the conditions prevailing in the district in question."

On the other hand, the Committee refused a similar application from the Engineering Employers' Federation for special consideration on behalf of federated firms in Ireland, and ruled that the whole of the 5s. advance awarded in November, like the 3s. awarded in July, must apply to Irish firms.

VIII. Conclusion.

Similar awards were again issued in the case of the shipbuilding trades on 23 November, the chemical workers, and other branches of the metal trades. On the whole, however, the Committee on Production was set free, through the system of national awards, for the consideration of questions concerning individual firms, of which a very large number were referred to it during the autumn. The question of parallel advances to women and to men munition workers was brought before it,[1] but was referred for special departmental decision, and the claim for equal increases was ultimately refused on the ostensible ground that women taking skilled men's work were, on the principle of equality of treatment, entitled to the skilled men's standard rates of pay but not to special war advances above these.[2]

The advances sanctioned and awarded in November, 1917, were disturbed by the echoes of the agitation caused by the $12\frac{1}{2}$ per cent. award to time-workers. In February, 1918, when the period came for a sixth cycle of claims for advances, the munition workers throughout the country were, almost to a man, receiving special advances of $12\frac{1}{2}$ per cent. on time-work, $7\frac{1}{2}$ per cent. on piece-work, calculated on their weekly earnings including the war bonus previously awarded. Further, owing to the system of price regulation adopted by the Government, the cost of living recorded by the Board of Trade index numbers was practically stationary. The Committee on Production accordingly refused all general claims for any fresh series of wage advances to take effect from 1 April, 1918. The rise in cost of living was, however, resumed, and in June and November the Committee awarded further advances of 3s. 6d. and 5s. respectively.

The above record of awards and arguments—awards affecting directly or indirectly two million munition workers and very large numbers of non-munition workers ; arguments repeated indefinitely in verbal and printed discussions—gives some indication of the work

---

[1] *e.g.*, by the unskilled unions when they claimed an advance of 1/6 per day or shift for *all* adult workers in the chemical trades in October.
[2] Vol. V, Part II.

of the Committee on Production in adjusting standard wages to cost of living in the munition trades. By the end of the year 1917, the rise in the cost of living was estimated at 103 per cent. over the level of July, 1914, while the rise in wages, apart from that acquired under the $12\frac{1}{2}$ per cent.[1] and $7\frac{1}{2}$ per cent. bonuses, for which the Committee on Production was not responsible, was 20s. a week in the engineering trades. Thus the labourer was very nearly recouped for the fall in the value of his pre-war wage of 20s. to 25s. a week—completely so if he received the $12\frac{1}{2}$ per cent. bonus—while the skilled workman had suffered a definite loss in real wages (although his actual earnings were normally much in excess of those which he took home in time of peace). It was, perhaps, with a view to his position after the war, when opportunities for extra earnings might have disappeared while high prices were still maintained, that the engineer still claimed at the beginning of 1918 a substantial increase in his standard rates.

The awards of the Committee on Production for the engineering and metal trades were, as has been said, largely copied by other trades, equally pressed by the effects of increased cost of living, and by isolated firms which often reached a settlement with their employees without recourse to arbitration, although, if controlled, they must apply for the sanction of the Ministry of Munitions. Apart from its awards on cases turning on cost of living, the Committee also did much to regularise industrial relations by awards which served as general precedents for the conditions of the wage contract, such as the settlement of overtime rates in different industries (especially for labourers), and the rates of payment for work at night, on Sundays and during customary holidays. It adjudicated on schemes for time-keeping bonuses, for the conversion of war bonuses into war wages, and for the merging of differential war bonuses (distinguishing, *e.g.*, between the allowances to married and unmarried workmen) into flat rates. The iron and steel trades, dependent primarily on sliding scale systems of payment, were under such a system of remuneration to a great extent outside its sphere. When, however, the sliding scale ceased to operate, owing to the fixing of steel and iron prices by the Government, the Committee issued various awards modifying the operation of the scales but maintaining their principle, or giving war bonuses to some extent similar to those of the engineering trades.[2] In the perplexing cases, on which so many fair wage claims turned, of " mixed trades "—the bricklayers in engineering works, the engineers in steel works, etc.—it maintained the principle that such workmen must receive the advances of the trade which it had been customary for workmen of their type to follow in their own firm or district, but that they must not vary between the systems of payment of two trades or claim the advances of both.

---

[1] The $12\frac{1}{2}$ per cent. bonus added 7/- or 8/- a week to the earnings of the majority of skilled workmen of the engineering trades, in so far as they were paid on bare standard time rates apart from overtime.

[2] Cf. Awards of 20 June, 1916 (Bolckow, Vaughan & Co.), and 30 March, 1917 (S. Wales Iron & Steel Trades), altering maxima; and 1 May, 1917 (S. Wales Siemens Steel Association), etc., awarding bonus. See also below, pp. 204-205.

By the end of 1917, the Committee on Production had, since its appointment, issued 1451 awards, by the end of 1918, 3,754. Although it had not propounded any very definite principles of action, it had defined the limits within which wage movements in the whole of the munition trades took effect. It had secured a more or less uniform series of changes in standard rates of wages, and it had inaugurated a very important movement for dealing with changes in such rates, nationally, and not only by craft or trade, but by industry. It had indeed only dealt partially with the difficulties surrounding the adjustment of piece-rates and of systems of payments by results, with which it had been brought into contact chiefly through disputes referred to it from individual firms. It had, however, either by award or by precedent, established the principles on which the "war wages" throughout the country were adjusted, and its work served to a very large extent as the framework within which the Ministry of Munitions dealt, under the limitations of the Munitions of War Acts, with the wages of workmen in the national factories and controlled establishments.

CHAPTER IV.

THE ORDINARY WAGES ADMINISTRATION OF THE DEPARTMENT.

I. Introductory.

The early administration of the Ministry was directed principally to the maintenance of recognised standard rates of payment, deviations from which were as far as possible to be prevented in the interests both of economy and of industrial peace. It was, therefore, carried on by means of a centralised staff, communicating with controlled establishments and national factories chiefly by letter and telephone, supplemented by interviews at headquarters with employers and workmen anxious to settle problems by word of mouth. From the first establishment of the Ministry labour officers and Labour Exchange officials obtained for the Department local information on definite questions concerning wages referred to them; at a later stage the investigation officers appointed in the autumn of 1916 performed the same office. Early in the spring of 1916, two engineers (the number was increased later) were attached to the Wages Section for the express purpose of visiting firms, collecting information, and giving expert advice on the many technical questions involved in the settlement of wages, while members of the administrative staff of the Section to an increasing extent visited districts in which special wages problems appeared. As a whole, however, the control of wages was definitely centralised. It was probably partly on this account that while rates of time wages (ascertainable by district standards) were dealt with on a consistent plan, on the lines laid down by the Committee on Production, the very difficult group of questions connected with payment by results (which had never been settled in detail in the engineering trades by standardised agreements between employers and workmen), received comparatively little departmental attention, except in the National Shell and Projectile Factories, until the year 1917.

(a) Effects of Dilution Policy on Wages.

Only in connection with the policy of dilution did the Ministry adopt a definitely constructive policy during the early months of its control of munition workers' wages. This group of cases, with the difficult and important related question of the rates to be paid under dilution schemes to men and women who undertook munition work without replacing individual skilled workmen, as has been shown above, was forced on the Ministry as an integral part of its dilution policy, and led to the taking of compulsory powers of wage regulation in the Amendment Act of January, 1916. With these powers, and with a relatively clear field of operations in the new national factories, the Ministry was able effectively to take the initiative in wages questions. The resulting policy affected women's wages much more directly than men's, and is described in connection with the history of women's wages.

(b) TYPES OF WAGES QUESTIONS BEFORE THE DEPARTMENT.

The following, therefore, were, apart from dilution questions, the chief classes of wage questions that came before the Department during the first summer and autumn of the imposition of control.

(a) Complaints from individuals, or from trade unions, that the district rate was not being paid for munitions work as required by the Fair Wages Clause;

(b) Applications from owners of controlled establishments for leave to pay higher rates to groups or classes of their workpeople, and to members of their staff;

(c) Demands from workers or their societies for a rise of wages on general grounds, which might end in a dispute and involve arbitration.

The three types of cases were obviously very closely connected. It was frequently difficult to say when a doubtful fair wage claim might not merge into a demand for arbitration, or reappear, after an amicable agreement, as a request from a controlled establishment for sanction to an advance of wages to its workpeople.

These remained the standing types of problems presented to the Departments in so far as men's wages were concerned. A great mass of problems connected with the settlement of piece rates, the spread of systems of payment by results, and the relations of piece and time-workers were later thrust upon it for solution, and additional statutory duties and powers were entrusted to it. But the general aim of its administration remained the same, the maintenance of recognised standard rates and relations in spite of the widening scope of the administrative activities involved in that aim. The rapid and continuous rise in the cost of living was all the time provoking wages demands, with which the Department had to deal; the danger that strikes, and serious discontent that did not issue in an actual stoppage, might hamper the production of munitions made the settlement of these demands urgent; the possibility of stimulating production by some change of methods of remuneration acquired an additional importance with the growing shortage of labour. The administrative task was the more difficult because the standard rates and conditions which the Department was engaged in supporting were outside its own control and were frequently disturbed by changes in the making of which it had no say. The Department was bound to accept the awards of external arbitrators under the Munitions of War Acts, and could with difficulty refuse to accept agreements made between representative organisations of employers and workpeople.

In the present chapter the administration of the Fair Wages Clause, the sanctioning of changes in wages under Section 4 (2) of the Munitions of War Act, the regulation of wages in connection with dilution so far as it is not dealt with in the account of women's wages, and the extension of awards under Section 5 of the Amendment Act of 1917, are described. The problems arising from payment by results and the grievance of the skilled time-worker are the subject of separate chapters, V and VI.

II. Administration of the Fair Wages Clause.

(*a*) SCOPE OF THE DEPARTMENT'S RESPONSIBILITY.

In the first departmental allocation of work in July, 1915, it was arranged that Mr. Wolfe's section of the Labour Department should administer the Fair Wages Clause, in so far as it applied to work done under contract or sub-contract on behalf of the Minister of Munitions ; and that claims made to the supply departments of the Ministry in connection with this clause in their contracts should be transferred by them to the Labour Department.

The section also undertook certain responsibilities in the administration of the clause on behalf of the Admiralty and War Office.

As early as 28 September, 1915, the Admiralty suggested to the Ministry of Munitions that in future all questions affecting wages paid in controlled establishments, including those involved in the application of the Fair Wages Clause, should be dealt with by the Minister of Munitions, since the latter had, in any case, to sanction changes of rates of payment in controlled establishments.[1] For this purpose it was necessary to inquire into district rates of wages, and in practice it was very seldom possible to say at once, if at all, whether a given complaint was one of which the contracting Department could or could not take cognizance as a breach of the Fair Wages Clause. With this suggestion the Ministry of Munitions was at first unable to comply, on the grounds of "the very grave pressure of work at present (30 October), in the department," and the fact that the responsibility of enforcing the Fair Wages Clause must ultimately rest with the contracting Department. On 26 January, 1916, however, after further correspondence, the Ministry intimated to the Admiralty that it would be prepared to deal on behalf of the latter with all questions concerned with the Fair Wages Clause and changes of wages in controlled establishments, on the assumption that the Admiralty would make arrangements to prevent overlapping between their respective officials.

It was subsequently arranged that the Admiralty should be responsible for the observance of the Fair Wages Clause by firms on its " A " list and in all uncontrolled Admiralty firms, while the Ministry

---

[1] M.W. 37682.

of Munitions continued to deal with claims in all other controlled establishments engaged on Admiralty work.

Shortly afterwards, in February, 1916, the Department undertook to deal with Fair Wages claims made to the War Office, and with all other questions of wages in connection with work done by army contractors in controlled establishments.[1] The Director of Army Contracts in return undertook that " steps would be taken to prevent any overlapping taking place, or any advice or sanction being given to employers, to make changes of or additions to wages, and which might conflict with action being taken by the Ministry of Munitions."

(b) Procedure.

In administering the Fair Wages Clause the procedure adopted, after consulting those Government Departments previously chiefly concerned with its observance, was as follows :—On receipt of a complaint from an individual or a trade union that a firm was paying below the local standard rates, the complainant was asked to supplement the scanty details usually given. If there then seemed to be a *prima facie* case, the employer was asked for his observations ; if necessary, local enquiries were made, and finally a letter was sent to the employer pointing out his obligations under the Fair Wages Clause of his contract, or alternatively intimating to the complainant that he had no case under the Fair Wages Clause, but that, if dissatisfied, he could appeal for arbitration under Part I. of the Munitions of War Act.[2] The ordinary sanction of the clause, the removal of an offender from the list of Government contractors, could hardly be employed in wartime; so that official remonstrance and the possibility of appeal to arbitration had to serve. The Department was " at all times ready to inquire into fair wage complaints," although such complaints were often based on misunderstanding, as when a workman complained on general grounds that his income was " unfair " by comparison with his deserts, or claimed as a right an advance in wages obtained by fellow workmen in another trade. In some cases, conferences on disputed questions of wages were arranged between employers and trade unionists, in this way anticipating the proposals for the better administration of the clause in all Government work, which were later urged on the Ministry of Labour by trade union representatives.

---

[1] M.W., 37682/2.
[2] A large number of complaints from individuals as well as from trade unions reached the Department during its early days, often addressed to the Minister in person. A number were received after the Minister's speech at the Trades Union Congress at Bristol. Thus, in September, 1915, a letter was received from a labourer at Johnstone complaining that only 23s. a week was paid for his class of work by his firm, whereas workers " no more loyal " at Paisley, a few miles away, got 27s. 6d. The employer was asked for his observations, and was able to convince the Department that the normal rate paid by the Local Engineering Employers' Association was 23s. for a week of 54 hours. Under the circumstances the complainant was informed on 9 October that the Minister could not intervene, as no breach of the Fair Wages Clause had taken place, but that the matter might be referred to the Board of Trade for arbitration. (C.E. 612/4.)

(c) PROBLEMS RAISED.

Fair wage complaints reached the Department in a fairly even flow, and were dealt with at the rate of 2,000 to 3,000 a year. They involved many complicated problems, including some of the most difficult arising in the Wages Section. The handling of them required much exact knowledge of district rates and conditions and much sifting of evidence. Sometimes the Labour Exchange officials were able to supply the exact information required or the labour officers, or investigation officers, of the Department made special inquiries into the local circumstances. Sometimes, as has been said, employers and workmen were asked to attend, separately or together, at Whitehall Gardens, to substantiate their written statements.[1] The Fair Wages Clause had presented many problems of interpretation before the war, especially in ill-organised trades and districts and classes of workers; and these were increased, like most other labour problems, by the new industrial conditions produced by the war.

The difficulties mainly fell into two classes, those connected with the interpretation of the phrase " district rate," and those arising from the employment of workpeople " outside their trade."

Employers undertook in their contracts to pay to their workpeople while on Government work either the trade union rate for their work or, if there was no recognised trade union rate, then that " in practice prevailing among good employers " in the district, or the nearest district in which the gèneral industrial circumstances were similar. There was little difficulty in interpreting the rate to be paid to workers in the original " munitions " trades of engineering and shipbuilding, in which trade unionism was strong and standard time rates were adjusted by formal agreements between associations of employers and workmen's societies. The Workers' Union and the building trades unions, however, constantly approached the Ministry with requests for the enforcement of the clause among the semi-skilled and unskilled workers and the highly localised classes with whom they were concerned.[2]

The difficulty of interpretation was particularly great in the case of women workers, especially of those who were doing munitions work but not as substitutes for men. In the case of these women " on women's work " there frequently was no local rate—or at least no adequate rate—" commonly recognised by employers and trade societies," according to which their remuneration could be fixed. The Fair Wages Clause was almost inoperative among women munition workers, and the Ministry realised by experience that, since it could not by means of the Fair Wages Clause secure, as had been at first hoped, adequate remuneration for these women, it must obtain powers to issue statutory orders regulating their wages.

---

[1] L.R. 1563/5. cf. C.E. 1401/4, for an account of a six months' controversy with Messrs. Edgar Allen of Sheffield over a fair wage claim for the skilled man's rate by an iron moulder in this firm's employment.
[2] M.W. 31572.

The same difficulty of interpretation, complicated by local custom, appeared among other ill-organised workers. Thus on 8 August, 1915, the Workers' Union wrote to the Ministry, complaining that a Halifax firm was underpaying the labourers in its engineering works. Skilled engineers on night shift worked 44 hours at day rates and were then paid at time and a quarter for the next two hours and time and a half for the rest of the time worked, whereas labourers (rated at 21s. plus 3s. bonus) never had more than time and a quarter rates for overtime work.[1] Repeated letters from the firm supplemented by a report from the local labour officer, alleged that this difference in the position of the labourer and the skilled worker was generally accepted locally, and the Department accordingly explained to the trade union concerned that no action was possible under the Fair Wages Clause.[2] Similar indeterminate customs about overtime allowances often recurred and were naturally important, owing to the great amount of overtime worked during the first two years of the war.

If, as in the case quoted above, no definite district rate existed, then the majority rate of employers in the neighbourhood had to be ascertained. Thus in November, 1916, the Edinburgh branch of the Associated Blacksmiths' and Ironworkers' Society complained that a Leith firm of engineers paid time and a quarter, instead of time and a half, for overtime work.[3] The Department made an inquiry from 62 firms in Leith and the neighbourhood. 70 per cent. of the employers, representing 73 per cent. of the blacksmiths in the neighbourhood, paid at time and a half. The firm was therefore instructed, under the Fair Wages Clause, to pay at time and a half.

If there were no similar firms in the district, as in the case, for example, of some small country firm engaged on woodwork for Government purposes, neither district nor majority rate could readily be discovered. In such a case the only possibility was to take as a standard the rates for country work " recognised or prevailing in the nearest district in which the general industrial. circumstances are similar." Fair wage claims often arose in rural districts or in small businesses owned by a self-made employer, and such common-sense applications of the principle of fair payment were not infrequent.

The other common type of problem, in which the difficulty consisted not so much in ascertaining as in selecting the district rate, was that of the workman employed outside his own trade, or in his own trade but under special conditions, such as the maintenance men, carpenters and others in engineering works or bricklayers in a foundry.[4] These men would frequently claim, under the Fair Wages Clause, the rates and advances proper to their own trade under their own conditions. From its inauguration the department controlling wages was confronted with such problems. Thus in October, 1915, a certain engineering

---

[1] M.W. 31572
[2] The firm reported in November to the Ministry that, owing to the importunity of the union, they had raised the labourers' overtime rates according to their request.
[3] M.W. 128963.   [4] M.W. 161178; C.E. 1434/4.

firm in Greenock granted a bonus of 1d. to its workmen, including plumbers; subsequently a general advance of ½d. was awarded to plumbers in the building trade by the Lord Provost.[1] Should the engineering plumbers gain under both advances? Conversely, carpenters in the same town, also employed in engineering works, had been granted a bonus—Did this extend, under the Fair Wages Clause, to carpenters not engaged in maintenance work? When firms had been accustomed to paying building trade rates,—normally higher than those for the more regular shop work—to their maintenance men, the Wages Section did not interfere. On the other hand, supported by awards on similar claims by the Committee on Production, the section did not attempt to enforce such rates on unwilling employers under the Fair Wages Clause, even in areas where considerable numbers of engineering firms were paying these men on the higher scale. Difficulties such as these often, as in the first case quoted, clustered round the position of the ubiquitous plumber, a constant source of industrial strife before the war. But they re-appeared in many forms before the Wages Section of the Ministry and the arbitration courts, as a result of the special transference of men to work outside their own trade, brought about by the war.

An allied case in which the provisions of the Fair Wages Clause were claimed and the same difficulties of interpretation arose was that of new trades which developed during the war.

Thus in September, 1916, members of the Furnishing Trades' Association complained to the Department about the rates paid both to men and women for making ammunition boxes. These had naturally been made to a very small extent in time of peace. Since the war, joiners, cabinet-makers, packing-case makers had all been employed on their manufacture, often by small firms of builders, or by other wood-working employers whose trade was slack. The skilled workmen claimed the rates of pay proper to their own trades. The Department, on expert advice, ruled that such manufacture was in most cases only packing-case makers' work, and to be paid at such rates.

In such cases the Department acted upon the principle that the standard rate to be paid must depend on the job, not on the man performing it, *i.e.*, that if a man took work in a less skilled trade than his own, he must descend to the lower rate of pay or of advances belonging to his present occupation. This was of some practical importance so long as the leaving certificate system obtained, and one of the grounds on which a munitions tribunal might, under Section 5 (5) of the Amendment Act of January, 1916, grant a leaving certificate refused by an employer, was a proof that the employer was paying the workman less than the standard rate of wages.[2] While the case

---

[1] Wages Section Report, October, 1915.
[2] Munition tribunals found, on occasion, the same difficulty as the administrative Department, in ascertaining the district rate payable. *e.g.*, the cases on appeal of Mullins v. London Brighton & South Coast Railway, 22 September, 1916, and Sabin v. British Thomson Houston Company, February, 1917.

of the man working in a lower grade of employment than that of his own trade was not definitely provided for, yet it was generally held by the Department that a firm (while not bound to pay an employee above the rate due for the work on which he was engaged) should not withhold him under such circumstances from getting better-paid work in his own trade, unless it was prepared to pay him at the higher rate.

Constant attempts were made by aircraft woodworkers to obtain for the members of the numerous woodworking trades of different grades drawn in to make aeroplanes a uniform rate under the Fair Wages Clause equal to that of the best paid trade from which workmen had been recruited for the new industry. This claim was for many months resisted by the Department and by the Committee on Production,[1] although it was finally granted in principle under the skilled aeroplane workers' wages Order of February, 1918.

The same mixture of occupations sometimes involved the Department in the determination of normal hours of work, the regulation of which according to local or trade standards is included in the terms of the Fair Wages Clause.

Thus the Department was consulted in the autumn of 1916 about the case of a firm of builders near Bradford who employed a number of joiners on their building work, while they also had joiners and cabinet-makers in an adjoining workshop making naval ammunition boxes, which were admittedly cabinet-maker's work. The joiners, after the custom of the building trade, worked only $7\frac{1}{2}$ hours a day for the six weeks before Christmas, whereas the cabinet-makers worked 10 hours all the year round. The secretary of the Joiners' Society claimed that the cabinet-makers also should work only $7\frac{1}{2}$ hours per day.

The Department ruled that as the work was cabinet-maker's by nature, the cabinet-makers should work their own trade hours. There was no objection to the firm employing some of their regular joiners on the cabinet-makers' job and paying them joiners' rates for joiners' hours if they liked to do so ; but there was no claim for the men under the Fair Wages Clause.

Such questions of working hours did not often appear, though they occurred periodically in the wood-working trades, and on at least one occasion, came before the Committee on Production. Such importance as they had, was due to the calculation of overtime payments and the effects on such calculation of the adoption of a short or long working week. There was much friction among aircraft workers in 1917-18 over this question.[2]

(d) EFFECTS OF THE APPLICATION OF THE FAIR WAGES CLAUSE.

The most important direction in which the Fair Wages Clause operated among munition firms was in the gradual levelling up of wages throughout districts and trades by the extension of new rates resulting

---

[1] Cf. Award 340 of the Committee on Production on the claim of the joint Woodworking Trades Aircraft Committee of the Glasgow district on July, 1916.
[2] See below, Chapter V.

from arbitration awards, or from agreements between the various employers' federations and trade unions. A very definite series of advances towards uniformity in standard rates, though not in actual wages, was thus secured.

The awards of the Committee on Production established new district rates, in so far as they applied to the differences between associations of employers and men, as distinguished from individual firms and groups of workers, and they could therefore be extended under the Fair Wages Clause. Other general advances however, such as the $12\frac{1}{2}$ per cent. bonus, and the rates fixed under the different women's wages orders, could not be so extended, since they were made under special conditions and were not held to establish new district rates.

In August, 1915, a number of trade unions claimed that awards of the Committee on Production made with regard to wages paid by members of an employers' federation were binding on non-federated firms in the same trade.[1] The Chief Industrial Commissioner's Department ruled that non-federated firms were not so bound. Any action therefore taken to extend such awards, which at this period almost always involved advances in wage rates, had to take the form of recourse by the workers to the Fair Wages Clause. The Wages Section when appealed to was able to rule in the case of individual employers working on munitions contracts that the wages paid by them —the aggregate wages including war bonus but excluding time-keeping bonus—" should not be less than the aggregate rates paid by the majority of similar firms in the district." From the point of view of organised labour, the procedure meant but a slow advance. However, it offered a sure if cumbrous process of extending the operation of awards in so far as Government work was concerned, until the process was accelerated by the powers conferred on the Department for the compulsory extension of awards in 1917.

With the constant increase in the volume of Government as compared with commercial work, the Fair Wages Clause also in some cases raised wages for non-munition workers in munition works.[2] If the standard rate of wages were perforce guaranteed by a firm—even a non-union firm—when doing Government work, obviously those of the same firm's employees who were engaged on commercial work might, untrammelled by leaving certificate restrictions, demand the extension of this rate to themselves. This attempted use of the Fair Wages Clause as a lever to raise wages apart from work done on Government orders had been common among workpeople for a number of years before the war. The war-time scarcity of labour increased the effectiveness of the lever. It was, of course, used for this purpose exclusively by the workers, not by any official department.

It was constantly urged by trade unions before the war (and the claim served as a standing motion at meetings of the Trade Union

---

[1] Wages Section Report, 27 August, 1915.
[2] M.W. 40193.

Congress), that the Fair Wages Clause should be so extended in operation as to enforce general acceptance of trade union standards ; Government Departments should not even permit tenders for their contracts to be made by firms unless the latter paid standard rates at all times to their workpeople, whether they were employed on Government or on private work. Two deputations to the Ministry of Labour in July and October, 1917, repeated this demand, urging first, that the burden of securing that a firm was giving fair pay should rest on those who gave out contracts rather than on the trade unions, which could only, under existing conditions, send in detached complaints to successive Departments ; secondly, that Government contractors ought to pay (as stated above) standard rates to all their workpeople, however employed ; and thirdly, that a list of fair contractors and sub-contractors tendering for, as well as obtaining, Government contracts should be published or should be supplied to the unions concerned.[1]

This important proposal was considered in detail at the end of 1917 by the interdepartmental Fair Wages Advisory Committee just reconstituted under the chairmanship of Sir George Askwith, but not adopted.[2] It was felt that the Ministry of Munitions, whose enforcement of the Fair Wages Clause had been conducted with singularly little friction was not very closely concerned with these questions, though the Department was represented on the committee.[3] The movement is interesting, as one phase of the attempt to universalise trade union standards of conditions of work and wages.[4]

---

[1] L.R. 1563/2 to /5., and quarterly reports of the Parliamentary Committee of the Trade Union Congress, 1917.

[2] L.R. 2723. and L.R. 4669.

[3] L.R. 1563/5.

[4] Decisions of the munition tribunals in 1916 and 1917 helped to extend the operation of the Fair Wages Clause in the direction desired by trade unions. Thus, on several occasions, in the Court of Appeal, Judge Atkins ruled that for the purpose of the leaving certificate regulations, the Fair Wages Clause operated, whether the firm was or was not engaged on Government contracts. Thus, if a firm was admittedly paying below the standard rates of the district or those commonly paid by good employers, this was a sufficient justification for the granting of a leaving certificate to one of the firm's workers (cf. Sabin v. British Thomson Houston Company, 22 February, 1917). A clause making this ruling general was included in the Dilution (Munitions of War Amendment) Bill of 1917, but did not become law because leaving certificates themselves were abolished.

Similar cases were those of F. Newport v. The Great Western Railway Company, and E. Bowell v. The Midland Railway Company (Locomotive Department), heard before the Bristol local munitions tribunal. In the latter case, on 16 February, 1917, the Tribunal issued a leaving certificate to the applicant on the ground that his employers, who were not engaged on Government work, were yet not complying with the Fair Wages Clause, since they were paying him less than the standard district rate for engineers. " I am of opinion," stated the chairman in his reserved judgment, " that the proper meaning to be given to Section 5 (5) of the Munitions of War Act, 1916, is that if a workman to whom that section applies desires to leave his employment, and a leaving certificate is refused by the employer, he is entitled to claim that this refusal is unreasonable if he has, in fact, been employed on terms as to rates of wages and hours of labour less favourable than those required by the Fair Wages Clause, and that it is immaterial whether the employer is or is not under contract with the Government to comply with the Fair Wages Clause." (*A.S.E. Journal*, April, 1917, p. 14).

III. Changes of Wages in Controlled Establishments.

(a) Procedure.

Section 4 (2) of the Munitions of War Act made the sanction of the Ministry of Munitions necessary for any change of wages or salary of any class of worker or person engaged in a Controlled Establishment, unless the change was necessary to give effect to the Fair Wages Clause.

The principle on which the Department acted in considering applications for advances in wages was that both employers and employed must ostensibly desire them. The Wages Section had from its inception a stereotyped form for explaining to employers and workpeople that any request for an advance must be " an agreed application, otherwise there was no action for the department to take."[1] Under no circumstances would the Department be led, under Section 4 (2), to arbitrate upon disputes, for this was the function under the first Munitions Act of the Board of Trade and later of the Ministry of Labour. It was not uncommon for a firm to refer to the Ministry a demand from some group of its workpeople for an advance of wages, without any expression of opinion beyond the desire that the Department would " deal with the case on its merits." In such a case an application was referred back for further discussion, often with an indication of the line of action taken up by some other firm similarly placed, which might form a precedent for an agreement between the parties concerned.

This necessity for previous agreement limited the number of applications which reached the Ministry. The numbers were also diminished as owners of Controlled Establishments realised that advances of wages might still be made, without reference to the Ministry, when they concerned the cases of individual workpeople marked out for promotion, and of managers, directors or foremen whose proposed salary did not exceed £250 a year ; or when they dealt with conditions to which the Fair Wages Clause admittedly applied, for example, after an arbitration award establishing a new district rate in the trade and locality, or an agreement for an increase of wages between a trade union and the employers' federation to which the controlled firm belonged.[2] In spite of these limitations a very large number of " agreed " applications for changes in rates of wages to classes of workpeople were received by the department from its first establishment, and were dealt with at the rate of from thirty to sixty a week. The numbers of persons involved ranged from five or six to five or six thousand individuals.

(b) Refusals of Advances.

It was difficult to refuse these applications, especially if they represented the result of negotiations between a firm and a body of organised workers, since if the Department withheld its consent the possibility

---

[1] C.E. 140/4.   [2] C.E. 541/4.

of arbitration (after the lapse of fourteen days from the date of application) was still open, and the resulting award might over-ride the Department's decision.[1] Definite refusals of sanction to proposed changes in wages in controlled establishments were at all times limited in number. They may be grouped as follows:—

(a) The first class consists of cases in which a proposed change conflicted with the Department's administrative policy. Thus in April, 1916, a proposal of the Fairfield Shipbuilding Company to pay for and compute overtime by the day instead of by the week was refused after consultation with the Admiralty, who "regarded the proposal as a retrograde measure" (on account of its probable effect on the workmen's timekeeping) and "supported strongly the opinion of the Minister that he should withhold his consent from the introduction of the new rule."[2]

(b) Cases in which men working outside their trade asked for the advances applicable both to their own trade and that with which they were working; such cases were liable to occur, for example, among engineers working in collieries or building workmen employed in munition factories. In such circumstances, as in the parallel claims under the Fair Wages Clause, the Department adopted the position that only the advance appropriate to one trade could be sanctioned and that the special advance to be followed must be decided by the previous custom of the firm. A bricklayer employed on maintenance work in a shell factory might receive the wage advances due to either the engineering or building trade, but was not entitled to both.

(c) Cases in which an application, if granted, would give the workmen of some one firm wages markedly in advance of the district rate. Thus in the summer of 1916, before the second period of general wage advances began, the Department refused claims for advances of 4s. to 6s. a week to toolroom men and fitters, already paid slightly in excess of the district rate, in several districts; and it subsequently refused similar proposals to raise other time rates without reference to neighbouring employers.[3] For the same reason in February, 1917, the Siddeley-Deasy Company, Coventry, was refused permission to raise the earnings of its tinsmiths from 1s. 4d. to 1s. 6d. per hour, "on the apparent undertaking to work harder in the proportion of 1s. 6d. to 1s. 4d." The proposal was not backed by any reference to the rates paid to tinsmiths by other Coventry employers nor by the consent of the local employers' federation, while earnings among others of the firm's employees were known to be large. "These considerations," it was explained to the firm, "are peculiarly important at the present time when rates are relatively very high in Coventry and the workpeople are apt to be disturbed by exaggerated rumours of the wages paid in local establishments."[4]

Similarly, in the following May, a proposed advance of 1d. per hour to all the employees of Messrs. Barr & Stroud, Glasgow, was refused. The labour officer reported that the firm had already given advances

---

[1] M.W. 51872.
[2] C.E. 432/22.
[3] C.E. 433/4 cf. C.E. 3359/4, and C.E. 4289/4.
[4] C.E. 894/4.

above those given by other firms in the local association, and " any further advance would lead to demands on associated firms."[1]

(d) Applications for " fancy " bonuses—such as those sometimes offered in the first year of the war distinguishing between the workers on the basis of number of dependents—for unworkable forms of premium bonus, or for inequitable piece-rates. Such proposed advances were at intervals refused, or their modification was suggested.

Refusals of advances were comparatively frequent in the case of proposals to raise the salaries of directors and managers; but these were, as has been said, negligible in number as compared with proposals in respect of workpeople's advances.

While point-blank refusals were rare, it was not uncommon for the Department to suggest modifications in proposed changes, by pointing out that, for example, an increase of 1d. an hour, bringing the wages of a firm up to the standard level of the district, would be accepted, while proposals for a higher advance would be refused. The effect of such suggestions, however, was not always in one direction. They often helped an increase, more especially for the lower-paid men, and were always in the direction of removing local inequalities of payment.

During the period of the suspension of advances in the spring of 1916, the Ministry, like the Committee on Production, refused various applications for advances in individual form, and shared the criticism levelled on the Committee by trade unionists.

" Where in Birmingham and Coventry employers have displayed a willingness to increase the bonus now being given, the Ministry of Munitions have stepped in with a veto. Employers report prospective changes in wages—if they have a slight upward tendency—with the keenest regard for the Minister's instructions and with perfect confidence that if anything can be put in the way it will be done. They fail to report much more important changes in which we are vitally concerned, and on which they have equally precise instructions, and apparently they are quite immune from the attention of the Ministry. If certain other sections of this department were half so vigilant and insistent upon the observance of the terms of the Munitions Act (Schedule II) and the circulars for which they are responsible, there would be less friction."[2]

(c) REGISTERING WAGE MOVEMENTS.

The necessity for applying for sanction to increases kept the Department informed of the general and highly complicated process of wage movements in the munition trades throughout the country. Roughly these corresponded with the cycles of advances inaugurated by awards of the Committee on Production, which have already been treated at

---
[1] C.E. 177/4.
[2] Birmingham District Delegate in *A.S.E. Journal*, April, 1916.

length. The first cycle of general advances in the engineering trades had begun definitely in February, 1915, and, as has been said, the principal districts had received their 4s. or 10 per cent. advance by the time that the Wages Section of the Ministry was established. There were, however, many applications for similar advances by skilled employees of individual firms and by labourers—and especially for sanctions to agreements regarding overtime rates for labourers—in the autumn of 1915 and the early months of 1916, while in some cases subsidiary awards of 1s. a week were granted to district associations where members had previously received only 3s., and advances hitherto given as war bonuses were transformed into war wages, with corresponding changes in payments for night work and overtime. The effects of such awards spread sometimes slowly, sometimes rapidly, like the circles made by a stone thrown into the water, and were visible in the applications for " agreed advances " in other trades than engineering which reached the Department. The weekly reports of the Wages Section's work illustrate this process of " permeation."

" The advance of 1s. and $2\frac{1}{2}$ per cent. to the Manchester engineers " (awarded on 13 April, 1916, by the Committee on Production) " has spread all over Lancashire. There has been a general movement in the galvanising trade for the commutation of existing bonuses. The Steel Company of Middlesbrough has fallen into line, and the commuted bonus is now almost universal in the trade. The advance of 1d. per hour recently given to bricklayers' labourers and general labourers in steel works in the West of Scotland has produced discontent among other classes of men in steel works and among the same class of men in foundries. The engineers in steel works in the West of Scotland have put forward a demand for an advance of 2d. an hour, and a demand for an advance of 1d. per hour comes from the foundry labourers in Glasgow." (27 May, 1916.)

" The advance of 1s. given by the Committee on Production to labourers in Glasgow has spread to Aberdeen." (20 May, 1916.)

" The advance of $12\frac{1}{2}$ per cent. in the Tinplate Trades is spreading through the Steel Trades in South Wales and is beginning to affect the engineering trades. One or two applications with regard to this have been referred to the Board of Trade." (July, 1916.)

In the first half of 1916, the Committee on Production, acting on the instructions of the Government, refused, in the interests of economy, the greater proportion of the applications for large scale advances in wages which it received. While, however, there was a pause in the advances of wages awarded by the Committee on Production or sanctioned by the Ministry for whole districts in the skilled trades, there was a rise in the wages of all workpeople in individual firms in many parts of England, and changes were made in methods of payment, such as the granting of special overtime allowances in districts and occupations where this had not been customary (as in some of the

Birmingham trades[1]), and advances in wages to apprentices.[2] These last advances became common, as wages for women and girls rose under the influence of the women's wages orders, and as apprentices were either promoted to responsible work, or put on to repetition work with little prospect of learning.

Mr. J. C. Smith thus described the attitude of the Wages Section towards the "embargo" in a minute to Mr. Beveridge on 15 June, 1916, during this solitary period when the Committee on Production tried to stem the tide of rising wages.

"We were, of course, aware of the instructions given by the Cabinet to the Committee on Production and were bound to act in the spirit of these instructions ; we were bound, that is, to scrutinise very carefully any proposal for a general advance, and not to assent to any such proposal without consulting the Chief Industrial Commissioner's Department. But as a matter of fact, we received comparatively few proposals for general advances, and I can recall no case of an agreement between an employers' federation and a union or unions covering a wide area that has been refused, though I remember two that have been somewhat modified in the course of discussion with this Department. The great majority of the proposals that come before us are from individual establishments dealing with particular classes of workers. Even in these cases, refusals have been rare when the proposals were made in the proper form. Our consistent endeavour is to preserve the wages balance in each district, to level up inequalities where they exist, but to prevent fresh inequalities from emerging by unjustifiable innovations on the standard district rates."

A second cycle of advances awarded by the Committee on Production began in July, 1916. They consisted of a 3s. advance to time-workers, primarily in the engineering trades, awarded on the application both of individual firms and their workmen and of employers' federations and groups of trade unions. These awards again spread in varying forms to firms and industries not covered by them, and the Department was much occupied in sanctioning them and interpreting their application to different trades and to different classes of workers, —especially at this time to unskilled workers.

The process of permeation again appeared clearly. "Proposals for a war bonus of 3s. a week" (reported the Wages Section in November, 1916) "are beginning to come in from the rubber trade in Lancashire. Proposals for advances in this district are generally measured by the standard of recent awards of the Committee on Production. Advances yielding an increase of more than 7s. weekly upon pre-war rates

---

[1] Cf. M.W. 95545 "Agreement of 3 March, 1916, on overtime, night-shift, and piece-rates, sanctioned as between the Metal Section of the Midland Employers' Federation," the Amalgamated Society of Metal Ware and Tube Drawers, the National Union of Gas Workers, and the Workers' Union.

[2] Cf. Award of Committee on Production for Manchester engineering apprentices.

are either refused or referred for arbitration. Piece-workers are generally excluded and in some cases a limit has been imposed to exclude the better paid classes of labour from the advance."

With the establishment in 1917 of the principle of national wage advances in the engineering and allied trades, in so far as they were employed by members of the Engineering Employers' Federation, the need for sanctions to piecemeal advances was to some extent diminished. The employees of federated firms received general advances, for piece- and time-work equally, of 5s. in April, 3s. in August, 5s. in December, 1917. Non-federated firms in these trades were warned by the Department before each of the two advances were due that they were expected to comply with these awards, and in many cases they fell voluntarily into line with them. Almost all the sanctions, except of individual proposals for the introduction of new forms of collective, time-keeping, or premium bonus (when the Department would offer advice from the experience of other munition firms), were after the first three months of 1917 on the general lines of these awards. The extension of the national awards of the Committee on Production by statutory order after the Amendment Act of August, 1917, to non-federated firms under contract with the Ministry of Munitions, further lightened (until the award of the $12\frac{1}{2}$ per cent. bonus in November, 1917) the administration of the "sanctioning" clause of the original Act.

(d) PROTECTION OF PIECE-RATES UNDER SECTION 4 (2).

It was not at first clearly realised that the "changes" which required sanction by the Ministry included proposed reductions as well as advances in wages. As early in the history of the Ministry as August, 1915, trouble was reported by labour officers in the London area and elsewhere, through the action of some controlled establishments in cutting down piece-rates. Could not some statement, it was suggested, be made through the press, explaining that any such change made without the Minister's consent was an offence under the Act, involving a fine of £50.

This difficulty was duly met by Mr. Lloyd George's reiterated statement at the Trade Union Congress in the next month that no cutting of piece-rates would be permitted, and by the issue in the Press of an official pronouncement to the same effect.[1]

"The Minister of Munitions has been informed that workmen employed in controlled establishments have been deterred in some cases from complying with the requirements of the Munitions of War Act that all rules, customs, or practices tending to restrict production should be suspended in such establishments by fear that any considerable increase in output might lead to a reduction of the piece-rates paid to them.

"In view of this the Minister desires to call attention to the fact that under the above-named Act no change in the rates

---

[1] This appeared in the daily papers of 13 September, 1915.

Сн. IV]   ADMINISTRATION OF DEPARTMENT   105

of wages, salary, or other emoluments to any class of persons employed in a controlled establishment can be made without notice to the Minister, who may thereupon withhold his consent to the change proposed, subject to the power of either party to demand arbitration.

"The Minister is prepared to exercise his powers, if necessary, in order to prevent the reduction of piece-rates as a consequence of the increase of output due to suspension of restrictions."

This statement was also supplied in poster form to controlled establishments, in order that there might be no further misconceptions among their employees.[1]

The unintended and disconcerting results of this pledge are dealt with elsewhere.[2] It was a turning-point in the history of wages, since it put a stop to the process of adjustment by which a stable relation is normally maintained between time and piece-rates and between the earnings of different classes of workers.

Comparatively few applications for sanction to proposals for reduction in piece-rates reached the Department, though a certain number were received and sanctioned in cases when the piece-rates for a new process had been admittedly fixed unreasonably high, or when an improvement in the means or method of manufacture had completely altered the conditions of work. The provision that all applications for sanction to such changes must be based on agreement between employers and employed, naturally limited the number of applications received.

Some examples of cases coming before the Department will illustrate the difficulty of the piece-rate problem and the limited powers of the Ministry in dealing with it.

In December, 1915, the firm of Wolseley Motors, Birmingham, asked leave to revise the piece prices on which they had worked for the last five months.[3] "When the manufacture of shells was first introduced," explained the firm, "we were compelled to utilise to a very great extent the services of persons who were unskilled, whilst to the toolsetters and foremen the work was a departure from that which they had previously dealt with, and also the material was difficult to machine." Since that time there had been an improvement in (a) the capacity of the workers, (b) the supply of machine tools and

---

[1] Some firms had anticipated the action of the Ministry. Thus, Messrs. T. Firth & Sons, of Sheffield, had on 1 August put up a poster (on the principles of which, they declared, they had acted since the beginning of the war), assuring their workmen that "no attempt would be made to restrict the amount of any man's earnings by cutting, when once fixed, piece-work prices for existing conditions of manufacture." (C.E. 439/2.)

It was reported that some firms were unwilling to put up the Ministry's posters, because they said nothing about the employers' corresponding safeguard, in the need for the Ministry's sanction to proposed advances, as well as decreases, in wages. These firms were, however, informed that the use of the posters was not compulsory. (M.W. 496/4.)

[2] Chap. V and VI.   [3] C.E. 1074/4.

(3130)   H

other tools, (c) the quality of steel and of lubricants procurable, and the percentage of bonus earned over the day rate had increased from 52 per cent. in July to 138 per cent. in November. This, urged the firm, surely represented a change in methods of manufacture, justifying a change of price, even if the machines on which the work was done remained the same. Semi-skilled men on shell-making were earning £4 10s. a week, and skilled toolroom men were endeavouring to enter the shell factory in order to earn higher wages there. The men were reported a few weeks later to have agreed to a reduction of 20 per cent. in piece prices, and this was accordingly sanctioned by the Department on 18 January. Similar " agreed reductions " in piece payments for other processes in shell production at these works were sanctioned during the next two months.[1]

If the process of manufacture was definitely changed, then fresh piece prices might be introduced by the firm, and these, as was suggested in the case of Wolseley Motors, did not require the sanction of the Ministry, though it was suggested at the outset by the Department that such changing of rates or fixing of new rates should be reported to the Department as " changes in working conditions," to be recorded under Schedule II of the Munitions Act.[2] Many firms took advantage of this provision to break free from high piece-rates rashly established.[3] Thus Messrs. Beardmore and Messrs. Mavor & Coulson of Glasgow, insisted, in correspondence with the Ministry, and in a case brought by the National Federation of Women Workers before the special arbitration tribunal early in 1916, that the women whom they employed on shell turning (at average piece-work earnings of 30s.) were not exactly replacing men. If they were paid at the men's piece-rates they would, owing to their special proficiency and absence of restriction of output, earn as much as £11 per week. But processes had been changed since the men left this work, and the firm was therefore not disregarding the principles of dilution by paying lower piece-rates.

A striking example from the experience of the Rudge-Whitworth Company, Sparkhill, Birmingham, illustrates the necessity, from the firm's point of view, of seizing the precise moment of the change of process in order to alter piece-rates, unless—and this was not very probable—there was a prospect that the workmen would voluntarily accept a reduction, after testing the results of the new process.

In March, 1917, the firm consulted the Department about the possibility of reducing the wages paid to a group of their labourers (four of whom were of military age and two just above it). The piece-rates for their work had been fixed when output was much less, and the men were now earning from £5 5s. to £9 per week. Would a reduction in their piece-rates be sanctioned?

---

[1] The negotiations with this firm suggested the departmental inquiry into the very varying scales of piece-rates for shell work in different parts of the country, which was carried out at the beginning of the year (1916).
[2] M.W. 53104.
[3] M.W. 53881.

An investigation officer of the Ministry reported on the situation as follows :—

"On 8 December, 1915, piece-work prices were arranged for trolleying ·303 cartridge caps at 2s. 4d. per ton, plus 4d. per ton bonus. The process of handling cartridge caps was as follows : they were filled in boxes (weight when filled, 1 cwt. 3 qrs.), then placed on four-wheel trolleys and trolleyed to the cleaning shop or muffles. This process was carried out up to August, 1916. About 16 August, 1916, alterations were made in production, but there was practically no difference in the distance to be trolleyed. Owing to the increase in output barrels were adopted instead of boxes, and two-wheel trolleys instead of four. The weight of the barrels when filled is 14 cwt. I examined the wage books from the week ending 7 January to 3 March (nine weeks). The average wage of the trolleyers was £2 13s. 2d. a week for 54 hours. From 5 January to 3 March, 1917 (nine weeks), the average wage was £6 1s. 2d., with 10s. a week extra for those on night work. There is no difference whatever in the distance to be trolleyed. The method was changed in August, 1916, by adopting barrels in place of boxes and two-wheel trolleys. I cannot understand why rates were not reduced. The men arrange amongst themselves to have a holiday in turns to suit their convenience, and even then they can earn over £6 a week. This is one of many cases of high wages for unskilled work in the district, which is causing considerable unrest among skilled workers."

On this report the Department could only reply to the firm that it was impossible now to regard the existing rate as other than an established rate. At the same time it was suggested that the firm should confer with the men on whom their employers' failure to question the rate in the previous August had conferred the present rate. Two months later the firm reported that it had conferred with the six labourers and with the Workers' Union to which they belonged, and that the men had accepted a reduction of their rates which would allow them to earn not less than 67s. 6d. a week. On 1 June, 1917, this arrangement was duly sanctioned by the Department as an "agreed reduction."

An isolated instance of the consequence of applying to articles produced in large quantities a piece-work price that had been defined for a small production is the following :—The works of Messrs. Webley & Scott, Ltd., Birmingham, produced before the war not more than 1,000 Very pistols per year. For rolling the firm's name and trade mark on the body, and the serial number on the body and barrel, the firm before the war paid a man, who did the work in his spare time, ·72d. for each pistol. In May, 1918, when 1,800 pistols were being turned out per week, this special work was done by a boy who, by whole-time work, earned steadily over £6 per week, including war bonus, for a week of 53–54 hours. The work was said to involve no skill or strength.[1]

---

[1] Weekly Intelligence Report, 11 May, 1918.

A more striking example of similar results from the same cause reached the Department in December, 1917, in the form of a strong protest by a large aircraft firm against any extension to piece-workers of the 12½ per cent. weekly bonus on earnings recently given to time-workers. The firm's description of the origin of the high earnings of piece-workers in their establishment would apply to many establishments throughout the country.[1]

They enclosed extracts from their last week's wages sheets, showing that some 60 of the fitters, turners and other skilled men in their aeroplane works were already earning over £10 a week. One fitter had earned £22 5s. 8d. during the week; a turner had been paid £20 15s. 3d.; a horizontal miller £18 2s.; and a grinder £17 6s. 8d.

"In ordinary times," explained the firm, "it was our practice to review our (piece) prices every six months, but since the war began we have been precluded from doing this by the fact that we are not at liberty to reduce prices unless by mutual arrangement with the workers, which, up till the present time, we have never been able to obtain. The reason that our workers have the high wages that are now paid them is that in the early days of the war the prices were fixed on the basis of a small weekly production, and nearly all the men had four or five different jobs in the course of a week's work. Now that we have a large output, all the men are specialising on one particular operation, and we have not been able to alter the prices. It practically amounts to our now paying jobbing prices for factory work, which you will no doubt realise is absurd.

"The payment of abnormally high wages has a very serious effect on production. Some men who can make a large wage in a very short time do not work steadily the whole week, simply because they have sufficient money, not only to live upon, but to enjoy luxuries without unduly exerting themselves. If the prices were such that they had to work reasonably hard to earn—say £6 or £7 a week, we are quite sure our output in this factory would be very greatly increased. We cannot repeat too often, or emphasise too strongly, the serious effect on production of abnormally high wages."

On the other hand, it was only by some such guarantee of piece-rates that workpeople could be reconciled to an extension of systems of payment by results. Errors like those just quoted could not have occurred if the extension of payment by results had not been pressed without regard to the difficulties of measuring and pricing new work. When the employers, therefore, in 1917, pressed for a further extension of payment by results, there could be no question of withdrawing the guarantee of prices. On the contrary, the Ministry found it expedient to give specific statutory form to the principle of the guarantee in Section 8 of the Amendment Act of 1917.[2]

---

[1] C.E. 140/4.   [2] Chap. II, Sect. 3.

The Minister's pledge and the powers he possessed of carrying it out were among the best known provisions of the Ministry's policy. The trade unions were constantly on the look out for breaches of it, to which they called the attention of the Ministry if a more direct remedy was not forthcoming.[1] The Ministry's powers were, however, negative; they enabled it to do nothing to remedy the inconveniences which resulted from maintaining piece-rates and premium bonus base times that had been fixed in a hurry. It took steps administratively to prevent such premature settlement in the National Shell and Projectile Factories, for which it was directly responsible, and it urged at times on controlled establishments the desirability of fixing rates and base times provisionally on new work. Beyond this it did not attempt any constructive policy for handling the problem until the end of the war.

(e) The Effect on Wage Advances of the Policy of "Sanction."

The provisions of Section 4 (2) of the Munitions of War Act safeguarded the maintenance of standard rates of (time) wages in controlled establishments, and checked to some extent any further dislocation of the rates of wages, already much disturbed in different firms by the middle of the year 1915.

Apart from the very limited extent to which the right of veto was used, the insistence by the Department on agreement between the parties concerned before permission was asked under the terms of Section 4 (2) to change existing rates of pay, prevented wholly irresponsible applications for advances. The administration of this Section of the Act therefore served as a steadying influence, in the interests of the taxpayer, on the rise of wages. It was, indeed, possible for firms to engage fresh labour at rates much above the district level without recourse to the Ministry, and the prevention of this was considered during the discussions of the Munitions of War Amendment Bill of 1918.[2] Further, employers could evade the need for official sanction by giving occasional unauthorised bonuses for good timekeeping, etc., and by special payments such as those known to shipyard workers under the names of " time and a bit," " hallelujah rates," " work on the corner," etc. Such evasions, however, were probably neither serious nor numerous, so long as the power of workpeople to exploit the shortage of labour was limited by the leaving certificate; and the Department only felt called upon to seek penalties before a munitions tribunal for unauthorised changes in wages in 53 cases (of

---

[1] Despite the general acceptance of the inviolability of piece-rates and premium bonus time allowances, there were frequent complaints that these were altered unjustifiably. Thus, an important strike of engineers at Vickers, Barrow, in March, 1917, originated in the men's resentment against the alleged cutting of time allowances under the premium bonus system. Normally such disputes involved disagreement as to whether the rates in question were or were not " fixed " before the change was made—the firm contending that they were experimental only, while the men maintained that they had become established by agreement or lapse of time.

[2] L.R. 5581/20.

which 50 were dismissed), involving fines of £28 in all.[1] After the repeal of the leaving certificate provisions, such evasions of the standard rate became more frequent and more serious in their effects. The Department was hampered in its efforts to check them, partly by the difficulty of discovering them until it was too late to take action, and partly by the wholly inadequate penalties which the courts inflicted when prosecutions were instituted. It had, therefore, sometimes to connive at, and even to suggest, time-keeping bonuses or other additions to the standard rate as the only way of enabling firms to retain essential men.[2]

The difficulties of the supply departments concerned with building labour, which only in exceptional cases came under the operation of Section 4 (2), and the chaos in the standard rates for building workmen produced by the absence of any powers of regulation, showed forcibly the advantages of central control, even on a limited scale, of standard rates of wages, under the special labour conditions produced by war.[3] The action of the Department in standardising rates of payment and in diminishing local and trade differences was of definite value, and synchronised with similar influences at work within associations of employers and workmen. Further, the Department gradually assumed advisory functions and was able to offer assistance in the construction and remodelling of a growing and varying series of systems of payment by results. But, in other respects, its lack of control of piece-rates, together with the fact that the main lines of its policy inevitably conformed to those laid down by the arbitration courts which were outside its sphere, prevented the Department from exercising any general control over the upward movement of wages. The influence which the Ministry was able to exert under Section 4 (2) of the Munitions of War Act over the exceedingly complex and difficult problems of munition workers' wages consisted in restraint rather than construction.

IV. Administration of Circular L.3 and the Dilution Policy for Men.

The administration of the Ministry's dilution policy for men has been described in detail elsewhere and its relation to wages problems will only be considered briefly here. It was embodied in Circular L.3, issued as a recommendation to controlled establishments in October

---

[1] To 30 April, 1918. One such case, that of Morris v. Rudge-Whitworth Ltd., was referred to the Munitions Tribunal Appeals Court on 31 July, 1917. Judge Atkin in this case maintained the finding of the munitions tribunal, which had imposed a £20 fine on the firm for changing its workers' piece-rates without sanction, and within fourteen days of application to the Ministry for such sanction. The Judge held that the absence of any expression of consent by the Minister for a period of fourteen days was equivalent to the definite " withholding of consent " provided for under Section 4 (2) of the Munitions of War Act of 1915. Within that period any unauthorised change of wages was a definite offence against the Act. At the end of fourteen days, such a change would still be an offence, unless the consent of an arbitration tribunal had been obtained.

[2] Interview with Management Committee of Engineering Employers' Federation, 4 October, 1918. (HIST. REC./R/342/14.)

[3] See below. Chap. VII, Sect. 3.

1915, and re-issued in February, 1916, as a statutory Order under Section 7 of the recent Munitions of War (Amendment) Act. It was sent to all controlled establishments, except those in the chemical, explosives, oil and seed crushing trades and a few firms in low-rated areas to which its terms were not applicable.

The history of Circular L.3 was uneventful compared with that of the twin Circular L.2, which prescribed the conditions under which women should take men's work in munitions. Both were set up as a fence, or rather a system of barbed wire entanglements, for the safeguarding of the skilled men's rates in exchange for the abandonment of practices and customs tending to restrict output and to limit the entry of untrained workers to the trade.

The tortuous history of L.2 may be traced in the account of women's wages.[1] Circular L.3, like L.2, was drawn up by the Central Munitions Labour Supply Committee in the weeks immediately succeeding the Trade Union Congress of September, 1915, and the conferences held by the Ministry of Munitions with the engineering trade unions. It contained three parts.

(i) The first re-enunciated the general principle of the Shells and Fuses and Treasury Agreements of February and March, 1915, and of Schedule II of the original Munitions of War Act, by stating that skilled men's work might be done by semi-skilled or unskilled workmen during the war, but that the latter should receive the time, piece or premium bonus rates customarily received by the former; that piece rates should not be altered after they had been established unless the means or method of manufacture were changed; and that the same overtime and other extra allowances should be paid to such workers as to skilled men.

(ii) It then prescribed the time-rate at which such work should be done in the processes of manufacture, the organisation of which was most prominent at the time. In the production of shell, fuses and cartridge cases (where the work was not previously "customary") machine men should receive the standard turner's rate less 10s., but their wage should in no case be less than 28s. per week including existing war bonuses, for a normal working week, except that a wholly inexperienced workman might start at 26s. per week. This lower probationary rate, however, was not to be continued for more than two months.

(iii) Thirdly, it defined the position of the toolsetter, again within this limited area of employment. Those engaged on fuse-making machines should receive 10s., those on shell-making machines, 5s., above the current district time-rates for turners.

---

[1] Vol. V, Part II, Chap. II and III.

The first part of these directions needs no further comment. It was at intervals quoted in complaints from unions of unskilled workmen, or unions with no very rigorous admission test, that their members were employed on skilled men's work, but were not receiving skilled men's pay.

Thus the Electrical Trades' Union from April to August, 1916, carried on negotiations with an important firm, concerning an ex-photographer and cinematograph operator employed on general electrical wiring at 30s. instead of 46s. the local district rate "in contravention of L.3." The firm said that the man was doing apprentice's or improver's work. Often before the war, they had, like other firms, taken on such men and given them a chance to improve their position. They had no intention of employing cheap labour. They fully intended, they explained to a representative of the Ministry sent to interview them, to pay the man full rates as soon as he had learnt his job,—and in August they reported that they were so doing.[1]

The case provided for in the second part of the directions was an instance of the process of partial substitution taking place all over the country in engineering works before and during the war. It illustrates the craftsman's distrust of the handyman as a possible source of cheap labour, and also the trade unionist's recurrent suspicion of any but the briefest probationary period. This attitude reappeared throughout the struggle over the introduction of women to skilled men's work (in which some period of probation was clearly necessary before the skilled man's rate could be fairly earned), and in the negotiations which began in 1917 for training disabled soldiers for certain occupations.

The circular expressly provided against the too great extension of probation. The actual minimum wage originally laid down, was based on the standard rates for fitters and turners in October, 1915.[2] No industrially important districts in the country except Mid-Lancashire, had less than a 38s. time-rate for their trades (though a lower rate was common in the low-paid districts of the South-West Midlands, East Anglia, Oxfordshire, etc.). Even in Mid-Lancashire, however, the rate in machine shops was 39s., (as against 36s. and 37s. in textile machinery shops). A few districts paid over 43s., while the rate in London was 47s. 6d., in Sheffield 46s., in Coventry 43s. But with these exceptions the highly rated districts were not of great importance for the purpose of regulation, and Sheffield was in any case excluded from the operation of the proposed circular, as shell had been made there before the war.

Therefore the 28s. rate was fixed on as a fair minimum which bore a reasonable relation to the unskilled labourer's rate, and, on the assumption that piece-rates would be fixed in relation to this, allowed the machinist to equal, but not exceed, the earnings of the skilled man.[3]

---

[1] C.E. 275/4.   [2] M.W. 92329.

[3] The piecework earnings of the male machine operator engaged on shell production were, in fact, normally greatly in excess of these rates.

Trade union officials were constantly on the watch against any possible undercutting of the standard rates by unskilled men who took skilled men's work, and against the acceptance of time-rates below the minimum laid down for machine workers.[1] But in fact the men brought into the engineering trade in the process of dilution of labour most commonly took semi-skilled work, and there was much less friction about their replacement of skilled men, even in "part or portion" of the latter's work, than was the case with the women "dilutees."

In one minor point of administration the interpretation of the principle of equal payment for equal work whether performed by the "skilled" or "unskilled" worker, differed as regards men and women under dilution.[2] In the case of women, the difficult question of deciding in marginal cases whether they were or were not employed upon work of a class customarily done by skilled men was in general determined by the custom of the country as a whole prior to the war. Where, however, it was claimed that an unskilled or semi-skilled man was employed on work which according to the custom of the establishment was previously done by a fully skilled man, the status of the substitute was, under paragraph 4 of the second schedule of the Munitions of War Act, regulated by the pre-war custom in the individual establishment concerned.

Thus in a case brought forward and contested by the Amalgamated Society of Engineers from March to October, 1917, and only terminated at the end of that month by one of the rare awards of the special arbitration tribunal for men's wages, it was urged that two unskilled workmen (an "ex-horizontal driller and an ex-labourer pensioner"), were employed at the Whitehead Torpedo Works on skilled work at less than the skilled man's rates. On investigation, it was found that the work on which the men were engaged, the internal circular shaping of torpedo air vessels, was work of a type on which the firm had normally employed skilled men before the war. "Shaping" was admittedly semi-skilled work, although it sometimes involved skilled handling ; but the firm had before the war employed shapers paid at turner's rates on all types of shaping work without distinction, and it was therefore directed to pay these men at the full turner's rates. Such payment conflicted with the practice of the great majority of the engineering firms of the country, but it maintained the principle on which the dilution of labour was based.

Problems such as the above were not often propounded to the Department, but the extra payments due to the toolsetters (engaged

---

[1] Thus in February, 1917, the North West Coast General Munitions Tribunal considered a complaint against a controlled establishment for employing a semi-skilled turner at 29s. instead of 35s. a week. He had signed on when engaged to work for two months at the lower rate, but it was held that as he had had previous experience and was therefore above the probationary stage, he was entitled to the 35s. a week. In this case the firm undertook to raise him to the higher rate, with back pay from the time of his engagement, and the summons was withdrawn.
[2] C.E. 1058/4.

on a limited class of munition work), caused some friction with firms, not so much on principle—since setters-up commonly received rates above those of the fitter and turner—as in practice.

Correspondence prolonged for fourteen months with Messrs. Firth, of Sheffield, and some half-dozen of their workmen illustrates the difficulty due to the limited application of the L.3. circular.

On 16 November, 1915, six toolsetters employed in this firm's new shell works, wrote to the Ministry, applying for the payment to them of the extra 5s. a week recommended in the new circular. The firm in January, 1916, pointed out they had made shell before the war, that they had customarily employed semi-skilled men in its production, and that therefore Circular L.3. did not presumably apply to them. They would gladly give these six men a rise in wages, if it were not that such a rise would only increase the existing discontent among their toolroom men as a whole. In March, 1916, the Ministry informed the men that they had no legal claim to the toolsetters' 5s., since L.3 did not apply to a firm in which shell had been made before the war. During the summer, however, the question was again raised, this time by the Sheffield District Committee of the Amalgamated Society of Engineers, which urged that as Messrs. Firth's shell works was a new building put up since the war, it formed a separate establishment to which L.3 must apply. The question was referred during the autumn to the special arbitration tribunal, which found (3 January, 1917), that the men's claims were not established. The conclusion of these negotiations is a testimony to the value of impartial investigation and arbitration. The men's correspondent wrote to inform the Department that the special arbitration tribunal had found against their claims, but that the men were quite satisfied with the results, since their fellow workmen could no longer upbraid them with working below the district rate. Further (and this probably affected their attitude towards the enforcement of the statutory Order), their manager had added 2s. a week to the 2s. above district rates which they already received, so that the loss of their claim only deprived them of 1s. a week.

Toolsetters taking charge of machines, and responsible for their good working condition, would probably in any case have received an addition to the ordinary fitters' or turners' payment. Sometimes, however, the Ministry was required, under the terms of its own order, to insist on special toolsetters' rates when these would not under normal conditions have been held to be justified. In well-equipped shell factories, the process of toolsetting was sometimes reduced to an operation described as being "as simple as that of putting a fresh needle into a gramophone," and involved no responsibility for the condition of the machines such as a toolsetter would normally assume. In spite of this, 5s. above the skilled man's rates had to be paid for such work.

Thus a group of workmen at the Keighley National Shell Factory, who from February to July, 1916, persistently claimed the established toolsetters' rates, were said[1] by the labour officer to be engaged merely

---

[1] C.E. 717/4.

in fixing cutters to the toolholders for single boring operations. The machines were of one type, specially built for the production of these shells, and fitted with special toolholders. The men concerned simply fixed the tools in place, and the girls often did it themselves. The management stood out staunchly against this claim, despite the agitation of the Amalgamated Society of Engineers, but the 5s. extra had eventually to be paid to these men.

Except for these special provisions for toolsetters—not wholly satisfactory, except in so far as they modified the " skilled man's grievance " among the producers of shell, fuses and cartridge cases— the administration of Circular L.3 and its succeeding statutory orders was virtually a " fair wages " question. The principle, that the " custom of the establishment " should decide what was or was not skilled work, was on the whole consistent with the principle previously quoted, that it was the job performed in an establishment, and not the original trade of the man performing it, that must settle the standard rate to which he was entitled. The enforcement of the Ministry's dilution policy turned ultimately, like its wages policy as a whole, on the maintenance of standard district rates, however great might be the changes of working conditions within the firm or industry concerned.

The scope of the Order embodying L.3 was also restricted by the increasing proportion of women and girls employed on the machining of shells and fuses. For the last two years of the war the greater part of this work was done by them.

V. The Compulsory Extension of Awards.

(a) THE DEMAND FOR EXTENSION OF AWARDS.

The process of adjusting local differences in wages by the methods described was laborious and comparatively slow. An advance in wages in controlled establishments was secured either by negotiations within a firm between the employer and workpeople—negotiations, the results of which normally received the sanction of the Department— or by direct award of the Committee on Production. If the decision of the latter concerned an individual firm, the parties concerned had no option but to comply, under heavy penalties. If again an arbitration award was made between a local association of employers and the trade unions representing their workers, its terms were binding on the whole association, while even a voluntary agreement was practically, if not legally, binding on its signatories and those whom they represented. This method of settlement, however, omitted all the non-federated munition firms, some of whom were geographically isolated, while others deliberately refrained from joining employers' associations. Often, indeed, they observed the same standard of wages as that of the federated firms and in some cases they paid regularly in advance of these ; but no compulsion could be brought to bear on them except through the Fair Wages Clause. And the Fair Wages Clause, as has been explained, only operated in such cases if the agreement signed by the local employers' association in the industry concerned covered the majority of local employers and thus established a new district rate. This was by no means always the case.

If then wages were to rise symmetrically, which was very desirable in the interests of industrial peace and of the maintenance of standard rates, this result was often only obtained after prolonged " heckling " of these outstanding firms by trade union officials.

Recalcitrant or dilatory employers could plead ignorance of Committee on Production awards (since they did not regularly read the *Labour Gazette* in which they were published) ; or the disturbance of their contracts by an unexpected change of wages ; or they would urge that some special privilege enjoyed by their employees more than compensated for a refusal to pay an advance accepted by other firms. Eventually, however, under the special relation of labour and capital produced by war, the advance claimed as a result of an important arbitration award had normally to be conceded by other firms in the trade or locality.

As early as August, 1915, and during the first eighteen months of the Ministry's operations, it was periodically urged by trade unions that awards of the Committee on Production should be binding on the whole of the trades concerned. With the movement for national advances in wages which took effect in February, 1917, it was possible to apply the principle of extension effectively, and then it appeared as a natural corollary to these general awards.

The opportunity was therefore taken of the Amendment Bill of 1917 to take powers to extend awards by Order.[1]

(b) EXTENSION BY ADMINISTRATIVE PRESSURE.

Meanwhile the Department had taken steps to ensure, among controlled establishments, the observance of the forthcoming clause in the Act.[2] Even before the introduction of the Amendment Bill, copies of the first national award of 1 March in the engineering and foundry trades were sent out, on 28 March, to all non-federated controlled establishments with the intimation that the Minister proposed, in a Bill shortly to be introduced into Parliament, to take power to extend its operation to non-federated firms in the engineering and foundry trades. Pending the issue of a Statutory Order to that effect, this intimation was sent in order that the necessary arrangements might be made to give effect to the award as from the first full pay day in April.

A similar letter was despatched on 23 July, containing a copy of the second national award of the Committee on Production for the engineering and foundry trades (3s. advance in weekly wages from 1 August[3]).

The great majority of non-federated employers in controlled establishments complied readily with these and similar general awards.

---

[1] See above, Chap. II, Sect. 5 (a).
[2] M.W. 172423/3 ; L.R. 5171/3 ; Circulars M.M. 122 and 122a.
[3] Circular M.M. 122b.

If they were recalcitrant, the Ministry could (if their works were in a district where the majority of firms in the same trade were federated) call upon them under the Fair Wages Clause to pay the advances to their workpeople.[1] To more isolated firms, the Department had to admit that they were not legally bound by such awards, but intimated that the expected compulsory powers for their extension would probably be applied retrospectively.

Parallel with this action by the Ministry was that of the Chief Industrial Commissioner's Department, which Sir David Harrel, Chairman of the Committee on Production, explained on 19 June to the great deputation of labour representatives who were then claiming a second general advance in the engineering trades; representatives of the ironfounders and of certain of the unskilled trade unions had complained of the difficulty of inducing firms to observe the recent awards except under compulsion.

"What we have done since the issue of the last national award is this, that where non-federated firms did not pay the award and the men concerned reported the circumstances to the Ministry of Labour, the latter declared that to be a ' difference ' and sent it along to us to be heard as a difference, and we did hear it, and we made awards. That is different from applying our general award to them, but it had to be done that way. On the other hand, I am bound to say that from the official information of which we are possessed, I think that the non-federated firms all over the country have responded very fully to the situation and have paid the award."

During the six months that elapsed between the issue of the first general award by the Committee on Production and the first extending order by the Ministry of Munitions, vigilant trade union officials were constantly on the watch to secure the general observance of all " national " awards. The tone of some of their comments in their reports to their members illustrates the desirability of action by some independent authority, to secure such observance.

"Almost all the various firms in the Division who refused in the first place to come within the terms of the March award are now brought into line, with the exception of a few whose cases are pending before the Ministry of Labour. Messrs. Lanston Monotype Corporation of Redhill had to be taken before the Committee on Production with the result we have secured the award. We are hoping now that the amending Act has passed that there will not be the same difficulty attendant upon securing future wages adjustments and although hopeful cannot help being somewhat sceptical of results but trust all recalcitrant firms will be early reported in order that they may be dealt with at the earliest opportunity."—(Delegate's report, Middlesex Division, *A.S.E. Journal*, September, 1917.)

---

[1] L.R. 2475.

"The national advance has been observed more readily on this occasion than on the last. Trouble has been experienced in one soulless concern which has two works. They complied readily when they received the men's ultimatum and even went to the trouble of posting notices throughout both works setting forth their good intentions."—(Delegate's report, Liverpool Division, *A.S.E. Journal*, September, 1917.)

"The majority of the Cork employers have not yet conceded the 3s. increase and notices have been handed in to cease work. We have only had satisfactory replies from two of the Limerick employers on the same subject and pressure is being brought to bear on the remainder. All the Newry employers have conceded the 3s. increase but only a few of the Portadown employers have come into line. I am at present dealing with the defaulters in these areas.—(Delegate's report, Belfast Division, *A.S.E. Journal*, September, 1917).

"If absolute control existed by the Government it would not be necessary for me to appeal to the Ministry of Munitions to apply the Wages Award of the Committee on Production *six* months after that award has been issued, yet I am engaged in that unenviable task to-day, and in a district where the salary of moulders was 5½d. per hour and that of labourers 3½d. per hour before the war ; and this is a controlled establishment. Did I hear someone assert that industrial unrest existed ? Perish the thought ; with a princely income like that he would be an ungrateful curmudgeon who would do other than *meekly wait and murmur not* ; and so I have undertaken the *duty* of revolutionary on behalf of these men."—(*Ironfounders Monthly Journal*, October, 1917).

(c) EXTENSION UNDER THE ACT OF 1917.

In September, 1917, the Ministry, equipped with powers under the Amendment Act just passed, could at last take action for the generalisation of wage advances, and under Section 5 of the Act it issued, between 27 September and 30 December, 1917, sixteen orders extending compulsorily the application of arbitration awards.

Two orders applied to the engineering and foundry trades.[1] They were sent in September and November to some 1,200 firms, almost all controlled establishments, calling on them to put the "national" awards (for the 5s. and 3s. advance of the previous April and August) into operation, if they had not already done so. Thus, including the members of the Engineering Employers' Federation, some 2,600 engineering firms came uniformly under the same group of awards.

The remaining orders covered a surprisingly small number of firms, some 80 in all. No. 7 was applied to 36 establishments in the Birmingham brassworking trade, No. 15 to 15 firms engaged in

---

[1] Circulars L. 103 and L. 104.

light casting; the remainder scheduled only 2 or 3 firms apiece. No. 4 was not issued at all, as all the establishments concerned complied voluntarily. No. 9 was applied on 30 September to a single dilatory brassworking firm which had not yet paid the 5s. advance of 1 March; No. 12 applied to one uncontrolled firm Sir W. Robinson's award of 14 May to the London building trade; No. 13 to a solitary shipbuilding firm the awards of 1 March and 14 July simultaneously.

The scantiness of the numbers of firms to which compulsion was actually applied under the Act of 1917 is explained partly by the fact that the principle of the general extension of arbitration awards was becoming known in the late summer of 1917. Further, the Department adopted the procedure of sending out to controlled establishments copies of " general " awards by the Committee on Production, asking firms to comply with these and to report when they had done so; and compulsory orders were only sent out to such firms as had not definitely stated that they had already complied.

Few formal complaints were received from those to whom the orders were sent. Such complaints as were received dealt, most comprehensibly, with the effect of the increased wages bill on costs of production. Thus a West Country shipping firm to which Order 16 was ultimately applied, but which for a year carried on an acrimonious correspondence with the Ministry and the Chief Industrial Commissioner, with regard to the application of awards, based its objection almost entirely on the effects upon its contracts[1]. On 2 April, 1917, it replied bluntly to the Ministry's circular with regard to the observance of the recent national award; " Please note it is not our intention to pay this," and explained that it held contracts to the value of £30,000 which would take eight months to complete " and this advance will mean £50 per week (£1,600) to us," while the prices quoted to the Government were based on existing prices. Reassured by the Department from which it held its contracts, that the increased expense of these would be defrayed, it applied the 5s. award to its workpeople at the end of April.

Later in the year, however, it again delayed with regard to the 5s. general advance of November, 1917, and after protracted correspondence with the Ministry, explained its position thus—" Kindly note that until we get the money refunded which we have paid out to our employees since April last, now amounting to over £4,000, we shall refuse to make this award, the amount of which up to date will be £6,000 to £7,000. We are not in a financial position to pay unless we get the outstanding money refunded. We have made repeated appeals to the Departments for the amounts on the different jobs we have in hand, but cannot get any settlement. They proposed a short time ago to give us an advance, but we hear now this is not forthcoming."

The gradual simplification of the process—to which this complaint refers—by which refunds for advances in wages were obtainable under

---

[1] C.E. 767/4.

certain conditions from the Departments responsible for the issue of contracts, is described elsewhere.[1]

When in July, 1917, intimations (M.M. 1226) were sent out to the engineering and foundry trade calling on non-federated firms to adopt the recent 3s. award, their attention was specially drawn to their position with reference to contracts. "If a contractor is of opinion that a claim arises for revision of prices payable in respect of direct contracts with Government Departments on the ground of increased labour costs due to the advance, such claim should be submitted to the Department from which the contract is held."

At the end of the year arrangements were made by the Ministry of Munitions, in conjunction with the Admiralty and the War Office, for the insertion in munition contracts of clauses providing for additions to contract prices "to meet additional labour costs arising from direct Government action." Under these circumstances, one valid objection of employers to the automatic adoption of awards was removed, and only two orders for compulsory extension were therefore issued in 1918.

The actual effects of the exercise of compulsory powers under Section 5 of the Act of 1917 were therefore very small, as measured by the number of firms scheduled under statutory orders. The desired extension of general awards was achieved far more by departmental circulars, urging a form of "voluntary" anticipation of compulsion familiar since the outbreak of war, than by exercise of the coercive powers given by the Act of 1917.

It is rather as introducing a new principle in the relation of the State to movements in wages, and so carrying still further the generalisation of trade union standards in industry, that the movement for the extension of awards is interesting. Its application laid down a precedent, which was followed in the Wages (Temporary Regulation) Act (1918), under which wages were regulated for twelve months after the Armistice, and the adoption of this principle in a permanent measure was urged by the Provisional Committee of the National Industrial Conference, convened by the Government in February, 1919. The experience of the principle in war-time was not, however, decisive. Employers on the whole were not reluctant to increase wages; they were able to recover the increase in their labour costs by a revision of their contract prices. These conditions were abnormal, and the intrinsic difficulties of giving effect to the principle under normal conditions, especially the demarcation of trades to which different awards were to apply, and the administrative enforcement of awards in marginal cases, were never fully tested.

---

[1] Chap. VII, Sect. 2 (b).

CHAPTER V.

PAYMENT BY RESULTS.

I. The Spread of Payment by Results, 1914-15.

(a) ATTITUDE OF LABOUR TOWARDS PIECE-RATES.

Of the incidental results of the demand for munitions, one of the most important was a wide extension of systems of payment by results. The industries affected by the demand were, before the war, mainly time-rate industries.[1] But methods of remuneration are closely connected with and dependent on methods of production, and the war demand, leading as it did to important modifications in methods of production, was bound to have an effect on methods of remuneration. The possibility of payment by results depends on the possibility of isolating and measuring the contribution to production of individual workers or groups of workers. By enormously increasing the proportion of repetition work of a uniform character, the munitions demand made possible this isolation and measurement over a largely increased proportion of the field of industry. The effect was the greater, because some payment by results was already in operation in most of the trades affected, and the decade before the war had been a period of much experiment in this direction. Employers had precedent to go on, and alternative systems to choose from, when the change in their output made the introduction or extension of payment by results a practical policy.

It is a common error to suppose that organised labour as a whole is opposed to piece rates. An intellectualist minority is opposed to any system of payment by results, and certain trades have always opposed it. But more unions, with more members, accept or insist on payment by results than resist it. The demand for munitions, however, affected particularly the trades that resist it. Thus the building industry (with which most, if not all, of the wood-working trades contributing to aircraft manufacture were connected), was essentially a time-working industry. The attitude of the chief building crafts to any system of payment by results is described later. They carried the same attitude of opposition into their ship-building work; while the other wood-working trades shared their traditional opposition to piecework. In the engineering and shipbuilding industries the current methods of payment varied. Of the workers in the shipyards probably at least 60 per cent were piece-workers in 1917.[2] The boiler-makers had for a number of years normally worked on piece-work, almost as sub-contractors, dividing the earnings of the squad between riveters,

---

[1] See above, p. 5.
[2] cf. Mr. Wilkie, before Committee on Production.

helpers and rivet-boys,[1] and the iron trades were to a considerable extent piece-working trades. " In most of the shipbuilding districts there are recognised piece-work price lists negotiated between shipbuilders and men's unions. In a few instances, the lists are not district lists but yard lists," explained the secretary of the Shipbuilding Employers' Federation at the beginning of 1917.[2] There remained, however, an irreconcilable minority among the shipwrights, shipspainters, carpenters, etc., while the blacksmiths, anglesmiths, electricians, coppersmiths, were also time-workers.

In the engineering trades payment by results was much less general. There had been an agreement, under which piece-work was allowed in the engineering trades, made in 1907 between the Engineering Employers' Federation and the principal engineering unions, but it was terminated before the war. The Secretary to the Engineering Employers' Federation thus described the position at a meeting of the Employers' Advisory Committee in July, 1917.[3] " The arrangement that we had with Trade Unions relating to piece work was embodied in the 1907 agreement which was terminated (cancelled by the A.S.E.) before the war. The arrangement that we have with the unions on the fixing of premium bonus basis times is contained in a memorandum which was not adopted by all the societies, and which is simply a recommendation. There is now no agreement except local agreements."[4]

Piece-work had been coming increasingly into engineering during the war, and even fitters and turners, and the skilled tool-room men, whose position caused so much unrest in the trade, had acquiesced readily, in many cases, in the introduction of some system of piece-work or collective bonus.[5] As a whole, however, probably, the majority of skilled men in the engineering trade looked with suspicion on

---

[1] The " gang " system adapts itself easily to piece-work. Thus brasscasters with one of the most elaborate and successful systems of settling piece rates in the metal trades of the country are piece-workers who share their large earnings with their helpers ; cf. the cautious statements of a delegate of the Brass Workers, and Metal-mechanics' Association, before the Committee on Production, 22 August, 1917. " I have two men and a boy at work for me. The boy gets £1 13s. 6d. a week. The two men pay income tax, so that they must earn £4 or £5. I pocket the rest,—a great deal but . . . I worked on an average 8½ days per week for 2 years."

[2] L.R. 141/2.

[3] M.W. 89791.

[4] The following is a typical example of such a local agreement. It is extracted from the working rules agreed to in March, 1916, between the Derby Engineering Trade Employers' Association, and the A.S.E., Patternmakers', Workers' Union, etc. " Employers and workmen are entitled to work piecework provided—

(a) Prices are fixed by mutual arrangement between the employer and workman.

(b) Each man's day rate is guaranteed irrespective of his piece-work earnings.

(c) Overtime and night-shift allowances are paid in addition to piecework prices on the same conditions as in each shop for time work."

These stipulations were the same in substance as those in the discarded general agreement of 1907.

[5] M.W. 89791.

systems of payment by results as applied to themselves, while—although the Amalgamated Society of Engineers was not officially opposed to payment by results as such, with due safeguards—the local trade union officials constantly threw difficulties in the way of its introduction in specific cases.

(b) Attitude of Employers.

Employers were predisposed to avail themselves of the opportunity afforded by the war changes in methods of production. The belief was general among them that payment by results was the most effective stimulus to exertion ; their effort for a generation before the war had been in the main to extend such systems, and that the extension had gone no further was due entirely to the opposition of the unions. Payment by results was not, however, the first thought of employers when the need of increased output became apparent. Dilution of skilled labour, the suspension of output and demarcation restrictions, and the removal of limits on earnings where systems of payment by results were already in operation were the first innovations proposed by them. The Shipbuilding Employers' Federation, it is true, suggested that the introduction of piecework would very likely meet the existing shortage of shipwright labour, but they did not press the point, and were more concerned to maintain the piece rate system where it was already established against the demand of the workpeople, which the latter were able to press with some success in the existing shortage of shipyard labour, for " piece-rate time rates," " lieu rates," and similar systems, under which the workman received for time-work an assured remuneration based on previous piece-work earnings.[1] In a deputation to the Ministry on 9 June, 1915, from the Emergency Committee of the Federation a statement of work done by eighteen squads of riveters in 1914 and 1915 was handed in, showing a fall in the number of rivets per man per day from 346 to 221 after the change to time-work. The work, it was stated, was of a lighter and easier character, and the employers, if they considered only their own interest, would raise no objection to the increased cost, since their contracts with the Government were on the basis of actual expenditure plus a percentage.[2] The parallel memorandum submitted to the Committee on Production by the Federation of Engineering Employers contained no reference to extending payment by results.

(c) Policy of the Government.

Nor did the Government in its early negotiations with the trade unions press for the extension of payment by results. Doubtless such an extension might have been implied in Mr. Lloyd George's appeal at the Treasury Conference to suspend all restrictions on output, and subsequently it was held in a number of arbitration awards that refusal

---

[1] Memorandum as to negotiations with the Shipyard Trade Unions handed in to the Committee on Production, 11 February, 1915. (Hist. Rec./R./180/4.)
[2] Memo. on Labour for Armaments, 9 June, 1915. (Hist. Rec./R./320/1.)

to accept payment by results did constitute restriction of output, but the actual examples of restrictive practices given by Mr. Lloyd George were limitation of number of machines which one man might work, opposition to the employment of semi-skilled labour, and opposition to the admission of female labour. It was realised that restriction of output might be practised as a method of protecting piece-rates. The Committee on Production in their second Interim Report, 20 February, 1915, called attention to this practice of workmen confining their earnings to " time and a half " or whatever the local standard might be. They understood that the practice was due to a desire to protect piece-rates, and suggested as a remedy that the Government should require firms engaged on the production of shells and fuses to give an undertaking that they would not take war-time earnings into account in fixing future piece-rates and would not cut piece-rates during the war unless some change in the method of production, such as the introduction of a new type of machine, justified the change. A little later Mr. Barnes called attention in the House of Commons to the effect of cutting piece-rates on output; a prominent employer[1] drew attention to the same evil; and a large Midland firm of explosives manufacturers complained that they could not induce their piece-workers to exceed 25 per cent. over time-work output, it being the custom of the district in the past to reduce rates if they did.[2]

Restrictions on output on systems of payment by results, therefore, was one of the evils which it was the object of the Munitions of War Act to remove.[3] No specific reference to this type of restriction occurs in the Act, so that to deal with it it would be necessary to refer to the Board of Trade or to arbitration under Section 4 (3) the question whether any rule, practice or custom of this kind did as a matter of fact restrict production. Similarly no specific provision was made to prevent the cutting of piece-rates or bonus times. The need for such provision had not been put forward at the Treasury Conferences and found no place in the Treasury Agreement on which the second schedule of the Act was based. Complaints, however, that restriction was practised to protect piece-rates continued to be made, and led to two attempts to reassure the work-people. In the first place the National Advisory Committee representing the unions attending the Treasury Conferences issued an appeal in July, 1915, in which after referring to cases of restriction of output reported to them and reminding their constituents that the Treasury Conference had decided that it was imperative that restrictions on output on war-work should be removed, they pointed out that the usual justification of such restriction, the fear that prices would be cut and the increased output made the standard, was no justification in view of the country's need and in any case had no ground since " under the Treasury Agreement

---

[1] Mr. W. L. Hichens, Chairman of Cammell Laird, in the Memorandum referred to above.

[2] Memo. on position leading to introduction of the Bill, June, 1915. (HIST. REC./R./221·1/6.)

[3] *Ibid.*

every conceivable safeguard was set up to protect the workman's interest when we return to normal times." In the second place, a press notice was issued in September, 1915, calling attention to the fact that changes in wages in a controlled establishment without the consent of the Minister were illegal, and that the Minister was prepared to use his powers to prevent the reduction of piece-rates as a consequence of the increase of output due to suspension of restrictions; a circular to the same effect was sent to all controlled establishments. Mr. Lloyd George gave the same· undertaking at the Trade Union Congress at Bristol. Mr. Isaac Mitchell had suggested investigation and action in one or two specific cases, and Mr. Owen Smith urged that it was necessary that all proposed alterations in piece-rates should be submitted to the Department for sanction; the number of piece-rate adjustments, however, as the volume of munitions work increased became too great for such detailed control.[1]

The importance of this pledge was hardly realised until its results began to be felt a year or two later. Employers made no organised protest at the time; doubtless it was accepted by them, as it was by all the officials concerned, as a reasonable concession to the workpeople's fears in return for the suspension of restrictions on output. Since the fixing of a piece-rate, or any other basis for payment by results, is difficult on all new work, and the production of munitions involved much new work, rates were fixed in many cases too high, and, reduction being prohibited, lucky individuals were enabled to make abnormal earnings, which led, gradually but inevitably, to a serious dislocation of the normal relations between the earnings of different classes and grades of workpeople. The guarantee did not even expressly exclude changes following on changes in methods of production. Changes of this character were not formally objected to by the unions and were allowed by the Wages Section of the Department; and this qualification gave some elasticity to the principle. But neither employers nor workpeople were satisfied with this carrying out of the pledge, and in the discussions which took place in the summer of 1917 on a proposed clause protecting piece-rates in the Munitions of War Amendment Bill of that year, employers attributed to the artificial fixity given to piece-rates much of the current ill-feeling and unrest in industry, while the trade unions accused employers of taking the opportunity afforded by trivial modifications in the methods of manufacture to force on their employees disproportionate reductions in piece-rates. By that time, however, the question of payment by results had become more important and more controversial. The manufacture of the more important types of munitions has passed from the state of experiment into that of routine production, in which the technical possibilities of payment by results were very much increased, and the combined increase in demand and reduction in the supply of all kinds of labour made the problem of finding a stimulus to sustained or increased exertion correspondingly more urgent.

---

[1] L.R. 2339. See also above, p. 104.

II. Official Propaganda before 1917.

The proposal of an organised campaign to extend payment by results, as distinct from measures designed merely to protect piece-rates and so stimulate output, appears as early in the history of the Ministry of Munitions as November, 1915, when the deputy labour officer for Scotland wrote to the Department from Glasgow, suggesting that shipwrights should be paid by piece-work. This could easily, he said, be arranged, "though the Ship Constructors' and Shipwrights' Association was against the proposal, and as firms were afraid that by moving in the matter they might hinder, rather than help, output, they were not prepared to do anything unless they had the sure backing of the Ministry of Munitions." Only one high-class firm of shipbuilders (William Denny, of Dumbarton) had introduced the system as yet. The Chief Labour Officer for Scotland in forwarding this letter noted that "many firms had lately said that output would be very largely increased by piece-work." The deputy labour officer, prior to joining the government service, had many years experience in various Scotch shipyards. He recommended the Ministry of Munitions to have a conference with leading officials of the Shipwrights' Association with regard to the proposal.[1] This communication was sent to the Admiralty who deprecated action.[2]

Incidentally the subject came up at conferences convened by the Admiralty[3] on 21 March and 1 April, 1916, at which representatives of employers, trade unionists and the Ministry of Munitions were present, in order to discuss (a) the question of "piece-work time rates," (b) the computation of overtime, with a view to improving time-keeping in shipyards. Much more emphasis was, however, placed on the latter question than on the former, and an elaborate scheme for improving time-keeping in shipyards was a few months later drafted by the Central Munitions Labour Supply Committee.

III. Propaganda by Employers.

Official propaganda achieved little in the field of private employment in 1916. Piece-work and other systems of payment by results were,

---

[1] M.W. 64440.

[2] The comment of the official to whom it went may be quoted:—

"In the Royal Dockyards, shipwrights have been on piece-work for many years, but they have been mainly time-workers with intermittent piece-work. Having regard to the present tendency of the workmen to insist on very high fixed time-rates as a minimum for piece-workers, it is considered that the present time is not the most suitable for attempting innovations of the kind. It is very desirable that the Ministry of Munitions should try to stop the exceedingly objectionable system known as 'made-up allowance, lieu rate, guaranteed day-rate, piece-work energy on time-rates, on the nod.' All these mean much the same thing: viz., that instead of a worker being paid according to the amount of work he has done, he has now secured that he shall be paid at a minimum rate, originally equivalent to, and now in many cases much in excess of, the previous average earnings under piece-work rates quite regardless of his output. This system encourages idling, and anything that can be done to stop it will have a greater effect in increasing output than anything that can be done in the direction of enclosed reports."

[3] M.W. 65058.

however, spreading all the time as a result of the pressure of employers. Most of the work undertaken by women and unskilled male dilutees in engineering shops was put upon some systems of payment by results as soon as the workers had become expert at it; the minimum time-rates assured to these workers by the Ministry's Orders were intended only as a safeguard during this period of training.[1] The work was repetition work, and lent itself to such methods of remuneration. With their skilled workers the employers were in many cases able to institute or extend piece-rates or premium bonus by agreement. The terms of the national agreement, regulating payment by results, from which the Amalgamated Society of Engineers had withdrawn just before war broke out, were re-embodied in local agreements in some cases, and served as the basis for private arrangements, even where no formal collective agreement was concluded. An inquiry made by the Ministry through its chief investigation officers early in 1917 indicated that about one-third of the general engineering shops of the country had adopted piece-work by that time; and skilled time-workers, fitters and tool-room men, whose work did not lend itself to a piece-rate basis, had in many cases acquiesced readily in the introduction of some form of piece-work or collective bonus. A circular inquiry addressed to secretaries of local Engineering Employers' Associations a little later (May, 1917) gave similar evidence of extension; Derby, for example, showed the large proportion of nine out of eleven firms with more than half their employees on some system of payment by results.[2] It was noted by the officers of the Wages Section of the Ministry that the Midlands were much further advanced than the North in the matter of piece-rates;[3] a difference that would be explained by the difference in the character of their pre-war production.

This policy of employers went beyond the limits of private negotiation and local agreement in three particulars. In the first place they used the possibilities of payment by results as an argument in arbitration hearings. It was frequently their practice to point out in replying to applications for increased wages before the Committee on Production and on other occasions that an acceptance of piece-work by the shipwrights', carpenters', cabinet-makers' and furniture makers' societies would, *per se*, increase the workers' incomes without forcing on the employers any increase of the district time-rate.[4]

---

[1] Vol. V., Part II., Chap. II.

[2] L.R. 3601, 1093.

[3] Wages Section Report, 8 June, 1917.

[4] Committee on Production Hearings, 22 March, 1915, 5 April, 1916, 23 August, 1916, 12 January, 1917, of the Shipbuilding Employers' Federation and the Shipbuilding Trades Standing Committee, with the Boilermakers.

At the second of these, the extra rates paid were incidentally discussed. Payments " on the nod " and lieu rates might (it was admitted by the men) mean an increase of " anything from 5 per cent. to 30 per cent. on existing piece-prices," given either to stimulate output or by way of compensation to the skilled piece-worker who through the admission of less skilled labour found that the " most intricate and least remunerative " portions of a job were left to him.

In the second place they claimed that a refusal on the part of workpeople to accept any system of payment by results amounted to restriction of output, and they referred such cases for arbitration under Section 4, Subsection (3) of the Munitions of War Act, 1915. This subsection made it illegal to persist in any rule, practice or custom, not having the force of law, that tended to restrict production, and left it to the Board of Trade, or on the application of either party to arbitration, under Part I. of the Act, to determine whether in any case the rule, practice or custom did tend to restrict production. It has been noted above[1] that this section and subsection constituted the only means in the Act of dealing with the practice of restricting output to protect piece-rates, which was so often referred to in the discussions preceding the passing of the Act; but there is no evidence that any compulsory change in methods of remuneration was contemplated when the subsection was drafted. The wording of it, however, gave employers the right to appeal, which they took in individual cases, and their contention was upheld.

Thus, Sir Thomas Munro, on 24 July, 1916, decided as a single arbitrator that the refusal of the electricians working in Messrs. Beardmore's engineering shop and shipyard to work on a premium bonus system (which had been accepted with a "very considerable increase in output" by other mechanics in other departments of the establishment), tended to restrict production, and he, therefore, prescribed in detail a system of premium bonus for the electricians, suspending their time system of payment for the period of the war.[2] Similar awards (with regard to joiners, etc.), were made by the Committee on Production on 22 November, 1 December, and 18 December, 1916.[3] While such awards may have contributed in some cases to the extension of payment by results, the opposition to such systems was much too deep-seated to be removed by such an indirect and incidental procedure. A case such as that of the Brightside Foundry & Engineering Company showed the impossibility of enforcing such an award where the opposition was determined, and Sir Thomas Munro himself pointed out the difficulty to the Employers' Advisory Committee.[4]

The system of recognising a "piece-work time-rate," was justified by Mr. Wilkie on the ground (often complained of by workmen at the time) that "the Government presses the employers to put twenty men on work where there is only room for ten, and it is done to enable them to make their money at the usual rates." Mr. Carter, President of the Shipbuilding Employers' Federation, denounced both systems vigorously. "The one thing that the shipbuilders in this country are against is this 'on the nod' and this 'piece time rate.' We have begged of the representatives of the Government to make it illegal. It is not the employers who want it, but it is certain trades have forced it on them by refusing to fix up piece-rates, and to get the work done for the Government some people have had to pay anything."

Such payments, it may be observed, offered a ready means of evading the spirit, if not the letter, of section 4 (2),—the "sanctioning" clause of the Munitions of War Act.

[1] p. 124.
[2] C.E. 185/5.
[3] Awards 585, 619, 642, 643.
[4] See Appendix II.

In the third place, an attempt was made to use subsection 5 of Section 4 of the Act, to compel the acceptance of payment by result. This subsection provides that—
"The employer and every person employed in the establishment shall comply with any regulations made applicable to that establishment by the Minister of Munitions with respect to the general ordering of the work in the establishment, with a view to attaining and maintaining a proper standard of efficiency, and with respect to the due observance of the rules of the establishment."

In order to make the Act effective, the Minister made the following regulations under this subsection on 14 July, 1915 :—

"(1) The owner of any controlled establishment shall as soon as practicable post rules relating to order, discipline, time-keeping and efficiency, conspicuously in his establishment, so as to bring them effectively to the knowledge of workmen employed therein. Copies of rules so posted shall be sent to the Minister of Munitions.

"(2) Every person employed in the establishment shall comply with any rule so posted, provided that no person shall be liable to a penalty under the Act for failing or refusing to comply with any rule, if the Munitions Tribunal is satisfied that the rule is an unreasonable one, or that the person had just cause for his failure or refusal to comply with it."[1]

The Engineering Employers' Federation therefore drew up a code of works rules, and circulated it to its members. Among these was the following :—

"5. *Piece-work or Premium Bonus System.*—All persons employed shall work on piece-work or the premium bonus system, as and when required by the Company, time-rates in the case of piece-work being guaranteed."

The validity of this rule, if challenged, depended on a munitions tribunal holding it "reasonable." The matter does not seem to have been tested, the direct appeal made by employers against the refusal to accept payment by results on the ground that such refusal was restrictive of production, raising the question in a different and more definite form. The result of that appeal has been given above. The mere posting of a rule, posted on the instructions of the Minister of Munitions, though not drafted or approved by him, may have had some moral influence in inducing men to waive their objections to payment by results ; but in practice it was found that the only rules that could be enforced were the Model Rules issued by the Ministry, which contained no provision of this sort.

IV. Payment by Results in National Factories.

While official action had little result in the field of private employment, systems of payment by results were generally adopted in the National Factories which began work in the course of the year. The

---

[1] Vol. IV, Part II, pp. 24–26.

Boards of Management of factories established in 1915 had no basis to go on in fixing rates except the schedules of Woolwich and the armament firms which had manufactured projectiles before the war. These were based on conditions of manufacture on which the new factories, just because they were new, had been able to improve, with the result that they enabled the workers to earn wages which excited the envy of more skilled time-workers. To meet this difficulty and to encourage other Boards of Management to adopt systems of payment by results, the department of the Ministry responsible for gun ammunition and the supervision of national factories (A.M.3) set up a section, which had the assistance of an expert from the firm of Messrs. Herbert of Coventry, which made a careful investigation into the pricing of shell operations and furnished information as to normal speeds for certain processes. Most of the National Projectile Factories on the strength of this information adopted piece-work for machine hands, with a bonus on output for toolroom operatives and other indirect producers, in the summer of 1916. National Shell Factories were recommended, early in 1916, to institute the system of overhead bonus, a recommendation adopted by the Huddersfield Factory, in February, and by seven or eight others soon after. In the summer the Director of Area Organisation decided that piece-work would increase output in Shell Factories also, and they were recommended to adopt piece-work, reporting their schedules to the Labour Department in order that a representative of that department might discuss the proposals with the management. Each Board, however, was left free to make its own decision, and while some changed from collective bonus to piece-work or adopted a combination of piece-work and bonus on output, others continued to rely on collective bonus. An inquiry in February, 1917, addressed to eight National Shell Factories with systems of collective bonus elicited very favourable opinions ; the system was said to increase output and reduce labour cost.[1] The National Factories were outside the control of the Wages Section of the Labour Department of the Ministry, until they became controlled establishments in February, 1916 ; the Royal Factories and Woolwich Arsenal were never under its control, their wages being settled by the Director of Munitions Finance with final reference to the Treasury.

After the first few experimental months the earnings of pieceworkers in national factories were not abnormal ; they were certainly moderate compared with some of the earnings in privately-owned works.[2] The substitution of women for men in shell factories in the course of 1916 (with alterations in the methods of production) did much to keep the piece prices for ammunition comparatively low. A section of A.M.3 worked out ideal costs which provided an exact and stable

---

[1] D.A.O. Committee and N.P.F. Committee Minutes, and C.E. 2266/4, 389/4, 492/4, 411/4.

[2] Hist. Rec./R./342/148. In the National Shell Factories in September, 1917, average earnings were as follows :—Fitters, £3 16s. 8d ; Turners, £4 4s. 5d ; Machine Operators, Men, £3 7s. 3d., Women. £1 18s. 3d.

In National Projectile Factories, July, 1917, average earnings of Machine Operators, Men, £4 4s. 3d., Women, £1 17s. 4d.

PAYMENT BY RESULTS

basis for piece-prices. Even before this an inquiry, arranged by the Wages Section at the beginning of 1916, had given a basis of definite information on piece-rate and piece-workers' earnings on shell, which was supplied to Boards of Management. During the autumn of 1915, the Department had received not a few complaints of the excessive earnings made by machine men on shell work. Thus at the Projectile Company, Wandsworth Road, it was shown that 57 machine men engaged on simple operations like shell boring and turning had for nine weeks been earning on an average £4 3s. 0d. a week, or nearly twice the wages of an ordinary skilled tradesman. These high earnings were felt to be objectionable from the point of view not only of national economy but actually of production, since " if a man could earn more than he needed in five days he had little inducement to work on the sixth."

It was therefore decided to hold an inquiry to find out how far the cause of the trouble lay in inflated piece prices and if so, whether it could be removed.[1]

The enquiry was directed chiefly to the manufacture of 18-pounder, 4·5 in. and 6 in. H.E. shell. By the end of February sufficiently detailed information had been obtained to serve as a basis for advice to the National Shell Factories and managers of certain other controlled establishments, though it was not definitely tabulated. Thus details of operation rates were sent in May to the Secretary of the Engineering Employers' Association for the North-West of Scotland, who applied to the Ministry for advice on behalf of his members, explaining that unduly high piece-rates for shell had been fixed early in the war by some local firms which had not previously made shell, and that the majority of shell-making firms (who were now preparing under pressure from their workers to fix their piece-rates) wished for a schedule based on that of experienced firms such as had been prepared for the National Shell Factories.[2] The results of the inquiry gave the Department a concrete basis for an estimate of piece-workers' earnings, and were therefore of value in negotiations for the improvement of the relative position of time-workers. On the whole, however, during the first year of the Ministry's existence, the Department was able to do little towards the systematisation of piece-rates. The only statutory power which the Department could use to regulate piece-rates was the power of requiring employers to submit changes in wages for its sanction under Section 4 (2) of the Act. This it used, as it had opportunity, to stabilise rates; but the power extended only to controlled establishments, a limited class in 1915 and 1916, and was further limited by the right of appeal to arbitration. And the Wages Section never possessed a staff that would have enabled it to scrutinise every change in a piece-rate or basetime.

The influence of the production departments was greater. They controlled the national factories, and were able by careful cost-accounting

---

[1] M.W. 76556.
[2] M.W. 112821, cf. Committee on Production award in the case G. & J. Weir, Cathcart (20 March, 1916). It was stated that pieceworkers earned up to £8 a week.

to find a satisfactory basis for piece-prices. In the light of the results of the national factories, they were able to criticise the costs, especially the labour-costs, of private firms, and to divert contracts for shell and other ammunition from those which were too, expensive.

V. Propaganda in the Shipbuilding Industry, 1917.

An organised campaign to extend payment by results was undertaken first in the shipbuilding industry as a result of a Cabinet decision early in 1917. The proportion of piece-workers here before the war was much higher than in engineering or woodwork, and the possibilities of dilution were much less.

The enemy submarine campaign in the winter of 1916-17, gave a new importance to any device for economising skilled labour or securing a larger output from the limited supply available. The Ministry of Munitions was not directly concerned in the negotiations with employers and unions, but the shipbuilding trades were so far identical with the trades engaged in the production of munitions under the Ministry's supervision, that any results achieved by the Shipyard Labour Department of the Admiralty and the Ministry of Labour, would have affected the work of the Labour Department of the Ministry of Munitions, and the mere negotiations helped to determine the attitude of unions and employers when they came to discuss the Munitions of War Amendment Bill in July and August. Some account of them is therefore given here.

On 5 January, 1917, a meeting of the Federation of Engineering and Shipbuilding Trades, which embraced some thirty trade unions, but did not at that date include the Amalgamated Society of Engineers, was held at Montagu House to meet the Minister of Labour.[1] The Minister of Labour intimated that it had been brought to his notice that differences had arisen in various parts of the country in the engineering and shipbuilding trades, in connection with proposals that had been made with a view to securing the maximum output in these trades by changing the method of remunerating labour from the time work system to that of payment by results. He had asked the Federation to meet him in order to put before them proposals which he intended to make, with a view to the matter being thoroughly investigated by a competent tribunal, under the guidance of a suitable chairman, with the assistance of persons having practical acquaintance with works management and industrial organisation, and he expressed the hope that he would secure the co-operation of the federation in the enquiry. The Minister's proposals were accepted " as a recommendation " to the executives of the affiliated societies, but it was decided to adjourn till January for any definite decision.

---

[1] See account pp. 197 ff. *A.S.E. Journal*, March, 1917, and *Boilermakers' Journal*; also the account with comments in *Carpenters & Joiners' Journal*, March, 1917, p. 197.

It was also decided to request the Minister to give a written statement, explaining his proposals in detail; he wrote as follows :—

"The proposals I made to the general meeting of the Federation are identical with proposals I submitted to the Engineering Employers' Federation and the Shipbuilding Employers' Federation, at conferences which were held earlier during the same day. Briefly I propose that in order to investigate certain points that have arisen in connection with questions of remuneration and systems of payment for securing increased output in the Engineering and Shipbuilding Trades, there shall be appointed by the Minister of Labour a special Committee consisting of representatives of the employers and of the Trade Unions, with an independent Chairman accustomed to industrial enquiries, the reference to the committee being to consider and report on the systems of payment now in operation in the Engineering and Shipbuilding Trades with a view to the adoption of the most efficient system, having regard to the interests of the State, the workpeople and the employers.

"It is intended that the Committee shall conduct their enquiry in the chief engineering and shipbuilding centres, and local representatives of the trades whose wages conditions are under review will be co-opted as members of the Committee, and will act whilst these conditions are being subjected to enquiry.

"The Minister will be glad to receive from the Federation of Engineering and Shipbuilding Trades suggested names of representatives from amongst whom he can select the persons to act on the Committee. It will probably be found advisable that the Committee should include three representatives of the workmen, and three representatives of the employers.

"A report of the Committee will be submitted to the Minister as early as possible, and he will be glad at a later date after receipt of the report, to discuss the matter again with the Federation of Engineering and Shipbuilding Trades."

The proposal of the Ministry of Labour was not received with favour. At the adjourned meeting, on 19 January, 1917, of the Federation of Engineering and Shipbuilding Trades, the meeting took the bit in its teeth and voted (by 38 to 29) in support of a motion of Mr. Dawtry of the Steam Engine Makers' Society:—

"That this conference of the allied trades, believing that the proposed enquiry into systems of payment by results cannot be of any value in assisting the successful prosecution of the war, and cannot profitably be discussed by Trade Unions except in conjunction with other controversial questions, we therefore agree that the time is not opportune for such an enquiry, and hereby affirm at this juncture that we cannot agree to the proposed enquiry."

The wording of this resolution was due to the Executive Council of the Amalgamated Society of Engineers, which, although it had dissociated itself for some time from the Federation of Engineering and Shipbuilding Trades on account of its constitution, had yet met the allied trades in the morning of 19 January, had represented the situation to them, and secured their support for the resolution adopted in the afternoon.

In a report by two members of the Executive Council of the Amalgamated Society of Engineers, the society explained its own refusal to co-operate in the proposed enquiry on the grounds that it referred more to post-war problems than the present, that it " could not be of any value in assisting the successful prosecution of the war," and could only be considered profitably in connection with the whole question of post-war restoration of trade union conditions. There was further in the mind of the Executive Council some anxiety lest the interests of engineering should be overshadowed by those of shipbuilding. No single enquiry, it represented, could possibly cover both trades.

At the same time the Amalgamated Society of Carpenters and Joiners, which had been engaged on canvassing its members with regard to the introduction of premium bonus or piece-work in connection with the shipbuilding and housebuilding industries, reported that out of 17,000 members a majority of 5 to 1 had voted against either system and for a strike if any employer attempted to change from the hourly system of payment. " Now," characteristically observed the society's Journal, " we can inform any employer or Government Department that if they attempt to introduce any departure from our present system of payment they will be courting trouble."[1]

Despite these rebuffs, the attempt was continued. On 7 February a general conference of the representatives of the trade unions concerned was held, when the Prime Minister and Admiral Jellicoe addressed the meeting on the urgency of increased shipbuilding. As a result on 27 February, 1917, the Federation of Engineering and Shipbuilding Trades accepted at their quarterly meeting the principle of payment by results " as the Government had determined that it was in the national interests that such a system should be adopted," and undertook to co-operate loyally " with a view to securing an increased output in the shipbuilding industry in order to meet the great national danger created by the wholesale attacks on shipping now being made by the German submarines."[2] It must be remembered, however, that the federation had no power to commit its constituent bodies.

On 12 March a letter was sent to the Council of the federation by the Minister of Labour, explaining the system proposed for the introduction of the change. Its proposals were as follows :—

(1) Proposals for the adoption of payment by results were to be made by the employer to the representatives of the trade union concerned.

(2) Counter proposals, if any, were to be made within 7 days by the workmen.

---

[1] *Amalgamated Society of Carpenters & Joiners' Journal*, February, 1917, p. 103.

[2] HIST. REC./R./342/121.

(3) In case of disagreement, a reference of the points at issue was to be made within 10 days to a district conference of employers and trade unions concerned, or to a local tribunal which would be set up in each district and would consist of two technical advisers for each trade (one appointed by employers and the other by the workmen in the district), with an impartial chairman appointed by the Minister of Labour. Any decision reached by such a tribunal would be made binding on non-federated firms.[1]

(4) The introduction of payment by results on such terms was to be duly recorded as a departure from trade union customs for the period of the war, with the usual implications:

(5) Any such agreement should " include provisions that the existing time-rates shall be deemed to constitute a guaranteed rate for all time worked, should this be desired by the workmen's representatives."[2] The district conferences included in the scheme should decide on general questions as to whether a system of payment by results should be introduced uniformly or by each shop concerned, and as to the method of its introduction. District committees of employers and employed should then be appointed for each trade or district, to draw up a schedule of the rates or prices for the trade in that district; or if no district committee or local tribunal took action, a shop committee (" of that trade in *each* shop ") should be set up to decide the matter.

" The local officials of the Ministry of Munitions and the Shipyard Labour Department of the Admiralty," it was added, " will be prepared to lend any assistance in their power," as would the Ministry of Labour.[3]

This scheme resembled the scheme of dilution commissions employed with considerable success the year before on the Clyde and elsewhere. Mr. Macassey, at this time head of the newly-formed Shipyard Labour Department of the Admiralty, was Chairman of the Clyde Dilution Commission.

It was arranged[4] that Mr. Macassey should hold meetings in the course of March, at Hull, Glasgow, Newcastle, Barrow, Liverpool, Cardiff, Bristol, where he should speak to delegates of all the trade unions concerned with shipyard work. After he had spoken in each place, members of this Department were to stay behind and attempt to

---

[1] The principle of extension of awards had just been decided on for inclusion in the (unsuccessful) Munitions of War Bill then before Parliament.

[2] The secretary of the Boilermakers expressly disclaimed for his members a guaranteed time-rate when on piece-work (cf. Committee on Production Hearing, 27 February, 1917). " We in our Society have never asked it, because where there are guarantees given, what happens very often is that the man is allowed only to earn something like time, time and a quarter, or time and a third."

[3] cf. *Boilermakers' Journal*, May, 1917. pp. 12–13.

[4] M.W. 167355/4.

induce the district committees of all the trade unions to enter into an agreement (a model of which was drawn up) for payment by results. A list of the Ministry's chief investigation officers was sent to Mr. Macassey at his request and it was agreed that the Wages Section of the Ministry should co-operate in the campaign.

Mr. Macassey was in favour of adopting legislative compulsion. On 27 April, 1917, he sent to Lord Curzon a draft of a Bill to be carried out by the Admiralty "to provide for the introduction of piece-work in shipbuilding and ship-repairing yards and marine engineering works,"[1] with a note that "inasmuch as what is to be given effect to is the decision of the War Cabinet, I suppose it is beyond my official duty to suggest the legislative machinery required, but still as the Department is vitally interested and I am satisfied that piece-work can be introduced successfully, I hope it will not be considered presumptuous in my submitting a draft Bill for the Act required." The Ministry of Munitions was then promoting an Amendment Bill to the Munitions Acts; it was a subject of consideration whether sections on the lines of Mr. Macassey's proposal should be incorporated. Mr. Wolfe and Mr. J. C. Smith, however, were clear that if this was attempted, it must be done through a separate Bill, not as an appendage to the Munitions of War Amendment Act, and the proposed Bill never passed beyond the stage of a draft.

Some agreements were secured.[2] An arrangement was made by the Shipbuilding Employers' Federation with the Shipwrights' Society through the Shipyard Labour Department that its members would work piece-work, and negotiations, it was repeated in June, had been taking place since, in the various districts, with reference to the framing of piece-work price lists. They were then proceeding on the North-East Coast. The Employers' Federation made an agreement also with the Woodcutting Machinists' Society on 5 June to the effect that so far as possible payments by result should be substituted for time-work, for the duration of the war. Piece-work prices were wherever practicable to be fixed by mutual arrangement between the employer and the workman or workmen who performed the job. But the electricians, the joiners, and other shipyard trades remained obdurate against any form of payment by results,[3] and the serious labour situation which the great strikes of May revealed made it undesirable to press to an issue so controversial a policy as the national adoption of payment by results.

---

[1] L.R. 141/4.
[2] L.R. 141/2.
[3] See *A.S.E. Journal*, May, 1917, pp. 16 and 17, for an appeal to A.S.E. members to accept piece-work, from Sir L. Macassey, Director of the Shipyard Labour Department of the Admiralty (4 May). "The scheme of the Admiralty has been constructed with assistance and advice from practical Trade Unionists lent to the Admiralty by their organisations. It contains every legitimate and reasonable trade protection. The scheme has been cheerfully and loyally accepted in many districts. In some there has been hesitancy in its acceptance because of its provision for payment by results. Let it then be clearly understood that no other system than piece-work will be introduced by the Admiralty."

VI. Negotiations with the Engineering Unions, and the Munitions of War Act, 1917.

In the engineering trades, with which the Ministry of Munitions was concerned, the statutory enforcement of payment by results was not seriously considered. The Ministry was engaged in negotiating with the unions to secure their support for the extension of dilution to private work, and the clauses in the Amendment Bill which did not bear on that proposal were all of them aimed at removing alleged grievances and so smoothing the passage of the unpopular clauses. The Labour Department neither opposed nor questioned the usefulness of the national propaganda of the Shipyard Labour Department; but just as it was not prepared to join with that department in pressing for statutory powers, so it was not prepared to follow its example in undertaking a national campaign. The reason for this attitude was brought out clearly in the negotiations over the Bill to extend dilution.

On the second reading Mr. Kellaway promised to propose in committee a new clause, which should be an addition to the second schedule of the original Act, prohibiting rate-cutting. The fear of rate-cutting still obstructed the spread of payment by results, and allegations of rate-cutting figured largely in the reasons given for the unrest that led to the strikes in May and the inquiry by the Unrest Commission in June. There was no other reference to payment by results in the draft; yet the Amalgamated Society of Engineers in bringing their proposed amendments before the Minister on 4 June included among them "that the question of 'payment by results' be not proceeded with on a national basis." The Minister stated that he had never asked for it. Mr. Brownlie explained that there was very strong feeling on the subject in the country, because the rules of the society required that a question of that type should be settled by the district. Dr. Addison thereupon said: "I never dreamt of it. So far as the Ministry of Munitions is concerned, I think you ought to pay by results when you can conveniently. I think it is an advantage to all concerned if you can, but I never proposed that it should be raised as a national issue, and I do not propose to do so." The policy of the Shipyard Labour Department was another and an independent matter.[1] At a subsequent conference[2] on 9 June reference was again made to the Shipyard Labour Department's propaganda. "A big effort," a delegate said, "is being made by the Shipyard Labour Department to get some sort of principle agreed as a national basis; but we say, with the best intentions in the world, we do not think it would be beneficial to you or to us to do such a thing. We know the forces which will be up against us and we ask that the question shall not be pressed on a national basis." Where employers wished to introduce a change they could ask for a local conference, and, if necessary, get the question referred to a central conference within six days. Mr. Brownlie confirmed this; the Shipyard Labour Department would never get

---

[1] L.R. 159/22.   [2] L.R. 139/36.

payment by results in the engineering trades on a national basis; they could get it through the machinery for negotiations between employers and the unions already in existence; progress would only be made if negotiations on a national basis were dropped.

The attitude of the Amalgamated Society of Engineers' executive on this occasion was quite consistent with their rejection of the Minister of Labour's proposals the previous February. Their opposition was clearly in part due to disapproval of the "means and method" of the introduction of the proposals. In the next number of their Journal[1] the General Secretary of the Amalgamated Society of Engineers discussed the question dispassionately from the point of view of his society.

> "It is necessary," he wrote, "that any system of payment by results will be one which in war time will give the workers a proportionate increase in wages for the extra work done, and at the same time secure that no advantage will be taken when the war ends to reduce prices. Suitable machinery must be set up whereby the Trade Union wage for the time-workers shall be the basis for establishing a minimum wage for piece-workers of not less than 25 per cent. over day wages."

This was the claim familiar to Mr. Macassey and others who had framed the women's wages Orders in the preceding and current year. The article proceeded to quote as follows from the August, 1911, number of the Society's Journal, issued under very different conditions but not in an atmosphere of industrial peace.

> "We are not suggesting that piece-work is the only perfect form of remuneration. We should much prefer an ethical condition of industry under which every worker would do a fair day's work and get a fair day's pay. But the time is not yet. We must take things as they are and try to improve them. The abolition of piece-work is out of the question nowadays. All theorising on the benefits of the system are fallacious and futile as long as the methods of using it are so divergent and contradictory in the actual experience of the workshop."

The Ministry concurred in the Amalgamated Society of Engineers' view of the situation, left the extension of payment by results to negotiations between the employers and the unions, and gave an undertaking not to press for the adoption of payment by results on a national scale.[2]

The clause in the draft Amendment Bill prohibiting rate-cutting was described by Mr. Wolfe in a conference of trade union delegates on 21 May as "a pure gift." The unions, however, did not hesitate to look the gift horse in the mouth. The clause provided that rates or basis-times once fixed should not be changed without *consultation* with the unions representing the workpeople concerned; the unions asked

---

[1] *A.S.E. Journal*, March, 1917, p. 48.
[2] L.R. 139/204. Cf. *A.S.E. Journal*, July, 1917, p. 11.

that for "consultation" should be substituted "consent"[1] and also that the consent of the Minister should be required to any change.

The Ministry took these suggestions up with the Employers' Advisory Committee, who strongly resisted them. The employers had no objection in principle to consulting the unions and securing their consent; but they argued that it was impossible in practice because the unions had not an adequate staff of officials to deal with the innumerable cases that occurred.[2] They were quite prepared to discuss changes with their employees and quoted the successful system of consultation and appeal in operation at Barrow as an example that might be followed; but they could not hold every change up for the attendance of a union official, and they did not like the possibility of national officials being brought into purely local questions. They objected also very strongly to the omission of any proviso limiting the operation of the clause to cases in which there had been no substantial change in the method of manufacture. It was explained to them that the unions attached very great importance to the clause. What the unions had in mind was indicated by a delegate at the conference on 9 June: "We are asking that the price of a job shall not be cut. You can make as many changes as you like in operation, but the fact that the firm alters a nut here or puts in a bolt there and then says that they have altered the method of manufacture is what we object to." What they desired was that they should be able to send to arbitration or appeal the question whether a cut in price was reasonable.[3] The employers' objection to the requirement of the Minister's consent was based on the same ground. Changes were too frequent—" every hour of the day "—to permit of it.

It proved impossible to draft a clause satisfactory to both parties. The Department therefore invited them to discuss the matter with each other and agree on a procedure for fixing and changing rates with due protection for the worker, which could be attached to the Bill as a Schedule and made compulsory. The Engineering Employers' Federation and the Amalgamated Society of Engineers agreed on such a procedure.[4] It was recognised that a different procedure might be required in shipbuilding; but it was hoped that a similar agreement might be reached there which could be embodied in the Schedule, and the employers' federation and the shipyard unions were invited to supply such an agreed procedure.[5] They proved unwilling to fall in with the suggestion. The Standing Committee of the parties to the Shipbuilding Trades' Joint Committee wrote that they were of opinion that their needs were amply covered by clause 5 of the second Schedule to the original Munitions of War Act, and that it would be better, in order to avoid friction and trouble, to leave existing practice and custom in respect of piece-rates undisturbed. The Admiralty had already[6] pressed for the exclusion of shipyards from the operation of

---

[1] L.R. 139/9.
[2] L.R. 139/28, 8 June. L.R. 5581, 17 July.
[3] L.R. 139/36.
[4] Appendix IV.
[5] L.R. 139/40.
[6] L.R. 139/32.

the clause. It became necessary, therefore, to frame it in such a way that it would not interfere with existing or proposed agreements. A further provision had to be made to meet the case of women workers, who had no agreements with employers regulating procedure in changing rates and whose wages were protected by directions given under Section 6 of the Munitions of War (Amendment) Act, 1916.[1] The clause as finally drafted and passed, therefore, read as follows :—

> "8.—(1) The undertaking which the owner of a controlled establishment is by virtue of sub-section (4) of section four of the Munitions of War Act, 1915, deemed to have entered into shall include an undertaking that piece prices, time allowances, or bonuses on output, or the rates or prices payable under any other system of payments by results once fixed in the establishment may not be altered except in accordance with any procedure which has been adopted by agreement between the owner of the establishment and the workmen or their representatives and is in force in the establishment at the passing of this Act or by the direction of the Minister of Munitions, which direction shall not be given except in accordance with an agreement between the owner of the establishment and the trade unions representing the workmen affected by the alteration, or failing agreement after consultation with the parties concerned.
>
> Provided that this provision shall not apply where the alteration is made in accordance with the directions as to the rates of wages of female workers given by the Minister of Munitions under section six of the Munitions of War (Amendment) Act, 1916, nor shall this provision apply to shipbuilding yards or ship-repairing yards, but as respects such yards the Minister of Munitions or the Admiralty may make rules regulating the alteration of rates or prices payable under systems of payment by results therein.
>
> (2) Where an alteration of the rates or prices payable under a system of payment by results is made in accordance with the provisions of this section, paragraph seven of the Second Schedule to the Munitions of War Act, 1915, shall not apply."

The view of the Wages Section of the Ministry on the problem raised by the clause is developed in some comments by its head, on the agreement reached between the Amalgamated Society of Engineers and the Engineering Employers' Federation.[2] He criticises the omission of the normal guarantee that the piece-rates or bonus system shall yield a percentage above time-rates, and the omission of any overt provision for any experimental periods, and for revision by consent. He regards Clause 5, which provides that no change shall be such as to effect a reduction in the earnings of the workers concerned, and Clause

---

[1] L.R. 139/185. See above, Chap II.
[2] L.R. 139/40, and Appendix IV.

7, which guarantees average earnings on new work as being open to the same objections as "lieu rates" ("piece-work time rate"). He objects to Clauses 3, 6 and 8, because they seem to contemplate the fixing of rates by the employer, while the essential thing is fixing by consent. The essentials of a sound scheme are in his opinion, (1) that no piece-rate having been fixed shall be altered except by consent; (2) that the time rate shall in all cases be guaranteed; and (3) that piece-rates, etc., shall be so fixed as to enable a workman of ordinary ability to earn at least 25 per cent. or $33\frac{1}{3}$ per cent. over his guaranteed time-rate.

Two of the officers of the section who had had considerable experience in assisting firms to instal systems of payment by results, emphasize the chief points in his comments. "Consent" covers the whole ground. The right of the workmen to negotiate piece-rates should be guaranteed. If it is, then the precise machinery whereby parties may confer had better also be left to their mutual agreement. If the workman has a legal say in the fixing of rates, he can see to everything else himself. They note as a result of their travels that employers everywhere realise that the old practice of fixing and changing rates behind the backs of the men was fatal to the best hopes of production, and that payment by results will only succeed if the workmen are given an equal joint voice in the fixing of prices. The guarantee of earnings, however, they regard as unnecessary and expensive.

VII. Payment by Results in the Aircraft Industry.

While the controversies in the shipbuilding and engineering industries turned on the extent to which systems already in use could be applied to work hitherto done on time, the war gave rise to a great industry in which all the workers practically who were taken over were accustomed to time-rates, while the actual processes of manufacture were mainly of a repetition character which lent itself to piece-rates or some other system of payment by results. The aircraft industry existed before the war, but only in the experimental stage; it went through a process of development in the course of the war which, under normal conditions, might have been spread over a generation. The dislocation of accustomed habits inevitably caused unrest among the workpeople, and disturbed relations between them and their employers. Their differences, due ultimately to the revolution in the character of the industry, focussed in two controversies, one on the admission of women to the industry; this has been discussed in the part of this history dealing with the control of women's wages; the other on the method of remuneration. A fuller account of the controversy over payment by results is therefore given in the case of this industry than in either of the other cases.

The manufacture of woodwork for aircraft was carried out by members of six or seven woodworking trades—carpenters, joiners, cabinet-makers, coach-builders, organ-builders, pattern-makers, wheelwrights, case makers—represented by at least ten different unions.[1] Each of these unions claimed to introduce into the industry its own wage rates and working rules, and raised difficulties as to " demarcation " and hours of work. The two points on which all the unions were agreed were (i) a claim for all workers to the rate of the best-paid trade engaged in aircraft in the locality concerned, and (ii) a combined opposition to any system of payment by results. These claims were inextricably intertwined, and the claim for a standard time-rate cannot be altogether omitted from an account of resistance to payment by results.

The claim to a standard rate and working conditions can be best followed in its early stages in the history of arbitration awards. It is to some extent a part of the department's administration of the Fair Wages Clause. In July, 1915, Mr. Mackenzie, at a hearing at Glasgow, rejected the claim of the workmen that " a rate of wages should be definitely fixed for all woodwork operatives in the Glasgow district, such rate to be the highest wage paid to any woodworking trade in the district." A similar claim (for the 11½d. an hour joiners' rate) on behalf of the Joint Woodworking Trades Aircraft Committee (Glasgow district), was refused by the Committee on Production in July, 1916 (award 340). The Committee was "unable to accept the contention that firms engaged upon aircraft manufacture should necessarily pay the rates of wages that may be agreed upon for the building and other trades, where many of the conditions of employment are dissimilar."

The claim to transfer the wage advances of one industry to another has been responsible for a large proportion of the difficulties of wage adjustment during the war, when very many workers have been transferred from their own work to something similar but not identical. The department in its fair wages administration and the Committee

---

[1] See *Amalgamated Society of Carpenters & Joiners Journal*, March, 1916, p. 151, and May, 1916, pp. 284–286, on the need for amalgamation and especially for a common policy re payment by results. See also report of U. K. Society of Coach-makers, November, 1915.

The following statistics of trade union membership are of interest in considering the claim for standardisation of conditions:—

End of 1914. Trade unionists in British Isles	3,919,962
Trade unionists connected with woodworking and furnishing	142,227
Trade unionist members of Amalgamated Society of Carpenters and Joiners	73,349
Trade unionist members of other woodworking unions	64,686
Total carpenters insured under housebuilding	123,722
Estimated number of Amalgamated Society of Carpenters and Joiners' members in shipbuilding	10,000
Estimated number of General Union of Carpenters	8,000—9,000
Estimated number of non-unionist building carpenters	52,000

" Some thousands of these non-unionists are only ' hammers and saw ' men, who during ordinary times would not be employed as carpenters."

" Our organising efforts in the future must be in the direction of closing up our ranks ; there are far too many unions catering for woodworkers." (*Journal of the Amalgamated Society of Carpenters and Joiners*, November, 1915, p. 560).

on Production adopted an identical attitude, *i.e.*, they insisted that payment for work should depend on the work done, and not on the original trade of the worker performing it.[1] The position was stated clearly in one of the "reasoned" awards issued by the Committee on Production on 12 January, 1916, after a hearing in the previous month of an application from trade unions including aeroplane operatives in the London district for a uniform minimum wage of 1s. per hour and a recognised code of working rules, including provisions relating to hours of labour, wages, overtime, notice of leaving, travelling allowances, limitation of apprentices and improvers, etc. The Committee after "detailed inquiry into actual conditions" and visits to a number of factories refused both applications, on the ground that the industry was still in an undeveloped state, and that it was much too early to stereotype it. A similar claim was refused on 17 July, 1916, with the additional reason that it was undesirable to apply the rates claimed in the building industry to aeroplane work.[2]

This defined the official attitude to the claim for a fixed minimum rate until the following year. Incidentally the Committee on Production noted that payment by results might be desirable.

" The increase in repetition work may be expected to make it practicable and expedient for piece-work to be applied to some portions of the industry. . . . The inspections which the Committee have made of various factories suggest to them that some of the processes involved could be performed on the piece-work system, and that the application of this system is likely to be of importance in the future development and progress of the industry.

" The Committee think that a properly adjusted piece-work system would probably lead to good time-keeping, efficient work and increased output (with higher earnings). The very close inspection both by the Government inspectors and the works' inspectors, and the checks provided at each stage by the fitting in of parts, ensure the maintenance of high quality in the work."[3]

Payment by results, however, was strenuously opposed by the workers. At a general meeting of aircraft workers as early as December, 1915, a resolution against the adoption of any system of payment by results, was passed.[4] The matter had been discussed in detail with the employers during the previous months. The comments

---

[1] Thus when in September, 1916, the Amalgamated Society of Carpenters and Joiners at Bristol claimed under the Fair Wages Clause the recent advance of $\frac{1}{2}d$. an hour granted by the local Master Builders (an advance which would secure their members a standard 11d. an hour, whereas the chief local aircraft firm only paid 10$\frac{1}{2}d$. *plus* 4d. a day war bonus), the Wages Section of the Ministry held that the claim was not justified, and quoted the recent decision of the Committee on Production. Weekly Sectional Report, 20 October, 1916. See also above, Chap. IV.
[2] Awards 151 and 340 of the Committee on Production, 1916.
[3] See Vol. V, Part II for illustration of the current change of processes.
[4] *Times*, December, 1915.

of the Amalgamated Society of Carpenters and Joiners in their *Journal* illustrate the hostility of the conservative worker, while the secretary's estimate that one-third of the woodworkers of the country were non-unionists partly explains his society's hostility to a system tending to weaken trade union influence.[1]

Unfortunately—from the point of view of the advocates of payment by results—there were departmental differences as to the policy to be adopted. Thus on 11 April, 1916, at an inter-departmental conference at the Ministry of Munitions on the payment of men and women in the woodworking trades, it was noted that the Admiralty employed aircraft workmen on time-work only, whereas the War Office permitted piece-work. It was agreed that this discrepancy might continue, since the Admiralty gave much fewer repetition orders than the War Office.

On 27 January, 1916, the Admiralty had sent out the following letter to 41 aircraft firms;—

"I have to inform you that the employment of piece-work or the premium bonus system in connection with any constructional portion of woodwork of aircraft is considered by the Admiralty to be undesirable and that such systems should not be introduced by you in connection with any Admiralty Aircraft Contracts.

If such systems are now in practice in your works in the above connection it is desired that they should be discontinued as soon as possible."[2]

On 5 May, 1916, the Engineering Employers' Federation asked for a reconsideration of this decision, on the ground that " the danger of faulty construction is just as great under pure time, as under piece or premium bonus systems." The remedy in either case was efficient supervision. To this the Admiralty replied on 1 July that it was impossible in Admiralty work to exercise the increased supervision which would be required. This decision was communicated to inquiring employers and trade unions.

The anomaly could not continue as the output of aircraft increased, and the shortage of labour became more and more pressing. In August, 1917, therefore, a committee was appointed to consider and report on the anomalies existing in the wages of aircraft workers. It was clear that the men's opposition to payment by results (a localised opposition, since the Coventry firms were almost wholly on piece-work or premium bonus, and it was estimated that the system covered 40 or 50 per cent. of the workers of the country),[3] and their demand for a standardised week and working rules, must be faced, in the interests of the trade and of output. The committee, of which Sir William

---

[1] See above, p. 142.
[2] M.W. 53250/2; M.W. 167355/4; M.W. 124283/2.
[3] " About 40 per cent. of the Contracts of the Air Board are on such systems and experience has proved that a change from time work to payment by results means an increase in production of from 25 per cent. to 50 per cent." (L.R. 4221, 22 September, 1917).

Robinson was chairman, contained the following members: Captain Little (Air Board) secretary; Mr. J. C. Smith (Ministry of Munitions); Captain Rogers (Air Board); Mr. A. G. Cameron (Amalgamated Society of Carpenters and Joiners); Mr. J. Compton (Coachmakers' Society); Mr Henson (Daimler Motor Co.), Mr. Sigrist (Sopwith Aviation Co.), the latter representing the National Aircraft Committee and the Engineering Employers' Federation respectively.[1] In September, 1917, it reported unanimously in favour of

(a) a standard rate;
(b) standard working rules and conditions;
(c) a maximum working week of 53 hours;
(d) the general institution of payment by results.

So far from effecting a settlement, however, the committee's findings precipitated a crisis. The last proposal—the institution of payment by results—was put to a ballot of the members of the unions and rejected by a very large majority. Shortly afterwards the Department was inundated with demands for the immediate putting into force of (a) (b), and (c). The situation became very critical in the Hendon district, and after a conference between the Minister and the National Aircraft Committee, a joint Committee of the unions, negotiations were entered into with the Committee which resulted in the signing of an agreement on 30 October.[2]

At a meeting on 22 October, 1917,[3] the secretary of the Amalgamated Society of Carpenters and Joiners reported the result of the vote of members of the ten unions affiliated to the Committee. The Minister pointed out the urgency of the German offensive in aircraft, and the desire of the Department to do its best for the industry. " We want," he said, " to make thoroughly good wage conditions and wages standards for your men, and we want you in return to make an absolute record in the output of aeroplane material." Sir William Weir admitted that there was some truth in the delegates' contention that the defective output was due to inefficient workshop management, but asked how the potential output of the workers was to be developed. The Union representatives refused a suggestion made by Mr. Kellaway that a statement should be sent to the press to the effect that (a) a standard rate would be adopted by the industry, and (b) the National Aircraft Committee would not resist the introduction of payment by results where the majority of men approved. The delegates, however, had no intention of interfering with existing systems, and would strongly advise their executives to that effect. Mr. Cameron himself was anxious to do all that was possible to help. He would go round to members throughout the country, urging them to do their very best for output, provided that the *standard rate* was secured. The best course would be to leave the question of payment by results and to go to the men and say: " The Ministry of Munitions has done all that they possibly can do to satisfy you, and they have established conditions

---

[1] *Weekly Intelligence Report*, 25 August, 1917.
[2] HIST. REC./R./342/134/9.
[3] L.R. 4914/8; 4914/2; 4914/5.

of employment which are satisfactory to the trade unions concerned and we appeal to you to do all that is possible to justify the efforts which we have made on your behalf."

The agreement of 30 October which was signed by the National Aircraft Committee embodied the recommendations of Sir W. Robinson's Committee with the exception that instead of providing for the general institution of payment by results, a clause was inserted confirming an understanding with the men that payment by results could be adopted where the employer and workmen concerned agreed.

> "The Minister would approve and support any satisfactory system of payment by results that might be mutually agreed between employers and employed. The Minister would in each case satisfy himself, before approving, that the system proposed was a satisfactory system proportioning reward to effort; and also that it had genuinely been mutually agreed between the employers and employed, *i.e.* is introduced by arrangement and with the general consent of the men concerned."

This amounted to an undertaking, in return for the promise of the long-desired standard time rate, that there should be (i) no interference with existing systems of payment by results; (ii) no opposition to new systems if agreed by the majority.

This compromise was received with little enthusiasm on either side. The irreconcilable workmen said that the results of their ballot had been ignored, and that the Ministry of Munitions—

> "instead of assisting the woodworkers to come to an amicable agreement, had provoked the woodworkers into adopting the 'down tools' policy by taking sides with the employers. We feel that this pernicious system, which will inevitably result in scamped and shoddy workmanship, should not be introduced into the manufacture of Aircraft. The lives of our Airmen are far too valuable to be exposed to such risk. As to the Ministry's charge of slackness of production, we answer that the principal causes are: (1) Allowing contracts for obsolete machines to be completed and then dismantled. (2) Inefficient inspectors in the Aircraft Inspection Department. (3) Shortage of materials. (4) Shortage of wood-working machinery. (5) Bad management.

> "The Ministry of Munitions and the employers have had ample opportunity of settling this matter, and have lamentably failed. We therefore have taken the only action possible, and have ceased work, and we are determined not to resume until a settlement has been arrived at."[1]

A serious strike was taking place at the Hendon works at the time of the discussion of the agreement, the signature of which had been hastened in consequence, and there was much unrest among aircraft workers.

---

[1] L.R. 4914/5. Manifesto of London District Aircraft Woodworkers' Council.

The employers and the Admiralty on the other hand also objected. Sir Lynden Macassey, head of the Shipyard Labour Department, wrote on 27 November to the Department protesting against the proposed Order fixing (under the Munitions Act of 1917), a standard rate and standard hours for aircraft workers. Such an order *must* affect wages in the shipbuilding trades, since a considerable amount of aircraft was being made in shipbuilding yards. "The recent experience of the futility of attempting to confine the 12½ per cent. bonus to the original recipients proved beyond doubt" that such extension must take place.[1] "Under these circumstances, the Admiralty could not be a consenting party to the making of any order which would give effect to the agreement already entered into, which they regard as most inexpedient and dangerous in its direct and indirect effects."

This protest was discussed with Sir Lynden Macassey by the Labour Committee on 27 November, and by the Employers' Advisory Committee on 6 December[2] and on 7 December, the Government Labour Committee decided to exclude shipyards from the operation of the proposed order. Accordingly the Order, when issued on 8 February, 1918, contained the following provision. (Clause 6.)

"These directions shall not apply to skilled aircraft woodworkers employed in a shipbuilding or ship-repairing establishment."

The Engineering Employers' Federation were equally hostile. The federation was not directly consulted before the signature of the agreement of 30 October. Only the London District Engineering Employers' Association were invited to discuss it (on 26 October), owing to the urgent need for a decision. The Engineering Employers' Federation refused to accept the agreement as the basis of a statutory order owing to the working conditions established thereby. "While admitting that their representatives had signed the recommendations of Sir William Robinson's Committee in favour of a standard rate, standard working rules and conditions, and the 53 hour week, they contended that the institution of payment by results was the price they were willing to pay. By the agreement on the other hand they had nothing to gain."

The difficulty again originated in the sources contributing to aircraft manufacture.[3] Aircraft woodwork was produced in (*a*) aircraft establishments; (*b*) engineering establishments; (*c*) establishments in the building trade; (*d*) establishments in the furnishing trade; (*e*) establishments in the coachbuilding trade; (*f*) shipyards; each of which had its own customs as to methods of payment, overtime rates, and hours of work.

---

[1] L.R. 4914/12.
[2] L.R. 4914/12, L.R. 5581/15 and minutes of Employers Advisory Committee, 6 December. The Shipyard Labour Department had, through Sir L. Macassey, protested strongly against the extension of the 12½ per cent. bonus to the shipbuilders (See L.R. 5581/11, etc.), but had to accept this in the December timeworkers order for shipyard men. It was correspondingly indisposed to accept this Aircraft Order.
[3] HIST. REC./R./342/134/9.

The proposed order gave (i) overtime rates on a more favourable scale than those common in engineering works, and also laid down 53 hours as the working week " or such shorter time as may have constituted the working week, in the establishment concerned immediately before the date of the order. This in a building establishment would mean a week of 44 to 46 hours for aircraft workers: (ii) it also secured to the workers the rate payable to carpenters, cabinet-makers, coachbuilders, " whichever is highest," employed on aircraft in a district.[1] The Engineering Employers' Federation strongly criticised both provisions, principally because the proposals would introduce alien wages and working standards into the engineering trades, already greatly disturbed by the $12\frac{1}{2}$ per cent. advance.

" This means," said Mr. A. Smith, at the Employers' Advisory Committee,[2] on 29 November, 1917, " that all the good work which has been done by the Committee on Production in order to take the manufacture of aircraft out of the housebuilding conditions is absolutely knocked on the head by this Order. We are not going to be a party to throwing back the aircraft industry into the building trade. We have the full support of the Committee on Production in this contention that it is a new industry and that it is more allied to the engineering industry than to building, in that it is not subject to climatic conditions, to short hours in winter, etc."

Again on 26 January, 1918, at a very full meeting of the Advisory Committee,[3] he repeated:

" You are wanting us to give to a certain section of the workpeople special rates of pay, special hours of working and special rates of remuneration for overtime, night shift and holidays. Once we agree to that we open the floodgates and we cannot deny it to any other section in the works. We are not going to do it. The Government has made this mistake and we are not going to get them out of it on that basis. . . . We are not going to be swayed by any considerations of the workpeople going on strike, because the issue is very much larger than whether they are going to work 53 or 54 hours."[4]

Meanwhile, workpeople were becoming exceedingly discontented, as November, December, and January passed without the issue of the Order, the *quid pro quo* for the acceptance of payment by results which they had very reluctantly and spasmodically permitted, and a formal letter of protest was sent to the Department by the National Aircraft Committee on 22 January.[5] It was clear that either an Order must be issued embodying the agreement in full, or a compromise providing that the present normal working week in each establishment should continue.

---

[1] Hist. Rec./R./342/134/9.
[2] L.R. 5581/14.
[3] L.R. 5581/17.
[4] The Clyde employers had protested against the 53 hours week as being an hour shorter than that of local engineering establishments.
[5] Hist. Rec./R./342/134/9.

The final decision was to exempt the engineering establishments in part from the operation of the order, by the insertion of a clause (5.B.) that:

" The allowances in respect to overtime and night shift shall not apply to establishments which prior to August, 1914, were recognised as engineering establishments, that is to say, which followed engineering practice and conditions. In such establishments, the allowances to be paid for overtime and night shift shall be those fixed by custom, in agreement between employers and Trade Unions, for men in the engineering trade."[1]

Still the situation was not clear. Trade unions continued their opposition, in practice if not officially, to new schemes of payment by results. These they said (at a conference on 13 March at the Ministry of Munitions) were being "introduced surreptitiously" by individual agreements between employer and workmen in contravention of the primary trade union principle of solidarity.[2] The spirit of the workmen, said Mr. Wolfe, at this conference, was all against the agreement of 30 October. "We find that you actually interfere in some cases with existing systems, but much worse you violently oppose the introduction of fresh systems of payments by results." On the other hand, the National Aircraft Committee said that on 14 February a National Employers' Conference had decided that all aircraft factories should come under clause 5.B. quoted above. "Every aircraft establishment was claiming to be an engineering establishment," in order to avoid the shorter working week, and so was "deliberately causing trouble."

The order, however, had been formally issued on 8 February, and applied to some four hundred aircraft establishments.[3] The basis of a settlement was there, and no Government Department could ensure its peaceable acceptance by compulsion. The double controversy over methods of payment and standardisation of conditions was carried on amid much overtime work, much unrest, but also a very great output of aircraft. Few industries can have passed through a more stormy period of adolescence than that of aircraft.[4]

---

[1] Order 187.
[2] L.R. 4914/30, of 1918
[3] Hist. Rec./R./342/132.
[4] Apart from the issue of the skilled aircraft order on 8 February, the appearance of aircraft manufacture as a separate industry was marked by a separate award from the Committee on Production on 18 March, 1918 (award 980). It had been part of the agreement of 30 October that in future aircraft workers should apply as a body for periodic advances in wages, and should not obtain them as part of the engineering, building trades, etc. This award, after a hearing of no less than twelve employers' associations and the National Aircraft Committee representing ten trade unions, (a) extended the 12½ per cent. and the 7½ per cent. bonus to aircraft workers on time or on systems of payment by results respectively, and (b) gave to workers in the majority of aircraft establishments the advance of 5s. per week from the beginning of December, 1917, already received as the third "national" advance by members of the engineering trades. This award was extended 11 June, 1918. (Award 1555) to semi-skilled and unskilled workers.

VIII. Departmental Policy, 1917–1918.

While the department did not undertake any organised campaign for payment by results, it must not be thought that its influence was negligible, or that the Wages Section had no opportunity of giving practical effect to its views. The provision in the Munitions of War Act (Section 4 (2),) under which any change in wages in a controlled establishment required the sanction of the Minister, was held by the Treasury Solicitor to cover changes in piece-rates.[1] Very many changes were doubtless made without that sanction; the view was even expressed by an officer of the department in May, 1917, that the section referred only to time rates;[2] but the existence of the rule acted as a check, and brought to the department a great many cases; it also enabled the department to interfere with effect when some disturbance, due to the unsatisfactory working of the scheme, brought to its notice a scheme which had not been submitted for sanction. The employers' while protesting against a reminder that the rule existed, and objecting that it was practically impossible to await the concurrence of the department in changes that were taking place every hour of the day, admitted that they were not permitted to make such changes[3] without that concurrence.

The submission of advances in time-rates for sanction was even more important. There were no doubts about the necessity of this, and the submission gave the Wages Section the opportunity of urging in cases they considered suitable, the substitution of some system of payment by results. The section had two aims before it in its decisions, first, to prevent any firm from "jumping" the standard rate under the pretext of granting some form of special bonus, and, second, to ensure that an advance should be adopted if possible to stimulate output. The variety and eccentricity of the bonuses proposed, afforded much scope for revision in the light of some such simple principles.

The department let it be known that it was in principle in favour of the adoption of payment by results, whenever this was practicable. Thus, when a protest against payment by results on the ground that such payments led to disputes was forwarded by a Lancashire Association of Brassfounders, Turners, Fitters and Coppersmiths, the department replied (6 June), that "in view of the vital necessity of increased output it favours the adoption of payment by results, and is of opinion that with proper machinery for discussion between employers and employed," disputes should be avoided.[4]

In May, a circular letter was sent by the department to secretaries of district engineering employers' associations, asking them how far methods of payment by results had been adopted in the engineering establishments of their district, and what extensions were possible.[5] This was followed up by visits from officers of the department

---

[1] L.R. 139/185.
[2] L.R. 139/9.
[3] L.R. 5581, 17 July, 1917
[4] L.R. 1966.
[5] L.R. 3601, L.R. 1093.

(Mr. Murray and Mr. Nance Williams), to a number of districts, Manchester on 7 June; Leicester, 8 June; Nottingham, 12 June; so that the policy and method of introducing payment by results (especially among the difficult class of tool-room workers), could be discussed in detail. " Employers," it was reported, " were surprisingly ready to commend the piece-rates circular, and to desire that the fixing of rates should be negotiated between the parties and be based on consent " (as in the shipyard scheme). " If the workmen's claim to be recognised were granted, employers and employed could settle the rest, much preferably without outside interference. The Midlands are much further advanced than the North about piece-rates."[1]

This gradual propaganda was making good headway, but was stopped towards the end of June by the recall of the two officers responsible. Mr. Wolfe shortly afterwards described the situation to Mr. Kellaway as follows :—

"A strong protest against the introduction of payment by results on a national scale has been entered by the unions. We have given an undertaking that we will not attempt this, and there is little doubt that what was done by the Admiralty Shipyard Labour Department in this respect, while perfectly justifiable and necessary, tended to create unrest. At the same time, particularly in aircraft, it is essential that some progress in this direction should be made, and we have found that by introducing payment by results quietly and locally, we have been able to accomplish a great deal. We have rather suspended work in this respect for the moment, and we shall be glad to have a decision to enable us to go forward."[2]

IX. Departmental Policy, 1918.

The issue of the Skilled Time-workers' Order, giving a 12½ per cent. advance, threw on the Wages Section an immense volume of work of application and interpretation.[3] It also imposed on the section the necessity of renewing, or rather increasing, its efforts, by personal propaganda and assistance as well as through correspondence, to extend payment by results. The necessity arose from two causes. On the one side the workpeople, in many cases in which piece-rates or bonuses were not very remunerative, decided that the enhanced time-rates were preferable and demanded a reversion to time-work, while in other cases they demanded a revision of piece-rates or bonuses to maintain the relative advantage of their position over time-work.

---

[1] *Wages Section Report*, 8 June, 1917.
[2] L.R. 139/204. Cf. *A.S.E. Journal*, July, 1917, p. 11. " A guarantee has been secured from the Ministry of Munitions not to press the demand for a general adoption of payment by results in all trades and districts." (Executive Council's report on negotiations re the Munitions of War Bill).
[3] See below, Chap. VI.

The employers on their side had a new incentive to extend payment by results, since by so doing they would avoid the necessity of paying the 12½ per cent. and secure additional output for additional payment ; even where economy in wages was not a sufficient motive employers were glad to avoid the invidious task of discriminating between one class of worker and another.

The Department used its influence to oppose any reversion to time-work and took the opportunity to install collective bonuses and substitute true bonuses on output, payment of which was contingent on and bore some relation to increase in output, for the fixed bonuses which had become common. Thus in the Manchester district, where there was great unrest among the lower paid piece-workers and among classes of skilled men who were excluded from the new bonus by reason of some small bonus on output, and in several cases where tool-room operatives were paid a fixed percentage over time-rates as " piece-time rates," an officer of the Department spent a good deal of time devising schemes of bonus on output, and, when the 7½ per cent. bonus to piece-workers made it necessary, revising these schemes. The schemes were generally entrusted to the supervision of a permanent bonus committee, representative of workpeople and management, whose function in supervising the scheme tended to stimulate interest in the production of the firm and to smooth over difficulties generally.[1] The Manchester Engineering Employers' Association preferred straight piece-rates to collective bonus ; but the workers were opposed to piece-rates in the tool-room. The Department had no strong prejudices either way, so long as the spread of fixed bonuses irrespective of output was stopped.[2] In the Midlands about the same time, it is noted, the Department endeavoured to use the grant of the 12½ per cent. to encourage the substitution of genuine output bonuses for the system of guaranteed percentage bonus that was becoming common in the district. They ruled that the existence of an " output bonus " with a guaranteed minimum of 25 per cent. was to be regarded as a fixed bonus such as disqualified for the 12½ per cent. bonus, and intimated that if the parties would substitute for this a bonus that rose and fell freely with the output, they would be regarded as qualified for the 7½ per cent.[3]

The Department looked to the spread of output bonuses to secure for it an increased effort that would correspond with the increase in wages, which became inevitable when the leaving certificate was abolished and labour became free to exploit its opportunities. Collective bonuses were preferred, since they went some way towards meeting the worker's traditional objection to ordinary piece-rates and premium bonus. At the same time it was recognised that a satisfactory collective bonus was even more difficult to devise than individual piece-rates, and cases occurred of schemes being dropped at the end of an experimental period because they cost too much or yielded too little. " The drawing-up of a good bonus scheme," the Section Report points out, " is in

---

[1] *Wages Section Report*, March, 1918.
[2] *Wages Section Report*, April, 1918.
[3] *Wages Section Report*, March, 1918. See below, Chap. VI.

reality a matter which would require weeks, if not months, of careful study, and it could hardly be expected that officers of the department in their hasty visits can be sufficiently acquainted with all the circumstances to design schemes with uniform success. It is remarkable how few employers have given serious thought to the question of stimulating output by methods of remuneration, and how few are capable of thinking out a successful scheme for themselves without assistance."[1] In this, as in other departments of its work, either the functions of the Wages Section were too large or its staff was too small.

The problem which the Skilled Time-worker's Order was intended to solve was created by the extension of systems of payment by results to occupations and processes in which a reliable basis in experience for fixing rates or base times did not exist. Rates yielding abnormal earnings to workers of a slight degree of skill were the inevitable result of such an extension, and it was impossible to deal with the problem as it arose on account of the pledge to maintain piece-rates once fixed. The employers who had been so anxious to extend payment by results endeavoured to meet the problem by a further extension. Opposed to any extension of the Ministry's power to fix wages, which was the correlative, they considered, of the Ministry's duty to insist on dilution and should therefore be confined to the wages of "dilutees," and fearing the extension of any special bonus granted until it covered all time-workers, they sought to restrict the concession to workers who had had the opportunity of working on "some system of payment by results and had refused to take it." Mr. Wolfe pointed out that such a provision would be, in effect, to make payment by results compulsory, and the Ministry refused to force by an indirect means a policy it had deliberately rejected on its merits.[2] When the propagandist work of the Wages Section was interrupted in July, 1917, the Department was beginning to consider the need of extending its statutory powers to fix the wages of skilled time-workers. The repeal of the leaving certificate section of the original Munitions of War Act, which had been decided on in June, made necessary some action to equalise the positions of the time-worker and the piece-worker. At this point the history of payment by results merges into the history of the $12\frac{1}{2}$ per cent. time-workers' bonus.

X. Some Questions of Principle.

(a) METHODS OF PAYMENT BY RESULTS.

There remains for consideration the question of principle involved in the extension to new processes of payment by results, and the issues which the Ministry was called on to decide.

Payment by results may, and during the war did, take a great variety of forms. Whatever form it took the object was the same— to stimulate the worker to larger production by making his remuneration depend more or less directly on his output. Under any system

---

[1] *Wages Section Report* for June, 1918.   [2] L.R. 139/193.

of remuneration, some relation between output and remuneration is assumed by the employer; but, whereas under time-rates the workman is assured of his hourly or weekly rate whatever the output resulting from his work, under payment by results his hourly or weekly earnings will fluctuate with his output. The applicability of payment by results obviously depends on the possibility of distinguishing the contributions of machinery and management, and of measuring and attributing to particular workmen the specific contribution of each. Where there is no difficulty in this, a price can be attached to each piece of work done, and the workman paid simply in proportion to the number of pieces done; this is the system of " straight piece-rates." But straight piece-rates are not always easy to adopt. The work of a group of men, or of all the workpeople in an establishment, may be so closely linked, that it is impossible to distinguish the specific contributions of each; some form of collective payment by results will then be the only alternative to time-rates. Or the work of an individual, although easily distinguished, may change frequently, so that it is difficult from want of experience to determine a piece-rate that shall at once offer an incentive to more than time-rate exertion without yielding a disproportionate reward to the increased exertion. The method by which this difficulty has been met has been to pay time-rates, and give a bonus on output supplementary to time-rates; the premium bonus system is a special variety of output bonus. Output bonus, like straight piece-rates, may be either individual or collective. These different systems may be explained in greater detail.

Straight piece-rates give satisfaction to both employers and workpeople where there is a large volume of work of a uniform and measurable character. The textile trades, and among munitions industries the boilermakers, normally work on a piece-list. The different classes of work have each their price; allowance is made for every variation in the operations performed; the " list " is established by collective bargaining for the district, or at least for a whole yard or factory; and no time-rates are guaranteed.

Where the work involves much repetition, but varies from worker to worker—so that uniform piece-rates cannot be negotiated for the whole establishment or the whole district—or the work changes frequently, to such an extent that the change involves the setting of a new price and cannot be met by a modification in the price for the previous job, there the system of output bonus is adopted. In ill-organised trades, it is true, straight piece-rates are employed; but where the trade union is strong, in such cases it either insists on time-rates alone, or makes a guarantee of the standard time-rate a condition of any system of payment by results.

(b) Premium Bonus System.

Of output bonus systems the premium bonus is the most interesting. Under this system a base-time is allowed for a job; then the worker is paid (a) his ordinary time-rate for the actual time he spends on the job, and (b) a further sum if he completes the job in less than the base-time; this further sum consisting of a proportion of his time-rate calculated on the difference between the time spent and the time allowed. A common proportion is 50 per cent.; under this a man rated at a shilling an hour, who did in three hours a job that was timed to take five hours, would be paid 3s. for the time spent, plus 1s. ($=$ 50 per cent. of the time saved), or 4s. in all. The effect of this system depends mainly on the fixing of the base-time. If the base-time is simply the time actually required by an average worker at time-rate speed, then the worker, although he can increase his remuneration by increasing his output, does not increase his remuneration *in proportion to* his increased output. If the premium were 100 per cent., the system would be equivalent to straight piece-rate; if it is less than 100 per cent. it amounts to an automatic reduction of the piece-rate as the output is increased. If, however, the base-time, after careful calculation of the time actually required by an average worker at time-rate speed, were fixed at something above this actual time, then the average worker would be assured of a bonus even if he did not exceed his time-rate output, and a bonus on the time saved of less than 100 per cent. could be justified. The fixing of the base-time above the time actually required, would guarantee a rate of payment higher than ordinary time-rate on all output below the point at which bonus became payable, and the employer would recover what he paid for this by paying at a lower rate for any output in excess of normal.

The spread of the premium bonus system would seem however to be due, not to any exact calculation of probabilities of this kind, but to its superficial advantages to both parties. The workman is attracted by the possibilities of augmenting his earnings without apparently risking his time-rate. The advantage to the employer is that the method allows a margin for error in fixing the base-time or piece-rate; a slight error in calculating the base-time (the alteration of which could not be effected without trouble) is not so serious when the bonus payable on the time saved is only 50 per cent. of the worker's time-rate, while it might be serious if he were paid straight piece-rates. For the same reason the system does not give rise to variations in earnings as great and disconcerting as result from straight piece-rates in trades where the precise estimate of probable output is difficult.

A special variety of the premium bonus system acquired considerable favour during the war, probably because it was particularly effective in levelling down inequalities in earnings. This was the Rowan system. Under this system the bonus payable varies with the output, the formula being

$$\text{bonus} = \frac{\text{time saved}}{\text{time allowed}} \times \text{time spent.}$$

In other words, hourly wages for the time spent are increased by 10 per cent. for every 10 per cent. saving on the time allowed. The object of the ordinary premium bonus system was to eliminate the necessity of cutting rates, by making it impossible for the workman to earn very much in excess of his hourly rate. This object the Rowan system attains with much more certainty. Under it the workman can never earn double-time (since that would mean that he had saved *all* the time allowed, and done the job in no time) ; the bonus increases (though at a diminishing rate), until the time saved is half the time allowed, after which it decreases. If the time-rate basis be ignored, and the relation of payment to output alone be considered, it will be seen that there is justification for the description sometimes given of the Rowan system ; " The rate automatically cuts itself."[1]

(c) OUTPUT BONUSES.

Another type of payment by results that may be mentioned is the differential piece-rate or bonus recommended by the advocates of scientific management. Under their system the timing of jobs is done with great care, the process being divided into unit operations and a time fixed for each of these ; by this method a standard time or output which should be attained without difficulty by the normal worker following instructions is established. On Mr. F. W. Taylor's system, when this output is reached the worker is paid at a higher piece-rate ; on later systems, which employ a modified form of premium bonus instead of piece-rates, the bonus jumps to a higher level at this point. The differential rate or bonus is intended to afford the stimulus necessary to induce the worker to bring his output or speed up to the pre-established standard ; the workman usually regards it as an arbitrary interference with the fundamental principle that remuneration for uniform work should be at uniform rates.

Scientific management as a system has not been adopted widely in this country. The method of detailed time-study by which it finds a basis for wages has however, been applied in a good many cases to the fixing of base-times for premium bonus with good results ; especially is the effect on relations good when the workpeople are given access to the materials on which a rate or base-time is fixed.[2] The device of offering a special incentive to induce the workpeople to attain a given level of output is a common principle in output bonus schemes. If an output bonus varies directly with output, it is equivalent to straight piece-rates with a guaranteed time-wage. Usually, however, the bonus does not vary directly, being adopted for the very reason that a satisfactory basis for piece-rates cannot be devised, and in consequence output bonus schemes have usually an element of arbitrariness in them.

---

[1] Abstract economic theory would seem to require that a bonus on additional output should not be at less than the hourly rate for normal output (as on all systems of premium bonus), but at a higher rate. The " disutility " of labour increases, so that increasing rewards would seem to be needed to overcome the disability. Examples of such increasing bonuses did occur during the war. (C.E. 488/4.) They were discontinued, because the high earnings of the workers under it caused discontent among the other workers in the firm.

[2] Cf. testimony by the delegate of the A.S.E. to a Manchester firm which had adopted the methods of scientific management. (National Advisory Committee Minutes.)

The systems of payment by results reported to the Ministry of Munitions have been analysed by the Intelligence and Record Section.[1] The output bonuses given are very numerous and based on a variety of principles. Some vary directly with output; the majority do not. The bonus in some cases increases as output increases, more frequently it decreases; sometimes the Rowan system was applied collectively. In many cases the bonus proceeds by a series of jumps, which may have been designed to lead the worker on from height to height in the curve of output. The variations are, however, frequently difficult to explain on any principle. While the bonus as a rule was a substitute for piece-rates, a bonus was in some cases given in addition to piece-rates as an incentive to reach a particular output, which, it was calculated, the factory should achieve. The bonuses were mainly "overhead" or collective bonuses; group, department, and works being taken as the unit in different cases.

The chief difficulties encountered were, first, to find a measure of output that would be fair both to the worker and to the firm; secondly, to establish a base time for the bonus that would provide an incentive to increased production without making it so easy to earn high wages that output was discouraged; and thirdly, to determine the basis of division among participants. To meet the first difficulty weight of output was sometimes adopted, but was satisfactory only in certain foundries; elsewhere, invoice value of product was taken, but this introduced into the problem of wages the factor of market fluctuations, and also subjected the worker's income to influences—ability of management and the like—over which he had no control; in other cases an attempt was made to estimate the relative importance of the firm's principal products, and allow a conventional value to each; or the bonus was made to depend on the relation between labour-cost and output value. It cannot, however, be said that any satisfactory basis, capable of general application, was discovered. The second difficulty was a difficulty that attached to all attempts to institute payment by results where there was little experience to go on. Just as individual piece-rates often yielded very large returns, so overhead bonuses often led to unexpected results. The third difficulty consisted in the difficulty of deciding the relative importance of different classes of workers in increasing a factory's output. On the one hand an overhead bonus had the advantage of enabling indirect producers—foremen, the important class of tool-makers, in one case sanctioned by the Ministry, welfare workers—to participate in the reward of increased production; on the other hand it was difficult to find a ratio of division which would satisfy the participants. Distribution in accordance with time-rate earnings was perhaps the most successful method.

In spite of the difficulties involved, collective output bonuses were widely adopted. This was due probably to two reasons: first, that an overhead bonus was possible where the unit of product was so large

---

[1] Completed and published when the section was transferred to the Ministry of Labour after the Armistice.

or the nature of the work so varied that individual payment by results was impracticable; and, secondly, that an overhead bonus did not give rise to the wide variations in earnings that individual bonuses or piece-rates did, where experience of fixing rates was limited and rates once fixed could not be cut. In addition it was claimed that an overhead bonus had a valuable influence in developing the team-spirit in a firm, and the directors of certain firms with successful systems pressed the claims of the overhead bonus as a remedy for the industrial unrest of the last eighteen months of the war.

The revision and sanctioning of output bonus schemes became an important and difficult part of the work of the Wages Section of the Ministry. The section encouraged collective bonuses, without insisting on them where individual bonuses or piece-rates were preferred. It endeavoured to insist that when a bonus was given at all it should afford a direct incentive to output, and not merely "jump" the district rate. It aimed also at separating output bonuses from timekeeping bonuses and other conditional grants, and, of course, at examining all complaints, and, if necessary, securing redress, when an individual thought that he was being deprived of some payment which was his due. The cases with which it had to deal under this head were one proof among many that simplicity and intelligibility are desirable features in any system of payment by results, a principle often ignored by production managers whose judgment was subtle rather than sound. Many of the systems in operation involved a great deal of clerical labour in the calculation of individual earnings, and the Department's officers, when advocating an output bonus, were on more than one occasion met by the reply that the firm could not afford the necessary clerical labour. Still greater was the difficulty in the shortage of men that marked the last year of the war, of introducing individual payment by results where there was any great variety of work.

(d) Opposition of Trade Unions.

The attitude of the trade unions towards payment by results is indicated in the negotiations that have been summarised. It was one of opposition to any extension at the expense of time-rates. This opposition was grounded in the fear that the security of the wage-earner's income would be jeopardised by any departure from the simplicity of standard hourly rates, a fear that expressed itself in the main in three ways. In the first place it was believed that rate-cutting was the invariable sequel to the introduction of piece-work or premium bonus into a field hitherto occupied by time-work. The Government's pledge doubtless prevented any overt cutting of rates; but the introduction of a clause making it specifically illegal in the Amendment Act of 1917 is evidence that the pledge had not been sufficient, and the discussions over the Bill revealed the suspicions of the workers. While an overt cutting of rates might not be attempted, any modification in the means or method of production enabled the employer to re-open the question and led, the men believed, to disproportionate cuts in the rate. The complexity of certain systems of payment by results, which the men did not understand, was a further cause of suspicion, and the premium bonus system, which withheld a portion of the return to increased output, and specially the Rowan system, which automatically reduced the return, gave further cause for fear.[1]

Employers in the early months of the war admitted that rate-cutting had been practised and was a cause of restriction of output. Later, they protested against the hard and fast rule that no rate once fixed should be cut unless there was a substantial change in conditions of production, on the ground that many rates had been fixed on very limited experience, or taken direct from Woolwich, which turned out to be far more remunerative than could have been expected. The Department admitted the difficulty, and regularly urged the need of experimental periods before rates were finally fixed; but the difficulty arose from the nature of the work, and the rate-fixer's mistakes pointed either to a large measure of truth in the workman's contention that the work was not suitable for payment by results, or else for the need of some different machinery for price-fixing.

The fixing of rates was a constant source of difficulty. The rate-fixer was the employer's agent, and although nominally a rate represented a mutual agreement, the advantages of knowledge and experience were all on the side of the rate-fixer[2].

District price-lists, such as obtained in the textile industries or boiler-making, were impossible at first owing to the variety of the work; even shop-lists were usually impracticable; individual arrangements were the result. As the volume of repetition work increased, district lists might have been devised. In the case of shell and projectile factories some approach to uniformity was made, and payment by results worked without friction. But no systematic attempt to draw up district or national lists was made. It was felt increasingly by workmen, and admitted by some employers, that some joint

---

[1] It should however be stated that many instances were quoted before the Committee on Production of antagonism to the premium bonus system which disappeared after experience.

[2] The working of the system under good conditions, but still from the point of view of the management, with no approach to "joint control" was thus described to the Committee on Production by a representative of Messrs. Beardmore, of Glasgow, in a premium bonus case in December, 1916. "Whenever we have introduced the premium bonus system, we have a special staff told off for this work. They are men selected as far as possible from the craft over which they are fixing rates. They are selected with a very great deal of care as being highly efficient tradesmen with some slight knowledge of arithmetic, in fact men who have not allowed themselves to go rusty since they left school. They estimate the times that it would take a man of average ability to do a certain piece of work—not the time that the quickest man would take or the slowest, but just a man of average ability. To that is added 50 per cent. and that is the time given to the workman to work upon and it is termed the basis time. Whatever the man saves from this time he shares with the firm." There was, he explained, a right of appeal from the rate-fixer to the chief rate-fixer and thence to the manager; but this right was very rarely used.

system of fixing rates, by which employers and employed were represented equally, should be devised. This was proposed during the discussions of the piece-rates clause of the Munitions Act of 1917, but no such provision was inserted, owing to the opposition of employers.[1] Both the men's and women's Trade Union Advisory Committees repeated the demand in 1918.

The fear that rates would be cut, the suspicion of complicated systems, the objection to existing methods of rate-fixing all sprang from a fundamental doubt whether standard rates, fixed by collective bargaining, could be maintained, if payment by results were permitted. Payment by results as practised in the engineering and aircraft industries cut across the practice of collective bargaining. Wages came to depend on a multitude of individual bargains, conditioned by innumerable variations in the kind of work, method and means of production, class of worker and the like. A guarantee of the standard time-rate, a definite arrangement that piece-rates or bonus times should be fixed to yield a definite percentage over time-rates, and care in the fixing of rates and times, might do much to conserve wages standards and remove the worker's fears; but these were not general, and, even if they had been, would have given no security that the fixing of wages by a multitude of individual arrangements would not have led sooner or later to a divergence of earnings, a breach in the solidarity of the group, and the disappearance of the district standard. Time-rates had the overwhelming advantage of simplicity.

The relation between piece-work earnings and time-rates where piece-work was in force went far to justify the workers' fears. No recognised proportion between piece-prices and time-rates was established in the country as a whole. Thus at Birmingham, shell machinists might be making double time, while the machine tool-workers on old established systems of piece-work earned barely time and a quarter.[2] At Manchester[3] a joint inquiry held by Mr. Mackenzie and Mr. Isaac Mitchell in February, 1917, after a disputed award of the Committee on Production, obtained the following returns for the earnings of some 9,000 piece-workers in the town :—

		Earnings above day rate.
530 men	(7.6 per cent)	12½ per cent. and under.
2,087 ,,	(30.6 per cent.)	12½ to 25 per cent.
2,730 ,,	(39.4 per cent.)	25 to 33⅓ per cent.
1,567 ,,	(22.6 per cent.)	over 33⅓ per cent.

A considerable number of the last class were on exceptionally important, hard or laborious work—such as smithy workers, who were allowed in some districts, according to the Amalgamated Society of Engineers' representative, to earn up to double time. Rates were specially low among most of the " exceptionally capable employees "

---

[1] See above, p. 50, and Chap. V, Sect. 6.
[2] C.E. 1031/4.
[3] Committee on Production Hearing, 11 April, 1917.

of the machine tool firms in the city, and also among the older locomotive shops and the textile engineers. Piece-work rates had been fixed in these trades for many years, but had been gradually " nibbled at," so that the surplus, if any, above the time rate was " hardly worth raising a hand for." " I have known," said the same delegate, " machine tool firms, whose highly skilled men work five hundred hours to draw a balance of 5d. over and above their day ratings."

It was said that conditions were exceptional at Manchester ; but experience in the older engineering shops of the Midlands did not predispose skilled workmen in favour of payment by results.[1] Objections might also be due to the high time-rates accessible for some sorts of war-work (as at Coventry where many firms paid above the district rate). Thus it was said that at the firm of Crossley Motors, Manchester, where the men were paid at time and a quarter on day rate, they did not want piece-work without a guaranteed minimum greater than the district rate.[2]

While fears for the standard rate were the important ground of opposition, there was frequent reference to other grounds. In the wood-working trades, where the handicraft tradition is perhaps stronger than in any other branch of great industry, it was argued that payment by results was inimical to good workmanship.[3] Generally, there was a fear of undue speeding up which combined with the resentment at being forced or tempted to do inferior work to make some of the most

---

[1] Committee on Production Hearing, 11 April, 1917.

[2] *Ibid.*

[3] The following extract from the *Journal of the Amalgamated Society of Carpenters and Joiners* gives a further illustration of the grounds of opposition to the system. " We submit that employers who desire to have the best class of craftsmanship put into any kind of joinery work, never request joiners to adopt premium bonus and piece-work systems, because all men recognise that either .... system inevitably leads to " rushing " and therefore necessarily " scamping " work, and consequently the demoralising effect in the long run hinders, instead of assisting, in increasing the output of the genuine craftsman's production. It is a well-known fact that much of the war-work produced on the premium bonus and piece-work systems has to be overhauled and rectified by men employed on the hourly system. ... It was during the year 1892 that our society decided to abolish piece work in our trade. Time has proved that the step then taken was in the interests of our craft as a whole, and we cannot now go back to the old·position simply because a few employers have pleaded that they do not get the maximum amount of production under the present method of payment. We, as craftsmen, must recognise that the employer desires quantity—without any regard for quality—when he speaks about introducing premium bonus or piece-work, and we must see that, whilst giving of our best as regards output, quality of work must be maintained, not only in our own interests but also in the interests of those who pay for and receive the products of our handicraft." (*Journal*, February, 1917, pp. 104–105.) The writer was considering shipbuilding and housebuilding, but the same arguments were reiterated with regard to aircraft. When this argument was put before the Employers' Advisory Committee, Mr. Allan Smith pointed out that bad workmanship was just as possible on time-rates and that employers did not find it any more practicable to omit inspection under time-rates than under payment by results,

skilled workers resist payment by results.[1] And a great deal of trouble was due to an incident of the system, which it was hard to avoid when the unit of work was large. This was the system of deferred piece-work balances. If a man were starting on a job which would last as much as two or three months, and would undertake to do it for a lump sum, he would draw his weekly wage till the job was finished, and might at the end find, if he had misjudged his time originally, that he was in debt to his employer.

Trade union representatives before the Committee on Production referred bitterly to the system of debit balances, which might leave a man permanently in debt (£70 in one case quoted) to his firm.[2] Or a mistake might be made the other way. At one time relations were strained in a Manchester armament works because the management were trying to induce the workpeople in one department to refund £130 paid in excess on account of piece-work balances through an error of a wages clerk, while workpeople in other departments were claiming a balance of £946 as due to them.[3] The model Wages Orders for women issued by the Ministry forbade the accretion of any debit balances.

(e) Difficulties of Settling Piece-Rates.

These objections, however, were incidental and could doubtless have been overcome, if the danger to collective bargaining and standard rates could have been removed; but that danger was inherent in the attempt to substitute payment by results for time-work. Time-work survived before the war in the main only where the work involved so frequent a change of product or method that a basis for payment by results was difficult to establish. The difficulty was one of measurement. Repetition work of a uniform character is easy of measurement, and experience makes it possible to adjust piece-prices so accurately that uniform remuneration for uniform effort is assured. In a textile piece-list all the factors that can influence output are set forth and allowance made for each. In engineering and most wood-work before the war there was no basis for such exact provision, and the worker

---

[1] The embittered statement by an A.S.E. representative before the Committee on Production, 11 April, 1917, illustrates the standpoint of the time-worker. "Ever since I can remember we have resented piece-work in the trade as it interferes with the technical ability of the man, because he is always more concerned about his prices than the real technical labour he is putting into his work.... The piece-worker is the keenest watched man in the trade; he is watched for output. Special men are employed to stand over him and see that the production is really every item that it is possible for a human being to put out. The output of a piece-worker really represents a man's limit, and employers of labour realise that.". . . "We will say a man has put in his best work, and he knows what time a job is going to take under ordinary circumstances to produce; then he finds ways and means of increasing the rapidity of production by attaching things to his machine and so simplifies the method of production, and, after all, instead of being complimented and compensated for his genius, he is punished by his price being lowered. This is continually done; it is the general workshop rule."

[2] Committee on Production Hearing, 11 April, 1917.

[3] Wages Section Report, April, 1918.

preferred the rough justice of time-rates, which were simple and could be upheld. Time-study, the resolution of complex processes into units, and the keeping of detailed records of jobs, might in time provide a basis for payment by results as exact as that embodied in a textile piece-list; but the empirical methods of the ordinary rate-fixer were as far removed as possible from anything of this sort; while the high rates in many cases fixed and the preference of employers for methods, like the Rowan system, which cover up the mistakes of the rate-fixer, are sufficient to show that the problem of measurement had not been solved. Even where the rate-fixing was scientific and an effort was made to allow for every factor that could influence output and earnings, the result was not satisfactory, because the process by which his wages were fixed became incomprehensible to the worker. He would need a professional expert agent to act for him, as the trade union official in the cotton industry acts for his members, and the area over which piece-lists or bonus times usually operate is hardly wide enough in engineering and wood-working industries to make the employment of specialised full-time officials for this work economical.

Even if the measurement of work had been achieved and the adjustment of prices to operations settled, the relatively frequent change of work complicated the problem. Payment by results on the whole caused little trouble in the case of the semi-skilled workers engaged on the routine repetition work connected with the shaping, assembling and filling of shells and shell parts. But skilled labour was too scarce to be left undisturbed at routine work; new rates had constantly to be fixed, and on occasion men had to be taken from remunerative piece-work and put on less remunerative but more important time-work. Such changes were difficult to effect, and the unions' claims to a joint settlement in each case, however difficult it might be to meet it in practice, was natural enough.

Allied to this difficulty was the difficulty of adjusting the wages of direct and indirect producers. Indirect producers (*i.e.* overlookers, setters-up, toolroom workers, general labourers) might do more than any other class to hold up or to accelerate the work of the plant; yet their work was usually of a nature hardly specialised enough, except in the largest plants, to permit of individual payment by results. The great advantage claimed for overhead bonuses was that it enabled the case of these workers to be met; but an increase in the time-rates of the more important of them was the device preferred by the Government when a decision could not be deferred. An overhead bonus to indirect producers, whether based on the output of the factory as a whole or on the piece-work balances of direct producers or on the total earnings or the output of direct producers—and all these methods were tried—had the defect that it made their remuneration dependent, not directly on their own efforts which it is the main object of payment by results to effect, but on the efforts of someone else.[1]

---

[1] A case, detected and stopped by the Department, may be worth noting, where a rate-fixer's bonus rose with the piece-work balances of the direct producers under him until these reached 25 per cent. of their time-ratings, but declined if their balances went above 25 per cent. C.E. 5172/4.

The trade union attitude towards payment by results during the war was consistent with its attitude before the war. It has been noted above that it is by no means the normal policy of unions to object to payment by results; many recognise it, and some insist on it. The attitude and policy of the unions depend on the nature and condition of the work. If the work is of a uniform and measurable character, so that a piece-list will ensure uniform remuneration for uniform effort, trade union policy will be directed to framing standard piece-lists; where the work involves a frequent change of product and method and piece-rates could be arranged only by a multitude of individual bargains, trade union policy will be directed to establishing and maintaining standard time-rates. In both cases the object is the same —the establishment of a uniform rate for the labour of the members, and the protection of it by collective bargaining. It happened that the Ministry of Munitions was brought most into contact with unions that preferred time-work; but that was because the engineering and woodworking trades, with which it had most to do, were, before the war, trades in which repetition work on a large scale was still the exception. The war resulted in a great extension of this kind of work, and the unions, especially the woodworking unions, in opposing a corresponding extension of payment by results were adhering to the letter and neglecting the spirit of their own principle. The employers' unqualified insistence on the need for payment by results provoked and in part excused their attitude.

(f) POLICY OF THE DEPARTMENT.

The situation then with which the Ministry of Munitions found itself faced in 1916, was one in which no policy would have avoided provoking dissatisfaction in some quarter. The change in the character of work in the engineering and woodworking trades made an extension of payment by results possible, while the growing shortage of labour in relation to the country's needs made it desirable. But payment by results was disliked by the workpeople, and regarded with suspicion by the unions in the trades in which the extension of it was most desired, and the attempt to secure formal agreement to it on the part of the trade union officials and executives, as agreement had been secured to dilution and the suspension of the right to strike, failed. Nevertheless, a great extension of payment by results was secured by the activity of employers, who had the sympathy and support of the department; the new repetition work was done mainly on some system of payment by results, and some extension of the principle was achieved even with the more skilled and varied operations.

The result showed that something more was needed than employers propaganda, departmental support, and even trade union approval, if the new methods of remuneration were to prove a success. The piece-lists of the textile industries, the tonnage rates of coal and iron trades, the collective agreements in the printing and boot and shoe industries, are the outcome of a generation or more of experiment. They represent, therefore, an exact adjustment of remuneration to work, which ensures a fair uniformity of remuneration and, while permitting exceptional industry or skill to earn exceptional wages, does not exaggerate individual differences, and allows no opening for the irrational, unjustified and disconcerting variations that follow inevitably from careless and inexperienced setting of piece-rates. In the engineering and woodworking trades there were few established piece-lists, and the work to which payment by results was extended during the war was much of it new or conducted under conditions so novel that previous experience was misleading. Even if all the conditions had been favourable to the introduction of payment by results in these trades—and the contemporary problems created by dilution, the rise in the cost of living and the increasing pressure of war demands made the conditions as unfavourable as they well could be—the task would still have been more difficult than in any of the old-established piece-work trades, because the work was so much more various.

Gradually a policy was shaped that embodied the experience of the best employers, and met many of the difficulties of the situation. At Barrow, after a strike due to the alleged cutting of rates, a successful scheme of control by a joint committee met some of the difficulties of rate-fixing. The same principle was applied elsewhere,[1] and was approved in principle by both unions and employers.[2] Local agreements of the engineering trades contained a provision that time-rates should be guaranteed. The Ministry's Women's Wages Orders, issued after prolonged consultations with employers and unions, carried the systematisation of payment by results still further. The Wages Section's power to require controlled establishments to submit all changes in wages for its sanction, became an important factor in the control of methods of remuneration as the class of controlled establishments grew in number. The section and the Ministry's local officials were also able to exercise a considerable influence by their advice. The policy of the Department, therefore, as expressed in the views of the section, may be taken as summing up the experience of the war.[3] The points insisted on were that there should be an experimental period before rates were fixed, and the pledge to maintain rates became operative, that time-rates should be guaranteed, that there should be some definite relation between piece-rates and time-rates, and that rates should be settled by full and sincere consent. The last was the most important point; the exact machinery did not matter so long as the workman was placed in a position to insist on his right to an equal voice in the determination of his rate; the complete fulfilment of the condition, however, would have required a drastic revision of the organisation and methods of his union.

These conditions were not fulfilled when the extension of payment by results began. The full effects of inexperience were felt, and the Government's pledge to prevent cutting of rates deprived employers of

---

[1] *e.g.* At the Phœnix Dynamo Company, Bradford (L.R. 3254/15).
[2] Cf. Employers' Advisory Committee Minutes (L.R. 5581).
[3] Cf. L.R. 139/40.

their usual resource in covering a mistake. The high earnings of pieceworkers represented so many mistakes in rate-fixing. If rates were not to be cut—and everyone agreed, when the pledge to prevent this was given, that the pledge was necessary—the old relations between the earnings of different grades of workpeople were bound to be upset. In the old-established piece-work industries like cotton, the relations between the earnings of different grades are as stable as in time-work industries. In the engineering trades by the middle of 1917, the extension of payment by results had relatively degraded the most skilled workers with the paradoxical result that the most essential work was the worst paid. The problem of the skilled time-worker was the inevitable outcome of the hasty extension of payment by results in time-work trades, and was only the most striking instance of a general dislocation of normal relations between the different classes and grades of worker. When allowance is made for the influence on production of the resentment, the friction and the unrest that this dislocation led to, a very serious debit must be placed against the increase in production that payment by results produced.

CHAPTER VI.
TIME WAGES AND THE "SKILLED TIME-WORKER" PROBLEM.

I. The Origin of the Problem.

The economic position of the skilled time-worker had became a problem before the Labour Department of the Ministry began its work in 1915. The great opportunities for repetition work afforded by munitions contracts enabled piece-workers to earn very considerably more than the more highly skilled time-workers, or than the "responsible" semi-skilled workers or labourers—enginemen, crane-drivers, etc.—who could not, if they wished, be placed on piece-work. Various complaints on this score reached the Department and the Committee on Production in the later months of 1915.

The enquiry into shell piece-rates at the beginning of 1916 referred to in a previous chapter was suggested by an application from the Wolseley Motor Company, Birmingham, for leave to change its piece-rates.[1] The firm stated that "semi-skilled men on shells earn £4 10s. a week; skilled men are getting from the toolroom into the shell factory among the semi-skilled, in order to earn the same wages."

Discontent among skilled workmen was reported periodically to the Department, especially from Sheffield, Birmingham and Coventry[2]. The Cabinet's "embargo" on a rise of wages in the early portion of 1916, and the Committee on Production's refusal of a series of applications for advances from skilled engineers[3] increased the time-workers' sense of injury.

On 1 March, a deputation from skilled day-workers at Sheffield waited on Dr. Addison, and explained the difficulty of their position and the need that they, who taught newcomers their work, should have increased rates. The average earnings of the skilled workers at Sheffield were a few months later, according to the Amalgamated Society of Engineers' representative at a hearing of the Committee on Production, £3 a week, whereas those of the semi-skilled workers (till lately "gardeners and coachmen") were at least £6.[4] Dr. Addison

---

[1] C.E. 1074/4.
[2] C.E. 1074/4, C.E. 1013/4, C.E. 541/4, CE. 847/4, C.E. 148/4.
[3] See Chap. III.
[4] Committee on Production Hearing, 9 August, 1916, on the claim of the Sheffield skilled engineers for an advance of 10s. a week. (The employers admitted the disparity of earnings between the two groups of workers, but as Sheffield had already the highest weekly rate (46s.) for fitters and turners in the country except in London, and as the cost of munitions had to be kept down, they could suggest no special remedy. The average earnings including much overtime were in May, 1916 in five local firms as follows :—

Fitters.	Turners	Slotters and Planers.
£ s. d.	£ s. d.	£ s. d.
3 12 0	3 6 0	3 0 5
2 17 9	3 13 0	2 18 0
3 7 0	3 11 8	3 6 0
4 1 0	3 15 9	3 0 9
3 17 9		

promised this deputation (the nucleus of a local organisation which asserted itself with much force subsequently) to appoint a small committee to visit Sheffield and go into the points raised by skilled day-workers and generally into the position with regard to dilution at Sheffield. This committee's report showed chiefly the complexity of the question and the need to deal with the time-workers' position nationally if at all.

From Coventry complaints turned on the position of the tool-room men, whose discontent at the higher earnings of piece-workers was affected, but not appeased, by the very different wages paid to their skilled workmen by different firms in their anxiety to attract and retain labour. In March and April two officers of the Wages Section (Mr. S. R. Davis and Mr. J. Murray) visited Coventry, " with a view to discovering if possible some means of standardising and stabilising the rates for this class of labour," and obtained statements of the actual rates paid. They subsequently visited Birmingham and other munition centres. The results of these enquiries were not very great. The Department was able to persuade a certain number of firms to experiment in granting a bonus on output to their tool-room workers. A few tried to introduce piece-work into their tool-rooms, but the great majority found this impracticable.[1] The mechanics in National Projectile Factories were so far as possible placed on systems of bonus on output, as these factories began work in the summer of 1916. Apart from this, the Coventry workers secured in June an advance of 12½ per cent. on their pre-war weekly rating of 38s.

In July the Committee on Production inaugurated its second cycle of advances, and gave an increase of 3s. a week to time-workers and premium bonus workers. Piece-workers received no advance. To some extent these awards improved the relative position of the time-workers, and employers, while vigorously opposing further advances to piece-workers, admitted before the Committee on Production that there was some justification for an advance on the grounds of cost of living to those on time-work. As the Amalgamated Society of Engineers' branches, however, were claiming 10s. a week advance for their members at the time, much discontent was expressed among the time-workers at the smallness of the results secured by arbitration.[2] The next general advance gave only 5s. a week in April, 1917, and both this advance and the two succeeding advances in 1917 applied equally to time and piece-workers. The 3s. awards of the late summer of 1916, therefore, represented, apart from extra payments for setting up, etc., or for teaching unskilled workers, the only relative gain of time-workers compared with piece-workers until late in 1917.

---

[1] Wages Section Reports, 3 and 18 March, and 1 April, 1916.
[2] *A.S.E. Journal*, September, October, November, 1916. October, 1916, page 32, Sheffield delegate's report. " A meeting has been held to consider the position of the day workers after the award of 3s. by the Committee on Production. After considerable discussion and great dissatisfaction at the smallness of the amount granted, it was decided to accept same for the present, but that an immediate demand should be placed for the balance of 7s. per week of our original demand of 10s. Resolutions were also passed calling upon the Government to take drastic steps to reduce the price of food-stuffs."

One result of their lower earnings was that tool-room workers were ready to work for very long hours (up to 80 or 90 a week on occasion) for at least the first two years of the war. The desire of the skilled workers to earn by overtime and Sunday work was given by various firms as a reason for not curtailing long hours, when this was proposed during the summer of 1916.[1]

II. Statutory Power to deal with the Problem.

The negotiations that led to the 1917 Amendment Act have been described in Chapter II. The disturbed industrial conditions of 1917 gave a new importance and urgency to the problem of the skilled time-worker. The Commission on Industrial Unrest, appointed after the engineering strikes in the spring, was instructed, in the terms of reference drawn up by Mr. Barnes, to enquire among other things into the alleged grievances of the skilled time-worker. Seven out of eight of the local Commissions set up under the main Commission recorded the opinion that the skilled time-worker's economic disadvantage was a fruitful cause of discontent; three of them recommended some supplementary payment to the skilled time-worker. The trade union representatives consulted in the negotiations over the Bill had also drawn attention to the grievance. Much more prominent, however, both in the Commission's reports and in the discussions over the Bill, was the objection to the leaving certificate system. As has been explained above,[2] the Ministry anticipated some of the recommendations of the Commission before they were published. It had decided to abolish the leaving certificate as part of the bargain embodied in the Amendment Bill, and the Department was carefully considering methods of meeting the time-worker's grievance. The findings of the Commission, however, constituted a weighty additional argument for the change. They formulated the munition worker's grievance with authority, and they were popularly taken to pledge the Government to action. Thus, when the members of the Amalgamated Society of Engineers rejected the proposed Bill,[3] it was politically impracticable to maintain the leaving certificate,[4] and the decision to abolish it was included by Mr. Barnes in his summary of the action taken to give effect to the Commission's recommendations, in the daily press, on 23 August.

Mr. Churchill, therefore, on assuming the Office of Minister of Munitions, found himself committed to action on the skilled time-workers' claims. The decision to abolish leaving certificates had been taken by the Cabinet, and the Ministry of Munitions was forced to devise some safeguard against a general movement of skilled men to less skilled but more remunerative piece-work, when they recovered their freedom to move. The first clause of the revised Bill was the safeguard adopted.[5]

---

[1] Vol. V. Part III, p. 101.   [2] Chap. II, Sect. 5.   [3] See above, p. 53.
[4] Cf. Minute by Mr. Kellaway in reply to memorandum by the chief officers of the Labour Department protesting against the abolition. See above, p. 53.
[5] See above, Chap. II, Sect. 6.

Mr. Churchill made it quite clear in conferences and in Parliament that this was the object of the powers taken by the new Act.[1]

> "There is another step which ought to be taken before the leaving certificates can be repealed. The swiftly developing conditions of labour during this war have led to the creation of great and invidious anomalies. We have seen—and there are numerous instances of it all over the country—highly skilled men, who have taught the others, working under time rates, at comparatively low wages, and who see side by side with them, in the same shop, newcomers whose skill, such as it is, has been hastily acquired, and who, on repetition work, and on non-repetition work, are earning wages far in excess of those paid to the skilled men. Let the Committee realise the seriousness of this. Supposing the leaving certificate provisions were abolished, while this anomaly remained unredressed, I am advised—and I believe I am rightly advised— that it might lead to a serious migration from the higher ranks of labour into the less highly skilled, though more highly paid, forms of labour."

General approval was expressed by the few speakers who took part in the debate on the committee stage of the Bill, Major J. W. Hills, who as chairman of the West Midland Commission into Industrial Unrest had heard many complaints about wages from the Birmingham district, in particular supporting the proposal.[2]

There was no debate on the proposed clause, which appeared as Section 1 of the Munitions of War Act issued six days later (21 August) in the following form.

> "(1) If at any time during the continuance of the present war the Minister of Munitions considers it necessary, in order to maintain the output of munitions, that directions should be given with respect to the remuneration to be paid for work (being munitions work or work in connection therewith or work in any controlled establishment) which at the time when the directions are given is paid at time rates, he may, subject always and without prejudice to any agreement made between employers and workmen with the consent of the Minister with respect to the remuneration of such work, by order give such directions with respect to the remuneration of such work as he may consider necessary for the purpose of the maintenance or increase of output.
>
> "(2) Any contravention of or non-compliance with any such directions shall be punishable in like manner as if the order in which the directions are contained was an award made in settlement of a difference under Part 1 of the Munitions of War Act, 1915, but where a difference has arisen respecting matters on which the Minister of Munitions has given directions under this section the difference shall be referred to a special arbitration tribunal

---

[1] *Parliamentary Debates*, 1917 (H. of C.), XCVII, 1305.
[2] *Parliamentary Debates*, 1917 (H. of C.), XCVII, 1316.

constituted under section eight of the Munitions of War (Amendment) Act, 1916.

" (3) Any directions given under this section may be varied from to time, but shall not continue in force after the termination of the present war."

Section 2 of the same Act gave powers to the Minister to repeal Section 7 of the Act of 1915, and measures were accordingly taken to withdraw the leaving certificate regulations from 17 October, 1917. This made it imperative to take action rapidly under Section 1.

While no criticism of the time-workers clause was made while the Act was passing through Parliament, the Employers' Advisory Committee protested against the Ministry's proposals when consulted by the Ministry in the six weeks during which the Act was under consideration. On 6 July they urged that great industrial unrest would be caused by the difficulty of determining what time-workers were to be entitled to an extra rate proportionate to the earnings of piece-workers, and that a new rate would be required for every kind of worker in the Kingdom. On 17 July the committee returned to the subject. The employers' representatives would not offer any counter-proposals to those of the Ministry, beyond suggesting the reference of the question to the Committee on Production, leaving employers to deal with separate cases. Both Mr. Allan Smith and Mr. Marjoribanks (secretary and president of the Engineering Employers' Federation) pointed out that any regulation would affect practically all time-workers, skilled and unskilled.[1] The necessity in the interests of output of limiting any bonus to men who had not had the opportunity of going on to some system of payment by results, and the impossibility of confining a time-workers' bonus to highly-skilled men, were urged at a further conference on 10 August. A draft clause embodying the employers' views was submitted to the Minister on 14 August,[2] and considered by him in conference with his advisers on the same day.

The Department, however, as has been explained,[3] could not accept the attachment of compulsory payment by results to its proposal for the improvement of the time-workers' position.

---

[1] The management committee of the Engineering Employers' Federation expressed their views on the first draft of the time-workers clause to the following effect:

"The committee desire me to say that in their view much of the difficulty which has arisen is due to the inflated earnings of piece-workers, brought about by the refusal of the Minister to alter piece-work prices or premium bonus basis times, arranged under stress of circumstances, and manifestly unreasonable. As to the proposed clause, my committee are of the opinion that on the understanding that the Ministry have decided that some such powers are necessary to enable them to deal with difficulties which have arisen and which they anticipate will be accentuated with the repeal of section seven of the Munitions of War Act of 1915, the responsibility of any such action as is contemplated should rest on the Ministry." (L.R. 5581. L.R. 5581/4.)

[2] HIST. REC./R./340/6.
[3] See above, p. 58.

III. The Skilled Dayworkers' Committee.

(a) The Committee's Problem.

On 4 August, while clause 1 of the Amendment Bill was under discussion, Mr. Churchill appointed a representative committee with the following terms of reference :—

> "To enquire into and report upon the rates of skilled men on munition work employed on day rates, with special reference to the discrepancy between such rates and the earnings of less skilled men engaged under systems of payment by results, and the possible effect of this discrepancy in view of the decision to abolish the provisions of the Munitions Acts dealing with leaving certificates, with due regard to the public interest both in the matter of expense and of increasing the output of munitions of war."

The committee consisted of Major J. W. Hills, M.P. (chairman), four representatives of employers' organisations, four representatives of trade unions and four official representatives, two from the Ministry of Munitions and one each from the Shipyard Labour Department of the Admiralty and the Ministry of Labour. Mr. John Murray, of the Labour Regulation Department of the Ministry of Munitions, was secretary. The committee assembled at 6, Whitehall Gardens on 27 August, and met on nine subsequent occasions, for about forty hours in all. No verbatim record of the discussions was kept. The question before the committee was one which implied measurement both of the numbers affected by the grievance and of the degree of improvement to their pay required as a remedy for the discrepancy in earnings. Unfortunately, the statistical information available in the Department was meagre and inadequate. The committee did not summon witnesses, and no comprehensive or detailed returns were procured showing the earnings of time-workers and piece-workers or numbers of workers in different categories. The committee's proceedings resolved themselves into a consideration of claims and counter-claims.

The obvious problems before the committee were to define :—

(1) The class of workers to whom the proposed advance should apply,
(2) the extent of the advance,
(3) the conditions, if any, to be attached to the bonus.

These three problems came up at once for decision.[1]

(b) Proposals Submitted.

The first proposals were submitted by the employers, through Mr. Allan Smith, on 28 August. As in the negotiations over the Amendment Bill in July, they proposed to make it a governing condition that men who were given the opportunity by their employers of working on a system of payment by results, and who refused, should not participate in the proposed bonus. Subject to this condition, skilled men

---

[1] Memo. by Major J. W. Hills. (Copy in Hist. Rec./R./342/10.)

employed on time in shops where manufacturing was done mainly on systems of payment by results were to receive the following bonuses in addition to time-rates :—

Gauge makers, while employed finishing guages ; *i.e.*, beyond ·002 of accuracy	2d. per hour.
Jig makers	2d. per hour.
Cutting tool makers while employed finishing tools ; *i.e.*, beyond ·002 of accuracy	1½d. per hour.
Inspectors, Examiners and Gaugers	1¾d. per hour.
Markers off	1¾d. per hour.
Charge hands	1d. per hour in addition to usual Charge hand allowance.
Setters-up (others than those engaged on shell fuses, etc.)	from 2s. 6d. per week according to the number of machines under their charge and the skill and amount of supervision and teaching of workpeople required.
Skilled men engaged in maintenance and repair of plant and machinery and in the production of light, heat and power.	1d. per hour in addition to any special shop allowance.

Semi-skilled and unskilled men on day work who were working as regular and constant assistants to skilled men on a system of payment by results, should receive a portion of the bonus earned on the job proportionate to their day rate ; other skilled men on time-work, no bonus. The proposals did not apply to shipyards.

The trade union representatives strongly opposed these proposals. They claimed instead a general advance of 20s. a week on time rates to all time-workers, skilled and unskilled, and that the position of the skilled piece-worker not employed on repetition work should also be considered. This was essential if the shifting of labour after the abolition of leaving certificates was to be avoided.

On the following day the representatives of the Department submitted an alternative memorandum, insisting with less rigidity on the alternative of payment by results, and substituting an even percentage of 10 per cent. advance on earnings to the same classes of workpeople, in place of the previous more elaborate scheme.

" It is considered," they said, " that any advice that is tendered to the Minister in accordance with the terms of reference to the Committee, must not discourage but must encourage by every possible means the stimulation of the increase in output, and therefore some system of payment by results should be adopted wherever practicable, with the introduction of such safeguards as may be agreed between the parties concerned.

" That any proposals that may be made should be limited to the skilled men in accordance with the original terms of reference."

They proposed to extend the bonus to skilled men employed in the maintenance and repair of plant and machinery, and in the production of light, heat and power, and to give a bonus of 5 per cent. to workpeople in the selected categories when employed in shops engaged wholly on time-work, in which the discrepancy in earnings was practically non-existent. They suggested that the committee should also consider the desirability of a general advance to all skilled time-workers, and expressed the opinion that the stimulation of output referred to in the terms of reference could be achieved only by some system of payment by results.

To this also the trade union representatives took exception, repudiating any association of payment by results with the problem of the time-worker.

> "In reply to the memorandum of the Ministry of Munitions representatives," they wrote, "we cannot accept the view that the purpose for which this committee was constituted, has anything to do with Payment by Results, and we therefore protest against any attempt to use this Committee in order to enforce the general adoption of payments by results. We hold that the question of any change in the methods of remuneration must be dealt with locally as at present, by District agreement, and we believe that negotiations on this matter would be most effectively carried on through Trade Union workshop committees acting under the authority of the District Committee."

The trade unionists recommended an advance of 20 per cent. on their day rate to the class of workers for whom the official representatives had proposed 10 per cent., and 15 per cent. to those for whom the official representatives had proposed 5 per cent.; and they added that "all other classes of skilled time-workers should receive a special advance of 15 per cent. on the same terms."

Further detailed proposals were made by either side, on the days immediately following. The employers, however, in a revised version of their first draft, insisted on a clause to the effect that the 5 per cent. and 10 per cent. bonus which they now proposed "should not apply in cases where workmen had been given the opportunity of working on a system of payment by results." The trade union representatives on 4 September refused to discuss any detailed proposals so long as this clause remained part of the employers' proposals. The employers' representatives refused to withdraw the clause, regarding it as a fundamental condition. It was decided, therefore, that the chairman should see the Minister, taking with him the amended form of the proposals of both sides, with a view to resolving the deadlock.[1]

The official representatives in an accompanying memorandum urged that the Trade Union Advisory Committee should be consulted with regard to the "payment by results" stipulation, and that if the provision was dropped any advance given to day-workers should be substantially less than the 25 per cent. above time-rates normally earned as a minimum by piece-workers.[2]

---

[1] This interim report, with the final memoranda submitted by the two sides, together with that of the official members, is printed in Appendix V.
[2] See Appendix V, p. 253.

(c) THE DEPARTMENT'S VIEW.

In acknowledging Major Hills' report, Mr. Churchill noted that it was proposed that the State should bear the cost of any bonus, and asked for an estimate.[1] Mr. Larke submitted an estimate to the chairman, which gave the cost of the employers' proposals as £3,200,000 per annum (or £4,643,000 if certain classes whom it would probably be found impossible to exclude were brought in), and that of the trade unionists' proposals as £10,400,000 per annum. He noted that there were no accurate data for estimating the numbers of the different classes of workpeople affected; the employers' proposals were found to be ambiguous in detail when examined critically, and it would be necessary for the committee to formulate its proposals in more definite terms. He found the number of male munition workers, as shown by the returns of the Munitions Area Recruiting Offices, was about 2,500,000. A census of 23,000 firms, to whom war-service badges were issued in December, 1917, showed a proportion of skilled men of 56 per cent., and a return from controlled establishments, in July, 1917, of 52 per cent., or roughly half; but the employers' representatives in the committee advised that this proportion should be discounted by a third, in order to allow for the tendency of employers, who were interested in returning as many men as possible as skilled, to include as skilled anyone who could not be replaced by a substitute with three to six months' training. In round numbers, therefore, there would be 800,000 skilled men. Of these the committee estimated that half were on some system of payment by results, leaving 400,000 as the number of skilled day-workers. The average earnings of these was taken as £3 7s. a week: 15 per cent. on this gave the cost of the trade union proposals. The cost of the much more restricted and detailed proposals of the employers was reached by taking each category separately and estimating the numbers in it and their average earnings.

On receiving the committee's interim report Mr. Churchill referred it to "L" committee (the Ministry's Labour Committee, of which Sir Charles Ellis was at the time chairman). In a covering minute, on 6 September, he asked this committee to make an independent estimate of the cost involved, and summarised his view of the problem.

" There is an admitted case of grievance and injustice in the disparity of wages between time-rate workers and semi-skilled piece-rate workers, which it is desirable in itself to remedy if the State or the employer, or both, can afford it. When it was decided to abolish the leaving certificate, it was strongly felt that the mitigation of this anomaly should, in the interests of the Government and of national output, precede such abolition; and we therefore delayed the abolition of the leaving certificate until we could take the necessary steps to improve the wages of the skilled time-rate workers . . . I consider, therefore, that we are morally bound to improve the rates of the skilled time-worker. I do

---

[1] For the discussion of the committee's proposals by the Ministry see L.R. 5997/5.

not consider that we are bound to equalise them with those of the piece-worker. The amount of improvement must be decided with reference to the interests of the State, as it is clear that the Treasury and the Cabinet have the final word . . . It is evident that the interest of the State in making such an advance will be powerfully affected by the possibility of obtaining an increased output, and if a large expenditure of money is required without achieving any special advance in this direction, the State would not be gainers except in regard to the greater contentment afforded. I am beginning to be rather sceptical of the degree of the danger which was so strongly impressed upon me, that there would be a violent movement from skilled to semi-skilled labour if the leaving certificates were removed while the wage anomaly remained unmodified . . . "

The departmental committee, on 8 September, endorsed the estimates of cost submitted by Major Hills, deferred any suggestions as to the form any advance should take, and advised on the point at issue that the advance should not be limited by the conditions the employers proposed. Mr. Churchill accordingly, on 15 September, replied to Major Hills that "the employers' suggestion that the advances proposed should not apply in cases where workmen had been given the opportunity of working on a system of payment by results, should *not* be adopted." The Committee was desired to make fresh recommendations to the Minister on this basis.

The committee met again on 20 September. The employers' representatives protested that " in the interests not only of increased output, but even of the maintenance of output, the principle contained in clause 7 of their proposals was fundamental. This did not provide that work should be done on payment by results. It simply provided that if the workmen would not by increased output on suitable work increase his earnings, he should not receive consideration." They therefore refused to sign the final recommendations of the committee ; these were based on proposals worked out by the chairman, and were signed by the official and trade union members of the committee, with the exception of Mr. I. H. Mitchell, and were dispatched to the Minister on 22 September.[1]

The report offered the following answers to the triple problem presented to it at the outset :—

(1) It recommended the inclusion of a limited class of skilled engineers on time-work, excluding those engaged on shipbuilding.
(2) It recommended an advance ranging from 10 per cent. to 15 per cent. on earnings.
(3) It refused to attach to the bonus any conditions as to alternative methods of payment.

Mr. Barnes, with whom Major Hills discussed the report on 22 September, expressed his approval, and promised to recommend the Cabinet to accept it.

---

[1] The Report is printed in Appendix V, p. 254.

IV. Adoption of the 12½% Bonus.

(a) CONSIDERATION BY THE MINISTER AND THE DEPARTMENT.

The recommendations of the Hills' Committee were in the main adopted, but not until they had been considered in detail and modified both by the Ministry of Munitions and by the War Cabinet. There was no time for further deliberate consideration, since the pledge to abolish leaving certificates could not be deferred; on the other hand, premature decision might prejudice the Government's policy on other wages questions. An additional difficulty was the necessity of ascertaining the views and securing the consent of a number of independent Departments and other authorities. An attempt had been made to anticipate this difficulty by making the Hills' Committee representative; but the employers' and trade union representatives had failed to agree, while the adhesion of the other Departments concerned, the Admiralty and the Ministry of Labour, had not been fully secured. The representative of the Admiralty Shipyard Labour Department did indeed sign the report, but, as afterwards appeared, his signature did not carry with it the full concurrence of that department.[1] The Ministry of Labour representative neither signed the report not indicated dissent.

The issue was clarified somewhat by an inter-departmental conference on 8 October; but it was re-discussed *ab initio* at the Cabinet meeting of 12 October, and the decision of the conference of 8 October was reversed by the Cabinet committee to whom the final decision was left.

Mr. Churchill, on receiving the final report of Major Hills' Committee, referred it to the departmental committee of the Ministry of Munitions for advice. The great inherent difficulty in the recommendations was apparent—where to draw the line in granting an advance. The committee emphasized the indefinitely wide character of the proposals and the slippery slope down which they beckoned.

" The primary difficulty really centres round the impossibility of defining what is a skilled man. The committee feel that the problem which the Ministry originally endeavoured to solve was to adjust a bonus in such a way as :—

(a) to prevent the highly-skilled worker from leaving his work and going to better paid piece-work on repetition machines when section 7 is abolished, and

(b) to remedy the sense of injustice felt by the skilled man at the inadequate reward which he receives for his high degree of skill.

" The Committee are in considerable difficulty in view of the recommendation of Major Hills' Committee that the bonus should extend to all skilled men. It is felt that this extension goes much beyond the limits of either of the problems which it was originally intended to solve by this order as set out above. In addition, if the advances are so extended, the Committee feel that it will appear

---

[1] Proceedings of Inter-departmental Conference, 8 October (L.R.5997/5).

that the Ministry are usurping the authority of the Committee on Production, as such extension would amount to a general rise of wages for all skilled time-workers in the engineering trades, such as Coppersmiths, Sheet Metal Workers, Foundrymen, etc.

" Further, the Committee have had impressed upon them that a similar demand is almost certain to be made by semi-skilled men employed on time-work in munitions, and that it would be very difficult to resist in the long run a general 15 per cent. increase of wages for all time-workers employed on munitions. If it is admitted that this wide extension is undesirable, it remains to be determined at what point a line should be drawn."

They therefore submitted two alternatives to the Minister ; one, known as schedule A, a narrower scheme making an advance of 15 per cent. on time-rates, and confining it to tool-room, supervising and maintenance classes ; the other, schedule B, proposing 12½ per cent. and extending it to all the classes covered by the Hills Committee proposals and also moulders. The reason for including moulders was that they worked in close conjunction with engineers and usually had their wages regulated with those of engineers.

They strongly recommended Schedule "A."[1] It may be noted that the Wages Section of the Ministry had, on 21 September, while objecting to the bonus as unnecessary, urged that if it were granted it should be restricted to a narrow range of carefully defined occupations.

Mr. Churchill again asked for estimates of cost. The committee replied that a narrower schedule " A " would cover approximately 165,000 men and cost £3,765,000 a year, the wider schedule " B " 250,000 men and £5,700,000 ; if ship yard and iron and steel workers as well as engineering were included, the numbers would be 315,000 and 400,000 respectively, and the costs £6,565,000 and £8,500,000. Mr. Churchill discussed the alternatives with the committee and Major Hills, and decided provisionally in favour of the limited schedule. A draft order was accordingly prepared, but the schedule was recast, after informal discussion with employers and trade union representatives, to include only those who by the nature of their occupation were prevented from working on a system of payment by results. As recast the schedule, referred to as schedule " C," covered approximately 207,500 men, and would cost £5,440,000 per annum.

Before coming to a final decision, Mr. Churchill decided to confer on the matter with the Ministry of Labour and Mr. Barnes. The conference was held on 8 October. In addition to Mr. Churchill and other representatives of the Ministry of Munitions there were present Mr. Barnes, Major Hills, Sir David Shackleton (representing the Ministry of Labour), and Sir Lynden Macassey and Mr. McElroy (representing the Shipyard Labour Department of the Admiralty). Mr. Barnes raised the preliminary point, that any advance ought to be first approved by the Committee on Production ; Mr. Churchill objected that this would cause delay and dislocation and was not necessary in the case of

---

[1] Cf. also memorandum of L. Committee's views printed in Appendix V, p. 255.

schedule C, which confined the advance to certain definitely limited special classes. Major Hills urged the adoption of the wider schedule B ; but the sense of the meeting was strongly in favour of the narrower schedule. Mr. Churchill said he would have preferred a general output bonus, but the general opinion was that this was impracticable, and he decided to bring schedule C before the Cabinet.

(b) DEPARTMENTAL DIFFERENCES AND THE CABINET DECISION.

Strong objection to the proposal was made by the Director of Shipyard Labour, Sir Lynden Macassey, in a memorandum to the Controller of the Navy, which was submitted to the Cabinet. The order would not, he argued, effect its object, since it would not remove the disparity between the earnings of skilled time-workers and semi-skilled piece-workers. It would extend to all classes of skilled men, in shipbuilding as in engineering, and would check the extension of payment by results, which the Admiralty had been successful in effecting. It introduced two novel principles ; first, a percentage wage advance " based not on the cost of living, but on a purely arbitrary percentage which cannot be tested on any economic grounds " ; this would undermine seriously the practice and procedure of the Committee on Production ; and, second, the principle that the day-rates of men not working piece-work speed should approximately equal piece-work earnings. As an alternative policy he suggested bringing skilled time-workers under some form of shop output bonus[1]. The possibility of intruding on the province of the Committee on Production had been considered by Mr. Barnes ; he decided it was not an objection, since the Minister of Munitions would be regulating wages in agreement with munition workers by statutory authority, while the Committee on Production dealt with wages only when a difference had arisen and arbitration was necessary. Sir David Harrel, the Chairman of the Committee on Production, however, objected that the Order would disturb existing wages relations ; that an accurate differentiation of the workers to be covered would be difficult, so that the bonus would tend to spread ; and that there would be confusion between this advance made by the Minister of Munitions' authority and the awards made by the Committee on Production. Already on 13 October, in a memorandum summarising his view, he suggested that it would be necessary for the Committee on Production to give all munition workers the $12\frac{1}{2}$ per cent.[2]

The proposal was discussed at a Cabinet meeting on 12 October.[3] Mr. Churchill explained the necessity of the proposal and the objection to using it to force an extension of payment by results. Sir Lynden Macassey repeated his objections. Sir David Shackleton urged that the proposal interfered with the relative position of piece-workers and time-workers. As such it raised pre-war controversies which hitherto

---

[1] An extract from this memorandum will be found in Appendix V, p. 256 ; L.R. 5997/22.
[2] L.R. 5997/11.
[3] HIST. REC./R./342/11.

the Ministry of Labour and the Committee on Production had refused to admit to consideration. Piece-workers would demand the restoration of the pre-war relation between their earnings and those of time-workers. Further, there were anomalies among piece-work earnings, and it would be impossible to resist the demand for revision of these. Sir George Askwith endorsed Sir David Shackleton's opinions. Mr. Churchill replied that no alternative proposal for dealing with the admitted grievance of the skilled time-worker had been put forward, and that the Admiralty and Ministry of Labour representatives had raised no objections on the Hills Committee. Mr. Barnes said that it was not proposed to help a single man who was likely to be put on piece-work.

The War Cabinet was impressed with the differences of opinion, but felt that it was impossible to disappoint the expectations raised. They referred the matter to Lord Milner and Mr. Barnes, who consulted the Departments concerned and the Chairman of the Committee on Production the same afternoon, and decided in favour of the wider Schedule B. The Cabinet thus confirmed the finding of the Hills' Committee, and over-rode the decision to confine the advance to a limited schedule of occupations in which payment by results was impracticable, reached by the Ministry of Munitions' Labour Committee, and supported by its officers, by the Minister himself, and by the inter-departmental conference held on 8 October. Lord Milner and Mr. Barnes were influenced by the Chairman of the Committee on Production, who advocated the wider schedule as a means of forestalling probable further demands, and who was supported by Sir David Shackleton. The decision was :—

> "that fully qualified skilled time-workers in the engineering and foundry trades should be granted an increase of $12\frac{1}{2}$ per cent. upon their weekly earnings, provided that their wages equalled or exceeded the district time-rate payable to fitters and turners. Such increase to commence in the first full week after the 14 October, 1917. This increase shall not apply to men with upstanding wage or salary covering overtime."

Mr. Churchill concurred in this decision. The order embodying it (1061) was issued on 13 October, and on 15 October leaving certificates were abolished.

V. Reception of the Bonus.

(a) Demands from Excluded Time-Workers.

The Skilled Time-workers (Engineers and Moulders) Wages Order, contained the following provisions :—

(1) A bonus of $12\frac{1}{2}$ per cent. on earnings was to be paid to fully qualified skilled engineers and moulders rated at or above the current district time-rate for turners or fitters while employed on or in connection with munitions work and paid at plain time rates.

(2) The term " plain time rates " excluded all the many forms of bonus in use at the time, except (i) a time-keeping bonus, (ii) a bonus (not being a bonus on output) less favourable to such workmen than the bonus payable under these directions, in which case the existing bonus should merge in the bonus payable under these directions, (iii) a war advance given to meet the cost of living as the result of or in conformity with arbitration under Part I of the Munitions of War Act, 1915.

(3) This bonus was not to affect time-rates, nor the basis of determining any system of payment by results.

(4) The bonus did not apply to " workmen paid an upstanding wage or salary which covers overtime or other allowances," *i.e.* it excluded foremen, etc.

(5) The order was applied only to workmen whose wages it " was the practice to regulate by the movements of wages in the engineering and foundry trades." Thus it was sent to engineering works, primarily, while the engineers employed in other factories, *e.g.*, in collieries and railway workshops, did not gain thereby.

The fears that it would be difficult to restrict it within its intended scope were quickly justified. In quick succession demands for inclusion came from border-line crafts in the engineering and foundry trades, from semi-skilled and unskilled time-workers, from allied industries such as iron and steel and aircraft, from branches of included industries not engaged on munitions such as agricultural machinery, and from piece-workers. In the end the bonus or its equivalent was extended to all, but reluctantly, and only after successive attempts to draw a line short of such comprehension.

Four days after the order was issued the Chairman of the Engineering Employers' Federation attended the Labour Committee of the Ministry to ask for a definition of the term " fully qualified engineer." He suggested apprenticeship as the differentia with a definite schedule of employment, including viewing and gauging when performed by skilled men. Logically the scope of the order could be very much extended and he suggested that unskilled time-workers might later receive an advance of perhaps 10 per cent.[1] The committee decided that no alteration in the scope should be made, claims being left to the Committee on Production to deal with: but it appointed a sub-committee to draw up an interpretative list of occupations based on circular W.M.V.33.[2] This list included men paid at or above the current district time-rate for fitters and turners in the following trades:—blacksmith, borer, core-maker, fitter, gauge-maker, gear-cutter, grinder, hardener and temperer, jig maker, miller, mill-wright, moulder, patternmaker, planer, shaper, slotter, toolmaker, toolsmith, turner. Also skilled men employed in the following capacities whose trade was one of those specified above :—charge-hand, draughtsman,

---

[1] L.R. 5997/2. [2] L.R. 5997/13.

examiner, foreman, gauger, inspector, marker off, rate-fixer, setter-up, viewer. It will be noted that at least two occupations normally classed as "semi-skilled," namely planers and slotters, were included in this list. The statement based on it was sanctioned by the Minister on 22 October.

The issue of the order at once excited unrest among excluded workers. On 25 October, it was reported that a large number of the representatives of the 47 unions attending a Committee on Production hearing of an engineering claim had expressed profound dissatisfaction with the order and anticipated a general strike. The Ministry's local representative in Sheffield reported mass meetings of unskilled workmen to demand the 12½ per cent., and said that the shop stewards, who had been organising for months with a view to such an opportunity, were encouraging the unrest. A stoppage was threatened at Nottingham unless the advance was extended to boiler-makers and coremakers.[1]

(b) Extension to Semi-skilled and Unskilled Workers and to Shipyards.

It was thought that the prompt enforcement of the order might still secure its object; arrangements were made for the administrative handling of the problems raised; and a press notice was issued on 27 October, explaining that the order was not a general wages order, but directed to remedying the skilled man's grievance alone; general advances were the province of the Committee on Production.[2] The difficulties of application and the demands for extension were, however, too great.

Three questions presented themselves :—

(a) Should men not strictly engineers but allied (e.g., plumbers, sheet metal workers, boiler-makers) be covered?

(b) Should the order be modified to include all men on timework who were skilled in their own trade (such as smiths, strikers, fettlers, core-makers and machinists) whether in receipt of the fitter's or turner's rate or not?

(c) Should it be extended to semi-skilled and unskilled workers?

In connection with the first of these, the Admiralty had to be considered, since at least as many men in some of the classes named were employed in shipbuilding and ship-repairing as in engineering establishments. To give these classes the bonus when employed in engineering shops would make it practically impossible for the Admiralty to exclude them when employed in shipbuilding and ship-repairing. The Admiralty were convinced that if these men had an advance, so must all the skilled men in shipyards, including shipwrights and joiners. Then it would be difficult to exclude joiners in engineering establishments, and then all skilled men throughout the engineering trade.

---

[1] L.R. 5997/10.　　　　[2] L.R. 5997/12, 23, 24.

CH. VI] PROBLEM OF SKILLED TIME-WORKER 183

The semi-skilled and unskilled workers claimed the bonus on the ground that, first, they were absolutely essential to production, secondly, they had been seriously affected by the increased production due to the war, in that they had to work with piece-workers at higher pressure and often with less staff than before, thirdly, they had been penalised as against new comers who had been placed on repetition work, and, finally, they had been neglected at the time of the Minister's pledge to skilled workers inasmuch as they had not, despite their representations, been consulted.

Their unions had not resisted piece-work or payment by results, but their special trades could not be placed on piece-work.

The following trades therefore, claimed inclusion under the bonus scheme (at an estimated annual cost of £4,500,000 for 300,000 workmen)—crane-drivers, slingers, boilermen, enginemen, some classes of electrical workers, beltmen and oilers, progress clerks, foremen's clerks, men in stores and warehouses, bogeymen, iron and steel dressers, core-makers, foundry labourers, smith's strikers and hammermen, woodworkers and others. They pressed these claims in a deputation to the Ministry on 10 November.

The Labour Committee recommended the immediate extension of the bonus to the " border-line " cases,[1] and the securing of the Cabinet's consent to an extension to all other time-workers over 18, skilled or unskilled, engaged on munitions work in the engineering, foundry and shipbuilding industries. The estimated cost was £750,000 to cover 40,000 time-workers, like coremakers and dressers, who claimed to be skilled but did not come under the existing order, and £6,500,000 to cover 562,750 semi-skilled and unskilled time-workers.

The grievance to be remedied, Sir Charles Ellis noted in forwarding these recommendations to the Minister on 17 November, was no longer a skilled man's, but a time-worker's grievance.

Before the Cabinet considered the matter a conference was held, at Lord Milner's request, of the Departments interested[2]—the Ministry of Munitions, the Ministry of Labour, the Admiralty—to consider the bearing of the problem on an award of 5s. a week just made by the Committee on Production to the engineering and foundry unions. It was recognised that the 12½ per cent. or its equivalent would have to be extended to all time-workers in engineering and ship-building, that the Committee on Production award would have to be extended to shipbuilding, and that the Committee in making its award had not taken into consideration the fact that it would prove necessary to extend the 12½ per cent. bonus to all time-workers. The representatives of the Ministry of Labour and the Admiralty thought that the bonus and award should be merged in a single advance; and the Admiralty proposed an advance of 7s. to skilled and 5s. to unskilled time-workers in preference to a percentage bonus, because it would be cheaper to extend such a bonus to piece-workers. ·The Ministry of

---

[1] Boiler-makers, armature-winders, coppersmiths, plumbers, sheet-metal-workers, brass finishers.
[2] Minutes of Conference, 19 November. HIST. REC./R./342/10.

Munitions on the other hand contended that the 12½ per cent. had been given as an unconditional bonus, and that its purpose would be negatived if it were merged in a general advance for all workers.

A further conference, at which employers were present, considered that the bonus must be extended to all time-workers on munitions in the engineering, foundry and ship-building industries, but that piece-workers' claims could be met by an adjustment of unfavourable rates and prices.

The Cabinet accepted this view on 21 November; Lord Milner and Mr. Barnes saw the representatives of the General Labour Unions the same day and announced the concession to them. The order embodying the decision was issued on 11 December.

VI. The Cabinet Committee on the Bonus.

At the time of the Cabinet decision on the first grant of the 12½ per cent., attention was called to the lack of co-ordination between different departments in dealing with labour claims.[1] After the decision to extend the advance at the meeting on 27 November, a Cabinet Labour Committee was set up under the Chairmanship of Mr. Barnes, to act as a general co-ordinating committee for labour questions. To it was referred the interpretation of the existing 12½ per cent. order, the drawing up of the order extending the bonus to semi-skilled and unskilled time-workers, and the question of the piece-workers' claims. The committee reported on 24 December, that the original order had started a wide-spread agitation which now involved the Government in the necessity of paying the 12½ per cent. or its equivalent to all classes of workpeople, or of facing wide-spread strikes. They would have preferred announcing that the bonus was a mistake and withdrawing the order, but they were informed that such a course was not considered practicable for political reasons. They therefore put forward a proposal drafted for them by a sub-committee representative of the Ministry of Munitions, Ministry of Labour, and engineering and shipbuilding employers. This was that piece-workers should be given a guarantee that their earnings should be made up in cases of deficiency to 12½ per cent. over time rates, that no further orders giving the 12½ per cent. should be made but all future general alterations in wages be submitted to the Ministry of Labour for remission to a re-inforced Committee on Production, and that an appeal be made to employers and workpeople to maintain and extend payment by results. The administrative difficulties of applying the 12½ per cent. order had simultaneously convinced the officers of the Ministry of Munitions of the need of some modification of policy. Claims were coming in not only from munition workers, but from makers of agricultural and textile machinery (which, not being munitions, did not come within the scope of the Minister's *statutory* powers), other munitions industries such as iron and steel, and from piece-workers. Mr. Wolfe in a memorandum on 15 December,[2] recommended as the only course now practicable the withdrawal of the 12½ per

---

[1] HIST. REC./R./342/11. [2] HIST. REC./R./342/10.

CH. VI] PROBLEM OF SKILLED TIME-WORKER 185

cent. orders on the ground that employers and unions had not accepted the principle of strict limitation on which they were based, and the conversion of the 5s. award first given by the Committee on Production into 12s. The head of the Wages Section, Mr. Campbell, a little later explained the difficulties of the department.[1] The ordinary work of sanctioning advances had been greatly increased since leaving certificates were abolished, and men could demand advances under threat of leaving. The extension of the Coal Controller's award meant additional work. The $12\frac{1}{2}$ per cent. bonus made such a further addition that effective control by the department over wages had practically ceased. The first $12\frac{1}{2}$ per cent. order might have been administered if it had been accepted by masters and men in the spirit in which it was intended; unfortunately the intention to remedy one grievance had been seized on as an invitation to demand remedies for many other grievances. The extension of the bonus had led to further demands, the concession of which merely defeated the original intention of the bonus. The result was general unrest, an unexpected situation which the section had not the staff to deal with : nor could the attitude of the Government, acting through the War Cabinet Labour Committee, on the many technical questions at issue, be sufficiently well defined to give the section the guidance it needed. He advocated withdrawing the orders and increasing the Committee on Production award to 12s., and then throwing back on to employers and trade unions the responsibility for dealing with wage anomalies by setting up joint wage boards in all trades. The Government, which paid practically all wages, could then indicate how far it was prepared to go, the Committee on Production would decide when a variation was necessary on the ground of change in cost of living, the joint boards would advise on the allocation of advances to particular grades and classes, and the Ministry would enforce their decisions. In subsequent memoranda (26 December and 1 January), he thought it would be necessary to extend the bonus to all time-workers on munitions, to press employers to revise piece-rates by local negotiations, and to deal with the iron and steel and aircraft industries by special trade conferences.

The Minister himself was of the opinion that it was possible to limit the advance by speeding up the application to the classes originally intended, and negotiating agreements in trade conferences where claims to it were pressed. An indiscriminate bonus would be unfortunate ; the right policy was to plough through the difficulties in detail day by day.[2] Piece-rates should be dealt with by local arrangement between employers and trade unions. In a memorandum urging this course on the Cabinet, Mr. Churchill insisted on his statutory responsibilities and powers, which could not be exercised by the Cabinet Labour Committee ; he asked for authority to extend the bonus to the remaining time-workers in the munitions industries at an estimated

---

[1] Memorandum of 20 December, 1917. Hist. Rec./R./342/134. cf. L.R. 5997/58.
[2] Hist. Rec./R./342/134.

cost of £8,000,000, and to negotiate settlements with outlying trades, especially iron and steel, building and aircraft.

To sum up, if the withdrawal of the 12½ per cent. orders was impossible for political reasons, two alternative policies were possible. One was that of the Minister of Munitions to persist in the original policy of the orders, extend the bonus to all time-workers in munitions work, adjust piece-work earnings where they were inadequate, using trade conferences to determine details, but to refuse any general advance. The other was that of the Cabinet Labour Committee and the Ministry of Labour, to extend the bonus generally, merging it in an ordinary advance, and so restoring the wages relations that had preceded the issue of the 12½ per cent. orders, and restore to the Committee on Production exclusively the task of dealing with claims for general changes in wages.

The War Cabinet adopted both alternatives almost simultaneously. It gave the Minister of Munitions the authority he requested almost in the form he suggested. He was authorised to negotiate a settlement within the following general limits :—

(1) extension of the 12½ per cent. bonus to all men in the engineering and foundry trades, including outliers ;
(2) settlement of any claims arising from the extension under (1), made in the chemical and building industries ;
(3) calling of conferences in the iron and steel trades and the aircraft woodwork industry, in order to discuss wage anomalies and devise remedies.

But the Cabinet also the following week on 7 January decided to extend the bonus to piece-workers, substituting at the same time the Ministry of Labour for the divided authority of the Ministry of Munitions and Cabinet Labour Committee as the authority for dealing with all claims arising from the 12½ per cent. bonus.

VII. The Spread of the Bonus.

(a) EXTENSION TO TIME-WORKERS IN OTHER INDUSTRIES.

The settlement with the aircraft industry is described elsewhere.[1] The negotiations with the iron and steel industry arose out of a claim by the Iron and Steel Trades Confederation, which was rendered urgent by a series of unofficial strikes in Sheffield and elsewhere. A conference was held on 3 January when a settlement was reached on the following lines :—

(1) That the Conciliation Boards, or the Employers in the case of Iron and Steel establishments not governed by such Boards, be informed that for plain time-workers employed in direct connection with the production of iron or steel, including those whose wages are governed by sliding scales, a bonus shall be negotiated on the following lines :—

---

[1] See above, p. 149.

(a) To workers who have received not more than 20s. war advance—the equivalent of 12½ per cent. on earnings.

(b) To workers who have received over 20s. war advance—sufficient to produce an equivalent to the 20s. plus the 12½ per cent. on earnings; that is to say, that in the case of workers who have received war advances in excess of 20s. such excess shall merge in the 12½ per cent. on earnings.

(c) Workmen who have received the equivalent of 20s. war advance plus 12½ per cent. on earnings, or more, are not affected by this settlement.

In calculating whether 20s. has been received, it shall be taken as 20s. for the normal week in the engineering department in the establishment, or in the absence of such engineering department, in the town or district.

(2) In respect of work done in an establishment both by plain time-workers and time-workers partly paid by results, the Conciliation Board, or the Employers, as the case may be, shall take into account any adjustment required to secure equitable treatment of the latter.

(3) As regards tonnage workers' helpers working as plain time-workers the Conciliation Board or the Employers shall consider and in conjunction with the workers' representatives agree how the bonus to which they are entitled under this settlement shall be paid.

(4) That in the case of workers whose wages are governed by sliding scales, advances accruing under the scales after the date of this settlement shall be merged in any advance arising out of this settlement.

(5) This settlement will operate as from the beginning of the first full pay next after 13 October, 1917.

(6) Agreements arrived at in accordance with these lines of settlement are subject to confirmation by the Ministry of Munitions.

(7) Any difficulty arising as to the meaning of the foregoing clauses or as to the carrying into effect of the principles thereof shall be referred to and settled by the Ministry of Munitions.

A settlement on similar lines was made with a number of allied metal trades :—nut and bolt, brass founding, bridge and constructional engineering, hollow-ware, springs, hot stampings, tubes, and wagon building. A pressing claim for the bonus from workers in electricity generating stations and sub-stations was settled by Sir George Askwith under authority from the War Cabinet.

(b) Extension to Piece-Workers.

The decision to merge the bonus in a general advance was made on 7 January and confirmed on 23 January. At the former meeting the Cabinet had under consideration two questions ; what authority should administer the bonus, and whether the bonus should be extended to piece-workers. Mr. Churchill urged that a single Department should have the administration instead of a Cabinet Committee, and that no general extension should be made; trade settlements should be negotiated in which particular classes of piece-workers were covered. If, however, a general extension were made he would prefer that the Ministry of Labour take all responsibility over from his Department. Against this it was urged that a settlement now with piece-workers could be made by conceding 7s. a week, a saving of 2s. 6d. a week a head, while if a settlement were delayed longer it would be necessary to grant $12\frac{1}{2}$ per cent. to all piece-workers.

The War Cabinet decided that:—

(1) "All applications for an increase in war advances and wage disputes arising therefrom shall be referred for decision to the Ministry of Labour, who may refer them to the Committee on Production.

The Ministry of Labour will have discretion to ask the department concerned to carry on any necessary negotiations, but the final decision will in all cases rest with the Ministry of Labour.

(2) "In deciding all claims for $12\frac{1}{2}$ per cent. bonus or its equivalent the adjudicating authority shall work within the limits and on the lines laid down by the following formula:—General formula for maximum concession for the settlement of the $12\frac{1}{2}$ per cent. question.

(i) To plain time-workers included in the concession:—

    (a) To workers who have received not more than 20s. war advance—the equivalent of $12\frac{1}{2}$ per cent. on earnings.

    (b) To workers who have received over 20s. war advance—sufficient to produce an equivalent to the 20s. plus the $12\frac{1}{2}$ per cent. on earnings; that is to say, that in the case of workers who have received war advances in excess of 20s. such excess shall merge in the $12\frac{1}{2}$ per cent. on earnings.

    (c) Workmen who have received the equivalent of 20s. war advance plus $12\frac{1}{2}$ per cent. on earnings, or more, are not affected by this settlement.

(ii) To premium bonus workers included in the concession—7s. on existing war advances.

(iii) To piece-workers included in the concession—7s. on existing war advances, or its equivalent in piece rates.

(iv) Any settlement under (ii) or (iii) shall be on the clear understanding that no one shall by the receipt of this concession in addition to previous war advances, receive more than $12\frac{1}{2}$ per cent. on his present earnings, or 27s. as a total war advance, whichever is the less.

(v) In all cases where war advances have been given otherwise than by the Committee on Production or similar award, re-adjustment must be made within the above limits.

(3) "The co-ordinating Committee on Labour Disputes should be replaced by the Ministry of Labour after dealing with any outstanding business.

(4) " Mr. Barnes should have full powers to decide on behalf of the War Cabinet in cases referred to him by the Ministry of Labour, bringing to the War Cabinet at his discretion only cases of extreme urgency or difficulty.

(5) " No proclamation should at present be made, but when a suitable opportunity occurred the Prime Minister might make a public statement on the general labour policy of the Government."

The substitution of the Ministry of Labour was announced in the press on 11 January. The decision to extend the bonus to piece-workers was not announced. On the contrary the announcement stated that the Minister of Labour proposed to deal with applications on the lines of a resolution passed by the Ministry of Munitions Trade Union Advisory Committee, viz :— that the 12½ per cent. should be extended to cover time-workers who had not yet received it in the shipbuilding and munitions trades, but that so far as piece-workers in these trades were concerned no 12½ per cent. should be given, but low piece-prices be revised and employers informed that this was the decision of the Government. The actual procedure would be by reference to arbitration under Part I and Schedule I of the Munitions of War Act, 1915. The decision to extend the bonus to piece-workers was, however, definite ; the Ministry of Labour was considering methods, and, as a result of their advice, Mr. Barnes suggested at the Cabinet Meeting on 21 January that a percentage bonus of 7½ per cent. be substituted for the flat rate of 7s. a week, as being easier to administer and a little cheaper. It was thought that the stimulus to output would more than justify the cost of the bonus, and the Cabinet approved Mr. Barnes' proposal.

Mr. Churchill's advisers had protested against the Cabinet's decision to extend the bonus as soon as it was made[1]. Mr. Churchill shared their view and took the occasion of the change in the form of the extension to raise the matter again. He circulated for the Cabinet Meeting of 23 January a memorandum by himself and a joint memorandum by Sir Stephenson Kent, Sir Thomas Munro and Mr. Wolfe. In the former he warned the Cabinet against the 7½ per cent. as unnecessary and expensive. " There is no excuse for shirking the laborious and practical business of insisting on the revision of low piece-rates and dealing with exceptional cases on their merits." The Department had succeeded in spite of interference in dealing with the 12½ per cent. They had given away only £1,000,000 in the last three months' negotiations, and had not yet applied the whole of the £14,000,000 authorised in November. It would be absurd to pay an increase to large classes of workers who at piece-rates were earning upwards of £5 per week, in some cases up to £25 a week, and to make such an advance in the form of a percentage would be to leave the grievance of the low-rate piece-worker practically and relatively unredressed. If it were extended to piece-workers generally the women

---

[1] L.R. 5997/79.

would be dragged in, which in turn would involve the extension of the 12½ per cent. to women. He offered to take back the whole problem from the Ministry of Labour and Committee on Production and wind it up. If his offer were refused, it would be necessary for him to give Parliament a full account and correct the impression left by Mr. Barnes' speech[1].

The memorandum by Sir Stephenson Kent and his colleagues stated at length the objection to the proposed extension, and laid particular emphasis on the danger of starting a new "vicious circle" by depriving the skilled time-worker of the relative improvement in his position given by the 12½ per cent.[2]

The Cabinet, however, confirmed its previous decision. It was argued that delay had made it impossible to resist, so many cases had accumulated; the extension would assist payment by results; in any case it was impracticable to undertake a revision of piece-rates.

The new bonus was announced in the press on 24 January in the following terms:—

(1) "The 12½ per cent. has been given, under existing orders and extensions thereof made by the Admiralty and the Ministry of Munitions, to workmen employed on munitions work (as defined in the Munitions of War Acts) and paid as plain time workers in engineering shops, boiler shops, foundries, ship-building and ship-repairing establishments, iron and steel trades, electricity generating stations and electrical contracting trades, nut and bolt trades, brass foundries and brass works, bridge-building and constructional engineering, hollow-ware trade, spring making works, hot stamping works, tube works, and wagon building works.

(2) "As from the beginning of the first full pay week which followed 1 January, 1918, a bonus of 7½ per cent. on their earnings shall be paid to all workmen of 21 years of age and over employed in establishments or trades (other than the iron and steel trades) covered by the existing Orders relating to plain time workers or extensions thereof, and engaged on munitions work as defined in the Munitions of War Acts who are piece-workers or are paid on a premium bonus system or any mixed system of time and piece or any system of payment by results including men working at augmented time rates fixed in lieu of piece-rates or by reference to results or to output of work.

(3) "The 7½ per cent. bonus shall be paid as an addition to any other bonus or war advances payable to the man concerned under any agreements or awards. Provided that any bonus

---

[1] Mr. Barnes at Glasgow had accused Mr. Churchill of "butting in" with the 12½ per cent. into the difficult task of adjusting wages to cost of living. He explained away his utterance in Parliament on the next day.
[2] L.R. 15726.

or war advance which in the case of timeworkers has merged in the 12½ per cent. shall merge in the 7½ per cent. and that no workman shall receive the 7½ per cent. bonus who has already received in some other form some equivalent consideration for the 12½ per cent. bonus. In any case where payment has been made to workmen pending the general consideration by the Government of the position of men paid by results, the amount of such payment shall merge in the 7½ per cent. bonus now authorised and such bonus shall as from this date be in lieu of and in substitution for any such other payment."

The extension to piece-workers in iron and steel was left over for a special conference. It was also stated that future claims would be referred through the Ministry of Labour to the Committee on Production. This was made legally possible by the nomination of the members of the Committee as a special tribunal under Section 8 of the 1916 Act.

VIII. Conversion to a General Advance.

(a) Procedure in Making Awards.

The day the press notice appeared the secretary of the Engineering Employers' Federation wrote to ask by what statutory authority the bonus to piece-workers was granted.[1]

The Ministry of Labour had apparently assumed that the Order could be made under Section 1 of the 1917 Amendment Act; that section, however, only gave to the Minister of Munitions power to regulate the wages of time-workers. A similar question might have been asked about the award made by Sir George Askwith on 7 January, of the 12½ per cent. for certain classes of electrical workers " under authority given " him " by the War Cabinet." The Engineering Employers' Federation did not press their question, a fact which illustrates the extent to which wages had become a question between wage-earners and the Government, with employers acting merely as agents of the Government. Under the procedure, however, adopted by the Ministry of Labour of referring claims as differences under Part I. of the Munitions of War Act, 1915, the extensions became legal and had binding force.

The chief steps in the subsequent extension of the bonus were as follows :—the explosives, chemicals and allied trades were awarded it by the Committee on Production on 5 February, sheet metal workers on 8 February, and building operatives employed by the Government on 21 February. A conference on 20 February drew up lines of settlement for the extension to piece-workers in the iron and steel industry. In the chain, wire and Sheffield light trades revised piece-rates or other special arrangements were substituted. Further extensions by Committee on Production awards were made to the metal trades, certain classes of employees of local Government Authorities and public

---

[1] L.R. 15726.

utilities, rubber, building (so far as not already covered), vehicle building, and smaller trades in the course of April, and a large number of awards affecting individual firms were made. The Committee was still busy extending the bonus all through May. Some of the awards affecting individual firms were important, for example, Messrs. Kynoch's, Birmingham, which was taken as a test case of the large composite engineering and chemical works, in which certain sections of the employees were covered by General Orders and Awards, but others not covered.

The delays inevitable in this piece-meal handling of the advance caused much jealousy and unrest; the actual awards, by making the bonus payable from different dates, did not allay such feeling. The press announcement of 11 January, although it stated that all claims should now be made to the Ministry of Labour for reference to the Committee on Production under the Munitions of War Act, 1915, did not relieve the Ministry of Munitions of a considerable share of the work involved. Weeks elapsed before claimants generally realised that they should not prefer their claim to the Wages Section of the Ministry, and every award left a margin of doubtful cases or difficulties of application which, in the case of munitions employment, came to the Wages Section for decision or advice. The section endeavoured to accelerate a settlement by advising employers and unions to submit joint applications to the Ministry of Labour and induced certain important associations, the National Employers' Federation and the Sheffield Light Trades' Association, to collect their members for uniform action[1].

Doubtful cases after an order had been issued granting the bonus were referred, in accordance with Section 1 (2) of the Act of 1917, to the Committee on Production, sitting as a special arbitration tribunal. Fifty-four appeals were dealt with in this way, most of them in the engineering and shipbuilding trades.

(b) CONCLUSION.

By June, the circles started by Order 1061 had spread to the edges of the pond. Isolated claims to the bonus were still being made when the Armistice came, but practically the whole field of munitions employment had been covered by order and award, while employers engaged on commercial work, even if no award had been made, had been compelled to grant the bonus in order to retain their staffs. The bonus had become, therefore, a general advance, and this was recognised in the Committee on Production awards, made at the regular hearings of the engineering and foundry industries in March, 1918; when the unions' claim to an advance on the ground of increased cost of living was rejected. This meant that the *status quo* in the relations of time-workers, skilled and unskilled, and piece-workers had been restored, and the grievance of the former remained unredressed. Members of the committee who recommended the original bonus defended it on the ground that their limitations had been ignored, and

---

[1] Wages Section Report for March, 1918.

complained that no extension should have been made without consulting them.¹ Mr. Kellaway in Parliament claimed that it had prevented the general migration of skilled labour, and consequent loss of production, that had been anticipated when leaving certificates were abolished. The effect had been thoroughly sound, and there were fewer strikes than at any period during the war.²

It has been necessary to give a somewhat disproportionate amount of space to the history of the 12½ per cent. bonus, because it became the subject of acute controversy and it has been necessary to make clear the attitude of the various contestants, and to bring out the limited effect of the order no less than the extent of its repercussions. Not every thing that happened between October 1917 and April 1918 is to be attributed to the issue of Order 1061. On the other hand the Schedule of Protected Occupations would have afforded a considerable safeguard against the feared migration of skilled time-workers to semi-skilled work, even if the bonus had never been granted. The "system of wages" on the other hand, which the Order was alleged to have dislocated, was not in fact a balanced system in October 1917. In any case the shock it sustained on the issue of the little-noticed Coal Controller's award of that month³ was much heavier than that which resulted from the 12½ per cent. bonus. The cost of the bonus had been much exaggerated. So long as it retained its original character of a special bonus to a special class its cost was moderate. When it lost that character it merged in the general advances, made at regular intervals to meet the rising cost of living, and was treated as such by the Committee on Production in March and April 1918.

From the point of view of the Ministry of Munitions, the bonus was an attempt to remedy an admitted grievance to a limited class of workpeople affected by the Ministry's contracts. The Hills Committee first widened the scope of the measure by including all skilled time-workers. When the administrative difficulties of confining it within even this extended scope became obvious, the Cabinet allowed it to be extended generally, and the Committee on Production covered up the failure to remedy the original grievance by treating the bonus in effect as one of their own periodical awards. The grievance itself arose from an earlier failure to deal with the anomaly of inflated piece-rate earnings, an anomaly that had already become obvious in the winter of 1915.⁴ The record shows the great practical difficulty of drawing sharp lines of demarcation in industry, and the impossibility of maintaining such lines, when drawn, if administration is divided among a number of authorities. The details involved in the application of the original Order alone were too numerous and complex for any merely advisory committee to define, and the Hills Committee may be taken as one further example of the difficulty of correlating the activities of advisory committees of busy men with the day to day necessities of departmental administration.

---

¹ Cf. Mr. W. H. Hutchenson's evidence before the McCardie Embargo Committee.
² *Parliamentary Debates* (1918). *H. of C.* CIII, 547.
³ Chap. VII, p. 212   ⁴ cf. p. 167.

CHAPTER VII.

THE PROBLEM OF CO-ORDINATION.

I. Introductory.

The Ministry of Munitions never possessed either the statutory powers or the administrative machinery needed for the systematic control of wages ; yet the control that it sought to exercise could be completely effective only if it were systematic and general. The Ministry's interference with wages was incidental to its main purpose of organising the production of munitions. It was limited to the minimum of interference with voluntary settlements that seemed from time to time to be practicable. It originated, as is shown above,[1] as a consequence of the limitation of profits ; it was continued and extended in the interests of industrial peace and output, since output was checked by discontent and restlessness of labour, stimulated by content and appropriate methods of payment by results. The expansion and exercise of the Ministry's statutory powers of wages control have been described above ;[2] in this concluding chapter, certain special problems and difficulties that arose from their limitations are considered.

These difficulties were mainly difficulties of co-ordination. The administration of the Ministry's statutory powers of wages regulation was necessarily in the hands of a special department, the Wages Section of the Labour Regulation Department ; but the Supply Departments and Finance and Contracts Departments had a direct influence on wages through the fixing of contract prices. Contract prices were related more and more directly to cost of production, in which labour cost was always an important element ; labour cost depended on rates of wages, which depended in turn, in part at any rate, on the regulation of wages by the Government. As has been explained above,[3] it was not the intention of the Government to regulate wages, but merely to substitute arbitration for the strike and lock-out ; employers, however, argued that the Government's interference deprived them of their normal power of resistance, that the Government was responsible for advances in wages awarded by the Committee on Production and other tribunals, and that therefore they could claim to be re-imbursed by the Government for any increases in costs due to such awards.

The immediate interests of the different sections of the Ministry were not identical. There was always a conflict between the Supply Departments and the Contracts and Finance Departments, since the former were inclined to subordinate economy to the need of securing supplies at any price, while the latter were primarily concerned with

---

[1] Chap. I.   [2] Chaps. II and IV.   [3] Chap. I, Sect. 4.

economy. The Wages Section was predisposed neither to favour wage advances nor to resist them, but to study the effect of any particular advance on the movement of wages in general and on industrial peace. The different grades and classes of labour are so connected, that a wages settlement in one grade or class has immediate reactions on others; wages demands, therefore, which seemed to concern only the employer to whom they were addressed, or the Supply Department for whom he was working, had to be considered also from the point of view of munitions wages as a whole, and it was to ensure this consideration that wages regulation was undertaken.

Even if co-ordination between different parts of the Ministry were attained, the regulation of wages was more than a departmental problem. Munitions labour was employed directly or indirectly by other Departments as well as the Ministry of Munitions. A settlement by the Ministry would not stand, if another Department authorised payment by its contractors of a different rate of wages to the same class of workers. Further, the rates of wages of different industries are closely connected and a change in one industry will invariably provoke demands for a corresponding change in industries that are either technically connected or customarily associated with it in the settlement of wages. Effective wage regulation, therefore, would require control by a single authority over all industries. Instead of this, the control of wages was divided between the Ministry of Munitions, the Ministry of Labour, the Admiralty, the War Office, the Coal Controller and the Railway Executive Committee. The Wages Section was struggling with a problem that stretched beyond its grasp or even the Ministry's grasp. The problem grew until it became one of the biggest with which the Government had to deal. It had not been solved when the Armistice came.

II. Wages and Contracts.

(a) LIMITATION OF WAGES.

There is no necessity under peace conditions to put pressure on Government contractors to keep labour cost down. The ordinary pressure of competition is sufficient inducement, and the purchasing departments find it more important to insist, through the machinery of the Fair Wages Clause, on contractors paying not less than standard district rates. Under the conditions of war, the force of competition operated in the opposite direction. Competition for labour was much stronger than competition for contracts, and the ordinary motives that lead employers to resist wages demands were weakened or neutralised. The pricing of contracts, therefore, was one method by which wages might conceivably be controlled.

The use of contract terms to control wages did not, however, figure prominently in the Ministry's policy. The difficulties of such a method were summarised by Mr. Campbell in a memorandum forwarded to the Minister by Sir Stephenson Kent on the eve of the Armistice.[1]

---

[1] L.R. 26039/2.

> "It is clear that so many factors enter into the question of what each firm could afford to pay in wages on contracts placed at a standard price and that the allocation of contracts on any rigid basis will be so difficult while the needs of the Army are constantly varying, as to make it impossible to maintain control over wages by such means. Such stipulation in a contract as that standard wages only should be paid in its execution are useless where standards are in a state of flux. In short, regulation of wages through contracts is a method too clumsy, dilatory, and indirect to be at all effective. Contract stipulations can only be used as auxiliary to other means for establishing wages. A very great deal could, however, be done by a system of allocation of contracts, which took closer regard of wages and other labour conditions, in particular man-power employed in relation to contracts to be placed, than has hitherto been attained."

Contractors regularly applied to the division from whom they held their contracts for instructions when a wages demand was made and the contracting division would either refer them to the Wages Section or consult that section and reply itself.

Where contract prices were based on costings, standard district rates were taken as the basis for estimating labour costs, and so long as district rates retained any definiteness and authority this served as a check on extravagance in wages. But after the middle of 1917, district rates lost their validity and the Ministry was forced to consider more direct methods of control. The attempt to keep down labour costs was not distinguishable from the constant effort of the Contracts Department to keep down costs generally.

So far as controlled establishments were concerned, no change in wages could be made without the sanction of the Ministry. But there were still uncontrolled firms engaged on munitions work in 1918, and the check was ineffective even with controlled establishments. It did not apply to advances to individuals, it did not prevent the employer from engaging new labour at an enhanced rate, and it was always possible for a firm, if an application for sanction were refused, to make of the proposed change a difference under Part I of the Act of 1915, and so in effect appeal from the Ministry to an arbitrator.

When the new national factories were beginning work early in 1916, a circular letter was sent to them calling attention to the danger of forcing up wages.[1]

> "With a view to avoiding competition for labour, it is in the view of the Minister, of great importance that no initial rate of wage should be fixed in any National Factories in excess of the standard district rate for each class of labour, and that no increase should be made in the rates once fixed (other than an increase necessary for giving effect to the Fair Wages Clause) without previous reference to the Ministry."

A similar letter was sent to building contractors.

---

[1] M.W. 95723.

Periodically, suggestions were made that maximum wages should be fixed for industries and districts and the payment of any wages in excess made punishable. Such a suggestion appears in the weekly sectional report for August, 1915. The Building Labour Committee which dealt with a class of labour, of which only a small proportion was employed in controlled establishments, while all the big contracting Departments had relations with it, considered the adoption of a maximum or flat rate for all building operations from its institution in the autumn of 1915. Its attempt to stabilise wages are dealt with below.[1] There existed, however, no statutory power to impose such a maximum until the Munitions of War Amendment Act was passed in 1917 ; the Building Labour Committee was not able to control wages through clauses in contracts, and it was not until the Building Wages Order (S.R.O.742 of 1918) was issued on 14 June, 1918, that any general regulation was effected. By this Order time wages for persons on building work, being munitions work or work in connection therewith, were limited to the district rate recognised on 15 April, 1918, or rates fixed by an award under Part 1 of the Munitions Act or by a decision of the Building Labour Committee ; deviation from these rates was permissible only with the sanction of the Department.

In 1918, when the abolition of leaving certificates had restored to labour its full bargaining power and standard rates were rapidly disappearing under an accumulation of special bonuses and allowances, an attempt was made to use the Minister's powers of restricting employment to control and limit indirectly wages. In the case of the London sheet metal workers, the following notice was sent to employers :—

" I am directed by the Minister of Munitions to inform you that he has decided under the powers conferred upon him by the Munitions of War Acts, 1916-1917, and the Defence of the Realm Regulations, to make requirements, regulations and restrictions with regard to the carrying on of sheet metal work in factories and workshops in the London area, and to regulate and restrict the engagement and employment of all skilled workmen employed upon such work, in that area. These requirements, regulations and restrictions are made with a view to securing a due efficiency and economy, and a proper distribution of the labour in that area, employed upon such work.

" I am accordingly to state that the Minister of Munitions, with a view to increasing the production of munitions, hereby regulates and restricts the employment and engagement of skilled sheet metal workers by you, and directs as follows :—

Conditions of Employment.

" (1) (a) You will not be permitted, without the written authority of the Minister, to engage or employ any skilled sheet metal workers in excess of the total number in your employment on the date of this communication.

---

[1] See below, p. 205.

"(b) Applications for authority to engage a number of workmen in excess of that employed by you on the date of this communication, must state in detail the circumstances justifying the engagement of an additional number of men.

"(2) (a) You will not be permitted to engage or employ any skilled sheet metal worker at a rate of wages other than the recognised day-work rate for the London area, plus war wages, as defined in paragraph 3, except in the circumstances specified in paragraph 2 (b).

(b) Any skilled sheet metal worker in your employment at the date of this communication, and paid at a rate of wages other than the recognised day-work rate for the London area, plus war wages, as defined in paragraph 3, shall continue to be paid by you while so employed such higher wages. The Minister will sanction the payment of wages higher than the recognised day-work rate for the London area, plus war wages, as defined in paragraph 3, to any workman engaged by you after the date of this communication (with the authority of the Minister, where such authority is required), who was receiving such higher wages from his last previous employer. When sanctioned, such higher wages will be payable as from the date of engagement of the workman, but pending sanction, he must not be paid in excess of the recognised day-work rate for the London area, plus war wages, as defined in paragraph 3.

"(3) By the term "recognised day work-rate" for the London area is to be understood the rate of 1s. 1d. per hour (or in the case of men engaged on panel beating 1s. 3d. per hour), and by the term "war wages," it is to be understood the war wages payable from time to time under general awards applicable to sheet metal workers."

The same powers could have been used, and their use was suggested,[1] to limit wages generally; but the exceptions allowed by paragraph 2 (b) of the regulations took away much of the effect of the embargo, and a necessary preliminary to any extended use would have been the re-establishment of definite and authoritative district rates.

The importance of restricting wages paid to the ordinary district rate attracted particular attention in the case of building, because a large proportion of the Government's building construction was undertaken by contractors on a cost and percentage basis, which gave employers a positive inducement to raise wages. In a return prepared for the McCardie Committee in November, 1918, it was shown that of production contracts outstanding on 31 August, only 1·44 per cent. of the total value were on a cost and percentage basis; of construction contracts, 57 per cent. of the total value were on this basis. It was the policy of the Ministry to restrict cost and percentage contracts as far as possible, and to grant them only in cases where it was impossible or very difficult to estimate a fixed price. On a complaint from a

---

[1] See above, Chap. II, Sect. 7.

Manchester firm that such contracts were causing unrest, Mr. Kellaway on 20 October, 1917, instructed the head of the Wages Section in conjunction with the Controller of Contracts to prepare a clause explicitly prohibiting any payment in excess of the district rates.[1] The following clause was drafted :—

"The contractor shall not, in the execution of this contract, pay to any class of labour employed thereon, or in connection therewith rates of wages, bonuses or allowances in excess of the standards current in the district for that class of labour without the previous authority in writing of the Ministry of Munitions.

The contractor shall be responsible for the observance of this stipulation by any other person or persons to whom this contract or any portion thereof is sub-let or assigned by the contractor."

The Controller gave instructions on 26 October, that it should be included in all contracts, and Mr. Kellaway minuted that attention should be paid to the observance of the clause in all audits of claims. The inter-departmental Joint Committee of Finance and Contracts Officers decided on 22 November, that the clause should be applied to existing as well as to future cost and percentage contracts.

(b) COMPENSATION FOR WAGE ADVANCES.

The employers claim to a revision of contract prices on the ground that labour costs had been increased by Government wage awards and orders, figured prominently in the negotiations between the Ministry and contractors.[2] On contracts entered into before war broke out, concessions were made on the initiative of the Army Council ; a more difficult question of principle was raised, when contractors began to ask for a revision of prices on contracts entered into in the war period itself.

A number of such demands were made as a result of the advances in wages awarded by the Committee on Production in the early months of 1915. The ground of the demand was that conditions were so unstable that it was impossible to make allowances for all changes in fixing prices, and that the Government, by compelling employers to accept arbitration so as to avoid stoppage of work, had thereby assumed an obligation to indemnify them against increases of pay awarded. It may be noted that labour spokesmen at Committee on Production hearings took the same view, arguing that employers could grant advances because the Government would re-imburse them. The pre-war rule was that existing contracts could be varied only with the consent of the Treasury in each case, and the Treasury's position was that a concession could be made only where the contractor proved loss on his Government work as a whole. The answer made to the earliest demands therefore, was an undertaking to consider

---

[1] Munitions Council, 200.
[2] Vol. III. Part II. Chap. III.

any representations that might be made if wages should change materially.

On the formation of the Ministry, the question was again raised, and a Committee appointed by the Treasury to recommend general terms on which contracts might be revised and to deal with individual appeals. This Committee, presided over by Mr. Lubbock, reported that there was a *prima-facie* case for revision of pre-war contracts, but no *prima-facie* case for revising post-war contracts; in the case of the latter, careful scrutiny of each claim would be necessary and the actual amount of profits made would need attention. They recommended that the appointment of the Committee should not be made public, since publicity might invite claims. The Treasury approved the report and the Committee proceeded to consider claims.

In the second report on 31 December, 1915, dealing specially with claims based on increased labour costs due to Committee on Production awards, the Committee recommended that contractors should be informed that the claims could not be admitted. The Committee on Production had never held out any hope that advances would be repaid, and there was no ground for the suggestion that wages would not have risen but for the Committee on Production's awards. If a contractor still pressed for revision, he should be told that the Government would consider cases where it could be shown that an actual loss had been incurred on Government work; but all work done for the Government must be brought into account and, if necessary, books examined. This report also was approved.

Contractors were not satisfied with this concession. In February, 1916, the Ministry negotiated an agreement with the chief armament firms for a substantial reduction in shell prices, and decided that it would be necessary at these reduced prices to make allowance for fluctuations in the cost of material or labour. Clauses making such provision were therefore attached to tender forms issued in May to these firms; and again in August when the provision for fluctuations in prices of materials was withdrawn, the provision for fluctuations in wages was repeated. In some contracts, schedules of price changes corresponding with different rates of wages were included.[1]

The concession of principle made to the armament firms could not be confined to them; nor could it be confined to shell prices. It was not, however, extended generally without hesitation and opposition from the Treasury. The first important extension was made on 1 November, 1916, when the Minister gave a pledge to the representatives of the Boards of Management to make good any increase in wages given on the direct instructions of the Ministry of Munitions. The pledge was subsequently defined to cover advances made as a result of an arbitration under the Munitions of War Acts, an order by the Minister under Section 6 or Section 7 of the 1916 Act, an agreement sanctioned or approved by the Minister, or an advance in the district

---

[1] Vol. III, Part II, Appendix VII.

rate required to be paid by the Fair Wages Clause. It was confined to contracts for shell placed by Boards of Management; it threw on the contractor the burden of proving an increase in costs of manufacture and reimbursed him the actual increase. Since this involved a separate examination of each claim and might result in different amounts of compensation for different firms, the system was changed in May following. A schedule of fixed equivalents was drawn up, providing for a definite alteration in the price of each kind of shell for each of the general changes in wages.

Direct contracts could still be varied only in accordance with the procedure laid down in the second Lubbock Committee report.

The Boards of Management, early in 1917, began to press for an extension of the concession to other stores. The claim had not the same force since their contractors had been producing shell under unfavourable conditions that did not apply to the other stores. The concession was, however, decided on in April, and Treasury sanction asked.

The Treasury referred the matter to the Lubbock Committee. The Committee considered that the Minister's pledge involved a complete reversal of the Government's policy. In the case of Board of Management contracts, they recommended that the Ministry should prepare scales, from data in its hands showing costs of production and the proportion which productive wages bore to the whole price, showing for each type of store the equivalent addition to the contract prices necessary to cover the rise in wages. In the case of direct contracts, they recommended that claims should be dealt with on the same lines as heretofore; the admission should not be made that an increase of wages awarded by the Committee on Production of itself afforded grounds for an increase in price. Where, however, a contractor could prove that the effect of an award was to deprive him of a reasonable profit, his claim should be considered subject to certain conditions. Since the number of claims to be dealt with would very much increase, the Departments should be authorised to deal with them instead of referring them to the Committee. In future contracts clauses should be incorporated providing for price variation in accordance with variations in labour costs. The Treasury authorised action on these lines, and the Ministry informed contractors.

There remained the claim of the direct contractors. This was pressed in the spring and summer of 1917, by the Association of Controlled Establishments, the Association of Chambers of Commerce and the Federation of British Industries. It was considered by a Joint Committee of Contracts and Finance Officers of the War Office, Admiralty and Ministry of Munitions, and was finally conceded in principle. Cost variation clauses were agreed on and brought into use on 17 December, 1917.[1] They were to be inserted in future contracts, but only if the contractor demanded them. The Ministry was prepared to consider their application to contracts of at least three months'

---

[1] Circulars M.C. 17, 18, and 19; Appendix VI.

duration, made between 1 September and 17 December; contracts made before 1 September containing no special wages or materials clause could be treated as cases of hardship and referred to the Lubbock Committee. The clauses provided that contractors might claim " the strictly net amount chargeable to the contract on account of the increased cost of labour properly employed in the execution of the contract "; no additions were to be made for establishment charges or profits, both of which had been claimed by the contractors. The advances on account of which claims could be made were limited to advances due to awards under the Munitions of War Acts or Orders or awards made by the Minister or any tribunal. Advances sanctioned by the Minister, under Section 4 (2) of the Act of 1915, had originally been included, but were excluded at the request of the Wages Section on the ground that their inclusion would make it more difficult to refuse advances proposed by employers. The Wages Section also objected to any bonus on output being included in the labour cost on which a claim was based; the responsibility for such bonuses should rest with the employer who would be recompensed by the additional output evoked. The Contracts Board agreed to exclude any bonus not approved by the Wages Section, and to take approved bonuses into account in fixing the amount of profit allowable.

It was found convenient to meet claims for reimbursement by the method worked out originally in the case of shell contracts. On the data possessed by the Ministry's costing departments, an estimate was made of the percentage or lump sum increase on each unit of product needed to cover a given increase in wages. Contractors were offered such increase in settlement of their claim; if they refused it, they could have their claim investigated as a "hard case" by the Lubbock Committee.

Thus, the pre-war position that a contract price included allowance for contingent changes in wages was given up, and the Government undertook to meet the full direct charges due to changes in wages consequent on Government interference with pre-war methods of settling wages. A proposal made by the Admiralty representative on the Joint Committee of Contracts and Finance Officers would have been a logical deduction from this change of policy; it was that wages should be standardised and all future changes be ignored by contracting departments, contractors being reimbursed by one central authority that also controlled wages. The proposal was rejected; the administrative difficulties would have been great; but the Government was, nevertheless, left with the sole responsibility for settling wages. Employers had no longer any immediate interest in resisting wages demands, though they might still be influenced by thoughts of the post-war wages situation. The introduction into contracts generally of these cost variation clauses represented the final repudiation of the principle on which the Government's interference with wages had originally been based, namely, that wages could be left to the ordinary processes of bargaining with the mere substitution of compulsory arbitration for the lock-out and strike.

(c) Limitation of Prices and Sliding Scales.

In the iron and steel manufacturing industries the contracts policy of the Ministry had a special and peculiar influence on wages. In these industries, which employed in controlled establishments 280,000 men in addition to 16,000 in tin-plate mills, the wages of the majority of workers were based on sliding scales.[1] The chief exceptions were the maintenance men and labourers, whose wages usually followed the settlements in the engineering and building industries. The wages of iron-ore miners, quarrymen in limestone quarries and blast-furnace-men were based on and fluctuated with the price of pig-iron, those of iron and steel workers on the price of specified kinds of manufactured iron and steel. The rise in the price of all these products which the war demand produced therefore raised wages. Some scales had maxima beyond which wages did not fluctuate; but it was estimated that wages had already advanced 30 to 40 per cent. by the end of 1915, and were likely to rise another 20 per cent. in the near future. The fixing of maximum prices by the Government stopped this rise. The desire to limit wages was one motive for fixing prices; an alternative proposal to limit the movement of sliding scales to 50 per cent. above pre-war level was discussed, but rejected as impracticable on the advice of the Chief Industrial Commissioner.

So far the Ministry's policy had merely put iron and steel workers into the same position as other munition workers; and new problems arose when it became necessary either to raise maximum prices or subsidise producers on account of increased costs. If prices were raised, the wage-earners would benefit again under their scales. If, on the other hand, a system of subsidies was adopted, the conditions under which the workers expected and were normally justified in claiming an advance in wages would have been established, and they would consider that they had a grievance if they received no advance; yet the rise in price would be due mainly to such factors as increased cost of imported ores, increased freight, increased insurance and adverse exchange, and it did not seem reasonable that the workers should receive a bonus on these national disadvantages.

On the whole, it was thought that a system of subsidies was preferable to an advance in maximum prices in the case of hematite iron, if the labour objection could be overcome. The Labour Department of the Ministry was consulted and advised that the matter be fully explained to the unions, emphasis being laid on the fact that the subsidy carried no profit with it for the employers on Government contracts. It was decided, therefore, to adopt the method of the subsidy and "to explain frankly and fully to the leaders of the trade unions that there would be no interference with the rights of workmen under sliding scale or other agreements."

Subsidies took the form partly of direct grants to meet increased expenses, partly of rebates on actual freights, insurance and exchange expenses. Direct subsidies were granted to meet the increased cost of

---

[1] See above, Chap. I, Sect. 1.

coal due to the Coal Controller's awards of 1s. 6d. per day to miners in October, 1917, and July, 1918, and to meet the cost of the $12\frac{1}{2}$ and $7\frac{1}{2}$ per cent. bonuses. The practice of employers varied in their treatment of bonuses for the purpose of wage determinations. The Scotch firms counted them as part of selling price for the purpose of the sliding scale; on the North-East and West Coasts they were excluded. The trade union leaders, in putting forward their claim on 24 December, 1917, to the equivalent of the $12\frac{1}{2}$ per cent. bonus granted to time workers in the engineering and shipbuilding industries stated definitely that "the sliding scales had been rendered inoperative by the fixing of maximum prices," and that in many cases the scale men were in a worse position than unskilled workers who had received war bonuses and than men in the engineering trades. The settlement of this claim marked the beginning of a restoration of the sliding scale system to its old predominance. Workers who had received not more than 20s. war advance, received the $12\frac{1}{2}$ per cent. on earnings; where the war advance exceeded 20s. the excess merged in the $12\frac{1}{2}$ per cent.; but there was also a provision that any advance accruing under sliding scales after the date of this settlement should merge in the advance granted by the settlement.

The general relation of subsidies to wages was settled on 5 February, 1918, after a series of conferences between the Ministry, employers and unions. All subsidies given to the manufacturers since the Coal Controller's award of October, 1917, were to be regarded as an advance in selling prices and so would affect wages under sliding scales. At the same time all war bonuses given since 1 March, 1917, to meet the increasing cost of living, were to be merged in the increased wages that resulted from the inclusion of subsidies in selling prices.

Before the sliding scale was restored to its normal position as the regulator of wages, the Committee on Production had in a number of cases to deal with applications from iron and steel workers. It dealt with them on three principles.

(1) It granted war bonuses. These were often initiated by the employers; examples were a bonus of 1s. to 3s. in March, 1915, raised two years later to 5s., in the South Wales and Monmouthshire iron and steel trade; a bonus of 6d. a day in March, 1915, to blast-furnacemen in Scotland; a bonus given by Messrs. Bolckow Vaughan to their Middlesbrough employees, raised by the Committee to 8s. a week in July, 1917. Bonuses consisting of a percentage on average earnings were fairly common. On the other hand the Committee refused to award bonuses, where in their opinion adequate advances had been secured by other means; examples were the applications from Cumberland blast-furnacemen, whose advances under their scale amounted to $28\frac{1}{2}$ per cent., and the West of Scotland manufactured steel trade, who had advanced $22\frac{1}{2}$ per cent. since war broke out, on 29 April, 1915.

(2) In a few cases the Committee's award removed maxima, which, under existing sliding scales, were preventing the further rise of wages. Thus, in the South Wales and Monmouthshire iron and steel trade, a maximum of 45 per cent. over the basis was agreed on in

July, 1915, in addition to which a war bonus was paid. This maximum was reached in January, 1916. On application to the Committee in March it was maintained, but on renewed application in March, 1917, it was removed and the scale extended for the duration of the war. In March, 1916, the maximum (55 per cent. above standard) in the Scotch pig iron (blast-furnacemen's) scale was extended 10 per cent.; in June of the same year a similar extension from 20 to 60 per cent. was granted for Messrs. Bolckow Vaughan's scale, but the following year, in July, 1917, instead of a further extension an increased war bonus was awarded.

(3) The Committee attempted an assessment of the advances which workers might have expected had prices and sliding scales been functioning normally. Thus, in March, 1916, on an application from the blast-furnacemen in the Scottish pig iron trade for the termination of their sliding scale, the Committee decided that the scale should be maintained during the war, but that the maximum should be extended and also an advance of 5 per cent. made on wages to compensate the workmen, most of whom were paid on tonnage, for the reduction in output due to difficulty in getting supplies; a minimum wage was also fixed. In October, on a renewed application a further advance of 15 per cent. on basis rates was awarded. A clearer case was the application of the blast-furnacemen at the Blaenavon Company for a payment of 10s. a week in compensation for the loss of percentage on the sliding scale due to the Government's action in fixing a maximum price for hematite pig iron in the middle of 1916. The Committee awarded an advance of $7\frac{1}{2}$ per cent. on the sliding scale.

The committee was reluctant to interfere with the normal working of sliding scales. It refused to authorise the transfer of blast-furnacemen from one sliding scale to another in the case of the South Wales and Monmouthshire iron and steel makers (24 July, 1916); in other cases it continued to the end of the war the operation of scales which were under notice to terminate. The result was a certain amount of confusion at the end of the war. Steel makers were generally on scales based on the price of open hearth steel; during the war there was a big expansion of production by the Bessemer process to which these scales were not adapted. Wages became adjusted to war prices which included subsidies that would cease with the war. In some cases, for example the Midland firm of Alfred Hickman, sliding scales were instituted during the war, which gave them an abnormal basis.

It should be noted that the Ministry did not require sanction under section 4 (2) of the Munitions of War Act, 1915, to changes in wages consequent on a rise in prices under a sliding scale.

III. The Problem of Wages in the Building Industry.

The attempts to control wages in the building industry illustrate well the difficulties and possibilities of inter-departmental action.[1] The services of the industry were required urgently and on a large

---

[1] HIST. REC./H./321/2.

scale by several Departments, especially the War Office for camps, and the Ministry of Munitions for factory construction and housing of munitions workers. There was a shortage of labour which made itself felt as soon as the Ministry programme of national factory construction was launched, due partly to unrestricted enlistment during the period of depression in the industry which followed the outbreak of war, and partly to the drift of building labour into the more regular and better paid work of munitions production; while wages standards were disturbed before any attempt at control was made by the competition of contractors, by varying local arbitration awards, and by the recruitment of navvy battalions by the War Office at rates of pay, 3s. a day and allowances, which gave the labourer with a family an income considerably in excess of his industrial standard.

Almost simultaneously attention was drawn to the need of systematic control by the Office of Works, which suggested subjecting building labour to the same limitations of movement as engineering labour, by the War Office, which forwarded to the Ministry a complaint by a contractor building hutments and paying $6\frac{1}{2}$d. to 9d. an hour that his labour was leaving him for Gretna where the rates were $7\frac{1}{2}$d. and 9d., and by the Treasury, which urged co-operation between the Ministry and the War Office in order to prevent competition for labour.[1] The matter was discussed at an inter-departmental conference on 22 October, 1915, which recommended the appointment of a small standing committee. This recommendation was accepted by Dr. Addison, the terms of reference of the committee being :—

"to consider and make recommendations with regard to the rates of wages and other questions arising in that connection with regard to the supply of building labour for Government purposes."

The Committee passed through the following stages in its first year in dealing with building wages :—

(1) It was decided at its first meeting (28 October) that no uniform rates, such as had been suggested, could be adopted for builders' labourers throughout the country; any such standards must be adopted locally if at all, and "the existing wage rates were the only possible basis." One reason given for this by the Committee was that the recent Gretna award as to labourers' wages, quoted above, had fixed so high a rate that it was quite impossible to bring the rest of the country up to its level.

(2) A circular was, on the recommendation of the Committee, sent out by the Wages Section in February, 1916, to Government contractors, urging them to refrain in future from paying more than the district rates to their workers, and to notify the Ministry of Munitions of any proposed changes in their rates of payment. Between thirty and forty replies to this circular were received, agreeing to its terms, and incidentally in several cases complaining of the degree to which their workers were unsettled by rates of pay offered by other Government contractors, especially those working for the Ministry of Munitions.

---

[1] Correspondence in HIST. REC./R./321/1.

(3) Could building contractors offering exorbitant rates of wages be " controlled " as a remedy ? The question was raised in January, 1916, with special reference to a group of firms in Coventry, who were said to be trying to outbid each other in securing labour. The Treasury solicitor gave, as his opinion, that the business of a builder could be declared a controlled establishment, and that by making establishments controlled it would be possible to prevent future increases of wages. He doubted whether any general regulation of building wages would be within the powers conferred by the Defence of the Realm Act.

(4) After two months' existence of the Committee, Mr. Morgan minuted to Mr. Rey, " the Committee suffers from lack of executive powers, and it is suggested that definite powers to require building contractors on works of all kinds connected with munitions to adhere to such scales as regards rates as it may lay down, should be delegated to the Committee." No executive powers with regard to wages were, however, at the time delegated to the Committee—this had been one of the obvious weaknesses of its position—and it had, therefore, to try perforce to regulate them by peaceful persuasion. This was done during its first year by an informal understanding among its members that they should report carefully on the contracts of their departments, and that no rates in excess of the district rates should in any case be paid, without the previous sanction of the committee. It was, however, only in February, 1917, that this procedure was formally recognised by a departmental minute.

(5) The informal understanding between members of the committee during 1916 to some extent kept building wages from being forced up merely by competition among impatient Departments and contractors, as distinguished from advances gained by arbitration awards, agreement with employers, and reasonable allowances for extra payments in the remote districts in which some munition works and soldiers' camps were placed.

The Departments concerned, however, sometimes omitted to consult the committee about wages to be paid by their contractors, and there were several fresh instances in the autumn of 1916 of overlapping between the firms working, for example, for the Army Contracts Department and the Office of Works. Accordingly, at the end of October, 1916, Mr. Johnston, on behalf of the committee, sent a fresh minute, this time to the Minister, explaining the utter inadequacy of its powers and asking for authority " to call on any Department to insist on its contractors reducing rates of wages paid by them . . . . in excess of the standard rate of the district, and further to insist that wages should not be raised above that rate " except with the Committee's fully considered consent. The Committee, it was explained, contained at the time representatives of every Department concerned with the erection of buildings for war purposes: the Admiralty, The War Office Contracts Departments, Explosives Supply, the National Shell Factories, the Office of Works, the Director of Factory Construction, the Director of Housing, the Road Board, with Mr. Vernon and Mr. J. C. Smith of the Wages Section.

As a result of these representations, instructions were sent to all the supply departments concerned within the Ministry, directing them to supervise the contracts of their departments in this way, while, after a good deal of discussion of the constitutional position involved, the representatives of the Departments outside the Ministry agreed, except in cases " of grave emergency," to be bound by the decisions of the Committee.

The Committee thus, after more than a year's work, obtained authority for the most important function laid down in its terms of reference—the control of wages.

As in the case of engineering labour, the question of wages could hardly be separated from the supply and movement of building labour. At its first meeting the Building Labour Committee considered the application to building labour of the leaving certificate provision of the Munitions Act. It was advised that the Act did not permit such an application. The Amendment Act of 1916 extended the definition of " munitions work " to the construction and repair of buildings for naval and military purposes or for munitions work, but this extension affected only a small proportion of the force engaged on building work. The regulations could still not be applied to the workers employed in preparing the ground for munitions factories and working on the early stages, and these were the building workers whose unsettlement gave most trouble in 1916. The leaving certificate provisions were unsuited to the building industry with its practice of short term engagements, and neither contractors nor committee pressed the Government very strongly for their extension to the industry.

An alternative method of restricting competition for labour was by restricting advertisement and other forms of " enticement," as had been done in the case of engineering labour by Regulation 8 B of the Defence of the Realm Act. This method was recommended by the Committee on 10 February, 1916, and subsequently,[1] but without effect.

A more drastic method was to prohibit or limit the employment of building labour on private work and so to release labour for Government work. The Admiralty representative urged this method on the Committee in view of the shortage of labour for work at Rosyth as early as 2 December, 1915, and the procedure was, it seemed, legal under Regulation 8 A (*b*) of the Defence of the Realm Act. Though not adopted immediately, this method was applied, in the first instance, to the work on the London County Hall, on 20 February, 1916.[2] This power was used sparingly, not merely because of the possible dislocation and expense of compensation, but because there was no security that the labour displaced would not be absorbed by other private work. Actual prohibitions were supplemented by a press notice on 29 March, 1916, advising private firms to commence no building operations without first consulting the Ministry of Munitions. The notice attracted a good deal of attention, and enabled the Building Labour Department to exercise pressure without actually invoking the aid of a compulsory Order.[3]

---

[1] L.R. 51873/16, 63.   [2] L.R. 51877/31.   [3] L.R. 51873/20, 25.

In spite of these measures, the Departments with building work on hand found themselves still faced with a shortage of labour. Both they and the Committee were of opinion that the only remedy was a general embargo on unregulated private building.[1] The Board of Trade's figures of employment pointed to the conclusion that there was still a reserve of labour on private work.[2] A special regulation, 8 E, was accordingly issued under the Defence of the Realm Act, prohibiting the undertaking or completion of any building contract of more than £500 in value, or involving the use of constructional steel, unless carried out under Government contract or by a local authority authorised by a Government Department to borrow money for the purpose, or unless licensed by the Ministry of Munitions.

Neither the co-operation of contracting departments through the Building Labour Committee nor the restriction of employment on private work checked the upward and irregular movement of building wages in 1917 and 1918. The Departments did not always consult their representative on the Committee, or send representatives regularly, or exercise complete control over their contractors.[3] Had they done so, rates were constantly being changed by arbitrations which, being local, were not co-ordinated and never final. Advances in the nominal rate were not large; the London increase, for example, between July, 1914, and July, 1917, was only 2½d. an hour; but earnings were driven up by the grant of extras, meals, fares, lodging money, special bonuses and, of course, by overtime and regular work.[4] The Building Labour Committee sought to check these allowances, but had not always the power. Thus an award by an arbitrator appointed by the Chief Industrial Commissioner at Hereford early in 1917, granted " wet money "—a special payment when wet weather prevented outside work—which the Committee had always opposed; the National Service scheme for volunteers proposed a lodging allowance of 17s. 6d., which the Committee had always opposed as unnecessary in the building industry, which involved migratory work in normal times; and double pay for Sunday work became a sort of special bonus on Government work until the Committee secured a special Order under Regulation 8 E, in July, 1917, prohibiting it except on sudden emergency. The rising cost of living provoked, and the growing shortage of labour enabled, building operatives to secure constant advances.

In the autumn of 1917 a new Department attempted to solve the problem of wages in the building industry. The National Service Department, in discharge of its obligation to economise man-power, organised joint committees of employers and workpeople to assist it

---

[1] L.R. 51873/26.
[2] Hist. Rec./R./321/2.
[3] Minute by Mr. Fane, 17·1·18 (L.R. 15945).
[4] The Journal of the Amalgamated Society of Carpenters of October, 1916, said: "Seventy-five per cent. of our members are at present engaged on war work, the majority of whom average £3 a week. . . . . It is a well-known fact that many of our members have taken up to £6 and £7 per week for periods of weeks, and others up to £4 and £5 for months in the last two years."

in considering the needs of each industry. At a conference promoted by that department, in October, 1917, it was decided to form such a joint board for the building industry, although members of the Building Labour Committee present took part only on the understanding that the conference was merely to discuss the question. The Board was to settle all questions of wages and conditions of labour as well as the economising of man-power and allocation of contracts in building.

The Building Labour Committee, whose members at the conference had refused to give their support to the proposal, at its meeting on 27 November passed the following resolution :—[1]

> "This committee desire to point out that they view with considerable alarm the suggestion that a committee formed, with the exception of the chairman, entirely of the representatives of the Masters and Men, should settle the question of wages and conditions of labour. The work of the present committee is to force adherence to standard rates, and the difficulties they have to contend with are not so much the demands of the men as the eagerness of the master builders to pay increased rates with the view of keeping the men together. At the present time, when practically all work is Government work, additional wages do not fall upon the builders, but upon the ratepayers, and a committee upon which there is no member of a Government Department to state the case from the Government point of view would have no interest in keeping rates down, and there would be a general rise all over the country."

The formation of a joint board was held up as a result of this opposition, but a renewed attempt was made in the New Year. Some of the principal contractors employed by Sir John Hunter's department pressed for the reference of all wages questions to it. Resolutions from trade unions and master builders' associations reached the Ministry in favour of it, and on 19 February a joint resolution from the National Federation of Master Builders and the trade unions, protesting against the delay in setting up the board was addressed to the Minister. Sir John Hunter himself, as a result of complaints about unequal conditions, put forward a proposal for a flat-rate for the whole country for each grade of building labour, and suggested the London standards as a basis. The chairman of the Building Labour Committee objected that this would be to attempt to apply equal conditions where equal conditions could not and did not exist;[2] new rates needed fixing, once they were fixed the committee could resume its work of preventing any departure from them.[3]

The opposition of the Ministry of Munitions to the proposed joint board was reinforced by that of the Ministry of Labour. At an

---

[1] L.R. 15745.

[2] Complaints were frequent against the contractors working for Sir John Hunter's own department: *e.g.*, Building Labour Committee Minutes, 12 February, where a contractor building an aerodrome was reported to be paying building labourers 11½d. an hour plus 5s. a week bonus, instead of the local rate of 7½d. an hour and 4d. a day bonus.

[3] Minute by Sir Ernest Newton, 21 January, 1918 (L.R. 15745).

inter-departmental conference convened at the Ministry of Labour, on 4 February, Sir David Shackleton stated that there was very grave objection to the kind of Wage Board proposed to be set up in the building industry, and that his department could not approve of such a board settling the wages in that industry as :—

(1) there was no check on the agreements they might make ;

(2) that it would inevitably lead to demands of other industries to be allowed to deal with their questions in the same way.

It was suggested by him that what was necessary was a committee with powers to see that departments did not outbid each other, and that employers were strictly limited to paying the standard rate of wages in the districts.

As a result of this conference the Ministry of Labour circulated a memorandum on the whole problem on 12 March. After explaining the need of control, it recapitulated the reasons for objecting to the joint board proposed by the Ministry of National Service, and supported by the trade. Such a board might make awards inconsistent with the policy of the Committee on Production ; whereas it was essential to maintain the position of the Committee on Production as the supreme co-ordinating authority, since one industry's settlements reacted on other industries. Moreover, the ordinary brake of competition being removed, there was nothing to prevent wages from being raised above an economic level at the expense of the State. The memorandum then summarised various alternative policies discussed at the conference: the reform of the Building Labour Committee, the use of local conciliation committees as advisory to the contracting departments, the unification of control by the concentration of all Government building work in the hands of a single building department, and the organisation of the building industry on the same lines as the engineering industry for joint submission of wages demands to the Committee on Production.

The Scotch building industry had, in January, made an agreement at the instigation of the Chief Industrial Commissioner for the submission of wage questions jointly at four monthly intervals to the Committee on Production. The Ministry of Labour's proposal, circulated with the memorandum, was that the national conciliation board of the building industry, which had ceased to function during the war, should be resuscitated; general wage applications should be submitted by this board to the Committee on Production at regular intervals, as was done in the engineering and other industries ; questions affecting district conditions or customs should be formulated by the local conciliation boards, and no change permitted without the concurrence both of the national board and of the Ministry ; the Ministry of Labour to consult contracting departments where changes were proposed, and, if they disapproved, to submit the case to the Committee on Production, the poaching of labour and excessive rates to be checked, if necessary, by the use of the Defence of the Realm Regulation, 8 A (*b*). The last point had been suggested by the Ministry of Munitions in a letter of 4 January.

The Ministry of Munitions, in reply, suggested two amendments of importance. The first was that the Minister of Labour should be assisted in considering changes by the Building Labour Committee, which embodied a wide experience and a detailed knowledge both of the building industry itself and of the reactions of building wages on other industries. The second was that local conciliation boards should refer proposals for changes direct to the Ministry of Labour. These amendments were accepted, slightly altering the balance of the scheme. In effect it now restored the authority of the Building Labour Committee, and gave it the means of making its decisions effective. On the one hand no change was to be considered, unless the representative organisation of the trade made itself responsible for it; on the other hand its decisions had a force they lacked when the committee was merely a piece of liaison machinery between contracting departments, since they had the authority of the Ministry of Labour, on which the Cabinet had imposed the duty of co-ordinating wage settlements generally. The building industry adopted the recommendation that general wage claims should be submitted to the Committee on Production at regular intervals; but these national settlements had not the same importance as in other industries, the chief occasion of controversy being local variations in special bonuses and incidental payments.

The Chief Industrial Commissioner took the chairmanship of the Building Labour Committee. To enable the Ministry of Labour to exercise its control, the Building Wages Order was issued on 14 June.[1]

The Order, after defining "building work," limited time-rates, working rules and conditions of remuneration, as from the date of the Order, to the wages fixed under any award made under Part I of the Munitions of War Act, 1915, or by a decision of the Building Labour Committee, or, where no such award or decision had been made, to the wages recognised by a Conciliation Board or collective agreement on 15 April, 1918. These rates and conditions could be varied only by an agreement between employers and workpeople approved by the Minister, or by an award under Part I of the Munitions Act of 1915. Any difference arising out of the application of the Order was to be referred to the Special Arbitration Tribunal appointed under Section 8 of the Act of 1917; in other words, to the Committee on Production sitting as a special tribunal. Any contravention of the Order was punishable in like manner as if the Order were an award under Part I of the Act of 1915.

IV. Extension of the Coal Controller's Awards.

The reactions on the Ministry of Munitions' work of other Departments' action in interfering with wages are illustrated by the Coal Controller's first award.[2] On 28 September, 1917, the Coal Controller agreed with the Miners' Federation of Great Britain to grant a special

---

[1] Statutory Rules and Orders No. 742 of 1918.
[2] See memorandum by Mr. J. H. Jones in Ministry of Labour, Intelligence Division papers.

war wage of 1s. 6d. a day to colliery workers of 16 years of age and over, and 9d. a day to those under 16. The award did not extend to tradesmen, mechanics and others who were already in receipt of similar war advances granted in respect of their particular trade or craft ; it was to be recognised as due to and dependent on the existence of the abnormal conditions then prevailing and was to be subject to revision in the light of changes in the cost of living. Where the customary number of days worked a week in any district was less than six, 9s. and 4s. 6d. a week were nevertheless to be paid. It was provided that the increase in the selling price of coal that the award would necessitate should not be made a ground for claiming a further advance.

The award immediately affected the Ministry of Munitions since the Miners' Federation asked that it should be extended to members of the federation in lead mines, ironstone and limestone quarries, coke-ovens, fire-clay and ganister mines. These, though few of them were controlled establishments, were working mainly for the Ministry of Munitions. Mr. McNair, of the Coal Controller's Department, took the matter up the same day with Mr. Craig, M.P., of the Iron and Steel Production Department, and with the Mineral Resources Development Committee early in October.[1]

Already, however, the Labour Committee of the Munitions Council had considered the wider aspect of the Coal Controller's action. A preliminary settlement of the Controller's with colliery engine winding men, made without consulting the Ministry, was expected to provoke a corresponding demand from shale oil mines for which the Ministry was responsible, and to cause discontent among other trades, since the war advances of this class were brought up to 29s. a week as against 15s. in the engineering and other industries. The Coal Controller's action was regarded as a claim to a jurisdiction over wages independent of the Ministry of Labour and the Committee on Production. The Ministry of Labour protested to the War Cabinet, and the Ministry of Munitions supported the protest.[2] The result of this protest was the formation of the War Cabinet Labour Committee referred to below.[3]

The Ministry first proposed that any claims to participate in the Coal Controller's award should be referred to the Committee on Production. The Coal Controller's Department stated that such a course would lead to strikes. The Ministry therefore agreed to negotiate corresponding advances. After conferences in which Sir Charles Ellis's Committee, the Ministry of Labour, the Coal Controller's Department, and the Labour Regulation and Iron and Steel Production Departments of the Ministry of Munitions took part, the following policy was agreed on :—

(1) All members of the Miners' Federation, whether coal miners or not, were to participate in the award ; the actual amount to be paid in each case to be adjusted by the Coal Controller and the

---

[1] L.R. 4647/7.
[2] Minute by Sir Charles Ellis, 24 September, 1917. (L.R. 4647/7).
[3] See below, pp. 221 *et sqq*.

Executive Committee of the Miners' Federation, and a payment on account to be made where necessary.

(2) Pending adjustment by the Coal Controller, any advance made since 1 March last to be merged in the advance of 1s. 6d. and 9d. a day.

(3) When a settlement had been reached with trades represented by the Miners' Federation, the Labour Regulation Department should negotiate corresponding advances in allied trades.[1]

At a meeting with the Miners' Federation on 17 October, a basis of adjustment was reached. It was embodied in the following memorandum :—

"1*st* : Advances in wages have since the beginning of the war been, generally speaking, given in two ways :—
  (*a*) As the result of increased selling prices (trade conditions).
  (*b*) To meet increased cost of living (War Wages).

2*nd* : The above award is a war wage.

3*rd* : The last advance to the colliery workers was in February, 1917.

4*th* : The present award is over and above all other advances, and a flat rate to all colliery workers.

5*th* : It is laid down in the award in the second paragraph as follows :—

'The advance shall not be paid to any workers such as tradesmen and mechanics who are already in receipt of similar war advances granted in respect of their particular trade or craft. Any question whether any advance so granted is such as to disqualify the class of workers concerned from receiving the war wage or part of it should be at once referred to the Controller.'

With these considerations in mind, the result of conferences with the Coal Controller, the Ministry of Labour, the Labour Council of the Ministry of Munitions, and the Executive of the Miners' Federation, has been to lay down the following principle for adjusting and harmonising the wages in allied industries to the Coal Controller's award.

  (*a*) 1 March, 1917, to be taken as the datum line ;
  (*b*) Advances taken before 1 March are not to be considered, except in so far as they are less than 12s. per week. (This 12s. is the amount which has been given by the Committee of Production to meet increased cost of living.)
  (*c*) Any amount less than 12s. advance given before 1 March to be regarded as arrears.
  (*d*) Any advance (war wage) which has been given since 1 March, after deducting arrears (*c*) to be merged in the war wage now awarded."

L. Committee approved this arrangement. The administration of the agreement when it was handed over to the Wages Section involved considerable difficulties. Five groups were found to be

---

[1] Memo. by Mr. Craig, 11 October, 1917 ; L.R. 4647/7. Cf. L. R. 7959.

affected: ironstone mines, coke-oven and bye-product plants, fireclay and fire bricks, limestone quarries and non-ferrous metal mines. The conditions in these groups varied from firm to firm and from district to district in respect both of commercial conditions and basis of wages.

Commercial conditions varied according as firms were working for the Government and could expect to secure compensation for increased labour costs or not. Employers had not been consulted when the award was made and the agreement come to to extend it, and in some cases refused to pay it. Such cases were referred to arbitration. In some cases the firm, if willing to pay the award to those of its workpeople who were on Government work, refused to pay it to other workpeople doing the same work on private contracts. In the case of lead mines it was necessary for the Ministry, not only to undertake to reimburse employers the cost of the award, about £150,000 a year, but to guarantee them against loss in general, before they were able to make terms with their employees which would secure the necessary output. The bulk of the work affected was, however, Government work, and the Iron and Steel Production Department instructed its contractors to pay the award as soon as the agreement to extend it was made.

The varying basis of wages was a greater difficulty. Coke-oven workers, for example, in South Wales and Derbyshire were in the Miners' Federation, and automatically received the award. In North Staffordshire, West Yorkshire and other fields, they were in a separate union, the National Union of Coke Workers, which became affiliated with the Miners' Federation, but not until after the agreement on 17 October; this union, however, received the same treatment as the Miners' Federation. In the Cleveland and Durham district, on the other hand, the workers in coke-ovens and attached to blast-furnaces were organised with the blast-furnacemen and received the same advances under the sliding scales and otherwise as blast-furnacemen. Clearly, therefore, they should not be classified with other coke-oven workers; but, unfortunately, they had been led to believe that they would receive the award,[1] which, moreover, had been given to Cleveland ironstone miners whose wages also moved with the sliding scale. The Lincolnshire coke workers were on the Lincolnshire blast-furnace sliding scale, but were also members of the National Union of Coke Workers, and therefore covered by the 17 October agreement. It was obviously not contemplated that their wages should move both with the sliding scale and with coal miners' wages, and the Ministry at first refused to sanction their claim, relying on the second paragraph of the agreement, which excluded workers whose wages customarily followed trades other than mining. It was impossible to persist in this course, however, and instructions were given to the firm to pay the award. The firm refused, partly because it had not been consulted when the agreement was made, mainly because it feared the reactions of the concession on blast-furnacemen's wages. The matter went to arbitration, and the men received the award.

---

[1] M.W. 184160.

There were similar variations among ironstone miners. In the Cleveland district they were on the sliding scale, but received the award by a special arrangement. In Cumberland and the Forest of Dean they received it as members of the Miners' Federation. In Oxfordshire, Northamptonshire and Lincolnshire they were organised separately and did not receive the award. Some clayworkers and brickmakers were in the Miners' Federation and got the award, the majority were outside ; limestone quarries and non-ferrous mines were in the same position.

The task of administration was eased by the agreement with the Iron and Steel Trades Confederation for the extension of the $12\frac{1}{2}$ per cent. bonus to those trades, reached on 3 January. By this, the bonus and the Coal Controller's awards were made alternatives, and both were to merge in future increases under sliding scales. Since Government subsidies at the same time were allowed to count as increases in price for the purpose of sliding scale determinations, the incentive to claim the Coal Controller's award was weakened.

The great majority of coke-oven workers received the award. Ironstone miners received either the award or the iron and steel trade's advances. It was extended to all non-ferrous metal mines except tin. In the case of clay, bricks, ganister and limestone, the principle on which the Ministry acted was to deal only with those parts of the industry's output in which the Ministry had an interest as consumer, to instruct employers to pay the wage within those limits, and to undertake to reimburse them. If the unions wished to extend the advance beyond these limits, they must do so by agreement.

On 12 June, the Miners' Federation demanded a second advance of the same amount as the previous award.[1] The Coal Controller, with the authority of the War Cabinet, offered an advance of 6d. and 3d. with the alternative of arbitration. The federation refused both offers, and the War Cabinet, against the advice of the representatives of the Ministry of Labour and the Ministry of Munitions, decided in the interests of output to concede the claims. The Prime Minister announced the award himself.

The Ministry of Munitions was able to settle its policy in regard to extending the award quickly in the light of its experience with the first award. It refused to be represented at the Coal Controller's conferences and insisted on discussing the matter of extension with the Miners' Federation itself. The federation's representatives visited the Ministry on 29 June, the day after the settlement with the Prime Minister, and stated that they insisted on the award being extended to all their members ; failing an immediate undertaking to this effect they should go back to the Prime Minister. They were persuaded to defer any action until a conference on 3 July. Before this conference the different divisions of the Ministry interested—Contracts, Iron and Steel Production, Explosives, and Wages—considered the claim and drew up a statement for submission, first to the Ministry

---

[1] Verbatim report of interview with Coal Controller in L.R. 4647/8.

of Labour and then to the Miners' Federation. Substantially, this statement was accepted by the miners at the conference on 3 July.[1] Agreement was reached, and, in a conference on 10 July, an agreement on identical principles with the National Council of Colliery Workers other than miners. It was decided that the Ministry of Munitions should notify employers of the agreement; the letter in substance reproduced the agreement and was submitted before issue to the unions for confirmation and to the Ministry of Labour for approval. The following are the effective clauses in the letter.[2]

"It has been explained that the Ministry of Munitions does not prescribe advances to wages for workpeople engaged in these industries. In certain cases, however, the product of these industries is sold at prices regulated by the Ministry; in other cases increased wages cannot be paid to the workpeople engaged on a product essential to the Ministry without financial assistance to the employers. In such cases the Ministry of Munitions has stated that it will be prepared to sanction approved increases in the fixed prices or to recognise approved claims to meet extra labour costs, provided the employer shows that he has paid to his workpeople a war wage or war advance on the conditions hereinafter specified. The Ministry reserves the right to examine the books of the employer in order to ascertain how much, if any, of the claim presented by him should properly be borne by the Ministry.

The amount of the war wage in respect of which the Ministry will be prepared to entertain claims under paragraph 2 hereof from employers, is as follows :—

(a) In the case of Ironstone, Limestone and Lead Mines— the same war wage as has been granted by the Controller of Coal Mines, subject to the understanding that the workpeople have received no advance (exclusive of advances on account of long service, individual merit or regrading) since they received the war wage previously granted by the Controller of Coal Mines.

(b) In the case of Fireclay, Silica and Ganister Mining—as provided in (a) except in cases where the wages of workpeople are governed by the award of the C.O.P. No. 1736 in the Fire-Clay Industry of Great Britain dated 28 June, 1918.

It is not intended that the war wage herein referred to should be paid to the workpeople whose wages it has been the practice to regulate according to the wage movements in a trade, not being the coal trade, other than that in which they are engaged, and no claims by employers under paragraph 2 hereof will be entertained in the case of such workpeople. Any case falling within this exclusion, in which, however, the war wage granted

---

[1] Verbatim Report in L.R. 4647/8.
[2] Circular M.M. 214.

by the Controller of Coal Mines as from 17 September, 1917, was paid may be referred to the Ministry for special consideration. It is not intended that any workpeople who received the war wage as contemplated in this letter shall also receive advances based on any other principle, *e.g.*, those whose wages have previously been regulated by a scale dependent on the selling price of pig-iron, if in receipt of the war wage, should not receive advances also due to movements in the scale.

In certain districts for example, Cumberland, Furness, Lincolnshire, Northamptonshire, Oxfordshire, etc.—wages in the industries referred to in paragraph 1 hereof have been regulated by special arrangements and in such cases it is not contemplated that the war wage shall apply.

In addition to the members of the Miners' Federation of Great Britain and the National Council of Societies representing Colliery workers other than Miners, members of other trade unions are employed in the industries specified in paragraph 1 hereof. Employers intending to submit a claim to the Ministry under paragraph 2 hereof in respect of the payment of the war wage to members of such other trade unions should, before payment of the war wage, communicate with the Ministry, stating whether they paid the previous war wage granted by the Controller of Coal Mines and ascertain from the Ministry whether in the event of payment they would be in order in submitting a claim under paragraph 2. Where the workpeople concerned are within the scope of the Committee on Production Award No. 1736 in the Clay Industry of Great Britain, dated 28 June, 1918, a claim by employers under paragraph 2 hereof would not be in order.

Employers concerned in non-ferrous mines other than lead mines who paid the previous war wage to their workpeople should submit particulars of their cases for consideration by the Ministry under paragraph 2 hereof in the event of the payment of the war wage referred to.

It is intended that the war wage herein referred to should, in all cases, be paid as from 30 June, 1918."

Workers in coke-ovens and bye-product plants received the award and in addition had a special grievance remedied. Under the first award the war wage did not count for overtime and was limited to six shifts a week. It happened sometimes in these continuous processes that the worker had to take a second shift immediately after the previous shift in order to act as substitute for an absentee in the gang that succeeded his own. The war wage of 1s. 6d. had not been payable on this substitute shift, because such substitute shifts could not legally be worked by miners who formed the great majority of the workers covered by the award; and the Coal Controller was unwilling to vary its terms. He did, however, in the following October, issue an additional award allowing payment of the war wage on both substitute shifts and overtime.

The expenses of the Coal Controller's Department were charged on the coal industry. The war wage was therefore charged on the levy made on coal to meet these expenses. The extension of the war wage outside the industry led to the extension of the levy to ironstone and clay got in connection with coal, but not in other cases.

The effect of the Coal Controller's action on the Ministry of Munitions' work was to force the Ministry to extend its regulation of wages to a new field, the industries intermediate between coal mining and iron production, and to throw on the Wages and Contracts Departments a great volume of detailed adjustments, in the one case of general awards to individual cases, in the other of prices to changed labour costs. Its effect on the regulation of wages generally was to compel the War Cabinet to take action to prevent unco-ordinated awards in future.

V. The Co-ordination of Departmental Action by the Cabinet.

The chaos of wages in the building industry, and the dislocation caused by the independent action of the Coal Controller, were only extreme examples of a difficulty that attended the administration of wage control throughout the war. A settlement in one trade or district was certain to have reactions on other trades and districts; an orderly adjustment of wages to changing economic conditions therefore was possible only if every settlement was co-ordinated with every other settlement. In practice, control was exercised and settlements made, not only by the Wages Section of the Ministry of Munitions and the Committee on Production and other tribunals to which disputes were referred under the Munitions of War Acts, but by the Admiralty, War Office, Post Office, Office of Works, Coal Controller, Railway Executive Committee, voluntary conciliation boards, single arbitrators appointed by the Ministry of Labour, and by the ordinary negotiations of collective bargaining in uncontrolled trades. The Wages Section always sought to correlate its decisions with those of the Committee on Production and special arbitration tribunals, it was in constant contact with, and was able to work in co-operation with the divisions of the Ministry that influenced wages by placing contracts. But there was no authority except the Cabinet that could guide and control the independent departments, and co-ordination between them depended almost entirely on consultation and agreement between them until towards the end of 1917.

The Ministry of Munitions naturally was in closest contact with the Shipyard Labour Department of the Admiralty, the War Office and the Ministry of Labour. Between these a fair measure of co-ordination was attained. They dealt with the same industries and classes of labour; the Munitions of War Acts were another unifying influence; and they accepted the Committee on Production as the ultimate authority on general wages questions. But there were differences; the Admiralty, for example, in 1916 resisted payment by results on aircraft construction when the Ministry was pressing it, and in 1917 pressed for statutory enforcement of payment by results generally when the Ministry preferred to rely on voluntary agreement. The sharp differences over the 12½ per cent. bonus have been indicated above. Again, on more than one occasion decisions which the Ministry had made under the sanctioning section (4 (2)) of the first Munitions of War Act were upset by single arbitrators appointed by the Ministry of Labour. And these departments even collectively did not cover the whole field of industry within which the settlements might be expected to react on one another. The difficulty with which they were faced was that there are no sharp lines of demarcation in the continuum of industry; demarcation is always in the last resort arbitrary; a classification that is satisfactory for one purpose will be unsuitable for others.

Thus, the provinces, with which the different departments of State were concerned, were not coincident with separate industries; all were concerned more or less with engineering and with building and with chemicals and with textiles. If a common policy in respect to a particular industry, however, were reached, it did nothing to solve the problems presented by the overlap of industries. Wages questions are largely questions of craft or occupation, and occupational lines of demarcation do not coincide with industrial lines. Any decision in engineering would affect shipbuilding; mechanics and building operatives were employed in large numbers as maintenance men outside the engineering and building industries; general labour and transport cut right across an industrial classification. Yet another cause of confusion is the relation of trade union organisation to industrial structure. Unions on an occupational basis, like the older craft unions, have interests in many industries, so have the unions of semi-skilled and unskilled workers. The trade card scheme of exemption from military service broke down, because union membership was not a reliable index of industrial status and function; the extension of the Coal Controller's award to all members of the Miners' Federation affected the Ministry of Munitions, because the federation had members among the ironstone miners, limestone quarrymen, coke workers, lead miners and others who thereby were able to claim the advance and, by getting it, enabled similar workers outside the federation to claim it. While, therefore, every authority that had to do with wages came to realise that no settlement could be made that would not have reactions on other wages, the practice of consultation between departments was not sufficient to ensure co-ordination, and some more effective means had to be sought.

The Ministry of Labour, to which the Chief Industrial Commissioner's Department had been transferred, was continuously occupied with this problem from its formation. Since it was not a contracting department, it stood in a different relation to labour from that of the other departments concerned. At the instigation of the Chief Industrial Commissioner a series of national agreements was negotiated early in 1917, to submit wages questions periodically to the

Committee on Production.[1] This arrangement did much to restore the committee's authority and power to control the movement of wages, since it was enabled to correlate local advances in each industry and advances in different industries ; and the effect went beyond the actual scope of the awards, since other trades, which did not come before the committee themselves, were guided by these awards. The Ministry of Labour was able further to exercise a co-ordinating influence, since all disputes which came under Part I. of the Munitions of War Act, 1915, and all disputes outside the scope of the Munitions Acts in which the parties agreed to arbitration or conciliation, under the Act of 1896, came to it for reference to arbitrators selected by it. By restricting the work of arbitration to a limited number of arbitrators of experience some check was placed on the tendency of rates to diverge.

This action of the Ministry of Labour was not sufficient. The Commission on Industrial Unrest, in the summer of 1917, received complaints from both employers and employed. Mr. Barnes, in his summary of the eight reports, said : " All the reports refer in general terms to what is called the want of co-ordination between Government Departments. The co-ordination of Government Departments dealing with labour is reported as an urgent matter." The reports themselves, however, confuse two things : the need of co-ordination and the need of decentralising labour administration. Much of the want of co-ordination was due to the large measure of decentralisation, which led to individual and divergent action. No further steps were taken to secure co-ordination until the Coal Controller's award in October.

The miners were not a party to the Treasury Agreement. They gave the Government an undertaking instead to utilise the existing conciliation machinery to prevent stoppages. It was in accordance with their usual practice that they refused to submit their claim for an advance in 1917 to the ordinary machinery of arbitration, and the mine owners supported them in their objection. The Coal Controller, as has been seen, therefore, acted without co-ordinating his action with that of the Ministry of Labour and Committee on Production, and arranged to give his first award.

The Minister of Labour brought the question before the War Cabinet who referred it to a committee on labour disputes consisting of Lord Milner and Mr. Barnes, who conferred with the President of the Board of Trade, Minister of Labour, Coal Controller and representatives of the Chief Industrial Commissioner's Department and Ministry of Munitions on 28 September. Their report was issued subsequently and considered by the War Cabinet on 18 October.[2]

The report pointed out that the demand for increased wages, stimulated by the concessions already made to the miners and worked up to some extent, at any rate, by people whose real object was to cause trouble and impede the conduct of the war, was perhaps the most serious difficulty then confronting the country. The attempt to remove discontent by keeping down the cost of necessaries and to stop

---

[1] See above Chap. III, Sect. 5.   [2] L.R. 4647/7.

"profiteering" had failed. If the pressure exercised on the Government by powerful unions was to be resisted, or in any degree controlled, it was necessary that there should be one authority dealing with all general demands for increases of wages; otherwise a concession in one case was apt to compromise the position in other cases.

The committee had come to the conclusion that there was in principle no justification for dealing with wages questions affecting miners by a different machinery from that provided for dealing with disputes about wages in other industries. The Coal Controller was not, as had been contended, in an impartial position between mine-owners and miners. The mine-owners, having a certain profit guaranteed to them, could not be relied on to resist wages demands. The real employer, in the mines as in the railways, was the State; and the natural third party to mediate was the Industrial Commissioner with the Committee on Production and other machinery for arbitration behind him. The argument for uniform procedure in all industries was strengthened by the fact that most of the demands for wages were put forward on the common ground of increased cost of living.

It was not suggested that every dispute should be referred to the Industrial Commissioner. The Coal Controller had reported that there was the strongest opposition on the part of both masters and men to any interference by the Ministry of Labour. They seemed to desire that the mining industry, by virtue of its great strength and peculiar character, should occupy a privileged position in this respect and be virtually left to itself. The committee was of opinion that it would be dangerous to admit this principle, since it would be difficult, if it were admitted, to refuse similar special treatment to other large and highly organised bodies of workers—for instance, the railwaymen. The broad proposition that there should be only one ultimate authority in all labour disputes seemed to the committee incontestable. The matter was, however, of such importance that it should be referred to the Cabinet for final decision.

The Ministry of Munitions was prepared to accept this report as being, indeed, little more than a description of their actual practice. The Ministry, in its capacity of virtual employer, was bound to deal with disputes as they arose in the works they controlled; but, if they were not settled immediately, they were referred as a difference to the Ministry of Labour. In regard to men's wages, the Ministry of Munitions was engaged merely in filling in and rounding off the decisions of the Committee on Production. The power to fix skilled time-workers' wages under Section 1 of the Act of 1917 was an exception; but this power was directed to dealing with a special case, in which the general considerations, such as cost of living, on which general awards turned, did not enter; and it was further co-ordinated with the Ministry of Labour's authority by the fact that the special arbitration tribunal to which differences under the section were referred was one of the tribunals recognised by the Ministry of Labour. In the same way the Ministry of Munitions' general control over women's wages was exercised on the advice of, and subject to reference to, a special arbitration tribunal recognised by the Ministry of Labour. Provided that its interests as employer were recognised and that the principle emphasised was that there should be only one ultimate authority for handling labour disputes and controlling wages, the Ministry of Munitions fully endorsed the report.[1]

The importance of the problem raised by the report was emphasised by the controversy over the $12\frac{1}{2}$ per cent. bonus to time workers, which was discussed by the War Cabinet on 12 October, and likewise referred to Lord Milner and Mr. Barnes. It was considered by the War Cabinet on 18 October. The representative of the Ministry of Labour stated that the Ministry had no desire to interfere in the many small disputes of a local and subsidiary character, in the settlement of which any delay was most undesirable, but in all these questions of a wider character which involved increases of wage to large classes of labour, it had now become essential, where State control of industries had been established, that the State, acting through some central authority, should be a party to any settlement. The representatives of the Ministry of Munitions and Shipyard Labour Department, while pointing out the special problems of their departments, expressed their anxiety to consult the Ministry of Labour. The Cabinet approved the report in principle, leaving it to the departments to arrange its application in detail with the Minister of Labour.[2]

The additional authority with which the Ministry of Labour was thus armed might perhaps have enabled it to ensure proper co-ordination had no new pressure come upon it. But the grant of the $12\frac{1}{2}$ per cent. bonus to skilled time-workers in the engineering and foundry industry had created a new problem, at once urgent and complicated, while the Cabinet was deciding the question raised by the Coal Controller's award. The difficulty of confining the bonus to the classes of workpeople originally covered and the equal difficulty of determining to what further classes to extend it, on which there were sharp interdepartmental differences, constituted a situation with which the War Cabinet was again forced to deal. On 27 November, a Cabinet Committee was set up to undertake the co-ordinating function previously entrusted to the Ministry of Labour. The composition and scope of the committee were embodied in a memorandum.[3]

The committee consisted of Mr. Barnes as Chairman; Sir Auckland Geddes, Minister of National Service, Vice-chairman; Sir George Askwith; Mr. I. Mitchell, Ministry of Labour; Sir Lynden Macassey, Shipyard Labour Department to the Admiralty; Mr. H. Wolfe, Labour Regulation Department of the Ministry of Munitions; Mr. Guy Calthrop, Board of Trade (Coal Controller's Department).

Negotiations in the departments for the settlement of disputes and of wages questions (whether by agreement, order or otherwise) were to be conducted with a view—(a) to confining concessions within

---

[1] Minutes by Mr. Kellaway, Mr. Wolfe and Labour Committee in L.R. 4647/7.
[2] M.C. 51. Hist. Rec.R./342/11.
[3] Hist. Rec.R./342/136.

the general limits of the decisions given by the Committee on Production, or (b) to dealing with inequalities within an industry or class, (c) to observing the general principle that no advance should be made that was likely to disturb the working conditions of any industry, trade or class, particularly by issue or administration of contracts which involved payment of wages exceeding the district rates. Where such advances were proposed the sanction of the co-ordinating authority should be given.

All settlements, however, were subject to ratification by the co-ordinating authority.

Failing a settlement on these lines and in the event of the claim still being pressed, negotiations were to be continued with a view to securing a joint reference to the Ministry of Labour for remission to arbitration.

Where a department found that in their opinion it was desirable to go beyond the limits proposed in paragraph 2 without having recourse to paragraph 3, the co-ordinating authority might confer with a consultative committee thereof with a view to final settlement, or, if necessary, submission to the War Cabinet.

A consultative committee representative of the following Departments should be appointed :—Treasury, Ministry of Labour, Admiralty (Shipyard Labour), Admiralty (Director of Dockyards), Board of Trade (Railways Department), Board of Trade (Timber Department), Board of Trade (Coal Mines Department), Ministry of National Service, War Office, Ministry of Munitions, Ministry of Shipping, Office of Works, General Post Office, Air Council.

The co-ordinating authority would have power to call on any Government Department to provide it with such information on matters falling within the sphere of that department as it might require. The co-ordinating authority would have power to appoint such officers as it might deem necessary.

The Secretariat was domiciled at the Ministry of Labour, and provision was made for summoning emergency meetings or an emergency sub-committee to deal with the matters demanding immediate decision. The representatives of each of the departments represented on the consultative committee were at liberty to send deputies when unable to attend personally.

The above principles and rules were to apply as far as they might be applicable to women's wages and to all differences other than wages questions.

The avalanche of claims that the $12\frac{1}{2}$ per cent. bonus had released could not, however, be stayed by a consultative body, and the Cabinet Committee never established an administrative machine capable of taking over from the Ministry of Munitions the work of dealing with them. The actual handling of the claims that came in in November, December, and January, fell on the Wages Section of the Ministry, as Mr. Campbell and Mr. Wolfe pointed out.[1] The Minister, indeed,

---

[1] L.R. 5997/58.

was the only person with statutory powers for dealing with the claims. The Cabinet Committee made one or two decisions on the extension of the 12½ per cent. but otherwise did not function, and the departments continued to act in their respective spheres in consultation with the Ministry of Labour, until the question of extending the bonus from time-workers to piece-workers had to be faced. This again was the subject of discussion by the Cabinet on 7 and 22 January, and resulted in the substitution of the Ministry of Labour again for the Cabinet Committee.

As is explained elsewhere,[1] there was a difference between the Ministry of Munitions and the Ministry of Labour. The former resisted the general extension of the bonus and was engaged in separate negotiations with the separate trades; the latter was in favour of extending the bonus, leaving the actual terms in each case to the Committee on Production. The Cabinet decision was that the bonus should be extended, but that the Ministry of Labour should at its discretion ask other departments to carry on any necessary negotiations. The Ministry of Munitions, therefore, completed the negotiations on which it was engaged, but referred all new claims to the Ministry of Labour, who referred them to the Committee on Production. At the same time the Co-ordinating Committee on Labour Disputes was to be replaced by the Ministry of Labour, and Mr. Barnes was authorised to decide himself or at discretion bring to the War Cabinet any cases which the Ministry of Labour referred to him.[2] Thus, the final position was identical with the original position; co-ordination depended on the loyalty of contracting departments in co-operating with the Ministry of Labour (formerly the Board of Trade), referring all disputes for arbitration to it, and accepting the rulings of the Committee on Production as the ultimate authority on general wage questions. The Minister of Labour informed the departments that he intended to continue in existence the consultative committee previously attached to the Cabinet Co-ordinating Committee; but in practice contact was maintained, at any rate with the Ministry of Munitions, by continuous informal consultation between the officials of the two Departments.

No further modification of the machinery for dealing with wages questions was made until after the Armistice; but it cannot be said that complete co-ordination was secured. Thus, almost immediately the Minister of Labour had to bring before the Cabinet the case of the London sheet metal workers who were trying to secure a district rate of 1s. 1d. an hour; they had already a war bonus of 40s. as against 27s. and the 12½ per cent. in the engineering industry, and they had refused arbitration six times. Now 44 firms had agreed to give them what they asked for without the Government's consent; three firms were resisting and the men were on strike. Sir William Weir pointed out that he was dependent on these men for an output of 280 aircraft a week, and in his view the Government was not warranted in incurring such a loss of output by withholding 2d. an hour from a

---

[1] See above Chap. VI, Sect. 6.   [2] See above Chap. VI, Sect. 7.

few firms.[1] Again, on 4 July, 1918, the claims of the National Union of Coke-Oven and By-Products Workers to time and a half for week-end work came up. It was resisted, because it was not the practice in continuous processes to pay these special rates, and a concession here would involve a similar concession in all similar processes. They had already got time and a quarter awarded by a special tribunal after the Committee on Production had refused it ; they now threatened a stoppage of all week-end work. The contracting department stated that they could not face the loss of output involved, 20 per cent. on steel and 40 per cent. on light oil. It was pointed out on the other hand that the concession would react very unfavourably on the position and authority of the Committee on Production, and that the Secretary of the committee had stated the previous day that the task of the committee had been made almost impossible by the action of the Government in superseding their awards and by the action of employers in giving sectional advances to special classes of workers. The Minister of Munitions had felt himself unable to decide between the claims of supply and the claims of wages regulation ; the Cabinet decided that the former must prevail and asked Mr. Barnes to explain their reasons to the Committee on Production.[2]

Even if this conflict between the immediate considerations of supply and the remoter considerations of wages control could have been reconciled, the multitude of claims coming forward was too great for any one authority to handle. Necessarily, therefore, the contracting departments were left to deal in the first instance with disputes that arose in connection with work for them ; they naturally heard of them first and could usually settle them most speedily ; but their independent action was a danger to co-ordination.[3] More important still was the number of independent authorities, the Ministry of Munitions, the Admiralty, the Coal Controller and the Railway Executive being all concerned in settling wages questions until the end of the war. The State as a whole, like the Ministry of Munitions in particular, became interested in wages only incidentally, so that the administrative provision made for handling wages questions was always a by-product of other activities ; its organisation was never governed by consideration of the wages question exclusively.

The difficulties of contracts departments charged with the question of reimbursing employers for additions to labour cost that could be attributed to Government action were another force tending to compel action on the problem.

The Select Committee on National Expenditure in their second report (13 December, 1917) referred to the lack of any single consistent policy in determining wages questions, and recommended that " a single policy, under the general direction of one authority, should be adopted in all industries in the determination of wages questions." They pointed out the bad effects of competition between different

---

[1] L.R. 15726.   [2] L.R. 10825/2.
[3] The Ministry of Munitions was dealing with 100 to 120 a month at the end of 1917. (L.R. 4647/7.)

trades for higher wages, the diversity of authorities making decisions, and the lack of any central control.

On 22 November, the Admiralty representative on the Joint Committee of Contracts and Finance Officers urged the desirability of centralising the control of wages, granting advances to meet the cost of living explicitly, in the form of Government subsidies, and authorising the authority that controlled wages to reimburse employers with money voted specially for that purpose by Parliament. The Controller of Contracts of the Ministry of Munitions favoured this solution, and the Munitions Contracts Board made recommendations to this end on 2 January, 1918.[1] The Council, however, preferred the method of making a fixed allowance on each class of product, a policy favoured also by the War Office, and that policy was adopted.

The responsibility, therefore, for economy in wages remained with the separate contracting departments. The prevention of unco-ordinated advances depended on co-operation and consultation between them, and on loyal support of the Ministry of Labour which was charged with a general supervision of wages. The Ministry of Labour sought to secure co-ordination by referring all crucial cases to the Committee on Production. But the Ministry of Labour had no powers that would enable it to prevent collusive arrangements to raise wages between contractors and their employees, and when an advance was proposed which might cause disturbance in allied or related trades, could only ask that the proposal be referred to the Ministry of Labour for settlement, or for reference to arbitration.[2]

The proposal to unify the control of all wages questions, considered by the contracting departments, was supported by Mr. Churchill himself. During the discussion over the 12½ per cent. and 7½ per cent. bonuses, he had been reluctant to relinquish the powers of wage regulation that the Ministry exercised, and looked forward to recovering and developing them when the bonuses had been settled.[3] But later in the year he came to the view that labour regulation should be separated from supply, and put forward a proposal for a centralised Labour Department as the correlative of a Ministry of Supply. Speaking on 4 October to the Management Committee of the Engineering Employers' Federation, who complained of the continuous and unco-ordinated rise of time-rates, and asked for drastic action to prevent it, he said[4]:—

" I have several plans which I have watched taking place in the first twelve months here for the reorganisation of Government Departments, with a view to arriving at unity of function. Obviously, the fighting services ought to fight, and the Ministry of Munitions ought to do all the supply, and there ought to be another department which deals with labour from one point of view, and one point of view only. I have thought it out very carefully, and I have not the slightest doubt that it is an absolutely certain solution of a great many difficulties. Just as you have a Finance

---
[1] Vol. III, Pt. II, Chap. III, p. 101.
[2] Ibid., p. 109.
[3] L.S. 8888/4 Minute of 19 January, 1918.
[4] HIST. R./REC./342/14.

Department of the country, the Exchequer, so you would have all these great blocks by functions, and then you would know to whom you had to go, instead of running round to each department, each department head having only a fragment of the power in his hands and only judging it during a period of his time. . . . . Personally, I have felt for a long time that the Government is strong enough, and the Nation is sound enough, for a definite advance to be made against this constant upward movement of wages, and the repeated threats we are getting of strikes here and there, and something in the nature of establishing a great national body, tripartite in its character, representative of both parties and of the State, which shall be the sole arbiter in all wages questions, coupling that with the fact that any person who disputes the decision or ruling of this authority will, *ipso facto*, be taken to enlist in the army if he ceases work. That, I believe, the country would stand and even welcome. I have never seen a strong measure adopted with a really good case behind it that has not been successful. It is very, very difficult to handle these matters. I should be quite prepared myself to assist any scheme worked out on these lines—something in the nature of saying : " We will form a body which will absorb the Committee on Production, and be a Wages Tribunal with district branches, and so on, for the whole country, with representatives of Labour, as well as employers on it, and say that their rulings are to be obeyed, and those who do not obey, if they are otherwise liable, must go and serve in another way."

After the Armistice, the Wages Section of the Ministry of Munitions, together with the rest of the Labour Regulation Department, and the Shipyard Labour Department, were amalgamated with the Ministry of Labour. The Committee on Production was reconstituted under the Wages (Temporary Regulation) Act as the Interim Court of Arbitration, and, a year later, under the Industrial Courts Act, as the Industrial Court. The embargo on strikes was removed, and freedom of bargaining restored subject only to the maintenance of the ruling district rates as legal minima for twelve months. The changes did not bring order into wages. The anomalies that had arisen during the war persisted. The committee of the National Industrial Conference convened by the Government in February, 1919, recommended that the Ministry of Labour should approach the different industries and urge them, through their ordinary conciliation machinery or in special conferences, to negotiate new standard rates in place of the existing mixture of rates and war bonuses, referring the decision to the Court of Arbitration if necessary. But action on the committee's report was delayed and little done. Such order as was restored to wages was due to voluntary agreement rather than official action, and the avoidance of serious and extended unrest in the process of readjustment was due mainly to the fact that prices continued to rise, so that there could be no question of removing the various general, sectional, and individual bonuses with which the war had overlaid the pre-war system of rates.

CHAPTER VIII.

CONCLUSION.

The control of wages was a task, it has been necessary to insist, which the Ministry of Munitions undertook reluctantly. It was incidental to the Ministry's main purpose of organising production ; it was not undertaken or developed in accordance with any preconcerted policy ; its sole objects were industrial peace, the enforcement of the limitation of profits and the safeguarding of munitions workers' interests under dilution. The Ministry's statutory powers were correspondingly limited, being taken piecemeal to meet new problems as they arose, and its regulative work was confined to munitions employment. The original policy of the Government, worked out by the Board of Trade and the Committee on Production, was to disturb as little as possible the ordinary methods of settling wages, to leave as far as possible all necessary changes to be negotiated between employers and employed, and to interfere only to accelerate negotiation and to substitute arbitration for the lock-out and the strike. The Ministry of Munitions' control of wages was undertaken within the limits laid down by that policy.

Wages, however, are not susceptible of sectional treatment. Munitions employment, wide as it became, was never so wide as the whole field of employment ; and the influences affecting wages could be controlled only if the whole field of employment was taken as the area of regulation. The relation between the wages of different classes and grades of workers is so intimate that interference at one point is bound to have reactions at others. The choice lay between the control of wages generally and a policy of abstention from the fixing of any rates. The original policy of the Government took the latter course. It sought to leave intact all the old relations, and, only substituting arbitration by a central authority for the strike and lock-out, to allow wages to be adjusted to changing conditions in the same way as in peace. Just as before the war, the Government relied on collective bargaining to fix rates. Arbitration acquired a new importance ; but it was free from any administrative control at first, and no other provision was made for the changes and adjustments that were to prove necessary.

The policy might have served if the duration of the war had been short ; it proved impossible to persist in it when the duration extended into years. The main influences that made it impossible to persist were two ; the economic changes to which wages had to be adjusted were too numerous, too rapid and too extensive for the machinery of collective bargaining and arbitration to cope with ; and the Cabinet, by its embargo on advances, in the autumn of 1915, stopped the process of adjustment.

The changes to which it was necessary to adjust wages affected women more than men; the conditions of women's employment were revolutionised. But the men's wages system was subject to unprecedented strains. On the one hand, the cost of living rose rapidly and compelled the most unselfish to seek advances; on the other, the demand for labour became, first, slack except in armament and shipbuilding centres, then keen for certain classes of labour, and finally intense over almost the whole field of industry. Old anomalies, such as the variation in rates from district to district or from trade to trade for roughly the same grade of skill, became exaggerated, and new anomalies, such as the skilled time-worker's grievance, were created. The first breach in the policy came at the point at which the greatest economic change had occurred, in the case of women taking skilled men's work. The circular L.2 was a breach in the policy because it substituted the fixing of wages by administrative order for the settlement of claims by collective bargaining and administration.

The embargo on further advances in wages stopped the process of adjustment, but it did nothing to stop economic change. The cost of living continued to rise and the demand for labour continued to grow. The awards of the Committee on Production ceased to be arbitration awards in the true sense. The committee became virtually an organ of the executive Government, giving effect to the executive's will in the guise of awards. A member of the committee pointed out the danger of this course;[1] and the workpeople whose claims were refused had no difficulty in perceiving the difference between the committee's hearings and awards during this period and the ordinary process by which an impartial arbitrator measures the strength of conflicting claims and anticipates by his judgment the stable compromise that would otherwise have been reached after a strike. They protested vigorously, and their faith in arbitration was permanently shaken.[2]

The embargo amounted to a further substitution of administrative control of wages, on considerations of financial policy, for arbitral determination by consideration of bargaining strength. It represented the second policy of the Government. The first had been to adjust wages from time to time to changing conditions; the second was to stop adjustment to general changes and to permit only the removal of small sectional and local anomalies. The economic changes that made it difficult to persist in the first policy, *a fortiori*, made the second impossible; the interruption in the process of judicial arbitration had produced a situation in which it was idle to attempt to revert to that method.

The rise in the cost of living and the growing strength of labour made it impossible to maintain the embargo for more than eight months, and the Cabinet authorised the Committee on Production to take into consideration in making its awards changes in the cost of living and other relevant factors. This initiated the policy which was to last till the end of the war. The committee instituted, or rather resumed,

---

[1] Sir George Gibb. (HIST. REC./R./342/7.)
[2] See above, Chap. III.

the practice of making advances to meet the increase in the cost of living; the Ministry of Munitions and other Departments and tribunals exercising functions of wage-control followed suit; and the policy was systematised in 1917 when the practice of periodical hearings and national awards was adopted.

In taking the cost of living as the main factor to be considered the committee was responding to the most frequent appeal made before it. By comparison no other argument brought by the work-people's representatives before the committee was of any importance. Simultaneously, the political spokesmen of the Labour Movement demanded Government action to check the increase in cost of living. The index numbers of food prices and cost of living published monthly in the *Labour Gazette* were the most frequently quoted figures in all arbitration hearings. A committee, of which Lord Sumner was chairman, appointed on 21 March, 1918, and reporting on 23 October, established the fact that the actual expenditure of the working classes had gone up less than the *Labour Gazette* figures indicated, and that the index number was based on family budgets that were no longer representative; but the report did not check the use of the *Labour Gazette* figures, and personal experience was a more important source of unrest than any figures.

A general policy of adjusting wages to cost of living and ignoring so far as possible all other influences was, therefore, almost forced upon the Government. The Committee on Production under this policy was something less than a judicial court, since the principles on which it had to make its awards were laid down for it by the executive Government; it was more than a mere part of the administrative machine, since it was free to interpret and apply those principles according to its own judgment. Thus it was able to smooth out a large number of inequalities, regularise advances, and check divergencies that free bargaining would have produced. It gave the workpeople less probably than they could have got had they been free to bargain; but the strike was illegal and the movement of labour in search of higher wages was checked by the leaving certificate provisions of the first Munitions Act. Where these did not apply, as in building, and in the munitions industries after they were repealed, the Committee on Production found it difficult to make its control effective.

The policy was difficult of execution for another reason. Its necessary basis was a system of wage-relations, generally accepted as fair, which only required adjusting to the increased cost of living. The pre-war system of rates and relations offered such a basis. Though it was illogical and full of anomalies and did not give the country the assurance of industrial peace, it had the sanction of custom and consequently a stability that made it a suitable basis. Had it been taken as a basis, wages effectively controlled, and comprehensive and uniform adjustments made over the whole field of industry from the outbreak of war, the policy might have been carried through. Then, too, it would have been possible at the end of the war to revert to the *status quo* by making any modifications in war bonuses called for by changes in the cost of living, and merging these in new standard rates, on the basis of which bargaining could begin afresh. Rates and wage relations would have been, as it were, frozen, and the influence of war conditions on wages, with the exception of changes in the cost of living, excluded. Some such ideal was implicit in all the attempts to control wages during the war.

Unfortunately, the policy was only reached after two or three years of experiment. Because State control of wages was undertaken reluctantly and piecemeal, the 1914 basis had been lost and no new basis, generally accepted as that of 1914 was accepted, established in its stead.

Three factors in particular combined to prevent any uniform relation of wages during the war to pre-war standards. In the first place, sections of workpeople exploited the bargaining power which the shortage of labour and the country's needs put into their hands, and secured advances far more than proportionate to the increase in the cost of living. The embargo was not completely effective. Strikes, though illegal, took place and attained their object. Employers " jumped " the standard rate by granting concealed advances in the forms of fancy bonuses to individuals and sections. In the second place, wide extensions of systems of payment by results, into fields in which there was little basis in experience for the setting of rates, resulted in fortunate individuals and classes of workers making earnings that bore no relation to their time-ratings and upset all established standards of the proper relations between the wages of different grades and classes of worker. No influence did more than this in the last eighteen months of the war to excite industrial unrest, by awakening cupidity and suspicion of exploitation, and the grant of the special $12\frac{1}{2}$ per cent. bonus to certain skilled time-workers failed to redress the disturbance in the balance between the wages of different classes. In the third place the immense transfers of workers from one occupation to another and from one district to another accustomed individuals to wages which they would never have commanded in their original occupations, and gave them new conceptions of their economic value.

These influences could not exert their full effect so long as the free movement of labour was prevented by the leaving certificate. So soon as that was removed, the Government found itself deprived of the power to impose any real control on the movement of wages. The industrial disorder of the winter of 1917–1918 was attributed to the $12\frac{1}{2}$ per cent.; but that bonus was only an attempt to anticipate a demand which was certain to be pressed and which the Government had deprived itself of the power to resist. Before any control of wages could be restored, power to restrict the movement of labour had to be recovered. The device adopted was the use of Regulation 8 A (b) under the Defence of the Realm Act, a device used only sparingly, but with the same result of labour opposition as the leaving certificate had provoked. The control of wages, indeed, could be effective only if the Government was prepared to control and " ration " labour, just as the control of food prices was possible only when the Government controlled and rationed the supply of food.

Any such policy was certain to receive the most violent labour opposition; but some such policy was being forced on the Government at the end of the war by the breakdown of the ordinary regulation of wages by competitive bargaining.

Finally, control was not applied systematically. There was no central authority endowed with statutory powers to regulate wages generally. On the contrary, the work of control was divided between the Committee on Production and half a dozen Departments, whose spheres of influence were not always clearly defined, and whose overlapping led to the Cabinet's attempts to compel co-ordination described in the last chapter. Had there been adequate administrative machinery, the intrinsic difficulties of the adjustment would still have been enormous, owing to the complication of pre-war wages. As the head of the Wages Section said in a memorandum on the situation created by the 12½ per cent. bonus[1]:—

" The Ministry is concerned in some ten principal industries and about 30 subsidiary ones. Wage systems involve technicalities, anomalies, complex inter-relations and illogical traditions, with which only some years' experience can bring any real acquaintance. The men with such experience simply do not exist. The staff to deal centrally with wages in 40 industries, therefore, cannot be found. But the trend of events in the last few weeks has been to bring an infinity of problems to London for instant adjustment."

It is not surprising, therefore, that the Committee on Production, even with the support of the Ministry of Labour and the Wages Section of the Ministry of Munitions, failed to control the movement of wages completely. From the middle of 1917 onwards there were increasing complaints of employers exceeding the district rate, workpeople extracting uneconomic wages, and normal relations between the wages of different grades and classes being disturbed.

As the difficulty of control became greater, the motives of control became stronger. At first an incident in a larger task, wages control became an end in itself. It was not merely industrial peace, but stimulus to output and financial economy that came to be considered, and the administrative organisation devoted to wages control grew correspondingly. The Wages Section of the Ministry of Munitions became a numerous and important section. It developed an extensive local organisation. A parallel development took place in the Shipyard Labour Department. A separate Ministry of Labour was established, and the problem of co-ordination taken up by the War Cabinet. The only change of policy, however, was an extension of direct control by administrative action in the issue of the 12½ per cent. bonus to timeworkers and the use of the Defence of the Realm Regulations 8 A (b), to compel employers to observe conditions and wages laid down by order. Every authority concerned with wages came to recognise that the difficulty of securing order and peace was that the pre-war rates

---

[1] L.R. 5997/58.

and relations had been upset, but no one could find a way of restoring them. The Ministry of Munitions' statutory powers were inadequate,[1] and the expert staff needed for systematic control could not be found. On the eve of the Armistice the Minister declared that the problem of control was insoluble during the war.

" Here we are in the fifth year of the war, and we seem to be muddling through once again ; but of course, we did not start on this war with cut-and-dried plans for dealing with the social and labour questions that might arise. We found our way into it, we wandered into it, and the great strength of the country and the individual quality which exists over the country have carried us along and we are coming through at an enormous cost with terrible waste and long delay—victoriously. But, looking round upon the field of battle in industry, I suppose you see what you see on every battlefield—chaos, wreckage, confusion and waste on every side. I do not believe myself that during the continuance of the war you will get a good solution of these labour difficulties ; for what are you going to base yourselves on ? Hitherto, there have always been the power of workmen to strike, the power of employers to lock out, and the power of the community to do without the product in the interval. That has been the foundation. But where is it now ? There is no such foundation. It has gone. As I have repeatedly said, a great many employers are not directly interested in keeping wages within reasonable bounds ; they are far more interested in boosting up their particular product. The workmen and even the large majority who are patriotic say : ' Why should we not get our share of all that is going ? ' and the State has not yet found itself capable or competent or strong enough to intervene with broad, clear rulings which have been obeyed. Even in Germany, with all their authority and power over the individual, they have had a good deal of industrial disorder. Here we have complete industrial disorder from that point of view. The only thing is, we have got great production, and we are winning the war. That is all there is to say on the other side. I tell you frankly (we are speaking quite confidentially) that in my opinion, until the conditions of economic bargaining are restored to their freedom, I doubt very much whether you will get a satisfactory result or a clear-cut basis."[2]

As the inadequacy of the existing policy became obvious, a new policy shaped itself in the minds of the officials of the Ministry of Munitions.[3] It consisted in establishing a new set of standard rates altogether, and so providing a basis on which effective control could be established. The same proposal had been put forward when the 12½ per cent. bonus had become impossible to administer in its original form ;[4] in the building industry, when the Ministry of Labour attempted

---

[1] See above, Chap. II.
[2] Interview with Management Committee of the Engineering Employers Federation, 4 October, 1918. Hist. Rec.R/342/14.
[3] See above, p. 61.   [4] L.R. 5997/58.

to systematise wages in the spring of 1918 ; by the Finance and Contracts Officers Committee in December 1917, when it was facing the difficulty of reimbursing employers for advances in wages due to Government action.[1] The contract officers suggested taking the rates of 31 December, 1917 ; the officials more directly concerned with wages control proposed to establish new rates to be determined by joint committees of employers and workpeople acting under the supervision of the Committee on Production as central co-ordinating authority. The war came to an end before any steps were taken to give effect to these proposals, and they involved perhaps, an overt and direct control of wages from which the Government might have shrunk. But they point to the fundamental difficulty of State control of wages—the basis, namely, on which rates shall actually be fixed.

Before the war, we saw, the Government carefully refrained from taking the responsibility of fixing rates. The responsibility was left to the employers who paid and the workpeople who received wages. The policy of making adjustments in pre-war rates was due to the same desire to avoid the responsibility of fixing rates. When it could not be avoided, as in the case of the Women's Wages Orders, the rates fixed had some relation to existing rates, established by the ordinary methods of bargaining, and were varied on the advice of a special arbitration tribunal. In all three Munitions of War Acts, careful provision is made for accepting the results of ordinary collective bargaining, wherever it could be preserved, and the proposal referred to above would have thrown on each trade the primary responsibility for establishing new rates in place of the pre-war standards that had been lost.

The war virtually forced the State to take this responsibility which it had so persistently avoided. The commercial conditions of war-time weakened the normal incentives of employers to resist wage claims. The munitions levy and excess profits duty still further weakened them. The arrangement by which Government contractors were enabled to claim reimbursement for any increase in cost due to wage advances granted by any Government authority finally destroyed the pre-war counterweight to the wage-earner's demands. The conflict of interests was no longer between employer and employee, but between the State, as the consumer of the greater part of the industry's products, and the worker. The employer working for profits is normally a shock-absorber, moderating and concealing the conflict of interests between worker and consumer ; the limitation and guarantee of profits turned him into a shock transmitter. The bargains by which wages were settled, in other words, had to be struck between workpeople and the State.

Now the Government cannot bargain about wages like a private employer. Once it begins to fix wages by administrative order, it has to accept responsibility for this administrative action, as for the rest of its administration. Anomalies which are tolerated, because they are traditionàl or customary, so long as wages are settled by

---

[1] See above, p. 202.

private bargaining, are no longer tolerated when the State has taken responsibility for them. Consistency is demanded in the action of Government Departments even when inconsistencies were tolerated in private employment. The State is expected to base its administrative action on some more or lees definite principles of justice or expediency, by reference to which its action can be justified if challenged.

The obstacle to any systematic settlement of wages by an administrative authority is the absence of any such principle, by reference to which services can be valued. People talk of a " fair wage," but no two parties to a difference agree, or can give a concrete definition of that wage. It is the absence of such a principle that explains the attitude of the State to wages before the war. The State would insist on uniformity of payment, as it did by the Fair Wages Clause in public contracts; it would enforce the determinations of representative industrial bodies called into being by itself, as in the case of Trade Boards; it would facilitate collective bargaining and supplement it by the provision of facilities for voluntary arbitration, as it did through the activities of the Chief Industrial Commissioner's department under the Conciliation and Arbitration Act of 1896. But the State, if it could avoid it, never fixed a rate; because the State is always expected to justify its decisions by reference to some generally accepted principle, and there are no such principles in the valuation of services.

Wages depended on the relative bargaining strength of the parties to the wage contract, which in turn was influenced by organisation, but depended ultimately on the need of the labour in the market and the possibility of securing a price for the industry's products that would cover the cost of meeting labour's claim. The conflicting interests of worker and employer—or, to go behind them, of producer and consumer—did not often result in an actual stoppage, because the two parties were in constant contact with each other and could gauge to a nicety the exact point to which it was possible to press a claim; and they could, sometimes with the aid of an experienced arbitrator or conciliator, ascertain the resultant of the forces in conflict without an overt trial.

There was and is no generally accepted answer to the question, " What is a just wage ? " There can be discerned in the decisions of the Committee on Production and the Government Departments tentative approaches to a determination of wages by reference to ethical or political principle. The award of flat-rate advances instead of advances proportionate to normal earnings was an advance towards equality of remuneration, the influence of which, in spite of the efforts of the higher wage workers to restore the pre-war disparity, is likely to be permanent. Again, in the choice of cost of living as the basis for war bonuses to the exclusion of other factors, a differentiation is implied of an element in wages that should cover and fluctuate with cost of living from another element representing the special economic value of a particular skill. Priority of importance for the purposes of the war, which might have provided a scale of absolute values on which the country might be taken as agreed, was used for the purpose of allocating men to the combatant forces and industry, but not as a basis of remuneration.

The absence of any agreed principle on which wages could be based by authority therefore compelled the Government to adopt its policy of accepting pre-war wages and making minor adjustments in them. In practice the influence of bargaining strength could not be excluded ; control and compulsory arbitration only veiled it and moderated it. A rigid control of all wages changes from the first, a single authority with statutory powers, an ungrudging grant of advances to meet the increase in the cost of living, and a strict limitation of profits from the first, might have made it possible to preserve the pre-war system of rates and wage-relations intact. Such a policy was hardly thought of, and the machinery for giving effect to it never created. The Ministry of Munitions was limited to piecemeal adjustments with its improvised machinery and an inadequate staff. Its opportunities of introducing any system into wartime wages were confined mainly to women's wages. Its wages administration was necessarily empirical and opportunist. That any limit at all was imposed on the influence of economic bargaining strength and any order maintained in wages through the succession of economic changes that the war entailed was due in the main to the action of the Ministry.

APPENDICES.

APPENDIX I.

(CHAPTER I, p. 26.)

Rates and Earnings in November 1915.

(Memorandum by Mr. J. C. Smith of the Wages Section, Ministry of Munitions.)

It will be well to lay a basis for conclusions as to the effect of the War on earnings by comparing the results shown in different parts of the country, first on the average earnings of all hands in a number of shops, and next on the earnings of particular trades.

1. WHOLE SHOPS.—Here are the average weekly earnings of all hands, for a pre-war month, and a month during the war for four shops totalling over 20,000 hands.

Name of Firm.	Average per man.		Percentage Increase per man.
	Pre-war £ s. d.	Now £ s. d.	
A. Harland & Wolff, Belfast	1 14 0	2 2 7	25·2 per cent.
B. Ruston Proctor, Lincoln	1 8 11	2 0 5	39·75 ,, ,,
C. Clayton & Shuttleworth, Lincoln..	1 9 5	2 3 7	48·2 ,, ,,
D. Whitehead Torpedo Works, Weymouth.	2 11 9	4 8 3	70·5 ,, ,,

These figures, it must be remembered, cover all classes of employees—Woodworkers, as well as Iron-workers, Labourers and Machine-men, as well as fully skilled hands. The excessive difference in shop D is unique, so far as is known, for a whole shop. The general average probably lies between A. and B.

2. SEPARATE TRADES.—The nominal increase in *rates* in the various Engineering and Shipbuilding trades has been fairly uniform, and, in view of the enhanced cost of living would not appear excessive. Here are the Birmingham Engineering Trade rates for July, 1914, and November, 1915:—

Trade Occupation.	July, 1914.	November. 1915.
	per week.	per week.
Toolmakers	38s.	45s.
Toolturners	38s.	45s.
General Turners	38s.	43s.
Toolfitters	38s.	45s.
General Fitters..	38s.	43s.
Planers	38s.	40s.
Shapers	38s.	40s.
Millwrights	42s.	45s.
Capstan Toolsetters	40s.	45s.
Borers and Slotters	40s.	43s.
Sectional Fitters	40s.	45s.
Gauge Makers	42s.	48s.
Universal Millers	40s.	45s.
Semi-Skilled.—		
Drillers	32s.	40s.
Millers	32s.	40s.
Capstan Operators	32s.	40s.
Brass Turners	35s.	80s. & upwards.

But as an index to actual earnings these nominal rates are fallacious, in as much as they give no indication of piece rates or of overtime. Here are comparative totals of actual earnings in four Engineering and Shipbuilding works, one in Belfast and three on the Tyne :—

Trade.	Workman, Clark.		Armstrong Shipyard.		Armstrong Ordnance.		Palmers.	
	Before War.	June 1915.	Before War.	Oct. 1915.	Before War.	Oct. 1915.	Before War.	Oct. 1915.
	£ s. d.	£ s. d.	£ s. d.	£ s. d.	£ s. d.	£ s. d.	£ s. d.	£ s. d.
Fitters	1 18 3	2 14 2	2 6 6	2 15 8	2 3 1	3 3 4	1 15 0	2 8 6
Turners	2 1 3	2 13 3	—	—	2 3 1	3 3 4	—	—
Labourers	1 0 0	1 6 3	1 5 10	2 0 1	1 4 9	2 2 1	—	—
Machinists	1 14 0	2 8 2	—	—	1 13 1	2 16 5	—	—
Sheet Iron Workers	—	—	—	—	—	—	3 2 7	4 6 4
Joiners	—	—	—	—	—	—	1 16 0	2 0 1
Painters	—	—	—	—	—	—	1 15 8	2 15 0
Angle Iron Smiths	—	—	3 11 0	4 17 9	—	—	—	—
Smiths	—	—	—	—	—	—	2 7 10	3 0 9
Plumbers	—	—	—	—	—	—	1 18 7	2 8 7
Platers	5 0 0	9 10 0	4 6 2	7 11 0	—	—	2 19 6	3 12 2
Rivetters	3 10 0	8 5 0	3 4 9	4 13 11	—	—	2 3 3	2 10 0
Drillers	2 17 6	4 17 6	3 10 7	3 14 11	—	—	—	—
Baulkers	3 0 0	5 2 6	3 3 10	3 6 10	—	—	—	—
Carpenters	1 14 0	2 18 0	3 1 11	2 17 10	—	—	—	—
Boilermakers	2 4 0	3 7 3	—	—	—	—	—	—

Of the above returns, those from Messrs. Workman, Clark's are complete, *i.e.* they comprise all hands ; the others show averages of groups or shops.

The returns for the Clyde Shipbuilding Industry are so complete as to deserve separate tabulation.

FOR CLYDE DISTRICT.

Trade.	No. of men.		Average wage per man.		Percentage of Increase per man.	Average No. of hours worked.		Percentage Increase.
	Before War.	War.	Before War.	War.		Before War.	War.	
			£ s. d.	£ s. d.				
Fitters	3,813	4,637	2 2 9	3 1 4	43·5	54·4	62·1	14·2
Turners	1,139	1,410	2 7 9	3 4 3	34·6	54·8	61·5	12·3
Shipwrights	2,125	2,287	2 4 4	2 13 6	20·7	53·8	56·1	4·2
Joiners	1,938	1,823	2 1 9	2 9 1	17·6	53·4	54·6	2·1
Cabinetmakers	34	23	2 0 2	2 5 1	12·2	52·1	53·0	1·7
Woodworking Machinists	291	252	2 0 1	2 6 1	15	53·4	54·6	2·3
Cabinet Machinists & Polishers	80	59	1 19 6	2 3 10	11	53·5	53·1	·8 Decrease
Painters	405	417	2 9 7	2 10 7	2	57·6	53·4	7·27 Decrease
Ships smiths	418	441	2 10 8	3 6 3	30·75	51·1	54·9	7·5
Sheet Ironworkers	269	423	2 3 1	2 12 0	20·7	52·0	54·1	4·1
Drillers & Hole Cutters	937	972	2 7 10	3 5 8	37·3	46·0	53·9	17·3
Tinsmiths	48	60	2 1 9	2 18 5	40	53·8	61·9	15·1

It will be seen that these figures account for more than 12,000 men. I have also before me a table showing the time-keeping and earnings of 495 riveting squads. These show an average of 48 hours worked per week, including overtime and Sunday work, and an average rate per hour per squad of 5s. 10d., which allowing for the Holder-up and Rivet-heater, leaves the approximate earnings per Riveter at 1s. 10d. per hour. These averages, however, are not wholly reliable, inasmuch as the hours worked—which range from 6¾ to 89½—may sometimes represent less than a week's work, and at other times more. A more reliable, if less succinct method is to take the "median range," *i.e.*, the range of weekly earnings, within which fall the majority of the men.

The median range here, which accounts for three-fifths of the squad runs from £2 19s. 4½d. to £5 9s. 4½d. per week, per Riveter, the actual median being £4 4s. 4½d.

Analysis of these tables and of others like them shows, in the first place, a wide divergence between nominal rates and actual earnings. Whereas the men at Workman Clark's during 1915 got a single rise in rates of 3s. to 5s. 6d. on time or ten per cent. on piece, their earnings show increases varying from 30 per cent. for labourers and machinists, to 90 per cent. for platers, and 135 per cent. for riveters. The Clyde figures show a smaller divergence between increased rates and increased earnings.

The causes of this are :—

(*a*) *Overtime.*—Here a singular fact comes to view. Though every class of men in Workman Clark's showed overtime during 1915, varying from three hours per week on an average for Labourers to 18 hours for Boilermakers, *not a single class* on the average made up a full normal week of 54 hours ; the Turners came nearest with 53 ; the Boilermakers had only 48. On the Clyde the Wood-workers all over show very little increase, Cabinet Machinists and Polishers show actual decreases in time worked. In spite of this all trades show an advance in earnings.

There has undoubtedly been some abuse of the overtime system, men working on Sunday and playing on Monday.

(*b*) *High Piece Prices.*—The main reasons for the abnormally high earnings of the Platers and Riveters at Workman Clark's probably lies in the fact that much of Workman Clark's work is Admiralty repairs on the "time and line" basis. There has been no such abnormal rise in these trades on Tyneside, nor in inland shops.

(*c*) *General Speeding-up.*—The confidence of the workers that piece rates would not be cut out as the result of increased production, has resulted in a general —though not universal—speeding-up, which has produced remarkable results in some ways.

At Messrs. Kynochs there are 212 Tool Makers, whose average earnings in July, 1914, were 38s. per week. In a recent week 57 of these men earned £5 and over ; 34 earned £7 10s. and over ; five earned £10 and over, and one earned £12 10s. The Manager attributes these results to speeding-up.

In the second place it is evident that even in the Engineering and Shipbuilding industries all trades have not profited equally by the war. Painters, Plumbers and Woodworkers generally have not advanced much. The Painters in the Clyde Shipyards have only advanced 1s., and the Carpenters at Elswick actually show a drop. Boilermakers have not advanced so much as might have been expected, except on Admiralty work.

At Ruston & Proctor's the Boilermakers show an advance of only 17·4 per cent., while Fitters, Turners and Machine-men show 38·4 per cent. Very large earnings are made by Tool Makers and Setters-up. One instance has been cited from Birmingham. The following table is for a London firm, Messrs. Vandervell and Co., of Acton.

AVERAGE WAGES EARNED BY VARIOUS TRADES.

	Ordinary 52 hr. wk.	Rate per hr.	Pay with Overtime.	Add extra for nightwork
	£ s. d.	s. d.	£ s. d.	s. d.
Toolmakers..	3 9 4	1 4	6 2 8	30 0
Fitters ..	2 6 7	10¾	3 9 7	30 0
Turners ..	2 16 4	1 1	3 15 3	30 0
Drillers ..	1 6 0	6	2 15 9	20 0
Setters-up ..	3 0 8	1 2	5 16 0	30 0

Toolmakers, of course, are highly skilled workmen, but it is doubtful whether the highly skilled workman in general has profited so much by the War as the unskilled or semi-skilled men, who have been put on to turning and other operations on shell.

Of 57 unskilled and semi-skilled men employed by the Projectile Co., Wandsworth Road, London, on Machine-men's work, such as turning and boring shells, fitting bushes, etc., the actual rate over an average of nine weeks ran from 1s. 3d. to 1s. 9½d.; the average earnings of each of these men was £4 3s. per week. These men comprised about a quarter of the hands employed by the Company on this work and doubtless were not the most inexpert; still the hourly rate runs very high for Machine-men's work.

3. INDIVIDUAL WORKERS.—For the sake of completeness I add a few instances of exceptional earnings made by exceptional men in favoured trades.

At the Westinghouse Co., King's Cross, the wages earned by the eight top men ran from £10 13s. 8d. to £19 10s. 2d. The most highly paid Riveters of the Clydeside squads, already cited, made £9 4s. 4½d., but this was for a week of 79½ hours.

A Toolmaker in Birmingham is known to have made £15 in one week, and now aims at £16.

Another Toolmaker in Coventry has made as much as £15 5s.

An Angle-smith in Dundee once made £19 16s. 3d. but from this his striker s pay had to be deducted.

These exceptional figures, however striking as they are, are of little value compared to the more extensive data given above.

APPENDIX II.

(CHAPTER II, p. 38.)

Circular L.3.

MUNITIONS LABOUR SUPPLY COMMITTEE.

Recommendations relating to the Employment and Remuneration of Semi-skilled and Unskilled Men on Munition Work of a class which prior to the War was customarily undertaken by Skilled Labour.

(*Note* :—These Recommendations are strictly confined to the war period and are subject to the observance of Schedule II of the Munitions of War Act, reprinted in the Appendix.)

GENERAL.

1. Operations on which skilled men are at present employed, but which by reason of their character can be performed by semi-skilled or unskilled labour, may be done by such labour during the period of the war.

2. Where semi-skilled or unskilled male labour is employed on work identical with that customarily undertaken by skilled labour, the time-rates and piece-prices and premium bonus times shall be the same as customarily obtain for the operations when performed by skilled labour.

3. Where skilled men are at present employed they shall not be displaced by less skilled labour unless other skilled employment is offered to them there or elsewhere.

4. Piece-work prices and premium bonus time allowances, after they have been established, shall not be altered unless the means or method of manufacture are changed.

5. Overtime, night-shift, Sunday and holiday allowances shall be paid to such machine-men on the same basis as to skilled men.

Time Ratings for the Manufacture of complete shell and fuses and cartridge cases, where not hitherto customary.

6. Where the manufacture of this class of munitions was not customarily undertaken by the establishment prior to the war, the following time ratings shall apply:—

(a) Semi-skilled and unskilled men of 21 years of age and over, when engaged as machine-men on the above manufacture, shall be paid a time rate of 10s. per week lower than the time rate for turners, including war bonuses, engaged in the engineering trade of the district, but in no case shall the rate paid to such men be less than 28s. per week of the normal district hours. This rate also includes all war bonuses already granted.

(b) Where a semi-skilled or unskilled man of 21 years of age and over has had no experience previously of the operation he is called upon to perform, his starting rate shall be 26s. per week, which shall be paid during his period of training, but such period shall not exceed two months from the date at which he commenced work as a machine-man.

(c) The time rates payable to setters up shall not be less than as follows :—

Setting up of fuse-making machines, 10s. per week over the current district time rate for turners.

Setting up of shell-making machines, 5s. per week over the current district time rate for turners.

These extras are in addition to any war bonuses which have been granted.

INTERPRETATION.

7. Any question which arises as to the interpretation of these recommendations shall be determined by the Minister of Munitions.

October, 1915.

Appendix.

MUNITIONS OF WAR ACT, 1915.

SCHEDULE II.

1. Any departure during the war from the practice ruling in the workshops, shipyards, and other industries prior to the war, shall only be for the period of the war.

2. No change in practice made during the war shall be allowed to prejudice the position of the workmen in the owners' employment, or of their trade unions in regard to the resumption and maintenance after the war of any rules or customs existing prior to the war.

3. In any readjustment of staff which may have to be effected after the war, priority of employment will be given to workmen in the owners' employment at the beginning of the war who have been serving with the colours or were in the owners' employment when the establishment became a controlled establishment.

4. Where the custom of a shop is changed during the war by the introduction of semi-skilled men to perform work hitherto performed by a class of workmen of higher skill, the time and piece rates paid shall be the usual rates of the district for that class of work.

5. The relaxation of existing demarcation restrictions or admission of semi-skilled or female labour shall not affect adversely the rates customarily paid for the job. In cases where men who ordinarily do the work are adversely affected thereby, the necessary readjustments shall be made so that they can maintain their previous earnings.

6. A record of the nature of the departure from the conditions prevailing when the establishment became a controlled establishment shall be kept, and shall be open for inspection by the authorised representative of the Government.

7. Due notice shall be given to the workmen concerned wherever practicable of any changes of working conditions which it is desired to introduce as the result of the establishment becoming a controlled establishment, and opportunity for local consultation with workmen or their representatives shall be given if desired.

8. All differences with workmen engaged on Government work arising out of changes so introduced or with regard to wages or conditions of employment arising out of the war shall be settled in accordance with this Act without stoppage of work.

9. Nothing in this Schedule (except as provided by the fourth paragraph thereof) shall prejudice the position of employers or persons employed after the war.

APPENDIX III.

(CHAPTER V, p. 128.)

Difficulty of Enforcing Awards on Methods of Payment.

A case which remained unsettled for some months during 1917, but ended in a tacit victory for the men, was that of the *Brightside Foundry & Engineering Company, Sheffield.*[1]

Here Sir W. Mackenzie had on 10 March, 1917, ruled, in deciding in a difference between the Sheffield Engineering Employers' Association and the Friendly Society of Ironfounders, that the refusal of the men employed by this firm to work piece-work in making ingot moulds exceeding four tons in weight, was a form of limitation of production.

On 25 March, a mass meeting of local iron-founders, considering this award, voted ; " Our members refuse to accept any further extension of piece-work in Sheffield ; further, if any action is taken to enforce this system of working, then the onus of responsibility will be on those who tried to enforce the award if any trouble arises." (The Investigation Officer who reported this to the Department added that the vote was taken at 3 p.m. on Sunday, just after many of the men had come out of their public-houses, and they were not unanimous. The firm wished to know where they stood. The shop stewards said that if piece-work were introduced, the men would strike). The following chronicle records the rest of the negotiations :—

18 *April*.—The men still refused to accept the award. Mr. Wolfe saw a deputation of them, and a letter was sent to the Secretary of the Society.

24 *April*.—The Ironfounders' Society replied that the matter was adjourned until after the National Conference on payment by results, which was being held that week.

29 *May*.—The Society again refused to accept the award.

20 *June*.—Mr. Kellaway saw a deputation of the men and explained that (*a*), the award must be obeyed, but that (*b*), conditions as to the safeguarding of the time-rate would be enforced, and that if after a reasonable trial objections continued, the question would be reconsidered.

22 *June* and 7 *July*.—Letters were sent by the Department to the Society urging the adoption of the award.

12 *July*.—The Society wrote that a ballot of the whole Society was to be taken on the matter.

29 *August*.—A letter was sent by the Department asking for the result of the ballot.

26 *September*.—The Society wrote that a ballot vote of the Society was being taken that day. (It was adverse to the award.)

3 *October*.—" L." Committee considered the case, and held that any attempt to introduce payment by results under Part I. of the original Munitions Act was most inadvisable.

19 *October*.—" L." Committee considered the refusal of workmen employed by the Brightside Foundry, Sheffield, to accept the award of Sir. W. Mackenzie, K.C. Attention was drawn to Sir D. Shackleton's minute of 16 October, expressing the opinion that in view of the difficulty (" which difficulty I think has been increased by the recent order relating to time-workers "), of enforcing awards introducing payment by results, and of the result of the ballot taken by the Trade Unions, no good purpose would be served by the

---

[1] C.E. 236/4 cf. the cases of Tweeddale & Smalley and E. Allen, Sheffield.

question being again raised. In view of the lapse of time since the date of the award, the Committee were of the opinion that no further action could profitably be taken."

22 *November.*—The Department informed the Engineering Employers' Federation, which had specially inquired into the matter on behalf of the Sheffield Engineering Employers' Association, that " after consultation with the Ministry of Labour," it was held to be unprofitable to do more in the matter.

29 *November.*—The matter was finally discussed by the Employers' Advisory Committee, when Sir T. Munro asked how it was possible to enforce the award. " I speak," he said, " with some feeling on the point, because I was one of the arbitrators who first gave a decision that if they did not go on piece-work it would mean a reduction of output, but I have grave doubts myself whether, if the men refuse to accept awards, the Government or anybody else can do anything to compel the men to go on piece." Sir George Carter, (Shipbuilding Employers' Federation), agreed that it was impossible to enforce such an award.[1]

---

[1] L.R. 5581/14.

APPENDIX IV.

(CHAPTER V, p. 139.)

Proposals for the Regulation of Payment by Results.

Agreed on by the Engineering Employers' Federation and the Amalgamated Society of Engineers, and suggested as a Second Schedule to the 1917 Amendment Act: 15 June, 1917.

SYSTEMS OF PAYMENTS BY RESULTS.

1. In all cases the time rate of the workmen concerned shall be guaranteed irrespective of earnings.

2. Over-time and nightshift and Sunday and holiday, and all other recognised allowances, shall be paid in addition to earnings under any systems of payment by results on the same conditions as already prevail in the trade and district in question for time work.

3. The price to be paid or basis time to be allowed either for a new job or for an altered job shall be fixed by mutual arrangement between the employer and the workman who is to perform the work or by such other methods as now exist or may hereafter be established by agreement in any trade or district.

4. No piece-work price, bonus or basis time once fixed may be altered unless the material, means, or method of production, is changed.

5. When the material, means, or method of production, is changed, and the employer desires a modification in price or basis time, the modification shall in no case be such as to effect a reduction in the earnings of the workers concerned.

6. When piece-work bonus or basis time system is in operation, and an employer desires a workman to undertake a job for which no price or basis time has previously been fixed, the employer shall, either before or as soon as possible after the job has been given out, see the workman with a view to agreement in accordance with the terms of this Schedule.

7. It is recognised that in the case of a new job or an altered job the workman may be unable to carry out the work as expeditiously as on repeat jobs. In all such cases the employers shall make an allowance on the job to the workman according to the necessities of the case. Such allowance shall be based on the average earnings of the workman concerned for the previous months.

8. In the event of a workman taking exception to any price or basis time allowed and being unable to arrive at a settlement, the matter shall be dealt with by a deputation of workmen consisting of the workman affected and two others engaged in the branch of trade in the shop concerned, who shall endeavour to effect a settlement with the management within seven days.

9. All settlements shall be retrospective to the commencement of the job on which the question is raised.

10. No debit balance shall be carried forward beyond the weekly or other mutually recognised period of settlement.

11. All balances and wages shall be paid through the office in proportion to the time and time rates of the workman or workmen employed on the job.

12. The employers shall in all cases supply the workman with a card stating the nature of each job and the price or basis time allowed, such card to be retained by the workman for reference until completion of the job.

APPENDIX V.

(CHAPTER VI, p. 174.)

Documents illustrating the Skilled ·Time-workers' Bonus:
1. Interim Report of Chairman of Skilled Day-workers' Committee.

1. The proposals finally put forward by the Employers are contained in Schedule A attached; those by the Trade Unions in Schedule B.

2. The differences between the two appear generally to be capable of adjustment on lines that would enable the Committee to present to the Minister an unanimous report, which would, it is hoped, remedy the grievance existing and also prove acceptable in the national interest. The obstacle in this is paragraph VII of the Employers' proposals which is as follows :—

" The foregoing provisions except those contained in Clause 1 shall not apply in cases where workmen have been given the opportunity of working on a system of payment by results, etc."

3. The Employers insist on this paragraph as a condition precedent; the Trade Unions refuse even to discuss it.

4. On behalf of the Employers it is urged :—

(a) That the paragraph is essential in the national interest in order to increase production.

(b) That it is the duty of the Committee to pass it seeing that the Committee is specially directed to keep down expense and to secure an increased output of munitions.

(c) That an extension of piece work can best be secured by a general bargain, covering the whole industry.

(d) That unless this paragraph is agreed to, the Trade Unions or their branches will prevent their members going on piece, even where they wish to do so.

(e) That the Employers only suggest piece work in cases suitable for that system, and that paragraph 7 safeguards this.

5. On behalf of the Trade Unions it is urged :—

(a) That an extension of piece work is outside the Committee's terms of reference.

(b) That even if it is within them it is not the business of a Committee, set up to deal with the question of the abolition of Leaving Certificates, to settle a big question like the extension of piece work.

(c) That the question can never be settled nationally or generally, but must be a matter of separate bargain in the districts.

(d) That the Trade Union representatives have no authority even to discuss it.

(e) That even if they agreed to it, their members would refuse to be bound by their decision, and

(f) That great unrest would be caused thereby.

6. At the same time the Trade Union representatives expressed themselves as favourable to the extension of piece work for the purposes of the war.

7. After trying all possible methods, I am satisfied that the difference between the two parties is incapable of adjustment, and until it is dealt with in one way or another no agreement can be reached such as would enable the Committee to make an unanimous report to the Minister. It therefore seems that the matter is one for the Minister to determine without the guidance of the Committee. That being so, it will be of great assistance to obtain the Minister's decision now.

8. My own views are :—
   (a) That the matter is clearly within the Committee's terms of reference ; but
   (b) That (leaving aside the question whether such a matter can be settled by a Committee set up to consider difficulties caused by the abolition of Leaving Certificates) I do not think it can be settled generally for the whole industry, but must be a matter of individual bargain in the localities.
   (c) I appreciate the difficult position in which the Trade Union representatives would be placed if they agreed to it.
   (d) Paragraph 7 would not effect its object. It would not be accepted by the men whom it professed to bind who would without hesitation throw their leaders over ; and the extension of piece work would be hindered rather than helped.
   (e) The unrest caused by paragraph 7 would more than outweigh the satisfaction given by the increase of wages.

9. Therefore whatever decision the Committee might come to I should find great difficulty in advising the Minister to incorporate paragraph 7 or anything like it in any Order he may make. An extension of piece work is urgent in the national interest, but it cannot be secured in this manner.

10. I suggest that the question is a proper one to be referred to the Advisory Committee.

11. This Memorandum is a personal one by myself as Chairman and has not been submitted to, and does not bind, this Committee ; but it expresses the views of the representatives on the Committee of the Ministry and of the Shipyards.

12. I shall be glad to receive the Minister's directions.

JOHN W. HILLS,
Chairman.

6, Whitehall Gardens,
 5th Sept., 1917.

(a) **Memorandum and Proposals by Employers' Representatives.**

Dear Sir,

REMUNERATION OF SKILLED MEN ON DAY WORK.

In view of the impossibility of arranging a further meeting at an early date I shall be glad if you will hand to the Chairman to give to the Minister the enclosed statement which explains the position of the Employers represented on the Committee.

Yours faithfully,
ALLAN M. SMITH.

MINISTRY OF MUNITIONS OF WAR.

DEPARTMENTAL COMMITTEE RE TIME RATES OF SKILLED MEN.
(MAJOR HILL'S COMMITTEE.)

REPORT BY THE REPRESENTATIVES OF EMPLOYERS' INTERESTS CONCERNED.

5th September, 1917.

1. We believe that the Committee have considered fully all the points which bear on the questions submitted. The problems arising therefrom are most difficult of solution on account of the complexity of the issues involved.

2. The discussion has demonstrated :—
   (a) The grievance alleged, owing to the difference in the earning power of the skilled man on time work and the semi-skilled man on systems of payment by results, was greater in the early stages of the war than at present.

(b) This is accounted for by the extent to which dilution has taken place on semi-skilled work and on the consequent elimination to a considerable extent of the large earnings of semi-skilled men who were skilled in the particular operation upon which they were employed

(c) In a great many instances skilled men on time work are earning greater amounts than semi-skilled men and women on payment by results.

(d) The extent to which the grievance alleged exists at this date is not such as to justify any measures of an heroic nature.

(e) The effect of the repeal of Section 7 of the Munitions Act, 1915, on skilled men on time work may cause a certain amount of migration of such skilled labour.

(f) The extent to which migration may take place is a matter of pure speculation.

(g) Many elements may contribute to or prevent migration—for example :—

(1) Workmen in lodgings may desire to return home even at less wages on account of the discomfort of the lodgings in the district in which they are working.
Men might be satisfied to remain if their families could be brought to the district in which they are working.
In some cases this is impossible owing to shortage of houses, in others, transport of furniture, etc., is preventative.

(2) Workmen at home may desire to leave their district in order to increase their wages.

(3) Time men may leave in order to obtain employment on payment by results.

(4) Men employed on systems of payment by results may desire to go on time, and so on.

3. The reference by the Minister requires the Committee to have regard to the effect which any report they may make will have on output.

4. We are convinced that any proposal which involves extra payment to time workers without relation to increase of output is fundamentally opposed to the National Interest which at this time demands, and is entitled to receive, the maximum effort of everyone concerned.

5. We have, therefore, maintained this principle as a cardinal principle of any arrangement to be made.

6. At the same time we recognise that to claim, arbitrarily to enunciate the principle, would be a mistake.

7. We therefore suggest that in certain highly skilled occupations an advance in wages should be given irrespective of the question of the difference in the earning power above referred to. (*See* Clause I of proposals attached.)

8. We also make further proposals for dealing with the difference in earning power. (*See* Clauses II to VI.)

9. The proposals must be read as a whole and are subject to the principle laid down in Clause VII.

10. It is to be noted that while maintaining the principle, we do not suggest that the exercise of the principle shall, at a time like the present, be in the absolute discretion of the employers. We provide machinery to ensure a war-time safeguard.

11. In conclusion, we desire to emphasise as strongly as we can the fact that all work of an engineering character is in some shop or other done on a system of payment by results. Where such a system is in operation the grievance alleged does not exist. It is, therefore, due to the Nation that the work-people should put no obstacle in the way of any reasonable system of payment by results being introduced as far as the work lends itself to such.

ALLAN M. SMITH.
D. S. MARJORIBANKS.
JOHN BARR.
A. WARNE BROWNE.

PROPOSALS BY EMPLOYERS' REPRESENTATIVES.

I. (1). Skilled men on promotion to the following occupations and while employed on time and not on system of payment by results shall receive :—

½d. per hour with a further ½d. per hour after six months' experience above the district rate for fitters or the time rate of the workmen concerned, whichever is the higher :—

(a) *Gauge Makers*, while employed finishing gauges, *i.e.*, beyond ·02 of accuracy.

(b) *Jig Makers*.

(c) *Cutting-tool Makers*, while employed finishing cutting-tools, *i.e.*, beyond ·02 of accuracy.

(d) *Inspectors, Examiners and Gaugers.*

(e) *Markers off.*

(2) Skilled men of the foregoing classes whose present time rates are not affected by the foregoing grading shall receive an advance of ½d. per hour.

(3) Skilled men on promotion to setting-up (other than on shell and fuse, etc., machines) shall receive

2s. 6d. per week or higher, above the district rate of their own trade according to the number of machines under their charge, and the amount of supervision and teaching of workpeople required.

II. In shops where manufacturing is done on a system of payment by results :—

(a) Skilled men of the foregoing occupations employed on time shall receive in addition to their earnings a bonus of 10 per cent. of their total earnings.

(b) Skilled men employed on time in maintenance and repair of plant and machinery and in the production of light, heat, and power, shall receive in addition to their earnings a bonus of 5 per cent. of their total earnings.

III. In shops where manufacturing is done on time the allowances provided in Clause I above shall apply.

IV. Skilled men transferred by the employers temporarily from a system of payment by results to time work shall in addition to their time rate receive a bonus equivalent to the average of the bonuses earned by them for the four weeks prior to transfer.

V. Skilled men engaged on factory production on time on work which is customarily done in the district on a system of payment by results shall receive in addition to their earnings a bonus of 5 per cent. of their total earnings.

VI. The foregoing provisions apply only to workmen engaged in the manufacture of munitions of war except the building of ships, and shall not apply to semi-skilled and unskilled men and women introduced on dilution to the foregoing occupations.

VII. The foregoing provisions, except those contained in Clause I, shall not apply in cases where workmen have been given the opportunity of working on a system of payment by results. Should a difference arise as to whether a job which, or similar to which, has not hitherto been so undertaken either in the establishment or in the district in question, is suitable to be done on a system of payment by results, the question shall be referred to the final decision of a Local Arbitration Court consisting of an employer and a workman of the trade concerned with an independent chairman. A system of payment by result so introduced shall be recorded as a change in terms of the Act. An extension of the introduction of such system shall not require a further reference provided the extension is in all essential respects of the same nature as the work covered by an award.

VIII. The additional labour cost entailed by the foregoing shall be borne by the Government.

(b) Memorandum and Proposals by Trade Union Representatives.

1. In reply to the memorandum of the Ministry of Munitions representatives, we cannot accept the view that the purpose for which this committee was constituted has anything to do with Payment by Results, and we therefore protest against any attempt to use this Committee in order to enforce the general adoption of payment by results. We hold that the question of any change in the methods of remuneration must be dealt with locally as at present, by District agreement, and we believe that negotiations on this matter would be most effectively carried on through Trade Union Workshop committees acting under the authority of the District Committee. As we understand that the question of Workshop Committees has been already referred by the Minister of Munitions to the newly constituted Advisory Committee, we shall not, in order to avoid overlapping, submit a detailed scheme.

2. The advance to the following classes of men employed in payment by results shops should be 20 per cent., and this advance should count on their day rate for overtime, night-shift and other allowances.

(a) Gauge makers, while employed finishing gauges, *i.e.*, beyond ·02 of accuracy.

(b) Jig makers.

(c) Cutting tool makers while employed finishing tools, *i.e.* beyond ·02 of accuracy.

(d) Inspectors, Examiners and Gaugers.

(a) Charge hands.

(b) Setters-up (other than those engaged on shell fuses, &c.).

(c) Skilled men engaged in maintenance and repair of plant and machinery and in the production of light, heat and power.

(d) And all other class of skilled time-workers should receive a special advance of 15 per cent. on the same terms as above.

The classes of workers referred to in Clause 2, who are employed in shops wholly engaged on time work, should receive an advance of 15 per cent. on the same terms.

The provisions of Clause 6 are covered by our reply in Clause 1.

August, 1917.

The Trade Union representatives on the Committee have to submit the following memorandum :—

(1) In our view, the Committee was constituted not for the purpose of enforcing or furthering the adoption of systems of payment by results but for that of finding some method of removing the inequality in the remuneration of skilled time-workers and semi-skilled and unskilled piece and premium bonus workers. The opposition to payment by results among our members is generally known, and we could not have accepted seats upon any Committee of which the object was to enforce its adoption. We mention this fact because we have felt that certain members of the Committee have throughout endeavoured to use it for the purpose of securing our acceptance of payment by results.

(2) We hold strongly that the right way of dealing with the situation is either by a bonus on the earnings of all skilled time-workers, or by an increase in the time rate of such workers. Should the latter method be adopted, it would be necessary to take into account the fact that many skilled time-workers are already receiving over the district rate, and therefore no flat increase in the district rate would at all meet the situation.

(3) We accordingly suggest that all skilled men who are employed on time should receive an advance of 15 per cent. on their present day rates, and that this advance should count on their day rate for overtime, night-shift and other allowances.

(4) These suggestions apply to establishments in which systems of payment by results are in operation, whether or not the majority of the skilled workers in the establishment are employed on such systems ; *i.e.* they apply wherever in an establishment the discrepancy in earnings forms a grievance. In other establishments in which time work prevails exclusively, the classes of skilled workers referred to in clause 3 should receive an advance of 15 per cent. on their present rates, payable on the same terms as are laid down in that claim.

(5) We believe that the foregoing recommendations, while they would by no means remove the discrepancy which is the reason for the deliberations of this Committee, would considerably improve the position. Any attempt, on the other hand, to enforce the adoption of payment by results or to exclude from participation in any advance recommended by the Committee workers who refuse to accept payment by results could only result in stirring up most serious unrest, and in making the present unsatisfactory position infinitely worse. In the course of the discussions, we suggested that the establishment of Shop Committees would serve to ease many of the difficulties that now stand in the way but we have no confidence in any improvement in the position unless the main lines of our recommendations are followed by the Minister.

Submitted 5 *September*, 1917.

(c) **Memorandum by Official Representatives.**

1. We consider that if we are to give full weight to the instructions in the reference that we are to have " due regard to the increased output of munitions of war " it is of first importance that nothing should be done which might tend to retard the extension of systems of payment by results. On the contrary we are of opinion that everything possible should be done to extend such systems to the utmost practicable limit.

2. The discussion made it quite clear that the Trade Union Representatives on the Committee could not agree to any recommendations which included a condition that any advances or bonuses proposed should not be granted in cases where workmen are given the opportunity of working on a system of payment by results. Further, even if they had been willing to agree, they could not guarantee that such agreement would be ratified either by the Executives of the Unions which they represented, or by the rank and file of their members. From this it follows that little advantage would accrue from a report from the Committee in which this was embodied as a condition.

3. We suggest that as this matter is one of national importance, the Minister should not announce any decision on the point at issue without first consulting his Trades Union Advisory Committee. In this connection it is desirable to point out that the A.S.E. is likely to be the Union most concerned and, whilst the Advisory Committee would no doubt offer advice and make suggestions, they could not in any way commit the A.S.E. to the acceptance of the principle which the Employers have advocated ; but they might point out the direction in which agreement would be likely to be reached.

4. If it be decided that an advance should be granted without the condition as to the extension of systems of payment by results, we submit that such advance must be on a less liberal basis than if the condition attached to it.

5. It should also be noted that the advance must be of such proportion that it does not prejudice existing systems of payment by results, nor tend to prevent the extension of such systems.

W. J. LARKE.
GORDON CAMPBELL.
J. M. McELROY.

7.9.17.

2. Final Report of Committee on Rates of Skilled Dayworkers.

The Committee make the following recommendations :—

I. The Committee have limited their recommendations to workmen employed in the engineering trades.

II. All skilled men employed on time (except those provided for in Clause III) shall receive the following bonus :—

(a) if employed in shops where systems of payment by results obtain—15 per cent. on their earnings :

(b) if employed in shops where manufacturing is done on time—12½ per cent. on their earnings.

III. All skilled men employed on time in maintenance and repair of plant and machinery, in the production of light, heat and power, and in setting up, shall receive the following bonus :—

(a) if employed in shops where systems of payment by results obtain— 12½ per cent. on their earnings :

(b) if employed in shops where manufacturing is done on time—10 per cent. on their earnings.

IV. The foregoing provisions shall become operative on the first pay after 6th October, 1917.

V. Skilled men transferred by the employers temporarily from a system of payment by results to time work shall in addition to their time rates receive a bonus equivalent to the average of the bonuses earned by them for the four weeks prior to transfer.

VI. The foregoing provisions apply only to skilled workmen employed on time rates in the Engineering Trades and engaged in the manufacture of munitions of war, and shall not apply to semi-skilled or unskilled men and women introduced on dilution to the foregoing occupations. With regard to the building and repair of ships the foregoing provisions apply only to members of the Engineering trades employed therein.

VII. Men who are at present in receipt of a bonus over and above their time-rates shall be paid either the foregoing bonuses or their existing bonuses, whichever are the higher.

VIII. The foregoing provisions shall not apply to women who receive the skilled man's rate under Order 489, Clause 1, (b).

IX. Nothing in the foregoing provisions shall affect the present basis of determining piece rates, premium bonus times, or any other system of payment by results.

X. The additional labour cost entailed by the foregoing shall be dealt with by the contracting Departments on similar lines to previous advances made by the Committee on Production.

XI. The Committee are greatly indebted to their Secretary, Mr. John Murray, whose skill and experience have been of the greatest assistance.

J. W. HILLS.
W. J. LARKE.
J. M. McELROY.
ALEC GORMAN.
W. H. HUTCHINSON.
W. F. DAWTRY.
GEORGE WILKINSON.
JOHN MURRAY,
Secretary.[1]

21 Sept., 1917.

---

[1] The representative of the Ministry of Labour did not sign, but made no protest.

3. Memorandum by the Labour Committee of the Ministry of Munitions.

ENGINEERING TRADE—SKILLED TIME-WORKERS' WAGES ORDER.

In forwarding this Order for the approval of the Minister the Committee has the following observations to make :—

1. The report of Major Hills' Committee recommended the following advances to all skilled men in the Engineering Trades employed on time-work :—

In Piecework Shops.
  (a) 15 per cent. to all such men except those included in
  (b) 12½ per cent. to all men engaged on the maintenance and repair of Plant and Machinery and the Production of Light, Heat and Power.

In Timework Shops.
Advances of 12½ per cent. and 10 per cent. respectively for the above classes.

When the L Committee came to examine Major Hills' report they felt that the distinction between men engaged on the maintenance and repair of Plant and Machinery, and on the production of Light, Heat and Power on the one hand and of all other skilled men on time on the other, was not a valid one, and they further came to the conclusion that the advances should be 15 per cent for all skilled men on time employed in piece shops and 12½ per cent for all skilled men on time employed in time shops.

2. The Committee considered the effect of the report in all its aspects and submitted a memorandum to the Minister on the subject of the classes of men which should be scheduled to the Order. One schedule A was prepared which limited the advances to those classes of men who were (a) most essential, (b) most closely associated with less skilled time workers and (c) least able to work on a system of payment by results. The other schedule B included practically all the skilled men in the Engineering Trade. The Committee's memorandum attempted to estimate the effects, both industrial and financial, of each schedule and asked for a decision from the Minister as to whether it should proceed on the basis of the limited A or the general B schedule.

3. The Minister after consideration of the memorandum decided in favour of the limited schedule.

4. The Committee then proceeded to draw up the Order.

5. The operative provisions of the Order did not present any great difficulties. The final form to be given to the limited schedule was, however, not easy to determine. After eliciting informally the views of representatives of Employers and Trade Unions on the terms to be used, the Committee has drawn up a further limited schedule C. This schedule is based on the logically defensible principle of including only those who by the nature of their occupation are prevented from working on a system of payment by results. In adopting this principle the Committee wish to make it clear that they do not conflict with the Minister's refusal to accept the Employers' proposal that the advance should be made conditional on the men accepting any reasonable offer made to them of working on payment by results. This proposal would have made the question whether in any particular case a man was or was not to receive the advance depend on the question whether an offer made to him was reasonable or not. Schedule C, on the other hand, includes definitely those for whom payment by results is generally impracticable.

Men employed in public utility undertakings have been included in Schedule C in consequence of representations to that effect made to the Committee by those undertakings.

6. The Committee recognises that the Order with Schedule C departs from the recommendations of Major Hills' Committee in favour of a general advance to skilled men. The Committee's objections to such an advance are (a) that it assumes a general grievance among all the skilled men and (b) that there is little prospect of confining such an advance to skilled men in the Engineering Trade.

The Order with Schedule C, on the other hand, recognises the specific grievance of the skilled time-worker who cannot increase his earnings by results and makes provision for that grievance.

7. The Committee has considered the Admiralty letter of October 5 filed in M.W.L.R. 139/256 and believes that its objections would not arise if the Order were made with Schedule C. Such an Order would not prejudice the introduction or extension of payment by results.

8. The Committee estimates that Schedule C covers approximately 207,500 men and that the cost of the advance prescribed by the Order would be £5,440,000 per annum.

CHARLES E. ELLIS.

4. Extract from a Memorandum by Sir Lynden Macassey, Director of Shipyard Labour.

* * * *

8. The intention of the proposed Order is two-fold :—

(1) To remove the difference in earnings between the time-paid skilled men and the piece-paid semi-skilled and unskilled operatives.

(2) To prevent skilled men leaving their time-paid skilled work on the abolition of the Leaving Certificates and taking up higher piece-paid semi-skilled work.

9. The proposed Order will not achieve these purposes. The grievance in many Engineering Shops is that certain semi-skilled and unskilled operatives working on piece-work make much larger earnings than the time-paid skilled men on whom they are dependent. The proposed percentage bonuses will not bring the earnings of the skilled men who receive them up to the level of the semi-skilled and unskilled operatives in question.

Secondly, as the earnings of the skilled men will remain lower than the semi-skilled and unskilled operatives even after the concession of the bonus, there will not be any financial inducement for the time-paid skilled men to remain at their skilled work and refrain from going on less skilled piece-paid work. If it is intended to prevent such waste of skilled labour Employers can and ought to be prevented, under No. 8a of the Defence of the Realm Regulations, from employing skilled men on semi-skilled work. That is the proper remedy.

The proposed Order gives a bonus to a certain number of time-paid skilled men and irrespective of whether they have been working in connection with piece-paid semi-skilled and unskilled operatives or not. It is obvious that the same bonus will and can logically be claimed and must ultimately be paid to all time-paid skilled men in the engineering trade because they all, like the limited class of proposed recipients under the Order, can point to some higher piece-paid semi-skilled and unskilled operatives. That this will be so, appears from the Report of the Committee, who apparently found themselves unable to draw any line and recommended a bonus to all time-paid skilled men in the trade.

11. Without question similar bonuses can logically be claimed and it would seem, on grounds of equity, must ultimately be paid to all time-paid semi-skilled and unskilled men in the Engineering Trade. These men naturally feel a grievance that they are not or cannot be put on piece-work and therefore cannot make the same high earnings as members of their own occupations make who are on piece-work.

12. Once the above-mentioned principle is admitted in the Engineering Trade it must ultimately be admitted in the Shipbuilding Trade. There is developing among the Boiler-makers a very strong movement for abandoning payment by results and introducing in its place a time-rate with a make up bonus to the approximate level of piece-work earnings. Further, by reason of the publicity attaching to the question in the Engineering Trade, semi-skilled men in the

Shipyards now paid on time and working with piece-workers are claiming bonuses on their time rates.

13. The proposed Order for the first time in the history of the Engineering industry gives effect to two new principles :—

(a) It provides for a percentage wage increase not based on any economic datum, as, for example, the increased cost of living, which has been the ground on which, up to the present, wage advances have been based, but on a purely arbitrary and empirical percentage which cannot be tested on any economic ground. This will undermine very seriously the practice and procedure of the Committee on Production which has now secured very general approval and authority in the industrial world. Once the percentage basis is adopted there will commence a regular agitation for the increase of the percentage and the amount of the increase will merely become a question of opportunism as to the amount from time to time requisite to keep the applicant trades quiet. There can be little question that the time-paid trades will ultimately claim as a minimum the highest general average earnings customary amongst piece-workers in their respective trades.

(b) It virtually establishes a principle that the day rates of men not working at piece-work speed, should approximately be the same as those now working at piece-work. This has long been the contention of an advanced section of the Trade Union movement but if adopted, would be a very serious blow to the Engineering and Shipbuilding industry.

14. A further effect would be to prevent materially the further extension of systems of payment by results as ordered by the War Cabinet (See War Cab. Decision No. 49 1 (1) & (2) Jan. 30 1917) which it is understood the War Cabinet regard as a matter of prime importance and which the Admiralty have been successful in effecting in the case of certain trades with most satisfactory results.

15. The time-paid skilled men generally have no grievance that a number of semi-skilled men are making substantially higher earnings. In cases where that occurs it is due to the fact that under the Treasury Agreement, the Munitions of War Act, 1915, and the documents known as L.2. & L.3. the piece-prices for semi-skilled and unskilled operatives doing skilled work are based on the skilled man's time rate. This was expressly provided to protect the skilled man's trade, and to keep up the price of his labour. The higher, therefore, the piece price the more is the skilled man protected. He cannot therefore on the ground of height of price make any legitimate complaint.

16. Apart from the general sentimental grievance in the Engineering Trade on the part of some skilled men who do not understand the reason that semi-skilled operatives in certain cases make higher earnings than a skilled man, the real case to be met in practice is the direct personal grievance and legitimate complaint of the time-paid skilled man working in tool-rooms and places of that sort in connection with piece-paid operatives, who finds himself with lower earnings than the semi-skilled and unskilled operatives instructed by, or dependent on him. The operatives make higher earnings for four reasons, because :—

Firstly, the semi-skilled operatives are prepared to go and do go on a system of payment by results.

Secondly, the price paid to them is based on the skilled man's high time-rate.

Thirdly, the rate of output of the semi-skilled operative has been much increased by the provision by the Employers of jigs, special tools, and other devices for making machines " fool-proof."

Fourthly, In some cases, before semi-skilled men went on to the work, the prices have been fixed much too high, owing to the skilled men holding back production or through mistake, both on the part of the Employers and of the Government Department concerned.

17. If then the time-paid skilled men desire to have their position remedied they, like the semi-skilled men, should be prepared to go on a system of payment by results wherever possible. It is wholly unreasonable for them to refuse to do so and at the same time claim time-earnings as great as the piece earnings of the

semi-skilled operatives. Where, therefore, it is practicable to put the skilled men on to a system of payment by results it is essential in the national interests of both production and economy that they should be so put and not paid a bonus independent of output. The order it is recognised, should not operate as a compulsory measure to substitute payment by esults, for payment on time, but at the same time it is submitted it ought not o prevent the introduction or extension of payment by results in proper cases. So long as the War Cabinet policy is payment by results in proper cases a potential piece-worker who refuses to go on to piece work should be refused a bonus.

18. The next question is the system of payment by results to be adopted. That should so far as possible be left to agreement between masters and men. On the general question of the system, this may be said : Strong objection would be raised by the skilled men to the premium bonus system. That, unless agreed between management and men, has to be excluded from practical consideration. The next system is piece-work. While that is much more acceptable to the skilled men, yet in some cases it would be impracticable. In such quarters as there are objections on the part of the men to piece-work they are usually based on the ground that each piece-worker tends to become a separate self-seeking unit, without any interest in the general life and welfare of the shop, keeping himself, his earnings, his tools apart, and often competing with his fellows for the use of necessary facilities and, if he is on day shift, working up to the limit of his time and therefore frequently not " dove-tailing " his work into that of his mate on night shift. The next system is shop output bonus or fellowship system to which no such objections apply. Under it the shop works as a united community and the output of a whole establishment or the respective output of the constituent parts, *e.g.* machine shop, smithy, foundry etc., are priced or a graduated bonus applied after the output exceeds a certain amount. The balance after payment of day rates to all operatives of every class concerned is carried to a common pool which is divided amongst them in proportion to day rates. To this system there is rarely any objection on the part of the skilled men. It is working with smoothness and success in a number of. large engineering establishments and would effectively meet the present case. It would ensure instruction by and co-operation on the part of the skilled men. The greater their efforts the greater the output and the more their bonus. Assuming the Government does not pay the bonus the only objection likely to be raised. to the shop output bonus or fellowship system would come from the semi-skilled operatives who would possibly object to any portion of their earnings being divided among the skilled men who instructed them, or on whom they were dependent for tools, etc. But the Government are in a strong position to deal with the semi-skilled operatives. They are nothing like so vital to the industry as the skilled men. The Government's pledge against reduction of piece-prices would not be affected. Strictly speaking, in almost every case, through changes in the mode of manufacture, since the piece-price was fixed, owing to the application of jigs, provision of special tools, and adoption of fool-proof devices, the Employers could without any violation of the pledge, if they had liked to enforce their right, reduce the price and therefore the earnings of the semi-skilled operatives. But no reduction of price whatever is involved under the shop output bonus, or fellowship system.

19. As it is recognised under the circumstances as they now exist that something must be done, it is urged, in view of the very serious industrial effects that would result from the operation of the proposed order, that the order be amended to provide that a bonus on the principle of the shop output or fellowship system (unless by agreement between master and man some other system is adopted) be paid to time paid skilled men in the engineering trade working for, with or in connection with piece paid operatives. This would meet the existing necessities of the case, and would appear fully to concede all that has been promised by the Minister of Munitions.

20. My opinion as to the serious effect of proposals such as are contained in the proposed order is I may say shared by the Shipbuilding Employers' Federation, and by Trade Unionists on the staff of the Shipyard Labour Department and also my by experienced local officers in the different districts.

LYNDEN MACASSEY.

5. The Skilled Timeworkers (Engineers and Moulders) Wages Order, 1917. (No. 1061).

Whereas the Minister of Munitions considers it necessary in order to maintain the output of munitions that directions should be given with respect to the remuneration to be paid to fully qualified skilled Engineers and Moulders of the class specified in this Order for work being munitions work or work in connection therewith which at the time when these directions are given is paid at time rates.

Now therefore the Minister of Munitions in pursuance of the powers conferred upon him by section 1 of the Munitions of War Act, 1917, and all other powers vested in him by the Munitions of War Acts, 1915 to 1917, hereby orders that the following directions shall have effect with respect to the remuneration to be paid to fully qualified skilled Engineers and Moulders of the class specified in this Order for work being munitions work or work in connection therewith which at the time when these directions are given is paid at time rates.

1. Workmen to whom these directions apply shall receive a bonus of $12\frac{1}{2}$ per cent. on their earnings which shall not alter or become part of their time rates.

2. The bonus payable under these directions shall accrue as from the beginning of the first full pay following the twelfth day of October, 1917, and the first payment thereof shall be made as soon as possible and not later than the first full pay day in November, 1917.

3. These directions apply, subject to the provisions of paragraphs 4 and 5, only to fully qualified skilled Engineers and Moulders rated at or above the current district time rate for turners or fitters while employed on or in connection with munitions work and paid at plain time rates without the addition of any bonus other than :—

(a) A bonus dependent on timekeeping.

(b) A bonus (not being a bonus on output) less favourable to such workmen than the bonus payable under these directions, in which case the existing bonus shall merge in the bonus payable under these directions.

(c) A war advance given to meet the cost of living as the result of or in conformity with arbitration under Part I. of the Munitions of War Act, 1915.

4. These directions shall not apply to workmen of the class specified in paragraph 3 of this Order whose wages it has been the practice to regulate by the movements in the wages of men employed in trades other than the Engineering and Foundry trades. An application may be made to the Minister of Munitions for special directions in cases where the existing basis of remuneration for such workmen is less favourable than that of workmen of the same class to whom these directions apply.

5. These directions shall not apply to workmen paid an upstanding wage or salary which covers overtime or other allowances.

6. Nothing in the foregoing provisions shall affect the present basis of determining piece rates or premium bonus times or any other system of payment by results.

7. Any contravention of or non-compliance with these directions is punishable in like manner as if this Order was an Award made in settlement of a difference under Part I. of the Munitions of War Act, 1915.

8. These directions may be varied by the Minister of Munitions from time to time but shall not continue in force after the termination of the present war.

9. Any question which arises as to the interpretation of these directions shall be determined by the Minister of Munitions.

This Order may be cited as "The Skilled Timeworkers (Engineers and Moulders) Wages Order, 1917."

Dated this 13th day of October, 1917.

WINSTON S. CHURCHILL.

APPENDIX VI.

(CHAPTER VII, p 201.)

Cost Variation Clauses in Contracts (Wages).

FORM M.C. 19.

Declaration by Contractor.
I. The Contractor declares that the price is fixed strictly upon the basis of present rates of wages, and that nothing had been allowed and no item included in the price covering the contingency of a rise in the cost of labour.

Contractor may claim.
II. If during the currency of the contract the cost of labour shall be increased by direct Government action (as defined below) the Contractor may claim and the Minister of Munitions shall repay any increased cost of production due to increased cost of labour, provided the following conditions are observed :—

Estimated claim to be lodged forthwith.
(1) Upon the announcement of any increase of wages resulting from such direct Government action as aforesaid paid or employed in the execution of this contract, the Contractor shall forthwith notify the Department of the estimated amount of his claim in respect of increased cost of production due thereto.

Clear records to be kept.
(2) If the Contractor shall so notify the Department, he shall keep his record in such form as to show clearly the amount of the extra cost due to the rise in wages.

Net increase.
(3) No claim shall exceed the strictly net amount chargeable to the contract on account of the increased cost of labour properly employed in the execution of the contract, i.e., no addition whatever in the name of establishment charges or profit or otherwise shall be admitted, but a claim for such increased cost shall not be excluded merely on the ground that the cost of such labour (including pay of foremen and draughtsmen) is brought into account in the cost accounts of the Contractor otherwise than as part of the direct cost of labour.

Choice of immediate or postponed settlement.
(4) Upon receipt of any such claim the Minister may either :—

(a) Agree with the Contractor the amount by which the contract price shall be increased by reason of such claim without awaiting the completion of the contract, or

(b) failing agreement, may postpone the determination of such claim until the due completion of the contract, provided that if required by the Minister any such claim must be supported by the certificate of a Chartered or Incorporated Accountant or by some other accountant approved in any particular case by the Minister that such additional wages have actually been paid and the accounts and figures upon which such claim is based shall at the option of the Minister be subject to independent investigation on his behalf. The decision of the Minister as to the additional sum, if any, to be allowed shall be final and conclusively binding on the Contractor.

Claims due on satisfactory completion.
(5) Except with the prior consent in writing of the Minister no claim shall rank as due for payment before the expiration of the contract, and the Minister shall not be bound to pay any claim unless the Contractor has duly fulfilled the obligations of his contract to the reasonable satisfaction of the Minister, and no claim in respect of any work, goods, or articles which are not completed or delivered within the date fixed by the contract shall be admitted unless the Minister is satisfied that the delay has been due to causes beyond the control of the Contractor.

Interpretation.	(6) For the purposes of this clause " direct Government action " means any award as to wages made upon any reference for settlement under the Munitions of War Acts, 1915-1917, or any order or award as to wages made by the Minister or by any Tribunal appointed for that purpose pursuant to any Act of Parliament, and
Decrease of costs.	III.—In the event of the cost of labour being decreased by direct Government action as above defined during the currency of the contract and of the cost of production of the goods ordered under this contract being in the opinion of the Minister thereby reduced, the Minister may withhold from the contract price an amount equivalent to the saving in the cost of production thereby effected on the contract, and in default of agreement as to the amount of such saving such amount shall be decided in the manner prescribed above for dealing with claims for increase.

APPENDIX VII.

Table of Statutory Wages Orders Relating to Men.

Statutory Rules and Orders Nos.	Date.	Description.
		Munitions of War (Amendment) Act, 1916, Section VII.
1916.—182.	24/2/16.	Application of Circular L.3 to Controlled Establishments. Order No. 1.
412.	26/6/16.	Employment and remuneration of semi-skilled and unskilled men on skilled men's work. Order No. 2.
589.	7/9/16.	The Munitions (Employment and Remuneration of Semi-skilled and Unskilled Men). Order No. 3.
1917.— 71.	24/1/17.	The Munitions (Employment and Remuneration of Semi-skilled and Unskilled Men). Order No. 4.
667.	26/6/17.	The Munitions (Employment and Remuneration of Semi-skilled and Unskilled Men). Order No. 5.
		Munitions of War Act, 1917. Section I.
1917.—1061.	13/10/17.	The Skilled Timeworkers (Engineers and Moulders) Wages Order, 1917.
1301.	11/12/17.	The Timeworkers (Engineering and Foundry) Wages Order, 1917.
1308.	11/12/17.	Timeworkers (Shipbuilding and Ship-repairing) Wages Order, 1917.
1918— 187.	8/2/18.	The Skilled Aircraft Workers' Wages Order, 1918.
742.	14/6/18.	The Time Workers (Building and Construction) Wages (General) Order, 1918.
		Munitions of War Act, 1917. Section V.
1917.— 938.	7/9/17.	The Munitions (Extension of Awards) Order, No. 1. (Engineering and Foundry Trades).
967.	20/9/17.	The Munitions (Extension of Awards) Order No. 2. (Light Castings Trade).
968.	20/9/17.	The Munitions (Extension of Awards) Order No. 3. (Light Castings Trade).
969.	20/9/17.	The Munitions (Extension of Awards) Order No. 4. (Stove, Grate and Light Metal Trades).
970.	7/9/17.	The Munitions (Extension of Awards) Order No. 5. (Light Castings Trade).
985.	24/9/17.	The Munitions (Extension of Awards) Order No. 6. (Chemical Trades).
986.	24/9/17.	The Munitions (Extension of Awards) Order No. 7. (Brassworkers—Birmingham and district).
1003.	30/9/17.	The Munitions (Extension of Awards) Order No. 8. (Dressers in Iron and Steel Works, Scotland).
1004.	30/9/17.	The Munitions (Extension of Awards) Order No. 9. (Brassworkers, Birmingham and district).

Statutory Rules and Orders Nos.	Date.	Description.
1047.	8/10/17.	The Munitions (Extension of Awards) Order No. 10. (Engineering and Foundry Trades).
1064.	15/10/17.	The Munitions (Extension of Awards) Order No. 11. (Scotch Steel Foundry Trades).
1137.	8/11/17.	The Munitions (Extension of Awards) Order No. 12. (Building Trade, London district).
1171.	20/11/17.	The Munitions (Extension of Awards) Order No. 13. (Shipbuilding Trades).
1172.	20/11/17.	The Munitions (Extension of Awards) Order No. 14. (Engineering and Foundry Trades).
1239.	6/12/17.	The Munitions (Extension of Awards) Order No. 15. (Light Castings Trade).
1258.	16/12/17.	The Munitions (Extension of Awards) Order No. 16. (Shipbuilding, Engineering and Foundry Trades).
1918.—180.	7/2/18.	The Munitions (Extension of Awards) Order No. 17. (Light Castings Industry and Ironmoulders and Dressers in Steel Foundries, Iron Works, etc., Scotland).
937.	12/8/18.	The Munitions (Extension of Awards) Order No. 18. (Engineering and Foundry Trades).

Contents of Volume V

Part   I.—The Control of Men's Wages.
Part II.—The Control of Women's Wages.
Part III.—Welfare : the Control of Working Conditions.
Part IV.—The Provision of Canteens in Munitions Factories.
Part V.—Provision for the Housing of Munition Workers.

Note.—The present issue is subject to revision and must be regarded as provisional.

CONFIDENTIAL
For Official Information only   *Crown Copyright Reserved*

HISTORY OF THE MINISTRY OF MUNITIONS.

VOLUME V

WAGES AND WELFARE

PART II

THE CONTROL OF WOMEN'S WAGES

VOLUME V

WAGES AND WELFARE

PART II

THE CONTROL OF WOMEN'S WAGES

CONTENTS.

CHAPTER I.
Problems and Powers of Control.

	PAGE
1.—Introductory	1
2.—The Initial Difficulties, 1915	2
3.—The Powers of the Ministry	4
4.—" Men's Work " and " Women's Work "	6

CHAPTER II.
Wages for "Men's Work," 1915–1916.

1.—The First Stage : Control by Recommendation	8
2.—The Central Munitions Labour Supply Committee	10
3.—The Issue of Circular L.2	11
4.—The Reception of L.2	13
5.—The Munitions of War Amendment Act : Statutory Control of Wages	14

CHAPTER III.
"Men's Work" in 1916.

1.—The Interpretation of L.2—

Work " customarily " done by Men	16
Allowances for Overtime and Night Work	17
Deductions for " Setting-up "	18
The Working Week	19
Alternatives in Substitution	20
(a) Women doing Boys' Work	20
(b) Girls on Boys' Work	22
(c) Girls on Men's Work	22
Probation and Split Jobs	23
2.—The Semi-skilled Worker and " Equal Pay "	30
3.—The Revision of L.2	33

CHAPTER IV.

"Men's Work," 1917-1918.

	PAGE
1.—Order 49 and its Reception	38
2.—" Skilled Men's Work "	38
3.—Intermediate Rates	44
4.—The Claim to Men's Advances	49
5.—Women on " Men's Work " in 1918. Summary	52

CHAPTER V.

Wages for "Women's Work."

1.—The Policy of Regulation	55
2.—The Preliminary Stages: 1915-1916	58
3.—The Special Arbitration Tribunal and " Women's Work "	63
4.—Order 447: Regulation by Statutory Order	66
5.—The Reception of Order 447	67

CHAPTER VI.

"Women's Work": The Extension of Regulation.

1.—Recommendations of the Special Tribunal	77
2.—The Revised Issue as Order 9 of January, 1917	79
3.—The Position after the Issue of Order 9: January, 1917–June, 1918	82
The Worker's Financial Position	82
The Further Extension of Regulation	83
The Consolidated Order: May, 1918	85
4.—Summary: 1915-1918	87

CHAPTER VII.

The Woodwork and Aircraft Wages Orders.

	PAGE
1.—Woodwork for Aircraft	89
2.—Other Woodwork	93
3.—Metal Work for Aircraft	94

CHAPTER VIII.

Rates and Earnings.

1.—Statutory Rates	95
2.—Estimates of Earnings	95
3.—Comparison with pre-War Earnings	105
4.—Wages and Prices	112
5.—Advance in Earnings in Non-Munition Trades	113

TABLES IN CHAPTER VIII.

I.—Rates of Women Munition Workers under Statutory Order (Dec., 1917) .. 96

II.—Rates of Girl Munition Workers under Statutory Order (Dec., 1917) .. 98

III.—Average Rates and Earnings of Women in :—
(a) National Projectile Factories .. 101
(b) National Shell Factories .. 101
(c) National Explosives Factories .. 102
(d) National Filling Factories .. 102

IV.—Average Weekly Earnings of Women in Controlled Establishments in Four Munition Areas between April and June, 1917 .. 106

V.—Average Earnings in certain Controlled Establishments, April-June, 1917 .. 108

VI.—Weekly Earnings of Women in the Light Metal Trades, 1914 and 1917 .. 110

VII.—Index Numbers of Retail Food Prices, 1914-1918 .. 112

VIII.—Women's Wages in certain Non-Munition Industries, January, 1918 .. 114

CHAPTER IX.
Some Results.

		PAGE
1.—A Definite Policy		115
2.—Methods of Payment		11*
3.—Changes in the position of Employers and Workers		117
1. Employers		117
2. Workers		118

CHAPTER X.
Questions of Principle.

1.—The Administrative Problem .. 121
2.—" Equal Pay for Equal Work " .. 125
3.—Alternative Policies .. 129
4.—The Differing Standards of Men's and Women's Wages 138

APPENDICES.

I.—Table of the Statutory Wages Orders .. 147

II.—Note on the Application of the Wages Orders .. 150

III.—Circulars and Orders relating to the Remuneration of Women and Girls on Munition Work .. 154
  1. L.2 .. 154
  2. No. 447 of 1916 .. 157
  3. No. 618 of 1916 .. 158
  4. No. 9 of 1917 .. 159
  5. No. 489 of 1917 .. 161
  6. No. 546 of 1918 .. 165

IV.—Two Illustrations of the Operation of Circular L.2 .. 173

V.—Agreements between the Workers' Union and Employers' Associations, 1915-1916 .. 177

VI.—Notes on the Work of the Special Arbitration Tribunal .. 181

INDEX.

Index .. 199

CHAPTER I.
PROBLEMS AND POWERS OF CONTROL.
I. Introductory.

The industrial position of women was an unsettled problem before the War. The mobilisation of women's labour for the production of munitions compelled the Government to become a party to its consideration. The problem focussed in the question of wages; the Ministry of Munitions, responsible directly or indirectly for the chief part of the increased industrial employment of women, found it necessary to control the wages of women munition workers and to develop a policy in accordance with which this control should be exercised.

Besides regulating the wages of large numbers of women in National Factories and Controlled Establishments, the Department influenced the earnings of many more for whom it was not directly responsible. Its orders served as precedents in other forms of employment, and (since the department dealt with "munitions" not with complete trades) the regulation of wages of one group of earners in an industry or factory inevitably affected those of the non-munition workers beside them. But wages problems could not be treated with uniformity in the country as a whole if only for the reason that no one authority was responsible for their handling. The powers which the Ministry of Munitions exercised for their determination among munition workers were given by special legislation, and were restricted in their application.[1]

The first Minister, in the month after the establishment of the department, acknowledged its responsibility for the wages of women engaged on munitions work, although the implications of this acknowledgment were not fully realised at the time. " . . . . We have agreed to pay exactly the same rate of wages for piece-work as to men . . . . " said Mr. Lloyd George to a deputation from a great gathering of women on 17 July, 1915. " For some time women will be unskilled and untrained, and they cannot turn out as much work as men can who have been at it for a long time. Therefore we cannot give the same time rate to them. Mrs. Pankhurst is perfectly right in insisting that whatever those wages are, it should be a fair rate of wages. . . . there should be a fixed minimum which would guarantee that we should not merely utilize the services of women in order to get cheap labour." Only 50,000 women, according to the official estimate, were engaged on munitions work as then defined. But as more women were transferred from other industries and called from other occupations to make munitions, and as the scope of " munitions work " steadily expanded, the permanent, and not only the incidental,

[1] For the range and industrial incidence of Wages Orders *see* Appendix II., p. 150.

importance of controlling their conditions of work became apparent. The introductory address of the fourth Minister of Munitions to an advisory committee of women trade unionists summoned in November 1917 to weekly meetings at the Ministry shows the Department's developed conception of its responsibilities:—

" I have come here to-day," said Mr. Churchill, " in order to meet the Committee at its first assembling and to say how strongly we here realise the importance of our work in regard to the employment of women. We are incomparably the greatest employers of women there has ever been in the world, we are the pioneers of women's employment in the industrial and even in the military field. Whatever may be the future position which women's labour will take after the war, it will be enormously influenced by the actual practice which has been followed when so much is in the making, and when so much control is vested in the organisation of the Ministry of Munitions. Therefore we are really at the head stream of history in regard to women's place in the industrial life of Britain, perhaps as far as this present century is concerned. The interests of women in industrial life must not be an incident of the Great War. Now is the time during the Great War for us to perceive, discover and proclaim the principles which should regulate, for perhaps the lifetime of a whole generation and perhaps for longer, the lines of advance on which women's industrial work should proceed."

II. Initial Difficulties, 1915.

The conditions were not favourable to the development of a wages policy, when the Ministry of Munitions came into being.

1. While endeavouring to secure good conditions for women munition makers, both for the sake of present and future needs, the Ministry was limited in action by the fact that the output of munitions was the primary end of its existence, and that regulation of labour must be directed to the increase of output. The establishment of a standard wage for women workers might be held to promote this end, but its enforcement had to be introduced with due consideration for employers and for existing working conditions.

2. Further, in dealing with the problems of women's wages, the Department had to cross an almost uncharted sea. Up-to-date information as to the conditions of women's work in the industries included in " munitions " was very inadequate—almost inevitably so owing to the absence of standardization in women's work. The only method of control of women's earnings already existing was that of the Trade Boards, and this was not wholly applicable to the needs of 1915-1916, partly on account of the time required by their procedure before wage changes became effective, principally because, as before said, the Ministry dealt not with trades or firms as a whole, but with " munitions." It was, for example, concerned with only a proportion of the employers and workers in the metal trades, according as their output was or was not destined for war purposes. Provisions such as those of the Trade Boards, which dealt with the whole of a trade equally, were therefore

clearly not appropriate to the circumstances. If the regulation of the wages of women producing munitions were necessary, new methods, which could be quickly made effective, were required.

3. Finally—and this was the most important factor in decision —many of the employers of women and most of the women engaged in munitions work were unorganised. Until two years after the passing of the first Munitions of War Act, the industry employing the second largest number of women munition workers had no employers' association which could produce a national policy for dealing with the workers, while the two trade unions which primarily concerned themselves with the wages of these women, had, in 1915 and even in 1916, enrolled only a very small proportion of the workers.[1] Women and girls came in the first year of the Ministry to make shells, explosives, etc., from the textile industries and the potteries in which "organisation" existed, and from other branches of the metal trades, in which they may have had opportunities of joining a Trade Union. But they came also from Scotch fishing villages, from Irish bogs, and the workrooms and villas of English provincial towns; they had little experience of the needs of the town factory worker employed at high pressure, and little idea of securing a standard wage corresponding with these needs; nor was there in 1915-1916 much opportunity either for employers as a whole or for workers to formulate such a standard.

It was largely for this reason that the skilled workman in the engineering trades tended to oppose the introduction of women into his trade. He had often a profound suspicion of the woman worker as a possible blackleg, accepting lower rates of pay than those laboriously acquired by trade union action.

The problem of women's wages was therefore very different at this stage from that of the wages of men munition makers. The latter had trade organisations of varying degrees of strength and comprehensiveness; the employers equally had organisations of their own. Although trade union influence did not cover the whole field of men's labour, even in the comparatively "well-organised" munition trades, such as shipbuilding and engineering, yet the principle of collective bargaining and of standard rates of payment was firmly established. For the first two years, therefore, of the Ministry's existence the principles adopted by the Department were that employers and men should settle wages between themselves; that where this was impossible either the established systems of arbitration and conciliation or the specially created Committee on Production should take action; and that the Ministry should only intervene in the settlement of wages to sanction changes, or in rare cases to disallow agreed changes, to insist, like other Departments of State, on the observance of the Fair Wages Clause by contractors, and to lay down standards of payment for

---

[1] The National Federation of Women Workers had 12,152 members at the end of 1913, the Workers' Union a female membership of 4,380; at the end of 1916 the numbers were 27,761 and 20,000. In 1913 the total female trade union membership was 356,963. Of these, 257,281 were in the textile, and only 99,682 in the non-textile, trades.

substitutes replacing skilled workmen under dilution. Most of these functions, however, presupposed organisation among workers, if not among employers, and recognised standards of payment ; these, as has been said, hardly existed in the case of women's work.

Despite the difficulties involved, some special form of regulation of women's wages was almost inevitable from the first establishment of the Ministry, both for the sake of the workers' efficiency and in the interests of industrial peace. It was required as a safeguard equally for the women, who, in theory if not always in practice, were until October, 1917, prevented by the leaving certificate regulations from changing their firm to better themselves ; for employers, anxious to know what they should pay to women taking the place of men, and what wages should be offered to women and girls imported from a distance for munitions work ; and for the men, whose fears of the effects of women's entry to their trades had to be dispelled. The established methods of arbitration and the checking of individual cases of underpayment by the enforcement of the Fair Wages Clause, were too slow in operation to solve the whole problem of women munition workers' wages during the war, even if standard rates for women had previously been in existence.

III. Powers of the Ministry.

Accordingly, the Ministry of Munitions was given special powers for controlling women's wages, under the Munitions of War Acts.

(1) Schedule II. (5) of the original Act of July, 1915, laid down in general terms the principle that women or men introduced to take men's work in the course of labour dilution, must not take lower rates than those previously earned by the men. " The relaxation of existing demarcation restrictions or admission of semi-skilled or female labour shall not affect adversely the rates customarily paid for the job."

Two other clauses affected the wages of women as well as of men munition workers. (1) Section 4 (2) provided that proposed changes of wages in controlled establishments must be sanctioned by the Minister before being put into effect. Section 7 forbade the employment of a person within six weeks of his or her leaving munitions work in certain establishments, without a certificate from the previous employer that the person concerned left work with the employer's consent. The first of these sections supplied a check on excessive increases in wages and on arbitrary changes in piece rates ; the second indirectly affected wages, especially of low paid workers, by making a change of employment difficult.

(2) The Amendment Act of January, 1916, provided as follows:—
    (a) *Section* 6 (1). " Where female workers are employed on or in connection with munitions work in any establishment of a class to which the provisions of Section 7 of the principal Act as amended by this Act are for the time being applied by an order made thereunder, the Minister of Munitions shall have power by order to give directions as to the rate of wages....
....of the female workers so employed."

(b) *Section* 8 (1). " The Minister of Munitions may constitute Special Arbitration Tribunals to deal with differences reported under Part I. of the principal Act which relate to matters on which the Minister has given directions under the last two preceding sections, and the Board of Trade may refer any such difference for settlement to such Tribunal in lieu of referring it for settlement in accordance with the first Schedule to the principal Act."

(3) The Munitions of War Act of August, 1917, provided (Section 4) that the regulation of wages, under Section 6 of the previous Act, should be extended to " female workers employed on or in connection with munitions work in establishments of all classes," when the leaving certificate regulations of the original " Section seven " should have been repealed.

The Statutory Orders made in accordance with Section 6 of the Act of January, 1916, were applied to individual firms by schedule. They did not cover all the firms in any one trade, nor did they necessarily apply to all munition firms. By the beginning of 1918, however, almost all controlled establishments employing women, and a large number of other munition firms and " certified undertakings " (gasworks, tramway companies, etc.) had received wages Orders. Their administrative enforcement was provided for departmentally by the Wages Section of the Ministry, and locally by its Labour and Investigation Officers. Uniform wage rates were prescribed by these Orders, which did not as a whole attempt to distinguish between the trade customs and local standards of living of the firms and workers to which they were applied.

The Special Arbitration Tribunal, established in accordance with Section 8 of the Amendment Act of 1916, provided a second and most important method of settling rates of wages. " Differences " between women munition workers and their employers, were, like those of men, reported under Part I. of the Munitions of War Act of July, 1915, to the Board of Trade or Ministry of Labour, and were thence referred for compulsory arbitration. The tribunal was independent in its awards, though subject to the Minister's interpretation of the Munitions Act, and its awards in individual cases constantly served as a basis for departmental administration. In this way, its position resembled that acquired by the Committee on Production on a very much larger scale in 1917, except that in addition to settling disputes and laying down precedents for payments in similar cases, it was responsible to the Department for advice upon the framing of Statutory Orders and any general problems of women's wages that might be referred to it by the Minister.

The awards of the Special Tribunal, and the provisions of the Statutory Orders, were enforceable by a Munitions Tribunal under a penalty of not more than £5 per head of the workpeople concerned for each day that an employer disregarded such awards or Orders, and of not more than £5 per day in the case of any employee disregarding an award.[1]

---

[1] To the end of 1918 one hundred and thirty-two complaints were heard, and fines were inflicted, in respect of seventy-five offences, amounting to £257 10s. 0d.

The history of the first two years of the regulation of women's wages is largely the history of the application of Statutory Orders to the heterogeneous mass of trades contributing to the supply of "munitions."

From one point of view the record is a confusing one, an example of what are called "bureaucratic methods." The quantity of Orders (increased in appearance by the practice of the Stationery Office of giving fresh numbers to re-issues of the same order) was complained of by employers and by workers alike. "With all these orders issued with regard to wages it wants really a lawyer, and a good one, to sit down and find out what they mean. Unless you study the things right out they are difficult to understand and we cannot understand them. An average Trade Union official has not time to devote to studying them. I will not say that the Orders are conflicting, but they are worrying," said the representative of a men's unskilled union which had lately taken up the cause of women workers, in a deputation to the Ministry in June, 1917.[1]

When, however, it is considered that by the middle of 1918 the wages Orders had been applied to firms in some eighty[2] different trades and occupations—each with its own traditions and requirements—while the pressing need for output and the employer's claims had constantly to be balanced with the demands of labour, the impossibility of complete simplicity is obvious. The greater part, indeed, of the difficulty of applying the Orders came in practice from the attempt to treat very varied trades with even a moderate amount of uniformity. The terms of the Orders were clear and simple when compared with those of many of the agreements reached independently by negotiation between employers and trade unions.

IV. "Men's Work" and "Women's Work."

Administratively the Orders fell into two main groups—those for "men's" and for "women's" work—and as such their history will be considered. The distinction is, to some extent, arbitrary. To the employer and the individual worker there was often no inherent difference between the two types of work, though in many cases the distinction was obvious, either from the degree of skill needed, and secured by the man's apprenticeship, or from the laborious character of the work done. Frequently, however, such distinction was only an instance of the conservatism of industrial life, the comprehensible exclusiveness of the male trade unionist, and the normal industrial woman's lack of initiative which had led her, in the century before the War, steadily to take the less skilled and worse paid work, as it appeared in the process of the division of labour.

When the first statutory circular was issued for women on men's work in February 1916, the officials of the Ministry and of the Board of Trade had frequently to disabuse workers of the impression that a uniform minimum wage had been prescribed for all women munition workers. In some ways it would have been much simpler if this had

---

[1] L.R. 142/4.   [2] See Appendix II.

been done, for, apart from the trouble of maintaining two, or more, sets of wages for " men's " and " women's " work, there was a border area in which it cost much labour to decide what was, or was not, substitution work. " The introduction of female labour would have been enormously simplified and extended had it been possible to protect the female workers first by fixing a minimum rate ; secondly, by providing due safeguards as to hours of working ; thirdly, by making no attempt to distinguish between what was women's work before the War and the contrary—although, doubtless, at this stage it is too late to reopen the question," wrote Mr. A. Herbert, head of the machine tool department of the Ministry, and himself a prominent engineering employer, when asked to comment on a proposed wage schedule in December 1915.

The two groups of occupation were, however, in so far as the Ministry was concerned, separated not only by custom and tradition and by the order in which it was called upon to deal with them, but by the specific obligations by which the Government was bound in the case of men's work under the Treasury Agreement of March, 1915. Wages for " men's work " had to be dealt with as part of the problem of labour dilution, in consultation with the men's trade unions concerned, and their settlement stood out against a background of generations of effort to establish the " district rates," which represented the standard of living of a skilled (or unskilled) workman and his family. Wages for " women's work " were controlled, in part at least, as an after effect—necessary but with less theoretical importance—of the substitution policy.

In regulating the wages of women when on men's work, the Ministry had, in safeguarding the men's established rates of pay, to interpret the principle of " equal pay for equal work." In dealing with those of women on " women's work," it had to attempt—though this was less categorically stated—to secure for the workers a " living wage." Both these phrases, apparently self-explanatory, are notoriously difficult to interpret in fact.

CHAPTER II.

WAGES FOR "MEN'S WORK," 1915–1916.

I. The First Stage: Control by Recommendation.

(a) THE NEED FOR A STANDARD OF PAYMENT.

In July, 1915, when Mr. Lloyd George promised that there should be no sweated wages for those who undertook munitions work, neither the normal employer nor the unorganised woman worker had any formulated standard as to what wages the women who took men's work should receive. Women in the metal and chemical trades before the War had been employed on unskilled work of a kind not commonly undertaken by men and paid for at low and varying rates; 12s. 8d. and 11s. 10d. were given in an official report[1] as the average weekly earnings in the two groups in September, 1906. The Trade Boards' minimum rates, though increased to 3d. and 3½d. an hour—some 14s. to 16s. a week—gave barely a living wage by July, 1915, when food prices had risen by a third above the level of the previous year; yet these were the only definite schedules for women's wages which could be quoted in any but a few trade groups. The unemployment and long periods of work on short time during the previous autumn and winter had shaken any standards of payment that had been growing up in those women's trades, such as dressmaking, that had suffered most from the War; while at the same time numbers of soldiers' wives and dependants with State separation allowances wished to go out to work, from the double motive of "helping to win the War" and of supplementing their allowances. There was great danger that partly from patriotism, partly from ignorance and lack of *esprit de corps*, the very varied types of new workers needed in the munition trades would accept too low wages and pull down the standard of living for themselves and for the men whose work they took.

The agreement between the Government and the Trade Unions, made in March, 1915 and embodied in the 2nd Schedule of the Munitions of War Act, had indeed laid down the principle that the admission of semi-skilled or female labour as a result of the relaxation of existing demarcation restrictions should not "affect adversely the rates customarily paid for the job." This was, however, rather a general statement of the fundamental principle of labour dilution from the craftsman's point of view than a definite direction as to what should be done, especially in the case of the woman taking

---

[1] Cd. 5814 of 1911, Cd. 6656 of 1913—"Earnings and Hours" Enquiry by the Board of Trade.

men's unskilled or semi-skilled work. Further, it was intended to refer directly only to piece rates, which varied from firm to firm, while the standard district time rates established in the engineering trades were unprotected. During the summer and autumn of 1915 it became increasingly clear that definite regulation of the wages of women on "men's work" was necessary if the opposition of organised labour to dilution was to be overcome, and the services of skilled workmen were to be made fully available for the greatly extended production of munitions required by the Country.

Only after full deliberation and after some months' delay did the Ministry decide on a policy of detailed regulation of women's wages. This caution was probably in part due to unwillingness to impede the all-important process of labour dilution by any restrictions the necessity of which was not proved, and in part to reluctance to embark on a new departure involving much administrative machinery. It was under strong Trade Union pressure that the compulsory regulation of wages for women on "men's" munition work was decided on at the end of 1915 and introduced in February, 1916, after the passing of the Munitions of War Amendment Act. During the previous six months, workers and employers as a whole, as well as the Department, were feeling their way to a settled wages policy.[1]

(b) Trade Union Representations, September, 1915.

Representations made to the Ministry soon after its establishment showed the prevailing uncertainty as to the payment of women workers. Thus, on 8 September, 1915, a deputation from the Workers' Union appeared before Dr. Addison, and asked that a minimum district time rate should be fixed for women in the engineering trades. The Union had agreed with the Midland Employers' Federation that women employed on the same work as men should have the same piece rates, but the non-federated employers had not come into line. Further, there was great disparity in the local rates paid to women munition workers ; thus, a great Sheffield firm paid a woman learner 8s. a week for shell work, while a Preston firm paid 16s. ; a large employer at Halifax paid 15s. a week to shellmakers for the morning eight-hour shift, 17s. for the afternoon shift, and 19s. for the night shift, while another Halifax firm paid 25s. for a 51 hours' week. The average earnings for women at one of the largest munition works in Birmingham reached 7d. an hour, while the rates paid by another large Birmingham firm worked out at $2\frac{3}{4}$d. an hour for the same operations. Dr. Addison, in replying to the deputation, said that the Ministry of Munitions had no power to fix a minimum rate of wages, but where any firm paid less for particular work than the district rate, the Department would be glad to be informed (since the Fair Wages Clause might be brought into operation). He asked for details of the agreement arrived at with the Midland Employers' Federation, and referred to the desirability of arriving at agreements

---

[1] Cf. Vol. IV., Part I., Ch. IV.

in the various districts for fixing a probationary rate of women's wages.

It was partly on account of this reliance on local Trade Union action and on the operation of the Fair Wages Clause—most valuable in some women's industries, but of little use in districts where new work or new processes were being introduced—that the compulsory regulation of wages was delayed during the autumn of 1915.

At the Trades Union Congress at Bristol in the same month, Miss Macarthur on behalf of the National Federation of Women Workers, moved the following comprehensive motion, which was carried unanimously, with regard to women enrolling for "war work" on the special register opened for them by the Labour Exchanges in the previous March.

> "In order to prevent the depression of the standard of living of the workers, adequate safeguards must be laid down for any necessary transference or substitution of labour.
>
> "The Congress therefore urges :—
>
> (a) That all women who register for war service should, as a condition of employment, join the appropriate Trade Union, and that Trade Unions which exclude women should admit them.
>
> (b) That equal pay for equal work shall be maintained.
>
> (c) That in no case should any woman be drafted from the War Register to employment at less than an adequate living wage, and that the stereotyping of sweated conditions must, at all costs, be avoided.
>
> (d) Adequate training with maintenance must be provided when necessary."

Miss Sloan (also of the National Federation of Women Workers), in seconding this motion, said that many women doing "war work" were getting very low wages, and that there were numerous cases where women were working seventy hours a week for 3½d. an hour.

II. The Central Munitions Labour Supply Committee.

Immediately after this Congress, at a Conference of Trade Union Executives at Central Hall, Westminster, the appointment was announced of the Central Munitions Labour Supply Committee. This Committee, as is explained elsewhere,[1] was called into being primarily to promote the dilution of skilled labour, but found itself compelled at once to deal with wages. Such action was contrary to the expectations of those responsible for its appointment. It was, however, wholly essential, if the Government's policy of dilution was to succeed, or even to receive the serious attention of the skilled workman, since the latter's reluctance to accept labour dilution was based fundamentally on wages, and on the fear that it would in the long run mean the degradation of the standard of living of his class.

---

[1] Vol. IV., Part I., Ch. III.

Although the wages policy of the Committee was not in itself remarkable, yet its few weeks' work was of great importance throughout the Ministry's subsequent control of wages. At its first meeting on 22 September, 1915, a wages sub-committee was appointed " to consider and report on the fixing of wages in connection with the introduction of semi-skilled or unskilled labour where only skilled workmen had previously been employed." This sub-committee, consisting of Mr. Allan Smith, Secretary to the Engineering Employers' Federation, Miss Macarthur of the National Federation of Women Workers, Mr Kaylor of the Amalgamated Society of Engineers, and Mr. Glynn West, representing the interests of the Supply Departments of the Ministry, drafted, on 24 and 27 September, recommendations for the payment of women and girls on men's work. These were accepted with one addition by the main committee, and were presented to Mr. Lloyd George, who wrote in reply on 14 October, " You will, of course, be aware that the Minister has no power to promulgate any binding regulations on these matters except as regards . . . the National Factories. He proposes to circulate these recommendations forthwith to the organisations representing the parties concerned for their information and . . . . to elicit criticism and suggestions. Pending the result of this step, the recommendations of the Committee will be provisionally accepted as far as regards establishments for which the Minister is directly responsible." The proposals, with some further modifications, were considered on 27 October, at a conference of the Central Munitions Labour Supply Committee with representatives of Amalgamated Society of Engineers, and were accepted (together with those issued as "Circular L.3," defining the wages of unskilled men under dilution schemes), as one of the conditions under which the Amalgamated Society of Engineers would agree to dilution. On 28 October, the agreed proposals were sent out as " Circular L.2 " to all the new National Factories and to controlled establishments. The circular was binding on the former, but was, as the Minister had explained, only issued by way of " recommendation " to the latter.

III. Issue of Circular L.2.

Circular L.2 acquired a unique position in the history of the dilution of labour. Officially, its original office heading was transformed four months later into that of "Statutory Order 181," of 1916, and it reappeared at intervals under the different numeration attached to successive issues of such Orders. To those sections, however, of the industrial world whom it immediately concerned, it was known familiarly as " L.2," and as such it will be referred to in the story of its difficult administration.

Circular L.2, like the twin circular L.3, was set up to provide a ring fence, or rather (as appeared later) a system of barbed wire entanglements, round the skilled workman's standard rates. Its main provisions were as follows :—

(1) Women introduced into munitions work " of a class which, prior to the War, was not recognised as women's work," should receive

the same piece rates and premium bonus allowances as were customarily received by men for the same job, on the principle that " on systems of payment by results equal payment shall be made to women as to the men for an equal amount of work done." (Clause 8). When, therefore, the new women workers were employed on any of the various forms of payment by results, the Circular, in so far as it was observed in the spirit as well as the letter, prevented the underselling of male by female labour.

(2) Piece rates and premium bonus systems were regarded as the concern primarily of the individual factory, to the needs of which they were adjusted. Time wages on the other hand were standardised throughout districts in the engineering trades. They embodied the results of years of collective bargaining, and represented a standard of living which the skilled workman expected to find unimpaired after the war, when the transitory woman worker, and the pressing demand for repetition work, with its opportunities for systems of payment by results, should alike have departed.' These time rates were therefore specially safeguarded by the stipulation that women employed on work customarily done by fully-skilled tradesmen should be paid the time rates of the tradesmen whose work they undertook. (Clause I.) It was not at the time expected that such direct substitution of women for skilled workmen would be common, if indeed it took place at all. For the very much larger class of women who were coming into engineering shops for shell production and other forms of work hitherto done by semi-skilled or unskilled men,[1] a conventional time rate of £1 a week, " reckoned on the usual working hours of the district for men in engineering establishments," was laid down, with overtime, night shift, Sunday and holiday allowances payable to men. The £1 time rate was below that of the unskilled labourer in practically all engineering districts. But it was not considered that one woman was the equivalent of one man. Further, the possible danger of lowering the rates payable for unskilled and semi-skilled male labour, was not considered at the time. This time rate was guaranteed to piece workers and those employed on premium bonus systems.

The circular thus established, or attempted to establish, a uniform standard time rate disregarding local differences in cost of living or in factory organisation, for women on " men's " munition work throughout the country—a method of payment which was, of course, wholly new to the engineering trades or, indeed, to any twentieth century industry except those covered by the Trade Boards. The Central Munitions Labour Supply Committee had inserted in its early drafts words fixing the £1 weekly wage for unskilled workers as a minimum, not a standard, rate ; and great stress was laid on this intention by members of the National Federation of Women Workers in discussion of the revision of L.2 just a year later. These words were, however, omitted from the circular on the recommendation of Dr. Addison, who urged that no ambiguous directions should be sent

---

[1] In fact, the majority of women introduced on men's work, at this time, did not displace or replace men, but started on new machines in new shops.

out. "What employers are asking," he wrote, "is how much they are expected to pay, and we must be able to give a definite answer to the question." Recommendations drawn up by the Committee for the payment of girls under eighteen, were also omitted by Dr. Addison's desire, since they presented many points needing further consideration, and the Committee had urged the speedy issue of the circular.[1] " L.2 " was a by-product of the dilution campaign, and was meant to be a simple weapon which could be placed quickly at the disposal of the promoters of dilution.

IV. Reception of L.2.

The " recommendations " of L.2 were by no means universally adopted by the establishments to which they were sent during the autumn and winter of 1915-16. Controlled firms were working at high pressure under very difficult conditions at the period, and it was easy to neglect or postpone the consideration of one among many official circulars, although the representatives of the women's trade union chiefly concerned agitated with much energy for the observance of L.2 by a number of leading firms. The scale of payments laid down in the circular met, even at this stage, with considerable opposition from employers, who in some cases said that it would not be worth their while to substitute women's labour for men's, under such terms. Various time rates, sometimes above the £1 standard, but more frequently 3s. to 5s. below, were being offered to and readily accepted by women on men's work at the time. Thus, at a National Shell Factory in which women were introduced with much success just before the issue of L.2, an initial wage of 17s. for a 54 hour week was given, and the management recorded that in the first fortnight after the women started work, six hundred applications had been received from other women for the fifty vacancies available.[2] On 8 December, 1915, the Central Munitions Labour Supply Committee received a deputation from the Coventry Engineering Employers' Association, whose members criticised the circular partly on the grounds of the disturbance of piece rates if women (who would presumably work more slowly than men) were yet to earn by piece work as much in excess of the skilled man's time rate, as the latter normally earned ; and partly on account of the effect of the high rates prescribed for " men's work " on existing standards of payment for women. The first of these criticisms was based on a misunderstanding of the circular. To the second the Committee replied that the recommendations were framed as a temporary measure with a view to facilitating the introduction of female labour during the war period for munitions. Where women were engaged upon work which was customarily recognised as women's work entirely different circumstances obtained, and L.2 would in itself provide no justification for an alteration of wages in the latter case. The deputation was said to be satisfied with this (perhaps unduly optimistic) statement.[3]

Apart from the low existing standard of payment to the woman worker, and her readiness to begin shell work at less than £1 a week,

---

[1] M.W/132834.   [2] C E. 717/4.   [3] C.M.L.S.C. Minutes.

there were other difficulties at this time in the observance of the L.2 rates. The women concerned were normally only learning their work, and employers were feeling their way, often amidst considerable opposition from their skilled workmen, both as to the processes on which diluted labour should be employed, and the level at which piece rates, perhaps for new work, should be fixed. This temporary uncertainty as to piece rates led to complaints which sometimes were, and sometimes were not, justified, that the Ministry's circular was being disregarded through the employment of women (especially on shell work) at rates lower than those paid to men. Thus on 17 November, the standing sub-committee of the Central Munitions Labour Supply Committee "considered the situation" at Messrs. Beardmore's Paisley Works, where a strike of the women workers was threatened owing to the refusal of the firm to adopt Circular L.2,[1] for which the National Federation of Women Workers was pressing; but the Ministry had no power to enforce its recommendations beyond despatching an official telegram calling the firm's attention to the "desirability of conforming with the terms of the circular."[2]

V. The Munitions of War Amendment Act, Statutory Control of Wages.

With these and other reasons for the non-observance of L.2, it became increasingly clear that the system of settling wages by recommendation was unsettling and unsatisfactory both to employers and employed. A demand for compulsory regulation was made at a conference with trade unions convened by the National Advisory Committee on 30 November, and the Amending Bill presented on 9 December contained a clause giving the necessary powers. Before the Bill became law there was a further very important conference on 31 December, 1915, between the Minister and representatives of the Amalgamated Society of Engineers, when cases were quoted of refusal by employers to apply the circular because it was not obligatory. The Society, through its executive council, promised its "active co-operation" with the Ministry's dilution policy "provided that the Government pledged itself to incorporate in the Bill the power to enforce the rates of pay and conditions of labour as set out in

---

[1] C.E. 187/5.

[2] C.E. 187/5, etc. One of the reasons given by the firm, and by another Clyde district firm, Messrs. Mavor & Coulson (who were equally met by difficulties as to their women workers' wages), for not complying with Clause 7 of L.2 as to piece work payments, was the fluidity of piece rates at the time. Both firms subsequently explained to the Special Arbitration Tribunal that their piece prices for shell work had been fixed too high in the pressure of the previous summer. Women on piece work at the second of the two firms could, it was stated, earn £2 5s. to £3 per week, whereas if paid at the men's temporary piece rates they would have to be paid £11 6s. per week. The points at issue in these two cases were difficult to disentangle. It was not ultimately claimed that the women must receive the men's piece rates, which had been in operation for too short a time to be established. The N.F.W.W. however claimed that the piece rates should be finally fixed so that the women shell makers should be able to earn as much above time rates as men would have received, if employed similarly on piece work.

documents L.2 and L.3 in controlled establishments." Little opposition was raised to this during the House of Commons debates on the Bill, and it was duly provided in section six of the Munitions of War Amendment Act of 27 January, 1916, that—

"Where female workers are employed on or in connection with munitions work in any establishment of a class to which the provisions of section seven of the principal Act......are for the time applied......the Minister of Munitions shall have power by Order to give direction as to the rate of wages of the female workers so employed."

Circular L.2 was accordingly after some slight delay reissued on 28 February, 1916, as a statutory Order. Its previous recommendations were, in accordance with the section just quoted, made mandatory on all firms within the ambit of the leaving certificate rules[1] to which it was applied by Order. Considerable impatience had been expressed locally at its non-appearance, since women had by this time been employed in certain districts for at least a year on "men's" munition work, without the protection of any authoritative scale of payment. This perhaps accounted for its final issue in the form in which it had been sent out in October, 1915, without further revision.[2]

---

[1] See Appendix I. The Order was not applied to explosives and chemical works (cf., L.R. 142/34).

[2] Mr. J. C. Smith (head of the wages section) wrote to the General Secretary of the Ministry of Munitions, on 21 February, 1916: "I have reason to believe that unless the main provision of L.2, the guaranteed time rate of £1 per week, is made statutory there will be an extensive strike in Manchester before the end of next week. I venture to ask whether it would not be possible to make this provision statutory forthwith, leaving the details to be elaborated by whatever machinery is set up under Section (6) of the Amendment Act. There are some details in L.2 with which I do not agree; there are others which I do not understand. But whatever one may think of the principle of a flat national rate, the £1 a week has caught the imagination of women workers and it is vain to argue the point." (M.W. 92329.)

It is worth while to recall the fact that, according to the Board of Trade, the £1 flat national rate, which women workers so greatly desired, was in December, 1915, worth only 13s. 8d. in food purchasing power, as compared with its value in July, 1914.

CHAPTER III.

"MEN'S WORK" IN 1916.

I. The Interpretation of L.2.

Few of the women who cheered Mr. Lloyd George on the Embankment on 17 July, 1915, can have realised the difficulties that would arise in applying the principle of " Equal pay for equal work," even within the limited field in which the attempt was first made. It may be doubted whether even the committee responsible for the drafting of L.2 foresaw what omissions and obscurities would be revealed, what conflicting interpretations would be offered, when the circular was applied to an industry so complex and opinionative as Engineering. The difficulties were partly genuine and inevitable, partly factious ; they sprang chiefly from the suspicion of labour dilution and all its concomitants felt by the skilled trade unionist ; and the suspicion was not at all allayed by the fact that the body that drafted the original recommendations for the payment of women substitutes on munitions work had as many representatives on it of Labour as of Capital.

A clause at the foot of Circular L.2 referred all questions of its interpretation to the Minister of Munitions, and much labour was required during the first year of its history to interpret the original drafting of the circular on the points that follow. The questions raised illustrate so fully both the attitude of the exclusive organisations of skilled workmen to the whole process of labour dilution during the War, and also the permanent industrial difficulties produced by the introduction to skilled work of unskilled or partly skilled workers, that it is worth while to follow them in some detail.

The difficulties occurred chiefly with regard to the apparently simple provisions of Clause 1.

" Women of eighteen years of age and over employed on time on work customarily done by men, shall be rated at £1 per week, reckoned on the usual working hours of the district in question for men in Engineering Establishments.

" This, however, shall not apply in the case of women employed on work customarily done by fully skilled tradesmen, in which case the women shall be paid the time rates of the tradesmen whose work they undertake. Overtime and night-shift and Sunday and holiday allowances payable to men shall also be made to women."

Work " Customarily " Done by Men.

In connection with the apparently innocuous word " customarily " it was possible to open up the whole question of the pre-war division of labour between men and women in the munition trades. Did " customarily " refer to the custom of the shop, the district, or the country as a whole? The answer was not easy. Thus, fuses had before the war been made by men at Woolwich but by women in the Midlands and elsewhere. In this case the Department and the Special Arbitration Tribunal held that fuse-making was not men's work, since its classification depended on the pre-war custom of the country at large.[1] This principle was applied in a number of similar cases, though it was necessary to modify it a year later in connection with women doing fully skilled work.[2] Thus, although at Sheffield, shell had, it was claimed, before the war been made by fully skilled men, it was held by the department, to the considerable discontent of some of the workers, that this practice was contrary to that of the country as a whole;[3] that the majority of shell-making processes were semi-skilled or unskilled work and entitled the woman employed on them to the £1 time rate of L.2, not to the full district rate for engineering tradesmen.

ALLOWANCES FOR OVERTIME AND NIGHT WORK.

Provision was made for overtime and night work in Clause 1, just quoted, and Clause 12, which laid down that " overtime... allowances shall be paid to women employed on piece work.... on the same conditions as now prevail in the case of men in the district in question for overtime work." This, however, left ambiguous the position of the woman doing a man's unskilled or semi-skilled work and paid at his piece rates, but not at his time rates, which would normally be considerably above hers. Should her overtime payments be calculated on the basis of the £1 a week time rate to which she was entitled? Or should they have some reference to the man's nominal time rates? Overtime was sufficiently extensive and prevalent in the first half of 1916 for the problem to have practical importance.

The question came before the Central Munitions Labour Supply Committee in January, 1916, with reference to a dispute between Messrs. Vickers, Erith, and the National Federation of Women Workers. The firm argued that the extra pay of women piece workers for night work and overtime should be calculated in accordance with their guaranteed £1 time rate. The National Federation of Women Workers, as represented by Miss Macarthur, said that this would not be giving equal pay for equal work; the Central Munitions Labour Supply Committee, however, upheld the firm.

The same question was brought forward on 24 February, 1916, in a communication from Mr. la Brooy, of Woolwich Arsenal.[4] Women workers making up cartridges in the Danger Building were, he explained, in calculating overtime[5] rated at £1 a week, even though they were

---

[1] M.W. 92329/3 and H.W. 64182.   [2] See page 42, Chapter IV.

[3] Cf., Conference, 25 October, 1916, between district representatives of the A.S.E. and the Special Arbitration Tribunal.

[4] M.W. 92329.

[5] The weekly average of overtime for all the women employed at Woolwich Arsenal was, a few weeks after this communication, 13½ hours. The question was therefore of considerable interest to those concerned. The employment of women at the Arsenal was being rapidly rearranged in the early months of 1916, and their payment and method of work under the special conditions prevailing there was the subject of much negotiation and discussion at the time.

actually on piece work, while men doing the same work and producing the same output had their overtime calculated on their time rating of 33s. The women's total weekly earnings were therefore 12s. 3d. less on night shift, and 5s. 3d. less on day shift than those of the men. This, they said, was in direct contravention of promises made in the House of Commons to the delegates of the various organisations who waited on Mr. Asquith. On this point Mr. Beveridge, Sir H. Llewellyn Smith and Dr. Addison successively argued that the woman's overtime rate must be calculated on her statutory £1 a week time wage. If the men employed by a firm were paid at "time and a quarter," "time and a half" or "double time" for such work, the women were also entitled to extra payments, but these were to be calculated on their guaranteed time rate only. This principle was incorporated in a series of "Rulings on L.2" sanctioned for departmental use by Dr. Addison on 7 March, 1916, and it reappeared in later statutory orders. The "unfairness" of this system of calculating overtime payments was periodically urged by women workers; its justification clearly depends on the hypothesis that the women's output would normally be less than the man's under the same conditions, so that she would obviously obtain special advantages, if paid for overtime at his time rates.

Deductions for "Setting-up."

The normal woman "dilutee" was unlikely, at least when she first began work, to be able to look after her own machine completely. "These recommendations are on the basis of the setting up of the machines being otherwise provided for," was the heading of the L.2 Circular. Did this stipulation mean that in the case of a woman who did a man's job except for the need of help in setting up her machine no deduction must be made from the prescribed wages? Clearly the standard rate of £1 a week was, under the wording of L.2, to have no deduction on these grounds. But was a deduction permissible in the case of a woman employed (like the majority of women shell-makers) on piece work in some form and paid at the man's piece rates or claiming the district rate for "skilled" work? Mr. Lloyd George in conference with the Amalgamated Society of Engineers on 24 February, 1916, argued that such deductions might fairly be made if the total cost of the job, as done by the woman with the man's help, remained what it was before the woman appeared in the factory.

On the one side it was sometimes urged by Trade Unionists that the employer who was introducing unskilled labour to fields hitherto barred should bear the cost of making this labour efficient in production. On the other side employers pointed out that a 10% deduction often by no means covered the cost of extra supervision and assistance and the replacing of spoilt material that was involved in the employment of unskilled male and female labour on skilled work.

The special Tribunal made a formal award on 17 January, 1917, for deduction up to 10% from the earnings of a woman needing special assistance for skilled work, in a test case put up by the A.S.E. with Messrs. Armstrong, Elswick (when the firm urged that the extra cost of supervision was quite 25% of the woman's earnings); and the decision was embodied in the same month in Clause 1.b (IV) of Order 49—a later version of L.2.

"In any case where it is established to the satisfaction of the Minister that additional cost is being incurred by extra setting up or skilled supervision due to the employment of women in place of fully-skilled tradesmen, the rates payable to women under these directions may, with the sanction of the Minister, be subject, for so long as such additional cost is incurred, to deductions not exceeding 10%, to meet such additional cost : provided that no women shall in any case be paid at lower rates than those prescribed by paragraph 1 (*a*) (*i*) of these directions "—the £1 rate for a 48-hour week.

THE WORKING WEEK.

What was to be the hourly rate, *i.e.*, what wages were to be paid where the three-shift system, or any other departure from the normal week of the district, was established for women ? The flat time rate of £1 a week was based on the usual working hours of the district in question for men in engineering establishments. These hours were commonly 53 or 54 a week. Should a woman working 48 hours a week be rated at proportionately less ? The question was frequently raised in the course of the year both before and after L.2 became obligatory ; it was addressed to the Department the day after the Order was issued.

Thus on 3 January, 1916, the Secretary of the Workers' Union wrote to the Ministry with reference to three employers at Halifax.[1] The Union had been trying unsuccessfully to arrange for the following wages for women employed on eight-hour shifts :—Morning shift, 20s. ; afternoon, 22s. ; night, 25s. Could the Department intervene ? The Ministry replied, quoting L.2 : the women were evidently entitled only to 48/53 of £1, since the normal working week in the district for the trade was 53 hours. The Workers' Union protested that such a decision would be most unfair ; engineering wages were never reduced because of reduction of hours ; the £1 in L.2 was clearly meant for an invariable minimum. A month later the same society wrote again to the Ministry of Munitions, to ask why no action had been taken in the matter, but the Ministry replied that they must stand by the terms of L.2 as indicated in their previous letter.[2]

The same complaint was brought forward at Manchester in March, 1916,[3] and frequently in the course of the year. It was specially unfortunate that the Order should appear to penalise the employees of the firms which had learnt the advantage of short hours of labour before the war, and of those, which, sometimes in response to pressure from the Ministry, were experimenting on a three-shift system. The Ministry, however, had no choice but to maintain its ruling that payment in such cases must be made at the rate of a proportionate fraction of £1, until the amendment of L.2 and its issue as Order 888 on 21 December, 1916. The amended Order directed

---
[1] M.W. 92329.   [2] M.W. 72357.   [3] See Appendix IV.

that the £1 rate should be paid where the working week was 48 hours; where the working week was less than 48 hours, the £1 rate was to be paid for the working week and for additional hours, if any, worked up to 48; where the working week exceeded 48 hours, 6d. an hour extra was to be paid up to 54 hours. Thus the amendment met the grievance of the women who were receiving less than the sum which they regarded as their legal minimum wage; in doing this, however, it abolished the flat rate of £1 a week, that sum becoming a minimum, and introduced the principle of hourly rate.[1]

ALTERNATIVES IN SUBSTITUTION.

(a) Women doing Boys' Work.

L.2 did not prescribe rates of pay for women doing work previously done by boys. This, however, was a very common form of substitution especially in the early stages of dilution, partly because the apprentice of two or three years' standing naturally knew more about his trade than the woman just introduced to it, and he could therefore frequently be transferred to a man's work leaving his own job to a substitute, partly because, by upgrading the seventeen and eighteen-year-old apprentice, even at the loss to him of a good deal of instruction in his trade, the workshop was spared the internal friction caused by the introduction of a girl at a statutory wage considerably above that earned by the boy of the same age.

At what rates should a woman or girl taking the place of an unskilled boy or of an apprentice under twenty-one be paid? If she replaced an apprentice, should the point be considered that the latter in theory had low pay on account of the instruction that he received (a sometimes doubtful quantity in war time), whereas the substitute would get no training beyond what was absolutely necessary? These problems were propounded to the Ministry from many sources in the three months after the issue of L.2 as an Order.

Thus a firm of electrical engineers wrote from Newcastle, in March, 1916, acknowledging the receipt of circulars L.2 and L.3 and adding, " What we are really doing is utilising women's labour, mostly girls under eighteen, for the purpose of replacing boys whose services it is now impossible for us to get. . . . Does the regulation as to paying women of eighteen years a minimum wage of 20s. a week apply?"[2]

A firm of ship repairers at Shields made similar enquiries a few

---

[1] The arithmetical calculations required for assessing women's wages on the basis of a weekly wage of £1 for a 53-hour week were a sufficient drawback to such a rigid basis. Thus when in April, 1916, a firm consulted the Department as to the weekly wages to be paid for a 45-hour week to its women employees on night shift (for which according to the men's custom 11½ hours were paid as 15), the conclusion was obviously that it should pay $\frac{45 \times 15}{53 \times 11\frac{1}{2}}$ of £1. The firm expressed its willingness to pay at the rate of 6d. an hour in lieu of this (C.E. 815/23).

[2] C.E. 559/22.

days later on receiving the circulars[1] : " We have been requested by one of your officers to endeavour to arrange to put female labour upon certain of our small machines, thereby releasing boy labour to take over other skilled work in our shops, and we shall be pleased to know if the Minister has issued any instructions with regard to the rates of pay for female labour which displaces apprentice labour."

Sir George Croydon Marks, then serving as Dilution Commissioner on the Tyne, reported periodical enquiries from the district on this apprentice question ; and special complaints from Manchester on the application of L.2 in the course of this spring were found to proceed largely from the same cause.[2]

The Department answered these questions by an age distinction. Dr. Addison ruled (in March, 1916) that " where work is habitually done by boys over eighteen and practically never by boys under that age, L.2 should apply," and that women doing the work of lads of eighteen to twenty-one came under L.2 ; and firms making subsequent enquiries were given this explanation.

In spite, however, of this office ruling, the payment of women replacing apprentices remained a difficulty practical and theoretical. The engineers on the Tyne raised a fresh problem (on which the Ministry refused to dogmatise) by asking whether the woman replacing a senior apprentice was not doing a skilled man's work and therefore entitled to more than her £1 time rate. In June Mr. J. B. Adams asked the wages section for a circular on this apprenticeship question, " a point raised so often and about which Trade Unions in every town say they have not a ruling," and in July the following minute from Mr. J. C. Smith was issued by Mr. Rey as a Labour Exchange Circular[3] to all Divisional Officers :—

" Women replacing apprentices : Application of L.2 :—

" The following rulings in connection with questions which have arisen as to the application of L.2 to women replacing apprentices are forwarded for your information :—

" 1. Women employed on work done by apprentices under eighteen years of age, do not come within the scope of L.2.

" 2. Women employed on work done by apprentices of eighteen years of age and over do come within the scope of L.2. The test of which particular time rate such women are entitled to, under Paragraph 1 of the Circular, depends upon whether the work on which they are employed is in fact skilled man's work or not. It is to be noted that apprentices towards the end of their apprenticeship are frequently employed on work not distinguishable from that of a skilled workman.

---

[1] C.E. 888/24.
[2] M.W. 123923/8 and /10. [3] E.D. 43062/1916. C.O. Circ. 2588.

"I should be glad if you would bring these rulings to the notice of Labour Officers, Labour Exchange Managers and any other officers dealing with dilution of labour."

In the course of the following year (1917), when the payment to women of "semi-skilled" rates of wages was, under certain conditions, recognised, various cases were reported to the Department and to the Tribunal, in which semi-skilled, if not skilled, rates of pay were claimed for women replacing apprentices in their last year or two of training, even if the latter had earned only 13s. or 15s. a week. The Department held that each case could only be judged on its merits, according to the actual degree of skill involved. Women taking the work of senior apprentices were on occasion held to be doing skilled work. Members of the Engineering Employers' Federation, however, repeatedly urged at meetings of the Special Tribunal and of the Employers' Advisory Committee that the work was normally semi-skilled and as such entitled the worker to a rate perhaps above the £1 basis of L.2, but emphatically not equal to that of the skilled workman.[1]

(b) Girls on Boys' Work.

The Ministry again did not definitely publish rules, such as the Munitions Labour Supply Committee had suggested in October, 1915, for the payment of girls doing the work of boys, whose labour grew constantly more costly with the growing scarcity of male labour. The special Tribunal issued one award (in April, 1916) prescribing the wages of girls taking unapprenticed boys' work,[2] and in the same month it recommended to the Ministry that girls' wages for such work should be fixed in any Statutory Order at 16s., 14s., and 12s., at the ages of 17, 16, and 15. No separate Order was, however, issued, and the ground was covered for girls as for women, by the later "women's work" Orders.

(c) Girls on Men's Work.

The wages of girls under eighteen[3] doing work "customarily done by male labour of eighteen and over eighteen years," on which the Wages Tribunal was asked in March to make recommendations, were fixed in July, 1916, by Order 456, at the following weekly time rates:—

18s. at 17.
16s. at 16.
14s. under 16.

Piece rates and premium bonus allowances were to be those given to men on the same work, less 10%, 20%, and 30% respectively at the three ages scheduled; time rates, as in the other women's

---

[1] M.W. 12329/4/5/10; M.W. 109452. Women doing the work of boys under 18 were subsequently paid under the rates described as governing "women's work" (*i.e.*, work *not* customarily performed by men). These rates, though below the L.2 scale were above the apprentices' and even the boy labourers' pre-war earnings.

[2] Cf., award for the Stalker Drill Works, Sheffield, 9 April, 1916.

[3] The number of girls under 18 employed on men's work at this time was, naturally, small; they were, however, engaged on some processes such as rough turning shells, previously performed by men, and a dispute at the works of Messrs. Vickers, Barrow, heard by the Special Arbitration Tribunal in July, 1916, turned in part on the rates of pay for such girls.

wages Orders, were guaranteed to piece workers. These deductions were authorised after discussion by the Special Tribunal, on the analogy of those made, in many trades, from apprentices when on piece work also performed by men. Lower rates of deduction were, however, fixed for girls than for boys on the principle that a girl was not normally passing through a prolonged period of training, and was therefore entitled to rather higher earnings than those of a boy whose " instruction was his hire " (in part, at least). Representatives of the National Federation of Women Workers protested when this order was issued—and their protests were repeated at intervals by other women's organisations—against this system of deduction. They urged that it was an infringement of the principle of " equal pay for equal work," and also that it encouraged employers to put young girls on to unsuitably heavy work on grounds of economy. It is difficult to refute these criticisms, except on the ground that the younger girls—never numerous in such employment—probably cost rather more to the employer in wasted material and in supervision than did their elders.

No special administrative difficulties appeared in connection with this Order. It reappeared as Order 48 of January, 1917, when the girls concerned profited by the calculation of their initial rate like that of their elders, on a 48- instead of a 53-hour week. It was re-issued as No. 490 in April, 1917, when each of the three age groups received an advance of 2s. corresponding to the women's advance of 4s. A fourth class of wage earners, consisting of those under fifteen, was then inserted at a starting wage of 14s.

Probation and Split Jobs.

There remained two much more complicated questions connected with the skilled worker, which beset the Ministry even before L.2 became compulsory, and were made a pretext on which to delay the process of " dilution " by its opponents. (As such, the negotiations over them in detail belong rather to the history of dilution than of control of wages.) These were the questions of the payment of women on probation during the period before they had really learnt their work, and the still more knotty question of " split jobs."

It had been generally agreed that a woman starting on unskilled work should, if on time work, have her £1 a week from the start, without any deduction for her waste of time and material while she learned.[1] Did the wording of Circular L.2 mean that a woman undertaking a skilled man's work should similarly start at his full time rate ? Or should she start as a probationer at the £1 standard time rate, working gradually up to the full rate ? Both on the Tyne and on the Clyde the Amalgamated Society of Engineers argued from the first issue of L.2 as a Statutory Order that a woman should start immediately at the full rates of pay.

Again, if a woman took part only of the work previously done by a skilled man—specialising on that part—should she be paid at his full time rates, and, if not, then what proportion should she receive ?.

---

[1] M.W. 92329/2/17/18.

The two questions were the subject of almost interminable discussion, and involved ultimately the whole question of the principle of the subdivision of labour and its relation to wages.

With the continued introduction of women into the engineering industry in the course of 1916, the position of the woman employed on a skilled man's work became of more than theoretical interest both to the more progressive woman worker and—much more obviously—to the craft unions, as well as to employers. The cases of women taking fully skilled men's work and claiming to step at once into the latters' rates of pay were numerically quite unimportant; and the trade unions' objection to any probationary period at lower wages in such work was apparently due, partly to a desire to block dilution, partly to the fear that standard rates would be tampered with, should such substitution take place. The A.S.E. representative on the Central Munitions Labour Supply Committee which was responsible for the original wording of L.2, admitted that the position of the fully skilled woman worker had been little considered in this direction.[1] " It is an utterly impracticable position," he stated, " to put a woman on to a fully skilled man's job, and it was never considered that such a contingency would arise when L.2 was drafted. At the beginning of L.2 we said, ' these recommendations are on the basis of the setting up of machines being otherwise provided for,' which is a definite and certain indication that dilution in our opinion was going to be confined to that class of work which lent itself to automatism and semi-automatism."

The women workers who entered the engineering trades in 1915 and 1916, if they were engaged on work said to be " skilled " (and the difficulty of defining the term is notorious), almost invariably performed only a part of the work of which the fully trained workman was capable. This form of substitution for the skilled workman involved a reorganisation of the engineering industry and a change in the employment of the skilled man, which obviously might become permanent. Employers constantly argued that " skilled " work when subdivided was no longer skilled; that women were normally only doing the " the semi-skilled part of a skilled man's job, and therefore did not deserve the tradesman's rate of pay." Workmen, on the other hand, feeling that by continued subdivision of processes almost all " skilled " work might on this basis become " unskilled," maintained that payment for such work should depend on the work done, not on the worker who performed it. Rightly or wrongly they held that the result to the employer was normally the same whether work was done by a number of " specialists " or by skilled craftsmen, and there was no justification in the capitalist's gaining by a reorganisation of industry due not to gradual evolution but to the pressure of war.

" There is a process of change going on continuously in normal times," said Mr. Ryder, the organising delegate of the A.S.E. for the Birmingham district, at a further prolonged conference on the payment

---

[1] Conference of Special Arbitration Tribunal, August, 1916.

for split jobs and probationary work held by the Special Tribunal in October, 1916, " in what is skilled man's work caused by automatic machinery and so on. But this is an entirely different question. This is a question of splitting up a job and giving part of it to women and part of it to the skilled man, who has hitherto done it all. Now that does not save time, it does not particularly increase production, because in a given number of articles the skilled man usually roughs down and finishes, but now a woman may rough down and the man finish. No time is saved, it is a mere matter of cheapening labour. If a skilled workman has done a particular piece of work in a certain shop the skilled rates should be paid to whoever does it under present conditions."

Representatives of unions which might be expected to be less exclusive in their attitude than the A.S.E., repeated this line of argument. Thus; Mr. Dawtrey, of the Steam Engine Makers' Society, who appeared with members of the United Machine Workers and the Toolmakers' Society at a later conference on the same day as that just referred to, assured the Tribunal that " the breaking up of work was common long before the war began, but because it was broken up into parts, that certainly did not mean that women and anyone else should come in, regardless of all considerations, and that is our position now. A skilled man's work is a skilled man's work, whether divided or undivided."

This remained the official view of the A.S.E. and of the engineering unions sharing its policy, although the skilled workman in various parts of the country showed a quite comprehensible readiness to claim rather more than the standard rates of pay and to insist on lower rates for his helper when the process of subdivision of labour gave all the hardest part of the work to himself.[1] In their negotiations over the application of L.2, however, the Central Executive Council of the A.S.E. and their orthodox members discountenanced such a system of payment. " The skilled man under present conditions " said one of their delegates in October 1916, " is willing to endure the strain (produced by sub-division) as long as he can, but his price is that the full rates for the other class of work shall be paid to whoever is put on the other operations."[2] They claimed the full standard rates for a woman taking any " part or portion " of a skilled man's work, and they opposed for a time at least, the establishment of any probationary period even for a woman taking skilled work in this highly limited form, on the ground that it might prove the thin end of the wedge which should introduce a separate and lower scale of payment for such work.

[1] Cf. the dilution agreement drawn up at Messrs. Beardmore's, Glasgow, early in 1916, etc.

[2] Gauge work was quoted as an instance of such sub-division in one of these prolonged discussions on the payment for split jobs in 1916. " The work," said a Trade Union delegate, " is done to an extremely fine limit indeed—a tenth of a thousandth of an inch. It is work which has to be done very minutely, and if there is not a little bit of easing off it is work which imposes an immense strain on the operative. Take screw gauges which have to be tested through a magnifying glass. The normal procedure is that the skilled man does his roughing-out as well as finishing, and it imposes a very severe strain on the man who has to keep to the one thing, when the ' roughing-out ' has been taken over by a woman."

Even before L.2 became obligatory the Department was called upon to consider both the recognition of a "probationary period" and the scale of payment for "split jobs" in the prolonged dispute at the machine-tool works of Messrs. John Lang & Sons, Johnstone, a *cause célèbre* in the history of dilution. Here after prolonged negotiations between the firm and the men concerned, a few women were being introduced at the beginning of the year to do certain work connected with the installation of lathes—the rough scraping and bedding of slides, planing and adjusting wedges for lathe saddles, etc.—hitherto performed by skilled men. The latter had been paid at or above the full district rate (they received 42s. a week plus bonus), while the women in part replacing them were paid at the £1 a week rate of L.2. The Clyde Dilution Commissioners[1] (who were engaged for some months of 1916 in fruitful negotiations for the introduction of female and unskilled male labour into the engineering works of the Clyde district) held that women were not entitled to the full district rate of pay unless they were doing " the whole of a fully skilled man's work," and further that a period of probation at less than district rates was permissible. The men would not accept this view, and accordingly, as the foot-note to L.2 directed, the Commissioners and the Paisley District Committee of the A.S.E. formally applied to the Ministry on January 27, 1916, for an interpretation of clause (1), paragraph (2) of L.2, *i.e.*, whether a woman taking the place of a skilled man on a job (*a*) part, (*b*) whole, was entitled to the full district rate, and, if so, from when?[2] On this the Minister issued the following formal interpretation, awarding a probationary rate for women doing fully skilled work until her output was fairly comparable to that of the man whom she replaced and pronouncing against the payment of the full district rate to women engaged on part of a skilled job, although such rates might be given eventually by agreement between employers and workmen.

" The Minister has carefully considered the questions submitted to him by the Paisley District Committee of the Amalgamated Society of Engineers, and by the Commissioners concerning the interpretation of certain points arising out of paragraph 1 of L.2."

" As a result the Minister desires me to state—

" (1) That where a woman is introduced to perform a part only of the work previously performed by a skilled man she is not, in the opinion of the Minister, entitled by the terms of L.2 to receive the full district rate customarily payable to that skilled man, inasmuch as she is not performing in its entirety the work customarily done by the skilled man. If, however, in the opinion of the employer and the representative of the men in the shop concerned, the nature of the work and the degree of efficiency acquired by the woman are such as to justify the subsequent application of the district rate there is nothing in the circular to preclude that rate being eventually paid.

---

[1] Mr. Macassey, K.C., Sir T. Munro, and Mr. I. H. Mitchell.
[2] M.W. 81953.

"(2) That where a woman takes the place of a skilled man on time rate and performs fully the work customarily done by such a man she is entitled to receive the full time rate customarily received by such a man as soon as her work can be regarded as fairly comparable to that of a man whom she has replaced.

"(3) As regards the further question raised—*viz.*, the date from when the woman is, in accordance with the above answer, entitled to receive the full time rate customarily received by the skilled man, the Minister desires me to say that the Circular L.2 does not fix the length of the period of probation. It seems, however, to the Minister that this period should be comparatively short and that during such period the woman should receive a rate of remuneration which, while being less than full time rate, should in no case be less than 20 shillings per week."

On receipt of this interpretation, which upheld the previous opinion of Mr. Macassey and his fellow Commissioners, four hundred of Messrs. Lang's men promptly went on strike (1 February). The situation was discussed at an evening meeting on the following day with representatives of the Executive Council of the A.S.E. in Dr. Addison's room, when the Chairman and Secretary of the Society undertook to secure a prompt resumption of work. They were informed that the Minister would give them an interview to discuss their objections to his interpretation of L.2 though this could not be promised " as a condition of the cessation of an illegal strike." Instructions were telegraphed by the Central Executive of the A.S.E. to their members at Messrs. Lang's, and by 7 February the strikers were back at work.

On 24 February the promised conference with the Minister was held at Whitehall Gardens, when, in a prolonged and argumentative discussion, the representatives of the Central Executive of the A.S.E. maintained that the Minister's interpretation " struck at the root of the whole of their existence as skilled craftsmen," that a skilled job however subdivided was always a skilled job and entitled its doer to skilled rates even if twelve women were doing different parts of the work of one man, and that in the work at Messrs. Lang's, scraping the saddle and bed of the lathes, etc., was " a fully skilled man's work, and it had never been doubted in any part of the country that it was the work of a fully skilled man."...."I submit to you," said Mr. F. S. Button (subsequently a member of the Committee on Production and of the Special Arbitration Tribunals for men's and women's wages), " that if we were to agree that by careful subdivision of our trade the work became unskilled or does not pass as that of fully skilled men, it means that the engineering trade will disappear entirely.... It is not the total cost of the job which you and your Department have to consider. You have to consider the time rate and having decided what was the time rate of the fully skilled man, you then have to decide whether the job now being performed by women was formerly done, although there were other jobs added to it, by fully skilled tradesmen. If it was, it seems to me there is no option but to agree with the interpretation which we venture to put forward."

The Minister, however, despite all criticisms, maintained his interpretation, and, in explaining this formally to the Chairman of the Commissioners on March 10th noted that his ruling overrode any possible decision of the Special Tribunal to which it had been suggested that the matter might be referred. " If any question as to wages to be paid to the women employed at Messrs. Lang's be reported as a difference to the Board of Trade and referred to an Arbitration Tribunal, it will not be open to the Tribunal to revise the Minister's interpretation of L.2 but (subject to the terms of the circular so interpreted) they will be empowered to make such award as to wages as they think just in the circumstances of the case. The principle adopted by the Minister is that the total cost of wages paid for the operation shall, as far as possible, remain the same after the introduction of women as before."[1]

The settlement of the dispute at Messrs. Lang's after this pronouncement from the Minister was complicated by the cross currents of opinion within the Amalgamated Society of Engineers and by the varying attitude towards the dilution of labour taken up by firms and their workmen in the Clyde Area. By 8 May, 1916, however, Mr. Macassey was able to report a successful settlement on the previous day, after a Sunday spent in eight hours' negotiations with the Paisley District Committee and the Executive of the Amalgamated Society of Engineers, " and the most strenuous opposition to the Minister's interpretation and to the acceptance of the probationary period."

" To eliminate controversy " the Minister's interpretation, that a woman undertaking a skilled man's work in whole or in part should be paid fully skilled rates after a period " agreed on between the employer and representatives of men in the shop," was superseded by arranging a definite period after which she should automatically receive the skilled man's pay.

In return for acceptance of the principle of probation under these conditions the men's claim for the payment of full rates for " split jobs " was accepted. The A.S.E. had clearly gained an important victory in the dilution contest, although it was at the time confined to a single firm. Some effects of this victory will be discussed later.

The text of the agreement is given below together with some comments by the Chief Commissioner.

"AGREEMENT BETWEEN THE EXECUTIVE COUNCIL OF THE AMALGAMATED SOCIETY OF ENGINEERS AND MR. L. MACASSEY AND SIR T. MUNRO, WITH REFERENCE TO THE CASE OF JOHN LANG & SONS, JOHNSTONE. (May 7, 1916.)

" In the case of women employed on part only of the work customarily done by fully skilled tradesmen, the women shall start and for a period of four weeks remain at £1 per week. They shall receive £1 5s. for the fifth week and then beginning from the sixth week rise by weekly advances so as to receive

---

[1] M.W. 81953.

at the end of the thirteenth week from starting the time rates of the tradesmen who customarily did the work.
" This arrangement is to be retrospective.
L. MACASSEY.
T. MUNRO.
J. T. BROWNLIE.
R. YOUNG.
" This is to be subject to confirmation by the Ministry of Munitions."

Mr. Macassey, in sending this agreement to the Ministry, added, " I am satisfied with the arrangement. If the Executive of the Amalgamated Society of Engineers agree formally, the Minister can if he thinks right...........make such an arrangement binding on all Controlled Establishments, as an addition to L.2. If I might suggest it, such an Order should be made at once, as many firms, I am informed, are starting women at the full district rate where they are doing part only of the work of a skilled man." " In this case, the difficulty at Lang's was largely caused because the firm started women on skilled work at £1 nearly four months ago, and have kept them at that." " Nothing could be more calculated to arouse bad feeling among the men."

This arrangement was confirmed by the Ministry on 23 May " on the clear understanding that it applied only to the establishment of J. Lang & Sons," and in July the Dilution Commissioners drew up similar agreements for the Tyne.[1] Meanwhile on 24 June the question of the extension of the compromise thus reached had, in accordance with Mr. Macassey's suggestion, been referred to the Special Arbitration Tribunal, which was asked to decide " Whether any, and if so what, directions should be given by the Minister of Munitions as to a probationary period, at specific rates of wages, for women employed on work customarily done by fully skilled tradesmen."

Pending the decision of the Tribunal with regard to a probationary period, which involved detailed consultation with representatives of the employers and workmen to whose conferences reference has already been made, and after the issue (in July) of Order 456 fixing the wages of girls on men's work, there came a temporary lull in the history of the interpretation of Circular L.2 and the payment of women replacing men. The Ministry, in the summer of 1916, was more immediately concerned with regulations for the wages of women on " women's work." Complaints reached the Department at intervals, chiefly through proceedings before the Special Tribunal, of " wholesale evasions " of L.2 in certain districts and trades (such as electrical engineering). In answer to general complaints, such as were raised by the delegates who came up to discuss the " split jobs " problem, the Chairman of the Tribunal, Mr. Macassey, could but point out that if any employer was in default in complying with the Circular, the right course for critics was " not to let the matter grow into a serious item

---

[1] M.W. 92329/15

of trouble but to report it straight away through the Chief Industrial Commissioner for remission to the Tribunal to consider the matter and give a decision. The Tribunal had jurisdiction and if complaint was made to it could remedy the matter." Only some half-dozen cases dealing with " men's work " and the application of L.2 were, however, brought before the Tribunal in the course of 1916.

II. The Semi-skilled Worker and "Equal Pay."

The position of the semi-skilled workers who, apart from those possibly involved in the special subdivision of skilled work, were becoming numerous by the summer of 1916, had hitherto been almost overlooked in all the controversy raised about the rights of the " skilled " man, and appeared as a new problem in the summer of 1916. Should " intermediate " workers receive more than the £1 weekly time rate, meant, it must be remembered, to be a standard, not a minimum wage ?

Already in May Mr. Macassey had drawn the attention of the Ministry to this point. " Semi-skilled men's work done by women is raising much controversy in Glasgow. The Glasgow District Committee (of the Amalgamated Society of Engineers) has steadily said that women on such work should start at £1 and rise to the semi-skilled men's rate, say 30s. to 32s. The Commissioners have told them that this was not provided by L.2. The Ministry must take some line on this point. . . . Something must be done to differentiate between women doing semi-skilled work from women doing unskilled work, in order to expedite and smooth difficulties out of the way of dilution. . . . I am quite prepared to recommend that women should after a period of qualification be allowed to work up to the semi-skilled man's time rate, say, after 4½ months."[1]

Just before this the National Amalgamated Union of Labour in the Shields and Wear district wrote to the Chief Industrial Commissioner's department that three local firms, all Controlled Establishments, had lately engaged female labour at 4½d. an hour for similar work to that done by the Union's members, fitter's mates,. etc., who would have received 29s. to 31s. per week. " This is a great injustice to female workers who are members of our organisation, and . . . absolutely contrary to the spirit of L.2. We think you ought to use your authority to increasing these women workers' wages to what would be paid to men."[2] Their complaint was forwarded to the Ministry, from which a reply was sent (on 3 June) to the effect that, " When women are employed in any Controlled Establishment on work customarily done by semi-skilled men, the Department has no power to insist upon payment of any higher time rate than that of £1 per week. Paragraph 8 of L.2 only refers to systems of payments by results, i.e., to piece work or premium bonus systems." A claim brought by this Union and the National Union of General Workers for

---

[1] M.W. 81953.   [2] M.W. 109430.

an advance on L.2 rates for their members was refused in December, 1916, by the Special Tribunal on similar grounds,[1] though the officials of the two societies urged that women in engineering and foundry works on the North East Coast were receiving at least 6s. a week less than men for the same work, ranging from the " semi-skilled category to that of heavy labouring in the shipyards in all weathers." Under the terms of L.2 there was no alternative to such decisions as these.

THE NATIONAL FEDERATION OF WOMEN WORKERS AND " INTERMEDIATE RATES."

On 28 July the National Federation of Women Workers, in the person of its secretary, Miss Macarthur, who had recently sent vigorous protests to the Ministry on the inadequacy of Order 447 just issued to regulate wages for " women's work," asked the Ministry of Munitions to receive a deputation to discuss the revision of the Order regulating wages for women on " men's work." The chief criticism of L.2 in the letter making this request turned on the position of the time worker, and especially of the time worker doing work intermediate between that of the craftsman and the lower grade of unskilled work, with no rating guaranteed to her but the £1 a week of L.2. The principle of L.2—" equal pay for equal results "—had, according to the writer, been attained for those on piece work or premium bonus, but not fully for women on time work. There were intermediate cases such as (a) that of women on jobs commonly performed by skilled men—a problem which had " engaged the Ministry of Munitions and the Amalgamated Society of Engineers and was understood to be in process of solution " ; (b) that of women on jobs formerly considered as belonging to semi-skilled and unskilled men, a question equally important in principle and perhaps concerning more people. With regard to these women, the £1 rate, if it was fair for the beginner, would, obviously, not be adequate payment to workers who had attained skill in a trade. " Time rates to semi-skilled men and labourers in engineering factories vary, but are everywhere above £1. Women have been very successful in shell work ; Sir W. Beardmore, among others, has put upon record his opinion that the output of women on shell work is not merely equal to but better than that of the men they replace. The National Federation of Women Workers, therefore, ask that women engaged continuously on time on a semi-skilled man's job, may receive the rate current in the district for semi-skilled men's work, and that those engaged on unskilled work may receive the district rate for labourers."

This last demand in Miss Macarthur's letter, raised an important question of principle, in the application of the theory of equal pay for equal work. Mrs. Pankhurst, on behalf of the women at the demonstration on the Embankment, in July, 1915, had specifically asked for equal

---

[1] In August, 1917, however, the Special Tribunal, in a case brought by these same Unions against two associations of employers on the North East Coast, awarded rates of 35s., 32s. 6d. and 30s. for a 54-hour week to semi-skilled (women) workers and labourers in these shipyards.

time as well as piece rates for women substitutes, and had been told by Mr. Lloyd George that equal piece rates only could be guaranteed. Obviously, insistence on equal time rates for labouring work might even in war time be a drawback to the employment of female labour, though it is doubtful if this was a very valid objection in the state of the labour market in the late summer of 1916. On the other hand, the continued payment of lower wages to women than to men when on time work might lead to a repetition of the underselling of low-grade male by female labour, which had been known in the past. Dr. Addison, in consulting the Labour Advisor on the point noted (8 September): " My own view is against making this change, which departs radically from the principle of L.2 and also from the Treasury Agreement." He suggested instead that higher rates up to a maximum of perhaps 30s. might be fixed for some of the semi-skilled workers, " in recognition of special ability or responsibility." Mr. Henderson, in reply, proposed that the revision of L.2 should be referred to the Central Munitions Labour Supply Committee, its authors and sponsors.

Conference with the N.F.W.W. on the Revision of L.2, September, 1916.

Before this step was taken, a conference on the revision of L.2 was held on 11 September, 1916, at Armament Buildings, in accordance with the request of the National Federation of Women Workers.[1] There were present at this conference, Dr. Addison and representatives of the Ministry, Mr. A. Henderson, Miss Macarthur, Miss S. Lawrence, Mr. J. J. Mallon, and four others representative of the National Federation of Women Workers, with Mr. Button and Mr. Kaylor of the Amalgamated Society of Engineers. Thus, the point of view of both the men's and women's trade organisations chiefly concerned in the payment of women substitutes was represented.

Miss Macarthur at this conference amplified the points raised in her letter of 28 July, and emphasised the disabilities of the woman time worker under the conventional rating established for her by the department. L.2 was being interpreted and administered " in a fashion never contemplated by the Labour leaders on the sub-committee which originally drew up the document."

The £1 weekly time rate should at least represent an absolute minimum, whereas numbers of time workers were receiving less than a pound a week. When the scheme was drafted in 1915, the two labour representatives on the Central Munitions Labour Supply Committee thought that £1 was to be a probationary rate, and certainly did not think that some workers would receive, as was the case, $48/53$ of £1 if they were employed for 48 hours instead of the normal engineers' working week. Cost of living had increased very considerably since October, 1915, and this was an additional reason for at least maintaining the level of the wage guaranteed to women on men's work. It was most unfortunate that the word

---

[1] M.W. 132834.

" minimum " had been deleted from the first draft of L.2, and that its intrepretation had been taken from the hands of those who drafted it.

It was therefore suggested, on behalf of the N.F.W.W. and the A.S.E., that an hourly minimum of 6d. should be fixed for women on men's work, with 7d. an hour for those employed at time rates for work done elsewhere " on piece," and an alteration on the same basis of the 15s. prescribed for " waiting time."

Mr. Button, of the A.S.E., in supporting this claim, raised the question of special payment to the semi-skilled worker, and urged that the position of " this big buffer class " should also be referred to the Central Munitions Labour Supply Committee, for up and down the country many difficulties on that point needed to be settled.

Dr. Addison in reply explained that he had considerable sympathy with the women who were being paid $48/_{53}$ or a smaller fraction of £1 ; it had never been intended that they should receive less than £1 for a full working week, though he must confess that he did not think L.2 said this. The Order might fairly be revised in this respect. The demand for an hourly payment of 6d. and 7d., instead of the fixed weekly rate, should also be referred, along with the other questions raised, to the Central Munitions Labour Supply Committee, though at the final stage the opinion of the Special Tribunal would also possibly be asked, and it was essential that the Minister should, as had been established some months previously, retain the right of interpretation of the existing Order or its amendments. The point raised with regard to the semi-skilled worker would also be referred to the same Committee.

The deputation, at the close of the conference, expressed its complete satisfaction with what had been arranged.

III. The Revision of L.2.

RETURN OF L.2 TO THE CENTRAL MUNITIONS LABOUR SUPPLY COMMITTEE.

Two days later, in accordance with Dr. Addison's undertaking, Mr. Henderson was formally asked to summon the Central Munitions Labour Supply Committee (whose meetings had been suspended for two months, and whose consideration of wage questions had ceased on the appointment of the Special Arbitration Tribunal in the previous March), to consider the following subjects of reference.

" (1) Variations in paragraph 1 of L.2 for
- (a) Women whose weekly rating is less than £1, because the number of hours is less than that of engineering men in the district.
- (b) Women on work involving special ability or responsibility though not customarily done by fully skilled men.
- (c) Women on time, on work in other districts customarily done on piece or premium bonus.

(2) Whether a variation in the general time rate of £1 per week is called for."

At meetings on 22 and 28 September, the Central Munitions Labour Supply Committee returned after nearly a year's pause to the consideration of its much discussed circular, and drew up recommendations for its amendment. These were substantially though not verbally the same as those later inserted in Order 49,[1] and on 25 October they were sent by the Department to the Special Tribunal for its final consideration, together with the question referred to it in the previous June, as to the probationary period for women employed on work of a class customarily done by fully-skilled men.[2]

In November the Tribunal reported, giving recommendations the same, except in detail, as those of the Central Munitions Labour Supply Committee both for the semi-skilled and unskilled worker, including the special case of the time worker on shell manufacture.[3]

On these two reports, a revised Order, varying slightly from both, was based.

A number of questions were asked in Parliament during November, as to forthcoming amendments of L.2 and on 15 November a statement was issued to the Press foreshadowing the issue of an amended Order and giving details as to its higher scale of wages.

ISSUE OR ORDER 888, DECEMBER, 1916.

At last, on 24 December, 1916, Order 888 was issued, and was hailed in the publications of the trade unions concerned as " an overdue but real advance" on " the first faulty charter of the woman munition worker."[4] It provided that the flat time rates should now be as follows :

For a week of 48 hours or less £1
49   ,,   £1 0s. 6d.
50   ,,   £1 1s. 0d.
51   ,,   £1 1s. 6d.
52   ,,   £1 2s. 0d.
53   ,,   £1 2s. 6d.
54   ,,   £1 3s. 0d.

It also made special provisions, though still in vague terms, for the semi-skilled or " intermediate " worker.
" Women employed on time
" (a) on work of a class customarily done by semi-skilled men, or
" (b) on work of an especially laborious or responsible nature, or
" (c) where special circumstances exist, shall be paid according to the nature of the work and the ability of the women, in no case less than the £1 a week minimum for a 48-hour week, rising to 23s. for 54 hours."

---

[1] The only difference of importance was a draft clause inserted to meet the point raised by the National Federation of Women Workers at their September Conference:—" A woman employed on time or work customarily done in the trade on piece work and premium bonus, shall after not more than four weeks . . . be paid 33⅓% above the statutory time rate."
[2] M.W. 132834.
[3] M.W. 92329/19.   [4] Cf. *Women's Trade Union Review*, January, 1917

In other respects the Order substantially repeated the original circular L.2. A foot-note was added to the effect that a further Order would shortly be issued with regard to women doing fully skilled work, and a heading which stated that the Ministry's sanction under Section 4 (2) of the Munitions of War Act must be asked for proposals to give higher rates of wages to women on semi-skilled, laborious or responsible work, as in the case of the ordinary advances of wages.

The proposal to fix a maximum wage for the "intermediate" workers was dropped, as was that for a higher minimum wage for women time workers on operations normally paid at piece rates when performed by men. The Department, however, discountenanced this method of payment to women under dilution when cases were reported to it, and only sanctioned it under special conditions.[1]

ISSUE OF ORDERS 48 AND 49 (JANUARY, 1917).

On 21 January, 1917, Orders 48 and 49 were issued consolidating and supplementing those of the previous year. The first was a repetition of Order 456 for the payment of girls on men's work, an order the application of which had given little trouble, despite the criticism raised by its regulation of piece work earnings. The second re-enacted the provisions of the Order issued in the previous month and gave detailed directions in eight subsections for the solution of the problem raised in many controversies over the position of the " skilled " woman worker.[2]

[1] Thus in June, 1917, considerable correspondence passed between the Department and a large rubber firm, consistently dilatory in applying the Ministry's wages regulations. On 19 June, the firm applied for leave to reduce the piece rates of the men in its balloon factory. When this was refused, they engaged women as learners to replace the men. These women they proposed to pay first at 27s., the minimum rate for unskilled women under the " men's work " Orders, then at the men's time wages. These amounted to 35s., whereas the men had frequently earned £4 at piece rates, which the women said they had been led to expect. " It is such actions as the above which go to make so much industrial unrest," commented the Chief Investigation Officer in reporting. The firm explained that their action was prompted by the certainty that the very high earnings procurable by these women on piece work would cause trouble and discontent in all the other departments of their works. The Department, however, refused its sanction to the employment of women on time in the manner proposed (C.E. 1153/4). In the case of a Lincolnshire firm quoted at the conference in September with the National Federation of Women Workers and Amalgamated Society of Engineers, the firm adhered to its method of payment by time to women shell makers, refused the demand of the National Federation of Women Workers for an 8d. hourly time rate to these women, but compromised by an undertaking to pay them 25 per cent. above the time rate laid down in the present and any future edition of Circular L.2 (C.E./565/4 II). On 9 January, 1918, the Special Tribunal awarded a rate of 7d. an hour for women employed on time on machine work on shell, plus the 3s. 6d. advance of the previous August (Cowlishaw, Walker & Co. and the N.F.W.W.).

[2] Order 49 was reissued in April, June, September and November, 1917, as Order 489, 539, 888, 1116. The wording was in no way altered except that the time rate for a 48-hour week became 24s. with corresponding increases for a longer week in accordance with the general rise of wages sanctioned for all women munition workers when on time work, in April, 1917. Order 48 similarly reappeared as Order 490, 540, 889 and 1120 with a rise of 2s. on the rates previously laid down. For the sake of clearness, however, each Order is referred to below under only one title.

1. The original direction given in October, 1915, for the payment of fully skilled work was made more precise by the insertion of three words. " Women employed on the work customarily done by fully skilled tradesmen shall in all cases be paid *as from commencement* the time rate of the tradesmen whose work they undertake " [1.b. (i)]. The A.S.E. had thus gained a point, for the clear statement of which they had pressed.

2. On the difficult question of the definition of "fully skilled work," the Order gave the following negative guidance. " A woman shall be considered as not employed on the work customarily done by fully skilled tradesmen but a part or portion only thereof, if she does not do the customary setting up, or when there is no setting up, if she requires skilled supervision to a degree beyond that customarily required by fully trained tradesmen undertaking the work in question." [1.b (iii).]

3. With regard to the payment during and after probation for women doing *part* of a skilled man's work, the Clyde Dilution Commissioners' agreement of 7 May, 1916, was inserted in substance.

" Women who undertake part or portion only of the work customarily done by fully skilled tradesmen shall serve a probationary period of three months. The wages of such women for this period shall be reckoned as follows : —

" They shall be rated for a period of four weeks at the time rate of wages to which they are entitled under those directions when employed on time, and from that rate shall then rise from the beginning of the fifth week until the end of the thirteenth week, by equal weekly increases, to the district time rate of the fully skilled tradesman, and shall thereafter be rated at the district rate of the tradesman whose work they are in part or portion undertaking." [1.b. (iii).]

No woman, it was provided, should be called upon to serve more than one such probationary period [1.b. (v)].

4. In cases where extra cost of supervision and setting up was required in the employment of women on skilled men's work, a deduction of not more than 10% might, as above stated,[1] be made from the women's rates of pay, provided that these in no case fell below the time rates (£1 to £1 3s. according to the length of the working week) laid down for the unskilled worker (1.b. iv).

Just before the issue of this Order, the Special Tribunal gave its award on the much-discussed Lang of Johnstone case, in which the men asserted that the agreement of May, 1916, about workmen's split jobs had not been carried into effect. The Tribunal gave the same ruling (with effect from 28 February of the previous year) as that contained in clause 1.b (iii), to which indeed it served in part as *raison d'être*. Thus the men's contention, that a woman time worker, taking a part of a skilled man's work should receive the man's time rate, was conceded by the Government. The controversy and the decision that ended it are important for the light that they throw on the

---

[1] Page 19.

skilled man's conception of the relation of pay to work ; they are relatively unimportant from the point of view of the number of women affected. The decision, however, probably had the result of discouraging the introduction of women to skilled time work, such as tool room work ; a woman who had served one probationary period could not be required to serve another, and a single probationary period would not give a woman the adaptability to new tasks which the skilled man possessed ; yet the frequency with which new tasks appeared was the principal factor tending to keep these occupations time work occupations.[1]

L.2 now disappeared into the well-filled ranks of obsolete Orders, although the principles which it established still remained the basis for the payment of " diluted " women's labour.

[1] Cf. p. 41.

CHAPTER IV.
"MEN'S WORK" 1917–1918.
I. Order 49 and its Reception.

The issue of Order 49, in January, 1917, closed the first period of difficulties in adjusting the wages of women on men's engineering work, difficulties caused in part by the faulty drafting of Circular L.2, but really inherent in any attempt to cover the highly debateable ground of "substitution work." It included most of the modifications and compromises in the interpretation of the principle, delusively simple in appearance, of "equal pay for equal work," reached in more than a year's experience of labour dilution. It supplied an obvious omission in L.2 by recognizing an intermediate grade between "skilled" and "unskilled" work, and it admitted the difficulty of even a triple classification of women's labour, as skilled, semi-skilled and unskilled, by providing for differential payments to different grades within each of these classes. It could not, however, by any amount of elasticity in definition, reconcile the fundamental opposition on some aspects of dilution between certain employers and employed; and its issue gave rise to protests from both sides (although the trade unions had obtained almost all their immediate demands in this direction during the previous year) as to the position equally of the woman doing skilled and of the woman doing semi-skilled or laborious work.

II. Skilled Men's Work.

In principle, the Order laid no new burden on manufacturers. It made, however, more precise the general undertaking on the grounds of which dilution had been accepted and L.2 had been made compulsory, and it accordingly attracted much more attention than previous orders. During the first year of the Ministry's existence, and even later, comparatively few women were doing skilled men's work on munitions. As late as the spring of 1917, in the North East Coast area, only 5, out of 150 firms employing women on men's work, reported that they had employees replacing fully skilled men, and these women numbered only 70 as compared with some 2,500 on semi-skilled and unskilled work. In the Birmingham district at the same time, out of some 900 munition firms making returns, only 39 by their own account were employing and paying women (680 in all) for fully skilled men's work. There was indeed a natural tendency among employers to class as "semi-skilled," work in which a group of women replaced a skilled man, although the Department could not necessarily accept such a classification.

Thus a well-known firm of electrical engineers,[1] in April, 1917,

---
[1] C.E. 254/4B.

wrote to the Ministry, explaining that though they were anxious to promote output in every way, they were not prepared to introduce women into their works under Order 49, as the high rates of pay (for work previously performed by men dilutees) would cause great discontent among the 1,000 women workers employed by them at present and paid either on the much lower " women's work " rates or on the rates for unskilled men. Instead, they proposed a scheme according to which a group of their women employees doing skilled work in gangs under the supervision of a skilled man, were to be rated as semi-skilled ; the work produced was to be paid for at the same rate at which it had always been paid for previously ; and the money was to be distributed to the members of the gang, " in accordance with their hours worked and in proportion to their time rates, the women so employed being rated at the same rates now applicable to women engaged on semi-skilled work." " This scheme," wrote the firm, " has brought forth protests from the local representatives of the Amalgamated Society of Engineers, and while we believe that they are in full agreement with the principle, as being equitable and just, yet they are not prepared to agree to it so long as Order 49 is in force. As we are of the opinion that the men's objections to such a procedure could be overcome, if adequate safeguards were introduced to protect the men against the continued employment of women in skilled occupations after the end of the war, except by subsequent negotiations, we beg formally to request that Order 49 be withdrawn from our establishment, and that we be given a definite instruction to introduce the ' gang ' system as described above, on the understanding that if any women were so employed at some fixed date subsequent to the declaration of peace—say, three months, such women should then be paid the time rates in accordance with Order No. 49."

In this case, in spite of the obvious practical advantages of such a gang system, the firm was informed that the Department was not prepared to exempt the establishment from the operations of Statutory Rule and Order No. 49 " unless some modification of the agreement with the skilled unions represented by that Order has been determined on which would be of national application. . . . The gang system proposed would be a contravention of the Order, in that women would be employed on work customarily done by skilled men, and would be receiving less than the skilled man's time rates."

In one of the most important engineering works on the Clyde a suggestion was formulated in March by the works dilution committee, at which for over a year representatives of the firm and of the operatives had met to settle problems of dilution. The scheme, which was sent up to the Ministry for sanction, proposed that women taking work previously done partly by skilled men, partly by apprentices, should receive wages based on an average of those received by their predecessors.[1] This compromise, however, the Department, in face of the principles established in its Order, could not accept. The

---

[1] C.E. 186/4B.

proposal was, indeed, although supported by the workmen concerned, opposed to the whole official line of policy of the Trade Union which mainly represented the interests of the skilled engineer in negotiation with the Government and with federated employers.

PROTESTS AGAINST ORDER 49.

During the spring of 1917 many employers protested collectively or individually against the application of the Orders made for the payment of women employed on skilled men's work. A meeting of twenty-five principal machine tool manufacturers convened by Mr. A. Herbert at the end of March to discuss the big gun programme passed a resolution that they would not employ women on the terms of the Order.[1] Equal disapproval was shown by the Executive Committee of Boards of Management at a meeting of the same date.[2] "The real effect of this circular," said the representatives of area organisation and of the Supply Department present, "would be to kill dilution. The principle of equal pay afforded labour its only chance of outing women after the war, as the payment of female labour at the rates entailed would saddle manufacturers with an intolerable burden of costs. Since the Circular laid down that if a woman did work which a skilled man had been doing, she was to get the same wages irrespective of whether the work required skilled labour or not, managers would not appoint women. . . . What was happening was this. They were now splitting up a man's task and allotting the skilled portion to skilled workmen and the unskilled portion to women, but because men happened to have been doing the unskilled portion also, it was laid down that women should get the same rate of wages as men. . . . In dilution women were not doing fully skilled work and to ensure their safety all kinds of foolproof devices had to be put in at extra cost."

The Employers' Advisory Committee, a small standing committee appointed by the Engineering Employers' Federation at the request of the Minister in the last days of 1916 for consultation with the Department,[3] considered in April, 1917, in conjunction with a number of representatives of the Labour Department of the Ministry, the application of Order 49. The employers agreed emphatically that the terms of the Order, and especially its insistence on the full rates of pay for split jobs, made the employment of women "expensive and unremunerative." They urged that (unless the Government would undertake responsibility for the whole extra cost involved in the payment of women on this basis) the portion of the skilled man's work given to women should be recognised to be, as indeed it normally was, "semi-skilled" and should be paid for at definite intermediate rates. They offered, however, no advice to the Department as to methods of reconciling labour to these proposals, which it was pointed out would clearly be looked on as "a thinly disguised scheme for taking permanently away from the skilled men a large portion of the work which they had succeeded in securing to the skilled unions alone before

---

[1] L.R. 179656.   [2] M.W. 92329/42.   [3] L.R. 5581; 5581/2, etc.

the War." In June and August of the same year, this Advisory Committee recurred to the question of women's wages (in relation to the proposed consolidated Order for their regulation, and to the vexed question of the application to women of the general wage advances prescribed by the Committee on Production). They again represented that the statutory wages payable were a definite drawback to dilution. "The skilled men," repeated the Secretary of the Engineering Employers' Federation, " are going to make the employment of women as expensive as possible so as to make it unattractive. . . . If that is the case the Department will not get dilution."

Other employers equally pointed out that the wages policy of the Ministry made dilution very difficult in any but repetition work, while from Manchester it was reported in July that " the position was very acute ; " that it would be impossible to dilute on the basis proposed because of the unrest caused in workshops by the payment of the same rate to women " dilutees " and to skilled men ; that it was impossible to pay wages under the terms of the Order, since " women could not possibly do as much in the time as highly skilled men," and that finally employers were prepared to take every " Order 49 " case before the Special Tribunal rather than comply voluntarily with its terms.[1]

The points at issue were clear and were irreconcilable. On the one side there was the irrefutable argument that a woman specialising on one part of the varied work of which a fully trained workman was capable, might, in course of time, get through her specialised job as quickly as the latter, or even more quickly, but that her potential value was less to the employer. She had not the man's " background " of workshop training, and was necessarily less adaptable. If the demand for the particular operation on which she was engaged fell off, she must learn the next process *de novo*, while a clause of the statutory Order under which she was paid expressly forbade her serving " more than one probationary period," at lower rates, for work which was in any sense skilled.[2]

This disadvantage in the employment of women at full district rates might never be felt unless an emergency arose. The vexed question of the comparative output of men and women on skilled work was the fundamental point of controversy, and on this employers naturally insisted. It was true that in many forms of repetition work, and in certain operations, such as those of oxy-acetylene welding, for which specially capable workers responding to intensive training had been secured, the skilled man's work was fully equalled under identical conditions by the woman substitute or " dilutee." Also, a concession had been made to employers by the much discussed provision that a woman doing part of a skilled man's work should serve thirteen weeks' probation, and that 10 % reduction of wages should be permissible to cover cost of supervision, etc., for the " skilled " woman worker.

---

[1] The Special Tribunal dealt with a number of " marginal " cases of split jobs in the course of this summer. (Cf. the case of Crossley Motors, Manchester, and the A.S.E.)

[2] Cf. L.R. 5581/2.

" The Department was given to understand that this would be accepted by employers, and not seriously objected to by the Amalgamated Society of Engineers, and that dilution would proceed satisfactorily," reported an officer of the Wages Section of the Ministry and of the Special Tribunal. Against this,[1] employers urged that the comparative value of women's skilled work measured by output ranged from 45 % to 64 % of the man's, and that an employer might have to " pay a woman for 60 % of the output of a skilled man on the easiest portion of his work the same rate as they paid to the skilled man who had served an apprenticeship at his trade, and was competent to do a wider range of work." This made the skilled man restive, and women—it was said—being guaranteed more pay than they needed, had no incentive to work. " Though technically a woman might be on part of a skilled man's work, she was in fact often doing work less difficult than that done by women who were technically on unskilled or semi-skilled work, while she was paid about twice as much. Other women were thereby dissatisfied."

On the other hand, it was frequently represented by the workmen's representatives that (despite the alleged slowness and inadaptability of the inexperienced woman worker on skilled work) " by improved methods and machinery, and acceleration of output, employers really had to pay no more for the same amount of work done." The workmen had made substantial and probably permanent sacrifices in accepting dilution, whereas the employers had not suffered thereby under the special condition of war contracts, and had good prospect of benefiting after the War by the changed organisation of the engineering industry. Even if the output and potential value of the woman substitute were less than that of the skilled workman, yet employers had had, long before the appearance of women in engineering workshops, to recognise the permanent difference in rates of output even among men paid at the same hourly wage, and to allow for the lack of adaptability of workmen transferred from different branches of the same trade. In so far as munitions were, temporarily, produced at greater cost owing to the attitude taken up by organised Labour—this must be accepted by the nation. " Our position on this subject," said the Chairman of the Executive Council of the A.S.E. when referring in October, 1916, to previous negotiations on the question with the Department and with employers, " was definite and emphatic, and it was in effect that that was the price the nation had to pay for dilution in the engineering establishments of this country."[2]

Some modifications of the terms of Order 49, in so far as it dealt with skilled work, were considered in the spring of 1917, but were held up by labour troubles, and its directions reappeared in substance in the consolidated Order for women on munition work, issued after much inter-departmental negotiation, in May, 1918. The Depart-

---

[1] M.W. 179656.

[2] See speech by Mr. Brownlie on 15 October, 1916, at the conference previously referred to, on the acceptance of a " probationary " period for women on skilled men's work.

ment, while admitting the inconvenience to employers in some cases, and the difficulties placed in the way of the free extension of labour dilution, yet held fast by the principles of the Order, on the assumption that it was bound by its pledges to Labour in the past.

A FURTHER PROBLEM OF INTERPRETATION.

The wording inherited from the original circular on women's wages of October, 1915, still presented problems in 1917, when questions arose for decision as to the grade of skill, and therefore the rate of pay, required in certain processes of work.

A special interpretation of the word "customarily," over which so much discussion had taken place in the previous year (cf. Clause 1 (b), of Order 49, concerning women employed on work "customarily done by fully skilled tradesmen"), was called for by the difficulty that a decision as to whether a job was skilled or not frequently depended on the custom of the separate shop, rather than of the district.[1] The Special Arbitration Tribunal, in reaching decision on claims for the skilled man's rate of pay, had constantly to take detailed evidence as to the custom not only of the trade, but of individual firms, of working a particular capstan, lathe, milling or drilling machine, by mechanics, labourers, apprentices or other semi-skilled workers. It was therefore suggested in April, on behalf of the Wages Section, "That the question of whether a particular job is a skilled man's job should be determined in the first place by the custom of the shop; if there is no clear and established custom in the shop, then by the custom of the district, and failing that, by the majority practice of the country." And the Special Tribunal in its function of advisor to the Ministry on women's wages, expressed its approval of this ruling, "on which in fact it had proceeded in several of its decisions." This, while a possible interpretation of the Circular, was not the principle on which the Department and the Tribunal had decided cases at first.[2]

It was explained to the Admiralty at the end of May that the payment of the skilled man's rate of wages to the woman substitute depended on whether the work in question was or was not customarily performed by men before the war. "Work," in this connection, covered not only the machine operated but the operation performed on the machine. In many cases women were using machines for simple work on which fully skilled men had customarily been employed for more difficult work, and in such a case the woman would not have the skilled man's wage.

The department steadily resisted in its rulings, both as to men's and women's wages, the position taken up periodically by trade unionists that a machine should be "rated" for "skilled" or "unskilled" work, without reference to the operative controlling it or the work turned out. The point is of obvious importance in the development of industry, quite apart from the special conditions produced by war.

---

[1] L.R. 142.   [2] See Ch. III, p. 17.

III. Women on Semi-Skilled, Responsible and Laborious Work.

A new group of problems developed in 1917 over the position of the large class intermediate between the unskilled workers whose time rates were fixed by statutory Order and the skilled women whose rates of payment had been the battleground of the skilled trade unions. Their position had, as has been explained, received preliminary consideration in the previous year. Order 49, repeating in this respect Order 888 issued on the previous Christmas Eve, substituted for the flat time rate of £1 a week laid down in Circular L.2 an elastic method of payment " according to their ability and the nature of their work," for women on semi-skilled, responsible and laborious work. The numbers of women so employed were, even in 1917, much larger than those of the much discussed substitutes (in whole or in part) for fully skilled men. In practice, special rates had frequently already been given to individual " intermediate " workers and had, in some cases, as in the National Shell Factories in the autumn of 1916, been officially recognised for groups of workers, such as gaugers.[1] The new clauses in the wages Order of 1917 authorised the payment of such special rates, which should be settled either by local agreement requiring the confirmation of the department under Section 4 of the Munitions of War Act, or by appeal to the Special Arbitration Tribunal, a large proportion of whose time was spent in the succeeding year in defining these intermediate rates. Experience has shown the extreme difficulty of distinguishing, especially in border lines cases, between " skilled," " semi-skilled," and " unskilled " workers ; and the position of the three types of intermediate work known to the Statutory Order :— " semi-skilled," such as the operation of various types of lathe ; " responsible," such as gauging and examining ; and " laborious," such as much of the labouring required in shell factories and shipyards—can be best considered *en bloc*.

A Standard Rate for the Semi-Skilled Worker.

The Labour department of the Ministry had sometimes been reproached for failing to consult employers in the application of its numerous wages Orders. In the group of cases above described, it received the advice, some three months after the issue of Order 49, of members of the Engineering Employers' Federation, through the special consultative Committee described above.[2] The latter repeated a suggestion frequently made by certain of their members before the Special Arbitration Tribunal since the previous summer, by proposing the adoption of standardised rates for the special classes of unskilled and semi-skilled workers, " since it was impossible to give the necessary time to gauge accurately the ability of each female

---

[1] Cf. also the circular issued in January, 1917, to National Shell and Projectile Factories, calling attention to the recent revision of L.2 and urging that in submitting further proposals for intermediate rates managers should consider the rates paid by local firms and by the Woolwich authorities to Government examiners.

[2] L.R. 179656. L.R. 5581, and sub-files.

worker." The following time wages were proposed for a 54-hour week, allowing for the 4s. increase on Order 49 rates just awarded to all time workers.

i. Labouring.
  (a) Unskilled : 27s. (i.e., the minimum officially permitted, corresponding to the £1 of Circular L.2).
  (b) Special : 27s. to 30s.
ii. Gauging and viewing, testing and inspection.
  (a) Preliminary unskilled operations : 27s.
  (b) Intermediate grade and ordinary testing : 29s.
  (c) Special gauging, final inspection and testing : according to skill.
iii. Work on power hammers : 28s. to 30s.
iv. Driving overhead cranes : 29s. to 34s.
v. Hand work not customarily done by skilled men.
  (a) Preparation and rough file and chisel work, wire splicing and assembling of interchangeable minor parts : 27s. to 30s.
  (b) Selected assembly of minor parts : 30s. to 32s.
vi. Machine work.
  (a) Simple operations—
    Setters-up provided : 27s. to 29s.
    Setters-up not provided : 2s. to 5s. extra.
  (b) Higher grade operations—
    Setters-up provided : 29s. to 34s.
    Setters-up not provided : 2s. to 5s. extra.

These rates approximated closely to those already arranged for some groups of workers, although in a few districts higher rates were obtained.[1]

The Ministry, in spite of such recommendations, deliberately left these payments for individual settlement and refrained from fixing statutory time wages for the semi-skilled workers as a class. The Trade Unions interested had, since the previous autumn, when the question was tentatively raised at the conference on L.2, shown that they would not accept a new general time rate or rates for such women workers which should be lower than men's ; while employers consistently maintained that the average woman's work in these grades was still markedly below that of men, in quantity if not in quality.[2] At the beginning of July, however, Mr. Kellaway undertook as the result of a deputation from semi-skilled and unskilled

---

[1] Thus at the end of May, 1917, the National Federation of Women Workers and the men's Unions concerned, made an agreement after prolonged negotiations with twelve principal engineering firms at Coventry for the following rates to be paid locally to women on men's work : unskilled workers, 26s. 6d.; semi-skilled workers, 32s. ; women doing part or portion of a skilled job, 40s. 6d. (the district rate of 45s. less 10%) ; those on fully skilled work to have the same rates as skilled men (L.R. 912).

[2] M.W. 132834 ; M.W. 109430 ; and conferences with Special Arbitration Tribunal, 28 July, 5 August, 25 and 26 October, 1916.

men on the North East Coast to recommend the insertion of a provision in the revised Wages Order then under consideration, that women doing the same work as the men represented by the deputation should have the same time rates, on the understanding that their output was the same.

Organised Labour and the Claims of the Intermediate Workers.

As the field of occupations entered by women widened, new industrial interests necessarily became involved. In its early negotiations with regard to the introduction of women into industry under War conditions, the Department had dealt so far as organised labour was concerned, almost exclusively with the A.S.E. and other skilled men's societies, and with one women's trade union, the National Federation of Women Workers. After over two years of war, however, unskilled and semi-skilled workmen, represented by the Workers' Union, the National Union of General Workers, the Dockers' Union, and the National Amalgamated Union of Labour, were becoming anxious lest the increasing number of women who were undertaking heavy labouring work in factory yards and shipyards or responsible work for which no payment by results was possible should accept lower wages than men (since in many cases they admittedly could do less work of this type in the same time), and should become the nucleus of a low grade class of blackleg labour. The risk of degradation of wage rates, already low in peace time for all such work, was probably greater in these groups of occupations than in the more highly organised skilled trades.[1]

This difficulty was constantly raised in different forms in the course of the year. Thus, at a conference on 1 August between the Minister of Munitions and trade union representatives[2] a workman's delegate drew attention to " a grievance of long standing." " Women doing men's semi-skilled and unskilled work (especially driving cranes) do not," he complained, " get the same rate as men, for *day* work. . . . All the men who are working about such a job regard this as a case of the employer getting cheap labour. Undoubtedly, if a woman is

---

[1] The interests of this very large group of workers had not been consulted in the original negotiations over L.2, which had become mandatory as a result of a bargain between the Ministry and the A.S.E. In 1917, however, the unions of labourers and semi-skilled workers were asserting their position beside the craft unions (in part owing to the " privileged position " said to have been conferred on the latter by the Trade Card Agreement at the end of the previous year) ; their representatives appeared with those of the skilled engineering unions in the applications for general wages advances heard by the Committee on Production during the year ; and in safeguarding the position of their members, the status of women workers in the same occupations became obviously important. The following *increases* in their female membership were recorded during 1916 by the unions chiefly concerned with women munition workers :—

National Union of General Workers	14,000
National Federation of Women Workers	10,000
Workers' Union	9,500
National Amalgamated Union of Labour	5,000

(*Labour Gazette*, May, 1918, p. 176.)

[2] L.R. 142/20.

doing the same work as a man and is not getting the same rate of pay as the man whose place she has taken, his case is being prejudiced. At present, the onus is upon the Trade Union officials to prove that the conditions are exceptional, or that the work is onerous, in order to get a higher rate of pay than the minimum set down in the regulations. I think the onus should be upon the employer of paying the rate that he formerly was paying for the work that he is now getting done by the woman, or of proving that the woman is not doing the same work and the same amount." This last point appeared not infrequently on labour platforms. The Department, however, held that it was impossible to make the employer normally responsible for equal time payments according to this suggestion. The principal of equal pay for equal work could be applied without difficulty to piece work, which gave an automatic measure of output ; equal time rates were guaranteed to the women who took the place of fully skilled men irrespective of the quality and amount of their work as the result of a definite bargain with the skilled men ; in the case of time workers the assessment of output and efficiency was so difficult that to throw on employers the burden of doing it by a general Order would have been to institute a ceaseless casuistical discussion. While they did not lay down the principle of equal pay for equal work in the case of time workers, the Orders did not exclude the application of that principle in a proper case. The proper method of making this application, however, was by local agreement or by establishing a case before the Special Arbitration Tribunal.[1]

WOMEN AS CRANE DRIVERS: AN ILLUSTRATION OF THE PROBLEM.

The position of the women crane drivers, to which the delegate referred, is of interest in the tortuous story of the settlement of the " intermediate " workers' earnings. Employers corresponding with the Ministry during the summer of 1917, estimated the industrial value of women as compared with men in these groups of occupations as 3 : 5 or 4 : 6. But in driving a crane, an occupation often described as a picturesque instance of labour substitution, an untrained woman's lesser strength or lack of experience could hardly tell,[2] although a beginner might from lack of practice mishandle heavy loads needing special judgment for their safe transference. The work involves nerve and good sense, but its accomplishment depends as much on machine as on personal capacity. The woman crane driver should, therefore, with some experience, be able to do as much work as the normal man, and accordingly should have his full time rates of pay. In a number of cases reported to it the Department maintained this view. Thus it was explained in July to the proprietors of a Middlesbrough Ironworks[3] that women should start at slightly above the minimum rate of 6d. per hour and after a short period of probation should have a man's time rates, less any extra cost of supervision. This, it was stated, had been the recent practice in various establish-

---
[1] L.R. 19160/2.
[2] The occupation was noted later in the year as one suited to disabled soldiers.   [3] C.E. 1421/4B.

ments employing crane drivers. To this recommendation the firm replied at great length, asserting that the general average of female capacity was in their experience between .65 and .70 of man's; that women substitutes had not the family obligations of men, and that the present demand of various labour bodies was clearly only advanced in order to block the system of dilution. Correspondence on the subject (which had been begun by the Union concerned in June) was prolonged until the case was referred to the Special Arbitration Tribunal, and an award issued on 14 November to the effect that women crane drivers employed by the firm under existing conditions should be paid at the men's rate of 8s. per shift after three months' probation.

A similar award was issued in the same month in a case brought against Messrs. R. Stephenson & Co., when it was settled that women employed by the firm on six-ton cranes should have 37s., and on ten-ton cranes 39s. a week, and in the case brought against Messrs. Harland and Wolff, at Belfast, when a woman crane driver employed on a 15-ton crane appeared before the Tribunal, and convinced its members that she was fully doing a man's work, and was entitled to his rates of payment, £2 4s. a week with extras.

Previously, on 9 August, the Tribunal had found, in a case brought against Messrs. Beardmore, that "women crane drivers after two weeks' experience, undertake the whole of the work previously done by men, and perform it as efficiently as the men. They are, therefore, to be paid, after two weeks (during which they should be paid at 6½d. an hour), the wages and allowances paid from time to time to men employed on the same work in the machine shops at Parkhead Forge, less any general advance payable to the women by order of the Minister of Munitions, so that the total payment to the women shall be the same as that to the men."[1]

The cause of the women crane drivers was espoused by no less a union than the Iron and Steel Trades Federation, as well as by the National Federation of Women Workers, and an award such as the above offered a useful precedent from the point of view of organised Labour. As an illustration of the Department's attitude towards the whole problem of time rates, these negotiations are worth noting, since the case of this group of workers served to point the moral of the necessity under normal conditions of equal output in return for equal payment.[2] The case was, however, exceptional,

---

[1] This rate was 10½d. an hour. "All our crane driver members should see that they are getting the men's rate," said the organ of the National Federation of Women Workers in commenting on this award. "If not they should let the Federation know at once. This should cheer our Woolwich members on whose behalf the Federation is at present negotiating."—*Woman Worker*, September, 1917; December, 1917.

[2] When women crane drivers did not undertake entire charge of cranes, but received help from men in oiling, greasing, etc., they were not necessarily entitled to a man's full rate of pay. Thus at a local conference held at Manchester on 21 January, 1918, after a hearing before the Special Tribunal between representatives of the Manchester Engineering Employers' Association, the Workers' Union, and the National Union of General Workers, it was agreed that the minimum rate for women crane drivers should be 34s. per week, plus the recent advance of 3s. 6d. to female workers.—*Workers' Union Record*, March, 1918.

as the work of women in crane-driving admitted of the clearest possible comparison with that of men in point of quality and efficiency.

LOCAL SETTLEMENT OF INTERMEDIATE RATES.

The Department, as has been said, maintained throughout 1917 its refusal to commit itself to any fixed time rate for the intermediate workers. On the whole, employers and workpeople settled special rates locally without much administrative direction from Whitehall Gardens. A certain number of proposed changes were duly referred for sanction under Section 4 (2) of Part II. of the Munitions Act. Thus in January, a rate of 26s. for a 53-hour week (3s. 6d. above the minimum then prescribed) was proposed and sanctioned for women viewers and examiners, and for drillers and rectifiers as being engaged respectively on responsible and on comparatively skilled work. In April, at the Rochdale National Shell Factory, 25s. was sanctioned for a 48-hour week for women employed on the "specially laborious" work of trollying. In July, a Sheffield firm of steel manufacturers received permission to increase from 26s. 6d. to 29s. (*i.e.*, 2s. 6d. above the new minimum for 53 hours' work) the wages of female labourers unloading bricks, an occupation fully deserving the classification of "specially laborious." There were not, however, very many applications to the Ministry for such "sanctions," since these rates were frequently arranged as individual advances which under the Act it was not necessary to report. After the general advances of April, 1917, to women on men's (time) work, a normal time wage for viewers and gaugers (on "responsible" work) and for women on semi-skilled machine processes, was 7½d. an hour—33s. 9d. for a 54-hour week, or 30s. for the 48-hour week under the three shift system.[1] These rates were adopted by the Minister as a basis in the National Shell and Projectile Factories, and served as a precedent to controlled establishments.

More valuable precedents were supplied by the Special Arbitration Tribunal, which was constantly occupied in the course of the year in defining rates for workers claiming special rates owing to their "ability" or "responsibility," and in deciding in a number of difficult cases whether work was or was not fully skilled. By December, 1917, it had confirmed the establishment of time wages of 7½d. to 8½d. an hour as a more or less recognised rate for "intermediate" workers. It was suggested that such rates might be inserted in a new wages Order either as a minimum or as a standard for local agreement. The consolidated order of the following May, however, left the position of the intermediate workers on "men's work" unchanged.

IV. The Claim to Men's Advances.

In 1917 a new and difficult problem arose, partly of interpretation, partly of policy. As a result of an agreement in February between the Engineering Employers' Federation and the Unions with which it

---

[1] C.E. 365/4B.; C.E. 3555/4; C.E. 1414/4B.

negotiated, the Committee on Production heard the claims of the engineering and allied trades together at four-monthly intervals and awarded national advances of 5s., 3s., and 5s. a week, in the course of the year. Were the women in receipt of men's " rates " entitled to identical advances ? Both the men's and the women's unions took the view that the women engaged on men's work at men's rates should logically receive any increase of pay secured by the men. The question had not arisen in the negotiations and discussions at which the principles on which women on men's work should be paid had been settled ; it was raised by a request from the Special Arbitration Tribunal for the Minister's interpretation of Clause 1b. of Order 49.[1]

The Department's view was that the Order did not require the payment of men's advances to women. The rate which the Government undertook to maintain was the standard rate which men were receiving when women were introduced. The object of the undertaking was to ensure that the men's permanent economic position should not suffer as a result of the temporary invasion of their work by dilutees. The advances awarded by the Committee on Production were temporary adjustments designed to meet the rise in the cost of living, without bringing into question the normal standard rate ; they were, in the words of the award, " to be regarded as war advances, intended to assist in meeting the increased cost of living, and .... to be recognised as due to and dependent on the existence of the abnormal conditions now prevailing in consequence of the War." Specifically, they did not affect the standard rate, they " are to be taken into account in the calculation of payment for overtime or night duty, or for work on Sundays and holidays, but they are not otherwise to apply to or affect present time-rates, premium bonus rates, or piecework prices, and are not to be taken into account as part of the time rates for the purpose of fixing new piecework prices or premium bonus rates." That they were not intended to affect the standard rate is shown also by the fact that they took the form of uniform advances for all classes and grades of workers, the only differentiation being by age between youths or boys and men, and that they were payable to pieceworkers in the form of a lump sum irrespective of their piecework earnings. In amount they were calculated to compensate the unskilled labourer for the increase in the cost of living ; the higher paid worker received an identical, not a proportionate advance. In their interpretation, the Department was upheld by the Law Officers of the Crown, to whom the question was referred at the end of the year.

The question of policy was distinct from that of interpretation, since the Department could by a new Wages Order have superseded or supplemented Order 49, on the basis of which the advance was claimed, and granted the men's advances. From the point of view of production it was held to be inexpedient to render the employment of women on " skilled work " even more expensive than it was already as a result of the prescription of full standard rates for what was often practically, if not technically, semi-skilled work. This was

---

[1] Cf. Appendix VI., pp. 189-191.

urged vigorously by the Employers' Advisory Committee when consulted on the subject by the Department in August[1] and was repeated to the Minister in November by the Chairman of L. Committee who stated that its members were " unanimously against such payment."[2]

Even more important was the reaction on other women's wages that might be expected from the grant of advances on the men's scale to the small minority of women doing skilled men's work and already enjoying exceptionally favourable terms of remuneration. If an advance not contemplated by the women's wages Orders were obtained by one section of the women, attempts to secure similar concessions would be made by other sections, and it would become impossible to maintain the system of wage relations established after such prolonged negotiations and embodied in the Orders. The policy of the Wages Section had been to guard against reactions of this kind by treating women's wages as a self-contained problem, and it would be impossible to continue to regulate women's wages, if these were to be controlled by every fluctuation in men's wages.[3]

The claim was not pressed with any great force either by men or by women trade unionists, until in October a formal complaint was received from the A.S.E. of a breach of faith on the part of the Department. The object of the stipulations for the payment of women on skilled men's work was " that there should be no economic advantage to employers in employing female labour in the place of fully skilled men." " The situation was now anomalous and one of the essential safeguards of dilution was removed if these women did not share in the men's national advances. It was no argument to say that periodic advances were not part of the district rate. Equality of remuneration was the point and this could clearly only be secured by making all advances granted to skilled men apply to women engaged on the work of skilled men under dilution."

On 19 March, 1918 (after intermediate correspondence), a detailed reply was sent by the Department to the General Secretary of the A.S.E. This sums up so fully the position of the Ministry with regard to a difficult aspect of the always difficult enforcement of " equal pay for equal work," that it is given almost verbatim.

.... " The Department does not agree that the view set out in your letter of 9 October correctly represents the intention of Circular L.2. The object of these words (" women on skilled work shall receive the rate of the tradesmen whose work they undertake ") was to protect the fully skilled tradesmen by securing that during the War the standard rate for his work should be maintained. The standard rate is the time rate, and that is the rate that is being maintained during the War. The Department required that the women should be paid the time rate of the fully skilled tradesmen immediately prior to April, 1917. The advances which have been given to tradesmen since that date have been war advances, due to and dependent on the exceptional conditions resulting from the War. The awards prescribing them have specifically stated that they are not to apply to or affect time rates while they are

---
[1] L.R. 5581.   [2] L.R. 4917.   [3] L.R. 142/5.

to be taken into account in the calculation of overtime.... There has been no intention of defeating the purpose of the Orders. On the contrary, the undertaking first contained in L.2 has been rigidly carried out."

In cases where firms spontaneously gave to their women employees the same advances as men, the Ministry did not refuse its sanction. The majority, however, of women on "skilled work" shared in the general advances of 2s. 6d. and 3s. 6d. a week given by statutory Orders to women munition workers in August and December, 1917, and not in the higher advances awarded to men by the Committee on Production.[1]

The Department maintained an attitude consistent with this in its administration of the $12\frac{1}{2}\%$ bonus given to men in the engineering trades in October and November, 1917, and L. Committee gave its full sanction to the refusal to extend this elastic bonus to women workers.[2] The question was formally considered on 9 May, 1918, by the Special Arbitration Tribunal, which had received various applications for the $12\frac{1}{2}\%$ bonus—notably from the women crane drivers who have been already described.[3] The Tribunal decided that the women's claim for the special bonus was not justified. This decision, if unsatisfactory on the basis of equal payment for equal work, was explained by an examination of the genesis of the $12\frac{1}{2}\%$ advance— an advance given to the male time worker by way of compensation for his lesser opportunities of earning compared with those of other men who were able to work on systems of payment by results. Such a consolation gift was not, it was held, required by a woman who had only entered the trade under special conditions in the process of labour dilution.

The claim of women to the same advances as the men engaged on the same work was pressed in the summer of 1918 in a number of industries outside the field of munitions. The claim was made not only to the same advances in respect of cost of living, but also to the bonuses awarded by the Committee on Production to men excluded from the original grants of $12\frac{1}{2}\%$ and $7\frac{1}{2}\%$. After the claims had led to a strike of women 'bus conductors in London, the whole question of the relations that should be maintained between the wages of men and women was referred by the Government on 29 August to a committee of enquiry presided over by Mr. Justice Atkin.

V. Women on "Men's Work" in 1918. Summary.

At the beginning of 1918, two years after the issue of L.2, the woman munition maker embarking on "men's work" had the following financial prospects before her:—

> (a) If she took a skilled artisan's work in full, a comparatively rare occurrence even in 1917, she received his standard wages in full, either on time or on any of the varieties of payment by results.

---

[1] The Special Tribunal, however, awarded the men's scale of advances to women crane drivers on several occasions in 1918.

[2] L.R. 5581.   [3] L.R. 142/100.

(b) If she took part of his work, *i.e.*, if she assisted in making the same product, even though the work was re-arranged and sub-divided so that she might specialise on a particular process, she still received the skilled worker's time and piece rates, subject to a possible deduction for a period of probation and for the cost of supervision if she needed direction or help in setting up her machine. Even if she worked more slowly than her predecessor, she was still entitled to his full time rates.

(c) If she were engaged, as the great majority of women munition workers were engaged, on machine operations involving pure repetition work or on "labouring" work in a factory or shipyard, she was entitled to a time rate of 30s. (including the war advances of 6s.) for a 48-hour or 33s. for a 54-hour week, or to the piece rates previously earned by a man, plus the 6s. bonus weekly. The latter was the more frequent and far the more remunerative alternative for her.

(d) If her work required greater skill, exertion or responsibility than that of the ordinary factory hand, without reaching that of the skilled tradesmen, her piece work rates, if she were paid by results, remained the same as those previously fixed for men, but on time work she might claim special rates of pay which would make her weekly wage some 6s. above that of her "unskilled" companions.

The woman munition maker on "men's work" was, therefore, guaranteed the opportunity of reaching a man's full earnings except in so far as she was engaged on :—

(a) Skilled work in which she could not work independently ; or

(b) Unskilled and semi-skilled work on time, in which case she might be awarded the time wages previously paid to a man, but could not claim them as a right and normally did not receive them. Further—and this was a most important exception—she did not participate in the war advances obtained by men in the organised trades but received separate, and smaller, advances under independent Orders. She also received, when employed on piece work in unskilled operations, lower overtime allowances, on account of her lower time rating, than a man would receive under similar conditions.

The consolidated Order of May, 1918, made the payment of the woman on men's work more easy to understand than it had become under the elaboration of the previous Orders. It did not, however, affect her financially, except that it prescribed a minimum rate of 6d. an hour instead of a standard weekly wage of 24s. for a week of 48 hours or less.

This was the position reached in the original munition trades after two years' statutory regulation of wages under the Munitions Act. The non-munition trades had in the same period met very similar problems to those surrounding the munition workers' wages as women were successively introduced in substitution for men ; and agreements had been duly drawn up " for the period of the War " between their employers' and workpeople's associations. Such agreements commonly stipulated that women should receive men's piece rates if employed, under similar conditions, on systems of payment by results. The much more difficult question of the time rates appropriate to the woman worker was often left unsettled. Each trade had to face its own difficulties of substitution sectionally, and could thus endeavour to insist on the safeguarding of its own established conditions. The problems, however, of payment under schemes of labour dilution in other occupations never approached the scope or the complexity which attended it in the " munitions trades," or rather in the munitions firms within those trades. The Ministry was able with effect to offer in 1917 to other Departments concerned in organising female labour its interpretation—not perhaps wholly consistent, but based on much concentrated experience—of the principle of " equal pay for equal work."

CHAPTER V.
WAGES OF WOMEN AND GIRLS ON "WOMEN'S WORK."
I. The Policy of Regulation.

DIFFICULTIES IN CONTROLLING WAGES FOR "WOMEN'S WORK."

It was only after a year's experience in organising the supply of munitions and of munitions labour, that the Ministry undertook the statutory regulation of wages for " women's work " (in the technical sense now attached to these words). The Order which fixed rates for women employed on " men's work " had already been in operation for some months, when the Department in July, 1916, took the further step of laying down standard rates for the payment of women in the heterogeneous mass of unskilled or semi-skilled occupations traditionally performed by women in the munition trades.

For purposes of administration it would clearly have been simpler to confine any regulation of wages to the women substitutes for whose introduction the Ministry was to a great extent responsible, and to let demand for labour drive up women's wages in certain underpaid industries. Meanwhile the operation of the Fair Wages Clause (which in principle secured to the employees of Government contractors either the district rate or that " commonly paid by good employers "), together with recourse to arbitration, might have been expected to secure a fair living wage in other occupations. Although the interpretation of the principle of " equal payment " for women substitutes undertaking " men's work " had produced a stream of administrative problems, yet the initial difficulties by which the Ministry was met were greater in connection with the wages of women munition workers doing work that had been done by women before the War. The reasons for this are obvious.

(i) The numbers involved in the first year of the Ministry's existence were very much larger in the case of women doing " women's work " than they were in the case of those taking the place of men, in spite of the fact that the manufacture of shell, which at this time absorbed a large proportion of the women recruited for munitions, was held to be men's work. The disturbance to industry resulting from regulation was proportionately greater. Employers who in a few months had trebled or quadrupled the number of women employed by them, were too much occupied with the technical problems of organising production to wish, even if they were recouped by the prices obtained for munition work, to change under a general statutory enactment the whole system of wage rates which they had used successfully before the War.[1]

---

[1] In the works of two firms in whose cases the Special Arbitration Tribunal issued awards on 9 April and 9 June, 1916, the number of women employees rose from 1,110 to 3,150 and from 210 to 2,040 between March and July of that year.

(ii) Circular L.2 dealt mainly with the women introduced, as part of the policy of dilution, into the engineering trades as a temporary expedient, and producing goods under abnormal conditions for the Government, which must accept high prices if these resulted from a minimum wage imposed by itself. Regulation of other trades and of work that was traditionally women's would in all probability involve changes that might be permanent after the War, and must affect quantities of women not engaged upon munitions, but working to supply the varying everyday needs of the home and foreign markets. Could the country, it was asked, afford to risk disturbing what remained of its foreign trade, after over a year of war, by suddenly raising the labour cost of goods produced for export ?

(iii) Further, the number of trades concerned in "women's work" on munitions was so great that any attempt to regulate them must involve the Ministry in all the difficulties due to variation in local custom, variation in rates and methods of remuneration, variation in the degree of skill required and training usually given, and in the difficulties due to the indifference of the woman worker, reconciled before the War, except in a few branches of the metal trades, to life at a wage level of 8s. to 15s. a week. When defining the payment of women taking men's work in whole or in part, the Ministry could to a considerable extent use men's recognised standards ; and the men's trade unions, notably the Amalgamated Society of Engineers, with occasional lapses, backed up the principle of a standard wage for women substitutes, based as far as possible on the skilled workman's district rate. With the women who were employed on "unskilled" work in electrical, chemical, rubber, soap, ammunition factories, or who packed and sorted goods in the warehouse departments of manufacturing firms, or performed any of the varied forms of press and lathe work common to the lower stages of most of the metal trades —work unchanged by the outbreak of war except perhaps in its intensity and its designation of "munitions"—low standards of wages were inherited ; and it was not, as in the newer forms of work, obviously to the interest of any strong trade union to support claims for higher rates. The National Federation of Women Workers, the union on which fell most of the brunt of the battle for increased rates at its early stages (in so far as it was carried on by organised labour at all), was not 20,000 strong in 1914.

Two other considerations obscured the position and impeded the fixing of a statutory wage for women's work.

(1) Previous experience of wage regulation for women in Great Britain had been drawn, as has been said, from the Trade Boards, which before the War secured to between 200,000 and 300,000 women workers minimum rates of from $2\frac{3}{4}$d. to $3\frac{1}{4}$d. an hour. The Ministry did not, and indeed could not adopt the procedure of the Trade Boards, either in their methods of establishing rates, or of intimating

prospective changes in wages.[1] Their "determinations," however, possibly suggested an unduly low standard when munition workers' wages were discussed, though both the type of worker and the rate of output required for munitions were different from those in many of the Trade Board occupations.

(2) The great and continuous rise of prices since the beginning of the War made necessary, as the history of men's war wages shows, a continual readjustment of standard rates of payment. By the autumn of 1915, and still more by the spring of 1916, a considerable number of war bonuses of from 1s. to 2s. a week had been given to women factory workers. These corresponded to the bonuses of 2s. and 3s. a week obtained at about this time in the same trades by male labourers, to whose imperfectly organised position, rather than to that of the skilled workers with their strong trade unions, women workers' industrial status was at all comparable. These increases, and the increase in earnings obtainable by overtime work, made both employers and workwomen slow to recognise the need for an increased standing wage on the score of cost of living alone.

REASONS FOR DEPARTMENTAL REGULATION.

Despite all these difficulties, and despite the governing condition that it existed to produce munitions, not to embark on a crusade for improving the industrial position of women, the Department was drawn into a system of regulating wages in "women's work" which in June, 1918, probably covered at least 300,000 women and girls and—with the "men's work" orders—extended to some eighty of the sub-divisions, known to the Employment Exchanges, in the metal, chemical, and "miscellaneous" trades. The Minister's system of regulation by Statutory Orders applied to employers of women munition workers in these trades[2] was, when it came into force, a natural complement to its policy about "men's work." But it was also due to the need to recruit women for munition work away from their homes, and to the sense that the Government should be a model employer directly and indirectly, or should at least secure a reasonable wage to workers from whom the leaving certificate regulations removed, in the public interest, the power to move freely from ill-paid occupations. The wages actually paid to women munition workers in the first two years of the War were very variable, sometimes high by pre-war standards, but often too low for the workers' efficiency or for industrial peace. The existing official machinery referred to above could not and was never intended to meet all the needs of all munition industries at the pace needed in

---

[1] Trade Boards had been formed in nine trades between the passing of the Trade Boards Act in 1909 and the establishment of the Ministry of Munitions. In order to bring a fresh trade under the operation of the Act, a Provisional Order confirmed by Act of Parliament had to be obtained in each case by the Board of Trade (by the Ministry of Labour since its formation). The Boards prescribed flat minimum rates for all workers throughout an industry scheduled. At least nine months must normally elapse, between the proposal of new rates and their general enactment, in order that objections from either side might be heard, and existing contracts might not be disturbed.

[2] These were chiefly controlled establishments.

war. Men munition workers at this time, if they were discontented with their wages, either obtained directions from Whitehall for their increase under the Fair Wages Clause, if this was applicable, or negotiated a rise with their employers, or, with increasing frequency, secured a general advance by an award of the Committee on Production for the whole of a "district." But women workers were far too sparsely organised for orderly negotiations of this sort, and awards, if applied to them, could only deal with the employees of individual firms *seriatim*. The Department in its wage regulation for women on their own traditional work supplied a rapid substitute for the collective bargaining to which only a small proportion of women munition workers had been trained when this policy was adopted.

Critics of the Department complained that such regulation when introduced was merely a belated fulfilment of Mr. Lloyd George's often quoted pledge on 17 July, 1915, to the effect that there " should be no sweated labour " among women coming forward to do munition work.[1] This interpretation is probably an instance of the evils of quotation apart from the context, for the Minister of Munitions was apparently speaking of women taking men's work, not of women employed on work done by them or by other women before the War, and no formal agreement such as that concluded in October and December, 1915, between the Ministry and the A.S.E. in regard to the enforcement of Circular L.2, safeguarded the position of the ill-organised women on " women's work." Doubtless from the point of view of the women themselves, especially if they were new recruits to munition making, the historic distinction between " men's work " and " women's work " was not very important, while the difference in remuneration came home to them closely. It was, however, more than once urged from within the Department that, while it was bound to secure standard wages for women substitutes, any regulation of wages for women on " women's work " should be accepted by them as an act of grace, not as the fulfilment of a pledge.[2]

II. Preliminary Stages : 1915-1916.

MEMORANDA OF THE CENTRAL MUNITION LABOUR SUPPLY COMMITTEE.

The Ministry did not definitely regulate wages for women on women's work till a year after its establishment. The first formal recommendation, however, from within the Department for the regulation of the wages of women munition workers *not* on men's work were drawn up by the Central Munitions Labour Supply Committee as early as November, 1915, just after the issue of its scale of payment for women on " men's work." One of its Memoranda, No. 44, dealt with the wages of women in the new Filling Factories, while Memorandum 43 attempted to provide for women described, in the cumbrous phrase stereotyped by future Orders, as engaged " on munition work of a class which prior to the War was recognised as women's work in districts where such work was customarily carried on," excluding those

---

[1] See Chapter I., p. 1.   [2] M.W. 92329/18.

engaged on shell filling, cartridge making, and fuse assembling. The main recommendations resembled those which were made obligatory in subsequent orders. According to both Memoranda the normal woman piece worker was to be rated at 4d. an hour, with higher time rates for the worker on dangerous processes—5½d. and 6d. an hour for fuse filling ; 6½d. and 7d. an hour for melting and running high explosives into shell. Piece prices were to be "such as to enable a woman of average ability to earn at least 33⅓%" (a fraction much discussed later) over the time worker. A flat rate time of 4d. an hour was, however, recommended in Memorandum 43, "to be paid whether the woman concerned was on time or piece work or premium bonus," *i.e.*, the distinction of ¼d. an hour between time rates for time and piece workers (4¼d. as against 4d.), which appeared in all subsequent Orders until May, 1918, and in almost all Special Tribunal awards, was not yet made.

These Memoranda were sent up for the Minister's approval on 17 November, with a covering letter from Mr. Arthur Henderson, as Chairman of the Central Munitions Labour Supply Committee, explaining the reasons why the Ministry of Munitions should embark on this extension of control.

"At first sight the subject of these recommendations may appear to be less directly connected with the Committee's work than the problems which have hitherto been dealt with by them. It was, however, found as a result of experience, that a statement dealing with this aspect of the wages of women was necessary, if women were to be employed in large numbers in Government factories and in Controlled Establishments on work which was not provided for in the Circular already issued (L.2). . . . The question of wages for women in Filling Factories other than those in the London area, or those existing before the War, was taken up by the sub-committee at the special request of Dr. Addison. The recommendations submitted have been the subject of consideration at a conference called by Dr. Addison and attended by Mr. West, Colonel Strange, members of the Health of Munition Workers Committee, and members of this Committee. I hope you will give your consent to the issue of these recommendations by the Ministry in the same form as the recommendations contained in Circulars L.2 and L.3, as I am convinced that pronouncements of this character will prove to be necessary if we are to succeed in effecting the employment of women on a large scale."[1]

Memoranda 43 and 44 were circulated for criticism to a number of the Departments concerned with munition workers' labour, and some attempt was made during December to secure statistics as to the wages actually paid at the time in Filling Factories and certain other munition factories (in the narrow sense of the word). These statistics were difficult to interpret and were drawn from a limited number of "samples," but indicated a marked discrepancy, common in most cases of unorganised labour, between rates paid by different firms in similar occupations. Thus, among the Filling Factories, an armament

---

[1] M.W. 62172/3.

firm reported that an average wage of £1 was paid for a 62-hour week in one of its numerous establishments; the Perivale National Filling Factory paid its workers, after four weeks' probation, 18s. at 18, 20s. at 19, 22s. at 20 and over; the Hayes Emergency Factory paid 20s. after training for a 49-hour week; while a firm at Erith paid 10s. 5d. to 15s. 8d. a week for filling bombs, with a normal week of 50 hours, and a Fulham factory paid 8s. to 10s. per week, with hours from 7.30 to 6.30.

In the miscellaneous munition works, rates were equally variable. Some specimens are tabulated below :—

Firm.	District.	Work done.	Wages.	Length of Week.
A.	Newcastle	Fuses, cartridge cases, etc.	Average earnings, 37s. a week (premium bonus).	53 hours with overtime.
B.	Manchester	Screwing fuse needles, machine operations.	14 yrs., 8s.; 18 yrs., 15s.; 21 yrs., 18s.; maximum, 24s. a week.	48 hrs.
C.	Dursley	Machining and viewing primers.	Average, £1 weekly.	51 hrs.
D.	Bow	Making bomb fuses.	Beginners: time rate, 14s.; piece rates, average, 19s. to 22s. 2d. a week.	55 hrs.
E.	Lincoln	Engraving, coremaking, mine assembling.	19 yrs., 11s. a week. 20 ,, 13s. ,, 21 ,, 15s. ,,	11¼ hrs. *net* per day.
F.	Croydon	Examining fuses	Recently 3d. per hr., now only 2d.	10½ hrs. *net* per day.
G.	Hayes	Gauging, etc.	3d., 3½d., and 4d. per hr.	52½ hrs. week.
H.	Liverpool	——	2d. per hr., rising to 4d., at 23.	——
J.	Coventry	——	2¼d. and 3d. per hr.	58½ hrs. when doing overtime.
K.	Stirling	Gauging and assembling fuses.	2¼d. per hr., and a service bonus of 1s. to 4s. a week.	——

Out of fifty-three firms reporting, only fourteen already paid at the rates suggested in Memorandum 43. These were widely scattered, four in Yorkshire, three in London, three in Scotland, two in Lancashire, one in the Midlands and one on the Tyne.[1]

In commenting on these statistics in a departmental minute in connection with Memorandum 43, Mr. Beveridge pointed out that the proposed rates were very much above those actually paid in many districts, and sanctioned for example in the recent agreement between the Midland Employers' Federation and the Workers' Union, under which a girl of 18 was to receive 13s. a week, as against 16s. 4d. to 18s.

---

[1] M.W. 62172/2/7. (The Co-operative Wholesale Society, consulted at the same time as to its minimum wage rates for women and girls, returned them as 5s. at 14, 13s. at 18, 17s. 6d. at 20, with a war bonus varying from 1s. to 3s. 6d..; but it pointed out that these were rates for distributive, not productive workers.)

under the draft recommendations.¹ He added :—" I do not think there is any case for making the proposed recommendations. There is no merit in having uniformity for all women's wages on munition work throughout the country. The only ground for which the recommendations could be really advanced is that they are necessary to prevent sweating. With regard to this (1) in the present state of the labour market sweating is extremely unlikely ; (2) the wage proposed of 4d. an hour is clearly unnecessarily high to prevent sweating ; (3) individual cases of sweating can be dealt with by arbitration under Part 1 of the Munitions of War Act, and should be so dealt with.

" The undertaking by the Ministry to fix women's wages generally will only lead to the diversion to other purposes of energy which is required for work more directly connected with the output of munitions."²

Further consideration of the two Memoranda was suspended during the negotiations for the Munitions of War (Amendment) Act, although the rates recommended in Memorandum 44 were adopted as the basis in the National Filling Factories as they successively engaged their staffs and settled their conditions of work. In the course, however, of its administration of Section 4 (2) of the Munitions of War Act, which entailed departmental sanction for changes of wages in controlled establishments, the Wages Section of the Ministry was often brought into contact with cases of low wages for women engaged in munitions work under pre-war conditions. Thus it was called on to sanction in November, 1915, an advance of time wages from 10s. to 14s. per week for women employed by a large firm on magnetos for the War Office and Admiralty³ ; an advance to $2\frac{3}{4}$d. per hour (and to $10\frac{3}{4}$d. per hour for toolmen) in the case of another firm at about the same time, and in the early summer of the following year increases of wages in some of the " marginal " munition trades, such as soap and porcelain, giving a weekly time rate of from 13s. to 16s. to adult workers.⁴ The readiness of women to work long—often over-long—hours at this period was, in part at least, connected with the rates of wages prevalent. The opportunity of earning higher wages was one of the grounds on which women agreed to change from an eight-hour to a twelve-hour daily shift in several instances reported to the Department in the first six months of 1916. The Department's " welfare " policy of improvement in hours and conditions of work in munition factories developed at the beginning of this year, and indirectly supplied an additional reason for control of women munition workers' wages.⁵

---

¹ See appendix V.   ² M.W. 62172/3.   ³ C.E. 253/4.

⁴ In June, the Luton Labour Advisory Board complained to the National Advisory Committee that girls in the fuse department of a local firm were paid only from 10s. to 17s. a week, and they had lately struck work owing to their low rating and also to their irregular earnings. The Department could, however, only reply that no regulation at present applied to their case.

⁵ The Sunday Labour Committee was appointed in December, 1915, and the Welfare Section was formed in January, 1916.

Powers under the Munitions of War Amendment Act.

The position of the low-paid women munition workers was brought forward in Parliament and elsewhere during the consideration of the Munitions of War Amendment Bill, and in January, 1916, Mr. Lloyd George, in answer to a question in the House of Commons by Mr. Cowan as to whether he was satisfied that women munition workers were being paid, generally speaking, a living wage, replied :—" No, I am not sure that I am. That is why further powers are being taken in the Government Amendment Bill."[1]

Section 6 of the Amendment Act of 27 January, 1916, gave power to the Ministry of Munitions to regulate women's wages in munition works which came under the leaving certificate regulations of Section 7 of the principal Act, while Section 8 authorised the Minister to constitute a Special Arbitration Tribunal (a) to arbitrate in differences concerned with women's wages or conditions of work ; (b) to advise the Department as to directions to be issued on such matters.

Effect on other Women Workers of the Issue of L.2 as Statutory Order 181, of 1916.

Under the powers given by the first of these Sections Circulars L.2 and L.3 were issued by the Ministry, and became obligatory from 28 February. The influence of Circular L.2 regulating the wages of women on " men's work " was at once felt, as the Coventry employers in their interview with the Central Munitions Labour Supply Committee in December, 1915, had pointed out would be the case, in producing demands for wages among women in other industries or departments of firms. Women fuse makers especially in many districts urged that it was unreasonable that they should earn less than women making shell in the same factory because the work of the latter was by tradition " men's," while their own had been " customarily performed by women " before the War. Thus on 17 March[2] the Labour Officer for the North East Area reported that " in this district the British Westinghouse Company (Manchester) have departments on shells, fuses and one on electrical work for war purposes. In shells I understand they are paying the girls on L.2, but in the electrical department, where work was partly done by women before, girls are being paid as formerly. This causes considerable unrest, the girls contending that while the rates in normal times may have been fair enough, they are quite inadequate at present. A good deal of unrest has been caused by the girls throughout the district having been informed that on the passing of the Munitions of War Amendment Act, £1 per week minimum would be paid to all girls of 18 and over engaged on munitions. . . .
The representative of the Women Workers' Federation tells me that she is sure, if the £1 per week minimum were applied to all female

---

[1] *Parliamentary Debates* (1916), *H. of C.*, LXXVIII. 872.
[2] M.W. 92329/6.

munition workers, she could almost guarantee their product would be doubled or trebled."[1]

After the issue of L.2 as a compulsory Order, the issue of some other statutory Order for munition workers not taking men's work became almost inevitable.

Meanwhile the Ministry could only decline to interfere directly in cases of low wages. Thus, when on 23 March, 1916, the Workers' Union wrote to complain of a firm at Camborne (Cornwall) said to be paying girls working on fuses at from 5s. to 9s. (plus 1s. 3d. bonus) a week, " contrary to L.2," the reply from the Ministry of Munitions was that as fuse work was women's work before the War, L.2 did not apply, but that any " difference " as to wages could be brought up for arbitration under Part 1 of the Munitions of War Act.[2] This was the procedure by which those reluctant to face a general statutory minimum wage hoped to avoid injustice to the ill-organised woman worker. A circular was, in response to many inquiries, drafted in March, 1916, for issue to Divisional Officers, and through them to Labour Exchange Officers, to the effect that where there was dissatisfaction as to wages among women on women's work, the women should first lodge a complaint with their employers, and then " be referred to " the Board of Trade, which would deal with the difference in accordance with the provisions of Section 8 of the Munitions of War (Amendment) Act. In other words, the dispute would, in the case of controlled and uncontrolled firms to which the leaving certificate regulations applied, be sent by the Chief Industrial Commissioner to the Special Arbitration Tribunal for settlement.

III. The Special Arbitration Tribunal and "Women's Work."

The first stages in the regulation of wages for " women's work " were secured, not by enactment but through the agency of the Special Arbitration Tribunal which was formally constituted by the Minister of Munitions in March, 1916.[3] After negotiations with the Central Munitions Labour Supply Committee it took over the latter's advisory functions with regard to wages, and at once embarked on the two lines of work laid down in its terms of reference.

---

[1] Two months earlier the Chairwoman of the " Manchester, Salford and District Women's War Interests Committee " stated :—" The average weekly wage paid in this district during this month to an adult woman working on munitions at a flat rate is under 14s. To this may be added 1s. to 1s. 6d. war bonus and a possible 3s. for overtime. We can only find five firms in this city who are paying the £1 per week flat rate minimum in L.2."—*Manchester Guardian*, 21 January, 1916.

[2] M.W. 99333.

[3] *See* Appendix VI. The Tribunal contained the Chairman of the Clyde Dilution Commissioners, then engaged in securing the introduction of female labour into engineering works on the Clyde, the Chairman of the Trade Boards, an ex-factory inspector, the secretary of the Engineering Employers' Federation, a member of the A.S.E. Executive Council, and the assistant secretary of the Women's Trade Union League, with a member of the Wages Section as secretary ; both the women members were members of Trade Boards. The Tribunal therefore possessed a great amount of concentrated experience of the conditions affecting women's industrial position.

(1) ADVICE.

On 10 March Dr. Addison had written to the Chairman of the Central Munitions Labour Supply Committee as follows :—

"Mr. Lloyd George proposes at an early date to refer to the appropriate tribunal the question of issuing any directions as to wages of women on munitions, not covered by L.2 ; the ground of memoranda 43 and 44" (as to the fate of which the Central Munitions Labour Supply Committee had inquired) "will be covered by such a reference." On 24 March the Tribunal was formally asked to advise the Minister :—

(1) As to the payment of girls under eighteen on men's work, and
(2) "Whether any directions should be given by the Minister under Section 6 of the Act fixing a minimum time rate for women or girls engaged on munitions work of a class which prior to the War was recognised as women's work in districts where such work was customarily carried on either generally or for particular trades or districts, or in the alternative, whether any question relating to the remuneration of women so engaged should be dealt with as and when it arises."

(2) AWARDS.

While considering these questions, the Tribunal in its other capacity was met by demands for arbitration on a number of "differences." A number of outstanding applications for hearings were referred to it *en bloc* by the Board of Trade, as soon as the appointment of the Tribunal was announced.

The first case on which it published an award was that brought by the National Federation of Women Workers against Armstrong's gauge, fuse and lyddite works at Newcastle. Here a specially organised local branch of the National Federation of Women Workers—strong for a women's Trade Union, since it contained 5,000 to 6,000 members—asked for a time and premium bonus minimum rate of 5½d. an hour. The Tribunal on 29 March, 1916, awarded 4½d. an hour to both time and piece workers (this was different from its later practice), with an extra ½d. an hour for the workers in danger zones and special rates for young workers. The Trade Union concerned congratulated its members on these results as a triumph of organisation, although its demands had not been wholly met.[1]

The next award, in settlement of a dispute between the National Federation of Women Workers and Eley Bros., Edmonton, laid down the terms which were subsequently crystallized in Orders 447 and 618, and formed a precedent for many other awards until these Orders were issued. Its terms were :—

Time rates guaranteed to piece workers.

For workers aged 18 and over .. 4½d. an hour .. 4d. an hour.
  ,,   ,,   ,,   17 ,,   ,, .. 4d.   ,,   .. 3½d. ,,
  ,,   ,,   ,,   16 ,,   ,, .. 3½d.   ,,   .. 3d.   ,,
  ,,   ,,   ,,   15 ,,   ,, .. 3d.   ,,   .. 2½d. ,,

with ½d. an hour extra in the danger zone.

---

[1] Cf. *Woman Worker*, April, 1916.

WAGES OF WOMEN & GIRLS ON "WOMEN'S WORK" 65

Similar awards were given in the cases of the Sterling Telephone and Electric Co., Dagenham, Essex, of Vickers, Dartford, and of Aerators, Edmonton (9/4/16). In the case of Messrs. Siemens' Electric Cable Works, Woolwich, alone, a time rate of 4d. an hour at 18, 3d. an hour from 16 to 18, 2½d. an hour from 14 to 16, was made for girls on rubber and braiding work. Practically the same terms as those of the Eley, Edmonton, case were awarded in the case of Messrs. Creed Bille, Croydon ; the Gramophone Co., Hayes ; Bradbury & Co., Oldham, Rudge-Whitworth, Coventry ; Coventry Ordnance Works, Coventry (19/6/16). All these cases were brought by the National Federation of Women Workers, while the Workers' Union, which had just concluded a general agreement with two employers' associations for women munition workers in the Black Country, extended its activities to Coventry and obtained on the same day a successful award, almost on the same lines, in the case of thirteen Coventry firms—an award which subsequently turned the flank of the position of the Birmingham and Black Country Employers, as represented by the Midland Employers' Federation, when they complained of the wage rates established in July by Order 447.

SHOULD THERE BE A FLAT RATE FOR " WOMEN'S WORK"?

Meanwhile the Tribunal was deliberating on the recommendations to be made with regard to the extension of the regulation of women's wages.[1] Should differential rates according to trade and locality be recommended for women munition workers, in order to maintain existing customs ? Should the Ministry evade the question of fixing time rates and their relation to piece rates, by prescribing, on the analogy of the Trade Boards, a minimum hourly earning, leaving the fixing of higher rates to be dealt with locally, if at all ? Both these questions suggested methods of treatment containing obvious advantages. They were considered in detail, but were, with some reluctance, answered in the negative, on the ground that employers needed definite directions at an early date as to the wages to be paid for munition work, that it would take too long to deal separately with all the trades involved, and that it was, as the Trade Boards had found after prolonged investigation, difficult to base any logical differentiation of women's rates on local standards, because so many external influences, such as the choice of employment available and the prevailing level of men's earnings, affected the wages accepted by the industrial woman, whose conventional payment was comparatively little affected by local variations in the cost of living.

It would have greatly diminished the subsequent opposition to the application of the Ministry's system of regulation, if some distinction in its terms could have been made according to the trade and locality dealt with, and it would have also removed the necessity felt by the Department of excluding certain trades and firms for a considerable period from any wage regulation. At the time, however, any policy of differentiation was clearly unworkable. It was essential to introduce regulation promptly, if at all, for the demands of the

---
[1] Cf. verbatim reports of the special sessions of the Tribunal, June, 1916.

supply departments were expanding with great rapidity, and more women's work was constantly coming under the elastic definition of "munitions." The Tribunal, therefore, decided that a flat national standard rate for all munition workers on "women's work" was the only alternative, and on 24 June formulated its recommendations, which were subsequently embodied in Orders 447 and 618. These were based partly on the industrial knowledge of its own members. No formal consultations with representative employers or workpeople were held before the issue of the recommendations. The hourly rates put forward were as follows :—4½d. for time workers, 4d. for piece workers, with 3d. and 2½d. respectively for girls under 16 (*i.e.*, they were a little higher than those suggested in the previous autumn by the Central Munitions Labour Supply Committee) ; time wages were to be guaranteed to piece workers, and piece rates were to be such as normally to produce 33⅓ per cent. above time rates ; overtime, night, and Sunday work were to be paid for on the same conditions as applied to men in engineering establishments in the district.

IV. Order 447 : Regulation by Statutory Order.

Order 447, involving the Ministry in the first stages of control and influence over women's wages as such throughout the country, was issued on 6 July, to take effect from 17 July.

Certain points specially are to be noted about the first issue of this Order.[1]

(1) It was applied only to a limited number of establishments, 1,373 in all. It covered, however, at this early stage, "90,910 women and 20,758 girls in private establishments, besides many thousands in national factories," according to the estimate of the Wages Section. It was applied (with 136 exceptions, 11 of which were in Ireland and 125 in rural districts in England) to all controlled establishments of the following classes :—

Armaments, ammunition, ordnance ; explosives ; Filling Factories (except one lately opened) ; mechanical, marine, constructional, engineering works ; machine toolmaking ; shipbuilding and repairing ; printing and textile machinery ; motors and cycles ; also certain iron and steel and aviation works, known to be concerned with engineering.

Each establishment to which the Order was applied received a copy of the Order with its name individually scheduled.

(2) It established time rates of 4½d. and 4d. for women, and 3d. and 2½d. for girls, according to whether they were employed on time or piece work. These were the rates recommended, as has been said, by the Special Tribunal.

(3) It contained, according to the precedents laid down by the Tribunal awards, clauses guaranteeing fixed time payments to piece workers and premium bonus workers (unable from

---

[1] M.W. 92329/18.

shortage of material or low pricing to earn up to the time workers' rates), and forbidding the carrying forward of debit balances of wages from week to week. These points were raised as contentious questions in their own case by men munition workers, when urged to accept systems of payment by results for their own work in the following year, and the operation of the women's wage Orders was quoted as a favourable precedent. These provisions remained unchanged in successive editions of the Order.

(4) It did not give effect to the recommendations of the Special Arbitration Tribunal on overtime rates and the relation to be borne by payment for piece work to time wages. The omissions and limitations in the Order, much criticised later, were deliberate. Those responsible for its enforcement knew well—and the almost interminable negotiations over payments for the postponed summer holidays brought this home at the time—that there were innumerable differences of local and trade custom as to overtime and other special payments for women, and as to the proportions between piece and time rates, and it was decided not to intervene at this stage in these questions, or in the detailed regulation of a large number of trades which were as much concerned in commercial as in munition work. Mr. Aves, with his experience as Chairman of Trade Boards, had emphasised the difficulties of such interference in June, when the recommendations of the Tribunal were sent to the Minister. It was further pointed out by Mr. Beveridge and Mr. J. C. Smith that the Department did not possess at the time, and could not be expected to possess, the knowledge of rapidly changing industrial conditions necessary for the application of a detailed and comprehensive Order. The primary object of the Ministry was to obtain munitions, and it was in no way clear that a general wages Order rashly issued might not "impede rather than promote the purposes for which the Ministry was intended."[1]

V. Reception of Order 447.

1. THE CRITICISMS OF ORGANISED WORKERS.

Order 447, issued under these conditions and with these limitations, was received with little enthusiasm. On the one side the National Federation of Women Workers demanded and obtained an interview with Dr. Addison, at which they expressed their "profound disappointment" at its terms, for the following reasons :—

(1) The wages prescribed were fixed rates, whereas they should have been minima. (Such standard wages were "worthy only of the Elizabethan period.") Women now earning above these rates might have their wages cut down as a result.

(2) No relation was laid down between piece rates and time rates. A 4d. time rate was prescribed for piece workers,

[1] M.W. 29329/18.

but, if no proportion were fixed between this and the rates paid for piece work, it would obviously be possible for the employer to exploit the worker by cutting down piece rates until they produced lower weekly earnings than those of the time workers.

(3) No provision was made for special rates for overtime and night work, nor for allowances, *e.g.*, for "waiting time,"[1] which had been carefully inserted in most of the Tribunal awards.

(4) The Order was applied to only a limited number of establishments, and omitted most of those whose wages were specially unsatisfactory, such as the electrical engineering and rubber works. "Women on munition work," said Miss Macarthur, "had awaited regulation of wages for a year, since Mr. Lloyd George's 'promises' on 17 July, 1915; the Federation's consistent demand was for 5d. an hour as a minimum, with piece rate earnings at least 33½ per cent. above this rate, and with safeguards for overtime, etc., and this order was satisfactory neither in principle nor in detail."

In reply to the deputation, Dr. Addison explained the grounds for the limited and experimental application of Order 447 and undertook that the Department would consider its extension as rapidly as the necessary inquiries would allow; he undertook also that consideration should be given whether some formula as to piece work rates could be devised, and whether instructions as to the payment of overtime, Sunday, and waiting time allowances in some conformity with trade customs could be issued; and he promised to send out instructions to prevent the use of the Order to reduce existing rates paid to individuals or to special classes of workers. The awards of the Special Tribunal, on which this Order was largely based, had equally prescribed fixed rates, not minima, for time workers. It was not intended that the rates laid down should necessarily and invariably be maxima, though (it was pointed out) except in the case of special individuals,[2] the sanction of the Ministry would have to be obtained for higher payments.[3]

SUPPLEMENTS TO ORDER 447. (L.67 AND ORDER 618.)

In fulfilment of these undertakings, two supplementary papers were despatched by the Ministry within the next month.

(i) A ruling by the Minister, issued as L.67, on the interpretation of Clause 8 just referred to, which removed all possibility that the

---

[1] This had been secured to the "men's work" group, by Clause 2 of L.2 which prescribed payment at the rate of 15s. a week for women "prevented from working owing to breakdown, air raid or other cause beyond their own control," "unless they were sent home." The stipulation was of much importance to the woman worker, in whose frequently irregular periods of employment "waiting time," both before and during the War, might mean a serious loss to an often scanty income. The Trade Boards Act of 1916 contained (Section 8) special provision for payment during such "awaiting time."

[2] Clause 8 of Order 447 allowed a limited discretion as to payments. "The foregoing rates shall not operate to prejudice the position of any person who has better terms and conditions, nor prevent employers from recognising special ability or responsibility."

[3] M.W. 92329/6.

WAGES OF WOMEN & GIRLS ON "WOMEN'S WORK" 69
CH. V]

Order as a whole might be used as an excuse for diminishing wages, as the trade union had suggested. "The intention of Paragraph 8 of this Order is that no person who has better terms and conditions than those prescribed by the Order shall be prejudiced either by a reduction in her existing rate of wages, or by her displacement by another person at any less rate of wages. And it is intended that the rates of wages customarily paid to any class of women or girls for particular work shall not be reduced."

(ii) A new Order, No. 618, which supplied the omissions of Order 447, by prescribing (1) that piece work prices and premium bonus basis times should be such as to enable a woman or girl of ordinary ability to earn at least $33\frac{1}{3}\%$ over her time rate, except in the case of an establishment where an application that this provision should be dispensed with was approved by the Minister, and (2) that additional payment for overtime, night shift, Sunday or holiday work should be made " in accordance with the custom of the establishment or district for the class of workpeople concerned in cases where such a custom exists," or, in the absence of established custom, " in accordance with the directions of the Ministry."

This Order, dated 13 September, was to take effect from 2 October.

The two Orders 447 and 618 were issued early in September to a large number of controlled establishments in addition to those which had received the first Order in July, with an intimation that the Ministry proposed to apply them to the establishments in question unless some special and valid reason against this could be shown by 18 September. " In such a case, the Minister would determine whether the circumstances were so peculiar as to justify him in referring the matter to the Special Arbitration Tribunal."

The two Orders together did not give all that this comparatively small body of "organised" workers demanded, and they left even those women and girls to whom they applied in a markedly inferior position to those engaged in " men's work." They represented, however, a distinct step both in the principle of State interference with wages, and in the practical work of standardising women's rates.

2. THE EMPLOYERS' ATTITUDE.

Meanwhile employers protested against Order 447 with vigour equal to that shown by the representatives of the workers whom it was intended to benefit. Thus the Chairman of the Central Council of the Association of Controlled Firms (Mr. W. L. Hichens) wrote to the Department on 9 September that its members had heard only on the previous day of the proposal of the Ministry to extend Order 447 to Controlled Establishments outside the engineering industries, unless good cause could be shown against this by 17 September. Very many firms to whom the Order was thus proposed were engaged on munitions work to a limited extent only of their output. The Order would have a most disturbing effect on their munition and non-munition work and on conditions generally in their industry and district. Could not the date at least be postponed, and could not opportunity be given for detailed protest against "the arbitrary course adopted by the Department"?[1] A reply on 23 September, after some intervening correspondence, explained that the Ministry was anxious to interfere as little as possible with the invaluable services of the controlled establishments, that the settlement of the wages of women and girl munition workers was urgent, but that protests against the application of the Order might still be made by letter. The Council accordingly undertook to instruct its members to forward their objections as soon as possible. Some hundreds of protests were received, and dealt with.

Other urgent protests were received from the Midland Employers' Federation and the Sheffield Engineering Employers' Association, which sent deputations to Dr. Addison on 13 and 24 September, when they expressed their criticisms of the Order with much pungency. Both these groups represented large employers of woman's labour, in a great variety of trades,[2] which in spite of alterations in the actual goods produced—helmets instead of dish-covers, aeroplane parts instead of cycle accessories, etc.—perpetuated the conditions of women's industrial life before the War. Such conditions even if accepted by the worker without apparent discontent, were from many points of view unsatisfactory.

Previous Agreements with the Workers' Union.

In addition to the extra wage cost involved by the Orders, there was an additional difficulty in that the larger of the two Associations, that of the Midland Employers, had in the course of the last year made successive agreements with the Workers' Union for scales of wages to women or girl munition workers, and its members were naturally reluctant that these should be set aside by Government regulation. It might fairly be urged that the results of collective bargaining were being set aside, in a way that would normally not be contemplated by a Department dealing with negotiations between organised employers and workmen.

Agreements between federated employers and women in the munition trades have been so rare that they deserve record. In the autumn of 1915,[3] while the Ministry was hesitating as to the adoption of the recommendations of the Central Munitions Labour Supply Committee, a series of agreements were drawn up by the Workers' Union,[4] the largest trade society dealing with both men and women workers in the munitions trades. The first was negotiated with the Midland Employers' Federation for the Birmingham Area on 10 November, 1915. It was followed by a similar agreement on 18 April, 1916, with the Manchester District Engineering Employers' Association, and was extended, with modifications, to the Black Country in May, 1916.

---

[1] M.W. 92329/17.

[2] A year later the Midland Employers' Federation, recently reconstituted as the "National Employers' Federation," contained sections for no less than 40 branches of the metal trades (M.L. 12214).

[3] M.W. 40941l.   [4] See Appendix V for text of agreement.

These agreements fixed wages at 16s. (Birmingham), 18s. (Manchester), and 15s. (Black Country) for women of 21 and over; 11s., 14s., and 12s. at 18; and 7s., 7s., and 6s. as starting wages for girls of 14 (about whose over-payment on Government work the employers felt strongly), and provided that piece rates should be settled on the assumption that the piece worker should be able to earn 25%—not, as in the Ministry's Order, 33⅓%—more than the time rate.[1] These rates for a 53- or 54-hour week obviously produced much lower earnings than those prescribed by Orders 447 and 618, earnings lower in some cases than the minima fixed by the Trade Boards, though the employers claimed that they represented local advances commensurate with the rise in the cost of living, and that it was unnecessary and unfair to supersede " agreements made so recently with a reputable trade union."[2]

GROUNDS OF COMPLAINT.

Both groups of employers accordingly complained of the issue of Order 447 on the following common grounds :—(i.) the want of proper consultation with themselves, and the short notice at which they were called upon to readjust their standards of payment; (ii.) the losses on running contracts, and disadvantage to themselves as against uncontrolled or foreign competitors ; (iii.) the excessive increases to young girls and consequent trouble with boy employees ; (iv.) the difficulty of distinguishing between munitions and non-munitions work, or of paying for the two classes at different rates in the same establishment.

Apart from these objections, common to employers in other districts, the statements made by the deputations illustrated the general uncertainty throughout the country, in times equally of peace and of war, about the basis on which women's wages should be fixed, and the extent to which the woman or girl worker ought to be financially independent. The speakers' arguments are, therefore, summarised at some length.

---

[1] Considerable bitterness against the Workers' Union, on account of these agreements, notably that secured at Manchester, was shown by other unions interested in women's organisation, and was recorded by the trade organs of the Amalgamated Society of Engineers and the National Federation of Women Workers. The Workers' Union, it was argued, was accepting a lower standard of living than that desired by the women's society for women on women's work, and was encouraging its members employed on the debatable ground between " men's work " and " women's work " to accept less than the rates authorised by L.2. In its *Record*, for August, 1916, the Workers' Union defended itself with vigour. " The crime we are guilty of is that we have improved women's conditions. We did not wait till the babel of discussion had evolved some plan, but we said to the others, ' go on talking, but the women need something whilst your interminable wrangles proceed ; and we will leave ourselves free to advocate all you are advocating whilst we are receiving.' That was the meaning of the Manchester agreement. It put shillings per week in the individual girl's and woman's pocket—and they needed it. And still they are free to go forward and obtain any other advantage which accrues from statutory orders. The other policy adopted by other unions was to go on talking, and whilst the talk was going on the money was in the employers' pocket." This war of words is not without interest in the process of trade union development during the War, and the relation of skilled to unskilled organised workers.

[2] M.W. 92329/17.

1. Deputation from Sheffield Employers.

There were present at this conference on 28 September, Dr. Addison and Mr. J. C. Smith, for the Ministry, and the presidents of the six local trade associations of the File, Machine Knife, Saw, Cutlery, Edge Tool Manufacturers, and the Master Silversmiths. They represented 259 firms concerned with the "light trades" of Sheffield.

The Secretary of the Chamber of Commerce, who accompanied the deputation, explained that only 10 per cent. to 20 per cent. of its members' work was for munition purposes, but that the "reflex action" of Order 447, if enforced, would go right through the trades concerned. If firms were called on to pay at the rates recently laid down for the small proportion of their work which was definitely "munitions," the whole of their work and workers would be affected. It would be impossible to separate the girls making munitions for these firms from those doing other work. "It is not likely," said the speaker, "that the latter would stand by and see some others getting an eclectic wage while they have to work without it . . . What we all object to about Order 447 is that it has obviously been drawn up, as so many of these documents are, I am sorry to say, in these days, by gentlemen who really have not any notion of the circumstances." The firms represented were already carrying on their general trade under great difficulties ; their selling prices were, in September, 1916, much what they were before the War, since the Americans were trading against them as keenly as possible in South America, South Africa, and Australia, and English firms were "trading with restraint as regards prices and conditions," because they were during the War working for good-will at a later date, in order, if possible, to capture trade. Increased labour cost would, therefore, have very serious effects on the prospects of the industries represented.

The speaker explained the many advantages provided by these trades for the women workers of Sheffield. "The employment of all these girls commences on their leaving school and with a few exceptions it ceases at marriage. I do not want to claim that these trades are benefactors, but they cannot help being benefactors in this sense, that the children employed by them learn orderly habits when they leave school and work on for the same firm until they are married, both in "productive" and "non-productive" work. All the work of the non-productive type is easy ; the hours are short and the work is conducted in warehouses which are light and airy and in which everything is healthy. As regards the workshop women's labour, that is also the lighter part of such work, and is excellently looked after as regards hygiene." "These girls—of whom there are 10,000 to 15,000—are as happy as queens." Their wages, he added, ranged from 5s. at fourteen (or thirteen since the removal of restrictions under the Education Act) to 10s. at eighteen ; for those aged eighteen to twenty-one, wages rose to about 16s. and in some cases higher, with a War bonus of 1s. to 1s. 6d. in many instances. The hours were 43 to 48 per week. If girls and women were paid at the rates laid down in Order 447, they would earn more in 47 or 48 hours than boys who were going to become skilled tradesmen, and were engaged on productive work, since a boy would start work at thirteen or fourteen at 6s. for a 53-hour week, rising to about 13s. at eighteen. The resulting friction might be imagined. Such a rise in wages would spread through the whole workshop to all the girls engaged in the same type of work whether for munitions or not, and thence to the boys and men. These girls, if not self-supporting, " do their work and have a bit of money in their pockets, all the time when otherwise they would be out of employment, and they are contributing very seriously to the household expenses, but they are not keeping house. There is not much married women's work in Sheffield."

If Order 447 were applied, it would be necessary to dismiss some girls and make the others work harder. Regulation would bear specially hardly on controlled firms if applied to them, because, as regards their general trade, they would be handicapped as against their competitors. The increased wages would permeate the whole place, and the burden would be put upon the backs of the lighter trades, and it would be a most severe burden.

" Is there any necessity " asked the speaker, " to apply Order 447 to the lighter trades represented before you to-day ? Where is the urgency ? Everybody was satisfied. Is it not reasonable that our light trades should be exempt from this order on the ground that there is no pressing necessity of any kind for it, and that everybody is well satisfied that the work is, even if it is a little patriarchal, very useful to these people ? It may be right to apply Order 447, like L.2, to the substitution of women for men and boys, but it is not necessary or reasonable, in the trades of which 80% is done in severe competition to-day, to impose a heavy advance in labour rates . . . . I put it to you that you should exempt these trades from the operation of the Circular, and if anyone wants to raise wages they must raise them, not on munitions grounds but on the ground of ordinary supply and demand. If not, a special local enquiry should be held, for the Order would affect these different trades very differently. It would bear specially hardly upon the silver plating trade and the silver trades, which have already suffered from the War, though they have given you a good deal of relief in the way in which they have tackled matters like helmet pressing and so forth, which was quite new to their trade. We think Sheffield is taking a very high and strong part in munitions work, and we are rather proud of ourselves. Anything we can do, you have only to ask us to do and we will try and perform it."

Discussion then turned on the points whether cutlery and other light trades were technically " munitions," and as such, subject to wages regulation; and whether, if so, Order 447 must be made applicable to all the firms in these trades, whether they were or were not controlled.

Dr. Addison finally promised to inquire from the Ministry's legal advisers and from the Board of Trade about these points, to report, and, if necessary, to hold a local inquiry. He thought that with the possible exception of files and edge tools, none of the work represented by the members of the deputation was "munitions" work, and in any case that Section 7 of the Munitions Act had not been applied in the trades concerned, so that Order 447 was inoperative. He had always been anxious to limit the application of the term "munitions." He would have these two points cleared up, and if that was not sufficient, would appoint someone to hold a special inquiry as to local rates of wages and conditions of employment as had been suggested.

"If, however," he concluded, "you have a large industrial area, as Sheffield is, with a large class of munition works—proper munition works without a doubt—to which the Order is applicable, there would have to be a very good case made as to why we should not apply it to munition workers generally in that place. We will first state definitely as to whether these firms are controlled, and then we will give you a definite reply as to whether the Order is to apply."

2. DEPUTATION FROM THE MIDLAND EMPLOYERS' FEDERATION.

The Midland Employers' Federation had in June sent a deputation to the Special Arbitration Tribunal, urging that it should be heard before any wage Order was issued, since it had within the past fortnight drawn up a special agreement with the Workers' Union, fixing a weekly minimum of 15s. for adult time workers in the Black Country on women's work "for the duration of the War," and that it had special claims for consideration, both because its members employed jointly the largest number of women on "women's" munition work in the country,[1] and because, unlike most manufacturers of munitions, they had dealt with women in the engineering trades long before the War. The deputation withdrew unsatisfied on this occasion, after unfavourable comparisons made by a member of the Tribunal between the rates agreed on by the Federation and those laid down by the Trade Boards for sweated workers, e.g., in the hollow-ware trade.[2] It had since then carried on an acrimonious correspondence with the Ministry with regard, first, to the composition of the Tribunal, and second, to the necessity for consulting employers of experience rather than officials before making wage regulations. These points were repeated at great length by their representatives at a Conference on the application of Order 447 at the Ministry of Munitions on 13 September, 1916, when Dr. Addison, with Mr. Primrose and Mr. J. C. Smith, met Mr. Harris Spencer, President of the Federation, with ten of its members. Mr. Spencer first complained strongly of the nature of the special tribunal for women's wages. The members of his association "would rather settle with the people than appear before the Tribunal, which in their opinion was not constituted so as to be

---

[1] Cf. Special Arbitration Tribunal hearing, 5 June, 1916. A year later, on munition work alone, approximately six times as many women and girls were employed in the controlled establishments of this district on "women's" as on "men's" work (M.M. 116 returns).
[2] M. W. 87395.

impartial."[1] In Birmingham they had settled with the representatives of the Trade Unions rather than subject themselves to appearing before this Tribunal. Order 447 had, he maintained, been issued like a good many other things since the War, without conference with the employers at all. It was absolutely impossible to distinguish between munitions and non-munitions work within a controlled establishment in such a way as to apply two rates of wages to women workers, and Order 447, if applied to women engaged on commercial work, would be "one of the most serious things ever done by the Ministry of Munitions." The rates established by Order 447 might apply under special circumstances such as those at Coventry,[2] where large numbers of women were being imported for munitions work and cost of living for such workers was high, but in Birmingham and the Black Country perfectly satisfactory agreements already existed between employers and employed. The increases suggested in this Order would amount in some cases to from 50 per cent. to 100 per cent. ; for girls of 14 it would be over 100 per cent., as they normally began at 6s., with 7s. 6d. a week at 15, and 8s. 6d. at 16 for a 54-hour week ; whereas the lowest rate prescribed in " 447 " was 13s. 6d. Women at 18, whose day rate was 12s., would now be raised to £1. The Order would create much discontent among boys, whose wages had not been proportionately raised, and cost of production would be indirectly as well as directly increased both in controlled establishments and in those which were partly controlled and partly uncontrolled. Midland Employers felt that they had had little consideration from the Minister since the War began, and thought that the time had come when they should be called into counsel.

The speaker concluded with an appeal to the Minister :—" We do ask you to get rid of this Special Tribunal, which is not satisfactory to us at all, or we ask you to dilute it so as to bring it into an impartial condition. We not only want you to withdraw this Order 447, but we want you not to issue such Orders in future without consultation with us."

Later speakers drew attention to other difficulties. Thus, at a very large Birmingham works in which 12,000 girls were employed most satisfactorily, in the majority of cases on a system of payment by results, their piece work earnings were much above, although their time rating was below, the level prescribed by the Order. If, however, the high time rates of Order 447 were fixed, and piece work earnings

---

[1] The only member of the Tribunal who could be held definitely to represent the employers' point of view (although in theory no member of the Tribunal was definitely "representative" of any party interest) was the Secretary of the Engineering Employers' Federation, which admittedly had much less pre-war experience of women's employment than had the Federation of Midland Employers. The Tribunal contained two Trade Union members.

[2] It had been pointed out to the Federation that the group of awards made in June by the Special Tribunal with regard to a number of important Coventry firms, had been on the same lines as those of Order 447, that their application must almost inevitably spread to Birmingham and the Black Country, and that opposition from these districts to the application of Order 447 was therefore misdirected.

had to be one-third above them, the whole basis of payment would be upset. Again it was argued that 90 per cent. of the women munition workers in the district lived at home, and therefore did not need the same high rates as imported workers ; and also that with much of the local trade, made to stock, it was impossible to tell if it was for the War Office or Ministry of Munitions, ultimately or not, *i.e.*, whether it was or was not " munitions " work and therefore subject to regulation.

Dr. Addison, in reply, first defended the Ministry warmly against the charge of neglecting the interests of employers, and then explained and justified in detail the composition of the Tribunal. He admitted that the scale of wages for the girls under 16 needed reconsideration. As to the older workers, " if you can show me," said Dr. Addison, " a munition contract which does not allow the employer to pay women more than 12s. a week, I will revise the contract." The Ministry would welcome a suggestion for distinguishing in the application of the Order, between " munitions " and " non-munitions " work, a distinction often exceedingly difficult to make in practice.

The delegates repeated their antipathy to the constitution of the Tribunal, but indicated that a probationary period before the payment of higher wages might partially solve the immediate question of the wages Order. Many of the " women " employed were, urged the deputation, very little more than children, who had not yet learnt to speed up and wasted their own and their employers' time, and the scale of wages proposed was quite inappropriate, unless substantial modifications were introduced in their case.

The Minister undertook to consider the points which had been brought forward and the conference closed.

CHAPTER VI.
" WOMEN'S WORK ": THE EXTENSION OF REGULATION.

I. Recommendations of the Special Tribunal.

The problems raised by the deputations described in the previous chapter were, on 3 October, 1916, referred by the Minister of Munitions to the Special Arbitration Tribunal, together with the protests sent in by firms which had been warned of the probable application of Order 447 to their works. The Tribunal was asked to advise whether Orders 447 and 618 should be applied in their entirety, or, if not, with what modifications, to controlled establishments in the following trades :—

1.*(a) Electrical Engineering, (b) Telegraphic Engineering, (c) the manufacture of Electric and Telegraphic Accessories.
2.*The Wire Rope Cable and Hemp Rope Trades.
3. (a) The Bolt and Nut Trade, (b) the Screw Trade.
4. The manufacture of Saws, Files, Cutlery and similar articles.
5.*The manufacture of Tubes.
6. The manufacture of Tin Boxes.

On October 17 this reference was extended to the following trades :

7.*Iron and Steel Works.
8.*(a) Iron and Brass Foundries, (b) Lead Works, (c) Copper Works.
9. " Sundry Mechanical Engineering Works," and the manufacture of sundry Mechanical Products.
10.*The manufacture of Scientific Instruments.
11.*Sundry Explosive Works.
12. Sundry Aviation Works.
13. Miscellaneous : (a) Woodwork, (b) Pottery, (c) Hollow-ware, (d) Paper,* (e) Rubber,* (f) Asbestos,* (g) Chemicals, (h) Soap, (i) Oil and Seed Crushing, (j) Glasswork, (k) Silversmiths,* (l) Emery,* (m) Mica, (n) Aluminium.

This truly miscellaneous collection of trades included those firms which had claimed exemption from the operation of the proposed uniform wages Order on grounds of special difficulties of industrial organisation or of local custom.[1]

---

[1] C.E. 1198/4B.—The objections raised by firms show the real difficulty of their position, in some cases. Thus a rubber firm in a small country town based its protest on the following grounds : The adoption of the Orders would raise rates for girl workers ¾d. per hour above their present rates, which produced on time work weekly earnings varying from 7s. plus 1s. 6d. war bonus for beginners of 14 to 14s. with 3s. bonus for the adult worker. This rate was already ½d. above the Workers' Union rate for the district. An advance would involve a

If the Ministry were to apply regulation to women's wages in all these trades, it would be invading the greater portion of the metal and engineering industries of the country, hitherto only in part affected by the application of L.2, together with the rapidly developing chemical industry and a group of varied occupations in which women had for many years been employed, but with the industrial conditions of which the Department had hardly come into contact, except through applications for sanction—often almost formal—to advances of men's wages by the firms included in them. It would also be cutting across trade agreements in certain cases, such as that of the Midland Employers' Federation, already often quoted, and of the hollow-ware and pottery employers, while it might also appear to supersede the Trade Board rates scheduled in the hollow-ware and tin box trades.

After some twenty meetings, at which representative employers and workers were heard in person, and detailed consideration was given to the protests sent in by the firms concerned, the Tribunal reported to the Minister as follows.

(a) Orders 447 and 618 should be applied to the trades marked with an asterisk in the preceding list, including certain silversmithing and mechanical engineering firms specially scheduled.

(b) They should *not* be applied to the following trades: Bolts, nuts, and screws; tin boxes, so far as they were subject to Trade Board rates; pottery, fire brick and fire clay; the paper mill board and paper mill trade; soap, oil and seed crushing, glass, glassworks, emery, aluminium.

(c) Woodworking should be brought under Order 621 issued for women on aircraft work.

(d) With regard to saws and files (No. 4 in the list), a sub-committee of the Tribunal would visit Sheffield, where this trade was mostly carried on, to decide whether Orders 447 and 618 should be applied to it.

---

similar advance to men workers, and would greatly complicate the system of premium bonus in use. Finally, and most important, only 45% of their work was " munitions."

C.E. 1153/4B.—Another rubber company, specially skilled in postponing the adoption of wages Orders for those of its 2000 workers employed either on " men's " or on " women's " work, wrote from Scotland complaining that it was impossible to comply with the Order, especially in its directions as to the ratio between piece and time earnings. Several thousand piece rates were in force in the establishment, and a fresh assessment of these would be most laborious and costly. In this case also, a large proportion of the firm's work was for private, not Government, orders.

C.E. 4946/4.—A firm of soapmakers, known for its detailed care for its workers, explained that its rate of pay for its women workers when on time work varied from 7s. at 14 to 17s. at 18 for a 45-hour week. This arrangement had been found to work perfectly.

C.E. 2776/4.—A small leather working firm at Birmingham asked for exemption on the ground that only 34% of its work was for Government, that its private trade must continue after the War, and that its existing wage rates ranged from 6s. for beginners to from 17s. to 19s. for adult women. These are typical of the representations made by protesting employers.

The Tribunal also made the following recommendations :—

(1) That lower time rates—2d. and 2½d. an hour guaranteed when on piece work, and 2½d. and 3d. when on time work—should be prescribed for girls of 14 and 15 respectively. (This met one of the objections raised at the two conferences described above.)

(2) That "there should be a probationary period of 1 month, 2 months, and 3 months, for workers of 18 and over, of 16 and under 16 respectively, during which ½d. an hour less should be paid." (This deduction during the probationary period had been agreed to in the case of the British Thomson Houston Co., of Rugby, brought by the National Federation of Women Workers in June, 1916, and in the award for the Hendon Aircraft Manufacturing Co., in the previous April. It corresponded to the probationary period of 13 weeks for women on skilled men's work which had lately been hotly debated before the Tribunal.)

(3) That in certain outlying districts, ranging from Cornwall to the Kyles of Bute, the rates should be reduced by ¼d. or ½d. an hour.

This proposal to grade rates downward represented an attempt to take into consideration local custom and cost of living when fixing rates of wages. A triple classification of districts and firms for purposes of payment had been considered by the Tribunal during its deliberations in June, but had been rejected as too elaborate.

(4) That where hardship was caused by the controlling of one or a small proportion of the total number of establishments engaged in any particular trade, such an establishment, if at all practicable, should be decontrolled. This suggestion met another of the Sheffield employers' objections to the Order.

On 18 January, 1917, the Special Tribunal finished its labours under the terms of reference of 3 October, 1916, by reporting on its visit to Sheffield. It recommended that the "light trades" of Sheffield and elsewhere, including the saw and file trades, should be scheduled under the amended Orders 447 and 618, *i.e.*, with the modifications suggested on 10 December, 1916, for young girls and learners, and with rates ½d. per hour less for the women and girls on "non-productive" work in warehouses, about whom such strong representations had been made.

II. Revised issue as Order 9 of January, 1917.

Orders 9 and 10[1] of 1917 (dated 6 January and 22 January, respectively) enforced these recommendations with some changes of

---

[1] Order 10, subsequently reissued as Order 493, was identical with Order 9, except that the rates contained in it were in each case ½d. per hour less. It was applied to a few outlying firms in which it was manifestly unreasonable to expect the same standard and cost of living as in the big industrial towns. The Special Tribunal had just before this dealt with the case of a small firm at Lutterworth, which employed ten women on wiremaking and insisted that 12s. a week was a high wage according to local village standards. The Tribunal's award of 4½d. and 3¾d. an hour in this case foreshadowed the rates of the new Order.

detail, and superseded Order 759 of 1916, which a month previously had consolidated the previous regulations about women and girls on women's work.

Just before the issue of Orders 9 and 10, another deputation from the Midland Employers' Federation was received at the Ministry on 3 January, 1917.[1] The deputation raised very similar points to those discussed in the previous September. Its members had heard of no action being taken on their representations at that date; the constitution of the Tribunal was still unsatisfactory; the difficulties anticipated about boy labour and apprenticeship were being experienced as a result of the Ministry's Order, since girls of 14 and 15 were receiving high pay instead of wages " proportionate to the services which they could render "; the provision that piece rates should produce earnings $33^{1}/_{3}$ per cent., rather than 25 per cent. above time rates, was needlessly setting aside a custom which had worked satisfactorily in 90 per cent. of the trades of the country; above all, there was no real demand for regulation at all among the operatives, whatever their so-called representatives, with whom alone the Ministry came into contact, might say. Once more the deputation complained that the Federation, representing very large employers with much experience of female labour, had not been consulted before the issue of the Orders. Mr. Kellaway, who received the deputation, pointed out that the new Orders met one of these objections by providing lower wages for girls under 16; that the rise in the cost of living justified a rise in wages; that the extension of Order 447 had been deliberately delayed as a result of the representations made by employers in September, and had only been applied to some—not all—of the trades with which the deputation was concerned, after most careful consideration by the Tribunal; and that the constitution of the Special Tribunal might possibly be amended if necessary.[2]

Complaints of the regulation of women's wages from the points of view of employers and of workpeople often coincided, in date if not in substance, Thus on 17, 20 and 21 December, 1916, and in January, 1917, a series of letters appeared in the *Times* denouncing the Ministry of Munitions for the low wages still paid in some controlled establishments —instances were alleged in which 8s., 9s. and 10s. a week were paid to women munition workers—and for the exclusion of certain occupations, the bolt and nut trade, the ammunition box makers, the electrical workers, from the operation of the Orders. Much had been done, it was admitted, in raising wages, but there were still inexcusable exceptions among women subject to the leaving certificate regulations, and therefore unable freely to change their work.

When the Special Tribunal, as a result of its autumn deliberations, issued its recommendations on the emendation of Orders 447 and 618 and their application, in the form of Orders 9 and 10, to certain fresh

---

[1] M.W. 92329/17.

[2] Mr. Warne Brown, Secretary of the Midland Employers' Federation, was shortly afterwards added to the Tribunal, together with Mr. Duncan, President of the Workers' Union.

industries, protests were made, in December, 1916, and January, 1917, by the National Federation of Women Workers and others, that these orders lowered the rates of pay for women, whereas they ought, owing to the increase of prices, to be raised. This was a fair criticism at the moment, but it had been deliberately decided by the Department to make these incidental reductions by way of adjustment, and to consider at an early date a general increase of wages to women munition workers as a whole.[1] Order 9 met the objection raised by the Sheffield and Birmingham employers, as to their warehouse girls, by providing that where it had been customary to pay special rates for such work—the lightness and cleanliness of which gave it attractions counterbalancing its comparatively low pay in the estimation of the young worker—these might still be paid with special permission from the Ministry, while girls of 14 and 15 were to receive 2d. and 2½d. an hour respectively instead of 3d., as in the first Order, and learners of different ages might be paid, for periods of from one to three months, ½d. an hour less than their appropriate time rates. The beginners fresh from school would thus still start work with 3s. or 4s. higher weekly wages than the normal rate in the Midlands just before the War, while a reduction of 2s. or 2s. 6d. from the full weekly wage, for a brief and limited period, was a very moderate reproduction of a common custom in training older entrants.

With regard to the ten trades excluded from the operation of the Orders by recommendation of the Tribunal in December, 1916, special reasons were given in a departmental memorandum.

(i) The Bolt and Nut Trade, about the standard of payment in which there had been frequent complaints both from workers and from outside sources, was partially covered by an Award (No. 549) of the Committee on Production on 27 October, which gave an advance of 3s. or 5 per cent. to the men in the trade (members of the National Union of General Workers) at Darlaston, leading to an equal advance of the women's wages from 12s. before the war to 15s., with 5 per cent. increase on piece rates. Further, an agreement with the Workers' Union had given an increase of 7½ per cent. to women in the area of the Yorkshire and Lancashire Bolt and Nut Union; while an arbitration case was pending with a representative firm in the trade (Guest, Keen & Nettlefold). For these reasons the Tribunal felt that further interference was at the time unnecessary. The award on this last case on 23 January, 1917, was for a time wage of 19s. per week for workers of 18 and over, 10s. for those under 15, with piece rates 25 per cent. above time rates. In the case of the Rivet and Nut Co., Gateshead, the National Federation of Women Workers had secured to the small number of women employed the ordinary Order 447 and 618 rates by an award of 12 December, 1916.

(ii) Tin box, hollow-ware, and paper box making firms (the latter represented by only two controlled establishments) were mostly under their respective Trade Boards, with initial wages of 6s. and wages for 18-year-old workers of 16s. 6d. and 12s. (rising to 15s. at 21),

---
[1] M.W. 92329/22.

respectively. A large number of these women were said to be earning comparatively good wages on piece work, and it was felt to be difficult to superimpose a second and higher set of official wages on these industries, especially as few firms were concerned from the point of view of the Ministry of Munitions.

(iii) In the case of pottery and hollow-ware, the workers came under a Trade Union agreement of 1 May, 1916, providing for warehouse women and girls 5s. at starting, rising to 12s. at 21, and for dipping-house women 10s. to 13s., with a 10 per cent. bonus ; " low rates, but the Tribunal thought that where agreements had recently been made for the whole of a very large trade there was no case for imposing a higher scale for the small proportion of women engaged on munitions work in the few controlled establishments." For similar reasons, the Tribunal refrained from interference with the other trades referred to it, except in the case of woodwork, for which a new special order was about to be issued on the lines of Order 621 already issued for aircraft workers.

III. Position after the issue of Order 9 (January 1917 to June 1918).

THE WORKER'S FINANCIAL POSITION.

After the issue of Order 9 in January, 1917, the position with regard to payment for women's work was as follows, in so far as the statutory wages Orders were observed in the establishments, ranging from 3875 in the spring of 1917 to some 6000 in the following year, to which they had been applied. On time work the woman munition worker received a standard wage (nominally only exceeded by permission of the Ministry) of $4\frac{1}{2}$d. an hour, or 20s. 3d. for a 54-hour week. Her minimum earnings on time work were therefore from 2s. to 3s. below that of the women on men's work. On piece work she was guaranteed a rate of 4d. an hour, and her piece work prices had to be adjusted so as to secure her at least $33\frac{1}{3}$ per cent. above this rate. She was, however, in an even less advantageous position financially compared with her neighbour on men's work when on piece work than when on time, since the latter's piece rates were based on those previously earned by men ; the normal woman on woman's work in January, 1917, however, under the regulations received at least 24s. for a 54-hour week when on piece work. These rates were raised in April, 1917, when the rate for time workers was fixed at $5\frac{1}{2}$d. an hour, and the guaranteed time rate for piece workers at $4\frac{3}{4}$d. an hour (Orders 492 and 493) ; the piece rates themselves, however, were not to be changed. In August, women on women's work shared the advance of 2s. 6d. based on the increased cost of living for all women workers, while in December they received another statutory advance of 3s. 6d. a week. At the end of the year, therefore, time workers would receive for a 54-hour week 30s. 9d., piece workers not less than 34s. 6d. with a guaranteed time rate of 27s. $4\frac{1}{2}$d.

No distinction was made, as in the regulations for women taking men's work, between different grades of work, but a probationary period of lower earnings was allowed for the munition maker on women's work. In danger zones an extra ½d. an hour was guaranteed, while extra payments for processes "dangerous or injurious to health," such as doping work on aeroplane wings, were sanctioned in principle. The actual rates for such work—dangerous to many workers despite the precautions enforced by the Home Office and the Ministry of Munitions—were fixed departmentally or by arbitration award in each group of cases brought before the Ministry. It was, however, urged by some of the women trade unionists that certain firms whose cases had not been so reported, did not give extra payment to these workers, and that some uniform rate should be fixed which should represent some sort of compensation for risk.

Deputations organised by the National Federation of Women Workers in the spring of 1917 called attention to the difficulties of the position of the women on "women's work" owing to the effect of the constant rise in the cost of living on the value of their comparatively low earnings. This bore specially hardly on the large numbers who were working at a distance from home, and were living in hostels or in lodgings. Board and lodging, said a Birmingham delegate on one of these occasions, cost a girl worker from 15s. to 18s. a week, and this, after payment for the extra food which the vigorous young munition maker expected during the day, for fares and other necessary expenditure, left little margin in the workers' weekly income. After the statutory increase of time rates in April, already recorded, the piece workers showed much discontent in some areas, especially in Coventry, already affected by the widespread strike of men in the engineering trades.[1] In this district, the employers offered to raise piece rate earnings by 4s. a week to correspond to the time worker's advance, and to the 5s. recently awarded to engineers of all grades by the Committee on Production. The Ministry, however, discountenanced such a form of bonus. Both in July and in November, 1917, a general advance of 10s. for all women munition makers was claimed by the Standing Joint Committee of Trade Unions representing women workers and was considered at length by the Special Arbitration Tribunal. As a result, statutory orders were, as has been said, issued by the Department, enforcing weekly advances of 2s. 6d. in August and 3s. 6d. in December (with half-rates for workers under 18) for women and girl munition workers whether employed on time or on systems of payment by results. The woman on "woman's work" had reached this financial position at the end of 1917.[2]

FURTHER EXTENSION OF REGULATION.

(a) *Outlying Trades and Establishments.*

The history of the Orders during the year was not eventful. The few controlled establishments making rope were brought under the

---
[1] L.R. 976.
[2] These rates were unchanged at the date of the Armistice, in November, 1918, except for an advance of 5s. to women and 2s. 6d. to girls in the previous August. (Cf. p. 99.)

women's wages Orders in the course of the year, though the hemp rope manufacturers were allowed, in view of competition from uncontrolled firms, especially in Belfast, to pay at the rates laid down in Order 9, instead of at the higher rates later due. Order 492 which succeeded Order 9 after the April advance, was applied in September (thus reversing the decision of the previous year) to controlled establishments in the bolt and nut trade, in which wages were as a whole notoriously low.[1] Its rates had in the previous month been made binding by the Special Tribunal on bolt and nut making firms in the Black Country and Smethwick area, while in November it was sent, along with the Orders for "men's" work, to controlled establishments in the same trade. This closed temporarily a lengthy period of intermittent warfare between firms in this localised trade and various bodies of organised workers.

During the summer and early autumn, the Orders were, under the powers of the Munitions of War Act of 1917, sent to certain other uncontrolled establishments and to the large number of "certified undertakings" (gas and electric works and tramways), brought under regulation for the purposes of "men's work" in September and November. The scope of Order 9 and its successors was, therefore, considerably widened. It still remained the only statutory source of control of wages in the chemical trade, since those of women on "men's work"—one-third of the whole number employed—had as yet been controlled only by recommendations from the Department and by precedents laid down by awards of the Special Arbitration Tribunal.

Optical and scientific instrument makers' wages were also regulated as "women's work" alone, since it was held that these were entering and learning the trade as a permanency, and not only as substitutes for, or competitors with, skilled men. A special arrangement existed by which after six months, women must receive at least 7d. an hour, and thereafter work up to the man's rate. The following munition trades alone remained exempt from the provisions of the "women's work" Orders; oil works and seed crushing, fertilisers, soap, glass, paper, leather, pottery, firebricks and fireclay, emery and aluminium, together with the tin box, hollow-ware, and paper box makers, in so far as they were subject to the Trade Boards Act. Except in the case of the tin box and hollow-ware makers (who received the statutory advance of August, but not the Ministry's Orders fixing standard rates), the number of women workers in these occupations who could possibly be said to be engaged on " munitions " was almost

---

[1] The piece work earnings of the Darlaston nut and bolt workers—many of them married women with inherited traditions of the trade which tended to remain in certain families—were returned in April, 1917, as ranging (for women piece workers) from 3·3d. to 4·6d. per hour (M.W. 180306). Timekeeping was noticeably bad in the trade as a whole.

The total number of women employed in the manufacture of bolts and nuts, rivets and screws for Government and other purposes combined was about 14,000 in July, 1917. (Report by Board of Trade on State of Employment, July, 1917.)

"WOMEN'S WORK": EXTENSION OF REGULATION 85

negligible. The Tribunal was, however, asked at the end of the year to advise on their inclusion also within the sphere of the Orders, and the majority of them were scheduled for regulation in June, 1918.

(b) Ireland.

In March, 1916, the position of twelve Irish controlled establishments, almost all in Belfast, was referred to the Tribunal for special consideration with regard to women's wages.[1] The Tribunal did not issue any formal report on the matter. There were obvious difficulties in extending an English standard wage to Irish works with lower wage standards and lower cost of living. The Trade Board authorities had realised this difficulty, and members of the Engineering Employers' Federation represented it emphatically to the Committee on Production when the claims for general advances to male workers were being considered in the following year. Just after the issue of Order 447 in July, 1916, eleven Irish controlled establishments were quoted as among the exceptions to which the Order was not applied.

On 6 March, 1917, in reply to a question by Mr. Anderson in the House of Commons why no wage regulations had been applied to Irish controlled establishments, Sir L. W. Evans stated, for the Minister of Munitions, that "Controlled Establishments in Ireland are very few in number and employ few women. The Orders regulating women's wages were made with regard to the conditions prevailing in Great Britain. Careful consideration is now being given to those prevailing in the controlled establishments in Ireland." As a result of this consideration, the wages Orders for women both on men's and on women's work were in June, 1917, applied to the four National Factories, and to fifteen out of the seventeen controlled establishments (excluding two soap works) in Ireland. Only some 2,000 women were contained in these two groups of munition makers. A few hundred women working for uncontrolled munitions firms remained at the time, like those in similar employment in Great Britain, without the protection of the statutory Orders.[2]

THE CONSOLIDATED ORDER (MAY, 1918).

The Consolidated Order for women munition workers' wages, issued in May, 1918, after nearly a year's discussion, modified the position of those on "women's work" in the following respects:—

(1) The normal rates prescribed were still, despite the reiterated criticism of the women's trade union representatives, "standard," not "minimum" rates. Directions were, however, inserted (paragraph 31) providing for the payment of higher rates under "special circumstances," to women employed "on specially laborious or responsible work or on work requiring special ability." The amount of extra payment was to be settled either "by agreement between the parties concerned with the sanction of the Minister of Munitions, or failing agreement, by arbitration." The capable worker, or the women who could take responsibility for others' work, need therefore no longer

---

[1] M.W. 88273/4, etc.   [2] M.W. 92329/41.

nourish a sense of injury by comparison with those "intermediate" workers whose position had been earlier guaranteed in order to promote dilution.[1]

(2) A somewhat complicated provision was introduced to remove the grievance complained of in some cases by piece workers. This was explained as follows in a covering letter sent out by the Department with the Consolidated Order.[2]

"The principle of differential time rates for time workers and those on systems of payment by results is abolished. The same time rates" (of $5\frac{1}{2}$d. per hour for adults) "are now prescribed for both classes of workers, but the percentage which piece work prices or premium bonus allowances are required to yield has been altered from $33\frac{1}{3}$ per cent. to 25 per cent." (the proportion upheld two years before by the Midland Employers' Federation on the experience of the Birmingham district). "Where prices or times already yield 25 per cent. over the new time rate no alteration in either prices or time is required. As the earnings of premium bonus workers depend on their time rate an alteration in the latter would mean an automatic increase in earnings for the same amount of work done. Piece workers on the other hand, whose earnings are now calculated in terms of their time rate, would receive no such increase. It has, therefore, been necessary to provide that the earnings of women and girls who are now employed on premium bonus systems shall continue to be calculated on the existing time rate" (of $4\frac{3}{4}$d. an hour) "provided their earnings reach the level of 25 per cent. over the new time rate." (Paragraphs 10, 13, 19 and 24.)

Thus the common pre-war ratio between time and piece rates was restored, while the piece worker was secured a position certainly no worse and probably considerably better than that of the time worker. Since the primary aim of a scheme of payment by results is to stimulate production, all piece work systems were probably intended to secure the piece worker such superiority. It had, however, rankled in the mind of certain piece workers—representing probably the great majority of women on "women's work"—that in the previous April, 1917, they had received no general advance comparable to that of women time workers or of the male piece workers who shared in the first general advance in the engineering trade of that month. The basis rate of premium bonus workers was left unchanged on the ground explained in the Ministry's letter.

---

[1] "This is an excellent and far-reaching provision . . . almost the only thing to be praised in the much-advertised and much-expected Order," was the comment of the organ of the Women's Trade Union League (*Women's Trade Union Review*, July, 1918). Efforts had been brought to bear on the Ministry during the year (chiefly by the National Federation of Women Workers) to introduce such a revised form of regulation. Without it special rates were sometimes, but rarely, sanctioned for classes of workers by the Department. Thus in the case of a large motor works where acute discontent was said to have been caused in a "formerly perfectly happy department" because the machine workers on "men's work" secured under the newly revised version of Circular L.2 higher wages than the upholsterers on "women's work," special rates for the latter were sanctioned by the Department in January, 1917 (C.E. 2182/4B.).

[2] Circular M.M. 194.

IV. Summary, 1915-1918.

The Ministry of Munitions, in the course of three years, thus established a system of regulation which covered "women's work" in some eighty occupations and sub-divisions of trades. It accomplished this gradually, passing through, first, a preliminary stage during which the need of regulation was argued out and accepted and the ground cleared by the early awards of the Special Tribunal; secondly, a period of revision and considered application of the first Order of July, 1916; and thirdly, a period of partial differentiation between employments and districts, ending in the Consolidated Order of May, 1918.

The difficulty of introducing such regulation into well-established women's occupations has been explained. It was compared in a departmental communication to the Press in January, 1917, to ".sticking a knife rashly into the works of a watch," and the delay in the prompt and general extension of the scope of the Orders to all women munition workers was due primarily to this cause, and to the effort, characteristic of the whole of the wages administration of the Ministry, to hold the balance true between the interests of employers and of labour. It was perhaps unfortunate that both parties were not consulted more before the successive Orders were issued, but modifications were made by the Department in answer to subsequent criticisms of either side as has been described.

The result secured by no means represented a revolution in industrial conditions. The 5½d. hourly rate (with 6s. war bonus) prescribed for time workers at that date only just equalled the pre-war Trade Board rate of 3d. an hour, if the calculations as to the rise in the cost of living quoted in the claims for advances before the Committee on Production are (though this is a debatable point) to be accepted.

The unskilled labourer in the engineering trades had by the same date more than doubled his weekly wage even when on time work (*i.e.*, he had received 20s. advance in his rate plus 12½ per cent. bonus on earnings). When amounts much above 30s. a week were earned on "women's work," as in some of the examples quoted on page 100, the workers were either doing overtime up to the full legal limit, or were employed on some remunerative system of payment by results. But the average earnings given on page 101 show (allowing for the fact that an average conceals the extremes at either end of the scale) that the general level of payment to these women was not high, even by a pre-war standard, if its real value be considered.

The regulations of the Department established no new principle in the very difficult problem, what should be the theoretic basis of women's payment. They secured, however, for the women making munitions, examining them, packing them, or performing the multifarious occupations involved in looking after the needs of others so engaged, a weekly income which, if work went on normally without broken time, represented a "living wage" to the self-supporting worker and a good deal more than a living wage to the girl living at home. The establishment and application of the Ministry's rates proceeded by piecemeal advances, often apparently as a result of external pressure. By the midsummer of 1918, however, the Department's system of wage regulation in these branches of munition work had produced the following results. It placed almost all, if not quite all, munition makers engaged on "women's" work in a financial position which on the whole secured, with a small margin over, their physical efficiency according to the standard most usually quoted ; it gave to employers a standard of payment and safeguarded them from " unfair " underselling by others who were ready to adopt a lower standard ; and it introduced the very important principle of State control of wages (hitherto confined to a limited number of low-wage industries) into occupations permanently performed by women and not only entered by them under the special limitations attached to " war work."

CHAPTER VII.
THE WOODWORK AND AIRCRAFT WAGES ORDERS.
I. Woodwork for Aircraft.

SPECIAL CONDITIONS IN THE AIRCRAFT INDUSTRY.

The manufacture of aircraft had developed so much during the War as to constitute practically a new industry. It had absorbed men from different woodworking trades—joiners, cabinet-makers, coachbuilders, organbuilders, etc.—together with numbers of women new to any kind of woodwork, and had had acute internal difficulties during its growth over questions of piece work, standard rates and working rules. Apart from a long-drawn battle over the introduction of systems of payment by results in aeroplane making, the main difficulty in settling rates of wages and conditions of work in the industry was due to the composite sources of its labour supply. Each of the six or seven trades and the ten or eleven craft unions drawn into the woodworking side of the industry imported its own standards of wages and hours, and was ready to give these up only if assured of the rates of payment and working conditions of the most favourably situated of the competing trades. The point of view of employers showed almost as much variety, for aircraft woodwork was produced in shipyards and in establishments in the building, furnishing, coachbuilding and engineering trades, as well as by firms which had given themselves up to the manufacture of aeroplanes. The difficulty of standardisation under these conditions is obvious. After much discussion, however, and sporadic strikes, the contest was, or should have been, ended by the issue, in February, 1918, of a Statutory Order prescribing a minimum wage (of at least 1s. an hour) and a normal working week for skilled men engaged on woodwork for aircraft.

Meanwhile, the position of the women engaged, in increasing numbers, on woodwork processes, remained on the whole less favourable than that of their neighbours in engineering works. No one union of men employed upon aeroplane woodwork had secured a position at all approaching that of the A.S.E. in the engineering industry; profound suspicion of dilution was frequently expressed by officials of the chief woodworking unions (notably the Amalgamated Society of Carpenters and Joiners); and in the first stages of the introduction of women, none of these societies insisted in advance, or at least insisted with the effect of the A.S.E. in another sphere, on the men's standard rates for women who performed similar work.

In April, 1916, a small inter-departmental conference was held at the Ministry of Munitions on points bearing on the organisation of the aircraft industry. Among other points discussed, this conference suggested a standard wage (of 3d. to 5½d. an hour) for women workers, whom, despite the opposition of the principal trade union concerned, it was held to be necessary to introduce into aeroplane work, and the subject was referred on May 4 to the Special Tribunal for further consideration. The Tribunal accordingly held a series of conferences in May and August with aeroplane manufacturers, and with five of the woodworking trade unions concerned. It was difficult to ascertain to what extent the employment of women on aeroplane woodwork could be based on pre-war experience. Women were actually engaged with success in the early summer of 1916 on various processes of the manufacture of aeroplane wings, the assembly and taping of ribs, finishing machine-made struts, polishing propellers, etc., while some half-dozen more operations in which they might be useful were, even at this date, suggested by employers and workmen. Before the War, the industry was largely experimental; a skilled workman, joiner or patternmaker, would make a " rib " by hand, and few women, if any, had been employed by members of the Society of British Aircraft Constructors. But when the rate of production multiplied a hundredfold, a subdivision of work became possible and necessary, and even in the work previously done by a skilled joiner, the use of " jigs " made the work practicable for quite untrained workers. In three days, it was reported on one occasion by the Admiralty representative who watched some of the early experiments in using female labour, women had learned to make perfectly serviceable ribs for seaplanes.

The woodworking trade unions showed as much reluctance as the engineers had shown to admit women into their side of the aircraft industry, the more so as, they urged, there was still unemployment among their members, some of whose original trades had been most seriously affected by the War. The same arguments as those of the engineers were produced about workers doing " part or portion " of a skilled man's job. It was impossible, said Mr. Bramley of the National Furnishing Trades Association at a conference with the Tribunal on 5 May, 1916, to distinguish finally between skilled and semi-skilled work in his trade. " You can take any piece of ordinary joinery or any piece of ordinary cabinet work and subdivide it into small sections, and by a process of sectionalising the trade you can almost describe it all as semi-skilled labour. The common practice in our trade is that as soon as a person picks up tools of any kind and begins to use them, they are in the skilled department of the industry. The only unskilled men we have are general labourers, who do not use tools at all." Women were already using hammers, saws and chisels, and were only assisted in their work by the provision of jigs and moulds such as carpenters had often contrived for themselves in their ordinary work. Clearly, then, such women at least should have higher rates of pay than those on merely " women's " work ; and the trade union representatives urged that the starting wage should be 6d. an hour, rising after a period of probation to the full district rate, while women whose work at the start was that of a fully skilled man should begin with the full district rate.

CH. VII] WOODWORK AND AIRCRAFT WAGES ORDERS 91

Incidentally, they urged very strongly that no women should be employed on woodcutting machinery because of the special danger involved, and that any introduction of female labour should be regarded as a temporary war measure only.

The employers maintained that a good deal of the work on which women were, or might be, engaged, was light repetition work suitable to young boys, and resembling toy making in some ways; and the workmen's wishes were not wholly met by the subsequent regulations for women's wages.[1]

THE WOMEN'S WAGES ORDERS.

On 17 August, 1916, the Tribunal issued detailed recommendations for the payment of women on woodworking processes in aircraft. The time rating was to be 5d. an hour for time workers and $4\frac{1}{2}$d. an hour for those on piece work, with $\frac{1}{2}$d. an hour extra for inspectors and gaugers; women on machine processes, after eight weeks' probation, were to be rated at $6\frac{1}{2}$d. an hour, but girls, for whom lower time rates were prescribed, were to be excluded from machine work. Night shift and Sunday and overtime allowances were to be the same as those " customarily prevailing among men in the establishment in question." Piece work prices and premium bonus basis times were to be fixed by mutual agreement between the employer and worker (a provision subjected to considerable criticism later), and were to be such as to enable a women or girl of ordinary ability to earn at least one-third above her time rates. In April, 1917, these hourly ratings were increased to 6d., 7d. and $7\frac{1}{2}$d. (thus corresponding roughly to the standard and " special " rates obtained by unskilled and semi-skilled women in the engineering trades), while, like other munition workers, women on aircraft work received a 6s. weekly war bonus in the course of the year.

The application of the Orders had some of the same difficulties as those surrounding Circular L.2, in so far as women were doing part of the work previously done by skilled men. No guarantee of the skilled workman's time or piece rates was given in the Order, but it was urged periodically on behalf of the women engaged in the industry that, at least in certain cases, they, like the women substitutes in engineering works, were entitled to the rates (however debatable these were at the time) of the fully skilled men whom they replaced. The question was raised at an early meeting of the Women's Trade Union Advisory Committee in December, 1917, when the Ministry was asked to secure to these workers " skilled " time rates by applying to them Order 489 (the contemporary version of L.2) instead of the special aircraft Order. Their position as substitutes for men, it was urged, was similar in the engineering and aircraft industries, whereas their financial position was quite different. A claim for advanced rates at Coventry had recently been refused by the Special Arbitration Tribunal, and much unrest was said to have been caused among women aircraft workers in that town, while their position—as " unwilling blacklegs,"

---

[1] Conferences of Special Tribunal, 15 and 16 May, 12 June, 2 August, 1916.

according to representatives of the National Federation of Women Workers—was becoming increasingly difficult in relation to men working in the industry.[1]

The Consolidated Wages Order of May, 1918, maintained the 6d. and 7½d. standard time rates, of which the women's organisations complained, and definitely excluded women on aircraft woodwork and allied processes from the provisions of Part I, which gave the skilled man's time-rate to women on work customarily done by fully skilled tradesmen. It met the Trade Union protests to some extent by providing (in Section 24) that " women or girls employed on piece work or premium bonus systems on work which in the establishment concerned was previously done by men " on such systems, should receive the same rates and allowances as men, and for payment in excess of the rates prescribed " where special circumstances exist."[2]

In spite of these concessions the separate time rating remained, and this differentiation between the treatment of women in the aircraft and engineering industries was vehemently criticised by the representatives of the National Federation of Women Workers, both in print and in dealing with officials of the Department at meetings of the Women's Trade Union Advisory Committee. It was pointed out that the introduction of women at special rates to do aeroplane work by simplified processes previously done experimentally by skilled men, offered an " ideal field for testing possible sex antagonism " ; that " no definite pledge of restoration had been given by the Government in this. case," and that a strong organisation of women as well as of men engaged in the industry was desirable so that employers might know with whom to negotiate in the " inevitable difficulties " after the War.[3] The protests of the wood-working unions were equally strong, and a demand was made in May, 1918, by the National Aircraft Committee for a minimum probationary rate of 10d. an hour for all women employed on woodwork and allied processes on aircraft, and for men's full time rates on completion of the probationary period.

The Department, however, adhered to the view that the wages of women on aircraft must be regulated in harmony with those of other

---

[1] The arguments produced at the hearing of this Coventry case, on 16 November, 1917, reproduced all those with which the Special Tribunal had become familiar in dealing with the engineering trade. Almost all the work now done by women at the aircraft factory of the motor company, against which proceedings were taken by the Coventry Aircraft Committee, had up to the early months of 1915 been done by skilled men, brought there from the carriage-building department, and put on to doping, varnishing and woodwork processes. Later, girls had replaced these skilled coachbuilders and painters in the aircraft works, but the trade union representatives claimed that they were still entitled to the coachbuilders' standard rates. " We are not concerned," said one of their officials, " whether these girls could paint coaches, we are saying that the point is that it was found necessary to take away men from coachpainting in order to perform the particular work they are now engaged in. As in engineering, specialisation has come into the industry to the advantage of someone or other, certainly to the advantage of production."

[2] There were other minor changes. The different time ratings for time and piece workers disappeared, but remained (at 5¼d. an hour) for those on premium bonus. Piece rates (as in the new " women's work ") regulations were to produce at least a quarter, not a third, more than time rates. Girls might undertake machine work, but only with the sanction of the Department.

[3] L.R. 4007.

women munition workers, and that the aircraft industry was not comparable with engineering ; the employment of skilled men before 1915 on work now given to women, was due to the experimental character of the industry then, and could not be taken to establish rates that must be observed now that it had become a manufacturing industry producing standardised articles by repetition methods. In this view they were on the whole supported by the Special Arbitration Tribunal, who were asked to advise on 29 August, 1918 ; the Tribunal, however, recommended that a restricted class of women— those engaged on certain finishing operations in the making of spars, the erection and trueing up of planes and fuselage, and the making of propellers—should be paid the time rate of the craftsmen whose work they undertook. No action had been taken on these recommendations when the Armistice checked the production of aircraft.[1]

II. Other Woodwork.

During the year 1916 complaints periodically reached the Ministry as to the underpayment of other women engaged on woodwork, such as those who were said to be making ammunition boxes at 2½d. and 3d. an hour. The work varied very much in its character, ranging from nailing together sawn lengths of wood for rough packing cases, to much more skilled operations akin to cabinet-making, such as making cordite trays, or teak boxes for the Admiralty. Woodwork was one of the trades the proposed inclusion of which under the " women's work " Order (No. 447) was referred to the Special Tribunal in the autumn of 1916. It was excluded from the revised edition of that Order in January, but in February, 1917, the Tribunal issued the following recommendations :—Time rates for women and girls to be from 4½d. to 2½d. for time workers, and 4d. to 2d. (according to age) for piece workers, " those on time on machine processes, or work requiring special ability or in processes of a specially laborious and responsible nature to be paid according to work and ability." On April 16, however, a simpler " interim " order was issued, laying down a flat rate of 6d. an hour as the minimum for women in such work. This rate did not satisfy some at least of the Trade Unions concerned, and in December they announced their intention of securing 10d. an hour as the minimum wage for skilled woodwork processes.

These workers gained under the Consolidated Order of May, 1918, by a provision with regard to piece rates similar to that which applied to the aircraft workers (Section 18), and by an elastic stipulation (Section 16) that machine workers should be paid, as the Tribunal had recommended, above the minimum rate, " according to the nature of the work and their ability." The standard rates for those not on machine work remained 6d. an hour, with 5d. an hour during the first eight weeks' work.

This Order was applied to all firms known to be engaged in making ammunition boxes. It had been difficult to secure payment of the standard rates laid down in the Order issued in the previous year, because the work was done by widely scattered firms, sometimes by small builders in country towns, who were not controlled under the

---

[1] L.R. 142/128.

Munitions Act. Special steps were, however, taken in the late autumn of 1917 to ensure that the terms of the Orders were observed by all firms employed on Government contracts.

III. Metal Work for Aircraft.

The introduction of women into the sheet metal trade for aeroplane parts had progressed far enough in 1918 to bring up the familiar problem of wage regulation for settlement. A special section of the Consolidated Order therefore prescribed standard rates for them as follows :—

(1) Women employed "wholly or mainly on hand processes in the beating of metal to shape from the plain sheet," were to be paid at the skilled man's rate, with the deductions sanctioned for setting up and during probation by the series of Orders which, since the issue of L.2, had provided for women employed on other forms of men's munition work. This applied whether women were performing the skilled man's work as a whole or, as was probable, in part, except that in certain specified processes, such as "the making of straight folds, straight bends and straight flanges," a lower rate of 7d. an hour, rising in eight weeks to 8d. an hour, was prescribed. On systems of payment by results, women were to receive the same piece work prices and time allowances as men.

Dilution had been vigorously resisted in the sheet metal trade, and the introduction of women was proportionately safeguarded.[1]

(2) Women employed either on time or piece work on machine processes (which had been to a great extent developed since the War) were to be paid at $5\frac{1}{2}$d. an hour, with $4\frac{3}{4}$d. as the time basis of premium bonus workers, according to the scale laid down in the "women's work" Orders.

The system of payment laid down for this group of trades stands midway between the "men's work" and "women's work" wages Orders. The employment of women had hardly existed in them before the War, while the methods of production in them changed so rapidly that pre-war conditions for men's work hardly gave a standard on which to settle the payment for woman's labour. The problems belonging to the rapid sub-division of processes and to the position of the specialist on certain of these processes, appeared in specially marked form in these trades, complicated by a set of industrial problems quite distinct from those of the engineering trades or indeed from "munitions" work as such. On the other hand, some of the operations involved were admittedly of the simplest kind of unskilled work, in no way above the level of that performed in many trades by women and girls before the War. The statutory regulations issued for wages in these trades therefore represented to some extent a compromise between the two series of Orders described in previous chapters.

---

[1] Cf. Tribunal award, November, 1917, of the skilled workman's rates for women (less any deduction for probation and supervision) in the case of the Scottish Sheet Metal Workers' and Braziers' Society and W. Harvie & Co.

CHAPTER VIII.

RATES AND EARNINGS.

The well-paid munitions girl has been a frequent subject of discussion in the press and elsewhere. Some measurements of her opulence are given below.

I. Statutory Rates.

The following tables (I. and II.) summarise the rates of payment —many of them previously quoted—guaranteed under Statutory Order to the women and girls making munitions, *i.e.* to those employed by firms which were subject to the Leaving Certificate regulations and had been scheduled by the Ministry or—after the Amendment Act of 1917—which were similar to firms already so scheduled. The proportion of munition workers so covered was estimated by the Department at 96 per cent, of the whole number employed on work for the Ministry. The period taken for this summary is December, 1917. In the second column is given the weekly wage for unskilled workers, according to the current Statutory rate and bonus. This is calculated on a 48-hour working week, the lowest weekly working period commonly provided under the three-shift system or in any Government Establishment. The recognised hours of work were occasionally less than 48 per week, but were normally considerably more, varying according to firm and industry, before the calculation of overtime began, and the average " unskilled " time worker therefore earned, apart from extra allowances for night work or overtime, more than the amounts given in column 2. The 48 hour basis, however, is taken for convenience.

II. Estimates of Earnings.

Tables I and II give only the *rates* payable by Statutory Order to women and girls on munition work. They represent, therefore, the normal wages due, at least to time workers, since, despite suggestions to the contrary, the Wages Orders laid down standard and not only minimum rates. Calculations of the earnings, however, as distinct from the Statutory rates of munition workers are complicated by various factors ; by variation in the working week ; by the variations of piece work rates and earnings and by the alteration from piece rates to " guaranteed " time rates ; by the payment of three-quarter time rates when no work was available, owing to break down in machinery, non-arrival of material, or air-raids ; by the complexities of premium bonus systems, with varying basis times and methods of calculation ; by extra allowances at time and a quarter, time and a half and double time rates for overtime, night-shift and Sunday work ; by higher rates permitted under " special circumstances ; " by time-keeping and other bonuses sanctioned and unsanctioned.

TABLE

Rates of Women Munition Workers

	Unskilled Work.		
	Hourly Rates.	Weekly Rate (48 hours).	Piecework or Premium Bonus Rates.
	1	2	3
"Men's Work"	6d. (24s. wage paid for less than 48 hours work if this was the recognised working week.)	24s., plus 2s. 6d. bonus.	Those earned by men in the same operation plus 2s. 6d. bonus. Time rate wages guaranteed as in cols. 1 and 2.
"Women's Work"	5½d.	22s., plus 2s. 6d. bonus.	Time rate of 4¾d. per hour guaranteed. Piece rates or premium bonus to yield at least 33⅓% above guaranteed time rate, i.e., at least 25s. 4d., plus 2s. 6d. bonus.
"Women's Work in low-paid areas."	5¼d.	—	As above, except that guaranteed time rate only 4¼d.
Aircraft	7½d. for machine processes, 6½d. and 6d. for other work.	30s. 28s. 24s. Plus 2s. 6d. bonus.	At least 33⅓% above time rates, i.e., 40s. to 32s., plus 2s. 6d. "The appropriate time rate," 7½d. on machine processes, 5¼d. on others, guaranteed.
Woodwork	6d. (Minimum).	24s., plus 2s. 6d. bonus.	—

CH. VIII   RATES AND EARNINGS   97

I.

UNDER STATUTORY ORDER (DECEMBER, 1917).

SEMI-SKILLED OR INTERMEDIATE WORK. Hourly Rates.	SKILLED WORK. Piece or Time Rates.	OVERTIME AND EXTRA WORK.	PROBATIONARY RATES.
4	5	6	7
"Special Rates" recognised by this date as from 6½d. to 8d. an hour, plus 2s. 6d. bonus.	(a) Skilled man's time and piece rates (b) if employed "on part or portion only" of fully-skilled tradesman's work the same rates, less 10% for supervision.	Same as men's for skilled workers; for other workers calculated in same ratio to normal rates as in case of men, but based on women's statutory time earnings.	For women on part of a skilled man's work, unskilled workers' rates (cols. 1 and 2) at start, rising in 13 weeks to fully skilled rates.
¼d. an hour *higher* rates to workers in dangerous areas; also in certain processes if sanctioned by the Ministry. *Lower* rates payable by special sanction to warehouse workers.	—	According to the custom of the establishment, trade or district.	1 month probation permitted at ¼d. per hour below statutory rates.
—	—	As paid to men, or, where no definite custom at time-and-a-quarter for first two hours, then time-and-a-half for overtime, double rates for Sunday work.	4 weeks at 5¼d. and 4 weeks at 6¼d. for machine workers: 8 weeks at 5d. for others.

V-2

TABLE

Rates of Girl Munition Workers

	Hourly Rate.	Weekly Rate. (48 hours). (*See Note*).	Piecework or Premium Bonus Rates.
	1	2.	3
Unskilled Work.			
"*Men's Work*"			
Age 17	5½d.	20s.	Those earned by men in the same process.
„ 16	4½d.	18s.	Less 10% at 17
„ 15	4d.	16s.	Less 20% at 16
Under 15	3½d.	14s.	Less 30% under 16.
	Weekly wage as in col. 2, payable for working week of less than 48 hours.	Plus 1s. 3d. bonus.	Plus 1s. 3d. bonus. Time rates as in col. 1 guaranteed.
"*Women's Work*"			
Age 17	4½d.	18s.	Time rate guaranteed at 3¾d., 3d., 2¼d. and 2d. an hour, according to age. Piece rates and premium bonus to yield at least 33⅓% above time rates. Plus 1s. 3d. bonus.
„ 16	3¾d.	14s.	
„ 15	3d.	12s.	
Under 15	2¼d.	10s.	
		Plus 1s. 3d. bonus.	
In low paid areas	All rates ¼d. per hour lower.	—	—
Aircraft.			
Age 17	5½d. & 5d.	22s. ; 20s.	Time rates guaranteed at 4½d., 3½d., 3d., 2½d. Piece rates and premium bonus to yield at least 33⅓% above time wages. Plus 1s. 3d. bonus.
„ 16	4½d. & 4d.	18s. ; 16s.	
„ 15	4d. & 3½d.	16s. ; 14s.	
„ 14	3½d. & 3d.	14s. ; 12s.	
		Plus 1s. 3d. bonus.	
Woodwork.			
Age 17	5d. (minimum)	20s.	—
„ 16	4d.	16s.	
„ 15	3½d.	14s.	
Under 15	3d.	12s.	
		Plus 1s. 3d. bonus.	

N.B.—The above wages were increased for time and piece-workers by 3s. 6d. a week for women and after December 1st, 1917. A further advance of 5s. to

II.
UNDER STATUTORY ORDER (DECEMBER, 1917).

SEMI-SKILLED AND INTERMEDIATE. Hourly Rates.	SKILLED WORK. Piece or Time Rates.	OVERTIME, ETC.	PROBATIONARY PERIOD.
4	5	6	7
——	——	As in Women's Orders.	——
——	——	As in Women's Orders.	Probation of 2 months at ages 16-18, 1 month below 16, at ½d. an hour below normal wages.
½d. an hour *higher* rates to workers in dangerous areas. *Lower* rates payable by special sanction to warehouse workers.	——	——	——
——	——	——	——
——	——	As in Women's Orders.	Probation of 2 months at 4d. an hour, 3d. an hour, 2½d. an hour, 2d. an hour, according to age.
——	——	——	——

1s. 9d. for girls, under Statutory Rules and Orders 31 of 1918, taking effect from the first full pay-day women and 2s. 6d. to girls was made in August, 1918.

The following extract[1] for the week ending June 30th, 1917, from the wage book of a firm employing some 12,000 women workers illustrates the difference to the individual between rates and earnings emphasized on page 95.

PUNCH GRINDERS IN FITTING SHOP (STANDING WAGE 6d. AN HOUR).

Case. (Every fifth quoted)	Normal hours worked at 6d. an hour.	Amount Due.			Overtime calculated in hours paid for.	Amount Due.		Output Bonus.			Time-keeping Bonus.		Total Earnings.		
		£	s.	d.		s.	d.	£	s.	d.	s.	d.	£	s.	d.
A.	60	1	10	0	18¾	9	4½	1	13	5½	1	6	3	14	4
B.	55	1	7	6	½		3		14	5	1	6	2	3	8½
C.	60	1	10	0	18¾	9	4½		19	0	1	6	2	19	10¼
D.	60	1	10	0	18¾	9	4½	1	3	10	1	6	3	4	8½
E.	45	1	2	6	—		—		15	1		—	1	17	7
F.	60	1	10	0	18¾	9	4½	1	6	0	1	6	3	6	10½

CAPSTAN HANDS.

Case.	Normal Hours worked at 6d. an hour.	Amount Due.			Overtime calculated in hours paid for.	Amount Due.		Output Bonus.			Time-keeping Bonus.	Total Earnings.		
		£	s.	d.		s.	d.	£	s.	d.		£	s.	d.
A.	55	1	7	6	—		—		19	5	—	2	6	11
B.	60	1	10	0	15	7	6	1	4	0	—	3	1	6
C.	40	1	0	0	—		—		4	6	—	1	4	6
D.	48½	1	4	3	—		—		16	0	—	2	0	3

Another firm's returns of the methods of payment illustrates the possible difference between a prescribed time rate and actual earnings as a result of war bonuses. The firm was a firm of Hollow-ware Manufacturers employing 50 women and 79 girls at the rates fixed by the Hollow-ware Trade Board on July 6th, 1914, with additions.

Workers over 18 :

	On Time.				On Piece.	
Wage	13	6	Wage		13	6
10% Bonus	1	4	5% Bonus			8
War Bonus	2	6			14	2
			16¾% Bonus		2	3
			War Bonus		2	6
	17	4			18	11

No wholly representative statistics as to actual earnings of women piece workers or total receipts of time workers are available. Returns have however been obtained periodically from the National Factories.

[1] C.E. 539/4.

Their wage rates cover a very large number of women munition workers, and are fairly representative of those paid and earned in non-government factories engaged on similar work. Samples are therefore given in some detail.

TABLE III.

AVERAGE RATES AND EARNINGS OF WOMEN IN

(a) *National Projectile Factories.*

	Oct. 1916. Earnings.	Feb. 1917. Earnings.	July 1917.		April 1918.	
			Rates.	Earnings.	Rates.	Earnings.
	s. d.	s. d.	s. d.	s. d.	s. d.	s. d.
Forewomen	—	49 4	41 9	49 4	49 8	64 2
Women in Tool Room	—	27 2	27 6	41 6	31 1	39 5
Machine Operators	30 9	39 10	26 1	37 4	34 1	62 5
Labourers	—	28 6	25 3	29 11	34 1	46 3
Viewers	—	32 6	27 11	34 4	35 8	45 2
Total (including certain workers not detailed above)	—	—	26 6	36 0	34 8	56 8

NUMBERS COVERED BY ABOVE AVERAGES.

Forewomen	Unweighted average of 9 factory averages	88	68
Women in Tool Room	4 ditto	110	4
Machine Operators	13 ditto	8,821	9,418
Labourers	10 ditto	2,899	2,858
Viewers	12 ditto	1,611	2,740

NOTE.—The total number of females employed in National Projectile Factories in April, 1918, was 20,667.

(b) *National Shell Factories.*

	October, 1916.	April, 1917.	September, 1917.		April, 1918.		
	Earnings.	Earnings.	Rates.	Earnings.	Rates.	Earnings.	No.incldd.
	s. d.	s. d.	s. d.	s. d.	s. d.	s. d.	
Forewomen	—	43 3	38 5	45 1	42 1	50 10	62
Women in Tool Room	—	35 2	32 6	39 1	32 2	34 9	127
Machine Operators	25 8	33 11	29 10	38 3	32 1	42 7	7,576
Labourers	—	29 1	27 9	35 6	31 4	37 9	1,315
Viewers	—	31 10	30 10	38 3	35 2	43 5	1,193
Total (including certain workers not detailed above)	—	—	29 11	38 1	32 0	42 4	10,618

NOTE.—The return for September, 1917, include 10,487 females. The total number of females employed in National Shell Factories in April, 1918, was 12,939.

TABLE III—*continued.*

(c) *National Explosives Factories.*

	July—August, 1918.		
	No.	Rate.	Earnings.
		s. d.	s. d.
Forewomen—Process	31	45 1	45 1
Maintenance	1	42 6	46 9
Transport Yard and General	9	40 3½	40 3½
Charge Hands—Process ..	637	46 10	48 7¼
Transport Yard ..	51	35 8½	36 4½
Power	10	34 11¼	35 8¼
Process Hands	9,919	30 11	32 5¼
Labourers—Maintenance	256	30 5	30 8
Transport Yard	1,294	30 0½	31 11
Power	235	35 6	36 4½

NOTE (1).—There were 12,448 females employed in National Explosives Factories.

NOTE (2).—The following earlier examples are given for purposes of comparison.

At Gretna in August, 1917, the wages for a 54-hour week ranged from 31s. 6d.-34s. 6d. in the Gun Cotton section to 39s. in the Nitrating House; 31s. 6d. for general workers on danger processes on Cordite; 32s. 6d.-34s. 6d. to those on acids. At Pembrey, earnings, fixed on the basis of an award by the special Tribunal a year before, were from 6¼d. to 7½d. an hour; 30s. 2d. to 36s. 3d. for a week of 53 hours paid as 58 hours, with the 2s. 6d. war bonus in addition. At Colnbrook and Queen's Ferry the weekly earnings varied between 25s. 8d. and 30s., with 2s. 6d. and 5s. bonus.

(d) *National Filling Factories.*

	July, 1918.		
	No.	Rates.	Earnings.
		s. d.	s. d.
Forewomen	165	50 5	60 8
Assistant Forewomen	195	47 6	55 9¼
Charge Hands	1,749	37 8	44 2
Filling Operatives	27,970	32 7	42 4
Labourers	5,156	32 5½	42 11

NOTE.—According to returns from 14 National Filling Factories in the period May-July, 1917 (*i.e.*, between the two general advances in women's wages) the average earnings of Filling Operatives were 29s. on the day shift and 32s. 6d. on the night shift.

CONTROLLED ESTABLISHMENTS.

More varied returns covering a very much wider variety of trades were obtained in April to June, 1917, from a circular sent out to all Controlled Establishments requiring them to report on the average wages and earnings of their women employees, according to the Statutory Orders then in force. The Schedule of questions was unfortunately not very clearly worded, and despite the assistance of the Chief Investigation Officers, through whom it was despatched to firms, it was not always clearly or accurately filled in. It served incidentally a useful administrative purpose, since those firms whose returns, on scrutiny at Whitehall Gardens, showed that the Statutory Orders were not being observed were required by the Department to comply with them in future. Valuable general information as to earnings can be gathered from them, though it is impossible to classify the returns accurately by trade groups or to distinguish clearly between piece and time earnings.

(a) In the North East Coast Area, out of some 150 firms circularised about 100 were employing women on "men's work." (The remainder were iron foundries and other works engaged in heavy forms of production in which dilution had so far been impossible.) Only five of these firms, by their own account, were employing women on skilled men's work—seventy-one women out of 2,500 employed in all. The average earnings per head of the semi-skilled and unskilled workers (over a large range of occupations) was 28s. 2d., whereas the corresponding average for the few skilled workers was 35s. The small number of women reported as on skilled work were engaged as follows :—[1]

		s.	d.	
Engineering	8 women at	32	0	time earnings.
Wire Rope	11 ,, ,,	30	0	,, ,,
Hollow-ware	5 ,, ,,	25	0	,, ,,
Chemical Works	35 ,, ,,	35	9	,, ,,
Forge	12 ,, ,,	44	0	,, ,,

(b) In the Yorkshire Munitions Area, a district including Sheffield, Leeds, Leicester, Nottingham, where women's work in the munition trades had been negligible before the war, two thirds of the women and girls employed were described as being on "men's work" (20,319 out of 30,442). Only 422 women and 5 girls were reported by their employers as being on skilled work, at average (adult) weekly earnings of £2 6s. 2d. for piece work, £2 1s. ½d. time work. The earnings of the women replacing unskilled and semi-skilled men averaged £1 18s. on piece and £1 8s. 7d. on time, as compared with £1 10s. 10d. and £1 6s. 1d. for women on " women's work " and £1 4s. 9d. and £1 3s. 9d. approximately for women on private work and " unregulated " munitions work.

(c) In the Bristol Area, covering the south-western district, in which the pre-war level of wages as a whole was low, and including Devon and Cornwall and firms in Southampton, Bournemouth and the industrial villages in the Stroud Valley of Gloucestershire, 5,037 women and girls, out of a total of 9,085 reported on, were engaged on " men's work," 76 women and 11 girls replacing skilled men. Their piece earnings were slightly lower than those in the preceding group, but the time earnings, which followed closely the standard laid down in the Orders, were similar in both districts.

(d) In the Birmingham and Midlands Area, a district in which women had long worked in many of the munition trades before they were called " munitions," some 220 munition firms out of 670 circularised were employing women and girls on " men's work." Out of

---

[1] These averages are based on a slightly different schedule of returns from that analysed on pp. 106-7.

over 11,000 women and girls so employed, only 671 were reported (by 39 out of 220 firms) to be engaged on skilled men's work. 9,758 women and 571 girls (the small number of the latter is noteworthy) were returned in the semi-skilled and unskilled class. At the same time 67,693 women and girls were reported by these firms as being occupied in "women's work" on the production of munitions.

A table (IV.) is appended[1] illustrating (a) the incidence of the different wages orders, and the numbers of women substitutes for men employed by the firms reporting; and (b) the average wages earned in these groups. The average, it must be explained, is an average of averages, being calculated on the average earnings returned by each *firm* as obtained by the women and girls employed by them under each heading; no more weight is given to a large than to a small firm in making up the figure. Moreover, both sets of figures must be received with some reservation since the definition of "skilled" work is admittedly somewhat arbitrary, and as explained above, the distinction between time and piece earnings was not always clearly made. They illustrate, however, the relative proportion of women on "men's" and on "women's" work in these districts—a distinction important administratively and socially—and the higher trend of the earnings of those on "men's" work. The small number of the girls under 18 employed by these munition firms, especially on "men's work" is noteworthy.

Some further returns, selected at random from those of firms employing large numbers of women in both categories, are given[2] to illustrate the operation of the Wages Orders on the wages books of individual establishments (Table V). The firms are all in the Birmingham and Midlands Area, except Nos. 4, 11, 22, 23, 24, 25, and 28, which are in the Yorkshire Munitions Area, and 26 and 27 in the London Area.

Statistics of average earnings are notoriously unsatisfactory, as illustrations of the position of the individual worker, and the averages quoted above inevitably conceal the exceptional cases of high and of low earnings which have been said periodically to be typical of the over or underpayment of the woman munition worker. Such criticisms could have been met statistically only by returns from employers, grouping much more precisely the weekly earnings received. The returns available are, as has been explained, of only limited value, but indicate that on the whole the statutory rates were adhered to pretty closely as a standard for the payment of women in controlled establishments and National Factories, although in certain forms of piece work, e.g., in shell and fuse making, the weekly wages and earnings were much in excess of the minimum prescribed.

The instances of low wages to munition workers quoted periodically were drawn almost invariably from firms to which Orders had deliberately not been applied, or which had ignored these Orders, or were experimenting on rates before the period.

In at least three cases of underpayment about which questions were asked in the House of Commons (Nobel's, Perranporth, at the end of 1915; Pirelli's, Southampton, in 1915 and 1916; and the North British

---
[1] See pp. 106, 7.   [2] See pp. 108, 9.

Rubber Works, early in 1917), it was shown on enquiry either that these rates were low because the firm had only lately started work in a low-rated neighbourhood, or that the firm had, inadvertently or otherwise, omitted to apply the Ministry's Wages Orders.

III. Comparison with pre-War Earnings.

A comparison with women's earnings before the war can only be of limited application, because conditions of women's work within the munition trades, and the personnel among the women actually performing such work, have changed so greatly during the three and a half years of the war. On the wage of 12s. 8d. a week, estimated by the Census on Wages of 1906 as the average for women in the metal trades, or on the more detailed averages quoted below, the increase of earnings would be over 100% among the lowest paid munition workers in these trades, even allowing for the slight advance in wages between 1906 and 1914.

A more precise indication of the advance in earnings for a normal week is given in Table VI,[1] which gives some of the results of an enquiry into earnings in the Midlands Light Metal Trades, some of which were affected by the Munitions Wages Orders, while others moved sympathetically, made in 1917 and 1918 by the Trade Boards Office of the Ministry of Labour.

The National Employers' Federation in a deputation to the Special Arbitration Tribunal in July, 1917, submitted the following statement as to the earnings of workpeople employed by its members in the Midlands in 1914 and 1917 :—

			Number.	Gross Earnings. £	Average Earnings. £ s. d.	Increase.
1st Week in	May, 1914	All Workers	56,800	76,500	1 6 9	66%
,, ,,	May, 1917		75,900	170,000	2 4 4	
2nd ,, ,,	May, 1914	Men & Boys	14,400	23,800	1 13 3	70%
,, ,,	May, 1917	(Piecework)	14,200	40,000	2 16 3	
3rd ,, ,,	May, 1914	Women & Girls	2,400	1,600	12 7	120%
,, ,,	May, 1917	(Piecework)	5,500	7,900	1 8 3	

It was stated by the Federation that these figures represented accurately the sums paid by their members, but that the sums represented comparative earnings, not wage rates, and included extra payments for overtime and night work in the second period.

The " Earnings and Hours " enquiry of the Board of Trade (Cd. 5814 of 1911) gave the following average full-time weekly earnings in September, 1906, of women in some of the trades contributing to the supply of " munitions " since August, 1914. They may be compared with the munitions workers' earnings quoted above.

	Women. s. d.	Girls. s. d.
Engineering and Boilermaking	13 1	8 2
Light Iron Castings, Stoves and Grates	10 0	7 5
Wire drawing and Metal working	13 2	7 3
Jewellery	13 6	6 10
Edge Tools, Spades, Files	11 7	6 10
Cycle making and repairing	14 4	9 1
Nails, Screws, Nuts	11 2	7 6
Scientific Instruments	12 8	6 9
Average for Metal Trades	12 8	7 4

[1] See p. 110.

TABLE

AVERAGE WEEKLY EARNINGS OF WOMEN IN CONTROLLED
APRIL AND

Area.	On skilled men's work.		Replacing semi-skilled or un-skilled men.		On woodwork for aircraft (C.)		On work not recognised as men's work (D.)	
	Piece.	Time.	Piece.	Time.	Piece.	Time.	Piece.	Time.
	£ s. d.	£ s. d.	£ s. d.	£ s. d.	£ s. d.	£ s. d.	£ s. d.	£ s. d.
Yorkshire	2 6 2	2 1 0	1 18 0	1 8 7	1 19 9	1 9 4	1 10 10	1 6 1
Bristol	2 0 0 (One firm only.)	2 10 6	1 13 6	1 7 0	—	1 7 7	—	—
Birmingham	1 13 5	1 9 1	1 12 6	1 7 6	1 15 5	1 3 7	1 9 0	1 3 7
Newcastle	—	1 10 9	1 12 0	1 7 0	—	—	1 6 6	1 4 0

NUMBER OF WOMEN

Area and No. of Firms.	On skilled men's work.		Replacing semi-skilled or un-skilled men.		On woodwork for aircraft.	
	Women.	Girls.	Women.	Girls.	Women.	Girls.
Yorkshire (377)	422	5	19,205	687	180	15
Bristol (94)	76	11	4,497	453	180	20
Birmingham (670)	964	86	9,758	571	114	7
Newcastle (90)	158	57	2,512	171	—	—

IV.

ESTABLISHMENTS IN FOUR MUNITION AREAS BETWEEN JUNE, 1917.

On munition work where wages are not regulated (E.)		On private work (F.)		Average rate before June, 1916, (i.e., before Statutory Regulation).			
Piece.	Time.	Piece.	Time.	C.	D.	E.	F.
£ s. d.	£ s. d.	£ s. d.	£ s. d.	£ s. d.	£ s. d.	s. d.	s. d.
1 4 9	1 3 10	1 4 10	1 3 3	19 10	18 11	11 8	17 0
1 3 1	1 0 5	1 9 4	1 1 6	1 1 0	18 2	17 9	14 5
1 4 7½	1 1 10	1 3 7	1 0 4	1 4 9	1 0 1	17 10½	16 3
1 4 9	1 3 0	1 0 9½	17 1½	—	17 10	14 4	15 1½

AND GIRLS EMPLOYED.

On work not recognised as men's work.		On munition work where wages are not regulated.		On private work.		Total.	
Women.	Girls.	Women.	Girls.	Women.	Girls.	Women.	Girls.
9,422	2,875	558	120	623	330	30,410	4,032
2,436	573	436	102	235	66	7,860	1,225
46,807	11,839	2,125	1,095	2,081	1,154	61,735	13,598
2,190	548	221	138	685	264	5,766	1,178

TABLE V.
Average Earnings in Certain Controlled Establishments, April-June, 1917.

	"Women's Work."				"Men's Work."			
	Women.	Girls.	Time Earnings (Adults).	Piece Earnings.	Women.	Girls.	Time Earnings. (Adult Workers).	Piece Earnings. (Adult Workers).
			s. d.	s. d.			s. d.	s. d.
1. Steel Tube Manufacturers	161	110	25 0	30 0	69	16	26 6	36 6
2. Chemical ,,	—	—	—	—	12	—	34 0	—
					12	—	—	—
					116	—	29 0	35 0
3. Electrical and Mechanical Engineers	16	5	27 6	55 0	26	5	27 0	34 0
4. Bombs, etc.	115	40	22 9	43 0	14	—	26 6	36 3
5. Tramways	—	—	—	—	1,143	—	29 3	—
6. (a) Rolling Mills	3,338	—	28 0	34 11	295	—	36 0	—
(b) Ammunition Loading	1,842	—	27 0	32 0	74	—	38 0	—
7. Motor Chains, Shell and Fuse Hole Plugs	193	94	27 7	29 5	53	6	30 0	—
8. Elec. Engineers, Shells, Primers, Mines	389	200	22 6	29 7½	25	—	—	44 5
9. Iron Foundry	31	18	{16 0 / 19 0}	—	147	3	27 0	37 2
					17	26	16 0 / 18 0	20 0 / 25 0
10. Engineering and Metal Work	—	—	—	—	39	1	—	45 6 (Skilled work).
					148	3	—	39 10 (Unskilled W'k)
					133	—	—	(Skilled Work).
11. Seed Crushing, etc.	—	—	—	—	138	39	34 0 (Min. for 48 hours).	35 0 (58 hours).
12. Engineers	690	—	—	35 0	84	—	—	—
	724	—	—	39 6	—	—	—	28 6

RATES AND EARNINGS

13. Cycle Works, engaged in Small Arms Ammunition	940 1061	—	25 3 28 5	—	—	—	41 0	—	24 11 35 0 40 0 48 9 45 0 50 0
14. Tubes	—	—	—	—	—	35 39 23 0 0 0	—	12 23	—
15. (a) Motors	—	—	—	—	—	—	—	—	—
(b) Woodwork	—	—	—	—	—	—	—	2	—
16. Cycle and Motor Works	363	213	33 0	49 0	—	26 26 6 6	—	—	—
17. Motors	—	—	—	—	8	30 0	—	—	—
18. Nuts and Bolts	206	217	19 6	24 5	10 (Semi-skilled) 317 28 17 1,096 274 (Unskilled)	—	40 0	—	32 6
19. Fuses	1,589	16	—	35 0		—		—	
20. Chains (Transmission)	609	192	—	29 0	31 (Skilled.) 27 (Unskilled.) 27	40 0	—	—	36 0 47 0
21. Engineering (Ordnance Co.)	2,174		—	38 6					
22. Shells	—	—	28 0 29 0	37 6 44 5½	4 (Skilled). 402 (Unskilled). 1,260	35 0 27 0	14	—	37 0 37 6
23. (a) Cycles and Ammunition	156	—	—	—					
(b) „	1,224 70 760	—	—	—					
24. Motors, Engines	—	—	—	35 8	2 (Skilled Welders). 40	40 0	6d. per hour, plus 2s. 6d. 32 0	—	—
25. Shells	—	—	—	29 0	91 (Labourers). 481	—	—	—	49 0
26. Small Arms	201	—	—	51 0	1,054 87 (Aircraft Worker).				39 0 38 3
27. Engineering	785	59	22 0 28 10 26 6	—	1,712 486	30 0 33 2	—	50	39 0
28. Iron Founding, Shells	1,168								

TABLE VI.

Light Metals—Wages, 1914 and 1917 (end).

Weekly Earnings of Women (over 18) in Exempt Occupations.

	Year.	No. of Workers.	Average No. of hours Worked.	Average Weekly Earnings.	Lower Quartile.	Median.	Upper Quartile.
Bolts, Nuts and Screws, Nails, Tacks and Rivets	1914	1,882	52¾	12 11	10 0	12 8½	16 3
	1917	718	52¼	24 8	18 9	25 3	29 9½
Metal Smallware, including Steel Pens, Pins, Hooks, Eyes, and Metal Buttons	1914	3,247	51	12 1½	9 7	11 10½	14 5
	1917	2,227	51¼	22 9	19 0	22 2	26 9
Cycles and Accessories	1914	960	52½	14 9	11 5½	14 3	17 0½
	1917	334	52¾	27 9	23 5½	27 6	31 6½
Needles, Fish-hooks and Fishing Tackle	1914	1,203	—	13 2	11 2	13 2	15 3
	1917	456	50	26 4	25 1½	27 6	29 1
All Groups	1914	7,292	51¾	12 9	10 2	12 11½	15 9
	1917	3,735	51¾	24 0	19 0	23 11½	28 10

The earnings tabulated in the preceding pages in the Birmingham district in the spring of 1917, may also be compared with those quoted for 1908 in " Women's Work and Wages in Birmingham " (Cadbury, Matheson and Shann). " In Birmingham for girls above 21, wages move near 10s. per week, while an unskilled man's wage is 18s. to 20s. at least. The following is an analysis of women's wages in the cycle trade (largely diverted to munition work during the war) :—For those over 21 the average wage is 10s. 6d. Nearly 50% of these are married women whose wages average 11s. Between 17 and 21, the average wage is 9s. 2d. ; below 17, 7s. 1d. Wherever women replaced men, the former always received a much lower wage—about 10s. to 12s. per week. The wage that the man previously received gave no criterion as to what the woman would get, though as a general statement, approximately correct, we may say a woman would get from half to one-third the wages of a man." (Pages 119, 121.) The following earnings are quoted for " typical " ammunition workers :—

	Minimum.	Maximum.	Average under 18.	Average over 18.
Cartridge Case-maker	3 0	—	8 9	11 0
Cartridge Cutter-off	3 0	18 0	—	8 6
Warehouse Worker	8 0	13 4	6 10	9 0
Cartridge Metal Drawer	6 0	18 0	7 0	12 6
Examiner	8 6	13 7	—	10 2
Filling Cartridges	7 0	18 0	—	—

THE YOUNG WORKER.

The rise in wages in the munition trades was specially noticeable among quite young girls, both the beginners of 13 and 14 and the girls of 18, classed for wage purposes as women. An effort was made by the Engineering Employers' Federation in the autumn of 1916 to postpone from 18 to 21, the age at which a munition worker became a " woman." Many trades and individual firms had, before the war, drawn up their scale of wages on the quite comprehensible assumption that a woman's full earning power in industry is not reached before she is 21. The lower limit of age, however, remained the dividing line in regulating wages for munitions purposes. With regard to the beginners, the increase in their wages over the pre-war level was to some extent paralleled by a corresponding increase in certain of the non-munition trades. Thus, the Trade Boards made provision for a definite increase in the minimum wages of learners, though these still in 1917 received, or at least were guaranteed, far less than munition girls. In other trades the reflex action of the high rates for girls employed on munition work and acting as substitutes for boys in other " unskilled " occupations, appeared in a different and probably more valuable form in the better provision for industrial training agreed on by various associations of employers for the benefit of their young workers.[1]

---

[1] Cf. an agreement of London Dressmakers in September, 1916, for the training and education of learners and apprentices.

IV. Wages and Prices.

To a considerable extent, the increase in the wages of women under the Munitions Acts was nominal only, and was neutralised by the increased cost of living.

The rise in the cost of food, if no allowance be made for change of dietary, between July, 1914, and December, 1917, was 106%. Even if allowance be made for a reasonable change of dietary, the rise in cost was 59%, in the light of which the purchasing power of the 30s. 0d. minimum time wage for women on "men's work," and of the 5½d. an hour plus 6s. 0d. a week bonus of women on "women's work," shrinks to very modest proportions.[1]

The rise in the cost of food is indicated the following table (Table VII). These figures are given, not as an estimate of actual increase in expenditure, but as the best known index number of food prices, to which most frequent reference was made in hearings before arbitration tribunals and other authorities charged with the fixing of wages.

TABLE VII.

Board of Trade and Ministry of Labour index numbers of retail food prices, showing percentage increase over level of July, 1914.		Purchasing power of £1 (in food) in towns of over 50,000 inhabitants.		
			s.	d.
January, 1915	18	July, 1914	20	0
July, 1915	32¼	December, 1914	17	0
January, 1916	45	June, 1915	14	10
July, 1916	61	December, 1915	13	8
January, 1917	87	June, 1916	12	4
July, 1917	104	December, 1916	10	8
January, 1918	108	June, 1917	9	8
July, 1918	110	December, 1917	9	6
		July, 1918	9	4

The most accurate measure of the increase in the cost of living is, however, afforded by the investigations of the Working Classes Cost of Living Committee, 1918, which reported on 23 October, 1918.[2] According to this report the general average rise in expenditure between July, 1914, and July, 1918, was 74%; the increase in weekly expenditure on food alone between June, 1914, and June, 1918, was 90%, the increase per man being on an average 5s. a week. The food requirements of a female over 14 years of age were taken as ·83 of those of a man.

The rise in money wages for women munition workers has been remarkable during the three year period under consideration; but the rise in real wages, difficult as this is to interpret, has been by no means so great, except in the case of certain piece workers. The journalistic picture of the opulent woman munition worker is largely due to the cumulative effect of family earnings, opportunities for which greatly increased during the war, to the combination of earnings from munition work with a separation allowance or pension among

---

[1] Cf. *Labour Gazette*, January, 1918, and the Second Report of the Select Committee on National Expenditure.

[2] Cd. 8980.

soldiers' wives, dependants and widows, and to the almost complete absence of periods of "slackness" and unemployment, which under normal conditions so greatly affect the average earnings of women in industry. While admitting the superiority of the woman munition worker's financial position by comparison with that of the non-munition worker, it was urged by successive labour deputations to the Ministry in 1917 that, except in certain forms of piece work, the normal woman munition worker at the time earned little more than enough to provide herself with a reasonable supply of the necessities of life, with small margin for other expenditure.

V. Advance in Earnings in Non-Munition Trades.

Probably in no form of women's industrial work did wages or earnings remain stationary between 1914 and 1917. Even in the unsusceptible trades of laundry and dressmaking, wages offered by London firms rose from 2s. 6d.–4s., to 6s.–8s. for learners, and from 20s.–25s. to 25s.–30s., for trained hands in the dressmaking trade, and from 12s. to 18s. for weekly workers in laundries. In the Trade Board occupations, the minimum wage was raised by 1d. and 1½d. above the 2¾d. and 3d. an hour pre-war rate, while in the three trades so regulated in which employment was good, earnings were increased to a considerably greater extent by overtime work and war bonuses. In domestic service and in the textile trades, from which large numbers were drawn to munition work, average earnings rose very considerably—in some branches of the woollen and worsted trade, piece work prices increased by 50%, while the earnings of women employed doubled. In spite of such advances, however, the munition trades on the whole offered the best financial prospects to the normal industrial worker, even if these prospects were coupled with very hard work ; and—quite apart from patriotic motives—the drift of the younger and more vigorous workers into amunition work from the occupations quoted above is explicable. The loss of women workers in these occupations, between July, 1914, and 1917, has been estimated approximately as follows :—[1]

Domestic Service	173,000 out of (?)	1,300,000
Shirtmaking	8,250 ,, ,,	75,000
Paper Box-making	2,660 ,, ,,	21,000
Lace finishing	2,310 ,, ,,	21,000
Confectionery and Preserving	13,600 ,, ,,	68,000
Laundry	16,000 ,, ,,	100,000
Dressmaking	22,600 ,, ,,	130,000

How far this superiority of earnings for women and girls on munition work was due to competition for reliable and accessible labour, how far to the effect of statutory regulation, it is impossible at present to estimate.[2] Some figures of women's wages in non-munition industries (in January, 1918) are given in the following table (Table VIII).

[1] See " Report of Occupations in the United Kingdom, July, 1917."
[2] See p. 161a for examples of some other wages of women employed by Central and Local Authorities.

TABLE VIII.

Women's Wages in certain Non-Munition Industries, January, 1918.

1. **Minimum Rates under Trade Boards Act of 1909.**
   Machine-made Lace and Net Finishing.—August, 1914—2¾d. an hour; raised in August, 1917 to 3½d. an hour.
   Paper Box Trade.—August, 1914—3d.; December, 1915—3¼d.; August, 1917—4d.; January, 1918—4¼d.
   Tailoring.—August, 1914—3¼d.; July, 1915—3½d.; February, 1917—4d.; November, 1917—4¼d.
   Sugar, Confectionery and Food Preserving.—June, 1915—3d.; August, 1916—3¼d.; May, 1917—3¾d.; October, 1917—4¼d.
   Shirt-making.—July, 1915—3¼d.; February, 1917—4d.; October, 1917—4¼d.
   Tin Box Trade.—November, 1915—3¼d.; March, 1917—3¾d.; October, 1917—4¼d.
   Hollow-ware Trade.—January, 1916, 3d.; July, 1917—3½d.; January, 1918—4d.

Weekly rates for learners [1]	January, 1916.	January, 1918.
	s. d.	s. d.
Under 15	6 0	6 6
„ 15	7 6	8 6
„ 16	9 0	10 6
„ 17	11 0	13 0

2. **Women's Army Auxiliary Corps.**
   Women engaged for technical employment with the R.F.C. and A.S.C.
   Forewomen (technical) 38s.-42s. per week with allowances, and board, lodging and washing at a maximum charge of 14s. a week, while in hostels or billets.
   Acetylene Welders (fully trained), magneto and scientific instrument repairers, fitters, machinists for capstan lathes, milling machines, drilling, slotting, grinding ("practically no repetition work"), turners, tinsmiths, coppersmiths, sheet metal workers, armature winders, aeroplane riggers 28s.-32s. per week with allowances, etc., as before.
   Dopers, painters, sign writers, 25s.-30s.; sailmakers, wing workers, upholsterers, 25s.-29s.; motor washers, 24s.-25s.; general unskilled labour, 24s.-26s. per week, with allowances.

3. **Women's Land Army.**
   Minimum weekly wage, 18s.; rising to £1 on passing a proficiency test, with certain allowances. Board and lodging guaranteed at not more than 14s. a week.

4. **Typical "Substitute" Wages.**

L.C.C. Tramway Conductors	42s. to 51s. for a 54-hour week.
London General Omnibus Conductors	5s. 10d. for a 12-hour day.
Railway Companies—	
(a) Midland : Cleaners	22s., plus war bonus of 8s. 6d. for a 48-hour week.
(b) G.W.R. : Porters	30s. a week for an 11-hour day.
Ticket Collectors	26s., plus war bonus of 8s. 6d. for a 10-hour day.
(c) G.C.R. : Cleaners	28s. 6d. a week for an 11½-hour day.

---

[1] Compare rates laid down by the Munitions Wages Orders for learners on munition work (pp. 98, 99).

CHAPTER IX.

SOME RESULTS.

I. A Definite Policy.

The policy of the Ministry of Munitions with regard to women's wages operated through its four groups of wages Orders, interpreted and applied by employers and employed, with ultimate recourse to the Department, and the Special Arbitration Tribunal. It was a policy of maintaining the standard rates acquired by men's collective bargaining and of supplying a financial safeguard to women workers in the absence of organisation—a safeguard as much from their own lack of industrial standards as from deliberate underpayment by employers. The degree to which this was accomplished has been estimated in previous chapters. It was a much more definite policy than the Ministry of Munitions attained with regard to the wages of men munition workers—more definite because the Department was able to deal with the problems of women's wages on a comparatively clean slate, whereas a multitude of schemes for the settlement of men's wages were already in operation when the Ministry was established. After four years of war, the problems of men's and of women's wages showed signs of converging in some respects, as women adopted men's work and to some small extent shared their organisations. But for the first three years of the Department's activity the problems and their settlement were almost wholly distinct.

II. Methods of Payment.

The details of the wages Orders may appear to have been given undue prominence in the foregoing account. They may be expected, however, to have a lasting importance over and above their influence during the War, in preventing or lessening wage disputes, in facilitating the dilution of labour, and in securing to the worker the remuneration specified—since they introduced a large measure of regularity and system into the chaos of women's wages. The following were some of the principles of wage payment enforced.

(1) The theory on which the payment for women taking the same work as men was regulated has been described exhaustively. But in addition to enforcing (with certain exceptions) equal payment for equal work, the principle of a minimum wage for women on munition work of any type was established by the later Orders. This was of obvious importance in the history of wages in the United Kingdom. It was largely because the original wage Orders of the Ministry prescribed standard, not minimum, rates, and therefore left no field for organisation to secure advances, that some women trade unionists criticised

them with vehemence, and compared them contemptuously to an Act passed three-and-a-half centuries earlier.[1]

(2) A relation—subject indeed to considerable elasticity in interpretation—between time and piece rates was prescribed, except for women on "men's work" in the engineering and allied trades who were intended to receive piece prices established for men. According to the proportion thus fixed, the normal worker must be able to earn at least 25 per cent. more when paid by results than when on time work. This provision overrode a large number of pre-war variations between districts, trades and firms, in fixing piece prices, which had been a cause of much difficulty in men's skilled work, and acted as an obstacle to the extension of payment by results.

(3) Overtime and other special allowances were similarly standardised (on the basis of those paid to men for work of the same class), although the provisions for the "women's work" group remained elastic. This standardisation of extra allowances had been spreading at the same time among unskilled male workers, who, like women, often had at the beginning of the War no agreement with their employers about such payments. A group of Committee on Production awards fixed these payments for unskilled labourers.

(4) Time rates were guaranteed "irrespective of earnings" to women and girls employed on piece work and premium bonus. This important provision served as a precedent when the extension of systems of payment by results in the engineering and woodworking industries was under consideration.[2]

(5) Piece work prices once established were not to be altered unless the " means or method of manufacture " were changed. This provision against the cutting of piece rates, was, again, obviously of the utmost importance for persons employed, like the majority of women munition makers, on systems of payment by results. The Ministry had, from the first acceptance of the principle of relaxation of trade union restrictions, given a general undertaking to all munition workers, that in return the cutting of piece rates would not be permitted, and had circularised controlled establishments to this effect in September, 1915. Men munition workers, it may be noted, only obtained explicit statutory recognition of this undertaking in the Munitions of War Act of August, 1917, although the principle was recognised in the second schedule of the first Munitions of War Act, and its observance coloured the regulation of munition workers' wages as a whole.

There remained a point in connection with the fixing of piece rates which left the workers' representatives dissatisfied. "Piece work prices and premium bonus time allowances shall be fixed by mutual

---

[1] The time rates prescribed for women on "women's work" and on woodwork, by the Consolidated Order of May, 1918, were still nominally standard rates. So much elasticity was, however, given for higher payments under special circumstances (see Chapter VI., p. 85, and Chapter VII., p. 92), that the " standard " rates were by this time virtually minima.

[2] Cf. the Trade Boards Act of 1909 (Section 8) and that of 1918 (Section 6).

agreement in accordance with these directions [summarised above], between the employer and the worker or workers who perform the work." (Section 36 of the Consolidated Order.)   An attempt was made in January, 1918, by the Women's Trade Union Advisory Committee to secure the insertion of the words "representative of" before "worker" in this clause, in order to introduce the trade union official into the process of rate fixing. Women, it was urged, were often inexperienced in estimating the prices due for a job, and needed outside help. This, it was frequently said, was specially desirable in the cases where women were engaged on "men's work," but were put on to new processes in such work. Such new piece prices might be underestimated and the prescribed relationship with the man's district time rate or the women's standard rate might disappear.[1] The same claim had been discussed previously with employers during the consideration of the clause concerning piece rates for men in the Munitions Act of the previous summer, and it had been rejected on the obvious ground of the very great administrative difficulties involved in each workshop by such an arrangement.

Apart from this debatable question, the provisions summarised represented a definite advance in systems of paying wages. Doubtless they coincided with the long-established practice of many employers; but they were valuable as standardising methods of payment in the country as a whole. The general recognition of them as conditions to be observed, whatever the rate of wages, would facilitate greatly the further differentiation of rates by trades or districts, which was inevitable when the distinction of "munitions" and "non-munitions" work should have disappeared.

III. Changes in the Position of Employers and Workers.

Some more general aspects of wage regulation may be suggested in their bearing upon employers and workers.

(1) THE EMPLOYERS' POSITION.

Manufacturers of munitions in controlled establishments found the wages which they had to pay to their women workers settled for them by an external authority. They complained, with some justification, of the extreme suddenness with which they were sometimes called upon to comply with Statutory Orders enjoining the payment of new rates of wages at a few days' notice. In so far as their work was for Government, however, as the greater part of it tended to be, the consequences of such changes were not so serious as they would have been in normal times. Not only did a firm's competitors, as a rule, labour under identical disabilities, so that there was no danger of contracts being lost owing to the competition of firms paying lower rates of wages ; but it was possible as a rule to recover any additional expense due to changes in wages from the Government that ordered

---

[1] Thus in a certain Lancashire district, as late as 1917, women piece workers on shell were said to have their prices fixed on the basis only of their guaranteed time wage of 26s. 6d., instead of on men's previous piece rates (L.R. 142/15).

the changes. The Ministry refused to commit itself to a general undertaking that a compulsory rise of wages should necessarily be refunded in full to a contractor by a revision of the terms of his contract. The Minister was prepared, it was explained to the Association of Chambers of Commerce in July, 1917, to take into consideration cases of grievances which might be brought to his notice, although a contract was supposed to allow a margin for wage fluctuations. In December, 1917, arrangements were made by the Ministry in conjunction with the Admiralty and the War Office for the insertion in future contracts—under certain conditions—of clauses providing for an addition to contract prices to meet the additional cost of wages " resulting from direct Government action."

The extension of the wages Orders to a large number of uncontrolled establishments in the autumn of 1917 removed, to some extent, grievances due to the payment of less than the statutory wages by firms free from control under the Munitions Act.

It may be possible at a later date to obtain, if not statistics, yet a body of opinion, on the important problem whether the increase in money wages for women was really an addition to labour costs, or whether the apparent loss to the employer was recouped by the better type of workers so obtained. At present no adequate data are available. Employers represented, during applications before the Special Tribunal for advances in women munitions workers' wages, that the height of their employees' wages might be dangerous to their trades after the War. The test of foreign competition was, however, to a great extent, absent during the War.

(2) The Workers' Position.

The position of the woman munition worker of July, 1918, had changed, like that of the employer, in the course of the past three years. A few months before the establishment of the Ministry of Munitions, she had, in many cases, been working short time, with memories of recent unemployment, in some other industry ; or she had been engaged in distributive or domestic work remote from the industrial world ; or she had been, technically at least, unoccupied. The Central Committee on Women's Employment at the beginning of 1915 was still considering the policy of relief workrooms and the provision of special assistance to transfer under-employed workers to other occupations. Three years later, unemployment, and the consequent disturbance of wage standards, had been a thing of the past for many months, at least for those who could move freely to take up work, and the competent woman munition maker was beginning to realise in some districts the increased commercial value of her labour as its supply at last grew short.[1] Her cash wages during these three years had frequently doubled and sometimes quadrupled,

---

[1] At the end of January, 1918, a period of unemployment began for women in certain filling and other factories, which were either closed down or worked short time owing to lack of material.

though their purchasing power had risen to a very much smaller extent, and her real earnings were normally by no means excessive, according to any fair standard of living. This increase was due partly to scarcity of competent labour, partly to the employer's desire to secure good conditions and efficiency in his factory, or to trade union agitation; but it was also definitely due to statutory regulation of wages on the part of the Ministry. For the first time in their lives, a very large number of women workers were earning a wage which made it possible for them, if they chose, to obtain at least the necessary minimum of food and clothes and rest, and in some cases very much more than this. Further, owing to the new mobility of women's labour, many women and girls employed on munition work (like the soldiers' wives in receipt of separation allowances) had become responsible, again for the first time in their lives, for the independent expenditure of an adequate weekly income. The social effects of the regulation of munition workers' wages were probably quite as important as the economic results. This, however, is a subject that it is impossible to pursue here.

In the course of the patriotic work of learning to make munitions, the woman worker had learnt, for better or worse, the value of a short period strike, and, to some extent, if not very profoundly, of organisation. Even the girl fresh from school, hitherto the cheapest and most insignificant factor in production, had found herself—perhaps not wholly to her advantage—guaranteed wages at fourteen, such as before the War she would have looked forward to as a possible maximum which she might reach as a grown-up worker; and on at least one occasion her grievances had been the cause of a strike which caused the employer to appeal urgently to the Ministry lest the output (in this case of tanks) should be indirectly affected.[1] The woman munition worker's "industrial sense" had developed, in part at least as the result of vigorous efforts by some four or five trade unions admitting women members, backed by the precept and example of unions, such as the Amalgamated Society of Engineers, which excluded women from membership.[2] These things were not necessarily the result of the Department's administration, but they formed the constant background to the Ministry's wages policy.

Although the scope and influence of the women's trade unions was in no way comparable to that of the men's unions, and their organisers admitted that the traditional difficulty of inducing the young worker to treat membership of her union as necessary and permanent still continued, the attitude of the Ministry towards the representatives of these unions was as cordial as that which it maintained towards the officials of the men's societies. An officer of the Women's Trade Union League was a member of the Special Arbitration Tribunal; the Secretary of the National Federation of Women

---

[1] I.C. 4386; C.E. 1460/5.
[2] The total female membership of trade unions at the end of December, 1915, was 405,000. At the end of 1916 it was 535,000. More than half of these members belonged to the textile trades.—*Labour Gazette*, May, 1918.

Workers had been placed upon the Central Munitions Labour Supply Committee and had shared in its discussions on wages in the autumn of 1915 and 1916 ; a body of representatives of women trade unionists was summoned by the Ministry in November, 1917, to advise the Department regularly on questions of women's wages and conditions of work. Complaints raised by these unions and by individual workers of the non-enforcement of the women's wages Orders were regularly and promptly investigated.

The new relationship between a Government Department and both employers and workpeople, established in three years' work of the Ministry of Munitions, was nowhere more tested than in the regulation of women's wages. The department, as has been said, created no revolution in the wages system of the country, so far as women were concerned. But this was clearly outside its province, which was, primarily, the output of munitions. The control of wages was only a bye-product of the manufacture of munitions, yet the effect upon the country's social and industrial life, thus incidentally produced, was remarkable and probably indelible.

CHAPTER X.

QUESTIONS OF PRINCIPLE.

I. The Administrative Problem.

In the preceding chapters an account has been given of the measures adopted by the Ministry of Munitions to control women's wages, the discussions and negotiations that led to them, and the results that followed on their adoption. There is another point of view from which the experience of the Department can be reviewed. The Ministry was continuously engaged in dealing with concrete issues, that left it little time for the consideration of questions of abstract principle. At the same time its work was beset with questions of principle, to which it had to find, and did find, answers in the course of its work. The experience of the Department, therefore, constitutes a contribution to the study of certain permanent problems arising out of wages that has something of the value of experiment in research into the problems of physical science. On two of these problems it may be permissible to summarise briefly the Department's experience; one, the practical problem of what is involved administratively in the control of wages by the State; the other, the theoretical question of the relations that should obtain between women's wages and men's.

On the first of these little need be said here, since the Department's experience in regulating men's wages has an equal bearing on the problem, and any final conclusions must be deferred until that experience has been recorded. The control of women's wages by itself, however, has been sufficient to establish two principles that were not grasped before the control was undertaken, first, that the problem of wages control cannot be dealt with piecemeal, since interference with the wages of one class of workers inevitably reacts upon the wages of other classes; and, second, that the fixing of wage-rates involves an elaborate administrative organisation, comprising not only a central department issuing the Orders, but local agents to enquire into questions of application, and some judicial authority to decide on disputed cases. That these implications of wages control had to be learnt by experience is shown by the scanty administrative provision originally made. The first suggestion was a committee, advising the secretarial officers of the Ministry, in the same way as a committee adjudicated on questions of transfer of War Munitions Volunteers; the actual provision made was the appointment of a single officer.[1] This was, of course, before

---
[1] M.W. 51,872 (Oct., 1915).

the Minister had taken power to regulate the wages of any class of worker by Order and before the actual issue of the recommendations that preceded the Orders ; but it was subsequent to the drafting and sending to the Minister of these recommendations, and it indicates how far removed from the original intentions of the Ministry was the detailed control of the wages of almost all women munition workers to which it was ultimately driven by the practical exigencies of its work.

It was, indeed, impossible in practice to draw a line, beyond which regulation should not extend, short of including all women munition workers. The policy of the Ministry at first was to rely on the Fair Wages Clause in public contracts to ensure fair wages, and on Section 4 (2) of the original Munitions of War Act to carry out the pledge that piece rates should not be cut. But the defective organisation of women's labour, as has been shown, compelled a positive policy. The Central Munitions Labour Supply Committee found that the regulation of the wages of women on men's work was essential to the smooth operation of dilution. From recommending rates the Ministry was led to take powers to order rates. From regulating the wages of women on " men's work," it was led to regulate the wages of women on " women's work." The fixing of rates involved decisions on all the incidental questions that the establishment of a standard rate involves—the rate of allowances for overtime, night work, and holiday work ; the relation of rates to hours ; the relation of piece work to time rates ; probationary periods, and rates during probation ; rates for juvenile workers ; allowances for waiting-time and stoppages ; differentiation between different grades of skill or exertion. Rates once established had to be adjusted to changes in the cost of living, which involved facing the problem of the relation between men's advances and women's.

The difficulty in drawing a line was due to the close inter-connexion of wages of different grades and different occupations. Absolute standards of fairness in wages there were none ; every wage-earner therefore tended to compare his or her position with that of fellow-workers in allied occupations. The restriction of regulation to women on " men's work," led to cases such as those quoted in Chapter V.,[1] where women on comparable work in the same establishments were receiving different rates of pay. Such comparisons aroused a sense of injustice, which practically compelled an extension of control in order to remove the anomaly. It is significant that when the Wages Orders expired and their place was taken by the Wages (Temporary Regulation) Act of 1918, the limits of control were widened still further, all standards rates made compulsory, and control unified in the Ministry of Labour.

Complaints were frequently made by Trade Unions and employers' spokesmen of the complexity of the Wages Orders. Yet the complexity was due very largely to a desire to meet or forestall difficulties raised by the same critics, and it would have been very much greater had their demands been conceded. As it was, only the activities

[1] p. 60.

of the local and central officials of the Department, supplemented by the Special Arbitration Tribunal, made it possible to cover such an immense variety of cases with such a limited number of Orders and such a limited number of clauses in those Orders. The history of Circular L.2 and its successors shows how impossible it is to forecast all the doubtful cases that may come under an Order and to provide for their decision. But the negotiations which led to the successive revisions of L.2 were only a part of the problem of application and interpretation. Industry does not afford the administrator the convenience of sharply defined categories and compact occupational groups ; on the contrary it offers a spectacle of infinite variety, in which every industry, district, and, one can almost say, firm, has its peculiar arrangements, and the categories, that one refers to so summarily by a single occupational term, prove in practice to be loose aggregations of very various units and to shade imperceptibly into one another. The number of problems presented by the application of general Orders to individual cases therefore is bound to be very great.

It must also be remembered that the Ministry's control of wages was undertaken and carried out under abnormal commercial conditions. The economic effort of the country was concentrated on a single task, the prosecution of the war, and the normal economic pressures, of competition on the one side and the possibility of unemployment on the other, were largely suspended. Had the Department had to allow in its control of wages for varying market conditions in all the trades it controlled and for constant fluctuations in these market conditions—had employers not had the possibility of throwing extra labour costs on to the Government, and workpeople not had the certainty of regular employment at rates much more remunerative than women were accustomed to before the war, the work of the Wages Section would have been infinitely more complicated. No such uniformity of basic rates as was achieved would have been practicable, the decision of what constituted a fair rate would have been much more difficult and arbitrary, and the explanation and enforcement of the multitude of different rates needed would have required a staff, at headquarters and in every industrial centre, such as the Ministry never commanded.

These considerations help to explain the difference between the State control of wages that existed before the war and that which the Ministry of Munitions was able to develop and exercise. Before the war, State control of women's wages was limited to eight trades, in which rates were regarded as exceptionally low. The characteristic that differentiated it fundamentally from the control established during the war, was that departmental action was directed not to *fixing* rates, but to *enforcing* rates fixed by Boards representative of the trades controlled. In other words, the State avoided the problems involved in fixing a rate and in making due allowance for all the varying factors that go to determine a rate, by throwing the responsibility on a body representative of the trade. In effect it provided, in certain ill-organised trades, a substitute for voluntary collective bargaining, and assimilated the condition of these trades in the matter of wage-determination to that of the majority of industries, in which standard rates are established without the aid of the State. By throwing this responsibility on to representative industrial bodies, the State escaped the necessity of laying down standards of fairness; it left to the representatives of the people most concerned the business of elaborating the provisions of an order so that it should cover all the contingencies that might arise under it; and, since the Trade Boards prescribed only minimum rates, it left an ample margin for adjustment by private arrangement to meet individual circumstances. The work of the Ministry of Munitions, it has been pointed out, has done much to introduce order and uniformity into the field of women's wages; to the extent that it has done this, it has facilitated the extension of control by Trade Boards and made the task of future Trade Boards much easier. If the differences between the general economic conditions of war and of peace, however, are borne in mind, too much will not be built on the Ministry's achievement in fixing rates as well as enforcing them when fixed. The conditions of war did not allow time for the lengthy process of collective bargaining; the conditions of peace require a much more delicate and precise adjustment of rates to market conditions. While there would seem to be scope for a considerable extension of State enforcement of standard rates, the actual fixing of the rates is best done by the representatives of the people who pay and receive wages.

The Absence of a Principle.

The Ministry's experience illuminates another difficulty in any policy of wages control by authority. Even if the Ministry had had the opportunity of treating women's wages from the beginning as an integral problem, instead of having it thrust upon it piecemeal, even if it had commanded from the beginning the services of a local and central staff, adequate in numbers and experience, the Ministry would still have lacked the essential condition of effective regulation, a clear and definite conception of the principles in accordance with which its control of women's wages was to be exercised.

The regulative activities of public Departments consist usually in the application to individual cases of general rules laid down by statute. The Department has usually a subordinate legislative function, since it can itself issue regulations interpreting and applying the general principle of the statute to which its administration is to give effect. But the statute itself settles the general question of principle; the discussions that usually accompany the passing of a Bill make clear its object, and give the Department time to consider its plans for administering the statute; and the Courts will interpret any point in the statute that has been left obscure. The Ministry of Munitions in its control of wages lacked this guidance. The general control of wages formed no part of the intentions of the promoters of the first Munitions of War Act; while the Amending Acts which empowered the Ministry to fix and enforce rates of wages for various classes of workpeople, gave no guidance as to the principles on which rates should be fixed.

Consequently, when the Ministry found itself faced with the question, what is a fair wage for a woman taking up unskilled repetition work in munitions manufacture, it could draw no guidance from the statutes under which its work was authorised, and had to frame a solution for itself.

The control of wages was, indeed, incidental. It arose from the exigencies of dilution, and the policy adopted necessarily followed the demands of the skilled men's Unions, who had it in their power to block dilution. There was no consideration of the problem of wages control on its merits; the principles on which the control should be exercised were largely determined by the need of finding an immediate solution to urgent practical problems, as in the Lang case. A decision might be taken, in order to secure an object to which the question of wages was only incidental, which would prevent a consistent treatment of a mass of wages questions in the future. Consistency, however, is essential to successful administration, and it can be attained only by settling the broad questions of principle, which come up again and again in the form of practical issues. The question, therefore, of the relation of women's wages to men's, theoretical and abstract as the discussion of it in the following pages may seem, has not only a practical importance for the future, but is an integral part of the history of wages control by the Ministry of Munitions, since it underlies most of the practical problems with which the Ministry had to deal.

II. "Equal Pay for Equal Work."

On one question the first Munitions of War Act purported to lay down a principle on the terms, namely, on which women should be paid who took men's work. Paragraph 5 of the Second Schedule laid it down that "The relaxation of existing demarcation restrictions or admission of semi-skilled or female labour shall not affect adversely the rates customarily paid for the job."[1]

Mr. Lloyd George, speaking as Minister of Munitions to a women's deputation on 17 July, 1915, gave a pledge to the same effect.[2] The Wages Section of the Ministry, therefore, could not in the field of "men's work" frame its own policy with the freedom it enjoyed in the field of "women's work." But how far the Treasury Agreement, on which the Schedule quoted above and the Minister of Munitions' pledge were based, was from affording a clear and definite principle on which the relations of women's wages and men's could be regulated is shown by the whole subsequent history of the Wages Section and especially by the negotiations that followed the issue of the Circular, L.2, intended to implement that pledge. The ordering of wages for "women's work" was straightforward and satisfactory by comparison with "men's work." The Schedule did not so much afford guidance for dealing with the problem as queer the pitch for the people who had it to deal with.

The pledge was generally interpreted as promising "equal pay for equal work," a formula that makes a popular appeal by its superficial

---
[1] Cf. pp. 4 and 8.   [2] Cf. pp. 1–2.

simplicity and obvious fairness, and it was the attempt to extend the pledge from piece rates to time rates that led to most of the difficulties. Mr. Lloyd George promised identical rates only on systems of payment by results, explicitly excluding time work ; the paragraph in the Second Schedule to the Act had, as the discussion preceding the formulation of it shows, the same limited reference ; and the paragraph on the subject in Circular L.2 (and its successors) is quite definite ; " the principle upon which the recommendations proceed is that *on systems of payment by results* equal payment shall be made to women as to men for an equal amount of work done." But these limitations are not inconsistent with a general application of the formula, " equal pay for equal work." The difficulty is that the formula itself constitutes a problem rather than a solution. The conflicting interpretations put upon it were a principal cause of the differences between employers and workpeople, and between both these classes and the Ministry itself, and its use has obstructed rather than assisted the development of a consistent policy of wages control.

Conflicting Interpretations.

The uselessness of the formula as a guide in administrative action is due to the ambiguity of the word " pay " and of the phrase " equal work," and to the absence from the formula of any reference to the element of time. Three different and conflicting interpretations at least can be put upon it :—

(1) The claim is made that women should be paid the same rate as men on the same work, time work as well as piece work, irrespective of output and of other differences between men and women which affect the value of an employee to an employer ;

(2) The claim is made for equal payment for the same work, due allowance being made for differences in output, expense of supervision, etc., where men and women are engaged on the same work *at the same time ;*

(3) The claim is made that women who have taken over work formerly done by men should be paid the same rates as the men *used to receive*, with due allowance for any change in the conditions of the work and for changes in the cost of living and other factors influencing wages that might have led to an alteration in the rates had men continued to do the work.

The first of these claims was the claim made by the engineers for women undertaking part of the work of a skilled time worker ; subject to a probationary period and a deduction for extra cost of supervision, it was conceded by the Ministry. The same claim was made for women on aircraft woodwork, but was refused on the ground that the industry had developed too recently and the nature of the work changed too much for any comparison to be drawn between men's work and women's. To this interpretation, employers always offered an uncompromising opposition, on the ground that equal time rates, since the women's output and general usefulness were less than the men's, represented unequal pay for equal work, and at various hearings they produced figures of actual expenditure to show that a woman's work in engineering or woodwork was the equivalent of only two-thirds or half of a man's.

The second and third interpretations were not usually distinguished, yet the practical importance of the distinction is very great. Equal pay for an equal amount of work is not only a practical policy, but the normal outcome of competition, when men and women are engaged on the same work in the same district *at the same time*. But it is comparatively rare in normal times to find men and women on the same work at the same time. Women are constantly displacing men, processes being adapted to make this possible, so that the really important comparison lies between the rates the women are receiving *now* and the rates that were *formerly* paid to the men before women undertook the work. The distinction is illustrated by the Special Arbitration Tribunal's recommendations after hearing the Aircraft Workers' claims on 10 and 11 September, 1918. The workers claimed that all work that had once been done by skilled men should be paid the full skilled rate ; the Tribunal did not allow this claim, but in the case of a limited class of women, doing work that was *still* being done by skilled men, it recommended that the women be paid the men's rates.

DIFFICULTY OF APPLICATION.

Even if these conflicting interpretations are ignored and the formula taken at its face meaning, an equal amount of pay for an equal amount of work, there are difficulties in applying the principle to actual problems. The measurement of output in time work trades is never easy or certain ; if it were, time work would almost certainly give place to piece work. Even equal piece rates do not give complete security that the choice of men's or women's labour will be a matter of indifference. Equal piece rates proportion payment to output ; but if the man's output is considerably more than the woman's, it will be more economical to employ men, since fuller use will thereby be made of the plant and organisation of the firm, and it will be possible to spread dead charges over a larger output. Again, the weight or quality of the work, or the conditions under which it is performed, may be different for men and women, whose work is apparently the same. The operations they perform may be apparently the same, and yet the men receive a higher rate of pay because the heavier, finer, or more responsible work is given to them, or because they perform for themselves incidental operations, such as setting-up a machine tool or "tackling" a loom, which the women do not perform. Or the men may command a higher rate, because they provide a necessary reserve of strength or skill. A woman may perform the ordinary routine of work as well as a man, and yet the man's services have a higher value owing to his capacity to meet more or less exceptional emergencies. A male porter's superior strength may be called for only occasionally at a railway station, but must be provided; a fully qualified tradesman's all-round skill may be required only occasionally in a machine-shop, and yet be indispensable. Thus an employer often commands in the case of men a reserve of strength or skill for which a charge is as reasonable as an insurance premium to cover contingent liabilities or an interest charge on reserve capital.

Thus the definition of " equal work " in the concrete is always a matter of difficulty. A great many cases in which there is apparently a disparity in the payment of men and women for the same work are found on examination to be due to such concealed difficulties in the nature or conditions of the work as are indicated above. The principle " equal pay for equal work " can therefore seldom be expressed in a single time rate or even in a single piece list ; it will usually involve the estimate and tabulation of a number of slight differences, each of which has to be allowed for in fixing the rate. Herein is the explanation of the workpeople's demand for a single rate, time or piece according to the nature of the work. They feel that every addition to the complexity of the wage formula, unless it can be made the subject of exact objective measurement, provides an opening for the employer to " nibble " at the rate. The employer has all the resources of his costing department behind him when it comes to making an estimate of the allowance to be made for any difference in conditions ; the workman has no such resource and is at a corresponding disadvantage in debate. The single rate on the other hand is a simple formula, easily understood and easily applied, that will rally all the workpeople concerned to its support ; that it may operate to the exclusion of women from many occupations is, if perceived at all, regarded as relatively a minor disadvantage.

The Unions have been able to make good this claim, however, in the main, only in industries like cotton, where all the factors influencing output can be tabulated, allowed for, and embodied in a piece list. Normally it is exceptional for men and women to do exactly the same kind of work ; but, where they do, equal pay for equal work, in the literal sense in which employers are prepared to apply it, tends to be the rule. For all the pressures to which competition subjects the employer tend to compel him to give equal pay for equal work. Labour cost is so important a factor in the economy of producing for the market, and the adaptation of work to the varying capacity of different classes and grades of workers is so important a factor in keeping labour cost down, that an employer could not usually afford to go on paying men at a higher rate than women for equal work in any numbers. If the women can do the work, they will tend to get it, driving out the men, whose different capacity will be employed on work which can be done only by workers with the longer training or stronger physique of the man. Inequalities of pay for the same work occur ; but so they do among men alone or among women alone. The rates of pay and allocation of work as between men and women vary from district to district ; but similar local variations are found in the pay and work of men alone or women alone. The principle of equal pay for equal work operates normally between men and women, with quite as much regularity as between men alone or women alone in ill-organised trades.

QUESTIONS OF PRINCIPLE

RESULTS OF SUBSTITUTION.

The more difficult problem, therefore, is that presented by the third of the interpretations of the formula given above, the relation namely of women's rates at one time with men's rates at another, earlier time. The real burden of the women worker's complaint, ill-expressed in the claim for equal pay for equal work, lies in the fact that when women have displaced men and the two are no longer engaged on the work together, the women do not usually get the same rates as the men used to get. There is usually some alteration in processes or conditions, that masks the drop in the rate of pay, and, strictly speaking, perhaps takes the work out of the category of " equal work," but the difference is usually too great to be accounted for by such changes. Women will accept and are therefore paid lower rates for the same or similar work than men, unless there are men actually engaged on the work with whom they can compare themselves and whose rates they can claim.

The formula, equal pay for equal work, does not then do much to answer the questions with which any authority or organisation attempting to control wages is faced. It merely slurs over and confuses two distinct questions, the question what should be the relation of women's wages to men's in cases in which men and women are doing the same or similar work at the same time, and the question what should be the relation, if any, of the wages of women who take over work formerly done by men to the wages the men used to receive. On the first question the formula of equal pay has issued in two irreconcilable policies, the trade union policy of the single rate irrespective of output or other circumstances influencing labour cost, and the policy of differential rates, corresponding with the differing efficiency of men and women, two policies that embody entirely different conceptions of the rights of labour in the economic organisation. The second question acquired a peculiar importance during the war, and, if we turn to the experience of the Ministry of Munitions, we find, not indeed an answer that was satisfactory either to the trade unions or the employers, but a policy that could be administered and a mass of evidence on which any better policy, if such can be devised, must be based.

III. Alternative Policies.

The war introduced two novel and exceptional conditions into the process of substituting women for men. In the first place, it speeded up the process. The usual motive that leads to substitution, the hope of reducing labour-costs, was weakened, since additional cost could be thrown in the case of so large a proportion of production on the State ; but the absolute shortage of labour and the withdrawal of men for military service together constituted an inducement much stronger than the usual motive. The consequences of this acceleration were, first that any difference between the rates paid to women after substitution and those paid to men before was much more noticeable ; and, secondly, that there were many more cases of incomplete substitution than usual and many more cases of women and men doing the same work at the same time. Hence the importance of the problem of the right relation of women's wages to men's, an importance which it will lose as these temporary conditions pass.

In the second place, the substitution of women for men was not contemplated as a permanent arrangement. In order to overcome the natural resistance of the men to a reorganisation of production which might weaken their bargaining strength, the Government gave pledges in certain industries to restore pre-war conditions, and private employers gave similar pledges in other industries. However complete therefore the substitution of women for men might be during the war, it could not have the same effects on wages as it would have had in normal times. The wages of the women substitutes were closely linked with the wages of the men whose places they had taken and to whom it was intended they should give place after the war.

POLICY OF THE MINISTRY.

The Ministry's policy must be considered in the light of these special conditions. The elaboration of it is detailed in Chapters II to IV ; it may be summarised briefly as follows :—

(1) Piece-workers were guaranteed the same piece rates, and premium bonus workers the same basis times, as men had received ;

(2) Time-workers doing the whole of a fully skilled man's job—a small class—were paid his full time-rate ;

(3) Time-workers doing part of a fully skilled man's job (owing to sub-division or other re-arrangement of work) were paid his time-rate, subject to (a) a single probationary period lasting three months at lower rates, and (b) a deduction not exceeding 10%, to be sanctioned in every case by the Minister of Munitions, for extra supervision ;

(4) Time-workers doing unskilled or semi-skilled men's work were not regarded as necessarily doing " equal " work, but were secured a minimum wage.

These regulations, with the possible exception of the last, were consistent with the principle of equal pay ; certain supplementary regulations made by the Ministry or based on decisions of the Special Arbitration Tribunal, excited more controversy. Thus :—

(1) Women piece-workers, although they received the same piece rates as men, had allowances for overtime or night shift calculated on the women's time rates, *i.e.*, on the rates guaranteed to women time-workers on men's work, not on the men's time rates ;

(2) Women did not participate in the bonuses and war-wage advances granted to men in 1917 and 1918, but received smaller advances at the same rate as women on work that was not done by women before the war.

The controversies on these points were complicated by the great practical difficulties met with in defining " men's work," because the customary distribution of work between men and women was different in different districts, and sometimes in different shops in the same district, and in drawing lines between skilled, semi-skilled, and unskilled work.

Thus, the women were given by the Ministry's policy the same or equivalent *rates* as the men who had done the work before them had received; they were not given the same *pay* as men would have received, had men continued to do the work, or as men were receiving when men had continued to do the same or equivalent work, because their bonuses, war wages and other allowances were different. The drop in rates that usually accompanies a rearrangement of work and the employment of women in place of men was prevented; but in the subsequent adjustment of wages there was differentiation between women and men. Thus, the principle of equal pay was not applied consistently in any of its three senses; and consistency was difficult to achieve, when the substitution of women for men was being treated as a temporary arrangement only, and the control of the wages of substitutes undertaken more in the interests of the men whose sphere of work was being invaded than of the substitutes themselves. The men's interests, it was considered, were adequately safeguarded, if the *rates* in operation when the women were introduced had not been cut by the time the women went out; bonuses and other adjustments in the interval did not affect the rate and could be left out of account, being equally temporary and specifically intended to meet the cost of living. The differences in overtime allowances for piece workers could be defended, when the woman's output was less than the man's, since her earnings in normal hours would be less and the reduced overtime payment roughly proportionate. Thus, the Ministry's policy was based on an attempt to "freeze" the system of rates in operation immediately before the introduction of women, and thenceforward to maintain a sharp distinction between these rates and any supplementary payments subsequently authorised to meet changes in the cost of living.

Even this policy, however, could not be carried out quite consistently. Thus :—

(1) The policy of encouraging systems of payment by results pursued by the Ministry (and by other Government Departments), and the stereotyping of piece-rates once fixed, had the effect of disturbing pre-war wage relations and establishing new standards of earnings, which had no relation whatever to changes in the cost of living.

(2) While the men's awards in the chief munition industries were intended specifically to leave *rates* unaffected, and therefore took the form of a single amount payable alike to all time-workers, skilled and unskilled, it was possible to argue that they did not leave the rates unaffected but were additions to them. For the awards to piece-workers took the form of percentages on earnings; and even in the case of the time-workers the war wage was to count for the purpose of calculating overtime and similar allowances. Thus, the women could argue that the men's rates on which their rates were based had been altered.

(3) While the great majority of the women on "men's work" received war wage advances in the same form as, but at

a lower rate than, the Committee on Production awards to men, the Coal Controller's award, when extended to allied trades by the Ministry of Munitions, did not discriminate between men and women on the same work. The number of women was no doubt small, but the case is important from the point of view of principle.

OBSTACLES TO UNIFORM TREATMENT.

The Trade Unionist criticism of the Ministry's policy and the Ministry's reply have been indicated in Chapters IV and VII. To have conceded the Unions' demand of equal war advances and of the $12\frac{1}{2}\%$ and $7\frac{1}{2}\%$ bonuses for all women on men's work would have involved the State in large additional expenditure. It must logically have led to conceding the same overtime, night shift and other allowances. By abolishing the distinction between the "rate" and war advances, it would have justified skilled workers, male as well as female, in refusing the flat bonus which they received in common with semiskilled and unskilled workers and in claiming larger advances proportionate to their higher normal rates. Its most serious effect, however, would have been its reaction on other women on "women's work," and on women wage-earners outside the munitions industries. The former could not have been expected to rest content with lower rates of pay merely on the ground of the historical accident that men had not done their work, much of it new work, before the war. They would have pressed for similar rates to those of their fellow women workers on munitions. Women working outside the scope of the Munition Wages Orders would have made similar comparisons, especially since the Wages Orders did not necessarily cover all the women in a given trade, and they, too, would have claimed advances that would at least maintain the existing proportion between their earnings and those of the two classes of women munition workers. Then, since male workers normally consider themselves entitled to rates higher, in some well-understood ratio, than those of the women in the same industry, they too would have presented their claims, and a new cycle of trouble would have begun. The Department's policy of treating the wages of all women munition workers as an integral problem and of placing on the pledge to the men's unions the interpretation that interfered with the uniform treatment of women's wages least is easily understood when the administrative problems that would have been raised by any other policy are considered.

On the other hand, the discrimination between men and women on "men's work" was resented by men and women alike. It gave rise to a sense of injustice among the women and a fear among the men that their economic position was being undermined, which had already produced serious industrial unrest and might have been expected to produce much more, when the Armistice was signed. Its inconsistency with the simplest and *prima facie* meaning of "equal pay for equal work" led the great mass of the workers concerned, who were ignorant of the strict limitation within which the Government had pledged itself to that principle, to impute a breach of faith to the Government. From the point of view of principle, what was perhaps of more importance was that it gave official recognition to a novel principle in the fixing of wages, by basing them on the assumed needs of the worker as well as on the work done ; if the lesser needs of the woman without dependants were to justify a lower rate for equivalent work than was paid to men who were presumed to have dependants, then a case would be made out for discrimination between women without and women with dependants, and between single and married men. The connection between value of product and labour cost would be severed, and demands would be invited for the application of the system of Army separation allowances to industry.

The root of the difficulty in which the Ministry of Munitions found itself was the difference in the general levels of men's and women's wages, and the obstacle in the way of a consistent policy was the pledge to the men's unions. Had no pledge to base the wages of certain women on men's rates been given, it would have been possible to treat women's wages as a self-contained problem, and to confine regulation to assisting collective bargaining and enforcing its results. Whether fixed by Order or by collective agreement, women's rates would have represented roughly the resultant of the bargaining strength of employers and employees ; and, where the substitution of women for men was complete, no question of the relation of the women's rates to those previously received by the men would have been entertained. But the pledge that women on "men's work" should receive the same piece rates as men had done, and the general undertaking that substitution should be temporary, precluded such a policy. The practical question was whether the men's position was adequately safeguarded by securing to the women who took their work at the rates in operation at that moment, or equality of pay, inclusive of all bonuses and allowances, was necessary.

The demand for the payment to women of the same bonuses, advances and allowances as men was in effect a demand for something more than "equal pay for equal work." As has been shown, equality of pay for equal work is normally established by the fixing of new rates after the introduction of women, which are either so high as to make the continued employment of women at them uneconomical to the employer, or so low as to render the occupation unattractive to men. The present demand in effect proposed that the rate should be determined on the assumption that the work was actually men's work, without allowance for the fact that women could do and were doing it. In other words, the demand was not for equal pay only, but for *equal pay at men's rates*, although the work had become women's work. When the women 'bus-conductors struck, what they demanded was not that the total sum that the industry could afford in bonuses should be distributed equally, which might have afforded a bonus of 3s. 6d. to men and women alike, but that the men should continue to receive a 5s. bonus and the women's bonus of 2s. 6d. be raised to the same amount. In the munitions industries, where the claim covered women in exceptional trades, in which they had completely, though only temporarily, displaced men, the basis of pay, had the claim been conceded, would have been entirely hypothetical; the women's pay would have been based on what men would have received had they continued to do the work, which as a matter of fact they had not.

The Ministry's policy of "freezing" the rates in operation when substitution began, was, however, only possible because substitution was being treated as temporary. As a permanent arrangement—and inevitably after four years' operation some of the war changes in the allocation of work must persist—it was impracticable. There was nothing sacrosanct about the rates in operation in 1914 and 1915, or whenever substitution began in a trade; industrial conditions are constantly changing, and wages must change with them. Once the war ended, the distinction between "rate" and "war wage," or "bonus," was bound to lose its force; the Wages (Temporary Regulation) Act, as we have seen, swept it away.

DIFFICULTY OF BASING WOMEN'S RATES ON MEN'S.

Under normal conditions, then, to base women's wages on men's, when women and men are no longer engaged simultaneously on the work, is not a practicable policy. It would require a continuation of State fixing of women's wages, since the problem would not arise if women could be relied on to stand out for equivalent rates to men's without assistance. State fixing of wages would not afford a certain guarantee of rates as high with women in a trade as they would have been with men; the authority charged with the task would almost certainly, like an arbitrator, be influenced by the probable results of free bargaining, which would certainly be lower rates for women, the general relation of women's wages to men's being what it is. Even if every care were taken to exclude that factor, the security would be incomplete owing to the intrinsic difficulty of the task placed on the State; it is a hard enough task for an ordinary arbitrator to estimate actual economic forces and reach a wage determination that will stand; to ask a State Department to fix women's wages on the assumption that men only are employed, a hypothetical and non-existent state of things, is to ask impossibilities.

The belief that women's wages can be based on men's, and the demand for a State policy of wage-regulation on this basis, would seem to be due to a notion that work has always a precise intrinsic value. The drop in wage rates that usually accompanies the complete substitution of women for men in an occupation is regarded from this point of view as an unjust abstraction by the employer—or, if the analysis is carried a little further, by the community in its capacity of consumer—of a part of the intrinsic value of the work; what the value of the work is, it is argued, could be ascertained when the men performed it, and the women who take their place should be paid that value.

Work, however, no more than anything else has intrinsic value. Every change in the demand for or supply of the product on which any kind of labour is expended influences the value of that product and indirectly of the labour. If a product is not wanted, then the labour that is specialised to it will not be wanted either, and its value will to that extent be reduced. Equally, if some change in the character, organisation or application of labour makes possible production at a reduced labour-cost, the value of the commodity will tend to fall. Profits act as a buffer between the value of the product and wages, bearing losses due to temporary reductions in value, and taking the gains due to temporary increases ; but competition and the advantages of large production, which can be disposed of only by keeping prices down, are usually sufficient to keep the value of the product and the wages of the labour expended on it in close and constant relation. Now the substitution of women for men usually does result in lower labour costs, because the women will not stand out for the same wages as men, and consequently if they displace men, get less for equivalent work. The substitution of women for men therefore normally leads not only to a lowering of rates of wages, but before long, to a lowering of prices of products—or, what amounts to the same thing, to a check to the rise in a time of rising wages and prices. Neither prices nor wages represent more than a temporary equilibrium of conflicting forces, and the women engaged on a low-priced product at a low rate of wages are just as likely to be getting the full market value of the work as the men who did the same work at a higher rate of wages before ; but the value of the work has changed.

THE DEMAND FOR THE SINGLE RATE.

Any attempt then to base women's rates on men's in occupations in which they are no longer working together is impracticable ; there remains the problem of the relation that should be maintained between men's and women's wages in work on which both are engaged at the same time. We have seen that all the pressure that competition exerts on employers will tend to make them give equal pay for equal work in this case. There will always be anomalies, because the pressure of competition is not uniform or always effective against customary standards ; but at any rate unequal pay is an unstable condition of things. Employers, as the experience of the Ministry and the Special Arbitration Tribunal shows, are willing to accept the principle of equal pay in this sense and to co-operate in giving effect to it where it is not already observed. But Labour, as represented both by the men's unions and the women's, will not accept this principle, and opposes to it the claim to the single rate for the job. It is necessary to consider whether that policy is practicable, and, if so, what would be its effects.

The policy is practicable in so far as any control of wages is practicable. A single rate or piece list for each occupation could be established and protected either by effective trade union organisation or by Statutory Order, and the Fair Wages Clause in public contracts could be made to give support to the principle in the former case. The effect would vary with the kind of work done. In time-work—except in rare cases of work for which men and women were equally fitted —the effect would be to exclude sooner or later the less efficient class ; in rare cases women would be more efficient, but in most cases the employer, having to pay the same rate in either case, would prefer the fuller training and stronger physique of the man. In the munitions industries, in spite of the shortage of labour of every kind and in spite of the possibilities of throwing on to the Government additional labour costs due to Government regulation of wages, employers were reluctant to employ women at men's rates, and the supply departments of the Ministry supported their protests on the ground that identical rates checked the employment of women ; the employment of women in the tool-room, for example, was hindered by the necessity the employer was under of paying the man's time rate (subject to a possible deduction for extra supervision) after the conclusion of a single probationary period, in which the woman would become expert at only one of the many tasks to which a tool-room hand might be set.

On systems of payment by results, the effect might be different in different cases. Where a piece list could be devised that made allowances for all the various factors that could influence output and gave therefore a wage that was exactly proportionate to the net output attributable to each worker, there women and men would continue to work together in the occupation ; cotton-weaving is the best example. Where, however, the measurement of output, with due allowance for every factor, is difficult—as is the case in most of the engineering occupations—a single piece list would probably have the same effect as a single time rate, and tend to exclude from the occupation the less efficient class of workers, which would in most cases be the women. The strong opposition of employers to the women's claim to identical overtime and other allowances for piece workers, backed up as they were by examples of the additional costs involved in employing women in the place of men, indicate that even on systems of payment by results an identical rate may tend to exclude women. The demand for identical rates for men and women was made most strongly, it may be noted, by those unions that offered the strongest opposition to payment by results.

The policy of the single rate would tend therefore to restrict the field of women's employment in time-work occupations, and to some extent in other occupations. It would hamper their entry into new occupations by imposing on employers who wished to introduce them the cost of maintaining them at the full rate during the period of training while their efficiency was less than normal. The restriction of women's employment in its turn would involve relatively an uneconomical use of men's labour, since they would retain work that could be done by workers of less complete training and weaker physique. It would also probably stimulate the search for processes and methods of organisation so different that they would enable employers to effect a substitution of women for men in the production of a given commodity without any comparison between men and women being instituted.

Another effect that the single rate might be expected to produce would be to stimulate the devising and extension of systems of payment by results. A system of payment by results as perfect as a cotton weaving piece list makes it almost a matter of indifference to an employer whether he employs women or men. If the men's production is greater, the employment of men will ensure a fuller use of plant and a lowering of overhead expenses per unit of product ; this, however, will not by itself be enough to counteract the advantages to an employer of women's labour. Women's standards of wages are lower than men's; the introduction of any considerable number of women to an occupation, therefore, will tend to lessen the pressure on the employer for higher wages. It must not be expected that the extension of systems of payment by results will be easy; the workers in what are at present time work trades will resist it, and their resistance will be valuable if it prevents the introduction of such systems in work in which the factors influencing the workman's productivity cannot be accurately measured and allowed for.

The chief result of the policy of the single rate, however, would be, for reasons already stated, to strengthen the tendency towards a division of labour between the sexes and their separation in different occupations. This division of labour will not necessarily be in accordance with the special capacities that distinguish men and women, owing to the hindrance the policy offers to the free entrance of women to trades at present confined to men; and the division would be to a large extent arbitrary in the large number of occupations in which women can do the work as well, if not as quickly, as men. But a division of labour would be effected, since it is unlikely that there would be many cases in which the work of men and women was exactly equivalent, or in which the inequalities in their work could be subject to continuous and precise measurement and allowance made for them all in a piece list.

These are grave objections to the policy of the single rate, from the point of view both of society, which requires the most economical application of the varying capacities of its members, and of women workers as a class, whose most pressing need is a wider choice of employment. But so long as the present disparity between the standards of men's and women's wages persists, the policy is probably open to less objections than any alternative solution of the problem Thus, while it restricts the field of women's employment, it does secure for them equality of pay in those occupations in which they are engaged along with men; and, unlike a policy of differential rates, it leaves no room for discussion and complaint as to the relative adequacy and fairness of the two rates. In the second place, by keeping men and women in the main in separate occupations, it lessens the opportunities of comparison between men's rates and women's, avoids all the awkward questions as to what constitutes " equality " of work, and offers no nourishment to that sense of injustice which, however illogically, is always found when men and women are engaged on the same or similar work at different rates. Nothing comes out more clearly from the Ministry of Munitions' experience than the administrative difficulties arising from any attempt to encourage the employment of women on " men's work " in " time work " trades. In the third place, it secures this convenient and desirable separation of the sexes in different occupations, without any overt or, indeed, any deliberate exclusion of women from any occupation; the rate discriminates automatically, just as a fixed price for any article determines the nature and amount of supply. Finally—and this is the consideration that commends the policy to Trade Unionists—it is the simplest policy to administer, whether rates are to be determined by collective bargaining or State control, and gives a security to the standard rate that would be difficult to attain with any other policy. The workman feels with justice that any additional complication in wages puts him at a disadvantage with the employer. Even if the workman's official can by some means compensate for his lack of access to the employer's cost accounts, and so secure differential rates that represent exactly the differing efficiency of men and women, he cannot count on the solid and unanimous support of the rank and file of the workers, when it comes to negotiating an advance, resisting a reduction, or adapting the rates to a change in conditions, as he could expect if his case were summed up in a single rate. Especially is this the case when the workers whom he has to rally include women as well as men; for women have not as a rule the same instinctive loyalty to their union as generations of Trade Union organisation have implanted in men, and women's standards of what they ought to receive and what they must at any cost stand out for, are lower than men's. If the policy of the single rate reduced the aggregate wealth of the community and the share of that aggregate that went to the wage-earning class, the wage-earner would still feel that the additional security that it gave to his rate was worth the sacrifice. And it is at least arguable that the reduction of friction in the relations of employers and employed, that the policy might be expected to yield, would be a contribution to production as considerable as any contribution that would be made by a redistribution of labour in industry carried through against the wishes of the workers. To be fair to the woman-worker, however, the policy of the single rate would need to be supplemented in two directions: first, by the provision of facilities for training that would enable women to qualify themselves for earning the full rate in the higher paid occupations, and, secondly, by the establishment and protection of minimum rates for women in lower paid occupations.

IV. The Differing Standards of Men's and Women's Wages.

Underlying every problem of the relation of women's wages to men's is the disparity between the general level of women's wages and the general level of men's. That fact was the reason why it was impossible to ignore the sex of the worker and consider only the skill required or the intensity of the work in deciding any question of remuneration. Some consideration may be permitted in conclusion of the reasons for this disparity.

It is not sufficient to say that wages are "customary" and that "custom" keeps women's wages down. It is true that custom makes change difficult, and that what has been for a long time comes to be regarded as ethically right. But to attribute the difference between men's and women's wages to "custom" means no more than that the difference is hard to remove and hard to explain. It is necessary to explain the "custom." Reasons are not really hard to find, although it is difficult to assess their respective importance. The most obvious is the restricted field of employment open to women. Women are excluded from certain of the better-paid manual occupations, such as coal hewing and iron and steel manufacture, by considerations of physique. In others the work requires a high degree of skill or an all-round capacity; these, women could attain if they went through the same lengthy training as men, but the average expectation of industrial life is so much less in the case of a girl than a boy that women rarely do undergo this training. From others, again, women are excluded by customary or Trade Union restrictions. The result of these restrictions is to crowd women workers into a relatively narrow range of occupations, within which competition for work is exceptionally keen.

But suppose these restrictions removed; suppose women had access to a range of occupations as wide, having regard to their respective numbers, as the range open to men. Would they then secure and maintain in their own field of work rates as high as men would have secured had they occupied the field? It is very doubtful. The restrictions on women's employment are no greater than those to which an unskilled male labourer of less than average physique is subject; yet women's wages before the war were much lower on the average than those of unskilled male labour. An explanation is needed also why competition for employment does not force workers, labouring under so many disadvantages as women, to accept even lower rates than they do. There is no common physical limit below which work could not be done; Mr. Seebohm Rowntree's calculations of a minimum wage give a figure far above the average woman's earnings, and in most countries wages are much lower than in England; even if there were a physical limit, charity, the Poor Law, and subsidies by relatives would enable a large number of workers to accept wages below it.

The explanation is probably to be found in a customary limitation of competition. Customary standards are established for which the great mass of workers in any grade or class will stand out. Wages tend to be pressed down by competition until this limit is reached, when competition ceases to operate. The great difference between labour and material commodities (in their reaction to changes in demand) is just this: in the case of a material commodity that, like labour, will not "keep," the price will usually if necessary be reduced until the whole of the supply is taken up, in the case of labour the seller will not reduce the price below certain customary limits, preferring unemployment in a sufficient number of cases to maintain these limits. The limit is fixed by the conventional needs of the workers concerned; *i.e.*, the customary limit is established by *the majority of the class*. Owing to competition among employers the minority who could manage on less will be able to get the rate; owing to competition for employment, the minority who have exceptional social liabilities and need more will be able to get no more.

Now, the majority of women have no dependants; the majority of men maintain a family. The customary standard in the case of women is therefore lower than in the case of men. Competition, as has been said, tends to go on till the customary standard is reached in each case, but the customary standard is different. It is through this influence on the customary standard of women workers that the fact that in the majority of cases women have no dependants influences wage rates ; whether it ought to do so, is an entirely separate question.

These customary standards are important because prices tend to be adjusted to a labour cost based upon them ; it is the consumer, therefore, not the employer in the last resort, who pays women less than men. They constitute a minimum supply price which has to be paid to get the work done, and in the long run the normal is not much above the minimum. In times of good trade, when labour is scarce relatively to the demand, wages will rise above them ; but the rise will not be permanent unless secured by organisation. Organisation substitutes conscious limitation of competition for the instinctive combination inspired by a customary standard ; consequently, it makes the standard more definite and can take advantage of any opportunity to raise the standard. Where the women are well organised rates high enough to attract men are maintained, and men and women are found on the same work. Whether established by conscious or unconscious limitation of competition, however, there is a rate for most kinds of labour, to which prices tend to be adjusted ; and this rate is usually lower in the case of women's work, because women as a rule can and will accept a lower rate than men.

If this analysis is correct, the lower general level of women's wages is the outcome of one of the most fundamental of social conditions, the economic unity of the family. There is nothing accidental or transient about it, and a Government that sought to ignore it would be continually brought back to a realisation of its fundamental character by the practical difficulties with which such a policy would find itself faced. The man's wage is a " family " wage, the woman's an " individual " wage. To say this is to state a fact, not to enunciate a principle. No Government authority or combination of employers before the war ever deliberately adopted the principle that women's wages *ought* to be less than men's, or consciously based women's rates on their individual needs, men's on a family's needs. Women themselves and men themselves have established the two standards, by standing out in each case for a wage that would meet the conventional needs of a normal member of the class.[1]

THE QUESTION OF SOCIAL PRINCIPLE.

Explanation, however, is not justification, and it is impossible to avoid the question—*Ought* women's wages generally to be lower than men's ?—or to put the problem specifically—Ought the Government, when it undertook the control of women's wages, to have accepted the fact of the difference between men's and women's wages without trying in the course of its control to eliminate the difference ? The answer given will depend not on any survey of facts, but on the political or ethical principle adopted by which to judge wage rates and wage relations.

---

[1] One important result of the War has been a raising of the conventional standard of life of the women workers. This is likely to be permanent, with the result, that the divergence between women's wages and men's is likely to be less. But there will still be a divergence.

Whatever policy the Government had adopted in regulating the relations of women's wages to men's, it would have met with an equal amount of criticism—not all of it from different quarters. For it is just on this point of principle, what *ought* to be the basis of wages, that the greatest and the least suspected differences exist. Thus, the implication underlying the claim to equal pay, when men and women are engaged on the same work at the same time, is one thing when the work is piece work and the pay proportionate to output, an entirely different thing when the work is time work and the pay independent of output. In the former case, the ethical principle adopted is that pay should be proportionate to output and should vary with the amount of work done; in the latter case, it is that a certain income should be attached to a certain industrial service, to be paid irrespective of individual variations in output, like the soldiers' pay or the salaried official's income. Again, when the claim is made that women should have the rates of men who formerly did the work before it became a woman's job, the implication is the same as in the former of the two cases given above, that pay should depend on output, and women should be paid the same proportion of the men's pay as their output bears to the men's output. But there is a further implication in this last claim, namely, that every kind of labour has an intrinsic value that ought to be secured to the worker in the form of wages, and that the payment for labour should not be affected by changes in the supply of labour in the way that the prices of commodities fluctuate with every change in the conditions of their supply. The criticism of the Ministry of Munitions' wages policy drew much of its acerbity from a feeling that its decisions were not merely mistaken or inexpedient, but actually unjust, because they infringed the principles of justice supposed to be inherent in existing wage rates and wage relations.

When we turn to the actualities of the wage system, we see that this criticism at any rate has no valid ground. Just as the principles on which the different critics based their claims were contradictory and inconsistent, so the actual rates and relations existing before Government control began are explicable by reference to no single ethical principle. Support can be derived from a study of the facts of wages for each of the principles indicated in the last paragraph; but taking a complete view, we find neither the uniform correspondence of remuneration with exertion required by the first theory, nor the guarantee of economic status by the second, nor the stable intrinsic values by the third. On the contrary, wages are seen to be the outcome of bargaining and to be liable to change with every change in market conditions and production methods, and generally with every change in the bargaining strength of either of the parties concerned.

So far as the influences determining them can be summed up in a single formula, wages would seem to depend on the relative indispensability of the labour for which they are paid. The demand for the product, the riches or poverty of the natural resources on which the labour will be employed, the extent to which capital is available, and the possibility of substituting some other labour, will condition the indispensability of any particular kind of labour ; combinations among the workpeople will largely determine the form and method of payment ; combination again, or in the case of unorganised labour an instinctive observance of common standards, will impose a lower limit below which wages will not be allowed to fall ; and no single formula can make due allowance for all the influences of historical conditions, perpetuated by custom, on wages. But analysis reveals among the factors no unifying ethical principle, because none such has ever been imposed. And the reason why none such has been imposed (and why the Government could impose none during the War), is that there is no agreement on the principle to impose. The whole system is empirical ; society pays through the employer what it has to pay in order to get the work done ; the worker gets from society through the employer just as much as he can for his work. There are no intrinsic values in the economic world, and labour, like the employer of labour, is left by society to make the best of its market.

No appeal to existing facts, therefore, will answer the question, *Ought* the general level of women's wages to be lower than men's ? All that the appeal to the facts shows is that the assumption of intrinsic value in work, on which the allegation of injustice rests, has no foundation.

No final answer to the question can be given, but a case can be made for the difference in the levels of men's and women's wages at least as strong as any case for equality. The benefit of the lower level of women's wages goes to the consumer ; otherwise profits in industries employing mainly women would be higher than in industries employing mainly men, of which there is no evidence. The majority of women wage-earners have not dependants, while the majority of men have ; a higher rate for men, therefore, is needed to secure anything like equality between the individuals dependent on wages. The difference in the levels, although it is not the outcome of any deliberate policy with this object, results in a closer approximation of income to needs and a greater equality of income among the individuals dependent on wages (as distinct from the actual recipients of wages) than would a single uniform level. Were the State to adopt the principle of the identical standard for men and women and to seek by authoritative control of wages to eliminate the present difference in the standards, it would not merely be introducing a new factor into the determination of wages, which would compel an indefinite continuation of the State control of wages; it would be establishing a new economic basis for the family, and it is from this point of view that any such proposal should be approached.

The experience of the Ministry of Munitions has afforded an object-lesson in the difficulties and problems attending any attempt to fix wage rates by authority. The relation that should be maintained between women's rates and men's was the problem on which the most numerous and the greatest difficulties centred. The controversies which the Ministry's decisions excited turn ultimately on differences of opinion on the question, What ought wages to depend on ? Until that question of ethical and social principle has received further elucidation and some general agreement on it has been reached, no satisfactory system of wage-fixing by authority can be substituted for the present system of wage-fixing by bargaining and private contract.

For this reason the experience of the Ministry affords no encouragement to go beyond the methods of State control of wages accepted in principle and already in operation before the war. These were to assist collective bargaining and accept its results, merely imposing such minima as the general wealth of the community permitted and public opinion demanded. To establish statutory bodies for collective bargaining, like the Trade Boards and the Agricultural Wages Board, to make the determinations of such boards and of voluntary joint bodies mandatory on whole trades, to assist collective bargaining by providing facilities for conciliation and arbitration, are all in line with this policy, and the experience of the Ministry has shown that a great extension of such activity is possible. The discussions over Wages Orders have also made it clear that a wages policy will not provide for all social needs, since it is impossible in establishing rates to make provision for every exceptional case, or even for such important groups as that of women wage-earners with families dependent on them; any wages policy therefore will form only a part of a general social policy. But with the actual fixing of rates in normal times, and especially with the fixing of rates for men and women on similar work, no Government that has studied the experience of the Ministry of Munitions and can by any means avert the necessity, will be inclined to meddle.

APPENDICES.

APPENDIX I.
Table of the Statutory Wages Orders.

NOTE.—Orders marked * are printed in Appendix III.

THE MUNITIONS (EMPLOYMENT AND REMUNERATION OF WOMEN ON MEN'S WORK) ORDERS.

Wage Order No.	Dated.	Date taking effect.	Remarks.	Statutory Rules and Orders No.
1	24/ 2/16	28/ 2/16	Circular L.2 in compulsory form. £1 a week for unskilled timeworkers, etc. (See Ch. II.)	(1916) 181*
2	26/ 6/16	3/ 7/16	Same as No. 181 applied to different firms.	,, 411
3	7/ 9/16	18/ 9/16	Same as No. 181 applied to different firms.	,, 586
4	28/ 9/16	16/10/16	Same as No. 181 applied to different firms.	,, 704
5	21/12/16	1/ 1/17	Provision for "intermediate" payments added. Amends and re-enacts previous orders. (See pp. 30-35).	,, 888
6	24/ 1/17	5/ 2/17	Amends and re-enacts No. 888 (Provision for probationary period and for recognition of the £1 a week as a minimum).	(1917) 49
7	16/ 4/17	8/ 4/17	Supersedes previous orders (24s. minimum for timeworkers, etc.).	,, 489*
8	30/ 5/17	18/ 6/17	Same as No. 489 applied to different firms.	,, 539
9	16/ 8/17	3/ 9/17	Same as Nos. 489 and 539 applied to different firms, including certified undertakings.	,, 888
–	7/11/17	19/11/17	Same as Nos. 488, 539, 888 applied to different firms.	,, 1116
–	31/ 5/18	——	Part I. of No. 546 applied to different firms.	(1918) 594

THE MUNITIONS (EMPLOYMENT AND REMUNERATION OF GIRLS ON MEN'S WORK) ORDERS.

Wage Order No.	Dated.	Date taking effect.	Remarks.	Statutory Rules and Orders No.
1	6/ 7/16	17/ 7/16	(See p. 22)	(1916) 456
2	7/ 9/16	18/ 9/16	Same as No. 456 applied to different firms.	,, 587
3	28/ 9/16	16/10/16	Same as Nos. 456 and 587 applied to different firms.	,, 703
4	22/ 1/17	5/ 2/17	Same as Nos. 456, 587, 703 applied to different firms.	(1917) 48
5	16/ 4/17	8/ 4/17	Supersedes previous orders. (See p.23)	.. 490
6	30/ 5/17	18/ 6/17	Same as No. 490 applied to different firms.	,, 540
7	16/ 8/17	3/ 9/17	Same as Nos. 490 and 540 applied to different firms (including certified undertakings).	,, 889
–	7/11/17	19/11/17	Same as Nos. 490, 540 and 889 applied to different firms.	,, 1120

THE MUNITIONS (REMUNERATION OF WOMEN AND GIRLS ON WORK NOT RECOGNISED AS MEN'S WORK) CONSOLIDATED ORDERS.

Wage Order No.	Dated.	Date taking effect.	Remarks.	Statutory Rules and Orders No.	
—	6/ 7/16	17/ 7/16	Hourly rate of 4½d. an hour on time, 4d. on piece, etc. (See pp. 64 *et sqq.*)	(1916)	447*
—	13/ 9/16	2/10/16	To be read in conjunction with No. 447	,,	618*
1	27/10/16	20/11/16	Consolidating Nos. 447, 618.. ..	,,	759
2	6/ 1/17	22/ 1/17	Amends and extends Nos. 447, 618, 759. (See pp. 77 *et sqq.*)	(1917)	9*
3	6/ 1/17	22/ 1/17	Amends and extends Nos. 447, 618, 759.	,,	10
4	16/ 4/17	8/ 4/17	Supersedes No. 9 (rates raised to 5½d. an hour on time, 4¾d. on piece).	,,	492
5	16/ 4/17	8/ 4/17	Supersedes No. 10	,,	493
6	30/ 5/17	18/ 6/17	Same as No. 492 applied to different firms.	,,	542
7	16/ 8/17	3/ 9/17	Same as Nos. 492 and 542 applied to different firms including certified undertakings.	,,	891
—	7/11/17	19/11/17	Same as Nos. 492, 542 and 891 applied to different firms.	,,	1119
—	31/ 5/18	———	Part II. of No. 546 applied to different firms.	(1918)	595

NOTE.—Statutory Rules and Orders No. (1917) Nos. 10 and 493 were only applied to a few firms in rural districts. The rates prescribed were a farthing lower than in Nos. 9 and 492, 542, 891.

THE MUNITIONS (EMPLOYMENT AND REMUNERATION OF WOMEN AND GIRLS ON WOODWORK FOR AIRCRAFT) ORDERS.

Wage Order No.	Dated.	Date taking effect.	Remarks.	Statutory Rules and Orders No.	
1	13/ 9/16	2/10/16	5d. to 6½d. an hour, etc. (See Ch.VII.)	(1916)	621
2	16/ 4/17	8/ 4/17	Supersedes previous orders (6d. to 7½d. an hour, etc.).	(1917)	491
3	30/ 5/17	18/ 6/17	Same as No. 491 applied to different firms.	,,	541
4	16/ 8/17	3/ 9/17	Same as Nos. 491, 541 applied to different firms (including certified undertakings)	,,	890
—	7/11/17	19/11/17	Same as Nos. 491, 541 and 890 applied to different firms.	,,	1117

STATUTORY WAGES ORDERS

THE MUNITIONS (EMPLOYMENT AND REMUNERATION OF WOMEN AND GIRLS ON GENERAL WOODWORK) INTERIM ORDERS.

Wage Order No.	Dated.	Date taking effect.	Remarks.	Statutory Rules and Orders No.
—	30/ 3/17	16/ 4/17	(6d. an hour minimum)	(1917) 313
—	30/ 5/17	18/ 6/17	Same as No. 313 applied to different firms.	,, 543
—	16/ 8/17	3/ 9/17	Same as Nos. 313, 543 applied to different firms (including certified undertakings).	,, 892
—	7/11/17	19/11/17	Same as Nos. 313, 543, 892 applied to different firms.	,, 111

THE MUNITIONS (EMPLOYMENT AND REMUNERATION) CONSOLIDATED WOMEN'S ORDER.

Wage Order No.	Dated.	Date taking effect.	Remarks.	Statutory Rules and Orders No.
—	8/ 5/18	———	Consolidates and amends existing Orders. (See pp. 51, 83, 90, 91).	(1918) 546
—	21/ 6/18	15/ 7/18	Same as No. 546 applied to different firms.	,, 743
—	30/ 8/18	1/ 9/18	Same as No. 546 applied to different firms.	,, 1103

ADVANCES IN WAGES OF WOMEN AND GIRLS.

Wage Order No.	Dated.	Date taking effect.	Remarks	Statutory Rules and Orders No.
—	31/ 7/17	18/ 8/17	Applied to all controlled and uncontrolled establishments to which wages Orders had been applied up to that date, 2s. 6d. advance to women, 1s. 3d. to girls.	(1917) 781
—	16/ 8/17	3/ 9/17	Same as No. 781 applied to different firms (including certified undertakings).	,, 893
—	7/11/17	19/11/17	Same as Nos. 781, 893 applied to different firms.	,, 1121
—	14/ 1/18	15/12/17 (first full pay-day after)	3s. 6d. advance to women, 1s. 9d. advance to girls.	(1918) 31
—	28/ 8/18	1/9/18	5s. advance to women, 2s. 6d. advance to girls.	,, 1073

APPENDIX II.

Note on the Application of the Wages Orders.

POSSIBLE SCOPE.

Under Section 6 of the Munitions of War Act of January, 1916, statutory wages Orders for women might be issued to establishments to which the leaving certificate rules applied—*i.e.*, to those engaged on "munitions" in the narrow sense of engineering and shipbuilding and the production of arms, ammunition and explosives. This definition did not, until May, 1916, include all controlled establishments, and the first issue of L.2 was therefore on a limited scale. After that date, the Department was able, if this appeared desirable, to apply the Orders to all controlled establishments.

Only about a dozen uncontrolled establishments had these regulations applied to them by special order during 1916. The question of their application to uncontrolled munitions establishments was discussed as early as April, 1916, with reference to the case of a small uncontrolled firm at Sheffield which was employing women on men and boys' work at less than the L.2 rates. It was, however, held to be impossible to regulate wages in uncontrolled establishments at the time, except by applying statutory Orders to individual works, since very large numbers of firms might be involved and only a Munitions Tribunal could say whether Section 7 of the Munitions Act applied to one of them or not ([1]).

In the summer of 1917 it was, however, decided to apply the wages orders to gas, water and electricity works and tramways, which, although not controlled establishments, had been classified as "certified undertakings" under Section 9 (1) of the Munitions Act of 1915. This was effected, despite the forthcoming withdrawal of the benefits of the leaving certificate regulations, which had been the immediate cause of the "certification" of these undertakings.

The Munitions of War Act of 1917 provided (Section 4) that the right to make statutory orders for women's wages should, if the leaving certificate regulations were withdrawn, be applicable to "female workers employed on or in connection with munitions work in establishments of all classes." In accordance with this provision the orders were sent during the succeeding autumn and winter to a considerable number of uncontrolled establishments (such as those producing bolts and nuts and—rather later—ammunition boxes) as well as to further "certified undertakings."

THE TRADES INCLUDED.

Circular L.2 in its obligatory form was sent primarily to controlled establishments engaged in munitions work in the sense described above. By February, 1917, the Orders regulating the wages of women and girls taking men's work (including those working on aircraft and paid under a separate Order) had been applied to 3,585 establishments engaged in the following trades :—

Arms, ammunition and ordnance ; mechanical, electrical, tele-

---

[1] M.W. 92329/32 ; C.E. 3845/4. Cf. Vol. IV., Pt. II.

APPLICATION OF THE WAGES ORDERS

graphic and marine engineering ; makers of electric and telegraphic accessories ; machine tool manufacture ; shipbuilding and repairing ; iron and steel works ; tube works ; tinplate ; lead and copper works ; foundries ; blast furnaces ; wire and cable works ; textile and printing machinery ; motors and cycles ; aircraft ; constructional engineering ; the manufacture of saws and files ; cutlery ; silver and electro plate.

Orders for women on men's work had not by this date been applied to the few controlled establishments in Ireland, although they were so applied in July, 1917. Explosive and chemical works, and munition works producing glass, optical and scientific instruments, tinplate, rubber, oil and seed-crushing were also excluded during the first two years of regulation.[1] The L.2 series of orders were; it was pointed out in an official memorandum (L.30) on the circulars bearing on dilution, intended primarily for the engineering and allied industries, though in other trades they might be used as a basis on which rates might be fixed. The most important exception to their application was the chemical and explosives trade group. This omission had been deliberate on the part of the Department, which, however, in so far as the national factories were concerned, endeavoured to secure at least as good conditions for the women so employed as for those in engineering works. Conditions as to daily shifts, the weekly hours of work and payment for overtime differed so much in the engineering and chemical trades that there were difficulties in applying the same wage regulations to both. Further, practically all work for women replacing men in such factories involved questions of payment under " special circumstances " or for special skill,[2] so that the application of L.2, even as modified in 1917, could settle little with regard to wages.

APPLICATION OF CONSOLIDATED ORDER.

The original application of the "women's work" Orders and their extension has been explained in Chapters V. and VI.[3]

The Consolidated Order of May, 1918, was applied to controlled establishments in the trades specified below, together with uncontrolled establishments known to the Department to be employing women on munitions work of a class similar to that performed in controlled establishments scheduled, and not known to be employing women on munitions work of a class which had been expressly excluded from the operation of the Order. An effort was made to cover all firms known to be producing guns, ammunition, ammunition boxes (wood) and aircraft.[4]

Metal Trades.

1. Metal manufacture :—Blast furnaces ; steel works ; iron and steel foundries ; forges ; stamps ; drops and dies ; rolling mills ; drawn rod and wire works ; tubes.

---
[1] L.R. 142/34, and Parliamentary Debates, 6 March, 1917.
[2] M.W. 92329/28   [3] See pages 55, 77.
[4] The number of women thus employed in April, 1918, was approximately as follows :—Controlled Establishments, 495,000 ; Government Factories, 133,600 ; Uncontrolled Establishments receiving orders, about 50,000 ; total 678,600.

2. Machinery :—Electrical and other machinery; factory equipment; machine tools.

3. Engine and pump building :—Steam turbines; steam, gas, oil and Diesel engines; locomotives (in controlled establishments—establishments other than railway workshops); pumps, compressors and condensing plant; aero-engines; motor vehicles, lorries and cycles (engines and chassis); tanks (engines and transmission gear).

4. Constructional engineering and boilermaking :—Constructional engineering; boilermaking; tanks (hulls and sponsons).

5. Vehicles and aircraft :—Aeroplanes, seaplanes and flying boats; airships; motor vehicles; lorries and cycles (bodies); railway carriages, wagon building, coachbuilding and wheelwrighting.

6. Arms and ammunition :—Guns, gun-carriages and parts; rifles, machine guns, revolvers; swords and bayonets; shells (excluding filling) and parts; fuses and shell accessories and cartridge cases; grenades, bombs, mines, etc.; torpedoes; rifle and machine gun cartridges and Q.F. cartridges; miscellaneous Trench Warfare (including steel helmets).

7. Miscellaneous :—Gas and water meters; cocks and valves; pipe fittings; ball and roller bearings; electric lampholders, installations, electric light and gas fittings and oil lamps; typewriters and duplicators; flexible metal tubes, etc., stoves, grates and ranges; field kitchens; small tools and gauges; " engineering and non-engineering implements"; scientific, surgical and dental instruments,[1] optical and glass instruments,[1] electrical and other instruments, screws, bolts, nuts; nails and rivets; springs; electric wires and cables.

Chemical Trades.

1. Explosives manufacture :—Nitrocellulose, gun cotton, R.D.B. and other propellants; T.N.T., ammonium nitrate and mixtures therewith; dinitrophenol and picric acid; gunpowder; blasting and other high explosives; fulminates.

Explosive filling :—Propellant filling (cordite, etc.); Q.F. cartridges; small arms cartridges; bad charges.

High Explosive Filling :—Shell filling (poison gas filling); fuse, primer and detonator filling; grenade, bomb, poison gas and other filling, mine and torpedo filling, cap and safety fuse filling and pellet pressing; fireworks, signal lights, flares, smoke-boxes, etc.

2. Other Chemicals :—Heavy chemicals, including poison gases; drugs and fine chemicals; fertilisers; dyes; dope; coke ovens; tar distilleries; refineries of tar products; seed crushing, oil extraction and refining tallow; seed cake production; animal and vegetable oil refining and tallow production; shale oil and petroleum refining.

---

[1] " Women's work" portion of Order only.

APPLICATION OF THE WAGES ORDERS

Miscellaneous.
Ammunition boxes; rope; rubber.

NOTES.

(i) Tin box firms, being under a Trade Board, did not receive the Consolidated Order, but in certain cases received the order of August, 1917, for a general advance of 2s. 6d. a week.

(ii) Hollow-ware firms, also under a Trade Board, received the men's work portion (only) of the Consolidated Order. They also received the orders for general advances of 2s. 6d. and 3s. 6d. a week, to be applied to women on men's work; in certain cases women on "women's work" had the 6s. special advance superimposed on their Trade Board rates.

(iii) Chain-making firms received orders for the special advances only.

(iv) Paper firms did not have the Consolidated Order, but continued to apply the advances in some cases imposed on them. A few paper box firms employed on cartridge cylinders got the order.

(v) Tinplate firms in S. Wales and firms who were members of the S. Wales Siemens Steel Association paid under special arrangements in lieu of the orders.

(vi) Certified undertakings and leather firms did not receive the Consolidated Order. The former remained under the separate "men's work" and "women's work" orders applied to them in the previous autumn.

APPENDIX III.

Circulars and Orders relating to the Remuneration of Women and Girls on Munition Work.

1. CIRCULAR L.2, OCTOBER, 1915.—Recommendations relating to the Employment and Remuneration of Women on Munition Work of a class which prior to the War was not recognised as Women's Work in districts where such work was customarily carried on.
2. STATUTORY RULES AND ORDERS, 1916, No. 447.—Remuneration of Women and Girls on Munition Work of a class not recognised as Men's Work, dated 6 July, 1917.
3. STATUTORY RULES AND ORDERS, 1916, No. 618.—Remuneration of Women and Girls on Munition Work of a class not recognised as Men's Work, dated 13 September, 1916.
4. STATUTORY RULES AND ORDERS, 1917, No. 9.—The Munitions (Remuneration of Women and Girls on Work not recognised as Men's Work) Consolidated Order, No. 2, dated 6 January, 1917.
5. STATUTORY RULES AND ORDERS, 1917, No. 489.—The Munitions (Employment and Remuneration of Women on Men's Work) Order, No. 7, dated 16 April, 1917.
6. STATUTORY RULES AND ORDERS, 1918, No. 546.—The Consolidated Women's Wages Order, dated 8 May, 1918.

Circular L.2.

MINISTRY OF MUNITIONS.

MUNITIONS LABOUR SUPPLY COMMITTEE.

RECOMMENDATIONS RELATING TO THE EMPLOYMENT AND REMUNERATION OF WOMEN ON MUNITION WORK OF A CLASS WHICH PRIOR TO THE WAR WAS NOT RECOGNISED AS WOMEN'S WORK IN DISTRICTS WHERE SUCH WORK WAS CUSTOMARILY CARRIED ON.

(*NOTE.—These Recommendations are on the basis of the setting up of the Machines being otherwise provided for. They are strictly confined to the War period and are subject to the observance of the provisions of Schedule II. of the Munitions of War Act reprinted in the Appendix.*)

1. Women of 18 years of age and over employed on time, on work customarily done by men, shall be rated at £1 per week, reckoned on the usual working hours of the district in question for men in Engineering Establishments.

REMUNERATION OF WOMEN AND GIRLS

This, however, shall not apply in the case of women employed on work customarily done by fully-skilled tradesmen, in which case the women shall be paid the time rates of the tradesmen whose work they undertake. Overtime and night-shift and Sunday and holiday allowances payable to men shall also be made to women.

2. Where women are prevented from working, owing to breakdown, air raid, or other cause beyond their control, they shall be paid for the time so lost at the rate of 15s. a week as above, unless they are sent home.

3. Women shall not be put on piece work or premium bonus systems until sufficiently qualified. The period of qualification on shell work shall not, in general case, exceed three to four weeks.

4. Where women are employed on piece work they shall be paid the same piece work prices as are customarily paid to men for the job.

5. Where women are engaged on premium bonus systems, the time allowed for a job shall be that customarily allowed to men for the same job, and the earnings of the women shall be calculated on the basis of the man's time rate.

6. Where the job in question has not hitherto been done on piece work or premium bonus system in the establishment, the piece work price, or the time allowed, shall be based on a similar job previously done by men, on piece work or premium bonus system as the case may be.

7. Where in the establishment in question there are no data from previous operations to enable the parties to arrive at a piece work price or time to be allowed, the price or the time to be allowed shall be so adjusted that the women shall receive the same percentage over the time rate of the class of men customarily employed on the job, as such man would have received had he undertaken the job on piece work or premium bonus system as the case may be.

8. The principle upon which the recommendations proceed is that on systems of payment by results equal payment shall be made to women as to the men for an equal amount of work done.

9. Piece work prices and premium bonus basis times shall be fixed by mutual agreement between the employer and the woman or women who perform the work.

10. On piece work, every woman's time rate as per Clause 1 hereof shall be guaranteed irrespectively of her piece work earnings. Debit balances shall not be carried forward beyond the usual weekly period of settlement.

11. On premium bonus systems every woman's time rate as per Clause 1 hereof shall in all cases be paid.

12. Overtime and night shift and Sunday and holiday allowances shall be paid to women employed on piece work or premium bonus system on the same conditions as now prevail in the case of men in the district in question for time work.

13. Piece work prices and premium bonus time allowances, after they have been established, shall not be altered unless the means or method of manufacture are changed.

14. All wages and balances shall be paid to women through the Office.

15. Any question which arises as to the interpretation of these recommendations shall be determined by the Minister of Munitions.

October, 1915.

APPENDIX.

MUNITIONS OF WAR ACT, 1915.

SCHEDULE II.

1. Any departure during the war from the practice ruling in the workshops, shipyards, and other industries prior to the war shall only be for the period of the war.

2. No change in practice made during the war shall be allowed to prejudice the position of the workmen in the owners' employment or of their trade unions in regard to the resumption and maintenance after the war of any rules or customs existing prior to the war.

3. In any readjustment of staff which may have to be effected after the war priority of employment will be given to workmen in the owners' employment at the beginning of the war who have been serving with the colours or who were in the owners' employment when the establishment became a controlled establishment.

4. Where the custom of a shop is changed during the war by the introduction of semi-skilled men to perform work hitherto performed by a class of workmen of higher skill, the time and piece rates paid shall be the usual rates of the district for that class of work.

5. The relaxation of existing demarcation restrictions or admission of semi-skilled or female labour shall not affect adversely the rates customarily paid for the job. In cases where men who ordinarily do the work are adversely affected thereby, the necessary readjustments shall be made so that they can maintain their previous earnings.

6. A record of the nature of the departure from the conditions prevailing when the establishment became a controlled establishment shall be kept, and shall be open for inspection by the authorised representative of the Government.

7. Due notice shall be given to the workmen concerned wherever practicable of any changes of working conditions which it is desired to introduce as the result of the establishment becoming a controlled establishment, and opportunity for local consultation with workmen or their representatives shall be given if desired.

REMUNERATION OF WOMEN AND GIRLS 157

8. All differences with workmen engaged on Government work arising out of changes so introduced or with regard to wages or conditions of employment arising out of the war shall be settled in accordance with this Act without stoppage of work.

9. Nothing in this Schedule (except as provided by the fourth[1] paragraph thereof) shall prejudice the position of employers or persons employed after the war.

STATUTORY RULES AND ORDERS.
1916, No. 447.
MUNITIONS OF WAR.

Remuneration of Women and Girls on Munition Work of a class not recognised as Men's Work.

Order, dated 6 July, 1916, of the Minister of Munitions made in pursuance of Section 6 of the Munitions of War (Amendment) Act, 1916 (5 & 6 Geo. 5, c. 99).

Directions relating to the Remuneration of Women and Girls on Munition Work of a Class which prior to the War was not recognised as Men's Work in Districts where such Work was customarily carried on.

1. Where women or girls are engaged on Munition work of a class which prior to the war was not recognised as men's work in districts where such work was customarily carried on, the time rates for pieceworkers and premium bonus workers shall be as follows:—

    Workers 18 years and over .. .. 4d. per hour
    ,, 17 ,, ,, under 18 .. .. .. 3¼d. ,,
    ,, 16 ,, ,, ,, 17 .. .. .. 3d. ,,
    ,, under 16 years .. .. 2¼d. ,,

2. The rates for such women and girls when customarily on time shall be as follows:—

    Workers 18 years and over .. .. 4½d. per hour
    ,, 17 ,, ,, under 18 .. .. .. 4d. ,,
    ,, 16 ,, ,, ,, 17 .. .. .. 3½d. ,,
    ,, under 16 years .. .. 3d. ,,

3. Women and girls in danger zones shall be paid ½d. per hour in addition to the above rates. Allowances for other processes which are dangerous or injurious to health will be decided on the merits of such cases.

4. The appropriate time rate shall, in the case of any woman or girl on piece work, be guaranteed irrespective of her piece work earnings. Debit balances shall not be carried forward from one week to another.

5. On premium bonus systems every woman's and girl's appropriate time rate shall in all cases be paid.

---

[1] Should be "third," and so amended in the Amending Act of 1916.

6. Women or girls shall not be put on piece work or premium bonus systems until sufficiently qualified. The period of qualification should not generally exceed four weeks.

7. The above rates shall be recognised as war rates, and as due to and depending on the exceptional conditions resulting from the present war.

8. The foregoing rates shall not operate to prejudice the position of any person who has better terms and conditions, nor prevent employers from recognising special ability or responsibility.

9. For the purpose of this Schedule the term "men" means males of 18 years of age and over.

10. Any question which arises as to the interpretation of these provisions shall be determined by the Minister of Munitions.

STATUTORY RULES AND ORDERS, 1916, No. 618.

MUNITIONS OF WAR.

Remuneration of Women and Girls on Munitions Work of a class not recognised as Men's Work.

Order, dated 13 September, 1916, of the Minister of Munitions made in pursuance of Section 6 of the Munitions of War (Amendment) Act, 1916 (5 & 6 Geo. 5, c. 99).

Supplementary Directions relating to the Remuneration of Women and Girls on Munitions Work of a Class which prior to the War was not recognised as Men's Work in Districts where such Work was customarily carried on.

1. Additional payment in respect of overtime, night-shift, Sunday or holiday work shall be made to women and girls employed on munitions work of a class which, prior to the war, was not recognised as men's work in districts where such work was customarily carried on. Such additional payments shall be made in accordance with the custom of the establishment for the class of workpeople concerned in cases where such a custom exists. Where no custom providing for such additional payments exists in the establishment, such additional payments shall be made at the rates and on the conditions prevailing in similar establishments or trades in the district. Where there are no similar establishments or trades in the district, the rates and conditions prevailing in the nearest district in which the general industrial conditions are similar shall be adopted. In the absence of any custom prevailing in the establishment, or in the district, or elsewhere, such additional payments shall be made at such rates and on such conditions as the Minister of Munitions may direct.

2. Piece work prices and premium bonus basis times shall be such as to enable a woman or girl of ordinary ability to earn at least

REMUNERATION OF WOMEN AND GIRLS 159

33⅓ per cent. over her time rate, except in the case of an establishment where an application that this provision should be dispensed with either generally or as regards any particular class of workpeople has been approved by the Minister of Munitions.

3. The foregoing conditions shall be recognised as war conditions and as due to and depending on the exceptional circumstances resulting from the present war.

4. Any question which arises as to the interpretation of these provisions shall be determined by the Minister of Munitions.

5. These directions shall be read in conjunction with the directions contained in Order 447 as if they were included in that Order.

STATUTORY RULES AND ORDERS, 1917, No. 9.

MUNITIONS OF WAR.
Employment and Remuneration.

The Munitions (Remuneration of Women and Girls on Work not recognised as Men's Work) Consolidated Order, No. 2, dated 6 January, 1917, made by the Minister of Munitions in pursuance of Section 6 of the Munitions of War (Amendment) Act, 1916 (5 & 6 Geo. 5, c. 99).

First Schedule.

Directions relating to the Remuneration of Women and Girls on Munitions Work of a Class which prior to the War was not recognised as Men's Work in Districts where such work was customarily carried on.

1. Where women or girls are engaged on munitions work of a class which prior to the war was not recognised as men's work in districts where such work was customarily carried on, the time rates for piece workers and premium bonus workers shall be as follows :—

Workers 18 years and over	..	..	..	4d. per hour
,, 17 ,, ,, under 18	..	..	..	3¼d. ,,
,, 16 ,, ,, ,, 17	..	..	..	3d ,,
,, 15 ,, ,, ,, 16	..	..	..	2¼d. ,,
,, under 15 years	..	..	..	2d. ,,

2. The rates for such women and girls when customarily on time shall be as follows :—

Workers 18 years and over	..	..	..	4½d. per hour
,, 17 ,, ,, under 18	..	..	..	4d. ,
,, 16 ,, ,, ,, 17	..	...	..	3¼d. ,,
,, 15 ,, ,, ,, 16	..	..	..	3d. ,,
,, under 15 years	..	..	..	2¼d. ,,

3. Women and girls in danger zones shall be paid ½d. per hour in addition to the above rates. Allowances for other processes which are dangerous or injurious to health will be decided on the merits of such cases.

APPENDIX III.

4. In an establishment in which a custom prevailed prior to the war of differentiating between the rates of wages paid to women and girls employed in warehouses and those otherwise employed, an application may be made to the Minister of Munitions for special directions as to the rates of wages to be paid to women and girls employed in warehouses.

5. Women and girls may be rated at ½d. per hour less than their appropriate time rate under these directions for probationary periods not exceeding :—

In the case of workers of 18 years and over				..	..	1 month
,,	,,	,,	16 ,,	under 18	..	2 months
,,	,,	,,	under 16 years		.. ..	3 ,,

Such probationary periods shall be reckoned from the date when women or girls are first employed, and no woman or girl shall be called upon to serve more than one probationary period.

6. The appropriate time rate shall, in the case of any woman or girl on piece work, be guaranteed irrespective of her piece work earnings. Debit balances shall not be carried forward from one week to another.

7. On premium bonus systems every woman's and girl's appropriate time rate shall in all cases be paid.

8. Women or girls shall not be put on piece work or premium bonus systems until sufficiently qualified. The period of qualification should not generally exceed four weeks.

9. Additional payment in respect of overtime, night-shift, Sunday or holiday work shall be made to women and girls employed on munitions work of a class which prior to the war was not recognised as men's work in districts where such work was customarily carried on. Such additional payments shall be made in accordance with the custom of the establishment for the class of workpeople concerned in cases where such a custom exists. Where no custom providing for such additional payment exists in the establishment, such additional payments shall be made at the rates and on the conditions prevailing in similar establishments or trades in the district. Where there are no similar establishments or trades in the district, the rates and conditions prevailing in the nearest district in which the general industrial conditions are similar shall be adopted. In the absence of any custom prevailing in the establishment, or in the district, or elsewhere, such additional payments shall be made at such rates and on such conditions as the Minister of Munitions may direct.

10. Piece work prices and premium bonus basis times shall be such as to enable a woman or girl of ordinary ability to earn at least $33\frac{1}{3}$ % over her time rate, except in the case of an establishment where an application that this provision should be dispensed with either generally or as regards any particular class of workpeople has been approved by the Minister of Munitions.

REMUNERATION OF WOMEN AND GIRLS

11. The above rates and conditions shall be recognised as war rates and conditions, and as due to and depending on the exceptional circumstances resulting from the present war.

12. The position of any person or persons whose existing rates of remuneration exceed the rates herein prescribed shall not be prejudiced by this Order either by a reduction in existing rates or by replacement by another person or other persons at lower rates, nor shall employers be prevented from recognising special ability or responsibility.

13. For the purpose of this Schedule the term " men " means males of 18 years of age and over.

14. Any question which arises as to the interpretation of these provisions shall be determined by the Minister of Munitions.

STATUTORY RULES AND ORDERS,
1917, No. 489.

MUNITIONS OF WAR.
Employment and Remuneration.

The Munitions (Employment and Remuneration of Women on Men's Work) Order, No. 7, dated 16 April, 1917, made by the Minister of Munitions, in pursuance of Section 6 of the Munitions of War (Amendment) Act, 1916 (5 & 6 Geo. 5, c. 99).

Directions relating to the Employment and Remuneration of Women of 18 years of age or over on Munitions Work of a Class which prior to the War was customarily done by Men of 18 years of age or over in Districts where such work was carried on.

NOTE.—(1) These directions are on the basis of the setting up of the machines being otherwise provided for.

(2) These directions are confined to the War period and are subject to the observance of the provisions of Schedule II. of the Munitions of War Act, 1915.

(3) Proposals under paragraph 1 (*a*) (ii) of these directions for advances to classes of women upon the time rates prescribed by paragraph 1 (*a*) (i) are proposals for changes in rates of wages within Section 4 (2) of the Munitions of War Act, 1915, and must accordingly be submitted to the Minister of Munitions for his sanction.

APPENDIX III

1. (a) (i). Women employed on time on work customarily done by men shall, except as provided in paragraphs 1 (a) (ii) and 1 (b), be paid :—

Where the working week is 48 hours, 24s.

Where the working week is less than 48 hours, 24s. for the working week and for additional hours, if any, worked up to 48.

Where the working week exceeds 48 hours, as follows :—

		£	s.	d.
For 49 hours		1	4	6
,, 50 ,,		1	5	0
,, 51 ,,		1	5	6
,, 52 ,,		1	6	0
,, 53 ,,		1	6	6
,, 54 ,,		1	7	0

(a) (ii). Women employed on time, (a) on work of a class customarily done by semi-skilled men, or (b) on work of a specially laborious or responsible nature, or (c) where special circumstances exist, shall be paid according to the nature of the work and the ability of the women, but in no case less than the time rates specified in paragraph 1 (a) (i).

(a) (iii). Overtime, night-shift, Sunday and holiday allowances as customarily paid to men shall be paid to the women to whom paragraphs 1 (a) (i) and 1 (a) (ii) refer. The basis for overtime shall be the working week for women in the establishment in question. For this purpose, the working week for women shall in no case be reckoned as less than 48 hours or more than 54 hours. The rate for overtime for women other than those referred to in paragraph 1 (a) (ii) and 1 (b) shall be computed on the basis of 24s. for 48 hours.

(b) (i). Women employed on the work customarily done by fully-skilled tradesmen shall in all cases be paid as from commencement the time rates of the tradesmen whose work they undertake.

(b) (ii). A woman shall be considered as not employed on the work customarily done by fully-skilled tradesmen, but a part or portion only thereof, if she does not do the customary setting up, or when there is no setting up, if she requires skilled supervision to a degree beyond that customarily required by fully-skilled tradesmen undertaking the work in question.

(b) (iii). Women who undertake part or portion only of the work customarily done by fully-skilled tradesmen shall serve a probationary period of three months. The wages of such women for this period shall be reckoned as follows :—

They shall be rated for a period of four weeks at the time rate of wages to which they are entitled under these directions when employed on time, and from that rate shall then rise from the beginning of the fifth week until the end of the thirteenth week by equal weekly increases to the district time rate of the fully-skilled tradesman, and shall thereafter be rated at the district rate of the tradesman whose work they are in part or portion undertaking.

(b) (iv). In any case where it is established to the satisfaction of the Minister that additional cost is being incurred by extra setting up or skilled supervision due to the employment of women in place of fully-skilled tradesmen, the rates payable to women under these directions may, with the sanction of the Minister, be subject, for so long as such additional cost is incurred, to deductions not exceeding 10 per cent. to meet such additional cost. Provided that no women shall in any case be paid at lower rates than those prescribed by paragraph 1 (a) (i) of these directions.

(b) (v). No woman shall be called upon to serve more than one probationary period.

(b) (vi). Every woman who has served the probationary period shall receive from her employer a certificate to that effect.

(b) (vii). Any time immediately before the date on which these directions take effect during which a woman has been employed on part or portion of the work customarily done by fully-skilled tradesmen shall be reckoned in diminution or extinction as the case may be of the probationary period prescribed by these directions.

(b) (viii). The same overtime, night-shift, Sunday and holiday allowances shall be paid to women employed on the work customarily done by fully-skilled tradesmen or part or portion thereof as are customarily paid to the tradesmen. The basis for overtime for such women shall be on the working week for the tradesmen in the establishment in question. For this purpose the working week for such women shall be the same as that of the tradesmen.

2. Where women are prevented from working owing to breakdown, air raids or other causes beyond their control, they shall be paid for the time so lost at three-fourths of their time rate unless they are sent home.

3. Women shall not be put on piece work or premium bonus system until sufficiently qualified. The period of qualification on shell work shall not exceed four weeks without the express sanction of the Minister of Munitions.

4. Where women are employed on piece work they shall be paid the same piece work prices as are customarily paid to men for the same job.

5. Where women are engaged on premium bonus systems, the time allowed for the job shall be that customarily allowed to men for the same job, and the earnings of the women shall be calculated on the basis of the man's time rate.

6. Where the job in question has not hitherto been done on piece work or premium bonus system in the establishment in question,

the piece work price, or the time allowed, shall be based on a similar job previously done by men, on piece work or premium bonus system as the case may be.

7. Where in the establishment in question there are no data from previous operations to enable the parties to arrive at a piece work price or time to be allowed, the price or the time to be allowed shall be so adjusted that the woman shall receive the same percentage over the time rate of the class of men customarily employed on the job as such man would have received had he undertaken the job on piece work or premium bonus system as the case may be.

8. The principle upon which these directions proceed is that on systems of payment by results equal payment shall be made to women as to the men for an equal amount of work done.

9. Piece work prices and premium bonus basis times shall be fixed by mutual agreement between the employer and the woman or women who perform the work.

10. On piece work every woman other than a woman to whom paragraph 1 (*b*) relates shall be guaranteed, irrespective of her piece work earnings, the time rate prescribed by paragraph 1 (*a*) (i), or where special circumstances exist such higher time rate as the Minister of Munitions may direct. Every woman to whom paragraph 1 (*b*) relates shall be guaranteed the time rate prescribed by paragraph 1 (*b*)

Debit balances shall not be carried forward from one week to another.

11. On premium bonus systems every woman other than a woman to whom paragraph 1 (*b*) relates shall, in all cases, be paid the time rate prescribed by paragraph 1 (*a*) (i), or where special circumstances exist, such higher time rate as the Minister of Munitions may direct. Every woman to whom paragraph 1 (*b*) relates shall in all cases be paid the time rate prescribed by paragraph 1 (*b*).

12. Overtime and night-shift and Sunday and holiday allowances shall be paid to women employed on piece work or premium bonus system on the same conditions as customarily prevail in the case of men for time work.

13. Piece work prices and premium bonus time allowances, after they have been established, shall not be altered unless the means or method of manufacture are changed.

14. All wages and balances shall be paid to women through the office.

15. For the purpose of these directions, the term " woman " or " women " means a woman or women of the age of 18 years or over, and the term " man " or " men " means a man or men of the age of 18 years and over.

16. Any question which arises as to the interpretation of these directions shall be determined by the Minister of Munitions.

REMUNERATION OF WOMEN AND GIRLS 165

STATUTORY RULES AND ORDERS, 1918, No. 546.

MUNITIONS OF WAR.

Employment and Remuneration.

The Consolidated Women's Wages Order, dated May 8, 1918, made by the Minister of Munitions in pursuance of Section 6 of the Munitions of War (Amendment) Act, 1916 (5 & 6 Geo. 5, c. 99), as amended by Section 4 of the Munitions of War Act, 1917 (7 & 8 Geo. 5, c. 45).

DIRECTIONS RELATING TO THE REMUNERATION OF WOMEN AND GIRLS FOR MUNITIONS WORK.

NOTE.—These directions are confined to the War period, and are subject to the observance of the provisions of Schedule II. of the Munitions of War Act, 1915.

PART I.—Work of a Class which prior to the War was customarily done by Men in Districts where such Work was carried on.

Time Workers.

1. Women employed on work customarily done by men shall be paid not less than 6d. per hour, with a minimum of 24s. per week. Where the working week is less than 48 hours, 24s. shall be paid for the working week and for additional hours up to 48.

2. Women employed on work of a class customarily done by semi-skilled men shall be paid according to the nature of the work and the ability of the women.

3. (*a*) Women employed on the work customarily done by fully-skilled tradesmen shall in all cases be paid as from commencement the time rates of the tradesmen whose work they undertake.

(*b*) A woman shall be considered as not employed on the work customarily done by fully-skilled tradesmen, but a part only thereof, if she does not do the customary setting up or, when there is no setting up, if she requires skilled supervision to a degree beyond that customarily required by fully-skilled tradesmen undertaking the work in question.

(*c*) Women who undertake part only of the work customarily done by fully-skilled tradesmen shall serve a probationary period of three months. The wages of such women for this period shall be reckoned as follows :—

They shall be rated for a period of four weeks at the time rate of wages to which they were entitled under these directions when employed on time, and from that rate shall then rise from the beginning of the fifth week until the end of the thirteenth week by equal weekly increases to the district time rate of the fully-skilled tradesman, and shall thereafter be rated at the district time rate of the tradesman whose work they are in part undertaking.

(*d*) In any case where it is established to the satisfaction of the Minister that additional cost is being incurred by extra setting up or skilled supervision due to the employment of women in place of fully-skilled tradesmen, the rates payable to women under these directions may, with the sanction of the Minister, be subject, for so long as such additional cost is incurred, to deductions not exceeding 10 per cent. to meet such additional cost. Provided that no woman shall in any case be paid at lower rates than those prescribed by paragraph 1 of these directions.

(*e*) No woman shall be called upon to serve more than one probationary period.

(*f*) Every woman who has served the probationary period shall receive from her employer a certificate to that effect.

(*g*) Any time immediately before the date on which these directions take effect during which a woman has been employed on part of the work customarily done by fully-skilled tradesmen shall be reckoned in diminution or extinction as the case may be of the probationary period prescribed by these directions.

4. Girls under 18 years of age employed as time workers on work customarily done by men shall be paid as follows:—

Working Week.	Age.			
	17 to 18 years.	16 to 17 years.	15 to 16 years.	Under 15 years.
	s. d.	s. d.	s. d.	s. d.
48 hours	20 0	18 0	16 0	14 0
49 hours	20 6	18 6	16 6	14 6
50 hours	21 0	19 0	17 0	15 0
51 hours	21 6	19 6	17 6	15 6
52 hours	22 0	20 0	18 0	16 0
53 hours	22 6	20 6	18 6	16 6
54 hours	23 0	21 0	19 0	17 0

and so on for working weeks in excess of 54 hours.

Where the working week is less than 48 hours, the rate above prescribed for 48 hours shall be paid for the working week and for additional hours up to 48.

Workers on Systems of Payment by Results.

5. The principle upon which the following directions proceed is that, on systems of payment by results, equal payment shall be made to women as to the men for an equal amount of work done.

6. Women employed on piece work shall be paid the piece work prices customarily paid for the same or similar work when done by men.

7. Women employed on premium bonus system shall be allowed the time customarily allowed to men for the same or similar work, and their earnings shall be calculated on the basis time rate used in the case of men.

REMUNERATION OF WOMEN AND GIRLS   167

8. Where in the establishment in question there are no data from previous operations to enable the parties to arrive at a piece work price or time allowance, the price or time allowance shall be so adjusted that a woman would receive the same percentage over the time rate of the class of men customarily employed on the job as such man would have received had he undertaken the job on piece work or premium bonus system as the case may be.

9. Girls under 18 years of age employed as piece workers or premium bonus workers on work of a class customarily done by men shall be paid as follows :—

(a) In the case of piece workers—
17 to 18 years—the piece work price paid or allowed for the same or similar work when customarily done by men, less 10 per cent.
16 to 17 years—Ditto, less 20 per cent.
Under 16 years—Ditto, less 30 per cent.

(b) In the case of premium bonus workers—
17 to 18 years—the time allowed shall be that customarily allowed to men for the same or similar work, and the earnnigs of the girls shall be calculated on the basis of the man's time rate, less 10 per cent.
16 to 17 years—Ditto, less 20 per cent.
Under 16 years—Ditto, less 30 per cent.

PART II.—Work of a Class which prior to the War was not recognised as Men's Work in Districts where such Work was Carried on.

Time Workers.

10. Women and girls shall be paid as follows :—

Women, 18 years and over	5½d.	per hour
Girls, 17 ,, ,, under 18..	4½d.	,,
,, 16 ,, ,, ,, 17..	3½d.	,,
,, 15 ,, ,, ,, 16..	3d.	,,
,, under 15 years	2½d.	,,

11. In an establishment in which a custom prevailed prior to the war of differentiating between the rates of wages paid to women and girls employed in warehouses and those otherwise employed, an application may be made to the Minister of Munitions for special directions as to the rates of wages to be paid to women and girls employed in warehouses.

12. Women and girls may be rated at ½d. per hour less than their appropriate time rate under paragraph 10 for probationary periods not exceeding one month from the date when they are first employed, and no woman or girl shall be called upon to serve more than one probationary period.

Workers on Systems of Payment by Results.

13. Piece work prices and premium bonus time allowances shall be such as to enable every woman or girl of ordinary ability in the establishment concerned to earn at least 25 per cent. over her

time rate, except in the case of an establishment where an application that this provision should be dispensed with, either generally, or, as regards any particular class of workpeople, has been approved by the Minister of Munitions. Subject to compliance with the foregoing provisions of this paragraph, the earnings of women and girls for work done by them in any establishment at the date of this Order on premium bonus system shall in that establishment be calculated on the basis of the following time rates :—

Workers, 18 years and over		4¾d.	per hour
,, 17 ,, under 18..		3¾d.	,,
,, 16 ,, ,, 17..		3d.	,,
,, 15 ,, ,, 16..		2½d.	,,
,, under 15 years		2d.	,,

PART III.—Woodwork Processes other than for Aircraft.

Time Workers.

14. Women and girls shall, for the first eight weeks, be paid as follows :—

Women, 18 years and over		5d.	per hour
Girls, 17 ,, under 18		4d.	,,
,, 16 ,, ,, 17		3d.	,,
,, 15 ,, ,, 16		2½d.	,,
,, under 15 years		2d.	,,

15. Women and girls shall, after eight weeks, be paid as follows :—

Women, 18 years and over		6d	per hour
Girls, 17 ,, under 18		5d.	,,
,, 16 ,, ,, 17		4d.	,,
,, 15 ,, ,, 16		3½d.	,,
,, under 15 years		3d.	,,

16. Women and girls employed on machine woodwork processes shall, subject to the provisions of paragraphs 14, 15 and 31, be paid according to the nature of the work and their ability.

17. No girl under 18 years shall be employed on any machine process without the sanction of the Minister of Munitions.

Workers on Systems of Payment by Results.

18. Piece work prices and premium bonus time allowances shall be such as to enable every woman or girl of ordinary ability in the establishment concerned to earn at least 25 per cent. over her time rate.

Provided that women or girls employed on piece work or premium bonus system on work which in the establishment concerned was previously done by men on piece work or premium bonus system shall be paid according to the provisions of paragraphs 5, 6, 7, 8 and 9.

Part IV.—Aircraft.

A. Woodwork Processes.

Time Workers.

19. Women and girls employed on woodwork processes for aircraft, other than machine processes, shall be paid according to the provisions of paragraphs 14 and 15.

20. Women employed on machine woodwork processes for aircraft shall be paid as follows :—

For the first four weeks of such employment.. ..	5¼d. per hour
For the second four weeks of such employment ..	6¼d. ,,
On completion of eight weeks of such employment ..	7¼d. ,,

21. Women and girls employed as inspectors and gaugers on woodwork for aircraft shall, after eight weeks, be paid at the rate of ½d. per hour more than the rates mentioned in paragraph 15 hereof.

22. No girl under 18 years shall be employed on any machine process without the sanction of the Minister of Munitions.

23. Where the employment of girls under 18 on machine woodwork processes for aircraft has been sanctioned by the Minister of Munitions they shall be paid as follows, on commencement, and shall receive an increase of 1d. per hour after the first four weeks and an additional 1d. per hour on completion of 8 weeks of such employment :—

Girls, 17 years and under 18	4¼d per hour
,, 16 ,, ,, ,, 17	3½d. ,,
,, 15 ,, ,, ,, 16	3d. ,,
,, under 15 years	2½d. ,,

Workers on Systems of Payment by Results.

24. Piece work prices and premium bonus time allowances shall be such as to enable every woman or girl of ordinary ability in the establishment concerned to earn at least 25 per cent. over her time rate.

Subject to compliance with the foregoing provisions of this paragraph the earnings of women and girls for work done in any establishment at the date of this Order on premium bonus system shall, in that establishment, be calculated on the basis of the following time rates :—

Workers, 18 years and over	5¼d. per hour
,, 17 ,, ,, under 18	4¼d. ,,
,, 16 ,, ,. ,, 17	3½d. ,,
,, 15 ,, ,, ,, 16	3d. ,,
,, under 15 years	2½d. ,,

Provided that women or girls employed on piece work or premium bonus system on work which in the establishment concerned was previously done by men on piece work or premium bonus system shall be paid according to the provisions of paragraphs 5, 6, 7, 8 and 9.

APPENDIX III

B. Sheet Metal Work for Aircraft.

(i) *Hand Processes.*

Time Workers.

25. Women employed wholly or mainly on hand processes in the beating of metal to shape from the plain sheet, except the processes specified in paragraph 26 (*a*) and (*b*), shall be paid according to the provisions of paragraph 3.

26. Women and girls employed on—

(*a*) the making of straight folds (whether beaded or not), straight bends and straight flanges ;

(*b*) the making of bends and flanges (if in one plane) on other than straight work ;

(*c*) hand processes other than the beating of metal to shape from the plain sheet,

shall be paid as follows :—

```
Women, 18 years and over      ..   ..   ..   7d. per hour
Girls,  17    „      „   under 18  ..   ..   ..   6d.   „
   „    16    „      „      „  17  ..   ..   ..   5d.   „
   „    15    „      „      „  16  ..   ..   ..   4½d.  „
   „    under 15 years   ..   ..   ..   ..   4d.
```

The rates prescribed by this paragraph shall be subject to an increase of ½d. per hour after four weeks' experience and to an additional ½d. per hour after eight weeks' experience.

Workers on Systems of Payment by Results.

27. Women and girls shall be paid according to the provisions of paragraphs 5, 6, 7, 8 and 9.

(ii) *Machine Processes.*

28. Women and girls employed as time workers, or on systems of payment by results, on machine processes shall, subject to the provisions of paragraph 29, be paid according to the provisions of Part II. of these directions.

C. General Aircraft Work.

29. Women employed as time workers on Aircraft work in any establishment wholly or mainly engaged in the manufacture or repair of Aircraft shall not in any case be paid a less rate than 6d. per hour after the first eight weeks.

PART V.—General Provisions.

30. The provisions of Parts I. and II. of these directions shall not apply to any of the work (other than General Aircraft Work) mentioned in Parts III. and IV., except in so far as those provisions are specifically applied by Parts III. and IV.

31. Where special circumstances exist, women and girls may be paid in excess of the rates prescribed in these directions. In particular,

and without prejudice to the foregoing provisions, they shall be so paid when they are employed—

(a) in danger zones,
(b) on work injurious to health,
(c) on specially laborious or responsible work, or
(d) on work requiring special ability.

Rates of wages in excess of the respective rates prescribed in these directions shall not be put into operation for any class of workers without the previous sanction of the Minister of Munitions.

32. The same overtime, night-shift, Sunday and holiday allowances shall be paid to women and girls to whom Parts I., III. or IV. (except paragraph 28) of these directions apply as are paid to men employed on work of the same class. For this purpose, the working week shall be the working week for women and girls in the establishment in question, but shall in no case be reckoned as less than 48 hours. Women and girls to whom Part II. of these directions applies shall be paid—

(a) in accordance with the custom of the establishment;
(b) where no such custom exists, in accordance with the custom prevailing in similar establishments or trades in the district;
(c) where there are no similar establishments or trades in the district, then in accordance with the rates and conditions prevailing in the nearest district in which the general industrial conditions are similar;
(d) where (a), (b) and (c) cannot be applied, such allowances shall be paid at such rates and on such conditions as the Minister of Munitions may direct.

33. Where women or girls are prevented from working owing to breakdown, air raids or other causes beyond their control, and no custom exists in the establishment as to payment in respect of time so lost in excess of what is hereby laid down, they shall be paid for the time so lost at three-fourths of their time rate unless they are sent home.

34. Where women or girls are employed on systems of payment by results their time rates shall be guaranteed and paid irrespective of earnings. Debit balances shall not be carried forward from one week to another.

35. Women or girls shall not be put on systems of payment by results until sufficiently qualified. The period of qualification on shell work shall not exceed four weeks without the express sanction of the Minister of Munitions.

36. Piece work prices and premium bonus time allowances shall be fixed by mutual agreement in accordance with these directions between the employer and the worker or workers who perform the work.

37. Piece work prices and premium bonus time allowances, after they have been established, shall not be altered unless the means or method of manufacture are changed.

38. These directions shall not operate to prejudice the existing remuneration of any person or persons.

39. All wages and balances shall be paid to women and girls through the Office.

40. For the purpose of these directions, the term "woman" or "women" means a woman or women of the age of 18 years or over, and the term "man" or "men" means a man or men of the age of 18 years and over.

41. In addition to the amounts payable to women or girls under any of the foregoing directions there shall be paid over and above those amounts to all women and girls whilst employed on munitions work, whether working on time or on a system of payment by results, an advance which in the case of women of 18 years of age and over shall be 6s. per full ordinary week, and in the case of girls under 18 years of age 3s. per full ordinary week.

This advance is to be taken into account in the calculation of payment for overtime, night-shift, Sunday and holiday work, but is not otherwise to apply to or affect time rates, premium bonus rates or piece work prices, and is not to be taken into account as part of the time rates for the purpose of fixing new piece work prices or premium bonus rates. This advance shall not apply in establishments where the payment of alternative war advances has been sanctioned by the Minister of Munitions.

42. These directions shall come into operation in each establishment named in the second schedule hereto as from the beginning of the first full pay occurring after either the receipt of the Order by the establishment or the 1st day of June, 1918, whichever may be the later.

43. Compliance with these directions shall exempt the owner of an establishment named in the second schedule hereto and any contractor or sub-contractor employing labour therein from the obligation to comply with any previous Order of the Minister of Munitions regarding the wages of female workers employed in that establishment on munitions work.

44. Any question which arises as to the interpretation of these directions shall be determined by the Minister of Munitions.

APPENDIX IV.

Two Illustrations of the Operation of Circular L.2.

1. WAGES QUESTION IN MANCHESTER.[1]

The purpose of our visit was to enquire into a number of cases in which it is alleged that the letter or the spirit of Circular L.2 is being evaded or defied in Manchester. Complaints involving about 16 different firms were made in a letter from Mr. Binns, the Local Delegate of the Amalgamated Society of Engineers, dated 7 April. Our visit was arranged for an earlier date, but was unavoidably postponed, and in the interval two events have somewhat modified the situation. There has been an agreement between the Employers' Federation and the Workers' Union fixing rates for women and girls of various ages on work outside the scope of L.2, an agreement similar to the Midlands Agreement but a little more generous in its terms. Neither the Amalgamated Society of Engineers nor the National Federation of Women Workers were parties to the Manchester Agreement, nor do they accept its terms. They regard it as a manœuvre of the employers to defeat their claims. All the same, it has in many cases improved the wages of women, and, as we pointed out, the Ministry can hardly avoid accepting its condition as " Fair wages " unless or until some other terms are awarded. The minimum wage it fixes for women of 21 is 18s. a week, but it provides for a probationary period of 2 months, during which they may be paid 3s. a week less.

Possibly, as a counterstroke to this Agreement, the Amalgamated Society of Engineers and the National Federation of Women Workers have written jointly to Sir H. Ll. Smith at the Board of Trade, reporting the same series of cases, and others, with a request for arbitration. What they desire is a visit of Mr. Lynden Macassey's Special Tribunal. It was, however, considered desirable that our visit of enquiry should proceed, in the hope that we might at least clear the ground for subsequent arbitration. In our opinion there will have to be arbitration, preferably on the spot, to fix rates for work not covered by L.2, especially for machine-tool work formerly done by boys or apprentices, but we can claim to have narrowed the issue so far that two or three test cases may now be expected to solve all the matters in dispute. In general, where L.2 is clearly applicable, it is being applied—*e.g.*, on Shell work. In one or two doubtful cases we were able to settle the doubt by reference to previous decisions of the Ministry, and in these cases our opinion was accepted. The interpretation that the

---

[1] This report was produced after a special enquiry made at Manchester in April, 1916, on behalf of the Wages Section, as a result of frequent complaints made in the Press and to the Ministry that the provisions of L.2 were not being observed.

age of 18 constitutes a " man " for the purposes of L.2 was new to the employers, and in one case they were inclined to contest it.

The only other point at issue in the interpretation of L.2, when it was admitted to apply, concerns the reckoning of hours per week. The great majority of engineering firms in Manchester work a 53 hour week normally, but one or two important firms work 48. One or two firms in the former class have adopted a shorter week for women, and have made a proportionate reduction in the 20s rate. Assuming that the custom of the district is to be determined by the practice of the majority, and that the standard week in Manchester is 53 hours, such a reduction is, as we told Mr Binns, in accordance with the terms of L.2 and with the general practice of the country. This, however, does not satisfy the Amalgamated Society of Engineers or the National Federation of Women Workers, who contend that the women ought at least to have the opportunity of earning 20s. even even if they have to work 53 hours for it, and that as firms working a short week have nevertheless to pay the full standard rate to men, they ought to pay full rates to women.

But the real kernel of the dispute lies in the Machine Tool trade, where girls and women are replacing boys and youths. Boy labour has been very freely employed on such operations as turning, shaping, slotting, drilling, and gear-cutting. In carrying out the Minister's instructions for dilution, apprentices (and men are called apprentices at Armstrong's up to the age of 23) have been moved up to replace skilled men, boys have taken the place of apprentices, and girls have taken the place of boys at similar wages. This would seem equitable enough at first sight, but the Amalgamated Society of Engineers is not content. The firm, they contend, is the gainer by the transaction and labour is the loser, because the promoted youth gains no promotion of wages, and the girl labour is too cheap. They probably fear that girl labour has come to stay. Most of the firms we visited declared that they much preferred boys, and had only introduced girls under pressure from the Ministry. In some cases they averred that they could still get plenty of boys and would turn the girls out if girl labour were made any more costly. In other cases, however, it was not denied that the girls would be retained if possible. It was made a charge against one firm that in engaging the girls foremen had told them that they were being taken on as apprentices. It appears to us that there is need for a test case on this point to award satisfactory wages to girls of various ages replacing boys and youths of various ages in this trade, and to fix some proportionate bonus or advance for the apprentice doing repetition work of a skilled character. The argument that an apprentice's wages cannot fairly be applied to a woman doing his work because the youth is paying for his tuition while the woman is not appeared to be new to the employers.

In some cases the claim was that a woman was doing skilled work and should have a skilled man's wage. We saw no clear cases in which a woman was doing the whole of a fully-skilled man's work.

But there were some dubious cases where a woman was doing very nearly the same work as a moderately-skilled apprentice of 20, or where work properly called skilled work was being done by women owing to certain alterations of the machine. In such cases we advised that the 20s. rate should be applied.

In general we found little to substantiate the charge that there had been a sort of organised evasion of the rules by employers in Manchester. There were several difficult border-line cases, but there appeared to be little foundation for the condition of "seething unrest" which we had been led to expect, nor did we detect any clear symptoms of such a condition. Undoubtedly there is a great deal of dissatisfaction against two of the largest firms, but this is probably due to a great degree to the unconciliatory attitude of these firms towards their employees and their representatives.

In our judgment the best way of handling the present situation would be for the Special Tribunal to visit Manchester as soon as possible and hear the claims against these two firms as test cases.

A detailed note on the various cases investigated will follow shortly. It was impossible to complete the investigation in a single week.

2. WOMEN OXY-ACETYLENE WELDERS.

The case of the *Women Oxy-acetylene Welders*, a few months later, shows the difficulty of defining the meaning of skilled work with regard to L.2, and of fixing the duration of a probationary period and the position of the semi-skilled worker, especially after training.

Women had begun to learn oxy-acetylene welding at a private training school in January, 1916; 27 of the pupils of this school started work in March at the Hendon Aircraft Factory. They received 7d. to 8d. an hour, while other women trained by the firm started at 4d., rising to 5d.

A trade union was formed among these trained women, which, in July, asked the employers for rates of pay "in accordance with L.2." They received 8d. an hour, whereas men were paid a starting wage of 10¾d., rising to 11¼d. The Society asked for a rise to similar rates for themselves, and that other women without training should, within a reasonable time, receive the wages of the male improver.

The London Engineering Employers refused to pay more than 8d. an hour, on the ground that the work was not skilled. On 7 August, the Women Welders' Society applied for arbitration to the Chief Industrial Commissioner's Department and were referred to the Special Wages Tribunal of the Ministry of Munitions, before which the secretary attended on 26 October to prove that her members belonged to a fully-skilled trade.

Two special investigations into conditions in the industry were made in August and October by officers of the Ministry. The main difficulty in the case was that oxy-acetylene welding was a new process, dating from about 1900, with very little regular apprenticeship. Men in the trade as a rule received 11d. or 1s. an hour, but this varied, and in a case heard in March, 1916, the Committee on Production refused to sanction the payment of the coppersmith's high rate of wages if he were transferred from his own trade to this process.

The investigators described the work done by most of the women as " not semi-skilled in the sense of tool-set automatic machine work, but of a somewhat higher grade of skill in which much patience, steady eyesight, and delicate and careful application are required in order to make a clean, smooth, and perfect joint."

Finally the Tribunal gave its decision on 17 February, 1917, deciding the question of skilled rates and probation.

> It awarded 8d. an hour to the trained woman on starting, rising after three months' probation to the fully-skilled man's rates ; and to the semi-skilled worker the £1 minimum, as in Order 491 (a) (1), rising to 8d. an hour after 6 months.

An identical award was secured by the same Society against another group of aviation firms in November of the same year.

APPENDIX V.

Agreements between the Workers' Union and Employers' Associations.

I. BIRMINGHAM.

MEMORANDUM OF AGREEMENT BETWEEN THE MIDLAND EMPLOYERS' FEDERATION AND THE WORKERS' UNION

with reference to Wages of Female Munition Workers in the Birmingham area, as defined in the Agreement of 4 January, 1915, between the Midland Employers' Federation and the Engineers and Allied Trade Societies' Federation.

(1) *Definition of Munition Worker.*—One who is covered by the provisions of the Munitions of War Act, 1915, and the Orders in Council.

(2) It is understood that the £1 minimum recently recommended by the Ministry of Munitions is to apply to women now doing work which prior to the War was done only by men.

(3) The Schedule agreed upon is as follows :—

Age.	Day Rate.
14 years	7s. per week
15 ,,	8s. ,,
16 ,,	9s. ,,
17 ,,	10s. ,,
18 ,,	11s. ,,
19 ,,	13s. ,,
20 ,,	15s. ,,
21 ,,	16s. ,,

All bonuses to merge.

(4) Where these day rates do not give to the day worker any advance, it is agreed that an increase equal to that recently given to boys and youths should be granted to such women, and to be regarded as a War Wage, viz. :—

Under 17 years	1s. advance on day rates
17 and under 19	1s. 6d. ,, ,, ,,
19 and over	2s. ,, ,, ,,

All recent advances to be considered as part of the settlement under this Clause.

(5) (a) No general advances on piece work prices.

(b) It is understood that the Munitions Act does not permit of any restrictions of earnings or output, but in the fixing of a piece price it is expected that the price will yield not less than 25 per cent. on day rates to a competent worker.

(c) Owing to the varying ages of girls and women employed on the same work, the usual balance on day rates for piece work can only be calculated on the schedule rate of wages for the girls and women employed on that work at normal times.

(d) If an operative working full time fails for some considerable period to make the day rate which corresponds to her schedule age, a certificate of release would not be withheld by the employer.

(6) The terms of this agreement are to remain in force and unaltered during the period of the War, and the new rates are to commence to operate from the last making-up day immediately prior to Saturday, 30 October, 1915, and will be paid as soon as practicable.

(7) This settlement will be communicated to the members of the Midland Employers' Federation if and when the Controlled Establishments receive the formal sanction from the Ministry of Munitions to the above terms.

Signed—

For The Workers' Union—
JOHN BEARD, *President.*
JULIA VARLEY, *Women's Organiser.*

For The Midland Employers' Federation—
T. HARRIS SPENCER, *Chairman.*
A. WARNE BROWNE, *Secretary.*

16 November, 1915.

II. MANCHESTER.

SUMMARY OF AGREEMENT BETWEEN THE MANCHESTER DISTRICT ENGINEERING EMPLOYERS' ASSOCIATION and THE WORKERS' UNION (16 April, 1916).

Agreement *re* Rates of Wages to female workers not covered by provisions of Circular L.2.

1. Wages.

Age	Rate
14	7s.
15	8s.
16	9s
17	11s.
18	14s.
19	16s.
20	17s
21 and over	18s.

2. All existing War bonuses to merge in the above.

3. The foregoing to be the minimum day rates. No alterations to be made in existing piece prices.

4. During a probationary period of two months, 2s. and 3s. lower wages to be paid.

5. Overtime payment. Time and a quarter for first two hours, time and a half after this, each day to stand by itself.

WORKERS' UNION & EMPLOYERS' AGREEMENTS

III. THE BLACK COUNTRY.

Tuesday, 16 May, 1916.

A MEMORANDUM OF AGREEMENT BETWEEN THE MIDLAND EMPLOYERS' FEDERATION and THE WOLVERHAMPTON ENGINEERING EMPLOYERS' UNION of the one part, and THE WORKERS' UNION of the other part.

1. The Workers' Union desired that the Agreement dated 16 November, 1915, between the Midland Employers' Federation and the Workers' Union in respect of Female Munition Workers in the Birmingham area should be extended to the Black Country.

The effect of such an extension would be to exclude from an increase of wages many women and girls employed on work identical with that being done by munition workers and under identical conditions in the Black Country.

2. This Agreement, therefore, refers to Women and Girl Workers in the Black Country engaged upon all classes of work whether for the purposes of war, civil or domestic use; whether for the Government direct, or for other contractors, and whether for this country or abroad.

3. The area known as the Black Country is that coloured pink on four identical maps supplied to the Chief Industrial Commissioner, the Ministry of Munitions, the Workers' Union, and to the Midland Employers' Federation, and embraces the towns and places shown in the Appendix "A" hereto.

4. The following is the Schedule now agreed upon :—

Age.	Day Rate.
14 years	6s. 0d.
15 ,,	7s. 6d.
16 ,,	8s. 6d.
17 ,,	10s. 0d.
18 ,,	12s. 0d.
19 ,,	13s. 0d.
20 ,,	14s. 0d.
21 ,,	15s. 0d.

and is hereby substituted for Schedule A. " Girls " in the Agreement dated 7 July, 1913, between the Midland Employers' Federation and Workers' Union and others.

5. (a) No general advance in piece work prices.

(b) It is understood that the Munitions Act does not permit of any restrictions of earnings or output, but in the fixing of a piece price it is expected that such price will yield not less than 25 per cent. beyond day rates to a competent worker.

6. Specific cases of inconsistency brought to the notice of the firms affected by this Agreement will receive proper consideration.

APPENDIX V

7. Nothing in this Agreement shall prejudice the right of the Union to apply for the enforcement of the provisions of Circular L.2 issued by the Ministry of Munitions of War, dated October, 1915.

8. The terms of this Agreement are to remain in force and unaltered during the period of the War, and the new rates are to become payable by all firms upon the usual pay-day first following the receipt of the official intimation from the Ministry of Munitions that same may be paid by the Controlled Establishments.

For The Midland Employers' Federation—
T. HARRIS SPENCER, *Chairman.*
A. WARNE BROWNE, *Secretary.*

For the Wolverhampton Engineering Employers' Union—
CHARLES MARSTON, *Chairman.*
JOHN T. BUCK, *Secretary.*

For The Workers' Union—
JOHN BEARD, *President.*
JULIA VARLEY, *Women's Organiser.*

Appendix "A" referred to—

BLACK COUNTRY.

Bilston	Halesowen	Stourbridge
Blackheath	Heath Town	Tipton
Brierley Hill	Himley	Walsall
Coseley	Lye	Wednesbury
Cradley	Old Hill	Wednesfield
Cradley Heath	Quarry Bank	Willenhall ; and
Darlaston	Rowley Regis	Wolverhampton
Dudley	Sedgley	

APPENDIX VI.

Notes on the work of the Special Arbitration Tribunal.

The history of the Special Arbitration Tribunal, though not part of the Labour Department of the Ministry, is interwoven with that of the regulation of munition workers' wages, and has therefore been already recorded in part. Some points, however, need further treatment, for the whole of the Ministry's policy towards women's wages was to a great extent influenced by that of the Special Tribunal.

TERMS OF REFERENCE AND CONSTITUTION.

When constituted in March, 1916, in accordance with Section 8 of the Munitions of War Amendment Act of January, 1916, the Tribunal was given the following terms of reference :—

(1) To deal with any difference reported under Part I of the principal Act which relates to any matter on which the Minister has given or is empowered to give directions under Section 7 of the Amending Act and which is referred to the Tribunal by the Board of Trade for settlement.

(2) To advise the Minister on any question referred to the Tribunal by the Minister as to what directions are to be given by him under Section 7 of the Amending Act.

The members of the Tribunal in its original form were the following, "chosen either for their official experience or their special knowledge of the interests of employers and workpeople respectively,"[1] were :— Mr. Lynden Macassey, K.C. (Chairman), Mr. Allan Smith (Secretary, Engineering Employers' Federation), Mr. Ernest Aves (Chairman of Trade Boards), Miss S. Lawrence (Women's Trade Union League), Mr. F. S. Button (Amalgamated Society of Engineers), Mrs. Deane Streatfeild (formerly H.M. Inspector under the Home Office). Later in the year, in-order to meet criticisms that the point of view of the employers—and especially of employers accustomed to deal with women's labour—was inadequately represented, Mr. A. Warne Browne, secretary of the Midland Employers' Federation, was added together with Mr. C. Duncan, M.P., general secretary of the Workers' Union. Mr. G. C. Campbell, then an officer and later head of the Wages Section of the Ministry of Munitions, was secretary to the Tribunal until the spring of 1917, when he became its vice-chairman. The Tribunal was constituted on parallel lines with the Special Tribunal appointed at the same time to deal with men's wages under dilution in accordance with Circular L.3. The two tribunals shared the services

[1] See description supplied to the Whitley Committee, 1-2-18, L.R. 142/82.

of several of their members, but the " L.3 " Tribunal was only on two or three occasions called into action.

Proposals were made during the summer of 1917 for the decentralisation of the work of arbitration, and for the establishment of panels of the Tribunal in some half-dozen districts, empowered to hear local disputes, and make recommendations thereon for awards by the central body, which would thus have more leisure for the consideration of general questions.[1] These proposals were not carried out; but the work was reorganised in the autumn of 1917, and the Tribunal reconstituted with the following membership :—The Hon. Alexander Shaw, M.P. (Chairman), Mr. J. C. Smith (late head of the Wages Section of the Ministry, Vice-Chairman), Mr. C. Kenrick (of the National Employers Federation), Mr. A. Glegg (of the Engineering Employers' Federation), Mr. G. Ryder (of the Amalgamated Society of Engineers), Mr. J. F. Cameron, Miss S. Lawrence, and Mrs. Deane Streatfeild, with Mr. F. S. Button, who was specially asked, in view of his most valuable service to the Tribunal as originally constituted, to serve as an advisory member in the intervals of his work for the Committee on Production. The members of the reorganised Tribunal agreed as far as possible to give whole time work in the provinces as well as in London, as required, and the Tribunal began a practice of holding arbitrations locally as well as in its London office.

FUNCTIONS OF THE TRIBUNAL.

As a court for compulsory arbitration under the Munitions Act, the Tribunal was to some extent a second version, on a different scale, of the Committee on Production, specialising on disputes over women's wages. Its position as a whole, was, however, different, first because it was possible under Section 6 of the Munitions Act of 1916 for the Ministry to issue statutory wages Orders, giving general application to the Tribunal's isolated awards ; secondly, because it possessed, under the second clause of its construction, advisory as well as judicial functions. Upon it fell the responsibility of framing suggestions for the wages policy of the Ministry, and to it were accordingly referred questions about the application of the women's wages orders to the different trades, such as the manufacture of rubber, soap, screws, rope, files, porcelain, some firms in which might be technically engaged in "munitions," but were reluctant to adjust their wages to the level of the statutory orders ; on the same grounds it dealt with problems about the inclusion under the Orders of different classes of workers— girls taking men's work, workers in low-paid country districts, warehouse women, fourteen-year-old girls just entering the trade—and of their payment at special rates, if included. It also considered the highly controversial proposals for the revision of Circular L.2, and claims for general advances of wages such as those made in April, August and December, 1917. The reference to its consideration of the scheme for a general consolidated Order to apply to the great majority of the munition trades, has already been recorded.

---

[1] See Reports of Employers' Advisory Committee, L.R. 5581, etc.

THE SPECIAL ARBITRATION TRIBUNAL 183

LIMITATIONS.

In two directions its functions were limited: (1) "Interpretations" of the Munitions Act and of the Statutory Orders were in the hands of the Minister, and must be observed by the Tribunal. This appeared in the labyrinthine discussion of Circular L.2. (2) The definition of the term " munitions," and therefore of the applicability of the leaving certificate regulations upon which depended the scope of awards and statutory orders, fell technically within the powers of a munitions tribunal, not of the special Arbitration Tribunal. Pending the pronouncement of a munitions tribunal, legal opinion might be taken as to the scope of regulation. Thus, in the case of girls engaged in an occupation apparently so remote from "munitions" as "wrapping up cottar pins" (for railway maintenance), the legal advisors of the Ministry ruled that such work was "Munitions work, or in connection with munitions work," and, therefore, however inappropriately, subject to Order 9 of 1917.[1]

RELATION TO THE WAGES SECTION.

The relation of the Tribunal to the Wages Section of the Labour Department was necessarily close, and was made closer by the fact that the secretary, subsequently vice-chairman of the Tribunal, was at the same time an officer of the Wages Section, and that the head of the Wages Section sat at first informally and from November 1916 until the reorganisation in the autumn of 1917 as a regular member on the Tribunal, when it met in its advisory capacity. The functions of the Wages Section and of the Tribunal were, however, quite distinct. those of the one being administrative, those of the other judicial and advisory. In practice the "rulings" of the Wages Section were accepted equally with the "findings" of the Tribunal, but the latter alone had binding force.

METHODS.

As a court of arbitration, the Tribunal proceeded mainly by hearing the verbal statements of the disputants who appeared with their witnesses to make representations of their case. If these representations, made by the workers themselves with no undue formalities, were inadequate to establish the point most commonly in dispute, namely, the grade in which the work in question should be classified, they were supplemented by special enquiries made locally by the Ministry's Investigation or Labour Officers or by the technical experts of the Wages Section. On occasion members of the Tribunal, instead of or in addition to such investigations, made personal visits to the works concerned, and examined the workers and operations in dispute. Once, but only once (in July, 1917), during the period the Tribunal prescribed piece rates in a case (that of Strachan & Henshaw and the National Federation of Women Workers) in which the dispute turned on detailed processes of shell making. Such detailed examinations were specially necessary in differences turning on the degree of skill involved

[1] C.E. 340/4.

in a special operation, or on the question whether such an operation was "men's" or "women's" work.[1] Some rulings of the Labour Department and decisions of the Tribunal in the course of the year February, 1916, to February, 1917, illustrate the technical character of this last group of questions, and the comparative artificiality of the distinction.

"*Men's Work.*"	"*Women's Work.*"
Shell—all operations.	Fuses—all operations (except possibly those on automatics). Hand Grenades—all operations. Rifle Grenades—all operations.
3″ Stokes Shell—machine operations on body of shell.	3″ Stokes shell—all operations on body of shell not on machines—all operations on cartridge containers. No. 2 Gaine (British) all operations. Primers—all operations (except possibly on automatics).
Steel Billets—sawing cold and loading into Lorries.	
Conduit Tubes—machining and packing.	
Conduit fittings—machining (Midlands).	
Turnbuckles—assembling.	
Adapters (steel).	Adapters (brass)—all operations (except possibly on automatics).
Shrapnel Shell—soldering inside over 4·5″.	Shrapnel shell—soldering inside up to and including 4·5″—filling. 3·7″ Trench Howitzer bombs—all operations.
2″ Trench Howitzer Bombs—Machine operations	2″ Trench Howitzer Bombs—all operations not on machines.
Tabor Pneumatic Toll-over ⎫ Prigmore Hand-ramming ⎬ Moulding machines Tabor Jarring (power). ⎭	Aircraft—fabric and dope work. Core making—small.
Oxy-acetylene Welding.	
Solid shop (for Admiralty)—machine operations	Solid shop—all operations not on machines.
Armature Bars—forming out of strips exceeding 1/16 sq. in. in Section.	Armature Bars—forming out of strips not exceeding 1/16 sq. in. in Section.
Armature winding—exceeding 10″ diameter.	Armature winding — not exceeding 10″ in diameter.

Requests for adjudication on this distinction between "men's" and "women's" work continued to be received in the later months of 1917. To some extent, however, the work of the Tribunal naturally changed in character. During 1916, when thirty-four awards were issued between its formation in March and the end of the year, the Tribunal was mainly concerned in arbitrating on difficult cases of firms employing women on "women's" work, either before the issue of

---

[1] See specimen awards at end of chapter; Rivet, Bolt & Nut Co., Dec., 1916, and Leyland Motors, June, 1917.

THE SPECIAL ARBITRATION TRIBUNAL 185

Order 447, or before its extended application. It was also occupied in detailed consideration as to the formulation and the application of this order for women's work, and in discussions at prolonged conferences with employers and trade unionists, as to payments to women employed on woodwork or taking a skilled man's work during a possible probationary period. Only a few of its awards concerned wages for " men's " work. During 1917, when it made just under a hundred awards, it was mainly occupied with questions about "men's" work—questions involving the assessment of special rates for intermediate workers, and adjudication on very difficult claims that work done by a woman was for purposes of the Orders the same as that done, possibly under different conditions, by skilled men.

Awards in Dilution Cases.

Some of the most difficult problems connected with the payment of " diluted " labour came before the Tribunal for decision, and its awards with regard to the payment for " skilled " and " intermediate " grades of work laid down valuable precedents for the administration of the later wages Orders described in Chapter IV. Some illustrations of this side of the Tribunal's work are therefore given.

1. " Intermediate " Grades.

The Tribunal broke fresh ground when in February, 1917, it began, in accordance with Orders 888 and 49, recently issued, to differentiate between the grades of skill involved in " men's work." In two cases then brought by the A.S.E. (against Messrs. Thwaites Bros., Bradford, and Crossley Motors, Manchester), it ruled that work on turning motor wheels and in the manufacture of hubs on a special form ("No. 9 Herbert ") of capstan lathe, "set up by fully skilled tradesmen and tooled for repetition work," claimed by the trade union to have been skilled men's work, entitled the women engaged on it to special rates of pay as semi-skilled workers. These payments were not, however, defined in the second case, and a long drawn-out argument between the firm and its workers as to the degree of skill involved and payment required[1] led to another adjudication in August when the second firm quoted was directed to pay 8½d. an hour (still the semi-skilled rate) to the workers concerned. The case heard early in the year, of the Society of Women Welders and the London Engineering Employers' Association, was the first when a definite rate was laid down, starting at £1 a week or the minimum time rate for women on men's work and rising to 8d. an hour for semi-skilled workers.[2] A few days later (February 21st) an award between the Llanelly National Shell Factory and the National Federation of Women Workers prescribed a weekly rate of 26s. (6s. above the statutory minimum for a 48-hour week) for examiners and machine operators.

In the case of women employed on 4½ in. and 6 in. centre lathes by the Caton Engineering Company, a rate of 8d. an hour was fixed

---
[1] C.E. 365/4B.   [2] See Appendix IV.

(instead of the fully skilled rates claimed by the N.F.W.W.) and the same rate was awarded at this time for women " employed in connection with furnaces and on or in connection with the operations on power presses," in the forging shrapnel shop of Messrs. Dorman, Long & Co., Middlesbrough. In the following year, an award of 8d. an hour was given for women employed as navvies in the construction of steel works at Openshaw, and to women furnace workers at Sir W. Beardmore's, so that they received 36s. a week plus war advances—a form of " laborious " work which clearly justified payments above the minimum of the Wages Orders.[1]

The hourly rates fixed for "intermediate" work varied, at the end of 1917 and during the following year, between 6½d. and 8d. As has been explained, 7½d. was the rate normally prescribed for gaugers and examiners at the end of 1917 and in the following year, with the general war advances in addition.[2]

2. *Skilled Work.*

Awards for intermediate rates of pay were frequently given after hearing claims from trade organisations for fully skilled rates for their members. The Tribunal maintained the principle, often exceedingly difficult to apply to actual workshop practice, that the mere sub-division of processes did not *per se* remove an operation from the category of " skilled work," but that any accompanying simplification of the method of manufacture through a supply of fresh appliances (" jigs," etc.) might fairly be held to place such an operation in the grade of " semi-skilled " work. Two examples, unimportant in themselves, illustrate the type of problem thus considered, when such marginal cases came up for decision.

(i) Messrs. Rolls-Royce, Derby (represented by the Derby Engineering Employers' Federation), and the Amalgamated Society of Engineers and National Federation of Women Workers (October 12, 1917).

Here the Tribunal had to consider a claim for the skilled rates by women taking men's work. In one group of cases, jigs and appliances had been introduced to assist the operation, in another no such appliances had been introduced. In the second case, the Tribunal awarded the skilled rates under Section 1b (iii) to (viii) of Order 489 (a successor to Order 49), but refused the claim where special devices had been introduced to facilitate production.

(ii) Another typical dilution case was that of a Scotch firm, Messrs. Keith & Blackman, of Arbroath.[3] In June, the secretary of the Associated Ironmoulders of Scotland claimed payment for women on a dozen moulding machines in this firm's iron foundry, as for work done by skilled men prior to the war. " Moulders " wrote the firm,

---
[1] Caton Engineering Co. and N.F.W.W., Oct. 3, 1917. Dorman, Long & Co. and N.F.W.W., Oct. 3, 1917. E. Nuttall & Co. and N.F.W.W., June 14, 1918. Sir W. Beardmore and N.F.W.W., March 16, 1918.
[2] Cf. North Eastern Railway Co. and N.F.W.W.
[3] C.E. 1319/4B.

"are not actually claiming that the work done on the machines is skilled, but that it was performed by skilled men prior to the war, but the fact that this was done was due entirely to the scarcity of apprentices and suitable unskilled labourers prior to the war." Other firms more fortunate in finding boy labour before the war, now, it was explained, used unskilled men and girls on such work. Why should one firm pay more for its work during the war owing to an accident of organisation in time of peace? The Department's enquiries confirmed the statement that the work was only incidentally done by skilled men, and when the case came up for arbitration in August, the Tribunal refused to award the fully skilled rates of pay.

In the course of the year 1917, the Tribunal adjudicated in some fifty such cases. Some of these were simple and quickly disposed of, and others involved highly technical questions, requiring detailed knowledge of parallel trade customs, and often requiring inspection of the actual process by members of the Tribunal, or by the Department's Investigation Officers, in addition to a hearing of representatives of the employers and workers at the Tribunal's office.

GENERAL ASPECTS OF THE TRIBUNAL'S WORK.

Apart from these technical questions, the Tribunal had focussed before it the essentially " human " background to the economic processes of dilution and wage regulation. The personal aspect, apparent in almost all industrial arbitration, was particularly prominent in many of the cases with which the Tribunal dealt—cases of the application of general principles to the wholly ungeneralised position of women in industry. Thus, it heard in the course of the very frank discussions held before it, the admission of representatives of the A.S.E., conscious of their craft and prolonged training, that despite their insistence on " fully skilled " rates for substitutes, it was impossible for complete substitution for the skilled worker to be achieved in engineering. Employers, such as the head of a Scotch firm who had employed a hundred women for four or five months in his machine tool works, "and none of them deserved more than £1 a week," agreed forcibly with the Trade Unionists that women would never as a rule do skilled men's work in their trade. It was only in the application of this opinion that employers and Trade Unionists differed, the men remaining obdurate that the woman substitute, even if, as was probable, only a partial substitute, must have the fully skilled rates of pay in justice to the skilled man if not to herself, the employers urging the absurdity of expecting them to pay a woman " who had never done any work but washing dishes in her life," the wages of a skilled artisan.[1] The decision of the Ministry on the controversy has been already recorded.

Other personal aspects of industrial problems came before the Tribunal, not only in the more formal hearings of employers and workers organisations, but in the normal routine of arbitration. It saw the cross-currents of opinion between the skilled and the unskilled unions with regard to the definition of skilled work, and the reluctance of

[1] Cf. Conferences, July 28th, August 25th, October 25th, and 26th, 1916.

such workers as slotters and drillers, to accept the designation of "semi-skilled," and it heard the recrimination of three overlapping unions engaged at cross purposes in securing agreements for women's wages.[1] It had to deal with the unwillingness of the woman worker to take reasonable care of her own strength, as in a case when the Right Hon. John Hodge attended as a witness, and stated, with much emphasis, that the sawing of cold steel into billets of 21, 43, and 56 pounds and loading them into lorries was not, and never had been, in his 45 years' experience, the work of either boys or women, despite the fact that women were then engaged on the work, in a controlled establishment, and were said to be volunteering to lift even heavier weights.[2] Or in a Lancashire case, when girls and women were said to be cutting up brass bars weighing 40 to 50 pounds and forging them into parts for fuses (at 16s. by day, 20s. by night, when on time work), and constantly, despite the management's advice, refusing to make these weights more manageable by asking for help in lifting them.[3] It had equally to consider the extent to which wages in a large explosives factory should be affected by the fact that the women, in this case admittedly of a poor physical type and unused to factory work, were suffering from their heavy and sometimes unwholesome employment, and to consider the probable financial results of shortening their hours of work and making better provision for their welfare.[4] It laid down in its early awards, the principle that no girls under eighteen should be employed on "dope" work, and that wages higher than the standard should be paid to women so employed. It was called upon to consider the precise cost of board and lodging for the woman worker at varying times and places, and the amount that munition girls of different ages should or would pay for this purpose to (a) their landlady, or (b) their parents, in relation to demands for advances of wages in a firm or district.[5] It heard, more than once, complaints by employers as to the paradoxical effect of increased wages on efficiency and output, so that, for example, in one very large firm the avoidable loss of time among pieceworkers was $4\frac{3}{4}$ hours per week, as compared with $2\frac{3}{4}$ among the less wealthy time workers, and it was urged that an increase above the weekly average of £1 10s. 8d. earned by pieceworkers in a particular group of large firms would only lead to increased irregularity and loss of time.[6]

Again, it heard the protests of employers over the application of the Wages Orders in marginal cases. Thus, in a rubber works, where the respective operations of making ground-sheets and hospital sheets or petrol tubing and garden hose, were identical, the extension of the

---

[1] Cf. British Westinghouse case, October 23rd, 1916.
[2] Beardmore, Moss End Steel Works and N.F.W.W., April 19th, 1916.
[3] Sutcliffe & Speakman, Leigh, August 2nd, 1916.
[4] Cf. Factory Inspector's Report in case of Nobel's, Pembrey, July-September, 1916.
[5] Cf. Armstrong, Whitworth & N.F.W.W., November 27th, 1916.
[6] Workers' Union v. Thirteen Coventry firms, May 22nd, 1916. The award in this case was celebrated by a concert and dance in the Trade Union's local quarters : *Worker's Union Record*, August, 1916.

THE SPECIAL ARBITRATION TRIBUNAL 189

Wages Orders to the makers of ground sheets or petrol tubing (which might be held to be "munitions" work) must inevitably raise the wages of the other workers equally by 10s. to 18s. a week, so that under competition the firm would be "ruled out of garden hose and hospital sheeting,"[1] It dealt with as much consideration as was possible in an era of collective bargaining for outstanding peculiarities in the relations of a firm to its employees; such as a custom of raising wages by individual merit rather than by groups of workers,[2] or supplementing a fluctuating war bonus and low standing wages by the provision of hot dinners in winter, and holidays in summer at the firm's expense.[3]

Its awards in some 320 cases (to November,1918), if fairly uniform in character were singularly varied in scope, ranging from decisions covering the whole of the women employees of Messrs. Vickers, at Barrow, or Messrs. Armstrong, at Newcastle, to provision for a case involving only two girls and one woman in a large Sheffield Works.

After the suspension of hostilities, the Tribunal ceased to operate as a Court of Arbitration under the Acts of 1915 and 1916, and was merged in the Interim Court of Arbitration set up under the Wages (Temporary Regulation) Act of 1918.

RESULTS.

The effects of sympathetic and impartial hearing of points such as these spread beyond the limited sphere indicated by the number of the Tribunal's "hearings" and the friendly attitude of employers and employed before the Tribunal as its methods were understood are a further illustration of the advantages of the conference method of settling industrial disputes.

GENERAL MOVEMENTS IN WAGES.

1. *Advances owing to Cost of Living.*

In addition to the very varied questions involved in its duties as a court of arbitration, the Special Tribunal had also to consider, in the course of the year 1917, applications for a general advance of women munition workers' wages, on the same lines as the similar applications made to the Committee on Production by men munition workers.

It has been recorded how the general advance of 5s. in April, 1917, to men in the engineering trade—given by the Committee on Production under a National Agreement between the Engineering Employers' Federation and some 40 skilled and unskilled men's unions—gave rise to a claim from "skilled" women workers for the same war advances as men. The claim was ultimately refused by the Department, though sanctioned in certain individual cases, partly on the ground that it was impossible to regulate wages by Statutory Order if they were

---
[1] Conference, July 12th, 1917.
[2] Marconi Wireless Works, Chelmsford, and the Workers' Union, December 6th, 1916.
[3] Nobel's, Linlithgow.

also liable to the influence of awards by another authority.[1] Apart, however, from any such claim on the basis of "equal pay for equal work," women began at this time to claim a general increase of wages on the score of increased cost of living.[2]

In April, 1917, new Statutory Orders were issued advancing the wages of women time workers by about 4s. a week[3] and the question of the need for a further increase owing to the cost of living was referred to the Special Arbitration Tribunal. A prolonged conference, typical of several held later on the same subject, took place on July 12th, 1917, between the members of the Tribunal, representatives of the National Employers' Federation, and of associations of India Rubber and Chemical manufacturers, cable makers and ironfounders (trades specially affected by the women's wages orders), and officials of a number of trade unions. The spokesman of the National Employers' Federation submitted the statement of wage increases given on page 105 and urged that women's wages had risen during the war in greater proportion than the cost of living, while employers profits were heavily and increasingly taxed. Quoting from a recent speech of Lord Leverhulme, to the effect that during the war " workers, most of them, have for the first time tasted and enjoyed the sweets of life. . . . and grown accustomed to a higher plane, its pleasures and advantages ; they will strive to remain on that level and if possible, rise above it," he commented—thus borrowing a phrase perpetually used by workmen in arbitration cases —" If that is not profiteering (on the part of the workers) I do not know what is." On the other hand, the representative of the joint committee of unions dealing with women's labour maintained that on principle, if a woman was to receive the same rate as the man whose work she took, she must have all the war bonuses which he would have got had he remained in his employment, and that organised labour viewed with apprehension the growing " economic difference " between the wages of men and women workers in similar employments. He urged that the women on piece work, and, in some cases, those on time work, had received no real advantage from the special advance granted in the previous spring ; and that both on grounds of equality and of the rising cost of living—which, he urged, clearly affected women as much as men—a full ten shillings advance in weekly wages was urgently required. According to the official index numbers of the Ministry of Labour, prices had risen 71%, and no less advance of time wages than ten shillings would fairly represent the increase.

The Tribunal, however, was not convinced by the trade union arguments, and in accordance with its advice, a new statutory order

---

[1] See pp. 49-52, Chapter IV.
[2] L.R. 142/5 and L.R. 142/100.
[3] The special Arbitration Tribunal refused such claims on January 8th, 1918, when it ruled in the case of the A.S.E. and Willans & Robinson, Rugby, that " it was advised " that women on skilled men's work should receive the women's advances, and not those awarded to men by the Committee on Production, and, it maintained this principle in awards made on February 19th in the cases of the Power Co. and the Coventry Ordnance Co.

was issued at the end of July, raising the wages of women and girls, both on time and piece work, on men's and on women's work by 2s. 6d. and 1s. 3d. a week from August 15th, 1917, when a second general advance—this time of 3s.—awarded by the Committee on Production to men in the engineering trades had been for a fortnight due. A further advance was claimed by organised women workers during the autumn in accordance with the fresh advance of 5s. awarded to men in November under the new system of a four-monthly revision of rates of engineering wages, and a general increase of 3s. 6d. and 1s. 9d. a week from the middle of December, 1917, was enforced by a Statutory Order sent to employers of women munition workers.[1] No fresh general advance in women's wages was enforced until the first pay day in September, 1918, when women munition workers, who had claimed 10s. at a hearing of the Tribunal in August, received a general advance of 5s.

2. "*Generalisation of Awards.*"

Proposals for the extension of the scope of the Tribunal's decisions appeared in 1917.

Hitherto the arbitration awards of the Tribunal had dealt only with individual firms or with small groups of firms, and other firms were often ignorant of the hearing of such awards in their own case until some vigilant Trade Union official drew their attention. The generalisation of isolated awards and agreements made for special sections of a trade was, however, the characteristic form of control of men's wages in that year, and powers had been given to the Department under the Munitions of War (Amendment) Act of August, 1917, to make awards or agreements affecting employers of the majority of persons employed in a particular trade or branch of a trade, binding on all or any other employers so engaged. This provision primarily affected men, since only one award against a federation of employers had at that date been secured by women workers.[2]

To a certain extent, it is true, the extension of awards had already been possible for women owing to the constitution of the Special Arbitration Tribunal, and Orders 447 and 618 had been virtually repetitions of awards previously made by the Tribunal. But by the summer of 1917, when general principles for the settlement of women's

---

[1] The recruitment of women members by several of the unskilled or semi-skilled men's unions brought about a growing tendency to include women with men in advances claimed on the score of increased cost of living. Thus at a hearing of the Committee on Production in October, 1917, when the National Federation of General Workers claimed from the recently formed Wages Committee of Chemical Manufacturers a general advance of 1*s*. 6*d*. per day or per shift for their members, a definite application was made by the labourers' unions concerned for an equal advance for women in the trade, whether on " men's" or on " women's " work. A much discussed award of the Coal Controller in the previous month had given an advance of 1*s*. 6*d*. a day to all adult workers.

[2] In the application of the National Union of General Workers, the Workers' Union and the National Federation of Women Workers against the National Employers' Federation for the extension of Order 492 to the Bolt and Nut Trade in the Black Country (August 9th, 1917).

wages had been established, the possibility of further extending awards of the Tribunal, and at the same time of providing for the needs of special trades within the scope of "munitions," came under consideration. It was discussed at length in two deputations to the Ministry on June 1 and 14, by the National Union of General Workers, the National Amalgamated Union of Labour and the National Federation of Women Workers.[1] The representatives of these Trade Unions urged that some sort of machinery should be set up, to which they could go regularly with their complaints representing the whole of the women workers engaged, e.g., in the filling factories, and put their case for a general advance. The Special Tribunal, it was admitted, allowing for the difficulties and limitations with which it was surrounded, "had done as well as any reasonable person could have expected from a Tribunal." But still, it could only give individual awards, and for general advances other than on grounds of cost of living an appeal by an organised deputation was necessary. The result, said the representative of the National Federation of Women Workers, "is, we have taken particular firms and by awards which have been given, they are paying really very much more than other firms. We say these other firms ought to be brought up to that standard." There should be some central body to which women could appeal, which would stop women's strikes ; perhaps, as an experiment, a standing joint committee of engineering employers and employed might be formed for this purpose on the analogy of the Trade Boards. Here, again, as in the first stages of the control of wages, the lack of organisation or the irregular distribution of Trade Unionism among women—75% of the munition workers in one area, and none at all in some other districts—stood in the way of adopting any scheme for women workers on quite the same lines that might be laid down for men. Such settlement of disputes and wage questions within the industries concerned, might possibly, it was suggested, be attained by "local conferences of the trades, both of employers and employed, district by district, and a central conference comprised of the principal representatives of local conferences, the latter to agree maximum and minimum rates for various grades of work, which might then be fixed by the Tribunal by order." This was again proposed in the following year, but action was delayed owing to the old difficulty of distinguishing between munitions and non-munitions work.

There was a special reason for some more simple system of extending the operation of the Tribunal's awards, and of the statutory wages Orders. The Fair Wages clause could not be interpreted to enforce the extension of awards of the Tribunal or of the statutory orders to firms to which they had not definitely been applied, since such awards and orders applied only to specified munitions works under the limitation of the leaving certificate regulations, until this qualification was removed by the Act of August, 1917.[2] If it were desired to ensure the payment of wages according to statutory order by firms to which these orders had not been specifically applied, then it was urged, a clause should be inserted in the contracts of such firms, binding them

---

[1] L.R. 142/4. [2] L.R. 3684. L.R. 173,874.

to pay wages at the rates prescribed by the Orders. Such a clause was actually inserted in the contracts of uncontrolled firms making ammunition boxes, in the autumn of 1917.[1]

To some extent the difficulty was met by the powers given to the Department by the Amendment Act of 1917, of making wages Orders for female workers " employed on or in connection with munition work of all classes." This did not, however, remove the employers' objection that uniform orders were being applied to munition workers in many different industries, regardless of the latter's special traditions and requirements.[2] This difficulty had been apparent from the first stages of wage regulation, but there was, as has been said, at that period no opportunity, and perhaps little necessity, for treating women munition workers' wages, industry by industry.

PROPOSALS FOR CONSOLIDATION OF THE WAGES ORDERS.

Both employers and workers had by the middle of 1917 criticised the complexity of the wages orders, and a promise was given that they should if possible be consolidated and simplified. This process was delayed by the changes in the composition of the Tribunal during the autumn; but in the middle of November, the reorganised Tribunal was duly requested to advise whether any, and if so what, directions should be given by the Minister consolidating and amending the existing orders relating to the wages of women and girls employed on munitions work, and to what trades, out of some fifty in an appended list, such consolidated directions, or the existing orders, should apply.

" The ideal," it was stated, " would be that all the trades affected should devise their own orders and leave it to the Department to administer in recalcitrant cases. But I think the functions of the Ministry of Munitions, the limitation of its powers to munition work, and the unorganised condition of women workers, render this ideal impossible for the Ministry to achieve and that a compromise as suggested would be best." That is, the issue of " one consolidated order applicable to as many trades as possible, and sufficiently flexible to permit of adjustments to meet the particular needs of particular trades."[3]

The Consolidated Order, issued after much discussion, on May, 1918, has been described under the different classes of work to which it applied. It was drawn up on the lines indicated in the preceding

---

[1] In November, 1917, on the application of the National Federation of Women Workers, the National Union of General Workers, the Municipal and Gas Workers' Union, and the Workers' Union, the Women's " Work " Order (492) with the Order for the 2s. 6d. and 1s. 3d. advance of the previous August, was made binding for all women and girls employed by the National Employers' Federation on munition work, other than " men's work." This was a further advance on the experiment recorded on p. 191, of issuing awards with general application.

[2] The same difficulty reappeared in the application of the $12\frac{1}{2}$% bonus to men munition workers in the autumn of 1917. Outstanding problems as to its application were settled by departmental conferences with separate trades.

[3] July, 1917. L.R. 142/16.

paragraph—probably the only form possible at the time. The desire both of employers and workers for collective treatment of their wage problems, and for the differentiation of these problems according to trade, is of interest in view of the official suggestions made during 1918 for the post-war settlement of women's wages (*i.e.*, by Wages Boards).

DUAL FUNCTIONS.

The double position of the Tribunal as a judicial and an advisory body had advantages and disadvantages. On the one hand the close contact into which it was brought in arbitration cases with the needs of employers and workers under special conditions, industrial or local, probably led to elasticity in the framing and application of the Statutory Orders. Thus in the case of a Cable Works with branches in rural or suburban districts in Lancashire and Cheshire, worked by " typical village people " according to the Dilution Officer's report, special rates, beginning at 1¾d. and 2d. an hour were laid down for beginners of 13 and 14, so as not to disturb too much the standard of living of the country girl. At a Linlithgow works, where 200 women and girls were employed on the manufacture of safety fuses at from 11s. 6d. to 17s. a week (including bonus) for grown-up workers, low rates in accordance, in some measure, with the local standard were again sanctioned. In the case of Siemens Bros., Woolwich, a flat rate was awarded for night and day work, in accordance with custom in cable works. These exceptions were stereotyped in the Statutory Regulations, subsequently issued with elastic provisions for overtime payments and for a lower scale of wages in certain areas.

On the other hand the Tribunal's advisory functions sometimes complicated its judicial work and led to delay. Thus in the autumn of 1916, certain cases brought by the National Federation of Women Workers against firms engaged in electrical engineering, in the manufacture of nuts and bolts, etc., were held up for several months, because the Tribunal was at the time considering the application of Order 447 to all controlled establishment in these trades. Delays such as these were almost inevitable, though they were much criticised at the time by those concerned.

As a whole, the peculiar constitution of the Tribunal, with its dual functions, was fully justified by the consistency thus secured to its awards and the weight acquired by its recommendations as a result of its members' arbitration experience. The effectiveness of its work is a testimony to the value of a standing court of arbitration for dealing with groups of cognate cases.

Examples of the Special Arbitration Tribunal's Awards.

NATIONAL FEDERATION OF WOMEN WORKERS
AND
THE RIVET, NUT & BOLT CO., GATESHEAD.

The Tribunal awards and orders that the following shall be the rates of wages to be paid by Messrs. The Rivet, Bolt and Nut Company, Limited, to the female workers employed in the establishments of the firm at Gateshead on munitions work of a class which prior to the war was not recognised as men's work.

1. The rates for workers customarily on time shall be as follows :—

Women of 18 years and over					$4\frac{1}{2}d.$ per hour	
Girls	„ 17	„ „ under 18			$4d.$	„ „
„	„ 16	„ „ „ 17			$3\frac{1}{2}d.$	„ „
„	„ 15	„ „ „ 16			$3d.$	„ „
„	„ under 15 years				$2\frac{1}{2}d.$	„ „

2. The time rates for piece workers and premium bonus workers shall be as follows :—

Women of 18 years and over					$4d.$ per hour	
Girls	„ 17	„ „ under 18			$3\frac{1}{2}d.$	„ „
„	„ 16	„ „ „ 17			$3d.$	„ „
„	„ 15	„ „ „ 16			$2\frac{1}{2}d.$	„ „
„	„ under 15 years				$2d.$	„ „

3. Women and girls may be rated at $\frac{1}{2}d.$ per hour less than their appropriate rate as prescribed by paragraphs 1 or 2 of the award for probationary periods not exceeding :—

In the case of women of 18 years and over .. 1 month.
„ „ „ girls „ 16 „ „ under 18 2 months.
„ „ „ „ under 16 years .. .. 3 months.

Such probationary periods shall be reckoned from the date when women and girls are first employed, and no woman or girl shall be called upon to serve more than one probationary period.

4. Any war bonuses already granted shall be deemed to be merged in the rates prescribed by this Award.

5. The appropriate time rate prescribed by this Award shall, in the case of any woman or girl on piece work, be guaranteed irrespective of her piece work earnings. Debit balances shall not be carried forward from one week to another.

6. On premium bonus systems every women's and girl's appropriate time rate as prescribed by this Award shall in all cases be paid.

7. Additional payments in respect of overtime, night shift, Sunday or holiday work, shall be made in accordance with the custom of the establishment for the class of women or girls concerned, or in

cases where no such custom exists then at the rates and on the conditions prevailing in similar establishments or trades in the district, or in default thereof then at such rates and on such conditions as the Tribunal may, on the application of either party, direct.

8. Except in cases where they are sent home, women and girls on piece work or premium bonus systems shall, between jobs, be booked on to and paid at their respective time rates as prescribed by paragraph 2, of this Award, and women and girls who are prevented from working owing to breakdown, air raid, or other cause beyond their control, shall be paid for the time so lost at the rate of three-fourths of their respective time rates as prescribed by this Award. This provision, however, shall not apply in cases where machines are stopped in the usual course of operations for setting-up, replacement or grinding of tools, or similar reasons.

9. Piece work price and premium bonus basis times shall be such as to enable a woman or girl of ordinary ability to earn at least $33\frac{1}{3}$ % over her time rate as prescribed by this Award.

10. The above rates and conditions shall be recognised as war rates and conditions, and as due and depending on the exceptional circumstances resulting from the present war.

11. The foregoing rates shall not operate to prejudice the position of any person who has better terms and conditions, nor prevent the recognition of special ability or responsibility.

12. This Award shall come into operation as from the commencement of the first full pay next after the date of this Award.

13. If any dispute arises as to the meaning of this Award, or as to the carrying into effect of the principles thereof, or as to the application of those principles to any cases covered by the Award but not specifically provided for therein, this Tribunal will decide it. Any application for a decision under this paragraph shall be addressed to the Secretary to the Tribunal, 6, Whitehall Gardens, London, S.W.

Dated the 12th December, 1916.

THE SPECIAL ARBITRATION TRIBUNAL 197

LEYLAND MOTORS (1914) LTD.
AND
EMPLOYEES OF THE FIRM AT LEYLAND AND CHORLEY.

The Tribunal finds and awards that women of 18 years of age and over employed on the undermentioned operations, in the establishment of Messrs. Leyland Motors (1914), Ltd., at Leyland and Chorley, shall be paid as follows :—

LEYLAND.

Motor Cylinder Grinding Machines	Under paragraph 1 (a) (ii.) (c) of Statutory Rules and Orders (1917) No. 489.
Cam Grinding Machines	Under paragraph 1 (b) (ii.) to (viii.) of Statutory Rules and Orders (1917) No. 489.
Norton Grinders	Ditto
Bevel Gear Cutters (Smith & Coventry Machines)	Under paragraph 1 (a) (ii.) (c) of Statutory Rules and Orders (1917) No. 489.
Stocking out Bevel Gear Wheels	Ditto
Broaching Machines	Ditto
Milling Machines	Ditto

CHORLEY.

Plain Grinders	Under paragraph 1 (a) (ii.) (c) of Statutory Rules and Orders (1917) No. 439.
Butler Shaping Machines	Ditto
Universal Milling	Under paragraph 1 (b) (ii.) to (viii.) of Statutory Rules and Orders (1917) No. 489.
Briggs Milling Machines	Under paragraph 1 (a) (ii.) (c) of Statutory Rules and Orders (1917) No. 489.
Pratt & Witney Vertical Shaper	Ditto
Potter & Johnson Automatics boring and facing exhaust flanges	Ditto
Churchill Grinder	Ditto
Centre lathe facing flange wheel caps for road wheels	Ditto
Oliver Turret Lathe. Boring and facing engine support cones	Ditto
Potter & Johnson Automatics. Turning pistons for engines	Ditto
Fly cutters Milling Engine bearings ..	Ditto

2. The Tribunal finds that the claim of the employees that women shall not grind or change tools on capstan lathes in the establishment of the firm at Leyland, is not justified in the light of the practice in this matter now prevailing in the trade.

3. The Tribunal finds that the claim made by the employees that girls under 18 shall not be employed in the Inspection Department of the firm at Leyland is not justified, but that in fixing rates for girls so employed, consideration should be given to the last portion of paragraph 9 of Statutory Rules and Orders (1917), No. 490.

4. Where this award prescribed that the rates of wages of women shall be determined under paragraph 1 (*a*) (ii) (*c*) of Statutory Rules and Orders (1917), No. 489, such rates shall be based on those prevailing for men employed on work of the same class less deductions on account of additional cost incurred by extra setting-up, or skilled supervision, due to the employment of women in place of men, regard also being given to the number of machines operated by the men and women respectively.

5. Nothing in this award shall prejudice or affect the right of the parties to have the nature of any departure from the conditions prevailing before the establishment became controlled recorded and dealt with under paragraph 6 of Schedule 2 of the Munitions of War Act, 1915.

6. Systems of payment by results should now be introduced in the establishments of the firm at Leyland and Chorley, based on the appropriate provisions of Statutory Rules and Orders (1917), No. 489.

7. If any dispute arises as to the meaning of this award, or as to the carrying into effect of the principles thereof, or as to the application of those principles to any cases covered by the award, but not specifically provided for therein, this Tribunal will decide it. Any application for a decision under this paragraph shall be addressed to the Secretary to the Tribunal, 158, Palace Chambers, 9, Bridge Street, Westminster, London, S.W.

Dated 7 June, 1917.

INDEX.

ADDISON, Dr. C., 9, 12, 18, 21, 32, 68, 74, 76.
AMALGAMATED SOCIETY OF CARPENTERS AND JOINERS . . 89
AMALGAMATED SOCIETY OF ENGINEERS, 11, 18, 19, 25, 28, 32ff, 36, 42, 51, 56, 71 (n), 89.
ANDERSON, Mr. W. C. 85 (n), 128 (n).
ATKIN, Mr. Justice 52
AVES, Mr. E. 65, 181

BEVERIDGE, Mr. W. H., 18, 60, 61, 67
BROWNLIE, Mr. J. T., 42 (n.), 181, 182
BUTTON, Mr. F. S., 27, 33, 60, 181, 182

CAMPBELL, Mr. G. C. . 181, 182, 193
CENTRAL MUNITIONS LABOUR SUPPLY COMMITTEE, 10, 11, 13, 32, 33, 58, 59, 63.
CIRCULAR L.2 . . 11ff, 16ff, 154ff
COMMITTEE ON PRODUCTION, 3, 5, 50, 85, 116, 182.
CONFERENCES—
Trade Union Executives (17/9/15) 10
A.S.E. (24/2/16) 27
N.F.W.W., etc. (3/8/16) . . 67
N.F.W.W. on Circular L.2 (11/9/16) 33
Held by Special Tribunal, 24, 25, 45 (n.), 91, 187.
Midland Employers' Federation (13/9/16) 74
Midland Employers' Federation (3/1/17) 80
Sheffield Employers' Federation (28/9/16) 72

DAWTREY, Mr. 21
DILUTION AGREEMENTS—
Clyde 26, 28, 36
Tyne 29
DOCKERS' UNION 46
DUNCAN, Mr. C. . . . 18, 80, 181

EARNINGS—
And Wages 95
Averages from Controlled Establishments, 106ff.
In National Factories 101, 102

EMPLOYERS' ADVISORY COMMITTEE, 22 40, 50, 182.
ENGINEERING EMPLOYERS' FEDERATION, 11, 22, 41, 44, 49, 75.
" EQUAL PAY FOR EQUAL WORK," 7, 16ff, 53ff, 125ff.
FAIR WAGES CLAUSE, 3, 4, 9, 10, 55, 58, 122.
GEORGE, Rt. Hon. D. Lloyd, 1, 6, 16, 18, 58, 62, 68, 125.
HENDERSON, Rt. Hon. A. . . 33, 59
HERBERT, Mr. A. 7, 40
HICHENS, Mr. W. L. 70
HOURS OF WORK 61
And payments under "L.2," 19, 33ff

IRON AND STEEL TRADES' FEDERATION, 48.

KAYLOR, Mr. 11, 33
KELLAWAY, Mr. F. G. 80

LANG, J. & J., & Sons . . . 28, 29
LAWRENCE, Miss S. . . . 181, 182

MACARTHUR, Miss M., 10, 11, 31ff, 68
MACASSEY, Mr Lynden, 28, 29, 30, 181
MIDLAND EMPLOYERS' FEDERATION, 60, 70, 74ff, 78, 80, 177ff.
MUNITIONS OF WAR ACT, 1915. . 4
MUNITIONS OF WAR (AMENDMENT) ACT, 1916, 4, 5, 62.
MUNITIONS OF WAR ACT, 1917, 5, 62, 192, 193.

NATIONAL AMALGAMATED UNION OF LABOUR, 30, 31 (n.), 46, 192.
NATIONAL EMPLOYERS' FEDERATION, 70 (n.), 105, 125, 190, 193 (n.).
NATIONAL FACTORIES, WAGES IN—
Explosives 102
Filling . . . 44, 59, 60, 61, 102
Projectile . . . . 44 (n.) 49, 101
Shell . . . . 44 (n.), 49, 101
NATIONAL FEDERATION OF WOMEN WORKERS, 2 (n.), 11, 15, 23, 31, 45, 46, 48, 56, 64, 65, 67, 71 (n.), 81, 83, 92, 110, 192, 194.

INDEX

NATIONAL UNION OF GENERAL WORKERS, 30, 31 (n.), 46, 192.

"PROBATIONARY PERIOD"—
  In "Men's Work" . 23ff, 37, 97
  In "Women's Work" . 79, 97, 99
  In Woodwork. 91, 99

RYDER, Mr. G. 24, 181

"SETTING UP," deductions for, 18, 19
SHAW, The Hon. A. 182
SMITH, Mr. Allan 11, 181
SMITH, Mr. J. C. . . 15, 21, 72, 182
SMITH, Sir H. Llewellyn . . . 18
SOCIETY OF WOMEN OXY-ACETYLENE WELDERS, 175
SPECIAL ARBITRATION TRIBUNAL—
  Awards—
    Aerators, Edmonton . . . 65
    Armstrong 18, 64
    Beardmore . . 14, 186, 188 (n.)
    Bradbury & Co. 65
    British Thompson-Houston Co., 79
    British Westinghouse Co., 188 (n.)
    Caton Engineering Co. . . 185
    Coventry Ordnance Works, 65, 90, 190 (n.)
    Creed Bille Co. 65
    Crossley Motors . . . 41, 185
    Dorman, Long & Co. . . . 186
    Eley Bros. 64
    Gramophone Co., Hayes . . 65
    Harland & Wolff 48
    Harvie, W., & Co. 94
    Hendon Aircraft Co. . . . 79
    Keith and Blackman . . . 186
    Lang, J. & J., & Sons. . . 36
    Leyland Motors 197
    Llanelly National Shell Factory, 185
    Mavor & Coulson . . . 14 (n.)
    Rivet, Bolt & Nut Co. . . 195
    Rolls-Royce 186
    Rover Co. 190
    Rudge-Whitworth 65
    Siemens 65
    Stalker Drill Works . . 22 (n.)
    Stephenson, R., & Co. . . 48
    Sterling Telephone and Electric Co., 65.
    Sutcliffe & Speakman . 188 (n.)
    Thwaites Bros. 185
    Vickers . . . . 17, 22 (n.), 65
    Willans and Robinson 190 (n.)
  Constitution . . . 5, 25, 75, 181
  Enforcement of Awards . . 5
  Functions 13, 63ff, 181ff
"SPLIT JOBS"—Payments for—
  In Engineering Work . . 23ff, 41
  In Woodwork. 91
  In Sheet Metal Work . . . 94

STATUTORY RULES AND ORDERS 147ff
  Nos. 9 and 10. . . . . 79, 159
  No. 48 . . . . . 23, 35, 36
  No. 49 . . . . . 35, 36, 38ff
  No. 447 . . . . . 66ff, 157
  No. 456 22
  No. 489 . . . . 93, 94, 161ff
  No. 490 23
  No. 546 (consolidated), 53, 85, 93, 94, 151, 165, 193.
  No. 618 . . . . . 68, 69, 158
  No. 621 . . . . . . 91, 161
  Enforcement by Munitions Tribunals 5.
  Summary of their Application 150ff
STREATFEILD, Mrs. 181
TRADE BOARDS, 5, 6, 8, 12, 56, 58 (n.), 65, 77, 78, 110, 113, 114.
TRADE UNION CONGRESS . . . 10
TRADE UNIONS—
  Number of Women Members, 3 (n.), 118 (n.).
TREASURY AGREEMENT . . . 7, 8
TRIBUNAL. See Special Arbitration Tribunal.

WAGE ORDERS, APPLICATION TO—
  Aircraft Work . . 89ff, 127, 169
  Bolt and Nut Trade . . 81, 84, 152
  Box-making 93ff, 153
  "Certified Undertakings," 84, 150, 153, 154.
  Chemical Trades . . 84, 151, 152
  Crane Drivers. 47ff, 52
  Fuse-making 62, 63, 184
  Hollow-ware Trade . . 82, 84, 153
  Oxy-Acetylene Welding . . 175
  Pottery Trade. . . . 77, 82, 84
  Rope-making 77, 83, 153
  Rubber Works 78, 153
  Scientific Instrument Making, 84, 151, 152.
  Sheet Metal Work . . . 84, 170
  Shell Manufacture, 12, 13, 14, 17, 55, 184.
  Tin Box Trade . . . 77, 78, 84
  See also Statutory Rules and Orders.
WAGES—
  And Prices . 66ff, 82, 83, 112, 190
  Claims by Women to Men's Advances 50, 52, 130ff, 190, 191.
  Clause in Government Contracts, 94, 118.
  Control in :
    Barrow . . . . . 22 (n.)
    Bristol 103
    Birmingham 38, 74ff, 103, 111
    Clyde District . . . 28, 30
    Coventry . . 13, 46 (n.) 83, 91
    Glasgow 25, 28, 36
    Ireland 85, 151
    Manchester 15 (n.), 19, 21, 62, 63, 173ff.

Wages—*contd.*
  Control in—*contd.*
    Sheffield . . . 72ff, 79, 103
    Tyne District . . . 21, 38
    Woolwich 17
  For Labourers on Time Work, 31, 33, 46, 49, 53.
  For Overtime and Sunday Work, 18, 68, 91, 116, 130.
  For Semi-skilled Work, 30ff, 44ff, 49, 53.
  For Skilled Work, 24, 36, 38ff, 53, 92ff, 103ff.
  For Women on Boys' Work, 20, 21, 174.
  For Young Workers, 22ff, 25, 72, 75, 79, 81, 111, 119.
  Pre-War 8, 105, 111
  See also Earnings, " Equal Pay," Fair Wages, Probationary Period, Split Jobs, Trade Boards.
WARNE-BROWNE, Mr. A. . . . 80, 81
WELFARE 61
WEST, Mr. G. H. 11
WOMEN'S TRADE UNION ADVISORY COMMITTEE, 91, 92, 117, 120.
WOMEN'S TRADE UNION LEAGUE, 63, 86.
WORKERS' UNION, 2 (n.), 9, 19, 46, 65, 70, 71 (n.), 81, 177ff.

www.ingramcontent.com/pod-product-compliance
Lightning Source LLC
Chambersburg PA
CBHW030420100426
42812CB00028B/3034/J